BANKING
REDEFINED

BANKING REDEFINED

HOW SUPERREGIONAL POWERHOUSES ARE RESHAPING FINANCIAL SERVICES

JOHN SPIEGEL

ALAN GART

STEVEN GART

A BankLine Publication

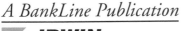

IRWIN
Professional Publishing®

Chicago • London • Singapore

A BankLine Publication

IRWIN
Professional Publishing®

HG
2491
S65
1996

Times Mirror
Higher Education Group

Library of Congress Cataloging-in-Publication Data

Spiegel, John.
   Banking redefined : how superregional powerhouses are reshaping
finance / John Spiegel, Alan Gart, Steven Gart.
     p. cm.
   ISBN 0–7863–0959–8
   1. Banks and banking—United States. 2. Bank mergers—United
States. 3. Banking law—United States. I. Gart, Alan. II. Gart,
Steven. III. Title.
HG2491.S65   1996
332.1'0973—dc20   96–3745

Printed in the United States of America
1 2 3 4 5 6 7 8 9 0 BS 3 2 1 0 9 8 7 6

CONTENTS

v

Chapter 10

First Union Corporation   223

Chapter 11

SunTrust Banks   259

Chapter 12

Wachovia Corporation   271

Chapter 22

Finale   459

PREFACE

The banking industry has gone through a period of unprecedented change during the 1980s and 1990s. Following a period of deregulation, massive bank failures, changing market demand, increased competition, and technological advances (that lowered costs and allowed firms to achieve economies of scale, and the development of alternative distribution systems), the banking industry became exceptionally profitable in the years 1994–1995.

The number of banks declined from over 14,000 in 1980 to just under 10,000 by the end of 1995, as did the banking industry's relative share of total financial intermediary assets. During this period there were dramatic shifts in the composition of both bank assets and liabilities. There were increases in the loan-to-asset ratio and in real estate lending. On the other side of the balance sheet, noninterest-bearing deposits as a percentage of assets declined substantially, while the equity-to-asset ratio and consumer-oriented interest-bearing deposits rose in importance. Banks began to emphasize generating fee income, improving productivity, efficiency, and risk management.

Bank mergers and acquisitions began to take center stage in a massive restructuring of the industry. Helped by a large increase in market capitalization of banking companies and changes in regulations, banks acquired other banks, thrifts, and nonbanking companies (e.g., mutual funds, asset management companies, finance companies, mortgage banking companies, and processing companies). Banks have reduced their credit risks with product and geographical diversification of their asset portfolios and reduced interest risk by the use of more effective and scientific asset/liability management strategies.

A number of regional banks have become prominent in the last decade because of their merger and acquisition activity. First Union, NationsBank, Banc One, KeyCorp, Norwest, First Bank Systems, First Chicago NBD, Fleet Financial, First Interstate, PNC, National City Corp, Mellon, CoreStates, SunTrust Banks, Wachovia, Barnett, Bank of Boston, Wells Fargo, BankAmerica, and Bank of New York have all become dominant players in the financial services industry. These banks are often referred to as superregional banks. With the exception of BankAmerica, Bank of Boston, Wells Fargo, and Bank of New York, most of these banks were not among the largest 25 banks in the country in 1980. Now all of these institutions, plus the money center banks, represent the key players in the banking industry of the United States.

Banking Redefined presents a study of the profiles and strategies of these superregional banks and their rise to power. In addition, the book explains why there have been so many banking mergers and how to place a value on a merger or acquisition. A model is offered to explain what has happened and what is likely to happen germane to banking mergers and acquisitions. Current trends, possible changes in regulation, and the salient financial ratios and characteristics that separate the good banks from the suboptimal performers are carefully explored and analyzed.

ACKNOWLEDGMENTS

The authors would like to thank James C. Armstrong and Robert J. Rhodes (Sun-Trust Banks), John R. Burke (Robinson Humphrey), John Mason (First Interstate/Johnson Lane), Jay Gould (KeyCorp), Edward Pierce (Nova Southeastern), Alex Anckonie III (905 Associates), Larry Frieder (Florida A&M), and A. Gilbert Heebner (Eastern University) for their insights and/or comments on earlier drafts.

John W. Spiegel
Atlanta, GA

Alan Gart
Huntingdon Valley, PA

Steven Gart
New York, NY

CHAPTER 1

Banks' Changing Franchise

Banks are empowered by their constituencies (shareholders, customers, employees, regulators, and legislatures) to provide specified financial services within limited geographic areas. Chartered under federal and state laws, banks have enjoyed a protected market during most of this century. Historically, banks' domains were partially protected from outside competitors and enriched by specific rights, including deposit insurance and fiduciary powers. The significance of the bank franchise is reflected in banks' stock values, funding costs, and quality of talent.

However, the relevance of banks and their share of the entire U.S. financial system are declining as the environment changes rapidly and as competition increases. Banks have moved from a majority to a minority position in the financial marketplace. Environmental changes have resulted in a fundamental alteration in the character of the banking franchise.

This chapter explores the major problems and challenges facing the banking industry and their impact on the bank franchise. In addition to other important factors, the ultimate success or failure of banks will rest on their ability to relate meaningfully to the consuming public, to capitalize on established customer relationships, to control their operating costs, and to make mergers with other banks work.

INDUSTRY PROBLEMS

Irrelevant, Restrictive Charters
The U.S. financial environment has changed dramatically over the years, but the banking industry continues to operate under legislation and regulations dating from

1

the 1930s. Although these rules have been amended over the years, they are substantially irrelevant and overly restrictive today.

Constrictive Bank Paradigms

The public, and even bankers, views banking according to historical, learned perceptions of what banks should do and how they should operate. These paradigms restrict the openness with which bankers and others view alternatives. They limit banks' exploration of new activities and operating processes.

Concentrated Business

Lack of diversification resulted in performance fluctuations that a broadened base of business and geographic coverage could have mitigated. Because of the legal restrictions on the products and services they could offer, banks sought growth by reaching more deeply into the approved markets and accepting exposure to risks that might have been unacceptable if alternate opportunities for expansion had been available.

Focal Point for Controlling the Economy

Although disturbances may originate in other areas of the U.S. financial markets, the banking industry is a conduit through which the Federal Reserve system can focus activity to influence the economy. When actions are needed, the Federal Reserve must act decisively. Federal Reserve activities affect banks earlier and more severely than they affect most competitors and other segments of the economy. Additionally, generally accepted accounting principles (GAAP) require banks to report the negative changes in the economy. Potential loan losses that might be incurred during a period of economic difficulty must be expensed and accumulated in a loss reserve. Front-ending these losses leads to claims of banks taking overt actions that intensify economic difficulties. Adverse bank publicity, occurring before Federal Reserve–induced economic changes, dilutes public appraisal of banks' interest in the general well-being of their constituencies.

Inefficient, Low-Margin Business

Banks must support volumes of activity at substantial expenditure to service customer needs. Products are thinly priced, and delivery systems and labor-intensive procedures are expensive. Returns on shareholders' capital have been moderately acceptable only because the amount of capital that supports banking activities is low compared to the capitalization of other businesses. Figure 1–1 displays the recent trend of bank profitability, measured both by return on assets and by return on equity for the industry as a whole.

Banks had a record net income of $44.7 billion in 1994. Higher net interest income and lower loan loss provisioning accounted for most of the improvement in earnings last year. Net interest income was up due to strong growth in

FIGURE 1-1

Bank Profitability, 1984–1994

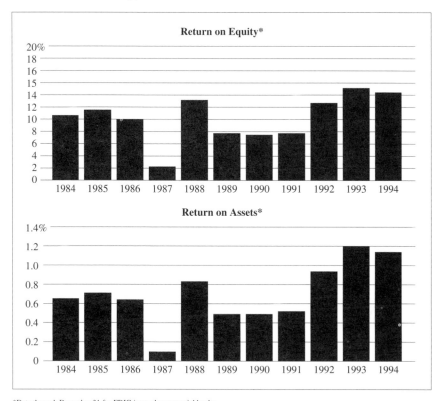

*Data through December 31 for FDIC-insured commercial banks.
Source: FDIC.

loans and other interest-bearing assets. More than half of all banks had higher earnings than the year before. With banks experiencing strong asset growth, return on assets declined slightly in 1994, in spite of record earnings. Nevertheless, the return on bank assets remained high relative to that experienced by the industry over the past 10 years.

Over the last few decades the banking industry's ability to maintain acceptable returns on equity resulted from increased leverage of capital, rather than from significant earnings growth. With capital levels now subject to minimum restrictions, maintenance of satisfactory returns on equity must come from improved operating efficiencies, thereby expanding banks' capacity to generate earnings from the services they render.

Lost Quality Reputation

Historically, the public perceived banks as solid, safe institutions. With high credit ratings, banks could acquire deposits and other funds at favorable rates and lend at positive spreads. During the last decade, banks lost much of this favored position as credit rating agencies reduced their ratings and the markets reflected lower quality-ratings in higher borrowing costs and lower price-to-earnings ratios. Now rating agencies consider many corporations to be of higher quality than banks, and those corporations can access national funding sources at lower rates than banks. Most Fortune 1,000 corporations borrow in the commercial paper market at rates substantially below banks' prime rates.

Perceived Public Entitlements

The legislative bodies that charter banks often hold them particularly responsible for carrying out legislative interests in exchange for the special franchise they are granted. Challenged to comply, banks must document their performance relative to legislative intent. Regulatory scrutiny ascertains compliance. Motivated by the embarrassment and costs associated with the collapse of the savings and loan industry, legislative bodies have now passed legislation that moves themselves and regulators deep into the operating practices and processes of individual banks. The resulting restrictions discourage banker experimentation with new processes, services, and activities. Compliance with the bureaucratic requirements is costly and a growing resource burden.

MANIFESTATION OF PROBLEMS

Recent manifestations of these problems of the banking industry have included slower growth, volatile earnings, failures, inadequate returns to investors, and little industry leadership. These conditions constitute a radically different climate for bank management from the accustomed stability during past decades.

Slowed Business Growth

Though the markets have grown, banks' loss of market position has lessened their rate of growth. Decreased participation in economic expansion and public reactions to industry problems have depressed the development of banking institutions. As reflected in the industry's low stock price/earnings ratio, investors do not believe banks can provide earnings growth comparable to that achievable in other industries.

In comparing the size of banks' balance sheet assets to those of other financial intermediaries, commercial banks' share of total financial assets fell from just under 40 percent in the 1960–80 period to under 30 percent by the end of 1994. Similarly, the share held by thrift institutions declined from just under 20 percent in 1960–80 to under 8 percent at year-end 1994 (see Table 1–1). Also, banks and thrifts have been losing market share in traditional lending and deposit functions, but they remain central to other, equally vital forms of financial activity. For example, banks provided over 35 percent of funds utilized by nonfinancial borrowers in 1973. At year-end 1994, commercial banks provided only about 22 percent of market share. Thrifts have also suffered a decline in market share from more than 20 percent in the late 1970s to under 10 percent in 1994 (see Figures 1–2 and 1–3). However, a few researchers feel that the official figures understate the amount of business done by banks. These economists feel that bank assets are growing faster than the rest of the economy, and, after adjusting for off-balance-sheet activities and other accounting issues, banks have lost little ground to other financial institutions. These researchers feel that banks are not dinosaurs, but are alive and well.[1]

Volatile Earnings

Over the last decade, few banks avoided a year or more of substantially depressed earnings. During the recent recession, sizable loan losses occurred in several segments of banks' loan portfolios (such as loans for commercial real estate and highly leveraged transactions) and resulted in major hits to earnings. The percentage

T A B L E   1-1

Relative Shares of Total Financial Intermediary Assets,
1960–1994

	1960	1970	1980	1990	1994
Insurance companies					
Life insurance	19.6%	15.3%	11.5%	12.5%	13.0%
Property and casualty	4.4	3.8	4.5	4.9	4.6
Pension funds					
Private	6.4	8.4	12.5	14.9	16.2
Public (state and local government)	3.3	4.6	4.9	6.7	8.4
Finance companies	4.7	4.9	5.1	5.6	5.3
Mutual funds					
Stock and bond	2.9	3.6	1.7	5.9	10.8
Money market	0.0	0.0	1.9	4.6	4.2
Depository institutions (banks)					
Commercial banks	38.6	38.5	37.2	30.4	28.6
Savings and loans and mutual savings	19.0	19.4	19.6	12.5	7.0
Credit unions	1.1	1.4	1.6	2.0	2.0
Total	100.0%	100.0%	100.0%	100.0%	100.0%

Source: Board of Governors of the Federal Reserve System, Flow of Funds Accounts.

FIGURE 1–2

Commercial Banks' Share of Total Nonfinancial Borrowing, 1960–1994

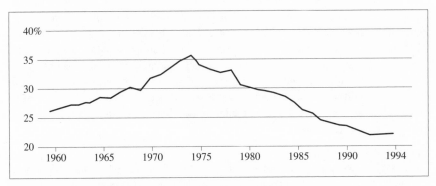

Source: Board of Governors of the Federal Reserve System, Flow of Funds Accounts.

FIGURE 1–3

Thrifts' Share of Total Nonfinancial Borrowing, 1960–1994

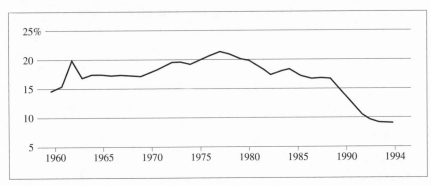

Source: Board of Governors of the Federal Reserve System, Flow of Funds Accounts.

decline in profits could have been significantly lessened if banks had been allowed to develop broader product lines and expand geographically.

Many banks, including Banc One, NBD, JP Morgan, Comerica, Norwest, Society, and Wachovia, came through the credit cycle virtually unscathed with respect to both earnings and credit quality ratio deterioration. Some banks survived with somewhat embarrassing but relatively minor damage: CoreStates, PNC, NationsBank, and SunTrust. There were serious doubts about the viability of the Bank of Boston, Shawmut, Midlantic, and some of the money center banks. Other banks failed outright, including Bank of New England, Southeast, and First City. Some banks had to cut or eliminate dividends, while others continued steady double-digit dividend growth right through the real estate debacle.

Total Failures
The collapse of the savings and loan industry and the failure of many banks caused great concern about the integrity of the whole financial system. Figure 1–4 shows the unprecedented frequency of bank failures in the late 1980s. Although the recent favorable interest rate environment provided a short-term improvement in earnings and a partial recapitalization of the banking industry, it has masked the significance of problems underlying the industry. Failures are reflected in liquidations, sales of institutions to others, and poor shareholder returns.

The current climate has provided many bank owners and managements the opportunity to exit the industry, thus stemming further deterioration. Figure 1–4 shows the extent of consolidation that has occurred over the last decade.

Inadequate Investor Returns
Shareholders' returns on investment in many banks have trailed returns available from other equity investments. The current price/earnings ratio of bank stocks is a reflection of the caution that investors have to investing in banks. The most significant disappointment in returns has come from investments in smaller, community banks. Dividend yield has been low, and earnings reliability and growth have been poor. Today, however, small banks can obtain significant one-time, sell-out premiums from banking companies wishing to expand geographically or add efficiencies to existing market delivery systems. Many investors in small banks are challenged to justify maintaining those investments instead of selling their holdings at a premium.

F I G U R E   1–4

Bank Failures, 1980–1994

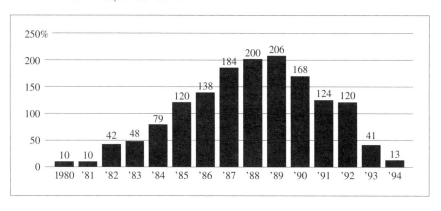

Little Industry Leadership

Banking leaders concentrate on challenges in managing their own organizations, spending little time on industry issues. They are perceived as having strong self-interests, which, at times, appear contrary to those of public policy makers. The industry's principal trade association, the American Bankers Association (ABA), must represent the interests of each member bank, large or small. Much of its thrust is diluted by this attempt to serve all. Thus, many of the ABA's positions are compromises from within the industry. Negotiating from a weakened consensus position is difficult and leads to further compromises with regulators, legislators, and Congress, which is less effective than if the ABA had initially taken a strong, one-sided position. Rather than be proactive, the ABA often finds the best course is to resist change as long as possible. Therefore, this lobbying organization often appears negative and resistant. Past industry failures to influence legislation and regulation have discouraged bank managements from being in the forefront of efforts to effect legislative change.

RESPONSES TO CHANGING CONDITIONS

Bankers and others have responded to the industry's problems by instigating actions contrary to the old paradigms of what banks are expected to do and how they are expected to operate. In the worst cases, management has significantly leveraged institutions and accepted speculative risks in hopes that their initiatives would save an inadequate or failing situation. Employees seek short-term, spectacular returns to boost compensation knowing that their careers are not tied to long-term dependency on one employer. Legislators and regulators have developed new controls to tighten their influence over the operation of individual banks, including requiring enhancement to specific services for advancement of entitlement goals. Customers are shopping for better and less expensive ways to satisfy their financial needs. Litigious customers have required banks to accept responsibility and liability for servicing their needs as professionals who deliver expert advice and commitments. Competitors, for decades satisfied with the specialization of function that existed in the financial markets, have developed new services expanding their entry into banking's domain. For example, mutual funds have attracted substantial consumer savings, and companies such as GM, AT&T, Sears, and Ford have become major issuers of credit cards. The declining attractiveness of banks as investments has resulted in the sale of many banking companies and lower price/earnings ratios for others.

Legislative Initiatives

Recognizing the weakened state of the banking industry, Congress and state legislatures moved to prevent taxpayer-assumed losses similar to those resulting from the collapse of the savings and loan industry. They have strengthened laws and regulations affecting the management of banks. Rather than freeing banks to grow and develop in response to the market changes, these legislators have focused on the processes that bank officials use in managing their institutions. Instead of being deregulated, banks are being reregulated with laws and regulations reaching deep into their organizations.

Bureaucratic Regulation and Supervision

Following the precepts of legislators, regulators have required banks to develop costly, unproductive bureaucratic processes that divert resources away from serving customers' needs. Supervision has become an enforcement process rather than a collaborative effort to improve individual bank practices and procedures. Instead of focusing on the result, supervision searches for failures to comply with regulations crafted by staffs distant from the business of banking.

Magnified Personal Liability

Bank examiners continually remind bank officers and directors of the significant responsibilities and liabilities they accept by agreeing to manage a banking institution. Banking laws and regulations identify specific legal obligations beyond those normally assumed by corporate officers and directors. Additionally, directors doing business with their banks face increasingly onerous conditions and are subject to standards, processes, and controls to which other customers are not subjected. Senior officers and directors are discouraged from doing business with the bank they serve in an official capacity. Thus, attracting significant business leaders to serve on bank boards of directors is becoming increasingly difficult and sometimes is in conflict with a bank's interest in generating business.

Lost Public Confidence

"Could my bank fail?" was a familiar question heard during the late 1980s and early 1990s. Many savings and loans ("banks" to most consumers) and banks did fail. With banks subject to the difficulties noted above, and losing market share among U.S. financial service providers, it was conceivable that a bank might be facing major adversities. Congress and the press heightened consumer anxieties by speculating on failures. Most notable was the often mentioned position that no bank was too big to fail and that some large ones surely would.

Erosion of the Customer-Bank Covenant

Historically, established banking customers received preference in obtaining credit and personalized service. Banks and their customers had relationships in which both parties anticipated that each would respect and, to the extent possible, accommodate the needs of the other. Banks assumed that borrowers would do their best to repay their loans, even in case of serious financial difficulties. Borrowers expected bank lenders to structure lending arrangements to meet their specific needs and, during difficulties, to work with the borrower to restructure the agreement to facilitate ultimate repayment. This covenant relationship has eroded, being replaced by contractual obligations in an increasingly litigious environment. The rights of the parties have become more important than the ethics and implied commitments underlying relationships. The diluted market-positioned bank has less perceived significance and thus less ability to hold on to covenant relationships. In many respects, banking is changing from a relationship business to a commodity business.

Increased Nonbank Competition

Nonbanks are entering the banking realm from all sides, and yet banks continue to be restricted from broadening their range of product offerings. Banks once had the exclusive right to offer demand deposit accounts (checking accounts), but now securities firms and mutual funds offer checking account equivalents. Auto manufacturers lend money to car purchasers. Mortgage bankers and brokers lend to home buyers. Investment bankers privately place debt for small commercial companies. There are now few significant services offered by banks where banks retain a competitive product or pricing advantage.

Life Saving/Threatening Risk Taking

Responding to the difficulties and challenges facing the banking industry, many bank managements have taken risks beyond those acceptable in the past. Some have been successful, while many have placed their institutions in jeopardy. During the 1980s and early 1990s, numerous failures occurred when banks reached for profitability and growth beyond that the normal business of banking provided.

DEVELOPING OPPORTUNITIES

The widespread recognition of the problems previously noted creates a banking climate more receptive to change, thereby facilitating efficiency and effectiveness improvements that affect personnel and imbedded corporate cultures. Opportunities to diversify geographically are growing, and regulators are allowing slow entry into new services and products. New management information systems facilitate the management of loan accounts, overall asset and liability management, and knowledgeable service of individual needs and insight into the customer's total relationship with the bank. Derivatives and asset securitizations are providing new ways to manage risks and liquidity, as well as new services for customers. Banks have strengthened loan loss reserve and capital positions and have begun to concentrate efforts on building greater operating efficiency.

The Competitors

Surviving U.S. banks face fewer domestic bank and savings and loan competitors. However, more nonbanks and foreign banks (in an age of globalization) have been attracted to compete for U.S. loans and U.S. dollar deposits or their equivalents. Although competition from remaining banking companies is significant, market competition among banks is becoming more rational. The surviving larger institutions have a higher level of professional management and processes that lead to more consistency and predictability. Thus, competition offers fewer wild pricing moves and risky service offerings.

Movable Quality Business

During a period of change and disruption, customers are more inclined to consider moving business to a competitor. Stable and strong banks are the beneficiaries of new ties to those seeking long-term relationships. Confidence that one's bank will continue to provide quality, personal service is important to many customers. Even if they do not change their primary banking relationship, many customers will establish secondary relationships to provide backup in case of difficulties with the primary service provider. If managed well, many of these secondary relationships can be converted into primary ones.

Rationale of Efficiency Building and Changing Paradigms

Obtaining internal support and commitments for major changes in established operating practices is often difficult, but change can be facilitated by adversity. Employees understand the need for change because they see the difficulties facing the banking industry. Similarly, old paradigms that restricted changing perceptions of appropriate bank activities and processes are more easily changed during periods of stress. The recent passage of the federal preemption of interstate banking barriers to interstate ownership of banks by bank holding companies is an example of changed opinions, at least partially arising from congressional belief that the banking industry needs aid to build strength.

Expanded Acquisition Opportunities

Strong banking institutions will continue to acquire others. Acquisitions provide survivors opportunities to expand, diversify, and add customers, while capitalizing on the survivors' delivery systems and professional capacities. Banks have also learned that there are noninterest cost savings often ranging from 25 to 50 percent in acquiring banks located within their current geographic markets and savings of about 10 to 20 percent in out-of-market mergers (see Table 1–2).

Greater Quality Differentiation

In the past, banks looked very much alike. Differentiating characteristics reflected the personalities of the individual bankers one encountered. Since few customers were exposed to a broad range of bankers, comparison differentiation was limited and difficult. Bank products and services were virtually the same, and bank facilities

T A B L E   1–2

Average Merger Noninterest Expense Savings

Area of Bank	In-Market	Contiguous	Out-of-Market
Branches	20%	10%	5%
Operations	30	25	15
Systems	55	50	40
Trust	25	20	15
Indirect overhead	60	40	15
Other	30	25	10
Weighted average	35	25	15

Source: First Manhattan Group.

resembled one another in location and appearance. Today, with the substantial publicity given banking activities and assessments of quality, there is a greater opportunity for differentiation.

ENVIRONMENTAL IMPACT ON THE BANK FRANCHISE

Banks receive their franchise rights and values from their various constituents: customers, shareholders, employees, legislators, regulators, and the public in general. With the interests of these parties changing over time, banks have faced and will continue to face evolving challenges, responsibilities, and opportunities. During the last few decades, the major environmental changes and banks' responses have been dramatic. The banking industry has experienced a significant decline in its representation and importance within the U.S. financial system. Banks have dropped from a position of dominance throughout the deposit and credit markets to a position of minority status. The impact of environmental changes on banking's publics has been significant, but the loss of market share has also stemmed from the growth of new competitors.

Technological developments in computers, communications, and software have provided companies with outstanding on-line information systems or databases, as well as the ability to utilize this information cheaply. These developments have allowed new entrants to come into the financial services industry with only modest costs and to have access to what was once proprietary information, helping make local markets regional, regional markets national, and national markets local. Advances in information technology and communications have reduced the costs of credit evaluations and made the information readily available. Banks no longer have as much of an advantage as they once had in developing the information needed to make a loan. Inexpensive information on company credit helped the commercial paper market develop and grow. This is one reason the banking industry has declined in relative importance as a commercial lender.[2]

Customers

Banks' greatest strengths may now rest on the marketplace's information and product delivery inefficiencies, rather than on their own value-adding capacities to satisfy customers' financial service needs. The banker-customer relationship carries inherent competitive advantages, providing the foundation for maintaining important positions of relevance in the U.S. financial systems. For example, if banks were permitted to underwrite and sell insurance, they should be able to increase fee income and sell insurance to consumers at lower prices than are currently available. Citicorp claims that because of lower distribution costs, it could offer bank customers insurance at premiums 10 to 15 percent below those available at most insurance companies.[3]

Shareholders

Shareholders seek a return competitive with alternate investment possibilities. Banks must continue to grow and develop profitably if shareholders are to receive respectable returns from dividends and market appreciation. Achievement of the required growth in business activity comes from providing value-added services to existing bank customers. Thus, the customer is king in the creation of shareholder value.

Legislators and Congress

Federal and state legislatures, as bank chartering authorities, have maintained control over permitted bank activities. The grant of specific banking powers, rights, and privileges carries legislatively determined limitations and responsibilities. Some legislators view banks as the proper instruments for helping social programs, and legislators also feel responsibility for the safety and soundness of the banking system. Legislation has become increasingly specific as to bank responsibilities and operating practices. The resulting burden of regulations and restrictions is far greater for banks than for insurance companies and brokerage firms, which now compete directly with banks.

Employees

Buyer-seller relationships are based on the associations people have with other people. Supporting a bank's customer-contact staff are many others who provide and deliver services and manage the corporation. With some difficulty, banking institutions seek to expand customer loyalties from individuals to the institution. Employees also relate to each other and to the institution from which they want security, competitive compensation, and an acceptable working environment. The more relaxed working conditions of the past have been replaced with increased activity, supported technologically by advanced information and processing tools. Compensation practices are increasingly becoming tied to each individual's performance, recognizing that attainment of corporate goals rests on individual commitment and achievements.

Regulators

Federal and state bank regulators, charged by legislative bodies to supervise banks, have focused increasingly on the control aspects of their responsibilities. Collaboration has given way to enforcement, and advocacy to compliance, as regulators faced significant legislative challenges to their supervision of savings and loans and failed banks, and the perceived lack of compliance with certain legislative initiatives, such as the requirement for increased lending in low- to moderate-income neighborhoods.

BANKING'S FUTURE

The future of banking depends on its ability, or lack thereof, to respond to the changing needs of customers. Limitations on product offerings continue to inhibit banks from fulfilling customer financial needs. The window of opportunity to develop competitive positioning is closing rapidly. However, the passage of the interstate banking act should augment geographic expansion and help to diversify risk.

With greater frequency, customers are seeking to fulfill their needs by moving away from traditional banking services, and in many cases to competitors outside the banking system. The most creditworthy corporate borrowers use the commercial paper markets to fund short-term working-capital needs; retirees seeking higher returns have turned to money market instruments and mutual funds; automobile buyers are financing and leasing their cars from manufacturers; individual borrowers are accessing credit through their nonbank credit cards; and, small to midsize companies are finding nonbanking lenders, helped by loan placement advisors. There are few bank services that are not available from lower-cost, more efficient providers. If success will come only to the financial service providers with the lowest priced, most responsive products, banks will face continued loss of their share of the market. Bank branches are expensive to operate, but they provide a venue for direct contact with customers. Increasingly, branches are delivering a broad array of financial services, building on the substantial fixed cost of the branch delivery system and on the convenience and comfort that customers have in visiting branch facilities. Banks will continue to exploit their advantage of established customer relationships, and the strength of these ties will continue to be tested.

Technological developments continue to bring fundamental changes to the financial services industry. Automated teller machines (ATMs) provide access to cash and deposit facilities that are not branch hour dependent and to interchanges that allow broad geographic access. Direct deposit and debit (ACH) services simplify routine, repetitive activity. The next major development will be management information and sales systems that assist customer-contact personnel in knowing their customers and in anticipating their individual needs. Home banking and expanded electronic funds transfer systems will provide more convenient services and products to consumers, both individual and corporate. On-line credit approval and documentation systems will remove the delays customers currently experience when obtaining credit. Image technology for processing checks and other paper-based services will improve customer service and reduce costs. Success or failure from a competitive standpoint could depend on the prudent investment in and proper application of technology with respect to retail banking, customer information systems, and risk management. Proper investment in technology is usually manifested in greater efficiency, better customer service, and more rapid earnings per share growth.[4]

New technology will aid new competitors entering the financial services markets by allowing for the development of cost-effective operations and by providing access to proprietary information. Additionally, advances in technology and communication will lead to new products and services.

Recently passed congressional legislation will allow bank holding companies to acquire banks without regard to past state barriers to ownership. Greater diversification in geographic coverage will strengthen banking organizations. According to a recent study by McKinsey & Co., the elimination of the barriers to interstate banking could cut total bank noninterest expenses by somewhere between $2 and $4 billion annually for the industry over a five-year period.[5]

Glass-Steagall Reform

If not Congress, bank regulators are likely to expand permissible banking activities before the year 2000. The 1994 election that resulted in a turnover in congressional leadership has led to selected initiatives to improve the competitiveness of the U.S. banking system. If House Banking Committee Chairman Jim Leach's (R-Iowa) bill on Glass-Steagall reform is passed, it should have a positive impact on easing the legal restrictions regarding certain commercial companies' (investment bank holding companies) ability to purchase banks or to establish an uninsured "wholesale financial institution." These types of organizations could not accept deposits of less than $100,000 deposits insured by the FDIC. Leach's bill would allow for the mergers of commercial banks with investment banks, not insurance companies.[6] In addition, Senate Banking Committee chairman Alfonse D'Amato (R-New York) and Congressman Richard H. Baker (R-Louisiana) have introduced similar bills in the Senate and House of Representatives that would allow financial institutions to own any type of business and vice versa. For example, under the D'Amato bill, AT&T could merge with a commercial bank, securities firm, or insurance company (see Table 1–3).

Treasury Secretary Robert E. Rubin proposed the elimination of legal barriers (Glass-Steagall Act) that have separated the nation's commercial banks, securities firms, and insurance companies for decades. The goals of Rubin's reform would be:

- To promote competition to lower customer costs.
- To promote a more stable banking system by introducing new sources of earnings, while diversifying bank activities.
- To enhance the international competitiveness of banks by making them stronger and more diverse at home.

Both Federal Reserve Board chairman Alan Greenspan and FDIC chairman Ricki Tigert Helfer support the repeal of the Glass-Steagall Act. Greenspan has argued that banks would be on a stronger footing financially if they could sell securities and insurance, while Tigert has argued that the banking system would be strengthened by allowing them to diversify.

The argument against the repeal of or amendment to the restrictive Glass-Steagall Act is that a combination of banking and other services, such as securities underwriting, would pose significant risks to the banking system. If a large securities unit of a bank were to run into financial difficulty, for example, the bank's financial resources might be used to bail out the securities unit, thus weakening the bank. The principal argument for modernizing the banking system is that the bank's traditional role of financial intermediation, acting as a middleman for the exchange of funds, has eroded as the marketplace has changed. Unless laws are changed, the competitiveness of banks will continue to decline, as the trend toward direct investor-borrower linkages expands.

T A B L E   1–3

Glass-Steagall Reform Proposals

	Current Law	Rubin Plan	D'Amato Bill	Leach Bill
Another bank	Yes	Yes	Yes	Yes
Securities firm	No	Yes	Yes	Yes
Insurance company	No	Yes	Yes	No
Other companies	No	No	Yes	No

Source: T.H. Hanley and P.J. Carter, "The Implications of Glass-Steagall Reform," *CS First Boston*, May 12, 1995, p.15.

The pendulum of government may be swinging back in favor of more open competition, as demonstrated by the passage of the interstate banking bill, as well as more regulatory relief measures. It is possible that some compromise bill on Glass-Steagall reform will be enacted in either 1996 or 1997 that will give banks greater latitude in offering investment banking and insurance services. Following the passage of a reform bill, banking organizations should be capable of offering a much broader array of products and services. Moreover, a change in Glass-Steagall could put more pressure on existing players who are not currently offering a full array of products. The reform of Glass-Steagall should also lead to a substantial acceleration in the consolidation between commercial banks, investment banks, and insurance companies. Banks may benefit the most from Glass-Steagall reform, given that they are better capitalized than nonbank competitors such as insurance agencies and securities firms. It would not be surprising to see an intermingling of banking and investment companies or banks and insurance companies before the year 2000.[7]

The reform of Glass-Steagall could possibly be held up by powerful special interest groups, particularly the Independent Insurance Agents of America. Insurance agencies have an extremely effective lobbying effort in Washington. Given banks' superior distribution channels, the agents consider banks' entry into insurance a threat to their livelihood. In terms of the securities industry, while it has traditionally opposed Glass-Steagall reform, several large securities firms now politically support Glass-Steagall reform. This is especially true since underwriting commissions on debt securities such as corporate notes and bonds (sans junk bonds), commercial paper, and municipal securities have declined substantially over the last decade and since many investment banking firms desire access to the federal funds market and immediate payment for securities purchased. Infighting among the federal regulators may also derail the reform process, as regulators continue to battle over postreform turf. Although passage of Glass-Steagall reform should not have a dramatic impact on the financial results of banking organizations for a few years, it should bolster existing strengths in debt underwriting and dealing at the money center banks and allow some superregional banks to expand through acquisitions of smaller investment banking, regional brokerage, and money-management firms. Under current banking law (Section 20 of Glass-Steagall), separately established securities subsidiaries of an organization can derive up to 10 percent of their total revenue from ineligible securities activities. This 10 percent limitation would probably be removed. Other expected benefits of reform include a substantial acceleration in the bank-consolidation process, as banks that can offer a full array of services continue to capture economies of scale and scope advantages.[8]

The banking industry also received some good news from the Supreme Court and the FDIC. The Supreme Court ruled that banks can sell annuities because they are investments and not insurance. The ruling upheld the comptroller of the currency's decision to allow annuity sales by NationsBank.[9] The FDIC proposed to slash the premiums that healthy banks pay for domestic depository insurance from 23 cents per $100 to 4 cents for each $100 of deposits. However, thrift insurance premiums are scheduled to remain unchanged. For those banks that do not offset the FDIC windfall with discretionary expenses or higher consumer deposit rates, the reduction in FDIC insurance premiums would add an average of close to 5 percent to 1996 earnings per share estimates for most superregionals (see Figure 1–5).

Regardless of what happens to Glass-Steagall reform, banks can be expected to sell a much higher volume of both life insurance and annuities over the remainder of the decade, as state regulatory and legal barriers continue to fall. Banks offer a lower-cost distribution channel compared with the existing independent agent insurance delivery system. In the long run, we are likely to see an increase in annuity/life insurance company acquisitions, which could also spread to acquisitions of specialty-insurance companies. Again, consolidation will become a necessity in order to achieve economies of scale and utilize technological advantages.[10]

Major industry consolidation will continue throughout this decade (see Figure 1–6). By the turn of the century, we are likely to see megabanks with assets in the neighborhood of $400 billion and a shrinking of the present roster of just

F I G U R E   1–5

Savings in Deposit Insurance Premiums

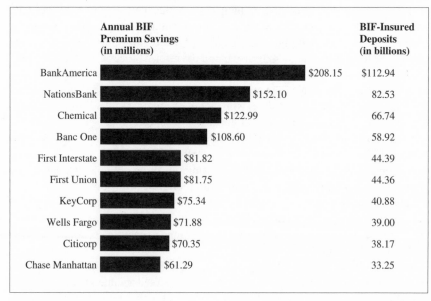

	Annual BIF Premium Savings (in millions)	BIF-Insured Deposits (in billions)
BankAmerica	$208.15	$112.94
NationsBank	$152.10	82.53
Chemical	$122.99	66.74
Banc One	$108.60	58.92
First Interstate	$81.82	44.39
First Union	$81.75	44.36
KeyCorp	$75.34	40.88
Wells Fargo	$71.88	39.00
Citicorp	$70.35	38.17
Chase Manhattan	$61.29	33.25

Source: Ely & Co., Inc.

F I G U R E   1-6

Insured U.S. Banks (in thousands)

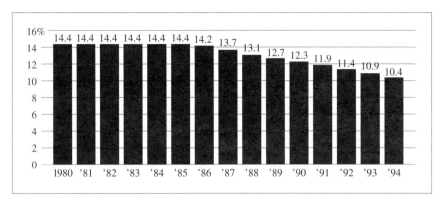

over 10,400 commercial banks to well under 5,000. With about 50 banks per million persons, compared with 8 banks per million in France and 6 per million in both Germany and Great Britain, the United States has an inefficient banking system with too many banks and too many underutilized branches. Given profitability pressures and low growth prospects, acquisitions should be an important source of earnings growth. Banks will need insightful acquisition and integration strategies besides just eliminating redundant capacity. It is hard enough to make a merger; it is more difficult to make it work. Bank management must focus on creating value for shareholders in each merger.

Bankers must also pay more attention to credit quality controls and the pricing of risk. The industry must learn to adopt the pricing and diversification of modern portfolio theory to the credit allocation and the discrimination process.[11] Banks must also pay more attention to training and developing their people at both the branch and future senior management levels. Gone are the days of the CEO whose most important talent was attracting borrowers and knowing a good credit risk. Far more than the industry traditionally required, bank CEOs now must respond to markets, innovate, and become organization experts, planners, strategists, human resource experts, and politicians, all the while creating value for shareholders. Management must be able to lead the transition of the organization through a changing environment.[12]

Costs must be managed, not merely cut. Distribution systems and relationship management must be redefined, improved, and perhaps even restructured. The business mix must also be better managed and controlled. Banks also need to synthesize their products and to deliver and maintain a perception of value to the customer, while concentrating on superior service. Bankers must be innovative and responsive to the markets, as well as being low-cost producers. Success may also depend on having the systems, technology, information flows, and infrastructure in place to capitalize on opportunities when they develop.[13]

ENDNOTES

1. M.E. Levonian, "Why Banking Isn't Declining?," *FRBSF Weekly Letter*, January 20, 1995, pp. 1, 3.
2. A. Gart, *Regulation, Deregulation, Reregulation: The Future of the Banking, Insurance, and Securities Industries* (New York: John Wiley & Son, 1994), pp. 21–22.
3. *Ibid.*, p. 232.
4. T.H. Hanley, P.J. Carter, and A.B. Collins, "Separating the Winners from the Losers in the Banking Industry," *CS First Boston,* February 14, 1995, pp. 4–5.
5. T.H. Hanley and P.J. Carter, "The Implications of Glass-Steagall Reform," *CS First Boston*, May 12, 1995, p. 2.
6. *Ibid.*
7. T.H. Hanley, P.J. Carter, and A.B. Collins, "The Competitive State of the U.S. Commercial Banking Industry," *CS First Boston*, March 24, 1995, pp. 5–6.
8. Hanley and Carter, "Implications of Glass-Steagall Reform," pp. 5–10.
9. A.G. Smith, "Bank Notes," *DLJ Credit Research*, January 20, 1995, p. 17.
10. Hanley and Carter, "Implications of Glass-Steagall Reform," pp. 1–2.
11. J.B. McCoy, L.A. Frieder, and R.B. Hedges, Jr., *BottomLine Banking* (Chicago: Probus Publishing, 1994), pp. 278–79.
12. *Ibid.*, pp. 339–40.
13. *Ibid.*, pp. 17–18.

CHAPTER 2

The Rise of the Superregionals

During the 1980s, we began to see the rise of powerful superregional banks. These are previously regional or large community banks (non–money center) that grew to achieve critical mass and economies of scale and scope, both by internal growth and through acquisitions, yet still emphasize their regional and local presence and flavor. They generally have community banking orientations, achieve general cost savings that are transparent to customers, and extend the product line throughout the branch system.[1] Typically, bank office systems are consolidated, including accounting, data processing, purchasing, payroll, financial management, treasury, strategic planning, and asset-liability management. Although the benefits of these consolidations are often not apparent to the public, these efforts at controlling overhead costs are the key to successful mergers. Local staffing usually remains stable, loan authorization remains at the local level, and the local bank president is typically maintained after the merger. Superregional banks are emerging as winners in the evolving financial services industry, as they utilize the community bank attitude and delivery systems, but also provide a breadth of product line and sophistication of service that is not available at most small, independent community banks.

A superregional bank couples the strong community orientation of a regional bank with the superior breadth of service of a large bank. "It is not too big to be small and not too small to be big. Its aim is to outlocal the nationals and outnational the locals."[2] A superregional takes advantage of size to offer in-house services that a small bank is incapable of offering because of cost, lack of expertise, or lack of a sufficient customer base.

Money center banks, on the other hand, often do not have the local presence to build relationships with many middle-market companies and individual

21

customers. Also, small and midsize companies often do not bring large business transactions to the bank, and some money center banks find that the cost-benefit relationships do not always justify the effort.

Community-oriented superregional banks can effectively serve select segments of the market that may be shunned by money center banks or small community banks. For example, although some midsize corporations play a key role in their local community, they may need foreign exchange transactions, advice services, risk management, or merger and acquisition assistance unavailable from a small community bank. A consumer-oriented superregional bank can provide the hand-holding appreciated by wealthy individuals and offer a more sophisticated package of products and services than a local community bank.[3]

As these large regionals become even bigger, they can take advantage of economies of scale, commoditized services, and low-cost production, as opposed to the personalized, customized approach of the traditional community bank. The product line and services offered tend to become more sophisticated, many of which require technological infrastructure and highly skilled and expensive talent.

Not all superregionals have maintained an emphasis on community-oriented retail banking or have retained the executive managements of acquired banks following mergers. Megamergers that emphasize local markets often create vacuums in customer service and displacement of customer relationships. On the other hand, community-oriented superregionals are positioned to capture those relationships by offering the level of service that customers crave without sacrificing the product breadth they seek. At the same time, they are under pressure to become more productive by slashing noninterest expenses to compete more effectively. Megamergers attempt to leverage both cost and product line to fulfill optimal opportunities. Following a few megamergers, some superregional banks are as large as or larger than some money center banks.

FAILURES SPURRED BANK CONSOLIDATION

The commercial banking industry has made a remarkable comeback over the last few years. After having the number of bank failures average over 100 per year from 1982 through 1993, from an average of less than 10 per annum in the 1946 to 1980 period, the industry had only 13 failures in 1994. Balance sheets at U.S. banks have been strengthened significantly as measured by asset quality, liquidity, and equity capital positions. Equity capital ratios are at the highest levels in three decades, and the book value at most banks is understated because of excessive loan loss reserve levels. Although liquidity ratios are likely to deteriorate during the mid-1990s as loan demand increases with a recovering economy and merger activity picks up, thus slightly increasing the risk profile of banks, profitability should continue to increase. Such increased profitability would lift the average ROA of superregionals from a healthy 1.23 percent and 1.25 percent in 1993 and 1994, respectively, to even healthier levels by 1996. ROEs are also expected to improve over that period from 16.05 percent and 16.80 percent in 1993 and 1994, respectively. These profitability increases are unlikely to be accompanied by an increase in the tangible common equity ratio of 7.07 percent in 1993 and 6.61 percent in 1994 as banks appear to be increasing dividends, repurchasing shares, and reducing loan loss provisions to levels below net charge-offs.

The consolidation process should accelerate, eliminating some overcapacity from the banking industry, as the barriers to interstate banking are removed. The inadequate capital of many of the money center banks during the late 1980s and early 1990s, which was brought about by huge loan losses to less developed countries (LDCs), highly leveraged borrowers, and commercial real estate investors, removed some of the weakened money center banks temporarily from the universe of acquiring banks. Also, many state laws excluded banks in New York from branching or acquiring banks in their state, which also kept money center bank acquisitions to a minimum. Of course, the merger of two weakened money center giants, Chemical Bank and Manufacturers Hanover, was an unusual case of enormous in-market, cost-cutting opportunities with the closing of duplicate branch locations and the layoff of about 10,000 employees.

However, many of the well-capitalized regional banks, with limited LDC exposure and heavily leveraged loans on the books, were able to take advantage of the weakened status of many community and regional banks, the Garn-St. Germain Act (permitting both in-state and out-of-state acquisitions of failing banks and thrifts), and interstate regional compacts to accelerate their acquisition programs. Many of the early acquisitions of troubled banks were made with considerable FDIC assistance and with little dilution of earnings per share. With most of the money center banks temporarily out of the acquisition game, superregional banks developed at a rapid pace (see Table 2–1).

IMPACT OF INTERSTATE BANKING ON SUPERREGIONALS

Beginning with the McFadden Act in 1927, there have been restrictions against both intrastate and interstate banking, as well as interstate acquisitions. In the early 1980s, bank holding companies (BHCs) were permitted to move across state lines to acquire financially troubled banks and thrifts following the passage of the Garn-St. Germain Act in 1982. The change in policy was implemented to increase the pool of bidders for failing financial institutions. This would reduce losses to the deposit insurance system. However, some states took major steps to tear down the geographic barriers to banking, while a few states allowed interstate branching on a reciprocal basis. These changes in interstate banking and branching regulations acted as a catalyst in the formation of many of the superregionals.

T A B L E   2–1

Total Assets of Banks (in billions)

Bank Holding Company	December 31 1984	December 31 1990	December 31 1993	December 31 1994	Average Annual Growth Rate (1980–94)
Superregionals					
Banc One	$ 9.1	$ 30.3	$ 79.9	$ 88.9	25.5%
BancAmerica	117.7	110.7	186.9	215.4	6.2
Bank of Boston	22.1	32.5	40.6	44.6	7.3
Bank of New York	15.2	45.4	45.5	48.9	12.4
Barnett Banks	12.5	37.9	38.3	41.3	12.7
CoreStates Financial	9.8	23.5	23.7	29.3	11.5
First Fidelity	10.7	29.1	33.7	33.9	12.2
First Interstate*	45.5	51.4	51.5	55.8	2.1
First Union**	4.3	52.1	70.8	77.3	33.4
Fleet Financial†	5.7	32.5	47.9	48.7	23.9
KeyCorp	5.8	49.9	59.6	66.8	27.6
Mellon	30.6	28.7	36.1	38.6	2.4
NationsBank	15.7	112.8	157.7	169.6	26.9
NBD Bancorp††	14.2	26.7	40.8	47.1	12.7
Norwest	21.3	36.9	50.8	59.3	10.7
PNC Bank	14.9	45.5	62.1	64.1	15.7
SunTrust Banks	9.4	33.4	40.7	42.7	16.3
Wachovia	8.7	33.3	36.5	39.2	16.2
Wells Fargo	28.1	56.2	52.5	53.4	6.6
Money centers					
Bankers Trust	45.2	63.6	92.1	97.0	7.9
Chase Manhattan‡	86.9	98.1	102.1	114.0	2.8
Chemical Banking‡	52.2	136.2	149.9	171.4	12.2
Citicorp	150.6	217.0	217.0	250.5	5.2
First Chicago††	39.8	50.8	52.6	65.9	5.1
JP Morgan	64.1	93.1	133.8	154.9	9.2

* First Interstate is likely to be acquired by either First Bank Systems or Wells Fargo in 1996.

** First Union agreed to acquire First Fidelity in 1995 with assets of about $35.4 billion at the time of the announcement.

† Fleet Financial agreed to acquire Shawmut National in 1995 with assets of close to $36 billion at the time of the merger.

†† First Chicago and NBD agreed to merge in 1995.

‡ Chemical Banking and Chase Manhattan agreed to merge in 1995 to form the largest bank holding company in the United States.

Source: Various company reports.

Various laws have forced BHCs that acquired multistate networks to maintain separate boards, administrative staffs, and sometimes even computer systems in each bank. An interstate banking bill was finally passed in 1994 that contained provisions effective in 1997 allowing owned banks to be merged into one. Consequently, BHCs would no longer have to incur the high costs of maintaining a separate banking infrastructure for each of their interstate affiliates, affording greater ease in making acquisitions. Although savings will vary among banks, those involved should be able to reduce annual noninterest expenses from between 5 to 20 percent. Aggregate savings for the banking industry should be at least $2 billion and possibly even $5 billion over the next five years. In addition, this legislation is likely to increase merger activity within the banking industry, resulting in a reduction in bank overcapacity. According to Christopher Flowers, a Goldman Sachs expert on bank mergers, the abundant capital position of many bank holding companies should spur merger activity, leading to more cash mergers.[4] Those banks wishing to establish national banking franchises such as BankAmerica, NationsBank, Banc One, KeyCorp, and First Union will have the opportunity to do so. As a matter of fact, interstate banking among the southern states became a reality when the southern regional compact allowed the entry of all banks in the takeover derby. Another catalyst was the passage of the aforementioned Interstate Banking Act. These factors should lead to an acceleration in the pace of bank acquisitions in the southeastern states.

Although most superregionals are likely to concentrate on in-market or adjacent-region acquisitions, there will probably be a few mergers of equals in more diverse geographic areas. Money center banks such as Chase or Citicorp are likely to bid for one of the large superregionals as soon as they can achieve higher capital levels and price-to-earnings ratios for their stock. If KeyCorp can demonstrate increased revenue generation of new products gained from its out-of-market merger with Society and a modest shrinkage of noninterest costs, we will see an increase in this type of consolidation activity. In the meantime, it is important that banks do not dilute earnings per share by overpaying for another bank franchise in their zealousness to outbid a rival in their acquisition programs. Growth for the sake of growth is the wrong approach—growth must be consistent with the strategic position, fundamental strengths, and culture of the bank.[5]

Cost reduction is a critical element of successful acquisition efforts. An example of a bank that has achieved excellent efficiency ratios by carefully closing redundant branches and eliminating excess personnel is First Fidelity. However, it has found additional cost savings in outsourcing technological development to experienced outside vendors rather than working through the consolidation and rationalization of the numerous disparate systems resulting from its previous acquisitions.

The evidence to date suggests that those banks that overpay for acquisitions and do not improve their efficiency ratios or increase revenues as a direct result of the merger reduce shareholder value. Some of the acquiring banks that failed to become more efficient and productive (e.g., C&S/Sovran) were themselves later acquired. Also, the era of consolidation activity has been accompanied by de novo bank activity: displaced bankers were anxious to participate in the opening of new banks in communities that had seen their independent banks sell out. Sometimes de novo banks were chartered with the eventual goal of a later sale at a healthy premium to an acquisition-minded financial institution.[6]

The usual concern about allowing interstate banking is that out-of-state controlled institutions will not provide the same level of service as "hometown" banks. At the extreme is the concern that out-of-state organizations will seek to raid local deposit markets and use the funds for lending in their home states. The empirical evidence suggests that interstate banking does not systematically reduce lending in the affected states, although there is some evidence that there is an increase in lending by banks in those states that allow higher interest rates. Interstate banking does appear to affect bank credit through its effect on risk. For example, an interstate banking acquisition can provide greater geographic and industry diversification and, consequently, less concentration of risk compared with the same banks operating separately. As a matter of fact, the spread of interstate banking has the potential to improve the allocation of credit and increase overall lending.[7]

Geographic diversification of the loan portfolio would be another advantage of interstate banking. Edward Crutchfield, Jr., chairman of First Union, believes that "if we had a national banking system 10 years ago, we would not have had a Texas bank crisis or a New England crisis . . . because geographically diverse banks could have absorbed the losses themselves." In addition, Crutchfield believes that 8 to 10 institutions will account for 50 to 80 percent of the nation's banking business before the beginning of the twenty-first century, up from less than 25 percent in 1994.[8]

Consumers, especially travelers and those who commute across state lines to work, should also benefit from nationwide banking because of greater convenience, ease of cashing checks, and lower prices from more efficient organizations. Bigger banks can raise money more cheaply, service credit cards and mortgages more efficiently, reduce administrative overhead, and undertake more effective marketing. Essentially, according to Goldman Sachs analyst Robert B. Albertson, there have been artificial impediments to interstate banking in the form of antiquated regulations that have imposed enormous costs on the industry, the consumer, and the economy as a whole: "It's like saying we shouldn't have supermarkets."[9]

SALIENT FINANCIAL RATIOS

A number of key financial ratios that consider issues of profitability, productivity, credit quality, capital adequacy and generation, dividend payout, and the generation of fee-based (noninterest) income aid in the understanding of banks. The ratios that we utilized to measure performance and make comparisons include profitability ratios (ROA and ROE), efficiency or overhead ratio, nonperforming assets to total asset ratio, net charge-off ratio, internal capital generation rate, tangible common equity ratio, dividend payout ratio, and noninterest income divided by total revenue.

Profitability Ratios

Return on Average (ROA) (net income/average total assets) reflects the profitability of a company's underlying business mix, as well as the effective deployment of assets. Historically, most banks have an ROA that falls within a range of 0.60 to 1.50 percent, reflecting wide margins on loans and other interest-earning assets and loss provisions attributable to improved asset quality. Regional and community banks, with a lower cost of funds and a higher-yielding loan mix, have higher net interest margins and tend to have ROAs in the upper part of the range.[10]

For 1993 and 1994, the average ROAs for superregional banks were 1.23 and 1.25 percent, respectively. An ROA of greater than 1.50 percent used to be considered stratospheric in the banking industry. This is no longer the case as a few banks achieved this lofty level of profitability in either 1993 or 1994, while a half dozen banks achieved a 1.40 percent return. Historically, between 1975 and 1985, ROAs averaged between 0.64 percent and 0.80 percent, while ROAs were more volatile between 1986 and 1993, running between 0.09 percent and 1.21 percent. This ratio tends to favor banks with strong levels of fee income and with high-yielding consumer, LBO, and commercial real estate loans during periods of strong economic growth; it hurts banks with high-quality, low-margin loans and securities. However, during periods of recession there is a much larger increase in nonperforming loans among riskier, higher-expected-yielding assets than among those banks that hold a high percentage of their assets in securities and less risky loans. Net interest margin, overhead costs, loan levels, credit risk, and interest rate risk all affect ROA and ROE.

Table 2–2 provides a glimpse at ROAs and ROEs for different sized banks over the last few years, whereas Table 2–3 shows profitability ratios for the 19 banks in our superregional universe. Only First Fidelity and Wachovia produced ROAs well above both industry and superregional bank averages during each of the last three years.

ROE (net income/total equity of a bank) can be calculated by multiplying the ROA times the leverage multiplier (assets divided by equity). It is often used as a benchmark, reflecting the positive working of financial leverage in using debt (i.e., stockholders' equity) to enhance revenue generation. ROE can vary widely from year to year, depending on such nonrecurring events as the setting aside of massive reserves for nonperforming loans, the selling or purchase of particular businesses or facilities, or major restructuring of operations and processes.

Since equity normally accounts for only a small fraction (5–10 percent) of a bank's assets, ROE is much larger than ROA, and ranges usually from 10 to 22

TABLE 2-2

Profits of Insured Commercial Banks by Asset Size, 1985–1994 (%)

Type of Return/Bank Size	1985	1986	1987	1988	1989	1990	1991	1992	1993	1994
ROA										
All banks	.69	.62	.09	.80	.48	.47	.53	.91	1.21	1.15
< $300 million	.85	.74	.64	.67	.74	.51	.61	.92	1.21	1.29
$6.5–$40 billion	.74	.72	(.09)	.81	.49	.24	.51	1.04	1.26	1.22
Ten largest	.46	.46	(.90)	1.07	(.19)	.48	.22	.61	1.13	.91
ROE										
All banks	11.2	9.9	1.4	13.0	7.6	7.4	7.9	12.6	15.5	14.6
< $300 million	13.0	11.1	9.5	10.0	10.9	7.4	8.6	12.2	14.9	15.4
$6.5–$40 billion	13.5	12.7	(1.7)	15.5	8.8	4.3	8.3	15.2	16.9	16.2
Ten largest	9.6	9.5	(18.1)	23.3	(3.9)	10.1	4.4	10.9	16.8	13.9

Source: Various Federal Reserve Bulletins.

28

T A B L E   2-3

Superregional Bank ROEs and ROAs

Bank	Net Income/Total Equity			Net Income/Average Total Assets		
	1992	1993	1994	1992	1993	1994
Banc One	14.87	17.19	13.14	1.20	1.50	1.15
BankAmerica	11.84	12.48	13.24	0.90	1.06	1.09
Bank of New York	11.54	14.98	18.49	0.85	1.20	1.49
Bank of Boston	12.53	12.44	16.53	0.76	0.78	1.01
Barnett Banks	8.27	16.02	16.70	0.55	1.13	1.28
CoreStates Financial	*11.21*	16.49	10.96	*0.81*	1.31	0.90
First Fidelity	*15.18*	16.94	16.71	1.06	1.27	1.34
First Interstate	9.55	20.76	21.35	0.58	1.43	1.31
First Union	9.14	17.42	17.04	0.63	1.20	1.27
Fleet Financial	9.67	16.07	18.77	0.62	1.06	1.27
KeyCorp	15.91	16.95	18.56	1.13	1.24	1.36
Mellon Bank	18.39	9.79	12.08	1.46	1.29	1.14
NationsBank	15.42	15.00	16.10	1.00	1.12	1.02
NBD Bancorp	10.44	15.46	16.49	0.76	1.20	1.23
Norwest	11.95	18.20	21.40	0.85	1.20	1.45
PNC Bank	12.43	18.40	14.10	0.95	1.44	1.00
SunTrust	14.99	16.48	17.66	1.14	1.22	1.31
Wachovia	16.69	17.13	17.41	1.36	1.46	1.46
Wells Fargo	8.70	16.74	22.41	0.54	1.20	1.62
Total/Average	12.56	16.05	16.80	0.90	1.23	1.25

Note: Items in italics are not comparable to current date because of restatements.

percent. Banks with ROEs in excess of 18 percent were in the top decile of bank profitability during 1993 and 1994. Historically, average ROEs for insured banks ranged from 10.52 percent and 13.90 percent between 1975 and 1985; average ROEs were extremely volatile between 1985 and 1993, ranging from 1.41 percent to 15.47 percent. Both ROAs and ROEs reached their highest levels in a decade during 1993–94, as good credit quality, increased loan demand, lower loan loss provisions, and wide interest margins led to good results at most banks. However, earnings suffered at some banks because interest margins declined, whereas other banks charged off losses in their investment portfolios as interest rates increased.

A popular measure of efficiency and noninterest expense control is the *overhead* or *efficiency ratio* (noninterest expense/interest and noninterest revenues).

Efficiency is likely to be one of the salient variables influencing the earnings prospects of the banking industry over the remainder of the decade. Aggressive cost-cutting and expense management will become a permanent secular change in the industry. Improved efficiency will ultimately replace the strong margins and credit-quality improvements that fueled earnings growth through 1994. More efficient back-office operations will provide the leverage to boost fee-based income and earnings performance through the remainder of the decade.

This ratio measures how efficiently a bank manages its earning capacity. Can it control noninterest costs? We have to recognize that there are spikes in noninterest expenses, which are related to significant investments in technology or acquisition and restructuring costs. The numerator measures personnel and occupancy expenses as well as other core costs. Banks with heavy off-balance-sheet activity often have high relative expense levels because it takes additional personnel to manage and operate this activity.

With fairly high technology costs and merger-related expenses in 1993 and 1994, banks maintained an intense focus on noninterest expenses. Overhead (efficiency) ratios at superregional banks were at an average 63.30 percent in 1993 and 62.27 percent in 1994 (see Table 2–4.) This ratio is expected to decline to about 57 percent by 1996–97, suggesting productivity improvements that will feature reengineering, benchmarking, outsourcing, and reliance on technological platforms.

Financial institutions such as Wachovia, Bank of New York, and Wells Fargo are among the most efficient of the superregional banks. Commercial banks that have made the investments in their support functions will be among the winners in extracting efficiencies, along with those institutions that can benefit from merger-related expense rationalization. In-market mergers allow for a reduction in noninterest expenses by between 30 and 50 percent of the acquired company's expense, while out-of-market mergers should generate savings of 5 to 15 percent, and adjacent-market mergers should generate 15 to 20 percent savings. Cost-cutting is being propelled by new interstate banking laws, increased competition, stalled revenue growth, and the losses suffered by some banks during 1994 that were related to the misjudgment of interest rates that affected the value of bonds and derivative securities. Banks will be able to consolidate interstate branch operations and eliminate many state-level back-office operations. According to Ashley G. Hilsman, a partner and banking law specialist at Marks and Murase, "the interstate banking legislation is intended to create efficiencies and those efficiencies are going to be accomplished by cutting staff." William Smart, president and CEO of First Interstate, estimated that employment in banking could decline by 10 percent, or nearly 150,000 people, before the end of the decade.[11]

The measurement of the adequacy of capital and the ability to generate capital are measured by the *tangible common equity ratio* and the *internal capital generation rate.*

T A B L E   2–4

Overhead Efficiency Ratios

Bank	1992	1993	1994
Banc One	62.91	63.00	68.59
BankAmerica	64.28	66.15	64.28
Bank of New York	58.00	58.45	54.76
Bank of Boston	72.82	70.76	61.62
Barnett Banks	73.75	70.50	64.89
CoreStates Financial	67.10	64.49	66.61
First Fidelity	58.01	58.41	58.74
First Interstate	75.03	69.41	64.60
First Union	70.27	67.37	65.40
Fleet Financial	69.17	68.30	64.79
KeyCorp	62.98	60.50	59.39
Mellon Bank	67.77	57.54	59.99
NationsBank	65.32	62.91	62.54
NBD Bancorp	63.12	61.70	60.10
Norwest	72.88	74.61	69.71
PNC Bank	55.76	52.40	64.77
SunTrust	61.80	59.66	58.93
Wachovia	57.96	59.18	56.86
Wells Fargo	54.15	57.70	56.60
Total/Average	64.90	63.32	62.27

Tangible common equity ratio equals tangible common equity/assets. This ratio is an indicator of how well capitalized a bank is and of an institution's strength and ability to withstand severe credit-quality problems that require huge write-offs. Regulators are now requiring a minimum 6 percent ratio before acquisitions are permitted. Consequently, this ratio also helps determine the likelihood of a bank participating in the consolidation process. In general, the higher the capital ratio, the more conservative the bank. High capital ratios can also indicate the ability of a bank to grow, either internally or through acquisitions.

Capital levels have been bolstered in the last few years because of new risk-based bank capital guidelines, increases in profitability that led to increased internal capital generation, and the raising of large amounts of both equity and debt in the capital markets. The average tangible common equity ratios for the superregionals were 5.16 percent, 5.56 percent, 6.05 percent, 7.07 percent, and 6.61 percent in 1990, 1991, 1992, 1993, and 1994, respectively. Wachovia (8.39 percent), Mellon (8.72 percent), and Banc One (7.73 percent) now have the highest ratios among the superregionals (see Table 2–5 and Figure 2–1).

With bank capital ratios at the highest levels in 30 years, the effective deployment of excess capital will be one of the key measures to separate the winners from the losers. Shareholders should benefit from increased dividend payments, stock buybacks, and cash acquisitions. The purchase of companies for cash should provide a way to buy smaller, fill-in banks with limited goodwill, to build assets and deposits, and to reduce overhead levels by consolidating operations concurrently.

The *internal capital generation rate* equals ROE × retention rate. This measures the rate at which a bank generates equity capital (retained earnings) and is computed by multiplying the return on equity (net income divided by equity) by the earnings retention rate (1 – dividend payout ratio). The retention rate is the proportion of earnings not paid out as dividends, while the dividend payout ratio is the

F I G U R E   2–1

Salomon Brothers Inc., Bank Composites—Tangible Common Equity Ratio, 1986–1994

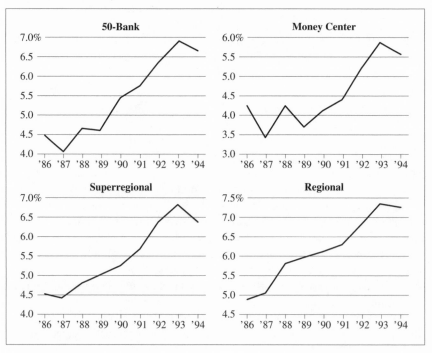

Source: Salomon Brothers Inc.

T A B L E 2-5
Miscellaneous Ratios

Bank	Tangible Common Equity Ratio			Internal Capital Generation Rate			Dividend Payout Ratio		
	1992	1993	1994	1992	1993	1994	1992	1993	1994
Banc One	7.52	7.96	7.73	10.80	10.91	6.41	38.90	36.52	51.24
BankAmerica	4.86	7.20	6.91	11.30	8.83	9.36	30.70	29.23	29.30
Bank of New York	6.59	6.99	7.40	7.90	10.27	13.02	36.30	31.43	29.59
Bank of Boston	5.31	6.00	5.52	12.80	10.20	12.34	2.20	18.02	25.34
Barnett Banks	5.45	6.65	6.31	3.70	10.39	11.00	66.70	35.16	34.12
CoreStates Financial	7.09	7.61	7.15	9.10	8.94	3.19	44.90	45.78	70.86
First Fidelity	5.85	6.53	5.68	9.40	11.71	10.95	31.60	30.90	34.44
First Interstate	4.77	6.52	5.28	5.30	17.05	14.61	37.20	17.86	31.57
First Union	5.57	6.42	6.07	6.70	5.75	3.90	57.40	66.96	77.13
Fleet Financial	4.74	6.92	6.28	5.50	10.60	11.76	46.30	34.05	37.33
KeyCorp	6.07	6.51	6.19	13.30	10.38	11.67	40.50	38.75	37.10
Mellon Bank	5.48	9.14	8.72	9.40	4.34	0.32	20.10	55.70	97.31
NationsBank	5.99	5.48	5.33	10.60	10.08	11.15	32.80	32.80	30.72
NBD Bancorp	6.53	7.37	6.50	4.90	9.91	10.44	54.50	35.90	36.70
Norwest	5.69	5.95	5.06	6.50	12.00	14.70	46.60	33.90	31.20
PNC Bank	7.11	6.97	6.82	8.80	11.50	6.90	45.80	37.50	51.20
SunTrust	6.97	8.40	7.57	12.20	11.40	12.30	29.90	30.60	30.10
Wachovia	8.22	8.26	8.39	10.60	10.40	10.60	39.80	39.50	39.40
Wells Fargo	5.09	7.38	6.60	4.80	13.00	16.40	33.80	22.30	27.60
Total/Average	6.05	7.07	6.61	8.61	10.40	10.05	38.74	35.41	42.22

proportion of net earnings after preferred dividends that is paid out as dividends to common shareholders. The internal generation rate varies widely. In 1991, the average internal generation rate for superregionals was 4.60 percent; it improved to 8.61 percent in 1992 and 10.40 percent in 1993 before slumping to 10.05 percent in 1994. For example, during 1994 Wells Fargo, Norwest, and First Interstate led the superregionals with internal generation rates of 16.40 percent, 14.70 percent, and 14.61 percent, respectively, whereas Mellon, First Union, Banc One, CoreStates, and PNC were at the low end of internal generation rates because of one-time charge-offs (see Table 2–5 and Figure 2–2).

The overcapitalized banks are expected to substantially increase their dividends, employ stock buyback programs, and utilize their excess capital for acquisitions to improve their ROE. The average dividend payout ratio for superregional banks was about 35 percent in 1993. The 42.22 percent dividend payout ratio in 1994 is distorted by special charge-offs at Banc One, CoreStates, First Union, Mellon, and

F I G U R E   2–2

Salomon Brothers Inc., Bank Composites—Internal Capital
Generation Rate, 1984–1994

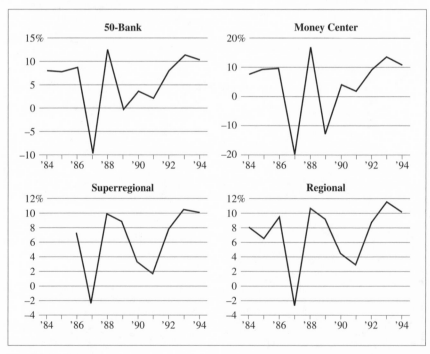

Source: Salomon Brothers Inc.

PNC, where dividends were not cut back when earnings suffered. There is a wide range in dividend payout ratios from a low of 27.60 percent for Wells Fargo to a 97.31 percent rate for Mellon. As expectations of earnings asset growth are lowered throughout the industry beyond 1995, commensurate with improved profitability and capital ratios, pressure will be placed on bank managements to raise dividend payout ratios (see Table 2–5 and Figure 2–3).

Asset quality is often measured by the *ratio of nonperforming assets to total assets*. This measures the dollar volume of assets past due or in arrears after 90 days delinquency divided by the total assets outstanding. Nonperforming assets include those in which income is no longer being accrued and for which repayment has been rescheduled. This indicator is a good signal of both asset quality and future losses. Although capital asset ratios and asset quality will improve steadily (as measured by a decline in the nonperforming asset ratio), the impact of these improvements will diminish over time. The level of nonperforming assets at superregional

F I G U R E   2–3

Salomon Brothers Inc., Bank Composites—Dividend Payout Ratio, 1984–1994

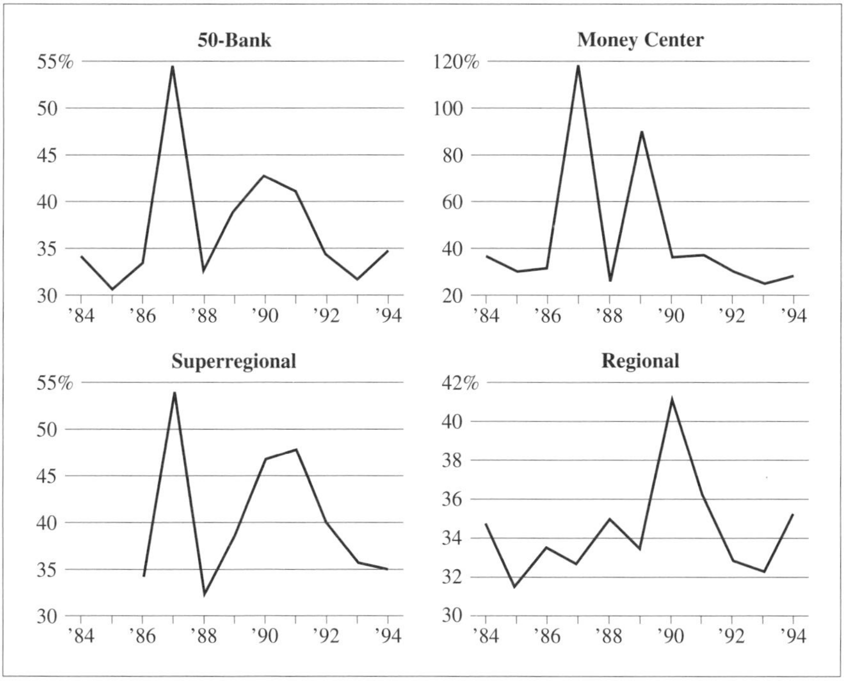

Source: Salomon Brothers Inc.

banks will diminish over time as the economy improves. The ratio of nonperforming assets to total assets normally ranges from 0.5 to 3.0 percent. When the
ratio exceeds 5 percent, which was the case at some banks between 1990 and 1992,
there is often a serious threat of bankruptcy. In addition to reducing the flow of
interest income, nonperforming assets represent potential charge-offs if their quality deteriorates further.

The ratio of nonperforming assets to total assets has declined from an average of above 4.0 percent in 1991 to 1.08 percent in 1993 and to 0.72 percent in 1994.
A percentage under 1 percent is excellent, from 1 to 3 percent is normal, and above
4 percent is an increasingly serious sign of trouble. Banks such as Norwest, NBD,
Wachovia, Mellon, First Interstate, and Key have low levels of nonperforming assets
and have high-quality loan portfolios (see Table 2–6 and Figure 2–4).

At many of the banks that sought merger partners or were forced to merge in
the early 1990s, this ratio had reached levels of close to 10 percent, a sign of unbelievably low asset quality and lack of appropriate credit controls. Bank of New
England, Security Pacific, and Valley National Corporation were among those with
such severe asset-quality problems. The consequences of the high levels of nonperforming loans for these banks was the failure of Bank of New England (Fleet
took over the franchise in a bidding war with First Boston and BankAmerica); the
serious wounding of Security Pacific (BankAmerica outbid rivals for Security
Pacific); and the weakening of Valley National (Banc One outbid rivals to acquire
Valley National).

Another important ratio is the dollar amount reserved for loan losses divided
by the nonperforming assets. A bank with a low ratio is likely to need an infusion

F I G U R E   2–4

50-Bank Nonperforming Asset Ratio, 1981–1994

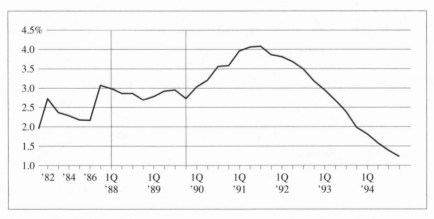

Source: Company reports and Salomon Brothers Inc.

T A B L E 2-6
Credit Quality Ratios

Bank	Nonperforming Assets/Loans + OREO			Net Charge-Off			Loan Loss Reserves/ Nonperforming Assets			Nonperforming Assets/ Total Assets		
	1992	1993	1994	1992	1993	1994	1992	1993	1994	1992	1993	1994
Banc One	1.78	1.15	0.76	1.25	0.73	0.53	106.10	197.40	235.30	1.12	0.79	0.53
BankAmerica	4.80	2.27	1.47	1.13	0.89	0.37	64.70	121.57	177.45	3.36	1.54	0.97
Bank of New York	3.33	1.20	1.10	1.68	N.A.	N.A.	101.50	206.90	224.40	2.34	0.88	0.72
Bank of Boston	5.28	1.61	1.40	1.22	0.54	0.40	68.40	163.80	154.20	3.62	1.23	1.02
Barnett Banks	3.19	1.76	1.02	1.00	0.55	0.34	64.90	171.00	250.00	2.14	1.20	0.70
CoreStates Financial	2.49	2.20	1.51	0.85	0.60	1.13	83.40	148.72	203.33	1.63	1.54	1.06
First Fidelity	3.75	2.30	1.38	1.42	1.23	0.55	87.70	159.00	253.00	2.21	1.47	0.91
First Interstate	3.08	1.28	0.90	1.79	0.60	0.46	142.20	323.95	362.02	1.48	0.60	0.46
First Union	4.26	1.95	1.03	0.86	0.51	0.40	52.20	111.00	175.00	2.82	1.27	0.74
Fleet Financial	3.68	2.27	1.88	2.05	1.10	0.38	104.00	166.39	183.98	2.11	1.25	1.06
KeyCorp	2.48	1.24	0.73	1.02	0.45	0.19	86.70	238.68	324.27	1.64	0.84	0.51
Mellon Bank	2.94	1.39	0.89	1.52	0.64	0.27	85.00	297.00	402.00	1.89	0.55	0.39
NationsBank	2.73	1.92	1.10	1.27	0.51	0.33	72.80	193.00	273.00	1.69	1.13	0.67
NBD Bancorp	1.63	1.05	0.64	0.81	0.31	0.12	101.80	157.28	238.64	1.00	0.45	0.44
Norwest	1.34	0.87	0.49	1.00	0.67	0.64	228.50	316.30	494.10	0.70	0.46	0.27
PNC Bank	3.15	1.65	1.25	1.15	0.66	0.29	109.30	253.12	314.17	1.60	0.89	0.69
SunTrust	2.28	1.62	0.96	0.66	0.46	0.23	87.10	214.39	344.91	1.43	1.01	0.64
Wachovia	1.25	0.67	0.39	0.48	0.41	0.29	143.00	372.00	516.00	0.80	0.46	0.27
Wells Fargo	7.19	3.59	1.59	1.98	1.44	0.70	76.80	176.83	357.90	5.13	2.98	1.63
Total/Average	3.19	1.68	1.08	1.22	0.65	0.40	98.22	209.91	288.61	2.04	1.08	0.72

37

of reserves at the next down cycle, which would penalize earnings. A bank with a high ratio has taken reduced earnings in anticipation of future need. Such a bank may be conservatively managed with a better opportunity to maintain higher earnings in the next down cycle (see Table 2–6 and Figure 2–5).

Another measure of asset quality can be found in the *net charge-off ratio*. Net charge-offs represent complete and unrecoverable loan losses or assets written down, which are essentially purged from the balance sheet. Banks that can keep their credit quality under control during a period of high loan growth will be rewarded normally with relatively higher earnings growth. The charge-off ratio measures the net charge-offs as a percentage of the average loans outstanding. The ratio attempts to measure asset quality and provides insights into how well the credit process has been managed. Charge-offs usually rise during a recession and decline only after an economic recovery is well under way. Prior to the industry's bout with problem LDC and commercial real estate loans, the ratio of net charge-offs to average loans ranged from 0.25 to 0.75 percent. The average net charge-off ratio in 1994 for our superregional universe of banks was 0.40 percent, while the ratio was 0.65 percent in 1993, 1.22 percent in 1992, and 1.38 percent in 1991. The lower the ratio, the better the asset quality at the bank; banks with higher ratios have more troubled loan portfolios (see Table 2–6 and Figure 2–6). Banks such as KeyCorp, NBD, SunTrust, and Wachovia have loan portfolios of pristine credit quality.

Noninterest income/total revenue represents the proportion of total income that is dependent on fees and noninterest income, that is, revenues that are not generated from interest payments earned from loans and investments. Examples of

F I G U R E   2–5

Bank Reserves to Nonperforming Assets, 1984–1994

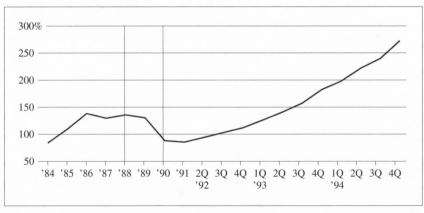

Source: Company reports, SNL Securities, and Salomon Brothers Inc. estimates.

F I G U R E   2-6

Salomon Brothers Inc., Bank Composites—Net Charge-Off Ratio, 1984–1994

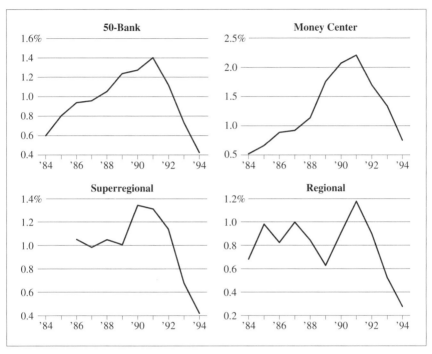

Source: Salomon Brothers Inc.

sources of fee income are safety deposit box rentals, deposit and checking account fees, trading account activity, mutual fund and annuity sales, mortgage banking fees, credit card fees, bounced check fees, lockbox fees, trust department fees, and investment banking activities. A more diverse and fee-oriented earnings stream enables a bank to generate a higher ROA than competitors because fee income is increased without a commensurate increase in assets. Fee income generation also makes a bank less sensitive to interest rate margins and movements.

The proportion of noninterest income to total income constituted close to 35 percent of net revenue income to total income at most banks in 1994 compared to about 19 percent in the 1960–80 period. In general, large banks have a greater proportion of fee income than do smaller banks, reflecting large banks' involvement in corporate finance, mortgage banking, investment banking, derivative securities, and other financial activities. We expect to see continued bank purchases of fee-generating businesses. Regional banks will continue to capitalize on their branch platform bases by offering fee-based products.

Superregionals and niche banks such as Mellon, Norwest, National City Corp., Bank of New York, Fleet, First Chicago NBD, and Northern Trust generate at least one-third of their revenues from fees (noninterest income), while banks (not in this study) such as State Street, Bankers Trust, JP Morgan, and Citicorp generate over 50 percent of their revenues from noninterest income. Trust income, asset management, mortgage banking, investment banking, mutual fund sales, and processing are key areas for generating fee income (see Tables 2–7, 2–8, and 2–9 and Figure 2–7).

Banks have muscled their way into the mutual fund industry through acquisitions and by establishing their own proprietary funds. Banks accounted for about

T A B L E 2–7

Noninterest Income/Total Revenue

| Bank | Fee Income/Total Revenue | | |
	1992	1993	1994
Banc One	25.50	26.63	25.32
BankAmerica	30.80	37.50	34.31
Bank of New York	39.10	46.84	42.88
Bank of Boston	28.00	35.66	34.49
Barnett Banks	24.90	28.14	25.83
CoreStates Financial	32.40	29.81	28.69
First Fidelity	24.90	22.08	22.90
First Interstate	28.70	32.59	30.99
First Union	27.50	32.01	28.32
Fleet Financial	30.90	41.28	36.71
KeyCorp	29.20	27.21	24.68
Mellon Bank	34.40	45.22	41.60
NationsBank	29.20	30.79	32.87
NBD Bancorp	27.20	27.30	25.20
Norwest	33.20	38.80	36.90
PNC Bank	29.70	34.10	30.10
SunTrust	32.00	33.40	30.80
Wachovia	34.30	31.90	31.50
Wells Fargo	32.80	29.20	31.50
Total/Average	30.25	33.18	31.35

T A B L E   2-8

Trust Income and Percentage of Total Revenues, 1990–1994 (in millions)

	1990 Trust Income	1990 Pct. of Tot. Rev.	1991 Trust Income	1991 Pct. of Tot. Rev.	1992 Trust Income	1992 Pct. of Tot. Rev.	1993 Trust Income	1993 Pct. of Tot. Rev.	1994 Trust Income	1994 Pct. of Tot. Rev.
Bank of New York	$ 357	15.07%	$ 110	4.38%	$ 113	4.51%	$ 131	4.57%	$ 126	4.13%
Bankers Trust NY	468	14.74	567	17.23	648	18.36	703	14.77	740	19.85
Chase Manhattan	401	7.45	375	6.69	407	6.76	465	6.80	567	8.38
Chemical Banking	345	5.36	344	4.92	361	4.72	406	4.68	421	5.08
Citicorp	513	3.50	551	3.73	666	4.26	785	4.88	462	2.75
First Chicago	168	6.84	175	7.46	190	7.02	201	5.79	199	6.17
JP Morgan	285	8.41	321	7.67	377	7.82	464	7.24	753	13.37
Republic NY	5	0.60	5	0.55	6	0.58	8	0.64	8	0.64
Money center composite	**$2,541**	**7.75%**	**$2,448**	**6.58%**	**$2,773**	**6.75%**	**$3,162**	**6.17%**	**$3,277**	**7.54%**
Banc One	171	5.04	185	4.38	205	3.85	225	3.81	226	3.96
Bank of Boston	152	7.51	157	8.29	166	8.20	178	8.46	202	8.38
BankAmerica	70	1.12	68	0.99	222	2.14	294	2.51	285	2.43
Boatmen's	107	10.87	121	10.68	138	10.15	150	9.95	156	9.87
Comerica	100	7.55	105	7.10	114	7.25	122	7.52	122	7.08
CoreStates Financial	N.A.	0.00	97	5.05	97	5.11	102	5.29	98	4.94
First Bank System	108	8.25	116	8.03	128	8.23	146	8.49	159	8.66
First Fidelity	83	5.82	84	5.60	86	5.47	105	5.90	106	5.73
First Interstate	159	4.47	173	5.23	170	5.79	177	5.83	193	5.68
First Union	105	4.08	133	4.30	177	4.89	202	4.97	225	5.24

Continued on next page

Table 2-8—Concluded

	1990		1991		1992		1993		1994	
	Trust Income	Pct. of Tot. Rev.	Trust Income	Pct. of Tot. Rev.	Trust Income	Pct. of Tot. Rev.	Trust Income	Pct. of Tot. Rev.	Trust Income	Pct. of Tot. Rev.
Fleet Financial	$ 77	3.84%	$ 119	4.71%	$ 160	4.78%	$ 174	4.90%	$ 175	5.47%
KeyCorp	217	8.06	236	7.69	251	7.28	245	6.53	220	6.05
Mellon Bank	239	13.88	270	14.60	584	23.49	853	28.59	953	30.08
National City Corp.	105	6.03	111	5.98	118	6.08	123	5.99	126	5.90
NationsBank	318	5.84	326	5.31	331	5.21	371	5.37	435	5.51
NBD Bancorp	118	6.75	130	6.84	140	6.60	150	6.75	157	7.04
Norwest	121	4.99	138	4.82	169	4.82	187	4.54	210	4.70
PNC Bank	217	10.31	238	10.31	260	10.06	274	9.73	292	10.56
SunTrust	178	9.11	200	9.62	226	9.80	247	10.46	250	10.54
Wachovia	100	6.08	103	5.82	110	5.79	120	5.97	128	6.30
Wells Fargo	143	4.39	138	4.02	165	4.39	190	5.07	203	5.33
Superregional composite	**$2,886**	**6.38%**	**$3,247**	**6.64%**	**$4,017**	**7.11%**	**$4,633**	**7.46%**	**$4,920**	**7.59%**
AmSouth	36	8.20	38	7.18	40	6.43	42	5.76	46	6.06
Bancorp Hawaii	25	5.64	27	5.17	31	5.47	41	6.75	49	8.38
Bank South	8	2.85	10	3.40	10	3.45	10	2.90	10	2.66
Barnett Banks	58	2.99	66	3.11	73	3.09	82	3.58	77	3.48
Crestar Financial	45	7.42	48	7.14	51	7.12	57	7.29	56	6.57
Fifth Third Bancorp	36	7.50	42	7.42	49	7.55	53	7.37	55	6.93
First American	13	3.65	13	4.27	15	4.43	15	4.27	16	4.37
First of America	51	5.51	61	6.15	69	5.93	77	6.35	82	6.59
First Security	15	3.48	17	3.57	18	3.43	19	3.28	21	3.08

First Tennessee National	18	4.13	21	4.25	24	4.11	27	3.76	29	3.74
Huntington Bancshares	24	3.54	24	3.21	25	2.61	28	2.51	28	2.84
Marshall & Ilsley	49	7.52	54	7.42	58	7.09	61	7.08	60	6.93
Mercantile Bancorp	47	9.85	49	9.20	58	8.85	61	8.61	60	8.45
Midlantic	53	4.70	56	6.37	47	5.77	41	5.91	43	5.42
Northern Trust	271	41.22	303	41.48	368	43.18	405	44.20	453	45.28
Old Kent Financial	36	8.49	35	7.64	38	7.37	40	7.18	42	7.07
Signet Banking	15	2.24	16	2.10	16	2.19	18	1.93	19	1.78
State Street Boston	381	47.99	442	48.50	545	54.60	628	53.60	717	52.29
U.S. Bancorp	38	3.62	40	3.37	46	3.41	49	3.26	51	3.52
West One Bancorp	10	4.03	11	3.86	12	3.53	14	3.21	14	2.98
Wilmington Trust	69	27.04	73	26.65	77	26.77	78	26.12	83	26.80
Regional composite	**$1,298**	**10.08%**	**$1,447**	**10.07%**	**$1,670**	**10.30%**	**$1,847**	**10.23%**	**$2,011**	**10.25%**
50-bank composite	**$6,725**	**8.15%**	**$7,141**	**8.07%**	**$8,460**	**8.40%**	**$9,643**	**8.42%**	**$10,209**	**8.70%**

TABLE 2-9

Banks and Thrift Companies That Manage Mutual Fund Assets (dollar amounts in millions)

Rank 6/95		Total Fund Assets			Fund Assets as of 6/30/95 by Type				Number of Portfolios as of 6/30/95 by Type				
		6/30/95	3/31/95	6/30/94	Money Market	Fixed Income	Muni	Equity	Total Number of Portfolios	Money Market	Fixed Income	Muni	Equity
1	Mellon Bank Corp., Pittsburgh, PA	$71,765.1	$68,032.2	$69,204.6	$40,385.0	$4,139.7	$16,416.0	$10,824.4	213	58	27	78	50
2	PNC Bank Corp., Pittsburgh, PA	23,981.0	22,414.4	21,522.7	20,000.2	1,006.4	347.3	2,627.1	120	56	19	14	31
3	NationsBank Corp., Charlotte, NC	14,907.5	14,688.8	14,132.3	8,633.3	1,782.9	983.1	3,508.2	143	15	28	74	26
4	BankAmerica Corp., San Francisco, CA	11,035.6	9,396.8	10,281.7	9,970.3	173.7	198.1	693.5	34	22	4	2	6
5	Wells Fargo & Co., San Francisco, CA	10,907.9	10,587.9	8,350.3	5,943.2	1,222.7	699.6	3,042.4	45	7	11	5	22
6	Banc One Corp., Columbus, OH	10,090.5	9,508.4	8,370.6	5,032.7	1,550.5	931.7	2,575.6	63	10	15	11	27
7	Northern Trust Corp., Chicago, IL	9,840.3	9,196.0	8,277.8	7,255.6	790.4	342.5	1,451.8	35	9	10	2	14
8	First Union Corp., Charlotte, NC	9,184.3	8,420.1	7,436.8	3,188.2	696.0	524.7	4,775.4	113	12	13	26	62
9	Norwest Corp., Minneapolis, MN	8,332.9	7,518.7	4,476.6	4,567.0	691.3	209.9	2,864.7	56	7	15	12	22
10	Chase Manhattan Corp., New York, NY	7,844.2	6,979.4	5,601.8	4,534.1	201.6	248.2	2,860.3	46	19	6	5	16
11	JP Morgan & Co., Inc., New York, NY	6,860.7	6,442.5	5,360.9	4,047.4	554.0	462.9	1,796.4	24	6	4	4	10
12	State Street Boston Corp., Boston, MA	6,548.0	6,416.8	5,932.8	4,410.0	1,347.8	6.0	784.2	13	5	2	1	5
13	NBD Bancorp Inc., Detroit, MI	6,395.3	6,065.9	5,611.6	3,094.1	992.2	116.2	2,192.8	29	5	6	4	14
14	Chemical Banking Corp., New York, NY	6,148.5	5,766.2	4,522.5	5,702.0	182.6		263.9	26	7	6	0	13
15	SunTrust Banks Inc., Atlanta, GA	5,960.5	5,657.9	4,874.0	1,711.9	709.3	158.6	3,380.7	39	6	9	8	16
16	First Bank System Inc., Minneapolis, MN	5,956.4	5,066.4	3,127.7	3,853.1	577.7	164.5	1,361.1	60	8	11	8	33
17	Fleet Financial Group Inc., Providence, RI	5,743.3	5,218.0	4,810.3	3,177.9	603.5	254.8	1,707.1	41	9	7	10	15
18	KeyCorp, Cleveland, OH	5,657.0	4,869.0	4,357.9	3,329.6	678.7	85.5	1,563.2	28	7	6	3	12
19	First of America Bank Corp., Kalamazoo, MI	5,089.9	4,800.0	4,538.1	1,586.8	1,137.3	363.1	2,002.7	52	8	16	8	20

No.	Company											
20	First Interstate Bancorp, Los Angeles, CA	5,030.1	4,967.0	4,291.7	3,367.1	414.0	286.2	962.8	42	9	10	8	15
21	Citicorp, New York, NY	4,759.9	3,861.7	2,982.5	4,108.0	100.9	88.0	463.0	16	10	2	1	3
22	Boatmen's Bancshares Inc., St. Louis, MO	4,738.5	4,345.1	3,436.9	3,484.4	356.9	336.6	560.6	31	11	7	5	8
23	Bankers Trust New York Corp., New York, NY	4,657.9	4,420.8	4,065.4	3,343.0	72.4	23.7	1,218.8	28	10	4	1	13
24	Comerica Inc., Detroit, MI	4,611.5	4,338.1	3,040.3	1,485.2	879.0	609.4	1,637.9	63	9	11	10	33
25	U.S. Trust Corp., New York, NY	4,268.7	4,051.1	3,694.7	2,657.5	208.4	467.3	935.5	35	4	5	4	22
26	Old Kent Financial Corp., Grand Rapids, MI	3,582.1	3,448.5	2,748.3	766.8	1,236.1	596.2	983.0	25	4	6	7	8
27	Barnett Banks Inc., Jacksonville, FL	3,581.4	3,389.7	3,413.1	2,912.5	189.4	136.7	342.8	32	11	9	3	9
28	Schroders Plc, London, UK	3,471.7	3,109.0	3,149.8				3,471.7	6	0	0	0	6
29	National City Corp., Cleveland, OH	3,104.2	2,883.4	2,389.0	2,380.4	420.8	75.8	227.2	22	8	6	2	6
30	First Chicago Corp., Chicago, IL	2,922.6	2,752.9	1,381.1	1,261.6	300.5	634.1	726.4	41	9	8	6	18
31	Great Western Financial, Chatsworth, CA	2,773.6	2,659.3	2,960.9	213.2	1,088.9	785.7	685.8	45	9	12	12	12
32	Societe Generale, Paris, France	2,748.3	2,421.1	2,066.5	12.2		36.1	2,736.1	4	1	0	0	3
33	First Fidelity Bancorp, Newark, NJ	2,729.4	2,312.0	1,983.3	2,227.3	199.3	23.8	266.7	13	6	2	1	4
34	Firstar Corp., Milwaukee, WI	2,657.9	2,398.2	2,392.9	1,246.2	471.0	108.3	916.9	15	5	3	1	6
35	Wachovia Corp., Winston-Salem, NC	2,648.1	2,462.8	2,027.8	1,590.8	295.7	66.6	653.3	18	7	2	3	6
36	Marshall & Ilsley Corp., Milwaukee, WI	2,426.3	2,297.9	1,875.7	1,061.1	531.3	142.4	767.3	12	2	3	2	5
37	Midlantic Corp., Edison, NJ	2,174.9	2,074.2	1,991.4	969.6	492.7	348.0	570.2	16	5	3	3	5
38	Bank of Boston Corp., Boston, MA	2,107.5	1,820.9	950.9	960.4	387.5	53.3	411.5	13	3	3	4	3
39	Crestar Financial Corp., Richmond, VA	2,089.6	1,831.7	1,323.8	1,585.8	171.3	13.3	279.2	25	7	6	4	8
40	Union Bank, San Francisco, CA	1,990.1	1,796.6	1,622.3	1,104.5	198.8	48.6	673.5	23	6	5	2	10
41	AmSouth Bancorp, Birmingham, AL	1,841.2	1,689.2	1,544.3	1,001.6	172.7	68.0	618.3	10	3	3	1	3
42	Mercantile Bancorp Inc., St. Louis, MO	1,820.8	1,693.9	1,655.9	954.7	200.5	972.4	597.6	27	7	6	2	12
43	Bancorp Hawaii Inc., Honolulu, HW	1,728.8	1,774.1	1,403.6	626.8	125.6	5.7	4.0	19	6	6	5	2
44	CoreStates Financial Corp., Philadelphia, PA	1,703.4	1,708.4	1,613.0	1,184.0	96.9		416.8	29	8	6	4	9
45	First Maryland Bancorp, Baltimore, MD	1,630.6	1,388.4	960.6	1,419.5	68.1		143.0	12	6	2	0	4

As compiled by Lipper Analytical Services Inc., Summit, NJ, from its mutual funds database.

Listed in order of total proprietary fund assets on June 30 compared with March 31 and June 30, 1994.

45

FIGURE 2-7

Salomon Brothers Inc., Bank Composites—Composition of
Revenue, 1986–1994 (in billions)

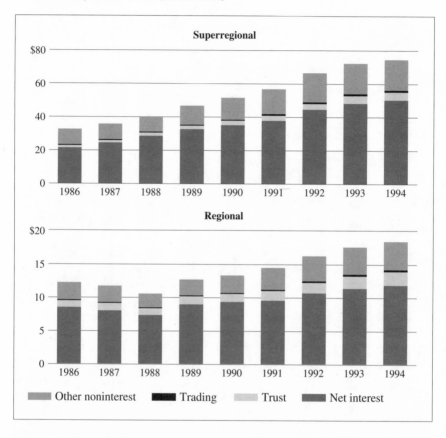

11 percent of total mutual fund assets under management in 1994, down from the
peak years of 1993 and 1992 when the banking industry's share of overall mutual
funds was at 15 and 14 percent, respectively. Among the mutual fund businesses,
banks are the primary providers of custodial services and trust operations. In addition, banks often provide fund accounting as part of their custodial services. Banks
can also provide transfer agency or shareholder services to mutual funds. Four of
the largest providers of mutual fund custodial services are superregional banks (see
Table 2–10). Since the mutual fund processing business is driven largely by
economies of scale, this sector is likely to remain under the control of a limited
number of players with intense competitive pricing.[12]

T A B L E   2–10

Top Mutual Fund Custodians (in billions)

Bank	Total Assets	Number of Funds Served
State Street	$774,063	2,246
Bank of New York	305,800	665
Chase Manhattan	264,428	383
United Missouri	162,648	476
Investors Fiduciary Trust	125,295	370
Brown Brothers Harriman	123,053	261
JP Morgan	120,859	162
Mellon Bank/Boston Co.	101,000	386
PNC	79,726	317
Bank of America	73,797	136

Source: *Journal of Mutual Fund Services.*

CHARACTERISTICS OF BEST SUPERREGIONALS

In most cases, the banks that continually achieve returns well in excess of industry averages are those that have garnered some strategic advantage, whether it is as a low-cost producer or an individual business with superior growth or return characteristics. The most profitable of the superregionals appear to be the niche banks, those with the highest percentages of fee or noninterest income, those that are extremely active in the fastest-growing segments of the financial services industry (such as credit cards and processing), and multibank holding companies that are committed to the service levels and culture usually associated with community banks (see Table 2–11). The latter banks take advantage of their asset base to achieve cost efficiencies without lessening the quality of service; they also offer customers scale-sensitive products that small banks cannot offer.

The most profitable banks gain competitive advantage over both large and small banks by creating a winning formula. For example, these banks may not be low-cost producers because they have ongoing technological expenditures for state-of-the-art information systems that enable them to offer superb service to their customers. However, this higher-quality service creates cross-selling opportunities that lead to substantial increases in revenues far greater than the additional costs of the service.

In addition, other salient characteristics distinguish winners from losers. The best banks usually possess at least five of the following six characteristics:

T A B L E 2-11

U.S. Bank Card Issuers—Top 50 Banks in Active Accounts, Ranked by Market Share, 1994 (dollars and account data in thousands)

Company	State	Outstandings Dec. 31, 1994	Pct. Change 1993-94	Market Share of Top 50	Total Accounts	Pct. Change 1993-94	Active Accounts	Pct. Change 1993-94	Charge Volume	Pct. Change 1993-94
Citibank	SD	$39,000,000	17%	17.38%	23,200	16%	18,046	15%	$70,000,000	27%
MBNA American (NB)	DE	17,558,000	52	7.83	11,079	37	8,261	43	24,162,000	40
AT&T Universal (NB)	GA	12,300,000	41	5.48	15,100	29	11,635	29	31,000,000	52
First Chicago	DE	12,153,471	18	5.42	12,225	19	7,115	11	29,328,938	27
First USA Bank (NB)	DE	11,004,323	103	4.91	6,387	67	4,519	67	10,421,586	68
Household Bank (NB)	CA	10,746,171	22	4.79	11,539	15	6,195	13	24,537,245	37
Chase Manhattan	DE	10,411,000	2	4.64	9,861	-18	6,594	0	13,299,000	11
Chemical Bank	NY	8,900,000	31	3.97	6,200	19	4,600	15	12,300,000	68
BankAmerica (incl. Seafirst Bank)	AZ	8,042,000	1	3.58	10,302	15	5,755	15	15,890,000	10
Capital One (NB, spin-off of Signet Bank)	VA	7,738,102	50	3.45	5,318	56	4,540	56	9,923,792	172
Bank of New York	DE	7,459,793	25	3.33	5,858	22	3,389	18	8,034,453	29
Banc One	OH	7,187,580	33	3.20	9,428	46	5,432	40	12,104,762	18
ADVANTA-Colonial National (NB)	DE	6,535,671	67	2.91	3,826	42	3,044	41	9,308,415	53
NationsBank	DE	5,865,461	20	2.61	5,449	34	3,165	25	13,528,733	53
Wachovia Bank	DE	4,073,000	31	1.82	2,528	10	1,683	19	4,916,981	25
First Union National	NC	3,979,044	84	1.77	3,150	45	1,577	43	5,198,112	79
Wells Fargo	CA	3,537,573	21	1.58	3,384	16	2,729	32	5,485,392	17
Ford-Associates National (NB)	DE	3,431,521	11	1.53	5,125	9	2,511	12	4,262,591	27

First Bank System	SD&CO	3,380,011	27	1.51	2,726	20	1,692	18	10,140,476	92
Providian National (from First Deposit Nat'l) (NB)	NH	3,100,000	19	1.38	2,390	37	1,200	28	3,400,000	42
USAA Federal Savings (NB)	TX	3,032,000	5	1.35	2,280	4	1,790	0	7,000,000	6
GE Capital Consumer Card (NB)	OH	2,391,900	14	1.07	3,208	11	2,511	10	3,911,000	26
Mellon Bank	DE	2,375,031	65	1.06	2,732	62	1,366	48	3,305,722	57
First National of Omaha	NE	2,346,000	33	1.05	3,255	25	1,610	6	3,033,000	32
Norwest Bank	IA	2,219,200	23	0.99	1,914	1	1,601	8	3,323,800	17
Marine Midland Bank	NY	1,686,315	21	0.75	1,415	25	844	10	3,290,601	49
KeyCorp (incl. Society National)	NY	1,661,765	16	0.74	1,610	15	1,046	6	2,242,000	-2
People's Bank (TH)	CT	1,548,579	48	0.69	1,101	41	844	22	2,032,177	29
Fleet Bank	RI	1,485,000	41	0.66	1,084	36	800	28	1,824,000	26
Crestar Bank	VA	1,484,439	51	0.66	867	43	676	48	1,515,975	82
Chevy Chase FSB (TH)	MD	1,400,000	26	0.62	823	18	634	24	1,964,000	19
Barnett Bank	FL	1,377,962	22	0.61	1,210	11	733	11	1,971,255	11
CoreStates Bank	DE	1,351,771	19	0.60	1,335	13	638	6	1,690,018	14
First of America Bank	MI	1,342,260	16	0.60	1,816	-2	933	1	2,531,694	8
First Interstate	CA	1,216,720	4	0.54	1,356	4	925	-1	2,500,137	2
Prudential Bank & Trust (NB)	GA	1,202,091	37	0.54	887	40	540	37	1,595,567	29
National Westminster	NY	1,069,557	20	0.48	827	42	545	25	1,753,361	57
National City Bank	OH	972,767	12	0.43	1,901	29	665	8	1,509,955	5
Harris Trust & Savings	IL	885,000	26	0.39	800	14	580	16	1,442,000	24
Mercantile Bank	IL	844,700	15	0.38	765	28	428	6	1,020,000	8
U.S. Bancorp	OR	827,150	-1	0.37	1,240	-1	773	-1	1,926,475	3
PNC Financial	DE	816,400	13	0.36	822	13	516	5	1,338,000	1

Continued on next page

49

Table 2–11—*Concluded*

Company	State	Outstandings Dec. 31, 1994	Pct Change 1993–94	Market Share of Top 50	Total Accounts	Pct. Change 1993–94	Active Accounts	Pct. Change 1993–94	Charge Volume	Pct. Change 1993–94
First Omni Bank	DE	$ 712,193	2%	0.32%	719	15%	439	9%	$ 930,054	3
SunTrust	FL	702,538	–1	0.31	798	7	441	–6	1,344,889	1
JC Penney National (NB)	DE	684,236	11	0.31	929	18	497	23	823,024	46
Firstar	WI	635,383	3	0.28	1,248	2	570	–8	1,515,724	–3
NBD Bank	IL	600,000	7	0.27	800	4	460	–4	1,385,000	9
Town North National (CU)	TX	497,447	10	0.22	521	–1	387	–1	910,273	2
American General Financial Center (NB)	UT	475,269	21	0.21	709	30	403	20	560,977	22
First North American National (NB)	GA	90,087	21	0.04	573	491	466	600	559,936	409
Top 50		$224,336,482	27%	100.00%	194,617	21%	128,341	21%	$377,993,088	35%
Bank card industry		$251,320,000	27%						$436,970,000	25%
Top 50's market share of bank card industry				89.26%						

Note: CU = credit union. NB = owned by nonbank parent. TH = thrift.

Source: *The Nilson Report*, no. 566, February 1994.

a diversified loan portfolio of exceptional credit quality, superior asset-liability management skills, a low overhead or efficiency ratio, quality management, superior merger and acquisition (M&A) skills, and intelligence-based information systems and profitability analyses that lead to more efficient marketing of products and services and an increase in fee income.

The ability to avoid bad loans, that is, to maintain a culture of credit quality through sound underwriting practices, is a salient characteristic of a superior bank. In the 1980s and early 1990s, when competitors expanded heavily into financing corporate takeovers and commercial real estate ventures that led to some banking disasters, the best management teams refused to succumb to the herd instinct.

Management really does matter. Bad management at many banks was clearly present during the 1980s and early 1990s, as can be seen in the relatively high level of banking failures. Subsequent examination reveals that many of the failed banks had a lack of loan documentation and poor credit control in basic loan underwriting. In some cases there was limited diversification in the loan portfolio. Some bank managements seemed oblivious to the ABCs of credit.

The troubles at some banks stemmed directly from a lack of managerial judgment and vision. Most bankers have learned that they cannot be all things to all people. Specialization and focus have their place in banking.

Management differs across institutions, and the differences play significant roles in the successes and failures of banks. A strategy that is appropriate for one bank may not be appropriate for another. Management must have the ability to direct the organization and focus the company toward what it does best, concentrating on its expertise. Also, the CEO must be able to make changes in strategy, culture, or organization when necessary, as strategic focus is critical for survival in the highly competitive financial services industry.[13] Executive management must be willing to discard or exit from businesses in which the company is not competitive or not earning sufficient profit. For example, the turnaround at BankAmerica has been associated in part with its exit from overseas wholesale banking and its concentration on consumer banking in the West. Similarly, the turnaround at First Fidelity can be attributed to the new CEO's improvement of the credit culture and quality of the loan portfolio at the bank, as well as the weeding out of unnecessary operations, the cutting of costs and payrolls, the development of a sound acquisition strategy, and a focus on potentially lucrative small-business and consumer loans.

Having superior merger and acquisition skills implies buying the right companies at nondilutive prices and properly integrating the acquired firms into the corporate culture and operating systems. A bank with strong merger skills also possesses a sound, effective due diligence process, especially in regard to the credit-worthiness of a merger candidate's loan portfolio and Community Reinvestment Act (CRA) rating. Once completing mergers, the best banks have integration strategies to reduce costs and generate additional revenues by leveraging the centrally managed products through subsidiary banks or branch systems. These banks generally build strong customer relationships that lead to the cross-selling of additional products and services.

TECHNOLOGICAL DEVELOPMENTS

Some of the best banks have developed or purchased advanced computer software and systems that have cut costs, increased productivity, and improved customer service. Banks appear willing to boost technological spending, particularly in back-office and consumer banking, as evidenced by an Ernest & Young survey that shows a projected increase of about 21 percent from 1994 to 1997 (see Figure 2–8).[14]

Most analysts believe that technology will be a critical factor in the long-term profitability of the banking industry. Improved technology should enable banks to lower their operating costs and have better information systems and customer profiles to boost the cross-selling of additional products and services, thus leading to greater profits. Bank managements are trying to pinpoint the profitability of each customer segment to tailor efficient and effective marketing strategies. Cross-selling is one of the most valuable uses of customer information files as banks hope to boost revenue growth. High-tech banks should begin to carve out a strategic advantage through their more efficient marketing efforts and lower costs relative to those of less technologically endowed banks.

Bankers expect to invest in the enhancement of automated delivery systems, including allocations for automating branches, improving phone-based customer service, and building home-based delivery. Customers are expected to become more

F I G U R E   2–8

Banking Industry Expenditure of Capital Dollars in 1994

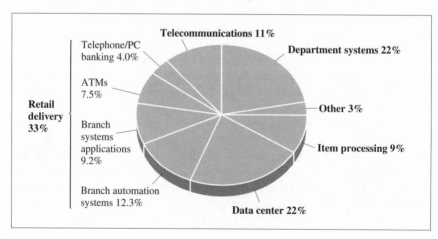

dependent on electronic-, computer-, and telephone-based banking during the remainder of the decade. Consequently, in-person and paper-based, customer-initiated interaction is expected to drop from 73 percent to 50 percent by the year 2000. Once a tangible symbol of soundness and the key point of contact between a bank and its customers, the bank branch is slowly becoming an artifact in an age of electronic banking. A fundamental shift away from the bank branch toward alternative, electronically driven channels, including PC-based home banking and telephone banking, can be expected. Lower-cost structures will lead to minibranches instead of full-service branches in high-traffic areas such as supermarkets and airports.

Some banks have begun to utilize image processing technology. Image processing refers to the transfer of traditional paper checks and other paper forms to electronic images that can then be manipulated. The technology provides customers with more efficient storage of checks and other records. However, the major leverage of this technology lies in the reduction of labor costs. Banks have been built on high-labor-intensive manual processes. The superregionals that have adopted image processing have used it to provide corporate customers with electronic records of checks via CD-ROM technology, charging a fee for this as part of their cash management function. It is expected that only 20–30 percent of the industry will have adopted image technology by the year 2000.

There has been much discussion about the productivity enhancement potential of image systems for some of banking's high-volume applications. Initially, technical difficulties have depressed the accuracy of reading handwriting and the magnetic inscripted character recognition (MICR) line, thus hampering the use of image technology for proof of deposit; but that has become less of a problem. The major inhibitor to technology's rapid development is that cost-benefit analyses have shown a lack of verifiable financial payback. Consequently, some banks are straddling the line on whether and when to install image processing capabilities. Image processing has been used effectively in lockbox applications, mortgage processing, and securities transfer and record keeping, but the cost-benefit jury is still out when it comes to check processing. Look for some banks to begin outsourcing or joint venturing their cash management, trade finance, clearing or securities services, and even check processing to avoid heavy up-front investments in image technology equipment and staffing.[15]

Banking has increasingly become a technologically driven business. Technology has also acted as a catalyst for consolidation, as more and more products and services, from loans to credit cards, are being marketed through computers and telephones instead of the traditional branch distribution system. Other bank products and services, such as derivative securities, securitization, securities processing, and trading, are even more technologically intensive. According to First Union's Edward Crutchfield, "this industry is on its way to eliminating the branch as a delivery system." Crutchfield acknowledges that the "cost of converting people to [electronic] banking is in the hundreds of millions [dollars]. We've now got the opportunity and the wherewithal to convert the system." Crutchfield has invested much time and money in technology to connect First Union's branches in a single reporting network. The appeal of acquiring First Fidelity by First Union was not to obtain 700 branches, but to add 2.5 million customers who could be sold First Union's advanced products through electronic channels as well as branches and telephones. The heavy spending on technology can be spread over a broader customer base. Similarly, according to David Vitale, vice chairman of the newly formed First Chicago NBD, an attraction of merging with NBD for First Chicago was the opportunity to leverage its advanced products and technology over a much larger base of potential customers.

Wells Fargo, with domestic branches only in California, has reached throughout the nation with mail and electronic offerings of retail banking products. According to President William F. Zuenatt, the bank became the first depository institution in the country to begin marketing nationwide preapproved small-business loans through the mail in 1995. In a similar manner, Banc One Corp. has spent heavily on technology, developing a new credit card processing system that it is currently licensing to four companies, including American Express, for $25 million each. Bank of New York also invested wisely in technology that would automate and lower its security processing costs. Then, the bank spent an additional $500 million to acquire a dozen securities processing operations from other bank trust departments, to add to its own sizable processing portfolio in order to gain further economies of scale in this heavily automated business.[16]

RETAILERS OF FINANCIAL SERVICES

The banking industry has an overcapacity problem both in the number of banks and branches as well as in its processing capability. For example, the industry processes about 200 million demand deposit accounts (DDAs), 85 million consumer loans, and 15 million commercial loans. However, it is capable of handling 280 million DDAs, 120 million consumer loans, and 25 million commercial loans. Therefore, there is overcapacity of between 10–40 percent in each of these product lines. This overcapacity continues to stimulate consolidation.

Thomas K. Brown, banking analyst at Donaldson, Lufkin & Jenrette, believes that the most successful companies will be those that transform themselves into successful retailers of financial services while controlling carefully the cost and credit risks in their commercial banking activities. Brown believes that banks that do not make dramatic changes necessary to become more competitive in tomorrow's financial services marketplace "will look out of sync in five years as most thrifts look today." According to Bill Gates of Microsoft fame, these banks will become "dinosaurs" or what others call "money mortuaries."[17]

Bank managements must recognize that the best growth opportunities lie in retail banking and asset management. As the baby boom generation ages and increases its savings, there will also be an incredible transfer of wealth through inheritance (see Table 2–12). The burden on individuals to save and to select their own investments will increase continually, opening up great opportunities for banks and nonbanks to provide a large variety of asset management services.[18]

In addition to displaying strong credit controls and processes, excellent expense management, and a proshareholder orientation, superior executive managements at superregional banks will develop skills that enable them to deal with change, have a focused but flexible strategy, and have a retail-merchandising orientation. The best banks will develop delivery systems with multiple distribution channels, develop multiple sales forces, combine sales and service for basic activities, develop segmented multiple products and brands, manage by local markets, and develop customer profitability and information systems that utilize database marketing skills. Easy-to-use customer profitability information systems will be installed at the point of customer contact, whether at the teller, on the platform, or over the telephone. The top-performing banks will be those that market intelligently and efficiently and that offer improved customer service. Banks will have to develop predictive models based on customer information, demographics, and psychographic information to help target the households that are most likely to become more profitable.[19]

There is usually not enough sales potential for complicated products (annuities, mortgages, mutual funds, other investment products, small-business products,

T A B L E   2–12

The Coming Boom in Wealth Transfer through Inheritance

Year	Total* (in billions)	Number of Heirs (in thousands)	Mean*
1990	$ 39.4	900	$43,814
1995	84.3	1,506	55,951
2000	143.8	2,202	65,289
2005	216.9	2,846	76,194
2010	286.2	3,255	87,918
2015	335.9	3,389	99,130
2020	334.5	3,135	106,717
2025	288.5	2,650	108,870
2030	201.6	1,881	107,180
2035	106.8	1,090	97,997
2040	40.7	417	97,636
Total	$10,365.0	114,953	$90,167

* Figures are in 1989 dollars.

and so forth) at every branch to justify the expense associated with staffing and training employees in all branches to handle these sales. Sales of complicated products cannot be efficiently and effectively handled by generalists in all branches, many of whom are consumed with processing routine transactions. However, studies have shown that customers are willing to drive longer distances for these transactions, use alternative delivery systems, or in some cases, have a bank employee visit at their home or office. Dedicated sales forces should be created for certain products.

In response to a study of its platform employees to determine staffing levels, Wells Fargo altered its branch structure by creating four dedicated sales forces aimed at small businesses, customers with more than $25,000 in savings, mortgage sales, and investment products. It funded these positions out of positions previously in the branches. Within branches, the position of assistant manager was eliminated and those of platform and teller employees were combined. There is now only one line for sales-service assistance at most Wells Fargo branches. Branch employees are trained to handle efficiently all basic transactions and sales, identify customer needs, and arrange meetings with product sales specialists for more complicated products (see Figure 2–9). How has this worked at Wells Fargo? The company has 8 percent fewer branch employees, handles more transactions than previously, and has increased sales across the board by about 30 percent.[20]

It has been almost a decade since banks and thrifts were hurt by interest rate risk problems. However, a number of banks suffered from suboptimal

FIGURE   2-9

Wells Fargo's Retail Banking Organization

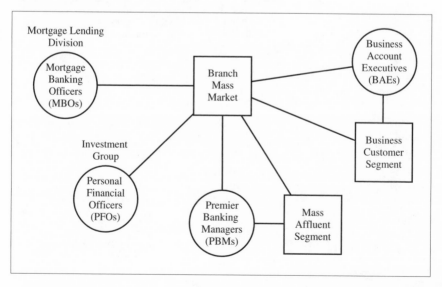

asset-liability management decisions during 1994. These banks had extensive losses in their bond and derivative portfolios when they misjudged the direction of interest rates. Furthermore, they had established negative gap positions and large fixed-rate security portfolios. Although only a handful of superregionals (PNC, KeyCorp, and Banc One) suffered large losses and a major decline in the market price of their common shares, it is noteworthy that the portfolio losses occurred during relatively good times in the banking industry.

Isolated banks have had problems related to losses involving the Mexican peso (Chemical Banking) or the lending of their cash balances from a securities loan for the intermediate term instead of short term during a period of rising interest rates (Mellon). After all, most of the banking industry went through tough times between the late 1980s and early 1990s. Banks had to raise capital to bolster their balance sheets and meet stricter regulatory requirements for capitalization. They suffered from bad real estate or LBO loans or some other malady during that period, such as a lack of geographic and industry loan diversification. Unfortunately, it seems as if the banking industry cannot stand success for more than a short period.

According to bank stock analysts at CS First Boston, the highest-performing products and services as measured by ROE include trading, credit cards, mortgage banking, trust and fiduciary, and foreign businesses. Each of these areas is expected to generate an ROE of 20 percent or more in 1996. Areas such as small-business lending, branch banking, and middle-market lending can be classified as attractive intermediation businesses, generating ROEs of about 15 percent. In the lower-performing categories are corporate lending to large companies and commercial real estate, both of which are expected to generate ROEs of about 10 percent. The growing investment management business is also in the lower category since banks allocated large expense dollars to build up this promising area (see Table 2–13).[21]

Repeal of Glass-Steagall

It seems likely that the Glass-Steagall Act will be repealed. This should enhance the efficiency of the financial system and be a positive influence for the banking system. Adding investment banking activities might make bank earnings more volatile, but the benefits of being able to keep growing the middle-market customers that banks would otherwise lose to the public markets are significant. In addition, repeal of the act should reduce the risks of most banks by providing the opportunity for further revenue diversification.[22]

INSURANCE AND ANNUITIES

According to banking analysts at CS First Boston, many banks can be expected to market a complete insurance product line within the next 5 or 10 years, as well

T A B L E   2–13

Projected Returns on Average Equity

Business Segment	1993	1996E
Trading	40%	20%
Credit cards	27	20
Mortgage banking	25	20
Trust and fiduciary	20	24
Foreign business	20	20
Small-business lending	18	16
Branch banking	18	15
Middle-market lending	16	14
Large corporate lending	11	10
Investment management	8	15
Commercial real estate	−10	10

Source: T.H. Hanley and P.J. Carter, "The Competitive State of the U.S. Commercial Banking Industry," *CS First Boston*, March 24, 1995, p. 41.

as perhaps even underwriting selected products such as life insurance or home-owner insurance on a limited basis. Both the Clinton-Rubin bill and the D'Amato bill have presented Glass-Steagall reform proposals to Congress that would, in varying degrees, allow banks to offer insurance on a nationwide basis. The aforementioned analysts feel that the increased insurance powers portion of the Glass-Steagall reform has a 25 percent chance for passage. Alan Greenspan, Federal Reserve Board chairman, and Eugene Ludwig, comptroller of the currency, have publicly supported increased powers for banks to sell insurance.

As of the first quarter of 1995, 21 states granted broad authority to sell life insurance and 11 others permit limited activities, while most of the remaining states (e.g., Florida, Texas, Colorado, Illinois, Massachusetts, and Connecticut) ban the sale of insurance through banks or make it extremely difficult. On the other hand, opposition to expanded insurance powers on Capitol Hill appears to be gathering strength, as Representative Thomas Bliley (R-Virginia) recently proposed a bill that would render the Variable Annuity Life Insurance Company (VALIC) Supreme Court decision moot, returning to the states the explicit authority to regulate anything they deemed insurance. However, Senator Christopher Dodd (R-Connecticut) decided not to attach an insurance-limiting provision to the 1994 interstate banking bill. Superregionals such as BankAmerica, Norwest, KeyCorp, and Wells Fargo, as well as money center banks such as Chase Manhattan and Citicorp, would be expected to benefit greatly by being granted expanded insurance powers since they already have active insurance units.[23]

In the shorter term, banks are expected to be selling a much higher volume of both life insurance and annuities as state regulatory and legal barriers fall. In the longer term, we can expect a number of annuity/life insurance company acquisitions as banks transform themselves from lenders to full-service financial product providers over the next decade. It is interesting to note that banks typically earn a commission of about 5 percent on annuity sales on the principal of the policy. Consolidation will become necessary to achieve economies of scale and to utilize technological advantages. Also, commercial banks can offer potential insurance customers convenience, accommodation, and lower cost-distribution channels compared to existing independent insurance delivery systems. We can also expect banks to establish more joint ventures or partnerships with insurance companies to sell insurance products through the bank distribution system. (Banks already achieved a 22 percent market share of individual annuity products in 1993.) These joint ventures will be similar to the partnerships that have already been formed between Chase Manhattan and CNA, Fleet and American Skandia, Norwest and Fortis, Wells Fargo and American Skandia, and National Life of Vermont and several Midwestern banks. The comptroller of the currency has permitted banks to lease space to insurance agents, who have offered an array of insurance products. A caveat has been that "some differentiation between the two must be made so that the public will understand it is not buying insurance from the bank."[24]

MERGER HISTORY AND OUTLOOK

Financial economists at both the Federal Reserve Bank of Atlanta (A. Srinivasan and L. Wall) and the Harvard Graduate School of Business (J.C. Linder and D.B. Crane) concluded that few mergers in the 1980s increased shareholder value, lowered costs dramatically, or raised profits significantly.[25] Another study conducted at the Federal Reserve Board concluded that "no more than one merged bank out of ten" became more profitable than banks that remained independent.[26] These studies showed how difficult it was during the early and mid-1980s to bring about successful mergers. Even the 1985 paragon of mergers (Wells Fargo and Crocker National Bank) demonstrated limited cost savings for the first six quarters. With the exception of the Wells-Crocker merger, most of the mergers studied were aimed at entering new geographic markets rather than cutting costs or enhancing profitability. Also, bank managements were more willing to dilute earnings per share in the 1980s than they are today. In addition, bank managements were less skilled in premerger due diligence work and in postmerger integration and cost-cutting necessary to make mergers accretive. The control of credit quality became more difficult in less familiar regions. During the late 1980s and the 1990s, M&A

became a way of not only growing assets, but of attempting to increase profitability. Banc One, PNC, Bank of New York, Norwest, First Union, SunTrust, CoreStates, and NationsBank have demonstrated superior skills in acquiring banks, while Mellon demonstrated skills in acquiring both banks and nonbanks such as Boston Co., Dreyfus, and mortgage banking companies.

The passage of the Interstate Banking Act and the losses suffered by some banks in their portfolios of securities during 1994 may act as a catalyst for mergers and acquisitions within the industry. (We know about the major losses suffered by PNC, Banc One and KeyCorp; what we do not know at the time of this writing is whether or not salient takeover candidates have suffered similar losses. We also do not know with certainty whether those superregionals that have announced losses and claimed them as one-shot deals will later be forced to take additional charge-offs.) Losses of this nature could bring these potential takeover candidates as well as "wounded" superregionals to the bargaining table.

Given the radical changes and expenses that will be necessary to reengineer retail banking and the relatively slow revenue growth anticipated, executive managements should begin to recognize the benefits to their shareholders of receiving a handsome premium for their stock and converting their shares, on a tax-free basis, into those of a stronger, more technologically advanced banking company, well ahead of the rest of the industry in adjusting to the new banking environment. When bank managements recognize that acquisition premiums and earnings per share (EPS) growth rates and other profitability ratios have probably peaked, we may see an increasing number of banking marriages.

If the Glass-Steagall Act is modified, some banks may reengineer themselves into financial services conglomerates. The need for capital may decline as banks exit risky, capital-intensive businesses, such as corporate lending, in favor of non-interest-intensive businesses (fee-income-generating businesses), which usually do not require as much capital allocation. Excessive capital at some banks may be utilized as a war chest to make both bank and nonbanking acquisitions. The recent consolidation process has not really been geared to adding branches, but to buying customers.

The economics of consolidation should come increasingly into play during the remainder of the decade, as larger banks develop the necessary scale advantages, while other banking organizations repeat past mistakes by excessively easing credit quality or pricing of loans. The banks that get into trouble may become tomorrow's acquisitions. In addition, while the managements of many of the banking industry's small- and midsize regional banks can still enjoy relatively strong returns over the near term, their competitive position in the long term and ability to generate substantial volume and profitability growth could be eroded steadily by large infrastructure barriers, including burdensome regulatory requirements, limited product offerings and marketing capabilities, and a lack of economies of scale in some business lines. Increased activism on the part of bank shareholders will almost certainly coerce some institutions to sell out to larger banks that best reflect their operating philosophies, at prices that benefit both institutions.[27]

ENDNOTES

1. A. Bird, *SuperCommunity Banking* (Chicago: Probus Publishing, 1994), p. 23.
2. Ibid., p. 25.
3. Ibid., p. 21.
4. G. Knecht, *The Wall Street Journal*, July 26, 1994, p. 2.
5. Bird, *SuperCommunity Banking*, p. 23.
6. J.B. McCoy, L.A. Frieder, and R.B. Hedges, Jr., *BottomLine Banking* (Chicago: Probus Publishing, 1994), p. 57.
7. F. Furlong, "Interstate Banking in the West," *FRBSF*, Weekly Letter, April 15, 1994, pp. 1–3.
8. Knecht, p. 1.
9. Ibid.
10. "On Solid Ground," *S&P Banking Industry Survey*, November 3, 1994, p. 30.
11. K. Holland, "Banker's Hours Don't Look So Good," *Business Week*, December 9, 1994, pp. 102–3.
12. T.H. Hanley, P.J. Carter, and A.B. Collins, "Separating the Winners from the Losers in the Banking Industry," *CS First Boston*, February 14, 1995, pp. 41–42.
13. D. Rogers, *The Future of American Banking* (New York: McGraw-Hill Book Co., 1993), p. 272.
14. K. Holland and A. Barrett, "A Delicate Balance at the Bank," *Business Week*, January 9, 1995, p. 93.
15. D.B. Glossman, "Technology and Banking: Another Step Forward," *Salomon Brothers*, February 23, 1995, p. 2.
16. K. Holland and R. Melcher, "Why Banks Keep Bulking Up," *Business Week*, July 31, 1995, pp. 66–67.
17. T.K. Brown, "The Future of Banking, Part II," *Bank Notes, DLJ*, February 10, 1995, p. 2.
18. Ibid., p. 7.
19. Ibid., p. 20.
20. Ibid., pp. 24–25.
21. T.H. Hanley and P.J. Carter, "The Competitive State of the U.S. Commercial Banking Industry," *CS First Boston*, March 24, 1995, p. 41.
22. "Repealing Glass-Steagall," *Banking Insights, Duff & Phelps*, March 1995, pp. 1, 8.
23. T.H. Hanley, "Commercial Banks: Insurance and Annuities," *CS First Boston*, April 13, 1995, pp. 1, 8.
24. Ibid., pp. 7–23.
25. A. Gart, *Regulation, Deregulation, Reregulation: The Future of the Banking, Insurance, and Securities Industries* (New York: John Wiley & Son, 1994), p. 354.
26. Bird, *SuperCommunity Banking*, p. 314.
27. Hanley and Carter, "The Competitive State of the U.S. Commercial Banking Industry," p. 12.

CHAPTER 3

A Primer on Bank Mergers and Acquisitions

Merger and acquisition activity continues to be an important force in the restructuring of the banking industry. Bigger, stronger banks continue to merge with or buy smaller depository institutions so that the number of banks and thrifts are declining.

A merger is generally a combination of two or more separate companies, typically involving the issuance of new securities. An acquisition occurs when one company purchases the stock of another. There is a clear buyer and seller germane to the transaction terms and the structure of the surviving entity.

Why do a merger rather than an acquisition? Mergers are cheaper; the buyer takes on no new debt and generally no goodwill is created (the premium a buyer pays over the book value of the target that must be written off over time against earnings). Also, there is a good chance that the buyer's earnings per share will not be diluted and that the EPS might even get a near-term or medium-term boost. There are often short-term costs associated with any merger or acquisition (such as computer software consolidation, branch closing costs, and personnel downsizing costs). The combined company is generally in a stronger financial position than it would be as a result of a premium takeover bid, and this increases the flexibility and financial wherewithal to do other things in the future. Also, in a merger of equals the stockholders of both companies tend to gain from consolidation. When an acquisition takes place with a large premium, often only the stockholders of the target company benefit immediately.

Prior to the 1980s, geographic restrictions, especially the prohibition against interstate banking, limited where and how banks could compete. Several states even restricted in-state branching. Often, the only way banks could expand was through multibank holding companies, formed to acquire banks and other non-banking companies in different geographic locations or markets. Bank regulators

63

evaluated all transactions closely to ensure that the acquiring company did not gain too large a market share on a "local market" basis. Although there is still some concern regarding market dominance and the lack of competition, in today's environment there are few constraints to consolidation.[1]

Consolidation within the banking industry has been dramatic over the past 10 years, and there are no signs that acquisition activity will be abating. The top 50 banks now account for over 75 percent of total U.S. banking assets. Banking analysts at C.S. First Boston suggest that before the end of the decade, the 50 largest banks could consolidate to 15 in the next wave of merger activity.

The number of bank acquisitions from 1983–94 totaled just under 3,100, with a low of 129 acquisitions in 1989 and a high of 441 in 1994. The average number of bank acquisitions per year was 256 in the 1983–94 period. So far in the first half of 1995, four of the largest banking acquisitions in U.S. history have been announced: Fleet Financial's acquisition of Shawmut National; First Union's acquisition of First Fidelity; First Chicago's merger with NBD; and Chemical Banking's merger with Chase Manhattan (see Table 3–1). First Union's acquisition of First Fidelity is similar in concept to the merger of Key and Society in that it is an out-of-market deal extending the scope of First Union's retail banking network from Florida to Connecticut. First Union paid 188 percent of book value in acquiring First Fidelity, the well-managed Midlantic bank with strong retail and middle-market franchises. First Fidelity should be able to add sales outlets for the growing number of superior products and services offered by First Union.

T A B L E   3–1

Ten Largest Bank Mergers (in billions)

		Announcement Date	Market Value
1.	Wells Fargo/First Interstate	October 1995	$11.6
2.	Chemical Banking/Chase Manhattan	August 1995	10.0E
3.	First Union/First Fidelity	June 1995	5.4
4.	First Chicago/NBD	July 1995	5.1
5.	BankAmerica/Security Pacific	August 1991	4.7
6.	NCNB/C&S Sovran	July 1991	4.5
7.	Key/Society	August 1993	4.0
8.	Fleet/Shawmut	February 1995	3.6
9.	PNC/Midlantic	July 1995	3.0
10.	CoreStates/Meridian	October 1995	3.0

E = estimated.

On the other hand, the Fleet/Shawmut merger is essentially an in-market deal (Fleet paid about 175 percent of book value for Shawmut), with many branch and back-office redundancies that will permit major productivity improvements; whereas the First Union/Fidelity merger represents fewer opportunities to reduce noninterest expenses, but an excellent opportunity to increase revenue growth (see Figure 3–1). The First Chicago/NBD merger creates some overlapping territory in Illinois and among corporate clients, which will enable noninterest expenses to be cut by about 10 percent as 1,700 employees will be trimmed from the payrolls in the trust, credit card, executive management, and corporate lending areas. There will also be large reductions of information system costs per dollar of deposits and savings and in the closing of some redundant branches in Illinois. There will be at least $200 million in cost savings in 1997. First Chicago NBD will emerge as the largest bank in the states of Michigan, Illinois and Indiana; it will have a huge

F I G U R E   3–1

Merger Market Overview

Characteristics of and motivations for transactions are varied and include...

Type of Transaction	Examples
In-market consolidation	Fleet/Shawmut
	BankAmerica/Security Pacific
	Boatmen's/Worthen
	Chemical Banking/Manufacturers Hanover
Market extension	First Chicago/NBD Bancorp
	First Union/First Fidelity
	BankAmerica/Continental
	Banc One/Valley National
	Comerica/Plaza Commerce, Pacific Western, Metrobank
	KeyCorp/Society
Merger of equals	Chemical Banking/Manufacturers Hanover
	KeyCorp/Society
	Dime/Anchor Bancorp
	First Chicago/NBD Bancorp
Business line extension	Mellon/Dreyfus and Boston Company
	Norwest/Island Finance
	NationsBank/U.S. West
	BankAmerica/Arbor National

credit card operation and be one of the largest corporate banks in the Midwest. First Chicago NBD will have a stronger core deposit base, excellent management, credit-quality expertise, and the opportunity to sell investment/capital market products to a much larger retail and corporate customer base.

Chemical Banking Corporation and the Chase Manhattan Bank signed a definitive agreement to merge in a stock-for-stock transaction that will create the largest bank in the United States. The new institution, which will adopt the Chase name, will have about $300 billion in assets and $20 billion in shareholders' equity. The new bank will have relationships with more than 25 million consumers from coast to coast and will be the lead bank to corporate America. It will also have dominant positions in mortgage servicing, mortgage origination, credit cards, and global finance. The estimated savings from the merger will be $1.5 billion, to be achieved over three years following the merger by consolidating operations, computer and information systems, closing branches, and laying off 12,000 employees, about 15 percent of the workforce.

In 1983, the industry was composed of approximately 14,500 banks. At midyear 1995, there were about 10,000 banks. Most analysts expect somewhere between 5,000 and 8,000 banks by the end of the decade after another wave of merger and acquisition activity.

Not only has the number of bank mergers and acquisitions increased between 1991 and 1994, but so have relative prices as measured on the basis of price-to-book values. The median price-to-tangible-book value for bank acquisitions at announcement rose from 137 percent in 1991 to 176 percent in 1994. The median price-to-tangible-book value for the acquisition of thrifts also rose during the same period from 104 percent in 1991 to 158 percent in 1994 (see Figure 3–2 and Tables 3–2 and 3–3). Price-to-book values appear to have moved even higher as evidenced by the three aforementioned 1995 acquisitions.

The takeover premiums paid for thrifts are less than those paid for banks. This has resulted from numerous differences between the traditional servicing approaches of banks and thrifts, including disparities in products and services offered, service fees charged, rates paid, investments made, and deposit composition. Additionally, concern over the attrition of business following acquisition has been important in dampening interest in paying high multiples for savings institutions. For example, thrifts tend to have a much smaller percentage of noninterest-bearing demand deposits or NOW accounts and a higher percentage of consumer CDs at near-market rates than their banking counterparts, eliminating their funding-cost advantage. There is also a tendency for thrift deposits to run off when repriced downward by an acquiring bank or when the competition offers a higher yield.[2]

Merger and acquisition initiatives, the main driver of the decline in the number of banks and the principal form of removing troubled banks and thrifts, were encouraged by the passage of the Garn-St. Germain Act and other legislation and

Median Price-to-Tangible-Book Value for Thrift and Bank
Mergers and Acquisitions

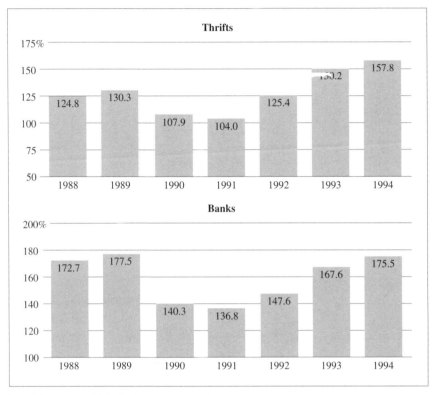

Note: Median price-to-tangible book value at announcement (%).

Source: Hovde Financial, Inc.

judicial rulings in the 1980s. During the 1990s, bank managements were searching for additional revenue growth (especially fee-based income), efficiencies in
operations, diversification of income (both productwise and geographically), sta-
bilized asset quality, and optimal deployment of excess capital (see Figure 3–3).

Banks have not only purchased depository institutions; they have also purchased mortgage banking companies, mutual funds, finance companies, brokerage
firms, and specialty finance companies to generate fee income and to diversify
away their dependence on interest income. For example, NationsBank has acquired
CRT, a leading specialty company in derivative securities, along with a number
of mortgage banking and mortgage servicing companies. Mellon has purchased
Boston Company and Dreyfus, the latter being the sixth largest family of mutual

T A B L E 3-2

1992–1995 Bank and Thrift Mergers Greater than $500 Million

Seller	Buyer	Date Announced	Aggregate Consideration ($ millions)	Price-to-Book Value	Price-to-Tangible Book Value	Price-to-Adjusted-Book Value	Price to LTM EPS	Premium to Core Deposits	Premium to Market
1995									
First Chicago	NBD Bancorp	7/12/95	$5,390	1.32×	1.40×	1.34×	8.75×	4.8%	3.0%
Midlantic	PNC Bank	7/10/95	3,000	2.12	2.29	3.14	10.8/14.2	15.6	34.0
CSF Holdings Inc.	NationsBank Corp.	7/05/95	516	1.84	1.84	1.83	12.4	7.5	26.9
First Fidelity	First Union Corp.	6/19/95	5,463	1.92	2.72	2.75	12.4	12.4	31.9
First Fed Michigan	Charter One Financial	5/30/95	556	1.19	1.19	1.09	11.0	3.1	12.6
West One Bancorp	U.S. Bancorp	5/08/95	1,575	1.94	2.13	2.15	13.9	14.7	46.0
Shawmut National Corp.	Fleet Financial Group	2/21/95	3,686	1.79	1.96	1.98	16.0	9.6	45.5
Michigan National	National Australia Bank	2/05/95	1,516	1.79	1.79	2.27	10.1	10.5	26.4
Median, 1995				1.81×	1.90×	2.13×	12.4×	10.1%	29.4%
1994									
Worthen Banking	Boatmen's Bancshares	8/18/94	$ 608	2.00×	2.20×	2.58×	14.0×	12.1%	11.8%
Anchor Bancorp Inc.	Dime Bancorp	7/06/94	552	1.10	1.36	1.11	11.4	2.8	20.4
Metropolitan Financial	First Bank System	7/01/94	874	1.72	2.19	1.88	14.3	9.5	58.7
Citizens First Bancorp	National Westminster	3/21/94	524	2.38	2.47	3.00	13.7	13.8	21.9
Continental Bank	BankAmerica	1/28/94	2,300	1.25	1.25	1.34	6.7	4.5	35.7
Median, 1994				1.72×	2.19×	1.88×	13.7×	9.5%	21.9%
1993									
Independence Bancorp	CoreStates Financial	11/19/93	$ 513	2.12×	2.13×	2.75×	47.1×	14.1%	30.6%
Liberty National Bancorp	Banc One Corporation	11/03/93	842	2.07	2.34	2.67	16.3	13.6	12.8
Society Corporation	KeyCorp	10/04/93	4,040	1.96	2.33	2.50	10.7	13.4	N.A.
Valley Bancorp	Marshall & Ilsley	9/20/93	803	2.34	2.60	2.91	17.7	13.9	5.5

Cragin Financial	ABN Amro	7/06/93	563	1.72	1.89	3.36	13.6	14.1	51.2
MNC Financial Inc.	NationsBank Corp.	2/18/93	1,361	1.40	1.50	1.45	39.9	1.6	16.7
National Community Banks	Bank of New York	1/29/93	652	2.60	2.60	2.74	30.5	11.3	30.7
Median, 1993				2.12×	2.33×	2.74×	17.7×	13.6%	16.7%
1992									
Colorado Nat'l Bankshares	First Bank System	11/09/92	$ 528	2.15×	2.35×	2.68×	18.9×	12.5%	35.0%
Dominion Bankshares	First Union Corp.	9/21/92	1,024	1.66	2.04	1.87	N.A.	6.4	30.6
Key Centurion Bankshares	Banc One Corporation	6/05/92	546	1.75	1.98	2.50	15.7	11.7	18.9
First Florida Banks	Barnett Banks, Inc.	5/18/92	885	2.43	2.69	2.72	N.A.	12.6	78.4
Valley National Corp.	Banc One Corporation	4/14/92	1,248	2.27	2.31	2.11	32.9	8.0	54.9
Team Bancshares	Banc One Corporation	3/23/92	782	2.49	2.63	2.52	22.9	12.5	N.A.
INB Financial Corp.	NBD Bancorp	3/18/92	912	1.90	2.08	2.21	18.2	10.4	36.0
Puget Sound Bancorp	KeyCorp	3/09/92	807	2.00	2.11	2.46	14.7	13.9	13.7
Median, 1992				2.08×	2.21×	2.48×	18.6×	12.5%	35.0%

T A B L E   3–3

Summary Statistics

Year	1992	1993	1994	1995*
Number of deals	397	477	562	206
Bank	318	372	441	154
Thrift	79	106	121	52
Total deal value ($ millions)	16,105	23,496	23,516	22,085
Bank	11,891	17,820	13,405	18,553
Thrift	4,213	5,676	9,111	3,531
Total assets ($ millions)	164,378	175,385	189,938	163,305
Bank	104,644	127,293	98,265	131,070
Thrift	59,734	48,092	91,673	32,235
P/E (median)	14.0	14.8	14.4	15.7
Bank	14.5	14.9	14.5	15.2
Thrift	12.8	14.1	13.8	16.5
Premium/core deposits (median)	4.14	6.38	6.71	7.57
Bank	4.50	6.88	6.68	8.38
Thrift	1.67	5.19	6.72	5.78

* Year-to-date, July 11, 1995.
Source: CS First Boston.

funds in the United States. Bank of Boston has acquired a number of finance companies and mortgage banking companies, including Ganis Credit, Century Acceptance, Fidelity Acceptance, and Bell Mortgage.

During 1994–95, aggregate bank earnings reached record levels, aided by strong loan demand, good interest rate spreads, and a reduction in the number of nonperforming loans. Consequently, this enabled some banks with excess equity to reduce loan loss provisions. However, banking ROA and ROE growth from mid-1995 onward is likely to dwindle, accompanied by a modest increase in credit problems related to the slowdown in economic activity. The broad trends of slightly declining net interest margins, slower revenue growth, and more difficulty in reducing expenses suggest a gradual erosion in profitability toward the 1.00 percent ROA level prevalent throughout the 1980s. These factors are likely to spur interest in increased merger and acquisition activity along with the passage of the Interstate Banking Act of 1994. Shareholder return based on dividends and market appreciation is dependent on a bank's EPS growth. Sustained and consistent earnings growth must be founded on revenue growth and good credit controls. For many banks, the search for sources of growth will focus largely on obtaining new markets and products through mergers and acquisitions.

F I G U R E   3–3

Drivers of Merger Activity

Promoting Factors	Potentially Inhibiting Factors
Recent stock market valuations	Increased ROI hurdles
Excess capital	Alternative businesses/acquisitions
Minimal organic growth	Stock repurchase programs
Projected cost savings	Antitrust issues
Disparity in product capabilities	Loan/deposit runoff
• Scale	Long-term views on delivery systems technology
• Customer bases	Volatile interest rates
Defense/improvement of market position	
Size for sake of size/leverage	
Hostile shareholder activity	
Product diversity	
Geographic diversity	
Legislation/judicial rulings	
Stabilized asset quality	
Attractive pricing in merger market	

Source: Goldman Sachs.

The large superregional banks have built their franchises through a combi-nation of internal growth and mergers and acquisitions. Although size and business concentration, deregulation, and competition helped change the banking industry rather dramatically, there has not been a great impact on investment return to the shareholder. The typical acquisition involved transferring capital in the form of cash or partial ownership of the acquiror to the shareholders of the acquiree. For this distribution of capital, the acquiree gave up to the acquiror some of the net worth and the franchise value of the acquired entity. Seldom was the transfer in perfect balance. One set of shareholders usually seemed to get a better deal; it was the shareholders of the acquired company who were paid a large premium over both market and book value. Because of competition for the "bride in marriage," the acquiring bank often bids aggressively, diluting future earnings per share with-out enough commensurate cost savings or revenue enhancements. Except in unusual circumstances, sellers expect and receive a premium over the predeal mar-ket price of the stock. Often the acquiror's market price adjusts to the potential for dilution prior to the occurrence of the merger.

Following the announcement of the Fleet/Shawmut merger, Fleet's stock declined by between 10 and 15 percent, but gained back 80 percent of the decline in the following four months. Following the announcement that First Union would acquire First Fidelity, the stock of First Union declined about 8 percent in the first two days after the announcement, roughly about the size of the potential forecasted dilution in EPS, before recapturing the entire price decline within three months (see Figure 3–4). Two days prior to the announcement that PNC agreed to acquire Midlantic at a premium larger than that paid by First Union to acquire First Fidelity, the price of PNC's stock started to decline and continued to decline for one week after the announcement. The decline in the price of PNC's common shares was about equal to the potential dilution in EPS forecasted by some bank analysts (see Figure 3–5). On the other hand, when the nondilutive merger of equals between NBD and First Chicago was announced, the price of both NBD's and First Chicago's stock rose because the merger was expected to be accretive to EPS (see Figure 3–6).

Following the announcement of the Chemical Banking and Chase Manhattan merger, share prices of both banks rose substantially in response to a deal which made good strategic sense and lent itself to in-market cost-cutting opportunities, as well as accretion in EPS. As a matter of fact, estimated future growth rates in EPS of the new company exceeded pre-merger growth rate estimates of the independent banks.

Although it is not always possible to forecast accurately the market price of stocks, when a large premium is paid for an acquisition that dilutes EPS substantially for more than one year, there is usually a decline in the stock of the acquiring company.

F I G U R E   3-4

Stock Price Reaction of First Union/First Fidelity Merger

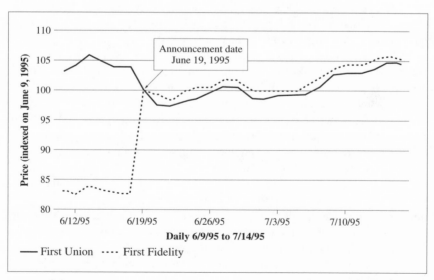

Source: Goldman Sachs.

F I G U R E   3-5

Stock Price Reaction of PNC/Midlantic Merger

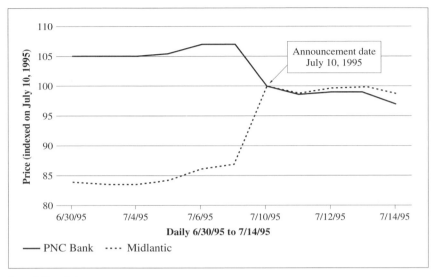

Source: Goldman Sachs.

F I G U R E   3-6

Stock Price Reaction of NBD/First Chicago Merger

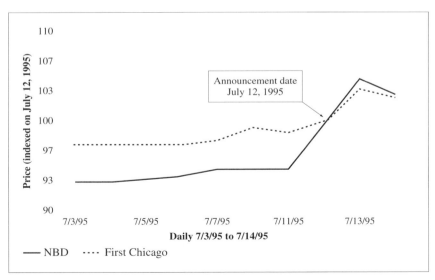

Source: Goldman Sachs.

On the other hand, the shareholders of the acquired company that have been offered a premium obviously benefit handsomely by the merger offer. Sometimes, when a merger is accretive immediately to EPS, the stock price of the acquiring bank also increases. There are situations in which future earnings and EPS grow beyond what the separate entities could have earned independently. This growth in value (synergy) is generated from operating efficiencies, cross-sales of products and services not otherwise provided by each unit, increased professional capabilities afforded by larger enterprises, and lessened loss vulnerability through increased diversification.

Investors must view the projections used to justify the purchase price to be paid for an acquisition with a fair amount of skepticism—particularly those forecasts that come from a management with an unproven or unsuccessful acquisition track record. In the words of Warren Buffet: "While deals often fail in practice, they never fail in projections. If the CEO is visibly panting over a prospective acquisition, subordinates and consultants will supply the requisite projections to rationalize any price." Also, beware of looking at any one deal on a stand-alone basis. For example, consider a company that announces an acquisition that is 5 percent dilutive initially and doesn't raise the growth rate of the company, but the dilution can be recovered over a two-year time frame. One deal like this may or may not be a mistake; however, one such deal every year would result in a no-growth banking company. Investors should concentrate on owning banks that have proven to be value-added acquirors or those that are unlikely to make value-destroying acquisitions. The goal of management should not be survival; it should be an attractive EPS growth rate, accompanied by strong profitability ratios.[3]

A company's ability to control its destiny in the banking industry may rest on its size and perceived strength, which help to build and sustain customer confidence in its survivability. Substantial size means an organization can spread fixed costs over a larger base and also permits it to increase its depth and breadth. Size does matter to those rating the strength of banks, and great size (large market capitalization) can act as a barrier to a takeover. For example, the chairman of one superregional bank seemed to be overpaying on an acquisition in 1992 in the eyes of most Wall Street analysts. This chairman indicated to analysts that he felt he had paid a fair price and predicted that bank takeover prices were going to accelerate over the next few years. Although his forecast proved accurate, he admitted privately that he made the acquisition for defensive purposes, as it was an in-market merger; he also felt that the bigger his company was, the better was the chance of remaining independent. Moreover, he indicated his board's awareness that executive management compensation was partially a function of size.

Although academic textbooks generally report that discounted cash flows represent the best valuation technique, the acquiror of a bank or any other institution is usually concerned with the impact on the current and next year's EPS and the future growth rate in EPS over the next five years from the combination of two firms. As a matter of fact, any competent, due diligence analysis will show numerous forms of analysis.

Sellers assess acquisition proposals by comparing what they can earn from continuing investment in their own bank ownership versus alternative investments. As a result of weak and in some cases uncertain returns from ownership, as well as the need to make large investments in technology, alternative delivery systems, and branch and systems modernization, many small banks and some large banks have been receptive to selling their organization to a friendly buyer or placing it into "play" (selling to the highest bidder). This is especially so when they feel that a large premium to the current share price may be available and that future growth prospects in a merger are considerably greater than if they remain independent.

A bank's board of directors and executive management are faced with the responsibility to maximize shareholder value and determine whether their bank should buy other banks, remain independent, or be positioned for sale. Each alternative has different implications regarding future growth in earnings, the security of jobs, future investment in technology and branching, and nature of services provided.[4]

How does an acquisition increase the value of the acquiring bank? Value is created if the combined bank is able to generate increased earnings or cash flow compared to historical norms. Such increases might result from (1) entry into attractive new markets, (2) stronger product lines, (3) cost-cutting (see Tables 3–4 and 3–5), (4) improved marketing and distribution of products, (5) risk reduction, and (6) improved managerial capability. Increasing market share and revenues create value. A buyer values a target's customer base and will often pay a premium to obtain core deposits or additional customers to whom products could be sold.[5]

T A B L E   3–4

Typical Savings from Mergers in Second Year (% noninterest expenses of acquired bank)

Functional Area	In-Market	Contiguous	Out-of-Market
Systems	6.1%	5.5%	4.4%
Branch networks	5.0	2.5	1.3
Trust and investments	3.9	1.4	1.1
Operations	3.8	3.2	1.9
Financial management	2.4	1.8	0.8
Marketing	2.2	0.8	0.6
Human resources	1.5	1.1	0.5
Sum of other sources	11.9	8.5	3.4
Total	36.8%	24.8%	14.0%

Source: BAI; First Manhattan; *Bank Consolidation Monthly,* CS First Boston, July 14, 1995.

T A B L E   3–5

Cost Savings (% noninterest expenses of acquired bank)

Functional Area	In-Market	Contiguous	Out-of-Market
Systems	55%	50%	40%
Branch networks	20	10	5
Operations	30	25	15
Financial management	60	45	20
Marketing	55	20	15
Trust	55	20	15
Human resources	60	45	20
Other	35	25	10

Source: *Bank Consolidation Monthly,* CS First Boston, July 14, 1995, p. 6.

VALUATION EXAMPLE

The example which follows is a summary of an analysis performed in late 1994 by SunTrust Banks to determine the maximum price it could afford to pay for the shares of an acquisition target, a bank holding company with roughly $18 billion in assets, without diluting its EPS. The multimethod study includes an incremental earnings valuation, EPS valuation with a short-term nondilution limit, a graph showing the dilutive impact of the target's anticipated slower growth rate on the EPS of the acquiror, excessive capital buildup at the target that would be paid to the acquiror in the form of dividends (could be used to buy back outstanding shares of stock), acquisition incremental cash flows, and a discounted cash flow model.

The price suggested by these models represents the maximum price that the acquiror would be willing to pay so that SunTrust shareholders would not be hurt by a dilution in EPS.

Some of the basic statistics and underlying assumptions, as well as background information on the two bank holding companies involved in the potential transaction, are summarized in the tables, figures, and paragraphs which follow. The acquiror would be SunTrust Banks, a $42 billion asset bank holding company with about 625 branches located primarily in Georgia, Florida, and Tennessee. SunTrust Banks was expected to earn $560 million or $4.85 per share, based on 115 million shares outstanding in 1995. At the time of the study the market price per share was $50, the price-to-earnings ratio was 10.3, and the expected long-term growth rate was 10 percent. On the other hand, the target bank had a large branch system in three states. Its 1995 earnings were forecast at $200 million and $3.40 per share based on 60 million shares outstanding. Its market price was $30 per share, price-to-earnings ratio 8.8, and long-term growth rate 5 percent. SunTrust had calculated a weighted average cost of capital of 13 percent and assumed that it could cut the target's noninterest costs by 20 percent (see Table 3–6).

The discounted cash flow model gave an estimated "Cap" offer pricing scenario that was modestly higher than the other methods. The maximum prices that could be offered to avoid dilution were just above $41 in the incremental earnings valuation model, $45 in the EPS valuation (short-term nondilution limit), and just over $47 in the discounted cash flow model. The maximum suggested premiums to be paid over the current market share price ranged from 37 percent in the incremental earnings valuation model to 58 percent in the discounted cash flow model (see Tables 3–7, 3–8, 3–9, and Figures 3–7 and 3–8).

What was the conclusion? The target chose to remain independent. SunTrust Banks chose not to pursue a hostile offer.

T A B L E   3–6

Acquisition Data

	Target	Buyer
Assets (in millions)	$18,000	$42,000
Earnings (in millions)	$200	$560
Shares (in millions)	60	115
Per share		
Earnings	$3.40	$4.85
Market	$30.00	$50.00
P/E ratio	8.8	10.3
Term growth rate	5%	10%

T A B L E   3–7

Incremental Earnings Valuation

20% Target cost savings (in millions)	$65
Buyer EPS	$4.85
Break-even shares (in millions)	13.4
Market value addition (in millions)	$670
Target's current market (in millions)	$1,800
Total market value exchanged (in millions)	$2,470
Target exchange value per share	$41.17
P/E of target	12.4
Premium paid	37%

T A B L E 3–8

EPS Valuation: Short-Term Nondilution Limit

Normalized 1995	Target
Earnings (in millions)	$200
20% Target cost savings	65
Adjusted earnings (in millions)	$265
Buyer EPS	$4.85
Break-even shares	54.6
Market value (in millions)	$2,700
Target no. shares (in millions)	60
Target exchange value per share	$45.00
P/E of target	13.3
Premium paid	50%

T A B L E 3–9

DCF Valuation: Nondilution Limit ($ millions)

	Cash Flow	P.V. at 13%
1995	$275	242
1996	308	238
1997	344	233
1998	382	228
1999	424	222
2000	469	216
Terminal 8.5× Alone	3,200	1,473
Total		$2,852
Buyer stock price		$50
Shares traded (in millions)		57
Premium over market		58%

VALUATION

Buyers must examine a variety of financial and nonfinancial factors when deciding whether to negotiate a deal and at what price. How do you put a value on an

F I G U R E   3–7

Dilutive Impact of Target's Slower Growth
Excess Capital Build Up Invested Wisely

F I G U R E   3–8

Acquisition Incremental Cash Flow (in millions)

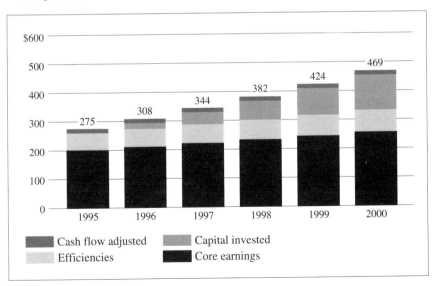

acquisition? The theoretically correct procedure for determining value is to discount expected cash flows from the new entities at the appropriate discount rate. The buyer projects future earnings that are then discounted at the required rate of return to determine the true economic value. Since this approach involves estimates of many key components of the present value model, market participants often use a variety of less rigorous techniques. Other procedures focus on recently completed transactions and average premium to book value or EPS ratios. These historic averages are then applied to a similarly structured and sized target bank's financial measures to estimate a range of potential prices, which are then used in negotiations with the bank to be acquired. The agreed-upon price will reflect recent market prices for similar acquisitions and adjustments for off-balance-sheet activities, each party's bargaining strength, and the nonpecuniary benefits that the negotiators include in the price: public recognition, ego, asset size, market share, potential cost savings, potential revenue enhancements, and so forth.

Since many of these ideas are discussed elsewhere in this book, we will only mention some of the adjustments that must be considered to help determine the fair premium to be paid. Adjusted book value can be obtained by adding to or subtracting from the stated book value changes in loan loss reserves, changes in other asset appraisals, value of off-balance-sheet activities, value of core deposits, and so forth.

For example, adjustments for changes in asset quality are often necessary. If asset value is lower than that reported, the loan loss reserve should be restated at a higher level such that net loans are lower than the reported figure. On the other hand, if asset quality is higher than reported, the loan loss reserve should be adjusted downward so that net loans are higher. There can also be changes in the market value of investment securities brought about by changes in interest rates. For example, if the market value of securities differs sharply from cost because interest rates have either increased or declined, that difference should be added to or subtracted from book value.

There can also be differences in the market value of other assets (such as real estate or stock acquired because of a loan default) and the costs reflected on the balance sheet. If the market value is above book value, the difference should be added to the book value of equity. There will also be adjustments to the book value of off-balance-sheet activities. Mortgage servicing, trust assets under management, and number of active credit card accounts may have a special value to the buyer that is not fully reflected in the stock price. An estimate of this market value should be added to the book value of equity. Core deposits are another valuable factor because of their relative stability and the fact that an acquiror can leverage them by selling additional products and services to the existing deposit holders. This value also incorporates the franchise value of the bank, or its value as an ongoing concern. However, this value is difficult to estimate.[6] It is interesting to point out that the stated book value per share for Norwest in 1994 was

$10.97. However, footnote 17 in Norwest's 1994 *Annual Report* shows a fair book value of $42.23 per share, almost four times the stated book value. The two largest positive discrepancies are the consumer finance network and core deposit valuation (see Figure 3–9).

Other factors that can influence the price premium include the amount of competition in the bidding for the takeover candidate, the size of noninterest expenses that can be cut after the merger, the overall quality and diversification of assets, the degree of interest rate risk, and hidden value in either the bond portfolio, loan portfolio, or other assets.

There are also substantive nonprice objectives that influence deals. Buyers generally wish to avoid postmerger financial and operational complications, hoping that the two banking cultures match and that the two managements can work together without major conflict. They want to retain the best employees and the best customers of the acquired bank, maintain the beneficial aspects of the acquired bank's culture, and minimize dilution of earnings per share. Sellers want to walk away from a deal without any residual risk, keep as many of the employees of the acquired bank employed by the acquiring bank as possible, and gain concessions from the acquiring bank to continue to support local community activities of the acquired bank.

POOLING OR PURCHASE ACCOUNTING

Reported earnings and thus EPS are impacted by accounting standards as well as the real economic return from an activity. The approach used to account for an acquired business can greatly affect the apparent profitability resulting from the transaction. Two accounting approaches, purchase or pooling, for an acquisition can result in materially different reported earnings of the acquiror.

Pooling accounting assumes that the two entities combine into one and are recognized as if they have never been separate. Prior period reports are restated to reflect this assumption. Under generally accepted accounting principles (GAAP), certain conditions must be met for an acquiror to elect this accounting treatment. The most important of these is that at least 90 percent of the remuneration must be paid to sellers in the form of "untainted acquiror stock." Pooling accounting assumes that essentially the entire transaction is paid for with added company stock. In addition, acquirors often prefer to avoid the tax consequences of a cash transaction. Also, pooling prohibits wholesale asset liquidation after the acquisition.[7] For there to be no postacquisition dilution in EPS, the return on the new shares must be at least equal to what the acquiror was earning on its preacquisition shares.

It is possible that a company can add to its capacity to use long-term debt for an acquisition by adding to its capital base throughout the transaction by using discounted cash flow valuation techniques. In most cases, such techniques result in

FIGURE 3–9

Fair Values of Financial Instruments and Certain Non-Financial Instruments

17 **NOTE** **Fair Values of Financial Instruments and Certain Non-financial Instruments**

Statement of Financial Accounting Standards No. 107 "Disclosures about Fair Value of Financial Instruments" (FAS 107) requires the disclosure of estimated fair values of all asset, liability and off-balance sheet financial instruments. FAS 107 also allows the disclosure of estimated fair values of non-financial instruments. Fair value estimates under FAS 107 are determined as of a specific point in time utilizing various assumptions and estimates. The use of assumptions and various valuation techniques, as well as the absence of secondary markets for certain financial instruments, will likely reduce the comparability of fair value disclosures between financial institutions.

Financial Instruments The fair value estimates disclosed in the table below are based on existing on and off-balance sheet financial instruments and do not consider the value of future business. Other significant assets and liabilities, which are not considered financial assets or liabilities and for which fair values have not been estimated, include premises and equipment, goodwill and other intangibles, deferred taxes and other liabilities. The estimated fair values of the corporation's financial instruments as of December 31 are set forth in the following table and explained below.

The following methods and assumptions are used by the corporation in estimating its fair value disclosures for financial instruments.

Cash and Cash Equivalents The carrying value of cash and cash equivalents approximates fair value due to the relatively short period of time between the origination of the instruments and their expected realization.

Trading Account Securities, Investment Securities, Mortgage-Backed Securities, Investments and Mortgage-Backed Securities Available for Sale Fair values of these financial instruments were estimated using quoted market prices, when available. If quoted market prices were not available, fair value was estimated using quoted market prices for similar assets.

Mortgages Held for Sale Fair values of mortgages held for sale are stated at market.

Loans and Leases and Student Loans Available for Sale Fair values for loans and leases are estimated based on contractual cash flows, adjusted for prepayment assumptions and credit risk factors, discounted using the current market rate for loans and leases. Variable rate loans, including student loans available for sale, are valued at carrying value since the loans reprice to market rates over short periods of time. Credit card receivables are valued at carrying value since the receivables are priced near market rates for such receivables and are short-term in life. The fair value of the corporation's consumer finance subsidiaries' loans have been reported at book value since the estimated life, assuming prepayments, is short-term in nature.

Interest Receivable and Payable The carrying value of interest receivable and payable approximates fair value due to the relatively short period of time between accrual and expected realization.

Excess Servicing Rights Receivable Excess servicing rights receivable represents the present value using applicable investor yields of estimated future servicing revenues in excess of normal servicing revenues over the assumed life of the servicing portfolio.

Deposits The fair value of fixed-maturity deposits is the present value of the contractual cash flows, including principal and interest, and servicing costs, discounted using an appropriate investor yield.

In accordance with FAS 107, the fair value of deposits with no stated maturity, such as demand deposit, savings, NOW and money market accounts, are disclosed as the amount payable on demand.

Fair Values of Financial Instruments

In millions

	1994 Carrying Amount	1994 Fair Value	1993 Carrying Amount	1993 Fair Value	1992 Carrying Amount	1992 Fair Value
Financial assets:						
Cash and cash equivalents	$ 4,024.3	4,024.3	3,608.0	3,608.0	3,428.0	3,428.0
Trading account securities	172.3	172.3	279.1	279.1	132.0	132.0
Investment securities	1,235.1	1,268.7	1,542.7	1,597.6	1,865.0	1,927.3
Mortgage-backed securities	—	—	151.0	153.1	165.9	167.5
Investment securities available for sale	1,427.6	1,427.6	2,001.2	2,260.9	1,573.6	1,815.7
Mortgage-backed securities available for sale	12,174.2	12,174.2	9,021.6	9,244.0	9,358.2	9,565.6
Student loans available for sale	2,031.4	2,031.4	1,349.2	1,349.2	1,156.5	1,156.5
Mortgages held for sale	3,115.3	3,115.3	6,090.7	6,103.4	4,727.8	4,727.8
Loans and leases, net	31,786.1	31,872.8	27,971.6	28,236.7	25,009.4	25,255.3
Interest receivable	367.7	367.7	300.8	300.8	330.9	330.9
Excess servicing rights receivable	98.9	139.4	54.4	86.7	9.0	20.7
Total financial assets	56,432.9	56,593.7	52,370.3	53,219.5	47,756.3	48,527.3
Financial liabilities:						
Non-maturity deposits	24,475.6	24,475.6	24,066.8	24,066.8	20,116.9	20,116.9
Deposits with stated maturities	11,948.4	11,696.9	11,909.7	12,074.5	11,492.5	11,687.9
Short-term borrowings	7,850.2	7,850.2	5,996.8	5,996.8	8,824.9	8,824.9
Long-term debt	9,186.3	8,825.5	6,850.9	6,928.7	4,553.2	4,645.2
Interest payable	259.0	259.0	238.4	238.4	263.8	263.8
Total financial liabilities	53,719.5	53,107.2	49,062.6	49,305.2	45,251.3	45,538.7
Off-balance sheet financial instruments:						
Forward delivery commitments	(2.3)	(2.3)	28.3	28.3	(35.7)	(35.7)
Interest rate swaps	(1.5)	(25.0)	11.2	14.8	0.7	(7.0)
Futures contracts	—	—	0.5	—	—	—
Interest rate caps/floors	5.8	12.5	2.4	17.2	23.4	36.3
Option contracts to sell	(4.6)	(4.6)	4.2	8.1	—	—
Foreign exchange contracts	0.6	0.6	(0.4)	(0.4)	—	—
Total off balance sheet financial instruments	(2.0)	(18.8)	46.2	68.0	(11.6)	(6.4)
Net financial instruments	$ 2,711.4	3,467.7	3,353.9	3,982.3	2,493.4	2,982.2

F I G U R E   3–9 (concluded)

Short-Term Borrowings The carrying value of short-term borrowings approximates fair value due to the relatively short period of time between the origination of the instruments and their expected payment.

Long-Term Debt The fair value of long-term debt is the present value of the contractual cash flows, discounted by the investor yield which considers the corporation's credit rating.

Commitments to Extend Credit, Standby Letters of Credit and Recourse Obligations The majority of the corporation's commitment agreements and letters of credit contain variable interest rates and counterparty credit deterioration clauses and therefore, the carrying value of the corporation's commitments to extend credit and letters of credit approximates fair value. The fair value of the corporation's recourse obligations are valued based on estimated cash flows associated with such obligations. As any potential liabilities under such recourse obligations are recognized on the corporation's balance sheet, the carrying value of such recourse obligations approximates fair value.

Forward Delivery Commitments, Interest Rate Swaps, Futures Contracts, Options, Interest Rate Caps and Floors and Foreign Exchange Contracts The fair value of forward delivery commitments, interest rate caps and floors, swaps, options, futures contracts and foreign exchange contracts is estimated, using dealer quotes, as the amount that the corporation would receive or pay to execute a new agreement with terms identical to those remaining on the current agreement, considering current interest rates.

Certain Non-Financial Instruments

Supplemental fair value information for certain non-financial instruments as of December 31 are set forth in the following table and explained below.

The supplemental fair value information, combined with the total fair value of net financial instruments from the table on page 67, is presented below for information purposes. This combination is not necessarily indicative of the "franchise value" or the fair value of the corporation taken as a whole.

In millions, except per share amounts	1994	1993	1992
Non-financial instrument assets and liabilities:			
Premises and equipment, net	$ 955.2	842.1	742.2
Other assets	1,927.8	1,452.6	1,538.5
Accrued expenses and other liabilities	(1,750.0)	(1,841.5)	(1,413.9)
Other values:			
Non-maturity deposits	2,684.1	1,265.1	1,150.4
Consumer finance network	3,207.1	3,128.5	2,374.0
Credit card	259.9	245.3	84.6
Banking subsidiaries' consumer loans	166.3	269.3	224.4
Mortgage servicing	867.0	431.4	187.2
Mortgage loan origination/ wholesale network	621.4	836.4	707.6
Trust department	709.8	631.8	570.0
Net fair value of certain non-financial instruments	9,648.6	7,261.0	6,165.0
Net fair value of financial instruments	3,467.7	3,982.3	2,982.2
Stockholders' equity at the net fair value of financial instruments and certain non-financial instruments*			
Amount	$13,116.3	11,243.3	9,147.2
Per common share at December 31	$ 42.43	36.59	30.33

Amounts do not include applicable deferred income taxes, if any.

The following methods and assumptions were used by the corporation in estimating the fair value of certain non-financial instruments.

Non-Financial Instrument Assets and Liabilities The non-financial instrument assets and liabilities are stated at book value, which approximates fair value.

Non-Maturity Deposits The fair value table of financial instruments does not consider the benefit resulting from the low-cost funding provided by deposit liabilities as compared with wholesale funding rates. The fair value of non-maturity deposits, considering these relational benefits, would be $21,791.5 million, $22,801.7 million, and $18,966.5 million at December 31, 1994, 1993 and 1992, respectively. Such amounts are based on a discounted cash flow analysis, assuming a constant balance over ten years and taking into account the interest sensitivity of each deposit category. During 1994, the corporation considered a greater percentage of the deposit rates to be fixed than in prior years.

Consumer Finance Network The supplemental fair value table includes the estimated fair value associated with the consumer finance network which is estimated to be $3,207.1 million, $3,128.5 million and $2,374.0 million at December 31, 1994, 1993 and 1992, respectively. Such estimates are based on current industry price/earnings ratios for similar networks. These current price/earnings ratios are industry averages and do not consider the higher earnings levels and the value of the data processing business associated with the corporation's consumer finance network.

Credit Card The fair value of financial instruments excludes the fair value attributed to the expected credit card balances in future years with the holders of such cards. The fair value of such future balances is estimated to exceed book value by $259.9 million, $245.3 million and $84.6 million at December 31, 1994, 1993 and 1992, respectively. This represents the fair value related to such future balances of both securitized and on-balance sheet credit card receivables based on a discounted cash flow analysis, utilizing an investor yield on similar portfolio acquisitions.

Banking Subsidiaries' Consumer Loans For purposes of the table of fair values of financial instruments on page 67, the fair value of the banking subsidiaries' consumer loans is based on the contractual balances and maturities of existing loans. The fair value of such financial instruments does not consider future loans with customers. The fair value related to such future balances is estimated to be $166.3 million, $269.3 million and $224.4 million at December 31, 1994, 1993 and 1992, respectively. This fair value is estimated by cash flow analysis, discounted utilizing an investor yield. The expected balances for such purposes are estimated to extend ten years at a constant rate of replacement.

Mortgage Servicing Mortgage servicing represents estimated current value in the servicing portfolio. The corporation estimates that the fair value of its mortgage servicing exceeds book value by $867.0 million, $431.4 million and $187.2 million at December 31, 1994, 1993 and 1992, respectively.

Mortgage Loan Origination/Wholesale Network The supplemental fair value table includes the fair value associated with the corporation's origination network for mortgage loans, which is estimated to be $621.4 million, $836.4 million and $707.6 million at December 31, 1994, 1993 and 1992, respectively. Such estimates are based on current industry price/earnings ratios for similar networks.

Trust Department The fair value associated with the corporation's management of trust assets is estimated to be $709.8 million, $631.8 million and $570.0 million at December 31, 1994, 1993 and 1992, respectively. Such estimates are based on current trust revenues using an industry multiple.

Source: Norwest Corporation, 1994 *Annual Report*

higher valuations than measuring capacity to pay based on the acquisition's impact on earnings per share. Buyers employing this broadly accepted form of price setting can rationalize paying a higher price than those focusing only on the impact on EPS. The highly respected consulting organization, First Manhattan Consulting Group, concludes that acquirors should use the discounted cash flow technique; but when the final valuation is made, the discounted cash flow forecast may be moderated to mediate the impact of the acquisition on EPS growth. In other words, a company could structure a deal in which the selling shareholders got the full benefit of the acquisition synergies, thus not adding to the buyer's EPS. Still, the transaction could be favorable to the receiving shareholders because of a positive return calculated in the discounted cash flow analysis. Buyers would be willing to pay a price up to an amount that would not dilute EPS, since the real economic return exceeds that reported in the income statement. The actual pricing results from negotiations between the seller and buyer to reach a price acceptable to both parties.

There are more than pure economic or financial factors that play a role in the final pricing of a deal. These factors include the personal interests of key shareholders and managements of both organizations. Regulatory pressures, strategic game plans, the personalities of the chief executives of the involved banks, and the historical treatment of the employees of acquired banks by the acquiring bank can also impact the final pricing of some deals. Strategic mergers were justified in the past, not necessarily on the financial return, but on the institutional positioning designed to carve out national or regional franchises, geographical diversification, and market share ahead of the competition. Future business opportunities rather than immediate increases in EPS justified the deals to the acquirors. Strategic value encompasses fundamental value plus potential strategic and operating advantages that a buyer can expect to gain from an acquisition. Hence, a buyer may be willing to pay an additional amount for an acquisition candidate.[8]

Purchase accounting assumes togetherness only from the point of combination. Under this approach, assets of the acquired bank are marked to market and added to those of the acquiror. The positive factors of purchase accounting are the avoidance of shareholder dilution from share issuances as well as the reduction of idle excess capital. On the negative side, "goodwill," an intangible asset, is created when the acquisition price exceeds the mark-to-market equity of the acquired. This asset is depreciated over time through an expense charge against ongoing earnings. Thus, purchase accounting normally results in reduced reported earnings and EPS until the intangible assets are fully depreciated (see Figure 3–10). This may stretch out for 15 or even 40 years.

The value of the assets on the balance sheet of the acquiring bank must be adjusted to reflect goodwill. The addition of goodwill onto an acquiror's balance sheet is generally unattractive to the acquiror. Also, any goodwill created affects tier 1 capital ratios in two ways: goodwill is deducted from the numerator and fully included in the denominator. Goodwill can become an asset burden, so companies use purchase

FIGURE   3–10

Management Note: Intangible Assets from Wells Fargo & Company and Subsidiaries

Wells Fargo's balance sheet shows both *tangible assets* (such as loans, buildings, and investments) and *intangible assets* (such as goodwill). Wells Fargo now carries $532 million of goodwill and $467 million of identifiable intangible assets on its balance sheet. Most came from its purchase of 130 branches of Great American Bank in 1990 and 1991, and Crocker National Bank in 1986.

These intangibles represent real value to Wells Fargo. For example, when Wells Fargo purchased the Great American branches, we paid a $465 million premium above the book value of the assets acquired in the transaction. We paid the price because Great American's Southern California franchise, with its excellent branch locations, strong customer base, and $6.2 billion in stable, low-cost core deposits, presented an important opportunity to strengthen our presence in Southern California and moved us to a number one market share in San Diego.

Wells Fargo's income statement is also affected by the level of intangibles. For example, for the first nine months of 1992, we incurred approximately $85 million of intangible amortization that appears as an expense on our income statement.

Intangible assets are typically created when companies pay a premium over book value to make acquisitions of businesses and use the "purchase" method of accounting. This is different from the "pooling" method in which the balance sheets of the two companies are added together on a line-by-line basis, thereby creating no intangible assets.

There are two types of intangibles. *Identifiable intangibles* are those that relate to the fair market value of specific customer relationships. Acquisitions of such items as core deposit liabilities, credit card relationships, and mortgage servicing rights create this type of intangible. We estimate the current value of future revenues attributable to such relationships in order to establish the amount of identifiable intangibles. Core deposits, for example, might be worth 2 to 7 percent more than the actual amount on deposit with the bank, depending upon the relative costs of other borrowing sources. This premium is the core deposit intangible. The identifiable intangibles created when purchasing other lines of business, such as credit card and mortgage servicing rights, reflect the present value of expected benefit from those relationships. The value of these intangibles is reassessed regularly. If we determine that the value of an asset is impaired, we make an adjustment to that asset on our books.

A second category of intangibles is *goodwill*. Goodwill represents the excess of the purchase price (premium) over the fair market value of the assets (including identifiable intangibles) and liabilities acquired.

Under accounting rules, intangibles are written off over a period of time and eventually disappear as an asset on the balance sheet. Some of the intangible amortization expense is deductible for tax purposes. The following simplified example illustrates the difference in balance sheet and income statement treatment of an acquisition under the purchase and pooling methods of accounting.

Assume Bank A, with $1,000 of loans, $950 of deposits, and $50 of equity on its balance sheet, acquires Bank B, an identical bank. The purchase price is two times book value, using all stock and no cash: that is, Bank A issues $100 of equity for the purchase. If each bank earns $10, they both look like this before the acquisition:

ASSETS	LIABILITIES	INCOME
Loans $1,000	Deposits $950	Earnings = $10
	Equity 50	ROA = 1%
		ROE = 20%

In purchase accounting, the newly issued equity of $100 is added to the equity of the acquiring bank, and the purchase premium of $50 is counted as an intangible asset on Bank A's balance sheet. (For purposes of illustration, the fair value of Bank B's loans and deposits is assumed to equal book value.) Earnings are reduced by the amortization of the intangible assets, which we have assumed to be straight line over 10 years ($5 per year) and not tax-deductible.

The resulting balance sheet and income statement would be:

ASSETS	LIABILITIES	INCOME
Loans $2,000	Deposits $1,900	Earnings = $15
Intangibles 50	Equity 150	ROA = .73%
		ROE = 10%

Under the more restrictive pooling method, the balance sheet and income statement of the combined company would appear as indicated below, with the balance sheets of the two banks added line by line with no resulting intangible assets.

ASSETS	LIABILITIES	INCOME
Loans $2,000	Deposits $1,900	Earnings = $20
	Equity 100	ROA = 1%
		ROE = 20%

Although Bank A issued $100 of equity to acquire Bank B, there is only a $50 increase in equity representing the addition of the book value of Bank B. It is as though the other $50 in equity issued to shareholders of the acquired bank was "written off" on the acquisition date without ever flowing through the income statement as amortization.

At first glance, two identical acquisitions would give dramatically different results based on the accounting method used, which depends on the particulars of each individual acquisition and how the accounting rules fit the specific circumstances. Earnings are higher under the pooling method because there is no amortization of intangibles. ROA and ROE are also higher because of both the difference in income and the lower equity base.

However, when considering cash flow and tangible net worth, the two companies are identical. Since intangible amortization expense is not a cash flow, the cash earnings for companies using either accounting method are $20 after the acquisition is completed. Tangible net worth (equity less intangibles) is also the same for both companies.

Source: 1992 Third quarter report, Wells Fargo & Company and subsidiaries.

accounting when the prospect of creating a lot of goodwill is low and when a merger generates significant cost savings and revenue enhancements.[9] Thomas H. Hanley, the eminent bank stock analyst from CS First Boston, has suggested that future deals may be structured as purchases to allow the carve-out and sale of undesirable assets, which would make acquisition success less dependent upon cost savings.

HYPOTHETICAL PURCHASE CAPACITY OF BANC ONE

For example, the hypothetical purchase capacity of Banc One is outlined in Table 3–10. Assuming capital adequacy constraints of a leverage ratio of more than 7 percent and a double leverage ratio of less than 1.125 times, and an internal growth rate for Banc One of 12 percent, Banc One can pay up to $1.2 billion for a nonbank (at 350 percent of book value) and up to $1.4 billion for a bank (at 175 percent of book value).

In the nonbank case, Banc One could add on additional $870 million in goodwill, which translates into a purchase price of $1.2 billion, assuming a purchase premium of 350 percent of book value. This purchase price assumes an equity-to-assets ratio of 5 percent, income growth of 20 percent, and a ROE of 25 percent.

Using the same analysis, Banc One could utilize its excess capital to purchase a banking institution for 41.4 billion, assuming the following minimum guidelines: a 7 percent equity-to-assets ratio, a 10 percent income growth rate, and a purchase price of 175 percent of book value. Through these assumption, Banc One could use up $600 million in excess capital (via goodwill), which translates into a $1.4 billion purchase price and an asset size of approximately $11 billion. An $11 billion bank is clearly not a big acquisition for the $88 billion Banc One, which demonstrates limitations of purchase transactions for Banc One and the relative attractiveness of pooling transactions.[10]

T A B L E   3–10

Purchase Capacity, Banc One ($ in millions)

	Acquire Nonbank	Acquire Bank
Equity to assets	5.0%	7.0%
Price/book value	350	175
Income growth	20	10
Purchase price	$1,218	$1,400
Goodwill	870	600
Book value	48	800
ROE	25%	15%
Pro forma double leverage	1.061×	1.026×
Pro forma leverage	7.0%	7.0%

Source: Banc One.

Table 3–11 details a bank merger that used the purchase method of accounting, while Table 3–12 shows a bank merger that used the pooling method of accounting. Table 3–13 shows the recent trend in bank and thrift mergers (pooling or nonpooling transactions) for deals larger than $100 million.

T A B L E   3-11

Example of Cash Acquisition—Purchase Accounting ($ in millions)

	Buyer	Seller	Combined
Assets, preacquisition	$4,000	$1,000	$5,000
Market adjustment		(50)	(100)
Goodwill		100	200
Assets, postacquisition	4,000	1,050	5,100
Liabilities, preacquisition	3,700	900	4,600
Market adjustment		10	10
Liabilities, postacquisition	3,700	910	4,610
Equity, preacquisition	300	100	400
Market adjustment		(60)	(60)
Sellers' price premium		100	100
Equity, postacquisition	300	140	440
Net income, preacquisition	50	12	62
After-tax interest cost		(9)	(9)
After-tax write-off			
Market adjustments		3	3
Goodwill		(6)	(6)
Net income, postacquisition	50	0	0
Outstanding stock (shares in millions)	10		10
Earnings per share	$5.00		$5.00

ROLE OF DUE DILIGENCE IN THE ACQUISITION PROCESS

Careful scrutiny of an acquiree's financial, contingencies, and operations is an important part of the acquisition process. This due diligence is often completed before any offer is made with only a few "outlines" that are well documented. The deal is subject to bonded values being uncovered for these items with a "price" incorporated to cover the case if the values are outside the bounds. The agreement is often confirmed in a letter of intent or in a purchase agreement. The deal may be protected from outside intrusion through various techniques, including an agreement to sell a large amount of stock to the planned partner in the transaction if an outside party attempts to acquire either party.

T A B L E   3–12

Example of Stock Acquisition—Pooling Accounting (in millions # of shares)

	Buyer	Seller	Combined
Assets, preacquisition	4,000	1,000	5,000
Market adjustment			
Goodwill			
Assets, postacquisition	4,000	1,000	5,000
Liabilities, preacquisition	3,700	900	4,600
Market adjustment			
Liabilities, postacquisition	3,700	900	4,600
Equity, preacquisition	300	100	400
Market adjustment			
Seller's price premium			
Equity, postacquisition	300	100	400
Net income, preacquisition	50	12	62
After-tax interest cost			
After-tax write-off			
Market adjustments			
Goodwill			
Net income, postacquisition	50	12	62
Outstanding stock (shares in millions)	10	3	13
Earnings per share	$5.00		$4.77

T A B L E   3–13

Recent Trends in Bank and Thrift Mergers Greater than $100 Million

	1991	1992	1993	1994	1995*	Total
Number of mergers announced	21	34	43	41	21	160
Number of pooling (stock) transactions	19	26	28	22	14	109
Number of nonpooling transactions[†]	2	8	15	19	7	51
Percentage of nonpooling transactions	10%	24%	35%	46%	33%	32%

* As of July 13, 1995.

† Includes transactions completed using a combination of stock and cash, and those in which there was a repurchase of shares equal to the amount issued in the transaction.

Source: Goldman Sachs, Project Soleil, July 21, 1995.

The examination process is necessarily tailored to each situation. Most regional banks, having conducted many due diligence studies, are able to complete the activity within a few days when the counterparty is a small local bank. However, when two large banks are being joined, the due diligence process may involve over 100 analysts for approximately two weeks. Since most of the risks in banking are centered in the loan and investment portfolio, significant time is spent examining major credit commitments and lending and documentation procedures. Following is an abbreviated list of basic information one regional bank requests of a small seller at the beginning of the diligence process:

1. Organization chart.

2. Audited financial statements or annual reports for last three years (consolidated and unconsolidated statements if multiple entities).

3. All quarterly reports since most recent annual report.

4. Call report—most recent.

5. Chart of accounts.

6. General ledger listing for most recent month.

7. Three years of tax returns.

8. Information on any dilutive securities, for example, stock options, warrants, or convertible preferred stock.

9. Severance agreements.

10. Board reports and minutes.

11. Name of DP servicers and termination penalties.

12. Summary breakdown of loans by category.

13. Summary of deposits by category.

14. Detailed listing of securities portfolio with mark-to-market values shown.

15. Listing of significant fixed assets owned and leased.

16. Service charge schedules.

17. Trust department financial and fee schedules.

The team conducting the due diligence effort is customarily composed of knowledgeable officers from a number of areas of the acquiror's institution, including auditing, taxes, credit review, lending, controllership, operations, and human resources. Consultants are often used to supplement the team, especially when an independent view is valued or when the "acquiring institution" may not have expertise in some areas of service of the "acquired" institution.

THE SUPERREGIONALS

The banks discussed in the chapters that follow have been major factors in consolidation activities during the 1980s and the first half of the 1990s. They will most likely play a salient role in shaping the banking industry through the remainder of the 1990s. Though they will continue to buy a few smaller banks here and there to fill in coverage in existing markets, increasing market share and consolidating operating efficiencies, the major transactions in terms of impact on share value and institutional development will come from entering new markets through sizable transactions, including the purchase of other large or superregional banking organizations such as the Fleet acquisition of Shawmut, the Key/Society merger, the First Chicago/NBD merger, or the First Union acquisition of First Fidelity.

It is highly likely that there will be several mergers among the banks mentioned in this book as the industry moves through this wave of consolidation. The new interstate banking bill facilitates this movement by eliminating regional compacts originally passed by state legislators to permit their regional banks the opportunity to merge and grow en masse prior to the intrusion into local markets by the few megabanks located principally in New York. These laws precluded entry by outsiders through acquisitions of banks within a defined region. Not only did these protective laws preclude entry by outsiders into the region, they also kept banks from within the region from making acquisitions outside of the designated region. Now that regional and superregional banks have grown materially in size, these protective laws have become detrimental to regionally domiciled banks. Therefore, a number of state legislatures moved in advance of Congress and eliminated the geographically restrictive expansion laws.

The federal interstate banking law change, though not terribly significant in itself, increased interest in and conversations about mergers across state lines and into distant territories, which in turn led to renewed appraisals of other lines of business that could be expanded through nonbank acquisitions. During the past few years, the focus has shifted away from just acquiring banks, to establishing sources of fee income in unregulated or modestly regulated markets that grow faster than traditional banking activities. There has been an attempt to diversify into new product lines and to obtain geographical diversification, while reducing credit and interest rate risks and increasing income.

Acting as a catalyst in the merger frenzy are the emotive forces of fear and ambition. The fear stems from the threat of an unwanted takeover and from the danger of being left behind as other banks become bigger and more powerful. Ambition has been an equally potent source, as personified by Edward Crutchfield, CEO of First Union. His philosophy can best be summarized in a comment made in 1994: "Size is the admission ticket to play the game."[11]

Other factors that are increasing merger activity are excess bank capital, the rapid changes and associated high costs of technological developments, and increasing competition in the lending and depository arenas. According to Richard Thomas, chairman of First Chicago NBD, "There is excess capital and capacity in the business . . . Large companies do not use bank credit any more . . . And the competition for those who do want to use banks is becoming more intense . . . The pace of technological change is so rapid that only big banks can afford the investment needed to keep pace."[12]

In support of this statement, David Vitale, vice chairman of First Chicago, has stated that "With more and more products requiring heavy technology spending, you are better off if you can spread the cost over a broader customer base." In addition, Gerald Smith, the head of investment banking in UBS Securities' Financial Institutions Group, has stated, "Technology is a new imperative. Those that can spend on technology are going to dominate the field." There is a major disagreement on whether asset size is the critically important factor in being able to afford the necessary technological expenditures. According to Chris Fornant, chairman of Coopers & Lybrand's global practice area for retail distribution, "Technology is relatively inexpensive nowadays. Technology is yesterday's argument." Blaming a bank's lack of competitiveness on its inability to invest large sums of money in technology is "a cop-out."[13]

Banks have not been losing market share because they can't afford the necessary technological investments. They have lost market share because of inferior strategy and execution. There is no question that most bank holding companies need major system upgrades and other technological investments, but it is not necessary that banks have asset bases in excess of $100 billion or even $50 billion to afford such investments.[14]

ENDNOTES

1. T.W. Koch, *Bank Management* (Fort Worth, TX: The Dryden Press, 1995), pp. 848–49.
2. J.B. McCoy, L.A. Frieder, and R.B. Hedges, Jr., *BottomLine Banking* (Chicago: Probus Publishing Co., 1994), pp. 180–81.
3. T.K. Brown, "Challenging Some of the Traditional Wisdom Surrounding Bank Consolidation," *DLJ Bank Notes*, August 18, 1995, pp. 2, 9.
4. Koch, p. 842.
5. Ibid., pp. 851–52.
6. Ibid., pp. 858–61.
7. McCoy, Frieder, and Hedges, pp. 163–64.
8. Ibid., p. 158.
9. T.H. Hanley, "Excess Capital at Commercial Banks," *CS First Boston*, May 31, 1995, p. 5.
10. McCoy, Frieder, and Hedges, pp. 164–65.
11. R. Waters, "Dash to Take Part in Mating Game," *Financial Times*, July 17, 1995, p. 13.
12. Ibid., p. 13.
13. Brown, p. 2.
14. Ibid., p. 8.

MIDWESTERN BANKS

Our universe of midwestern superregional banks consists of First Chicago NBD Corporation, Banc One, KeyCorp, Norwest, and PNC Corp.

First Chicago NBD is the largest of the group, with about $120 billion in assets. It was formed as a merger of equals between First Chicago Corporation, a leading wholesale and credit card bank, and NBD, which has both a strong retail and corporate banking presence in the Midwest. The new bank is currently the seventh largest bank holding company in the nation, with over 750 domestic banking offices; the bank also maintains an international presence in London, Tokyo, Beijing, and other cities. First Chicago NBD is number one in Midwest large corporate banking and middle-market banking; number one in consumer banking in the tristate area of Michigan, Illinois, and Indiana; number four in credit card issuance nationwide, with $14 billion outstanding; number three in the cash management business; and a leading trust bank, with $62 billion in discretionary assets under management. Prior to the merger, both banks were highly efficient and exhibited exceptionally high credit quality in their loan portfolios. Operating independently in 1994, NBD and First Chicago had ROAs of 1.08 percent and 1.21 percent and ROEs of 16.10 percent and 15.50 percent, respectively.

Banc One, headquartered in Columbus, Ohio, is the second largest of the group and has one of the premier banking franchises in the country, operating in 12 states with over 48,000 employees and 1,300 banking offices. Banc One had stellar 1993 financial ratios with an ROA and ROE of 1.53 percent and 17.81 percent, respectively, before slumping in 1994 as a result of misjudging the direction of interest rates. The first decline in earnings in over a decade cost the bank its premium price-to-earnings multiple and handicapped the bank in its 1994–95 acquisition programs. A salient characteristic of Banc One is exemplary credit quality.

Banc One also has a history of acquiring healthy and profitable banks and improving their performance germane to revenue enhancement and expense control. As a matter of fact, since 1984 Banc One has acquired approximately 75 banking organizations. Banc One is extremely well capitalized, with a 1994 tangible common equity ratio near the top of the list of superregionals and an above average internal capital generation ratio. John McCoy, a third generation banker and an admired CEO, was named "Banker of the Year" by the *American Banker* a few years ago.

PNC Bank Corp., based in Pittsburgh, was the nation's 11th largest banking organization, with assets of $62 billion, in 1994. It merged with Midlantic Bank ($14 billion in assets) in 1995, becoming the second largest bank in both New Jersey and the Philadelphia area. PNC operates community banks in Pennsylvania, New Jersey, Delaware, Kentucky, Ohio, and Indiana and is the sixth largest bank asset manager in the country. It had a return on assets of 1.48 percent in 1993, second only to Banc One, while having the lowest expense ratio among our universe of superregional banks. However, PNC's earnings and profitability ratios fell in 1994 as the bank also misjudged the direction of interest rates and was hurt by the precipitous rise in that year. The bank has fine credit-quality controls and has demonstrated the ability to make good acquisitions and to make them work. It is also a technological leader in retail banking.

Norwest is a quiet giant, headquartered in Minneapolis, with about 2,900 stores operating in all 50 states, 10 Canadian provinces, and abroad. It owns 88 commercial banks serving 16 states and operates mortgage banking offices in all 50 states and consumer loan companies in 46 states. Norwest achieved healthy ROAs of 1.20 percent in 1993 and 1.45 percent in 1994, generating more than 36 percent of its revenues from fee or noninterest income. Its ROE was 18.2 percent in 1993 and 21.4 percent in 1994. The company has demonstrated superb acquisition skills and has grown from regional status to become a backyard financial institution nationwide. The holding company has generated growth in operating earnings that has averaged 17 percent per year over the last five years. The consumer finance unit and mortgage banking units are among the fastest growing and most profitable in the industry. Loan losses have been among the lowest in the banking industry, whereas profitability ratios have been among the highest.

KeyCorp, headquartered in Cleveland, was formed by the merger of Society and Key. It had $66.8 billion in assets at year-end 1994 and more than 1,300 offices in 22 states, making it the fifth largest branch network in the country. The bank is concentrated along the northern tier of the nation, with offices stretching from Alaska to Maine. It concentrates on consumer, farming, trust, investment management, and small-business banking activities. KeyCorp had an ROA of 1.39 percent in 1994 and an ROE of 19.3 percent despite misjudging the direction of interest rates. The company is concentrating on expanding revenues by selling already existing products to customers in newly acquired banks, cutting costs, and growing both internally and through acquisitions. The company sold its mortgage banking unit in

1995 as it could not reach critical mass and generate a corporate goal of returning 20 percent on equity. The company has introduced a new game plan called First Choice 2,000 in an attempt to increase revenue and operating efficiency.

CHAPTER 4

Banc One Corporation

Banc One, headquartered in Columbus, Ohio, had assets of approximately $89 billion and restated net income of just over $1 billion in 1994. The net income represented the seventh highest total among U.S. banks. However, net income declined from $1.14 billion in 1993. During the fourth quarter 1994, Banc One incurred after-tax charges of $220 million reflecting sales of securities to reduce its exposure to rising interest rates and for costs relating to bank acquisitions and restructuring.

Fortune magazine hailed Banc One as the second most admired banking company in the top 10 U.S. banking companies, while *American Banker* named Chairman John McCoy, a third generation banker, as "Banker of the Year." Over the past 10 years, Banc One has recorded the highest return on assets and second highest return on equity, while maintaining the highest ratio of equity to assets among the largest 25 U.S. banking organizations (see Table 4–1).

Banc One's ROA in 1994 was 1.15 percent (1.39 percent excluding securities transactions and other charges) compared with 1.20 percent in 1992 and 1.53 percent in 1993. Its 1993 ROA represented the first time a U.S. banking company with assets in excess of $50 billion earned over 1.5 percent on assets. Its ROE was 13.35 percent as reported in 1994 (16.1 percent as adjusted), compared with 17.81 percent in 1993 and 15.21 percent in 1992. The corporation reported a strong average common equity-to-asset ratio of 8.50 percent and a Tier 1 ratio of 9.93 percent in 1994. It increased its cash dividend by close to 10 percent in early 1995, making the 24th consecutive yearly dividend increase. As a matter of fact, its dividends have grown at a 13.6 percent compounded annual growth rate over the last 10 years.

Banc One employs over 48,000 employees and operates more than 69 banks in 14,000 banking offices in 12 states, augmented by 1,900 ATMs. During 1995, about 100 redundant facilities or marginally profitable locations will be eliminated

T A B L E 4–1

Performance Consistency, 1985–1994

Average	Banc One	Median 25 Biggest U.S. Banks	Banc One Rank
ROA	1.38%	0.72%	1
ROE	16.41	13.41	2
Average equity to assets	8.24	5.88	1

Source: Banc One, 1994 *Annual Report*, p. 3.

to help improve the efficiency ratio. The franchise is predominantly retail and small- to midmarket commercial.

The Banc One strategy as noted by its chairman is to develop advanced products and provide exceptional service for a fair fee. Banc One operates affiliate banking organizations in Arizona, Colorado, Illinois, Indiana, Kentucky, Ohio, Oklahoma, Texas, Utah, West Virginia, and Wisconsin (see Table 4–2).

Banc One also engages in data processing for other banks and healthcare-related organizations, venture capital, investment and mortgage banking, trust, brokerage, investment management, equipment leasing, consumer finance, insurance, and mortgage banking. Banc One Mortgage Corporation services mortgage balances in excess of $14 billion. The corporation focuses on the consumer, small and middle-market businesses, and certain niche lending businesses. The loan portfolio had $19 billion in consumer loans, almost $6 billion in credit card loans, $11 billion in residential mortgages, $5.6 billion in commercial real estate loans, $2 billion in construction loans, $16.6 billion in commercial, financial, and agricultural loans, and $1.3 billion in leasing loans. Credit quality remains excellent throughout the loan portfolio. The company anticipates expanding its direct leasing business on a nationwide scale. During 1994, Banc One introduced two new Visa credit card programs, which have a combined customer base exceeding 1 million accounts. It also has cobranded a BP oil card and a TravelPlus card. The latter earns users free travel on any domestic airline, whereas the former earns points for free gasoline and other automotive services from BP oil.

Banc One's long-term record shows growth in size, expansion in markets served, improved profitability, increased capital strength, and consistent performance. These positive results were achieved through pursuit of the company's past strategies:

- Serving retail and middle-market customers through community banks that operate with local autonomy, coupled with strong, central financial and credit controls.

T A B L E   4–2

Banc One Markets, December 31, 1994

	Assets (in billions)	State Rank
Arizona	$11.9	1
Colorado	3.2	3
Illinois	4.3	8
Indiana	8.7	2
Kentucky	6.8	1
Ohio	21.6	2
Oklahoma	0.5	7
Texas	18.4	3
Utah	0.9	4
West Virginia	3.1	2
Wisconsin	7.7	3

Source: Banc One, 1994 *Annual Report*, p. 7.

- Continuing to invest in technologies that enhance production, create competitive advantages, provide operating efficiencies, and generate nontraditional bank revenue sources.
- Treating bank acquisitions as an ongoing line of business, requiring rigorous pricing and management disciplines, which permit market expansion and provide economic diversification.

Throughout the years, including the recession of 1991–93, a salient characteristic of Banc One has been exemplary credit quality. The bank has had a steady decline in the ratio of nonperforming assets as a percentage of total loans, from 1.12 percent in 1993 to 0.75 percent in 1994. In addition, its loan loss reserve as a percentage of nonperforming loans was at a conservative 235 percent at year-end 1994, while the reserve to ending loan ratio was at 1.45 percent.

Under William T. Boardman, Banc One's "Mergermeister" and a senior executive vice president, Banc One has a history of acquiring healthy, respectably profitable banks. Over a few years, Banc One has usually improved profitability from 70–90 basis points to 150–160 basis points through revenue enhancement and expense control. The efficiency ratios of the banks acquired by Banc One prior to 1992 equal about 55 percent. In contrast, the banks acquired since then have an efficiency ratio of much more than 60 percent, leaving the total corporation in 1994 with a 62.3 percent efficiency ratio. Of the 175 banks it has acquired in its franchise areas, it has consolidated 54 percent of them over the years; this remains an ongoing process. The longer Banc One owns a bank, the more products and efficiencies the company can bring to bear. For example, every 1 percent decline in the efficiency ratio below 60 percent is worth approximately $0.10 per share on an annualized basis. This will remain a salient catalyst for earnings growth and should offset any erosion in net interest margin. According to John H. McCoy, "The biggest reason we spend so much time on acquisitions is to increase earnings for our shareholders . . . . What we've done is to establish a philosophy: finding well-run banks, paying a fair nondilutive price for them, and using our systems to improve their performance. Because our buys are nondilutive, those gains are funneled directly into improved earnings for our shareholders."[1]

John Fisher, a retired Banc One senior vice president, referring to the company's acquisition of 112 banks over the last two decades and its above-average efficiency ratio, stated: "I wonder if these guys are building such layers of management that eventually they'll become lethargic or expensive... That changes 'The Uncommon Partnership' [a term coined by Fisher in 1968 and the Banc One credo through 1994]...to leave affiliates autonomous to cut costs, set salaries, hire, and market." The idea is to engender loyalty and pride in local employees and preserve Banc One's nice-guy image for future merger candidates. However, it is sometimes difficult to force individuals to consolidate and eliminate redundancies immediately because local managers do not want to cut their own staffs. McCoy agrees that cost-cutting is slower, but that the executives make smart moves when they get around to dealing with the problem of overhead and their efficiency ratio.

The uncommon partnership is now undergoing significant redefinition. McCoy pointed out that the bank cut at least $150 million in expenses in 1995 and has already consolidated 12 credit card centers into 4: "There is not a market we're in where we're not improving the efficiency ratios."[2] Banc One announced a program to streamline operations in November 1994, to improve its corporate efficiency ratio. The company indicated that it would cut its workforce by 8.6 percent (4,300 jobs) and close 100 out of 1,425 branches, primarily in Ohio, Illinois, and Wisconsin. Banc One had been a bit negligent over the last decade in not cutting overlapping jobs and marginal operations in many of its 100-plus acquisitions until now. These cutbacks resulted in a $65 million charge against earnings in the fourth quarter of 1994. Banc One took an additional charge in that quarter of $170 billion to liquidate fixed-rate securities whose prices were battered by rising interest rates during 1994. These charges resulted in the first decline in earnings in over 15 years at Banc One. The key restraint to operating improvement has been the corporation's liability-sensitive gap position through the 1994 rising interest rate environment. Reflecting this position, net interest margin declined by about 100 basis points from the first to the fourth quarter of 1994. During this period, Banc One has reduced its gap to within 1 percent of neutrality, management's stated goal.[3]

At the end of 1994, Banc One operated 248 different proof, item capture, and deposit and loan centers. The company operated only 69 at the end of 1995. By the end of 1997, all state banking operations should be on common, updated systems. In the second half of 1995, Banc One announced the closing of 100 branches in 1996 and a further reduction in headcount of 3,500, which should lead to greater progress toward a 56–57 percent efficiency ratio. This new program should generate incremental pre-tax earnings of about $1.5 billion by 1999.

Banc One used to allow local banking affiliates autonomy to maximize marketing effectiveness and product pricing. However, to control local autonomy and maximize overall returns, Banc One monitors performance through detailed MIS data and largely consistent profiles for all 81 affiliates. When variables are under target, including pricing, Banc One management uses peer pressure to focus affiliates to recapture levels of the high achievers in their system. In addition, Banc One will directly prescribe goals for affiliates in larger cities, particularly in low pricing.[4]

In April 1995, President Richard Lehmann introduced a new strategy for growing revenues, controlling costs, and improving shareholder value. Although Banc One used to be managed as a group of separate affiliate banking organizations through a management vision termed the "uncommon partnership," the company will now be managed as a "national partnership" of financial services providers of exceptional banking services. This revised focus is aimed at consolidating banks and standardizing products and services across the entire organization, creating a more efficient and profitable national financial services provider. Upon completion, Banc One's efficiency and sales should be enhanced greatly, along with medium-term EPS growth. As a result of the new process, management expects to realize $1.15–1.75 billion of pretax earnings enhancements by 1999, mostly on the revenue side. An essential feature of the new national partnership is to instill a sales culture in all banks and branches and among customer contact people. Being relieved from responsibility for back-room operations, bank and branch employees should be able to concentrate on more efficiency, selling, and customer service. There will also be a sales incentive program that rewards productive employees and improving revenue-generating activities.

Banc One should return to its historical levels of performance as measured by ROA and ROE. As seen in Figures 4–1 and 4–2, Banc One has achieved consistently superior returns over the past 10 years, while experiencing compound annual growth in net income of 30 percent during the same period.

Although management will continue to focus on the company's historical strengths in retail, middle-market commercial, and small-business banking, consolidation into a single banking charter per state and standardization of products and services are the cornerstone of the new strategy. The consolidation-standardization strategy should enable Banc One to deliver products and services in a substantially

F I G U R E   4-1

Net Income and Return on Average Common Equity, 1984–1994

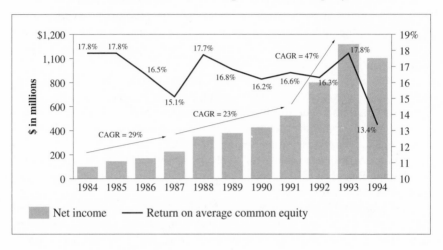

F I G U R E   4-2

Return on Average Assets, 1984–1994

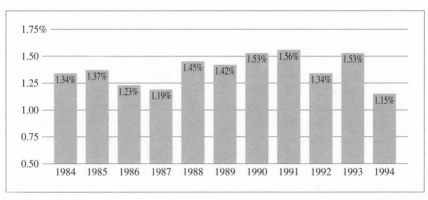

Source: CS First Boston/Banc One Corporation.

more cost-effective manner. The company will no longer offer differing products to each market it serves. The prime markets will remain mass retail and middle market. In addition, businesses such as mortgages, leasing, trust, securities, and credit cards will be removed from the disparate banks and run on a line-of-business basis. In the Lehmann's words, Banc One will be "run like a national company rather than a mutual fund of banks."[5]

HISTORY

Banc One was founded by John H. McCoy in 1934. The founder and his son, John G. McCoy, saw City National Bank of Columbus (the predecessor bank) expand rapidly during the 1950s and 1960s. Banc One was originally incorporated in 1967 as First Banc Group of Ohio, Inc., for the purpose of becoming a bank holding company. The present name was adopted in 1979.

In 1968, the company acquired control of City National Bank and Trust Co. and Columbus and Farmers Savings and Trust Co. (Mansfield, Ohio). Between 1970 and 1980, the bank acquired approximately 20 more Ohio banks, including Coshocton National Bank (Coshocton), First National Bank of Cambridge, Barnitz Bank of Middleton, Peoples National Bank and Trust Co., Security Central National Bank (Portsmouth), First National Bank of Wapakoneta, Citizens National Bank of Wooster, Lucas State Bank of Lucas, Clermont National Bank (Milford), Ashland Bank and Savings Co., Liberty National Bank (Freemont), First National Bank and Trust Co. (Ravenna), First Citizens Bank of Oxford, Athena National Bank (Athena), Citizens Baughman National Bank (Sidney), Citizens Bank and Trust Co. (Wadsworth), and Sterling State Bank. Additionally, in 1974, the bank formed First Trust Co. to provide trust services in all parts of Ohio as well as reinforce services already provided by the company's member banks.

Between 1984 and 1990, Banc One made approximately 54 bank acquisitions in five states. These banks included Hardin National Bank (Kenton), Pomeroy National Bank, First National Bank of Fairborn (Fairborn), Lake National Bank (Painsville, Ohio), Firestone Bank (Akron), Union National Bank (Youngstown), First National Bank (Sardina), Citizens State Bank (Somerset), Chardon Savings Bank Co., Heritage Bancorp, Tower National Bank (Lima, Ohio), Winters National Corp. (Dayton, Ohio), First National City Bank of Alliance (Ohio), Peoples Bank of Mt. Gilead (Ohio), Tri County Bank in Coolville (Ohio), First National Bank of East Liverpool (Ohio), Union Savings and Trust Company of Warren (Ohio), Waverly State Bank (Ohio), Union Bank and Trust Co. (Franklin, Indiana), First-Union Bank of Bellaire, First American National Bancorp (Plainfield, Indiana), KYNB Bancshares, Inc. (Lexington, Kentucky), Purdue National Corp. (Lafayette, Indiana), Money Management Corp. (Merrillville, Indiana), Citizens Northern Bank of Elkhart (Elkhart, Indiana), Carmel Bank and Trust Co. (Carmel, Indiana), United Bank (Uhrichsville, Ohio), Marion Bancorp (Marion, Indiana), First Crawfordsville Corp. (Crawfordsville, Indiana), Citizens State Bank (Sturgis, Michigan), Spartan Bancorp, Inc. (East Lansing, Michigan), the $4.9 billion asset, 71-office American Fletcher Corp. (Indianapolis, Indiana), First National Bank (Fenton, Michigan), First National Corp. (Bloomington, Indiana), Charter 17 Bancorp Inc. (Richmond, Indiana), Northwest National Bank (Rensselaer, Indiana), the $4.1 billion asset Marine Corp. (Milwaukee, Wisconsin), Universal Corp. (Yipsilanti, Michigan), First National Bank of Knightstown (Indiana), and Weaver

Brothers, a mortgage banking company in Chevy Chase, Maryland. Additionally, in 1988, Banc One merged First Municipal Leasing Corp. into the company.

In 1990, Banc One acquired from the FDIC Bridge Bank in Dallas, formerly M Corp. and renamed it Banc One Texas. They also acquired about $217 million of deposits and certain assets of the former Bright Banc Savings Association of Dallas from the Resolution Trust Co. (RTC), certain assets and certain liabilities of Community Savings and Loan Association (Fond du Lac, Wisconsin) in an RTC-assisted transaction, Metropolitan Bancorp, Meuse-Rinker-Chapman-Endres-and-Brooks (an investment banking firm in Columbus, Ohio), Capital City Federal Savings Association (Austin, Texas), and DSB Bancshares (Randolph, Wisconsin).

In 1991, Banc One acquired over $1 billion in certain assets and liabilities of Benjamin Franklin Federal Savings and Loan Association (Houston, Texas), and four Ohio banks from Central Trust Corp. (an affiliate of PNC Financial Corp.) with $2.1 billion in assets.

In 1992, Banc One Mortgage Corp. purchased five Diamond Savings mortgage offices located in North and South Carolina. Banc One acquired the $1.7 billion asset First Illinois Corp. (Evanston, Illinois). Also in 1992, Banc One Middleton consolidated with Banc One Cincinnati. Also, Banc One acquired First Security Corp. of Kentucky with $1.6 billion in assets. Banc One completed its affiliation of Jefferson Bancorp., Inc. (Peoria, Illinois) and Bedford National Bank joined Banc One (Bloomington, Indiana). Further 1992 acquisitions included the purchase of most of the deposits and offices of Diamond Savings and Loan Company; Affiliated Bankshares of Colorado (Denver), with assets of $2.8 billion, and changed its name to Banc One Colorado; 60 offices of Team Bancshares Inc. (Dallas), with assets of $5.65 billion; and Valley National Corporation (now known as Banc One Arizona Corporation), with assets of $12 billion, which operates banks primarily in Arizona, but also in California and Washington. In addition, Banc One, CoreStates, PNC, and Society (now KeyCorp) signed an agreement to combine their ATM systems in a joint venture called Electronic Payment Services, Inc. Banc One customers can access their funds electronically through the MAC network, which has more than 15,000 ATMs in 16 states.

New affiliates in 1993 increased Banc One's asset base by over $16 billion. In that year, Banc One acquired Key Centurion Bancshares (now known as Banc One West Virginia Corp.), with assets of $3.3 billion; First Community Bancorp, Inc. (joined Banc One Illinois Corp. as Bank One Rockford, N.A.), with $791 million in assets; Colorado Western Bancorp, Inc.; First Tier Financial Inc.; Central Banking Group Inc. (Oklahoma City, Oklahoma), with assets of $537 million; and First Financial Associates, with assets of $388 million. First Financial Associates affiliate First National Bank of Kenosha became Banc One Kenosha.

In 1994, Banc One completed the acquisition of the $6.4 billion asset Liberty National Corporation, renaming it Banc One Kentucky Corporation. In fact, the combination of Liberty's 40 percent market share in Louisville with Banc One's market dominance in Lexington created the largest banking institution in Kentucky. Furthermore, the addition of Liberty's Indiana branches bolstered Banc One's number two position in that state. Other announced acquisitions include Parkdale Bank (Beaumont, Texas), with assets of $60 million; Mid States Bancshares, Inc. (Moline, Illinois), with assets of $192 million; Capital Bancorp (Salt Lake City, Utah), with assets of $117 million; and American Holding Company (Highland Park, Illinois), with assets of $229 million. In addition, Banc One acquired $1.2 billion of Great American Federal Savings Bank's deposits in a regulatory-assisted transaction.

In February 1994, Banc One and First Tier Financial, Inc. (Omaha, Nebraska) terminated a merger agreement. The agreement to merge First Tier into Banc One was reached when bank stocks were at all-time highs. Since that time, Banc One and other banks have witnessed a large decline in the market value of their shares. Rather than increase the exchange rate of Banc One shares to reach the dollar value anticipated by First Tier, the agreement was terminated. A similar termination agreement was reached in the case of a previously announced intention to merge with $95 million asset Nebraska Capital Corporation. These termination agreements were reached because Banc One has a policy of protecting current shareholders by not accepting dilution in an affiliation transaction. The potential mergers with Tier One and Nebraska Capital Corp. represented new state expansion for Banc One with little room for cost-cutting or ROA improvement. Therefore, the deal was tightly priced to still provide upside accretion. The act of termination by Banc One management should be considered a positive display of takeover discipline. Additionally, Banc One sold its $1.03 billion student-loan portfolio in the third quarter of 1994, generating a $49 million capital gain. Banc One signed a definitive agreement for the sale of its Michigan banks with assets of $614 million. The company also completed the sale of its Fresno, California, bank in 1994 for a $3 million profit. In addition, the bank reduced its indirect auto portfolio by $1.2 billion to $10.8 billion to remove low-yielding paper.

Banc One, exercising a 1991 option, agreed to purchase Premier Bancorp (Baton Rouge, Louisiana) in a stock transaction valued at approximately $700 million in July 1995. With its entry into Louisiana, Banc One bought the third largest bank in the state, with assets of $5.5 billion and close to $3 billion in loans and $4.5 billion in deposits. Although the original agreement was for 1.25 times book value, Banc One paid about 1.44 times book value because Premier had improved its credit quality and expanded in size, while Banc One's price-to-earnings ratio had declined since the original agreement was reached in 1991. Banc One repurchased 18 million shares in 1994 to finance the purchase. This purchase represented Banc One's initial foray into Louisiana. Premier is the third largest bank in Louisiana, with $5.5 billion in assets and 150 branches. It holds the leading market share of deposits in the state outside of New Orleans.

The decline in Banc One's P/E ratio and the loss of its premium valuation were in part related to uncertain future earnings, possible losses in derivative securities, and a shrinking net interest margin (see Summary section and Figures 4–3, 4–4). The lower P/E ratio makes it more difficult for Banc One to grow by acquisitions, a business line in which Banc One has participated for over 20 years. Also, potential

F I G U R E   4–3

Banc One Assets (in billions)

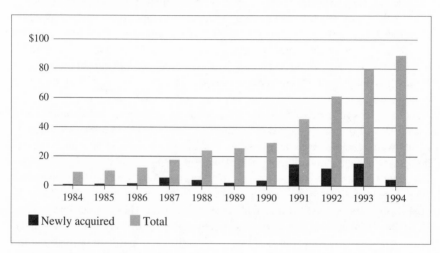

F I G U R E   4–4

Stock Price as a Percentage of Book Value

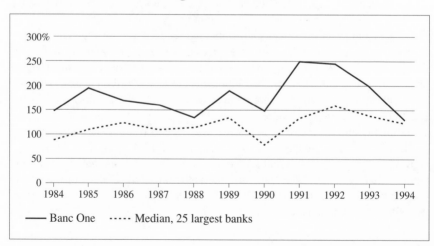

acquirees have to consider whether to affiliate with a company whose performance and outlook may have diminished. The timing of the share price decline was suboptimal since Congress passed a nationwide interstate banking bill in 1994.

Despite the decline in the P/E ratio and termination of the Nebraska deals, the flow of acquisitions has not abated, although the level of the stock is a braking influence. In total, acquired assets in 1994 will be close to $6 billion, or 7.5 percent of beginning-year assets. Banc One's acquisition strategy has been cyclical and the current slow period of acquisition is not a major concern. The periodic lapses in acquisitions are effectively filled, in the case of earnings, from the momentum of previous acquisitions coming to full performance standards. Although acquisitions have clearly added to earnings growth, periods of sparse deals have not produced much slackening in the growth rate (e.g., EPS growth in 1994 was 11 percent) as these are also digestive periods during which optimization of acquired banks takes place.[6]

TECHNOLOGY

John H. McCoy described the process of investing in the franchise as involving the continual use of information and the company's processing capability in the creation of new products that add value to Banc One. For example, on the fee side, fiduciary, mortgage banking, insurance, securities, investment banking, and credit card processing that accounted for $64 million in the first quarter of 1989 have grown at a compound rate of 21.7 percent since then. Many of these products in insurance, securities, and investment banking were developed during that five-year time frame.

There are two ongoing technological developments that should help improve earnings and information flows at the bank. The customer information position of the Strategic Banking System, jointly developed with EDS, is being installed in all the bank's data centers. Triumph, jointly developed with Andersen Consulting, is a completely new credit and debit card processing system that is currently operational and installed for use by the company's bank affiliates and other processing customers. This system represents major advances in the use of technology and will enable the bank to improve service and operating efficiency throughout the corporation. The acquisition of Crogham and Associates, now called System One Corporation, is a data processing company that specializes in the development and delivery of medical payment services and related electronic data interchange services. Banc One continues to look for ways to leverage its expertise in processing credit and debit card transactions and providing data interchange service.

Banc One has centralized as many back-office operations as possible and has utilized technology to help it gain a competitive edge. The company uses state-of-the-art software to improve its cash management system and to achieve a leading credit card position. Technology has been in the forefront of the bank's information system, so that Banc One receives immediate information on where it stands with select products, markets, and banks. Banc One commits 3 percent of its net income to research and development, which is an industry high.[7]

Banc One has been slower to consolidate its back-office operations than PNC, Fleet, and First Union. However, the comprehensive program to achieve commonality was begun in early 1994 and should be completed in 1996. This should slow expense growth, helping the organization reduce expenses by $150 million in both 1994 and 1995. Centralization of function under the holding company umbrella has been standard operating procedure for many years, including MIS, and parts of treasury, credit, and loan administration. In addition, the adoption of common systems and standardization of operations will allow customers crucial access to banking 24 hours a day, seven days a week, and provide detailed, current information to management about market share and product sales.

NONINTEREST INCOME

A major effort under way by Banc One's management is to increase noninterest income. As can be seen in Table 4–3, service charges on deposit accounts, loan processing and servicing income, and fiduciary activities are the salient providers of fee income. Noninterest income, excluding securities transactions, actually increased to about $1.7 billion in 1994 from $1.5 billion in 1993. Currently, the mortgage servicing portfolio of $25 billion is still relatively small. It would not be surprising to see the company acquire a mortgage servicing company or assets to increase fee income and achieve greater economies of scale. Other potential fee-income acquisitions would include additional credit card assets, a money management or investment company, and a finance company. Banc One has a lot of excess capital, so the acquisition of a nonbanking company would be a reasonable expectation.

T A B L E   4–3
_____

Noninterest Income (in millions)

Source	1994	1993
Fiduciary activities	$ 226	$ 225
Service charges/depository accounts	484	451
Loan processing/servicing income	484	465
Securities gains (losses)	(261)	17
Other	487	395
Total	$1,420	$1,554

Source: Banc One, 1994 *Annual Report*, p. 23

SUMMARY

Banc One's "uncommon partnership" linking 85 autonomous banks across a dozen states ended in late 1994. This strategy was successful over much of the past 25 years, producing compound annual earnings growth of 13 percent between 1968 and 1993. As nonbank competition intensified in the late 1980s, the bureaucratic, redundant characteristics of this approach began to outweigh the benefits of local market focus. Top management has implemented a new "national partnership" strategy, which, as indicated by the latest results, has Banc One back to its historic levels of profitability. With the fourth quarter 1995 acquisition of Premier Bancorp, its first major deal in more than a year, Banc One is back in the acquisition arena, an area in which it has great expertise.[8]

With robust profitability ratios over the last 15 years, Banc One produced higher earnings per share every year with the exception of 1994. The company is unquestionably one of the highest-quality banking organizations, with a good record of enhancing shareholder value across various economic and business cycles.[9] The cornerstone of the bank's success can be found in operations, research and development, management information systems, marketing, and a generally quick response to changing conditions. Commitments to technology, autonomy, accountability, and service, as well as strategic focus, have provided the foundation for Banc One's good performance in such areas as consumer and middle-market banking and bankcard operations. For example, although Banc One has done a better than average job in the bank credit card business, with outstandings, number of accounts, and net income that have grown at 20 percent, 19 percent, and 38 percent, respectively, compounded over the last five years, the goal of management is to produce 30 percent asset growth. The company estimates that this will produce a 20 percent income growth along with a 10 percent productivity improvement. Credit card, especially private label, along with point of service and consumer finance, are expected to provide a potential of $550–900 million of incremental pretax earnings over the next five years.[10]

The company has demonstrated excellence in credit-quality control and in making successful acquisitions. Banc One is an example of how a superregional can stay close to its communities as it grows to be a megabank.[11] Most analysts expect the company's future growth in EPS to average in the low teens.

Banc One experienced nearly a 30 percent decline in its stock price during 1994 as well as a major decline in its price-to-earnings and price-to-book ratios from 1993 levels. Much of this decline is probably related to industrywide concern surrounding derivative exposure and the ability to manage interest rate risk. Banc One's large derivative position and the fact that it had deferred $814 million of net realized losses on derivatives at the end of the second quarter of 1994 were of concern.[12] The bank also misjudged the direction of interest rates in 1994, experiencing some other asset-liability management problems as a result of having a negative gap during a period of rising interest rates. In reaction to rising interest rates in 1994, and in a move to become less liability-sensitive and more neutral in terms of gap measurement, Banc One chose to reduce its exposure to derivatives and fixed-rate notes and bonds. This resulted in the aforementioned charge-off in the fourth quarter of 1994 and a decline in EPS for the year from the record level established in 1993. Management's goal is to achieve a gap position that is within 1 percent of neutrality, reducing the corporation's exposure to any future interest rate changes.

To regain its premium P/E ratio and lost earnings momentum, Banc One will have to:

- Sustain loan growth without compromising price or quality.
- Stabilize its declining net interest margin.
- Continue to expand the franchise in markets where solid returns are both attainable and sustainable.
- Expand high-margin products and technological developments.
- Combine and centralize processing functions and some national lending functions.
- Develop standardized, high-quality financial products nationally, emphasizing the mass retail and middle markets.
- Install a superior sales and service culture throughout the company, measuring and compensating service people on sales success.
- Develop common systems, financial products, and operations.
- Continue to improve corporatewide integration and cross sales of products and services.
- Develop customer segmentation geared toward customer profitability.
- Substantially reduce its efficiency ratio from 1994's level.
- Replace full-service branch banking centers with alternate delivery systems such as Banc One Express centers, ATMs, computerized banking, and telephone banking to help reduce costs.
- Reduce shares outstanding as promised in the announced share repurchase program.[13]

Banc One's past acquisitions were accretive primarily from revenue enhancements. While management waits for a more appealing stock price before making additional acquisitions, a substantial cost savings from the existing affiliate structure is underway.[14] Consequently, the "Mergermeister," Senior Executive Vice President William Boardman, indicated that most banks have lower growth rates than Banc One, so that any bank acquisition must necessarily be nondilutive or even accretive over a short period of time. On the other hand, if Banc One were to acquire a company whose underlying growth rate was substantially above that of Banc One, it might necessitate taking dilution over the near term, but would be additive to the long-term earnings growth of this company. In all likelihood, Banc One will acquire a consumer finance, credit card, asset management, or mortgage servicing company, or all four, to augment its internal growth rate.[15]

Banc One has taken the necessary actions to generate a return to excellent levels of profitability by aggressively cutting overhead and concentrating on cross-selling and the generation of fee income. According to management, fee income is expected to rise from 27 percent of revenues in mid-1994 to 35 percent within a few years, as the company has targeted additional income from trust, service charges, and loan processing. This management target will be difficult to accomplish without a major acquisition such as a mutual fund, mortgage bank, or some other nonbanking entity that generates fee income.

Even though Chairman McCoy has moved to consolidate back-office operations throughout the system and reduce the number of banks from 69 to 13, while closing redundant and unprofitable branches and laying off 8,000 employees, some on Wall Street remain skeptical about the bank's regaining its cherished profitability ratios and market premium. According to Dennis F. Shea, Morgan Stanley bank securities analyst, there is a crucial question that must be answered: "Can the bank hit the high-return numbers without [Banc One] being the independently managed [nearly autonomous system] it was?" Even McCoy admits that Banc One will have to prove itself "by putting numbers on the board."[16] If management can accomplish what it has promised—that is, reducing overhead and generating additional fee-based income, while reducing its liability sensitivity—the company should be able to return to low-double-digit EPS growth beginning in 1995.[17]

First-half 1995 evidence indicated a turnaround in earnings, an ROE of 16.16 percent, and an ROA of 1.42 percent. Credit quality and efficiency ratios also improved. This confirms tighter expense management and a down payment on the promised back-office consolidation program. The efficiency ratio declined to 60 percent in the third quarter of 1995, down from 61.2 percent in the second quarter and 65.2 percent for 1994.

In an on-site analysts' meeting in early June 1995, Chairman McCoy stated that Banc One would continue to be a high-performance company dedicated to the bottom line, management would continue to emphasize shareholder interests and not asset size for its own sake, and substantial growth in EPS and high ROE from a strong capital base were still the goals of the bank. He also reiterated the superior credit culture and technological leadership as foundations of the bank's operations.[18] The standardization and consolidation of company systems and products nationwide should generate substantial cost savings and revenue-generating opportunities. There will also be better brand identity and a streamlining of the decision-making process throughout the entire organization.

With the purchase of Premium Bancorp announced in mid-1995, Banc One is likely to seek an additional bank in Louisiana. Acquisition candidates in that state include First Commerce Corp., Whitney Holding Corp., or Hibernia Corp. Banc

One placed a bid for Bank of Boston in July 1995, quickly withdrawing the offer because of cultural and control differences. Among other potential acquisition candidates are Barnett, Boatmen's Bancshares (Missouri), CoreStates (Pennsylvania), or Old Kent (Michigan). In the past, Banc One made only nondilutive acquisitions. McCoy has indicated that he would consider a dilutive acquisition only if the bank were to buy a company with double-digit growth that could erase any dilutive effect quickly.[19]

ENDNOTES

1. A. Bird, *SuperCommunity Banking* (Chicago: Probus Publishing Co., 1994), p. 76.
2. G. Stern and C. Ansberry, "Growing Pains," *The Wall Street Journal*, April 11, 1994, pp. A1, A6.
3. T.H. Hanley, "Banc One," *CS First Boston*, December 23, 1994, pp. 3–4.
4. R.B. Albertson, "Banc One," *Goldman Sachs U.S. Research*, August 16, 1994, p. 6.
5. T.H. Hanley, "Banc One," *CS First Boston*, May 10, 1995, pp. 3, 7.
6. Albertson, pp. 1–2.
7. Bird, pp. 76–79.
8. A.R. Davis, "Banc One Corporation," *Dean Witter Equity Research*, October 27, 1995, p. 1.
9. T.H. Hanley, P.J. Carter, and A.B. Collins, "Banking Weekly," *CS First Boston*, June 2, 1994, p. 14.
10. C.S. Berger, "Banc One—Beyond the Bump," *Salomon Brothers Research Report*, June 6, 1995, p. 9.
11. Bird, p. 82.
12. K. Blecher, "Banc One Corp.," *Gruntal Research*, August 25, 1994, p. 5.
13. T.H. Hanley, "Banc One," *CS First Boston*, September 13, 1994, p. 4; and "Banking Weekly," *CS First Boston*, May 25, 1995, p. 4.
14. R.B. Albertson, "Banc One Corp.," *Goldman Sachs U.S. Research*, January 17, 1995, p. 6.
15. Berger, pp. 12–13.
16. Z. Schiller, "Banc One Faces a Rocky Act Two," *Business Week*, December 5, 1994, p. 86.
17. C. Kotowski, "Banc One," *Oppenheimer & Co.*, November 22, 1994, pp. 1–2.
18. Berger, p. 3.
19. M. Murray, "Banc One Jumps Into the Hunt for Acqusitions," *The Wall Street Journal*, July 24, 1995. p. B4.

T A B L E   4–4

Banc One Financials

	1990	1991	1992	1993	1994
Earnings per share	$1.81	$2.13	$2.38	$2.93	$2.42
Assets (in millions)	$27,654	$33,861	$58,249	$74,716	$87,090
Net income (in millions)	$423.37	$529.47	$781.28	$1,139.98	$1,005.11
Return on assets	1.53%	1.56%	1.34%	1.53%	1.15%

	1994 (in millions)	%
Average earning assets	$79,270	100
Securities	18,342	23
Loans	59,815	75
Other	1,113	1
Loans	62,265	
Construction and land	2,195	
Commercial mortgage	5,571	
Highly leveraged	0	
Commercial loans and leases	17,958	
Other foreign	273	
Term LCD	0	
Credit card receivables	5,924	
Other consumer	19,070	
Unearned discount	0	
Corporate	25,997	42
Consumer	24,997	40
Mortgages	$11,274	18

	1990	1991	1992	1993	1994
Efficiency ratio	56.18	56.51	57.25	60.46	62.33
Shareholder equity (in millions)	$2,614	$3,306	$4,950	$6,554	$7,650
Preferred	$24	$203	$265	$253	$250
Common	$2,590	$3,103	$4,685	$6,301	$7,400

F I G U R E   4–5

Banc One Financial Charts

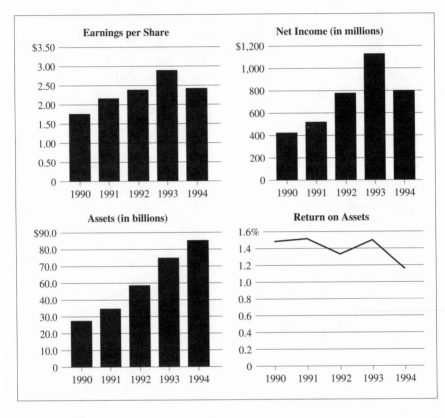

F I G U R E   4–6

Banc One Financial Charts

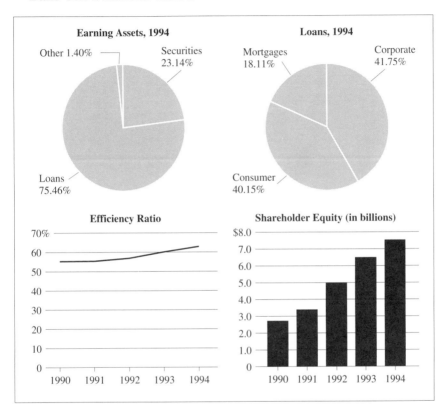

CHAPTER 5

First Chicago NBD Corporation

On July 12, 1995, First Chicago Corporation and NBD Corporation announced a merger of equals (one of the largest mergers in U.S. banking history) to form First Chicago NBD Corporation, the seventh largest bank holding company in the nation. The new company will have approximately $120 billion in assets, $10.7 billion in market capitalization, over 750 domestic banking offices, and $62 billion in discretionary trust assets under management. It will be the third largest cash management business and the fourth largest credit card bank ($14 billion in outstandings) in the United States; the number one banking company in Illinois, Michigan, Indiana, and Chicago; the number one, large corporate banking and middle-market banking company in the Midwest; and the number one consumer bank in the tristate area of Michigan, Illinois, and Indiana. In addition, excluding the impact of client overlaps, the new bank has dominant shares in the Chicagoland middle market (33 percent), small business (25 percent), and primary household relationships (18.8 percent).

This new company represents the merger of two midwestern powerhouses. The pro forma balance sheet and financial performance for the first quarter of 1995 can be seen in Table 5–1. Germane to earnings after synergies, large corporate banking should account for 25 percent of earnings, credit cards 24 percent, consumer banking 22 percent, middle market 18 percent, and other 11 percent (see Figure 5–1). Figure 5–2 shows the geographic diversity of earnings. The national credit card should produce 24 percent of earnings, national corporate 14 percent, Illinois banking 17 percent, Michigan banking 27 percent, Indiana banking 7 percent, and other 11 percent. About half of the customer base is midwestern, with the remainder either national (wholesale or credit card) or international. The combined organization is more diversified in both geographic source of earnings and

T A B L E   5–1

Pro Forma Financial Performance Ratios and Balance Sheet, 1995 First Quarter*

	FNB	NBD	Pro Forma
EPS**	$1.98	$0.88	0.99%
ROCE	18.9%	16.1%	17.7%
ROA	1.13%	1.18%	1.16%
Adjusted NIM	3.87%	4.02%	3.96%
Efficiency ratio	56.0%	57.0%	57.0%
NPA/loans + ORE	0.5%	0.6%	0.5%
Reserves/loans	2.79%	1.49%	2.10%
Reserves/NPL	618.0%	275.0%	447.0%
Net charge-off ratio	0.68%	(0.01)%	0.31%
Tier 1 risk-based capital	8.60%	8.2%	8.4%
Total capital	13.0%	12.1%	12.7%
Leverage	7.7%	6.8%	7.3%
Loans	$27.0	$30.7	$ 57.7
Securities	$ 2.5	$11.6	$ 14.1
Other earning assets	$28.8	$ 0.9	$ 29.7
Other assets	$14.1	$ 4.5	$ 18.6
Total assets	$72.4	$47.7	$120.1
Deposits	$32.2	$31.6	$ 63.8
Borrowings	$22.7	$ 8.9	$ 31.6
Other liabilities	$12.8	$ 3.8	$ 16.6
Common equity	$ 4.1	$ 3.5	$ 7.6
Preferred equity	$ 0.6	$ 0.0	$ 0.6
Total equity	$ 4.7	$ 3.5	$ 8.2

* Without synergies.
** Billions except EPS and financial ratios

customer segments. First Chicago brings its expertise in capital markets and risk management and its credit card business to the table, while NBD brings its expertise in credit analysis, credit quality, and management, and its Woodward family of mutual funds.

Richard L. Thomas (FNB) will become chairman of First Chicago NBD until his retirement in May 1996. Verne G. Istock (NBD) will become president and CEO; Thomas H. Jeffs II (NBD), David J. Vitale (FNB), and Scott P. Marks (FNB) will become vice chairmen.

F I G U R E   5–1

First Chicago NBD Diversification of Earnings by Customer
Segment after Synergies

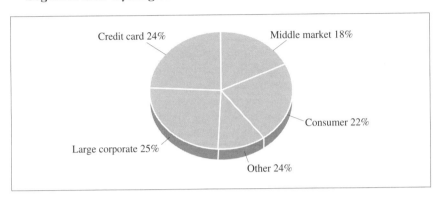

F I G U R E   5–2

First Chicago NBD Geographic Diversification of Earnings

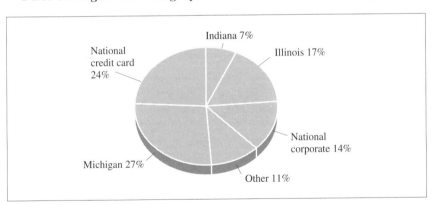

The merger combines two companies with exceptional customer franchises, both with overlapping and complementary businesses, establishing a platform for future growth and high profitability. The merger also improves economies of scale to support business expansion and technology investments required to be a highly effective and successful competitor.

Following the merger, there should be immediate EPS accretion in 1996, a restructuring charge of $225 million at closing for First Chicago, expense savings of $200 million per year (largely through job cutbacks of 1,700 full-time employees, or 5 percent of the bank's 35,000 employees, and the closing of 20–25 branches in Illinois), and an increase in targeted revenues of $50 million by 1997 from product synergies. Fully phased-in cost savings and revenue enhancements (totaling $250 million) represent 13 percent of First Chicago's noninterest expense base. Most of the cost savings ($110 million) will come from the elimination of redundancies in consumer banking. Commercial banking should cut about $45 million in expenditures, with another $45 million in cost savings coming from corporate staff and support areas. Examples include the consolidation of offices in London, Hong Kong, Sydney, and Tokyo, along with a reduction in international divisions and overlapping industry specialties.

Since First Chicago relied heavily on purchased funds, the bank maintained a rather large, liquid investment portfolio. Since NBD has a strong and growing core funding base, the combined company should be able to reduce gradually its liquid and trading assets by about $25 billion without jeopardizing its liquidity position. There is also the distinct possibility of asset securitization opportunities. First Chicago had authorized about $300 million in stock buybacks before the completion of the merger; excess capital of $1 billion should be available for reinvestment or return to shareholders by 1997. First Chicago NBD will also have a wider array of corporate products available for customers. The merger was accounted for as a pooling. Following the announced merger terms, the stock prices of NBD and First Chicago closed at premiums of 6 percent and 1.4 percent, respectively.

FIRST CHICAGO

First Chicago National Bank (The First) opened its doors on July 1, 1863, the day the Civil War battle of Gettysburg began. At the turn of the century, the industrial revolution created an unprecedented demand for credit. To help meet this demand, The First joined with the Union National Bank in 1900. The assets of the combined bank jumped from $56 million to $76 million. Two years later, the bank merged once again with the Metropolitan National Bank, raising its assets to $100 million. The First opened the First Trust and Savings Bank in 1904 as a separate corporation to serve the noncommercial members of the community. Within two years, the new savings bank had more than 10,000 depositors whose balances totaled nearly $18 million.

During World War I, in a period of lagging consumer purchases of Liberty bonds and other Treasury securities, the First and its savings bank responded by purchasing $10 million of U.S. Treasury securities for their own portfolios to help support the war effort and to draw attention to the U.S. Treasury's need for financial support. During the 1920s the bank grew steadily. In 1925, the Union Trust Company merged with the First Trust and Savings Bank.

During the Great Depression, the First never skipped an interest payment on savings deposits. Its financial strength permitted it to merge with Foreman State

Bank in early 1931, accepting all the latter's deposit liabilities. Because the savings bank was not a Federal Reserve member and had run into some difficulties during the depression, The First decided to absorb the First Union Trust and Savings Bank's business to retain its customer loyalty.

During the 1950s and 1960s, The First enjoyed a period of sustained growth as it continued to build its reputation as both a specialist and innovator in business loans. It turned to international expansion, establishing offices in London in 1959, Tokyo in 1962, and Beijing in 1980. It was the first American bank to open an office in China.

In 1969, The First was reorganized as a wholly owned subsidiary of First Chicago Corporation, a bank holding company. The new holding company broadened the scope of its activities worldwide under a new chairman, Gaylord Freeman. Freeman followed an aggressive plan to increase the bank's assets through the acquisition of more loans. The size of the bank doubled in five years. Unfortunately, the program of rapid growth produced a loan portfolio with 11 percent in nonperforming loans in 1976, double the national average. A. Robert Abboud replaced Freeman in 1975. Abboud's methods are described as tyrannical and intimidating. Over 100 officers left on their own volition, as did hundreds of customers, who were forced to pay above-average fees and provide interest-free deposits, called compensating balances, during the Abboud regime.

Continental Illinois, the chief competitor of First Chicago, was of about the same size and makeup in 1975 when Abboud took over as CEO. By 1980, Continental's loan volume had grown by 73 percent compared with only 4 percent at First Chicago. To catch up, Abboud decided on a risky strategy: fixed-rate loans and arbitrage in the Eurodollar markets. These risky decisions cost the bank dearly during a period of rising interest rates.

Barry Sullivan, a Chase Manhattan executive vice president, replaced Abboud in July 1980. With better people skills and a track record of righting a floundering bank, Sullivan helped the bank rebound. Unfortunately, the bank got into credit trouble once again with heavy losses in agricultural and energy lending, as well as a bad investment in a Brazilian bank.

In 1985, The First purchased American National Corporation. By 1986, earnings had reached record levels with the help of that acquisition, a prosperous and growing credit card division, and major payoffs from its venture capital stock portfolio. By 1987, First Chicago was back in the red again because of nonperforming Brazilian, real estate, and other problem loans.

Recent Developments

In July 1987, First Chicago acquired Beneficial National Bank for $258 million in cash, renaming it FCC National Bank. This purchase enabled First Chicago to become the third largest bank credit card issuer in the country. Later that year, First Chicago acquired First United Financial Services. In the summer of 1988, First Chicago purchased about 95,000 retail customer accounts from Continental Bank, $100,000,000 in loans, and $90,000,000 in deposits. The First also acquired Gary-Wheaton Corp., a holding company with four banks. The First made four acquisitions in 1989. It acquired Morgan Shareholder Services Trust Company from JP Morgan; Winnetka Bank (renamed First Chicago Bank of Winnetka); Ravenswood Financial Corporation; and Midwest Mortgage Services. During 1990 and 1991, The First acquired $500 million in assets and $500 million in deposits from the RTC, followed by $550 million in assets and $1.5 billion in deposits. In 1994, it acquired the Lake Shore Savings Bank. In July 1995, The First announced a merger of equals with NBD, catapulting the bank into the position of the seventh largest bank in the United States and the number one banking company in the states of Illinois, Michigan, and Indiana.

First Chicago has had an erratic profitability record over the last 15 years. Under Richard Thomas, who became CEO in the early 1990s, the bank returned to banking basics, credit quality, growth in fee income, growth in retail and middle-market banking, and greater stability in profits. There were numerous small retail acquisitions in Chicago and its suburbs. This gave the bank a stronger core deposit base, making it less vulnerable to the vagaries and volatility of the money markets. The bank achieved the following ROAs during the 1990s: 0.47 percent in 1990, 0.22 percent in 1991, 0.17 percent in 1992, 1.42 percent in 1993, and 1.08 percent in 1994. The accompanying ROEs were 9.4 percent in 1990, 3.2 percent in 1991, 1.8 percent in 1992, 24.2 percent in 1993, and 17.0 percent in 1994. By the end of the first quarter of 1995, credit quality was no longer a problem. As a matter of fact, it was exemplary. The ratio of nonperforming loans to total loans plus ORE was 0.5 percent; the charge-off ratio was at a low 0.69 percent; reserves to total loans was at 2.79 percent; while reserves to nonperforming loans stood at 6.18 percent. This represented a major turnaround from the mid-1980s when nonperforming loans had exceeded 9 percent.

Always a strong and innovative corporate bank, it became a major player in the national credit card industry. The bank is one of the Midwest's leading participants in the money and capital markets, foreign exchange, and derivative securities. It has a large correspondent banking network and utilizes this group effectively when it participates in the underwriting of government, corporate, and municipal securities. Fee income has always played a key role at the bank. For example, fee income as a percentage of total revenues was 41.8 percent in 1990, 44.5 percent in 1991, 48.1 percent in 1992, 55.3 percent in 1993, and 56 percent in 1994. Its larger percentage of fee income differentiated First Chicago from other superregionals. First Chicago ($72.4 billion in assets prior to the merger with NBD) was more of a money center bank and entered the superregional category only after it merged with NBD.

NBD

Prior to its merger with First Chicago Corporation, NBD Bancorp was the 18th largest bank holding company in the United States, with $47.1 billion in assets at year-end 1994. The bank was incorporated in 1972 as National Detroit Corp. Its present name was adopted in 1981. Through its 20 bank subsidiaries and 646 offices in Michigan, Illinois, Indiana, Ohio, and Florida, NBD provides domestic retail banking, worldwide commercial banking, cash management, trust, investment management services, mortgage lending and servicing, insurance, leasing, discount brokerage, and data processing activities. NBD also operates banking offices in London, Melbourne, Adelaide, Sydney, Frankfurt, Tokyo, Hong Kong, Toronto, and Windsor.

Under former Chairman and President Charles T. Fischer, the bank garnered a reputation for a high-quality loan portfolio and efficient expense control. NBD is affectionately referred to as the bank with "no bad deals." Fischer was fond of saying, "We don't know how to run a troubled bank . . . and we don't want to learn how." An analyst once said of Fischer: "He has taken what has always been a first-rate bank and made it into a superregional bank that will survive into the next century."[1]

NBD is eyeing Illinois, Ohio, Florida, and Wisconsin areas for additional acquisitions, as well as seeking potentially meaningful stakes in Kentucky, Missouri, and Tennessee. It is interesting to note the bank's shift of asset concentration away from Michigan into other areas of the Midwest (see Table 5–2).

The loan portfolio of the bank has always been of the highest quality and consisted of 62.3 percent commercial-related loans and 37.7 percent retail-oriented

T A B L E   5–2

NBD's Assets by Booking Entity

	December	
	1994	**1985**
Michigan	65.9 %	100.0 %
Indiana	22.3	
Illinois*	11.2	
Ohio**	0.5	
Florida	0.1	
Total	100.0 %	100.0 %

* Upon closing of pending acquisitions, assets will increase from $5.3 billion to $7 billion.

** NBD sold its Ohio branches in late 1995.

loans at the end of 1994. Commercial and industrial loans accounted for 53.1 percent of the loan portfolio, while consumer loans other than residential mortgages accounted for 26.2 percent (see Table 5–3).

T A B L E   5–3

NBD's Loan Mix, December 31, 1994

	Actual Outstandings (in billions)	Loan %
Commercial and industrial	$15.5	53.1%
Real estate construction	0.8	2.7
Lease financing	0.4	1.4
Foreign loans	1.5	5.1
Commercial subtotal	18.2	62.3
Residential mortgage	3.3	11.3
Consumer loans	7.7	26.4
Retail subtotal	11.0	37.7
Total loans	$29.2	100.0%

Source: NBD, 1994 *Annual Report*.

NBD Bank, N.A.

NBD Bank, N.A., Michigan, is the principal subsidiary of the holding company, accounting for approximately 67 percent of the company's consolidated assets and 71 percent of its consolidated net income in 1994. NBD Bank was organized in 1933. With 332 banking offices located in the lower peninsula of Michigan, it is the largest bank in the state of Michigan and the 20th largest bank in the United States.

In 1974 through 1976, the holding company acquired or formed five banks in Michigan and established NBD Mortgage Company: Grandvalley National Bank (Grandville), National Bank of Dearborn, NBD Commerce Bank (Lansing), NBD Troy Bank, and NBD Port Huron Bank.

NBD acquired First State Bank of Saginaw in 1978 and Peoples Bank and Trust Co. of Alpena, Michigan, in 1979. In addition, NBD formed NBD Portage Bank (Portage, Michigan) in 1979. During 1980, NBD acquired Farmers and Merchants National Bank (Benton Harbor, Michigan) and West Michigan Financial Corporation of Cadillac and its subsidiaries, Cadillac State Bank and Michigan Capital of Ann Arbor (now sold), all in Michigan.

During 1981, NBD established National Bank of Detroit, Canada, head-quartered in Toronto; it also acquired National Ann Arbor Corporation and its subsidiaries National Bank and Trust Company of Ann Arbor and Monroe County Bank, Dundee Co. In addition, NBD acquired Roscommon State Bank (Roscommon) and Wolverine State Bank (Sandusky). These acquisitions were followed by the establishment of NBD Northwest Bank (Kalksaska) and NBD Insurance Agency, Inc., in 1982.

NBD acquired Corporate Funding, Inc., a commercial leasing company headquartered in Grand Rapids (now sold) and received approval to establish a consumer credit bank in Delaware in 1983. During 1984, NBD formed NBD Equity Corp. and NBD Management Corp.; it also acquired Pontiac State Bank, with assets of $555 million. In 1985, NBD acquired United Michigan Corporation, with assets of $1.1 billion. During 1986, People's Bank merged with NBD's subsidiary, NBD Port Huron Bank, to form Peoples Bank of Port Huron, N.A. NBD Securities was also formed, and NBD acquired Midwest Commerce Corp. (assets of $556 million), Union Bancorp, and Omni Bancorp.

In 1990, NBD assumed deposits of New Guaranty Federal Savings and Loan Association of Taylor, Michigan, and Mid-America Savings and Loan Association of Columbus, Ohio, all from the RTC. The latter company now operates as NBD Bank.

Florida Subsidiaries

NBD formed a new trust subsidiary, NBD Trust Company of Florida (West Palm Beach) in 1982. Almost a decade later, in 1990, NBD assumed the deposits of First Venice Savings and Loan of Venice, Florida, from the RTC. In 1991, NBD acquired First Fidelity Trust, N.A. Florida in Boca Raton. First Fidelity had assets of $84 million under management at the time of the acquisition, bringing NBD's total assets in Florida to about $440 million. First Fidelity was then merged into NBD Florida. A new banking and trust office was opened in Naples in 1992. During 1994, the trust company and savings bank were merged for greater operating efficiency and improved customer service. NBD now has offices in six Florida communities that continue to attract customers from the Midwest.

Illinois Subsidiaries

In 1987 and 1988, the holding company acquired U.S. Amberibancs Inc. ($1.86 billion in assets), State National Corp. ($699 million in assets), and Charter Bank Group ($382 million in assets). This was followed by the acquisition of FNW Bancorp of Mount Prospect, Illinois, a holding company of about $1.5 billion in 1991. In December 1992, NBD Bancorp merged 17 of its Illinois banks into a single bank

(NBD Illinois), with assets of close to $4.4 billion, making it the seventh largest bank in Illinois. In January 1995, NBD announced plans to acquire Deerbank (Deerfield, Illinois) for $120 million, or 193 percent of third quarter 1994 book value. The savings and loan had assets of $766 million and 15 branches in suburban Chicago. Deerbank had generated an ROA of 1.07 percent and an ROE of 13.7 percent in the third quarter of 1994. In addition, NBD announced the completion of its merger with AmeriFed Financial Corporation of Joliet, Illinois, in January 1995. AmeriFed, with $910 million in assets and 10 offices, was acquired for approximately 5 million shares of NBD stock. NBD repurchased an equivalent number of its common shares before the closing of the acquisition. In the middle of the first quarter of 1994, NBD ranked as one of the largest banks in suburban Chicago, with more than $6 billion in assets. Following the completion of the merger with Deerbank, NBD will have 68 branches and $7 billion in assets in the Chicago area.

Indiana Subsidiaries

In 1986, NBD Bancorp acquired Midwest Commerce Corp. In 1992, the holding company acquired three more holding companies in Indiana: Gainer Corporation of Merrillville, a one-bank holding company (assets of approximately $1.5 billion); Summcorp, a five-bank holding company headquartered in Fort Wayne (total assets of $2.6 billion); and INB Financial Corporation, a six-bank holding company (total assets of $6.2 billion). These four Indiana acquisitions make NBD the largest bank holding company in the state of Indiana. NBD was given permission by the comptroller of the currency to merge its separate Indiana banks into a single national bank during 1993. Twelve banks with close to 200 offices and $9.5 billion in assets were consolidated into NBD, N.A., a wholly owned subsidiary of NBD Bank Indiana, Inc. Almost 2 million deposit and loan accounts and 200 software applications were consolidated into a standardized system. This consolidation began to produce cost savings in the second half of 1994 as some branches were closed.

At the end of 1994, NBD had assets of $10.4 billion in its Indiana banks. The only bank in Indiana that was not consolidated was the $685 million asset Elkhart Bank, which retained its state charter to preserve its ability to offer selected insurance products. This bank sells property and casualty insurance to business customers.

Trust Activities

At year-end 1993, the corporation's trust activities included investment management or administration of more than $103 billion in assets. The Woodward family of mutual funds had $6.0 billion under management at year-end 1994, making it the tenth largest family of bank proprietary mutual funds in the United States. NBD continued to rank among the nation's larger providers of master trust services. Total assets held and administered in this specialized custodian service for employee benefit, institution, and foundation customers at year-end 1993 was $65 billion.

Financial Highlights

NBD has one of the industry's exemplary expense control and credit-quality records. The bank has consistently maintained an efficiency ratio under 60 percent, varying only because of seasonal or merger-related expenses. As soon as the latest group of mergers is fully absorbed and consolidated, the bank is expected to reach an efficiency ratio of 55 percent by 1996. The ratio stood at 58.3 percent in 1994. NBD has begun to realize the full benefit from the cost synergies associated with the multiple Indiana acquisitions. The new management team, led by Verne G. Istock, is striving to make NBD more streamlined and efficient. The head count and the number of branches are likely to be reduced further. During 1993 and 1994, two dozen offices were consolidated; noninterest expenses were reduced by $17.5 million in 1994 compared to 1993. Management is also attempting to make the company more marketing oriented, attempting to achieve greater fee income by cross-selling products and services to the current customer base. The company generated just over 16 percent of its total revenue from fee income in 1994. Key sources of fee income came from trust, deposit, and service charges, credit card fees, data processing, letters of credit, mortgage servicing, insurance premiums, and foreign exchange. The company sells annuities and credit life and mortgage life insurance. It will be expanding into the sale of term, whole life, and universal variable life insurance directly through Charterpoint investment centers located in NBD branch offices (see Table 5–4).

SUMMARY

NBD has a stellar reputation for consistent profitability, a strong capital foundation, and a portfolio of earning assets of the highest quality. Asset-quality measures remained exceptionally strong during the recent business cycle, underscoring the bank's conservative credit culture and solid underwriting standards. The new management team is committed to focusing the company's efforts on anticipating the needs of customers and providing high-quality service to them at their convenience, while consistently exceeding their expectations. NBD wishes to build total banking relationships with its customers.

Germane to credit quality, the bank achieved a ratio of nonperforming loans to total loans and leases of 0.62 percent during the fourth quarter of 1994, among

T A B L E   5-4

Noninterest Income, 1994 (in millions)

Deposit service charges	$160
Trust	157
Credit card fees	39
Data processing fees	32
Letters of credit	23
Other domestic/international fees	20
Mortgage loan servicing	18
Insurance	15
Foreign exchange	14
Retail banking fees	13
Rental income	10
Mutual fund/annuity fees	7
Other	38
Total	$546

Source: NBD, 1994 *Annual Report.*

the lowest in the banking industry. As a matter of fact, NBD has not reported loan losses greater than 0.50 percent in any year since 1960. Additionally, the loan loss reserve to nonperforming loan ratio was a conservative 241 percent.

The capital ratios of the bank are exceptionally strong, with the Tier 1 ratio at 8.44 percent and a total capital ratio at 12.5 percent (December 31, 1994). All of these factors plus a wide net interest margin contributed to NBD's net income of $531.6 million in 1994 compared to $485.8 in 1993. NBD achieved a 16.49 percent return on average shareholders' equity in 1994 before extraordinary items and accounting changes, compared with 15.46 percent in 1993. The return on average assets for 1994 was 1.25 percent before extraordinary adjustments, compared to 1.20 in 1993.

The Midwest region is healthy, growing, and providing good lending opportunities for NBD. The bank has historically produced consistently good earnings growth through booms, busts, wars, market crashes, and recessions. NBD is also actively involved in technology-based cash management services for business customers.

Earnings should continue to remain strong as good loan demand and the realization of further cost savings associated with the consolidation of the 12 Indiana banks into a single operating system should offset modest contraction in the net interest margin during 1995.

THE NEW CORPORATION: FIRST CHICAGO NBD

Although many First Chicago investors were disappointed with the "no-premium" merger with NBD, after dreaming about a takeover-premium of 30–40 percent as suggested by some on Wall Street, most analysts believe that the First Chicago/NBD merger should work out well for shareholders in the long run. Two great banking companies have merged. The corporate lending and credit function will be directed by NBD people, whose institution has an enviable history of excellent lending and credit practices (remember…no bad deals).

The credit card and capital markets functions of both banks will be combined and led by the much larger First Chicago group. The trust departments will also be combined. Cost savings will result from elimination of job duplication and branch closings around Chicago that will lead to layoffs of about 5 percent of the total number of employees. Both banks have a clear understanding of how to run an efficient bank. The large corporate and retail customer base of NBD will be sold some of First Chicago's best products and services, and the huge technological development costs that lie ahead can be spread over a much larger customer base. There will be no dilution in earnings per share brought about by the merger, and the average growth rate of the two companies should exceed the anticipated growth rate had the companies remained independent. The combined profitability ratios should also rise following consolidation, as the core deposit base at NBD will enable First Chicago to reduce its borrowed funds position and its low-yielding liquid assets by $25 billion within two years. There will probably be more in-market retail acquisitions and, perhaps, some contiguous-market acquisitions into neighboring states before the end of the decade.

ENDNOTE

1. NBD, 1993 *Annual Report.*

T A B L E   5–5

NBD Bancorp Inc. Financials

	1990	1991	1992	1993	1994
Earnings per share	$2.47	$2.43	$1.84	$2.95	$3.35
Assets ($ millions)	$27,290	$37,125	$39,624	$39,992	$43,934
Net income ($ millions)	$288.84	$361.53	$300.13	$485.79	$531.66
Return on assets	1.06%	0.97%	0.76%	1.21%	1.21%

	1994	
	(in millions)	%
Average earning assets	$39,971	100
Securities	12,195	31
Loans	26,790	67
Other	986	2
Loans	29,228	100
Construction and land	817	
Commercial mortgage	1,591	
Highly leveraged	364	
Commercial loans and leases	13,934	
Other foreign	1,470	
Term LCD	3	
Credit card receivables	642	
Other consumer	5,795	
Unearned discount		
Corporate	18,179	62
Consumer	6,437	22
Mortgages	4,612	16

	1990	1991	1992	1993	1994
Efficiency ratio	60.68	60.94	59.02	58.91	58.13
Shareholder equity (in millions)	$1,875	$2,660	$2,876	$3,120	$3,305
Preferred					
Common	$1,875	$2,660	$2,876	$3,120	$3,305

F I G U R E   5–3

NBD Bancorp Inc. Financial Charts

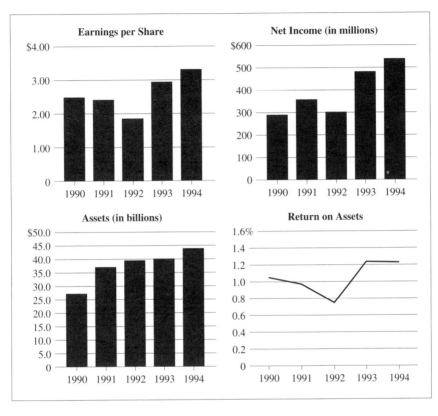

FIGURE   5–4

NBD Bancorp Inc. Financial Charts

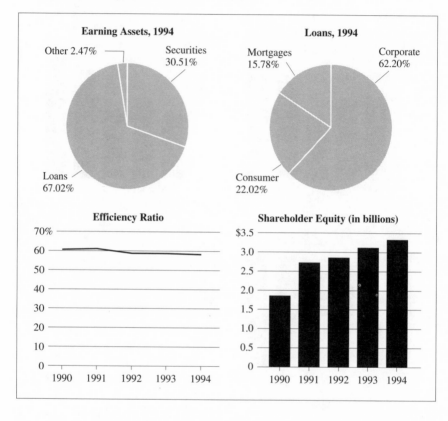

T A B L E   5–6

First Chicago Corp. Financials

	1990	1991	1992	1993	1994
Earnings per share	$3.35	$1.15	$0.64	$8.43	$6.88
Assets (in millions)	$50,779	$48,963	$54,768	$56,864	$64,138
Net income (in millions)	$249.30	$116.30	$93.50	$804.50	$689.70
Return on assets	0.49%	0.24%	0.17%	1.41%	1.08%

	1994	
	(in millions)	**%**
Average earning assets	$52,627	100
Securities	2,537	5
Loans	23,293	44
Other	26,797	51
Loans	25,974	100
Construction and land	256	
Commercial mortgage	2,240	
Highly leveraged	3,923	
Commercial loans and leases	7,806	
Other foreign	1,832	
Term LCD		
Credit card receivables	6,337	
Other consumer	3,580	
Unearned discount		
Corporate	16,057	62
Consumer	9,917	38

	1990	1991	1992	1993	1994
Efficiency ratio			73.2	54.2	59.9
Shareholder equity (in millions)	$2,812	$2,970	$3,401	$4,264	$4,533
Preferred	$419	$569	$669	$761	$611
Common	$2,393	$2,401	$2,732	$3,503	$3,922

F I G U R E   5–5

First Chicago Corp. Financial Charts

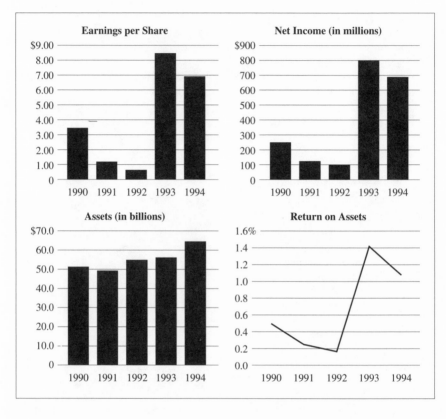

F I G U R E   5–6

First Chicago Corp. Financial Charts

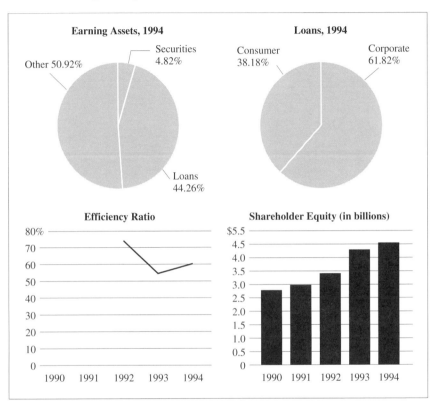

Earning Assets, 1994

Other 50.92%
Securities
4.82%
Loans
44.26%

Loans, 1994

Consumer
38.18%
Corporate
61.82%

Efficiency Ratio

80%
70
60
50
40
30
20
10
0
1990   1991   1992   1993   1994

Shareholder Equity (in billions)

$5.5
4.5
4.0
3.5
3.0
2.5
2.0
1.5
1.0
0.5
0
1990   1991   1992   1993   1994

CHAPTER 6

KeyCorp

The merger of KeyCorp (Albany, New York) with Society Corporation (Cleveland) in 1993 created the tenth largest bank holding company in the United States, with assets of $58 billion and more than 1,300 offices in 22 states. KeyCorp is the nation's fifth largest branch network with massive retail distribution capacity. An important question that must be answered is whether or not this merger creates value for stockholders. With little geographic overlap, there will be limited cost savings (about 5 to 10 percent) from the elimination of redundant operations. Essentially, Society Bank was rich in developed products and desired a broader distribution system to generate additional income. On the other hand, Key Bank had about 800 branches throughout the northern section of the United States and desired additional products to sell through its branches to embellish revenues. The synergy of the merger must therefore come from additional revenue growth within the new company, leveraging their different products and services over a much broader geographic area. For example, Society's Prism 401(k) products, other trust department products, automobile leasing, real estate and finance products, and new capital market products have been targeted for sale to KeyCorp customers.

Some bank stock analysts question the synergy and additional revenue-generating capability at KeyCorp. The skepticism stems from disappointments in revenue growth through the first quarter of 1995. The basic concept of improving revenue growth is centered on using information technology to reconfigure the key business segments, that is, segmenting customers into targeted client groups and changing materially the marketing to these segments to alter dramatically the profitability of these businesses. Most bank stock analysts are supportive of the merger and see enhanced growth in the period ahead. If this merger of equals meets or exceeds expectations, it could be a harbinger of other such deals between banks located in different markets.[1]

KeyCorp operates primarily in northern states in less competitive, smaller towns from Maine to Alaska, concentrating on consumer, agricultural, and small-business banking activities, as well as mortgage banking, securities, and insurance brokerage capabilities. On the other hand, Society is more a big-business bank with strong trust, investment management, and cash management business. Society maintains offices in Ohio, Michigan, and Indiana, and a savings bank in Florida. Its strengths lie in investment and trust activities.

At the end of February 1995, KeyCorp had a well-diversified asset base with $20.4 billion in assets in the Northeast, $30.8 billion in the Great Lakes region, $5.2 billion in the Rocky Mountain region, and $12.4 billion in the Northwest (see Table 6–1). Of the $68.8 billion in assets, about $47 billion was in loans. About 47 percent of loans was in real estate; 27 percent in commercial, financial, agricultural, leasing, and foreign loans; and 22 percent in consumer loans (see Table 6–2).

T A B L E   6–1

Regional Distribution of Assets and Branches, December 31, 1994*

Region	Bank Assets (in billions)	Branches
Northeastern Key Bank of New York Key Bank of Maine Key Bank USA Key Bank Vermont	$20.4	452
Great Lakes Society National Bank (Ohio) Society National Bank (Indiana) Society Bank (Michigan) Society First Federal Savings Bank (Florida)	$30.8	441
Rocky Mountain Key Bank of Wyoming Key Bank of Utah Key Bank of Idaho Key Bank of Colorado	$5.2	143
Northwest Key Bank of Washington Key Bank of Oregon Key Bank of Alaska	$12.4	290

* Adjusted for acquisitions completed as of February 28, 1995.
Source: KeyCorp, 1994 *Annual Report*.

T A B L E   6–2

Pro Forma Loan Portfolio, December 31, 1994

Type of Loan	Amount (in billions)	% of Total
Commercial, financial, and agricultural loans	$10.1	21.9%
Construction loans	1.3	2.8
Commercial mortgages	6.8	14.7
Residential mortgages	11.0	29.4
Credit cards, consumer	10.2	22.1
Student loans held for sale	1.8	4.0
Leases	2.3	5.0
Foreign	0.1	0.1
Total	$46.3	100.0%

Source: KeyCorp, 1994 *Annual Report.*

KeyCorp had combined trust assets of more than $64 billion at year-end 1994, with $31 billion being managed and $33 billion being nonmanaged, placing it among the top 20 banks in the country. Of the managed portion, the bank had $14 billion under management for wealthy individuals and corporate and institutional clients. In addition, Society Asset Management (SAM) has $20 billion in private wealth, corporate, and institutional money under management. KeyCorp also operates the nation's 13th largest bank mutual fund business, with 25 proprietary funds and assets of $5 billion. SAM, a wholly owned subsidiary of KeyCorp, provides money management, agency accounts for clients who do not require fiduciary relationships, and manages the investment process for the trust department.

Key sold its $25 billion mortgage-servicing portfolio, the 17th largest in the nation, to NationsBank in early 1995 for $350 million. The company also sold to NationsBank other servicing-related assets, such as receivables and advances for an additional $150 million. Key exited the mortgage-servicing business because the ROE in this unit would remain well below KeyCorp's 20 percent corporate average. Mortgage origination fees are also highly cyclical. The sale of these servicing units provided a $70 million capital gain in the first quarter of 1995, which offset a $49 million loss related to the sale of investment securities and interest rate swaps, as well as certain severance and disposition expenses related to the sale of the mortgage company and certain other expenses connected with KeyCorp's First Choice 2000 program. These unusual first quarter gains and losses should roughly offset each other. However, the sale of KeyCorp Mortgage should provide about $10 million to its 1995 operating earnings since revenues will decline by about $45 million while expenses fall by nearly $55 million. This estimate includes the expected benefits of reinvesting the $500 million generated from the sale as well as the future income from the sale of new mortgage servicing that is originated through the branch network.[2]

The merger combines specialty-product strengths, a vast tract of geography north of the Mason–Dixon line, and extremely capable management determined to make the deal work. Merger integration is a core competency of both constituent companies: both management teams have a history of generating accretive mergers and delivering on promised merger milestones. President Robert G. Gillespie's plans lie beyond the integration of Society and Key. He has indicated a desire to expand into markets such as Minneapolis or St. Louis. Gillespie also pointed out at an institutional investor conference in August 1994 that successful banks were those with merger and acquisition skills, good cost controls, superb credit management, properly utilized technology, high-quality service, and strong marketing skills. He made it clear that KeyCorp was customer- and not product-focused. He emphasized the seamless integration and delivery of four salient elements:

- Impeccable, consistent, and professional service at all points of contact.
- Innovative superior products and service, which are customer driven and focused on building and deepening relationships.
- Distribution through a variety of delivery methods, providing choice and convenience to the customer.
- Practical, well-integrated application of technology and operations that anticipate customer and employee needs.

At the aforementioned conference, KeyCorp's management also described how the company worked to optimize net interest income within the constraints of interest rate risk, liquidity, capital adequacy, credit risk, and regulations. In the process, the balance-sheet management team assisted the asset-liability management group with pricing and allocation models. Although management showed that more than 90 percent of the time the asset-liability management group's actions have been highly effective, that was not the case in 1994. KeyCorp announced a pretax loss of about $100 million.[3]

Other elements of First Choice 2000, the internal strategic plan, seem to be the emergence of national consumer lending as a major priority, an emphasis on Key's national specialty-lending businesses (including healthcare, leasing, agriculture, marine, and recreational vehicles), and small-business lending, especially since 1.5 million small businesses operate in the company's current banking region. Branchless banks will also be emphasized through advanced ATMs and 24-hour customer call centers.[4]

Following the merger, all the systems and processing centers were selected, and operating platforms were being consolidated and put in place; all synergies appeared to be on target. Bankcard operations, ATMs, mortgage company operations, and call centers were immediately combined. The company is working on reengineering back-office processing, completing the systems conversions, and leveraging technology across the company's businesses. KeyCorp management also indicated that it would employ alliances and vendor partnerships to accelerate and maximize its own capabilities.[5] The newly designed "virtual" call center serves customers and prospects via the phone, handling sales, service, and support activities, treating several physical sites as one logical entity. This delivery system, which won a gold medal from *Teleprofessional* magazine, is expected to be one of the keys to bringing down baseline costs, while simultaneously improving efficiencies.[6]

The bank has begun to develop a resource center in Seattle that should aid in transferring products from the old Society to the old Key territory. The center is staffed with experts in large corporate, healthcare, and trust employee benefit areas, cash management, international banking, foreign exchange, institutional investment products, public finance, and specialty consumer credit. Initial results are extremely encouraging germane to new revenue generation.

SOCIETY

Society Corporation, headquartered in Cleveland, Ohio, is a bank holding company with 437 full-service branches in the Midwest, including 309 offices in Ohio, 91 in northern Indiana, and 37 in Michigan. Society's nonbanking subsidiaries provide insurance sales services, reinsurance of credit life and accident and health insurance on loans made by subsidiary banks, securities brokerage services, corporate and personal trust services, venture capital and small-business capital services, mortgage banking services, and more.

Society was organized in 1958 to acquire the capital stock of Society National Bank, as an incident of the combination of Society for Savings, a mutual savings bank organized in 1849, and its subsidiary, Society National Bank. Since 1965, Society acquired or merged with numerous banks. Major transactions include the acquisition of Interstate Financial Corp. (Dayton, Ohio), with $1.2 billion in assets in 1984, and Centran Corporation (Cleveland), with $3.1 billion in assets.

Society acquired TrustCorp, Inc., in 1990, merging five of the TrustCorp banks to form Society, Indiana. The merger with TrustCorp helped Society build its trust and asset management business as well as increase its geographic presence in the Midwest. During 1990 and 1991, Society sold the following subsidiaries of Society Bancorp of Indiana: Trustcorp Bank (Huntington), Trustcorp Bank (Hartford City), Trustcorp Bank (Columbus), Trustcorp Bank (Dunkirk), and Trustcorp Mortgage Co., all in Indiana. It also sold certain assets and agency businesses of both Saint Joseph Insurance Agency and Trustcorp Agency of Society Bancorp of Indiana. In addition, Society sold Trustcorp Bank, Indianapolis, in 1991.

Society merged with its crosstown Cleveland rival, Ameritrust Corp., in 1992 in a stock transaction valued at nearly $1.4 billion. This merger created the largest banking company in Cleveland, with more than $23 billion in assets and 26 percent of the deposits in that city. This compared with only a 15 percent market share of deposits by rival National City, the closest competitor. National City was responsible for putting Ameritrust into play when it made an unsolicited bid for the company. Prior to the acquisition, Society had been one of only a handful of banks among the top 50 in the country to have reported 10 consecutive years of increasing earnings on an originally reported basis. This acquisition boosted Society's trust business to $29 billion in managed assets, placing the bank among the top 12 banks, with over $200 million in annual revenues. Trust fees now represent about 14 percent of the bank's total operating revenue. The acquisition of Ameritrust (assets of $10 billion) solidified further the position of Society as a midwestern banking power and helped move the company into a national prominence in regard to trust services and investment assets under management.

An additional merger in 1992 came into being when Society acquired First of America Bank, Monroe, Michigan, from First of America Bank. Society also acquired First Federal Savings and Loan Association of Fort Myers, Florida (24 offices with $1.1 billion in assets) in 1993. In addition, Society completed the merger of its three banking affiliates in Michigan into Society Bank, Michigan.

KEY

KeyCorp is a registered bank holding company engaged in the general banking business. It is headquartered in Albany, New York. Through its subsidiary bank, Key operates 657 offices throughout New York, Alaska, Maine, Oregon, Utah, Washington, Wyoming, and Idaho. Key refers to itself as "America's neighborhood bank," but others sometimes refer to it as the "Wal-Mart of banking" because it serves many small towns and has cultivated a folksy image, similar to Wal-Mart's.

Key dates back to 1825 when New York's governor Dewitt Clinton signed a bill chartering the Commercial Bank of Albany, the direct ancestor of KeyCorp. Commercial Bank was reorganized under the National Banking Act of 1864, and its name was changed to National Commercial Bank of Albany. The National Commercial Bank consolidated with Union Trust Company to become National Commercial Bank and Trust Company in 1920. The latter bank merged with First Trust and Deposit of Syracuse in 1971 and became known as First Commercial Banks, Inc. The name was changed to Key Banks, Inc. on April 23, 1979, and then to KeyCorp on August 27, 1985.

In 1971, KeyCorp (then First Commercial) acquired all outstanding capital stock of National Commercial Bank and Trust Co. (which later became Key Bank, N.A.) and First Trust and Deposit Co. (currently Key Bank of Central New York) in stock swaps. In 1972, Kingston Trust Co. (which became a part of Key Bank of Southeastern New York) was acquired through another stock swap. In 1973, Key formed FCB Leasing, Ltd., and subsequently merged it into the Key Bank of Southeastern New York. Continuing their acquisition binge, Key acquired Homer

National Bank and merged it into Key Bank of Central New York in February 1974. Additionally in 1974, not only did Key form FCB Advisory Services (currently Key Advisory Services), a consulting firm for corporate financial activities to businesses and individuals, but it also acquired part of Oystermen's Bank and Trust Co., which ultimately became part of what is now Key Bank of Southeastern New York. In 1975, Key formed FCB Life Insurance Ltd., an underwriting and reinsurance firm. In 1976, Key acquired Chester National Bank of Monticello, New York, which became a part of Key Bank of Southeastern New York. In 1978, Key acquired National Union Bank of Monticello, New York.

Key then merged with the then Chester National Bank. In January 1979, Key Trust Co., Albany, New York, a wholly owned subsidiary, was formed. In 1979, the now Key Bank of Central New York merged with Genesee Valley National Bank and Trust Co. of Genesee, New York.

In November 1980, National Bank of Northern New York merged with Key Bank of Northern New York through an exchange of stock. In 1981, Key acquired First National Bank in Greene. In 1982, Key acquired Lyons Falls National Bank and Farmers National Bank of Malone. Both banks were then merged into Key Bank of Northern New York, which was subsequently merged into Key Bank of Central New York. In 1983, National Bank of Pawling merged into Key Bank of Southeastern New York. In 1984, Key acquired Depositors Corp., now called Key Bancshares of Maine. Other 1984 acquisitions included 25 offices from the Bank of New York, the First National Bank of Red Hook, the Columbus Trust Company, and five other banking offices. These were all merged into existing New York State Key banks.

RECENT ACQUISITIONS

After numerous New York and New England acquisitions, Key began a westward expansion under Victor Riley's leadership and between 1985 and 1990 quintupled its assets from $3 billion to $15 billion. He anticipated increased trade with Asia and a commensurate improvement in the economies of the Western states and Alaska. Key focused its efforts on Western areas of low but growing population in which banking services were scarce and bank prices were relatively cheap. Riley began to gobble up promising and inexpensive banks in Wyoming, Idaho, Utah, Oregon, Colorado, Washington, and Alaska.

On July 1, 1985, KeyCorp acquired $508 million asset Alaska Pacific Bancorporation (Key Bancshares of Alaska), including its two banks, which were merged to form Key Bank of Alaska, and another bank in Oregon, which became Key Bank of Oregon. In January 1986, KeyCorp formed Key Pacific Bancorp to oversee activities in the Pacific Northwest.

Other 1986 acquisitions included Northwest Bancorp (Albany, Oregon) and Pacwest Bancorp (Portland, Oregon), whose four banks were merged into Key

Bank of Oregon; and four savings bank offices in the mid-Hudson Valley region of New York State and the Beaver State Bank in Beaverton (Oregon), which were merged into Key Banks in New York and Oregon.

In July 1987, Key acquired the Seattle Trust and Savings Bank and the First Northwest Bancorporation. The two were merged to form Key Bank of Puget Sound. Also in 1987, Key formed de novo Key Bank USA, N.A., a bank-by-mail organization, and Key Atlantic Bancorp to oversee Northeast activities; it also acquired Western Security Financial Corp. and the Commercial Security Bancorporation (now Key Bank of Utah) in a pooling of interests. Additionally, Key Bank of Northern New York was merged into Key Bank of Central New York.

In January 1988, Key purchased eight Maine branches from Fleet/ Norstar Financial Group and merged them with Key Banks in Maine; it also acquired the Bank of Casper, Wyoming. Additionally in 1988, Key Bank of Long Island merged into Key Bank of Southeastern New York, and Key acquired IB&T Corp. in Boise, Idaho, and renamed it Key Bancshares of Idaho. In December 1988, in another transaction deemed a pooling of interests, First Wyoming Bancorporation (Cheyenne, Wyoming) was merged into Key Bancshares of Wyoming, and four Key Banks in Maine were merged to form Key Bank of Maine. In 1989, Key acquired the American National Bank of Powell, Alaska Statebank, and B.M. Behrends Bank.

Key began 1990 by acquiring Washington Community Bancshares, Inc. ($91 million in assets). Later in 1990 Key Bank, N.A., headquartered in Albany, and Key Bank of Southeastern New York, based in Newburg, were merged to form Key Bank of Eastern New York, N.A. Additionally in 1990, Key acquired several branches of Mountain West Savings and Loan ($67 million in assets); Permanent Savings Bank, headquartered in New York ($317 million in assets); and Wyoming-based Provident Savings Association ($162 million in assets). In September 1990, Key acquired 40 branch offices ($3.1 billion in assets) of Empire of America Federal Savings Bank (New York State) and merged Key Bank, N.A. (Albany) with Key Bank of Southeastern New York (Newburgh). Now Key Bank of Eastern New York is headquartered in Newburgh.

The following year, Key acquired $7.3 billion of assets from weakened Goldome FSB, a Buffalo-based savings bank. Then Key merged its three New York State banks into a single financial institution. Key Bank of Eastern New York–Albany, Key Bank of Central New York–Syracuse, and Key Bank of Western New York–Buffalo became a single, nationally chartered bank named Key Bank of New York State, N.A., headquartered in Albany.

In 1992, Key acquired Valley Bancorporation of Idaho Falls ($221 million in assets) and purchased 48 former Security Pacific Bank branches in Washington State from BankAmerica ($1.4 billion in assets). In 1993, Key completed the acquisition of Puget Sound Bancorp in Washington State ($4.1 billion in assets); acquired National Savings Bank of Albany, New York ($701 million in assets); purchased 40 branches from First American Bank, New York ($700 million in assets); and acquired Home Federal Savings Bank in Fort Collins, Colorado ($246 million in assets).

In 1994, KeyCorp acquired Commercial Bancorporation of Colorado ($400 million in assets and 10 offices), Greeley Bank of Colorado, and Omnibancorp (18 offices in the Denver area). These acquisitions increased KeyCorp's presence in Northeast Colorado and increased Key Bank of Colorado's total assets to about $1 billion during 1994. Additionally, in mid-1994 KeyCorp acquired Bank of Boston's Vermont and Maine operations for just under $200 million (paying about 11 percent of assets), continuing Victor Riley's "frost belt" strategy of buying banks in the northern tier of the country. Although Key paid a premium for these banks compared with other recent purchases in the area (which averaged about 8.4 percent of assets), the acquisition should not be dilutive and in fact should add about six cents a share to earnings in 1996. The acquisition of $660 million asset Bank of Vermont marked Key's initial entry into Vermont, while the addition of Casco Northern Bank in Portland, Maine ($1.1 billion in assets) lifted Key into the position of the number one bank in Maine (postmerger assets of $3.7 billion), ahead of archrival Fleet. Key paid about 1.9 times adjusted book value for these acquisitions. There will certainly be cost savings in Maine in the neighborhood of 30–60 percent, normal for an in-market merger. Although the Bank of Vermont does not represent an in-market merger, the bank is contiguous with KeyCorp's New York State franchise, so that there should be substantial cost savings. Both of the acquired banks have hefty efficiency ratios at 80 percent or higher, so that there will be the opportunity for enormous cost cutting upon consolidation of those units (see Tables 6–3 and 6–4).

KeyCorp's 14-state, coast-to-coast franchise may be the closest thing yet to a nationwide branch network. However, it has a lot of room left for in-market expansion in such states as Colorado and Michigan. In Michigan, in particular, where Key has barely a 1 percent market share of deposits, at least two $10 billion acquisition candidates remain: Michigan National Corp. and Old Kent Financial. To achieve critical mass in Michigan, KeyCorp will need to make a major acquisition.[7]

Prior to the merger with Society, with only one exception did Key make any loans greater than $20 million, while its average commercial loan was about $2 million. The company refrained from making loans to third-world nations and instituted rigorous financial and credit controls. These are the reasons for the bank's low loan losses. Key installed a Vision 2001 computer system at a cost of close to $20 million to help branch bankers market a wide range of credit services. The system allows users to input new loan information, forward loan applications to managers, and access credit scoring data; it also aids in loan servicing and collection.

After selling its mortgage banking unit in early 1995, KeyCorp agreed to acquire AutoFinance Group Inc., of Westmont, Illinois, for $316 million in stock, and Spears, Benzak, Salomon & Farrell, Inc., a New York–based investment management firm. Spears, Benzak had aggregate assets under management of about $3 billion.

T A B L E   6–3

Key Bancshares—Acquisition History, 1990–1995

Company	State	Asset Size (in millions)	Date
Washington Community Bancshares	WA	$ 91	January 1990
Branches of Mountain West S&L	WY	67	May 1990
Permanent Savings Bank	NY	317	July 1990
Provident Savings Association	WY	162	August 1990
Part of Empire of America FSB	NY	3,115	September 1990
Branches of Citibank	UT	130	October 1990
Treasure Valley Bancorp	ID	69	May 1991
Portions of Goldome FSB	NY	7,296	May 1991
Branches of Casco Northern Bank	ME	260	December 1991
Valley Bancorporation	ID	221	June 1992
Branches of Security Pacific Bank	WA	1,400	September 1992
Puget Sound Bancorp	WA	4,700	January 1993
National Savings Bank of Albany	NY	701	February 1993
First American Bank, New York	NY	700	March 1993
Home Federal Savings Bank	CO	246	June 1993
Northwestern National Bank	WA	46	July 1993
Commercial Bancorp, Colorado	CO	409	March 1994
State Home Savings Bank	OH	321	September 1994
First Citizens Bancorp Indiana	IN	347	December 1994
Bank of Greeley	CO	60	December 1994
Bank of Vermont	VT	660	January 1995
Casco Northern	ME	1,100	February 1995
Omnibancorp	CO	500	February 1995

Source: Company reports.

FINANCIAL RATIOS

Although all of the aforementioned acquisitions improved shareholder value, they also left Key and Society with certain asset-quality burdens that required immediate attention. The managements of both banks were up to the task, and now the combined bank is in the forefront of credit quality. By the second quarter 1995, Key's nonperforming loans to total loans had declined to 0.65 percent from a peak of 2.05 percent in 1991, while nonperforming assets to period-end loans plus OREO and other nonperforming assets declined to 0.73 percent. Loss reserve coverage also increased from 109 percent to 324 percent of nonperforming loans from

T A B L E   6–4

Key Bancshares—Banking Offices, March 31, 1994

State	Number of Branches	Rank*	Market Share
New York	331	6	3.2
Ohio	291	2	10.4
Washington	193	3	10.7
Maine	92	2	13.2
Indiana	84	4	4.2
Oregon	79	5	6.1
Idaho	46	3	10.1
Michigan	36	15	0.8
Utah	37	3	6.2
Wyoming	27	1	17.9
Florida	24	N.A.	N.A.
Alaska	20	4	12.8
Colorado	15	13	1.1
Total	1,276		

*As of June 1993. N.A. = not available.

Source: Company reports.

1991 to the fourth quarter of 1994. The ratio of reserves to nonperforming assets was also at 237 percent at the end of the second quarter of 1995, while net loan charge-offs stood at 0.17 percent for the second quarter of 1995.

In addition to the improvement in asset quality, there was a commensurate improvement in operating efficiency; the efficiency ratio dropped from 65.3 percent in 1991 to 60.5 percent in 1993 and to 59.1 percent in 1994. Management expects to reduce this ratio to 57 percent in 1997 through consolidation of the two companies and a program to trim noninterest expenses. To aid in cost reduction, Key merged its operations into two computer centers and its four mortgage companies into one. The bank also sold unprofitable car leasing and financing companies and announced a corporatewide plan to cut 3 percent of its workforce, or almost 1,000 employees. The latter move should lead to a reduction of $100 million in costs over a two year period that began in mid-1994. KeyCorp appears well on its way to becoming one of the nation's most efficient producers of financial services.

Key's ROA and ROE improved from 1.26 percent and 18.7 percent in 1992, respectively, to 1.36 percent and 18.9 percent in 1994. Excluding the nonrecurring items, the 1994 ROA and ROE were 1.39 percent and 19.2 percent, respectively. During the first half of 1995, ROA averaged 1.16 percent, while ROE averaged

16.53 percent. Continued improvement in these profitability ratios is anticipated as the company attempts to leverage the respective product strengths across its extensive distribution network, thereby gaining revenue-enhancement opportunities.

Fee Income

The emphasis on marketing its fee-producing products throughout the franchise (see Table 6–5), controlling credit risk, and reducing inefficiency throughout the system should lead to recognition of KeyCorp as one of the top superregional banks in the country. The company has taken appropriate actions to cut noninterest expenses to improve its operating efficiency and to generate additional revenue from the sale of some of Society's products that were not available at Key, such as automobile leasing and financing services and trust products, to customers within the old Key branch system.

Prior to the detailed release of First Choice 2000, management had promised to produce revenue enhancements of $30 million per year by mid-1995, with 57 percent coming from small-business initiatives and 38 percent from corporate banking. Management seems to be taking advantage of its new size and financial strength to prepare for the changing demographics of the next decade, positioning the institution for greater efficiency and increased revenue growth.[8] For example, KeyCorp has begun to offer mutual funds with wrap accounts, charging fees

T A B L E   6–5

KeyCorp Noninterest Income (in millions)

Source	1994	1993
Charges on deposit accounts	$263	$ 252
Trust/asset management	220	245
Mortgage banking	88	128
Credit card	76	74
Insurance and brokerage	59	66
Special asset management	17	46
Net securities gains	(15)	28
Gains, asset sales		29
Venture capital	17	(.8)
International fees	17	21
Miscellaneous	140	113
Total noninterest income	$883	$1,002

Source: KeyCorp, 1994 *Annual Report*, p. 48.

of 1.25 percent of assets. This is a bridge product between the retail bank and the trust account. The bank also intends to quadruple its private-banking staff over the next five years to help generate additional fee income from wealthier customers. In the credit card area, where Key has 1.4 million cards and $1.4 billion in loans outstanding, a new experienced credit card executive has been hired to boost sales and use of the product.

KeyCorp has installed point-of-sale terminals in 18 BP Express stores (convenience store chain run by BP Petroleum in conjunction with service stations). The new debit terminals will permit customers to use ATM cards to pay for goods at these stores.

KeyCorp has also introduced a program aimed at making financial planning easier for consumers by offering a seven day per week toll-free hotline, which can be used by customers to answer questions about their finances. The program, called Key Solutions, will also give customers a five minute analysis of their financial needs.

The noninterest earnings are uncertain, and management will have to pay more attention to these important sources of revenue. The financial impact of the sale of the mortgage company to NationsBank; the acquisition of Spears, Benzak, Salomon & Farrell, a money manager; and the acquisition of AutoFinance Group will materially alter the earnings equation in 1995 and beyond. One of the salient goals of First Choice 2000 is to increase fee income substantially.

1995 ANNOUNCEMENTS

Aside from the sale of its mortgage banking unit and Society First Federal Savings of Fort Meyers, Florida, asset-liability management problems, and the unveiling of First Choice 2000, KeyCorp began to show strong loan growth of 15 percent in the first half of 1995. Unfortunately, net interest margin in the first half of 1995 declined from 4.92 percent to 4.49 percent, causing a decline in ROA from 1.43 percent in 1994's first half to 1.19 percent in 1995. Similarly, ROE declined from 19.43 percent in 1994 to 16.63 percent in the first half of 1995. However, Dennis Shea, bank stock analyst at Morgan Stanley, considered the second quarter of 1995 as the most encouraging since the merger with Society because of the large increase in loan growth and increases in other revenues. The results in the second quarter of 1995 revealed that KeyCorp rebounded successfully from the net interest margin troubles experienced during 1994 and the first quarter of 1995.

KEYCORP VISION

The merger between Society and Key has created one of the strongest and best diversified financial service companies in the country, with assets of $66.8 billion and net income of $854 million for 1994. These figures compared with total assets of $58.3 billion and net income of $710 million in 1993. KeyCorp is the ninth largest provider of corporate bank financing, the fourth largest agricultural lender, and the operator of the fourth largest bank-affiliated leasing company in the United States.

The vision of the company is to be the *First Choice* of those seeking world-class financial products and services.[9] The company's objectives are to achieve double-digit earnings growth in the coming years. Along with the aforementioned efficiency and credit-quality improvements, improved cross-selling of products and services, loan growth, and noninterest revenue increases from trust, investment management, card services, insurance, and brokerage businesses are likely to become significant drivers of earnings expansion in the years ahead.[10]

KeyCorp has aggressive marketing plans designed to exploit the company's extensive distribution channels in the areas of trust, investment management, and credit cards. It is also likely that Key will continue to make additional in-market and adjacent-market mergers that are accretive. This will fill in geographic gaps, further diversify risk, and expand the distribution system. However, another merger of equals is a distinct possibility before the end of the decade, and even a reasonable possibility under the tenure of current chairman Victor Riley. Riley would also like to boost Key's noninterest income to 40 percent of revenues from the 1994 level of 25.5 percent. This would require either another bank or nonbank acquisition that would strengthen Key's fee-based revenues.[11] Another asset management company or a bank with substantial trust or mutual fund assets under management would seem to fit Key's needs. Riley has also expressed interest in purchasing a financial institution with a strong international division.

KeyCorp decided to increase its dividend payout ratio from its historical 35 percent to 40 percent over the next several years. The company's board of directors announced a program to repurchase up to 12 million common shares, approximately 5 percent of its common stock. Of that total, 5.5 million will be reissued to pay for pending acquisitions. On the negative side, the unrealized pretax loss in KeyCorp's total securities portfolio stood at $467 million, while the unrealized pretax loss on the company's interest rate swap portfolio was $400 million at the end of the third quarter of 1994. Key took security losses of $24 billion in the fourth quarter of 1994 and $49 million in the first quarter of 1995 to help reduce the company's exposure to further changes in interest rates. The company also indicated that it was allowing certain fixed-rate loans and securities to mature without reinvestment. Counterbalancing some of these unrealized losses is the increasing value of Key's extensive core deposit base within a rising interest rate environment, which keeps the company's funding costs well below wholesale levels.[12]

KeyCorp had originally told analysts that it could survive its interest rate gap sensitivity problem without taking any unusual charges or losses. However, following the Fed's increase in short-term rates by 75 basis points in November 1994, management decided to incur a pretax loss of about $100 million, taking one-third of the loss in the fourth quarter of 1994 and the remainder in the first quarter of 1995. The company also experienced a one-time gain in the first quarter of 1995 on the sale of its mortgage banking and servicing business; that gain was expected to offset some of the losses taken in that quarter. KeyCorp felt that it could not reach enough critical mass in the cyclical mortgage banking business to warrant holding the company; it also needed to balance the major portfolio loss that occurred due to mismanagement of interest rate risk.

FIRST CHOICE 2000

Under the leadership of its president and CEO Gillespie, KeyCorp unveiled a plan called "First Choice 2000." The company intends to leverage the earnings capacity of its extensive banking franchise internally by reallocating resources and investment spending to certain businesses with potential for high revenue growth, while at the same time exiting its slower-growth business segments or improving their operating efficiency. First Choice calls for a reduction in expenses by $100 million annually (about 5 percent) by the end of 1996 and a doubling of earnings to $1.54 billion by the year 2000. First Choice 2000 is geared to raise 1994's net income of $870 million by 12 percent annually through reengineering, better and more focused marketing, greater cost controls, and strategic planning. The strategy supports the company's long-term objective to be the first choice of its customers and a top-tier financial services company; to achieve top-tier profitability and top-quartile productivity; and to produce double-digit earnings growth and superior returns to shareholders.[13]

Under the plan, the company's focus will be on selling more retail, finance, corporate, and private banking services to existing customers and attracting and building a more profitable customer base. Building on KeyCorp's core competence, information advantage, strong name recognition, local market presence, and broad-based product capabilities, management's assessment of the company's long-term competitive outlook has led them to focus on four strategic businesses, each with a nationwide scope: community banking, private banking, national consumer finance (auto loans and leases, credit cards, educational loans, marine and recreational vehicle loans, and direct lending from the branches), and corporate finance. Within each of these businesses, management is undertaking a substantial reconfiguration, either of the delivery system, the product profile, the approach to marketing, or the management information system needed for accurate assessment of performance and the competition.

In an attempt to optimize revenue-expense relationships, Key has developed a comprehensive marketing strategy for each segment, focusing on type of product offered, selling techniques, delivery channels, and extent and type of customer contact. Executive management is counting on an important change in the mix of its employment base: fewer clerks and more highly trained and financially motivated salespeople, who will spend more time selling to carefully targeted customers. The target is to move from 1.9 product relationships per household to 3.8 over five years. These actions have costs, but management believes other cost-saving efforts combined with higher overall product sales will make the actions self-funded. In an era when most banks are reducing the sizes of their branch systems, Key, despite its massive reconfiguration plan, currently does not plan any such reduction. Similar massive reengineering efforts are slated for the private banking and small-business sectors. Management took a major step toward growing the national consumer finance segment with its announcement to acquire AutoFinance, Inc., a leading national automobile lender. Jim Wert, KeyCorp's CFO, stated that AutoFinance would produce a return on investment of 15 percent after two full years of operating within KeyCorp. Management has also stated that this acquisition should position KeyCorp among the country's largest noncaptive auto finance companies, complementing their leadership position in specialty consumer finance businesses, such as marine and recreational vehicle leasing and educational lending. Management also left the door open for other types of nonbank acquisitions, given the nationwide scope of their operations.[14]

SUMMARY

The earnings momentum at Key should be driven by moderate revenue growth, improving operating efficiencies, and the deployment of excess capital into acquisitions or share buybacks. Although the management of KeyCorp may be on the leading edge of structural change, many on Wall Street are sitting on the sidelines until management executes flawlessly its five-year plan. The company intends to leverage the earnings capacity of its extensive banking franchise by reallocating internal resources and investment spending to certain businesses with high revenue growth potential, while exiting or vastly improving the operating efficiencies of its slower-growth business segments. Management is also focusing on improving marketing techniques through based strategies. The company has adopted a new model that is bank-based, nationally oriented toward consumers and commercial financial services, and characterized by technology, marketing, and service excellence. The engine of growth is likely to be in the national consumer finance business. The company's core strategic theme is to build a multiproduct, multichannel, national consumer finance entity. The mission remains to move KeyCorp's technology from the traditional back-office to a delivery mechanism for their customers. Management has accelerated technology and marketing strategies, realigning the organizational structure to decentralize product delivery and sales, while centralizing standards in product development, delivery, technology, and R&D.[15]

A rebound in revenue growth remains uncertain in the eyes of some analysts who have lost faith in this management team because of failures to deliver on past promises. For example, management suggested in 1995 that during the past several years the true underlying growth rate was only about 6 percent when all nonrecurring items and merger synergies were removed and when normalized net interest margins were utilized. However, investors had been told by the management teams at both the old Key and the old Society that existing EPS growth goals were in the low double digits. There was also an implicit admission by management that the net interest margin was overstated at the old Society because of higher than normal interest rate risk. In short, the credibility of the new KeyCorp management was frayed somewhat by the lack of revenue growth and higher than expected losses due to interest rate risk. Thus, although the new management's strategic initiatives may be comprehensive and well thought-out, and despite the merger being described as a revenue synergy deal and as creating an institution with superb asset-liability management skills, many analysts will probably take a "wait and see" approach. Clearly, there is uncertainty surrounding the KeyCorp plan among bank stock analysts.[16]

We can expect KeyCorp to make fill-in acquisitions whenever they can be made without diluting EPS. The company is also likely to make at least one more large acquisition or merger of equals. The candidates include Bank of Boston, Comerica, First Bank Systems, U.S. Bancorp, or Huntington Bancshares. Mr. Gillespie, the new CEO, indicated an interest in acquiring nonbanks with a preference for aspects of money management and credit cards. KeyCorp is also interested in acquiring companies that either brought specific customer segments or product expertise it did not already have, or acquiring companies with technological advantages and/or marketing know-how. The company also announced a new phase, "Resource '96", which represents additional consolidation cost savings (of up to $80 million) and revenue enhancements (of up to $20 million) that will be implemented in 1996 in order to allow substantial reinvestment in targeted growth initiatives. By the year 2000, a combination of "Resource '96" and "First Choice 2000" should provide a near doubling of KeyCorp's underlying current core EPS growth of 6 percent to a level of 10–12 percent. Gillespie also believes that the national consumer finance group represents the true engine of growth for the entire corporation and that community banking revenues and profits should be expected to grow at double digit rates.[17]

ENDNOTES

1. C.S. Berger, "KeyCorp Rolls Out First Choice 2000," *Salomon Brothers*, March 3, 1995, p. 3.
2. T.H. Hanley, "KeyCorp," *CS First Boston*, February 24, 1995, p. 1.
3. C.S. Berger, "KeyCorp," *Salomon Brothers*, August 28, 1994, pp. 2–3.
4. T.H. Hanley, "KeyCorp," *CS First Boston*, November 16, 1994, pp. 2–4.
5. Berger, August 28, 1994, p. 3.
6. Ibid., p. 4.
7. T.H. Hanley, P.J. Carter, and A.B. Collins, "Bank Consolidation Monthly," *CS First Boston*, October 1994, p. 7.

8. Berger, August 28, 1994, p. 2.
9. KeyCorp, 1994 *Annual Report*.
10. Hanley, "KeyCorp," *CS First Boston*, September 29, 1994, p. 3.
11. M. Murray, "Key Remains at a Crossroad after Bank Merger," *The Wall Street Journal*, November 23, 1994, p. B4.
12. Hanley, November 16, 1994, p. 9.
13. Berger, "KeyCorp Rolls Out First Choice 2000," p. 3.
14. T.D. McCandless, "KeyCorp," *Paine Webber Research*, March 24, 1995, p. 2.
15. C.S. Berger, "KeyCorp—Designing the Bank of Tomorrow," *Salomon Brothers*, October 3, 1995, pp. 1–2.
16. McCandless, pp. 1–2.
17. T.D. McCandless, "KeyCorp," *Paine Webber Research*, September 21, 1995, p. 2.

T A B L E   6–6

KeyCorp Financials

	1990	1991	1992	1993	1994
Earnings per share	$2.36	$2.45	$2.52	$2.93	$3.45
Assets (in millions)	$47,442	$51,996	$52,353	$57,051	$62,561
Net income (in millions)	$256.10	$313.70	$592.10	$709.90	$853.49
Return on assets	0.54%	0.60%	1.13%	1.24%	1.36%

	1994	
	(in millions)	**%**
Average earning assets	$56,916	100
Securities	13,309	23
Loans	43,463	76
Other	144	0
Loans	46,579	100
Construction and land	1,287	
Commercial mortgage	6,775	
Highly leveraged		
Commercial loans and leases	12,498	
Other foreign	97	
Term LCD		
Credit card receivables	1,652	
Other consumer	10,348	
Unearned discount		
Corporate	20,657	44
Consumer	12,000	26
Mortgages	13,922	30

	1990	1991	1992	1993	1994
Efficiency ratio	66.81	63.57	59.28	59.84	59.32
Shareholder equity (in millions)	$3,045	$3,369	$3,723	$4,189	$4,599
Preferred	$75	$166	$244	$184	$160
Common	$2,970	$3,203	$3,479	$4,005	$4,439

F I G U R E   6–1

KeyCorp Financial Charts

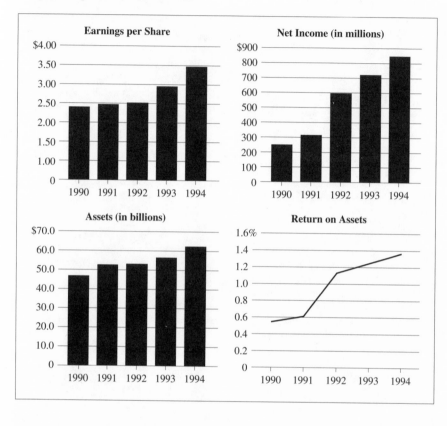

F I G U R E   6–2

KeyCorp Financial Charts

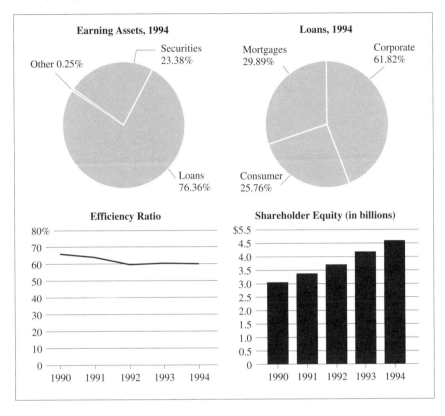

CHAPTER 7

PNC Bank

PNC Bank Corp., formerly PNC Financial Corp., is a broad-based financial services company with assets of $64.1 billion at year-end 1994. PNC had 1994 net income of about $610 million, compared to $726 million in 1993. In mid-1995, PNC announced an agreement to acquire Midlantic Corp. (headquartered in Edison, New Jersey) for $2.84 billion in stock. Following the merger, PNC would serve more than 3.8 million households and more than 100,000 small businesses. In addition, PNC should have lower funding costs, a reduction of liability sensitivity, and an improvement in its capital ratios. The Midlantic acquisition would make PNC the number two bank in New Jersey and in the Philadelphia region, as well as the 11th largest holding company in the United States, with assets of about $76 billion.

PNC operates one of the largest student-lending businesses in the United States and maintains a national presence in mortgage banking through an origination network that spans 33 states. PNC currently operates 550 community banking offices in Pennsylvania, Kentucky, Indiana, Ohio, Delaware, and New Jersey. In addition, PNC owns small banks in West Virginia and Michigan. PNC is also the largest bank manager of proprietary mutual funds ($26 billion in assets at year-end 1994) and the sixth largest bank asset manager (more than $213 billion in assets under administration, with discretionary authority over about $53 billion). PNC is also among the largest mutual fund service providers, with more than 300 mutual funds, assets of about $104 billion under administration, and 2.2 million accounts. The company also provides custodial services to more than $17 billion in assets. In addition, the trust department sells economic and investment research services to more than 245 financial institutions, including brokerage firms, insurance companies, pension funds, and correspondent banks.

The executive offices of PNC are located in Pittsburgh, Pennsylvania. The company's principal activities include retail banking, corporate banking, investment management and trust, and investment banking.

HISTORY

In January 1983, PNC Financial Corp. was organized from the consolidation of Pittsburgh National Corp. and Provident National Corp. Although the assets of the commercial banking subsidiary of the Provident Bank were not particularly large, given its location in Philadelphia, the trust assets under management and the management contracts with mutual funds placed it among the top five trust management banks in the United States. The merger of Pittsburgh National and Provident was the largest in the history of the U.S. banking industry at the time. PNC became the 27th largest bank holding company in the nation in 1983, with assets of $12 billion and earnings of $117 million.

PNC Corporation's forerunner, the Pittsburgh National Bank, was incorporated in 1959, but its roots can be traced back to 1852. At that time, steel magnates James Laughlin and B.F. Jones opened Pittsburgh Trust and Savings. PNC's other predecessor, Provident National Bank, was founded in the mid-1800s. In 1847, the Trademen's National Bank opened in downtown Philadelphia. After a century of acquisitions and name changes, it became Provident National Bank in 1964. In five years, PNC more than doubled its assets from its 1983 merger base to more than $36 billion in 1988.

In 1984, PNC acquired Marine Bancorp with assets of $757 million and its principal subsidiary Marine Bank (Warren, Pennsylvania). In 1985, PNC acquired Northeastern Bancorp Inc., and its principal subsidiary, Northeastern Bank of Pennsylvania. In 1986, PNC acquired the Hershey Bank ($146 million in assets) in Pennsylvania and sold Kissell Company, a mortgage banking company, to City Federal Savings. In 1987, PNC merged with Citizens Fidelity Corp. of Louisville, Kentucky ($3.9 billion in assets). In 1988, PNC merged with the Central Bancorporation and First Bancorp on the same day, February 29. In 1989, PNC merged with the Bank of Delaware, headquartered in Wilmington, Delaware (assets of $1.8 billion).

In 1991, Pittsburgh National Bank acquired approximately $2.7 billion of performing assets and retail deposit liabilities from the RTC as receiver for First Federal Savings and Loan Association of Pittsburgh. Additionally in 1991, PNC's Citizen's Fidelity Bank and Trust Co. acquired selected assets ($300 million) and retail deposit liabilities of Louisville-based Future Federal Savings Bank from the RTC. In the same year, it completed the sale of four Ohio bank affiliates.

During 1992, PNC completed the acquisitions of six financial institutions with assets of about $2.6 billion. It acquired Pro Group, Inc. (Bradford, Pennsylvania) and the $1.2 billion asset CCNB Corporation of Camp Hill (Pennsylvania). CCNB then merged Gettysburg National Bank and parent Federal Savings Bank into CCNB Bank N.A. Shortly thereafter, PNC acquired Sunrise Bancorp Inc. (Fort Mitchell, Kentucky) and Sunrise's subsidiary and merged them into PNC's Central Trust, Northern Kentucky, N.A., and Flagship Financial Corp. (Jenkintown, Pennsylvania) and its two thrift subsidiaries, First American Savings, F.A., and Brandywine Savings Bank, which were merged with PNC's Provident National Bank. In late 1992, PNC received approval from the Federal Reserve Board to form Electronic Payment Services, a joint venture between Banc One Corp., CoreStates PNC, and Society Corporation. It is the holding company for Money Access Service, Inc., a processor of ATMs, and for BUYPASS Corp., an electronic point-of-sale (POS) transaction processing service. The new company, 31 percent owned by PNC, is one of the largest processors of ATMs and POS transactions in the country.

RECENT DEVELOPMENTS

In January 1993, PNC introduced a package of 16 mutual funds to address the investment goals of a broad range of investors. With an increase in its licensed sales force from 125 to 500, PNC plans to boost these assets to $16 billion by 1997, from $5.3 billion at year-end 1994.

During 1993, PNC's total acquisitions had assets of approximately $12 billion. United Federal Bancorp, Inc., a State College, Pennsylvania–based savings bank (assets of $812 million) was acquired by PNC as was The Massachusetts Company, a bank and trust company (Boston), from the Travelers Corporation. The purchase of the State College Bank would make PNC the market share leader in central Pennsylvania, while the addition of The Massachusetts Company added efficient delivery of wholesale financial products to PNC's capabilities. PNC completed a merger with Gateway Fed Corporation of Cincinnati (assets of $503 million), the largest thrift in that market. Following the merger, Gateway Federal Savings Bank was merged into PNC Bank, Ohio. PNC also acquired the $2 billion asset Eastern Bancorp (Wilkes Barre, Pennsylvania). This acquisition made PNC the deposit share market leader in northeastern Pennsylvania.

Additionally in 1993, PNC acquired Sears Mortgage Banking Group (Vernon Hills, Illinois) from Sears, Roebuck and Co. The acquisition of the mortgage banking company positioned PNC as seventh in mortgage origination and ninth in mortgage servicing in the United States. In addition to accelerating mortgage banking revenue, the Sears mortgage customers provide a long list for cross-selling opportunities. The Sears acquisition gives PNC a banking presence in 33 states, with 117 offices. At year-end 1993, the mortgage-servicing portfolio totaled $36 billion, including $27 billion serviced for others.

In June 1994, the company announced two acquisitions: a $10 billion residential mortgage-servicing portfolio from Dallas Associates Corp. of North America, a subsidiary of Ford Motor Company, and BlackRock Financial Management, a New York–based asset management firm. The BlackRock deal ($240 million) would create one of the nation's largest institutional fixed-income, asset management companies, with $23 billion in assets managed for institutions and total assets of $75 billion under management. This acquisition is expected to increase PNC's investment management and trust income by 20 percent, while being nondilutive to shareholders. The PNC family of funds, which has 29 mutual funds, surpassed the $5.3 billion mark in assets under management in 1994. At the same time, the acquisition of the mortgage servicer increased PNC's servicing portfolio to approximately $41 billion, which would rank it 10th in the country (see Tables 7–1 and 7–2). These acquisitions should help expand the percentage of fee income from 31 percent in 1993 to 34 percent in 1995. PNC announced a letter of intent to form a

T A B L E   7–1

Top Mortgage Originators, 1995 (in millions)

Lender	1993 Volume	1994 Volume	1st Half 1995 Volume	1st Half 1994 Volume
Countrywide Funding	$ 49.48	$ 32.42	$ 19.59	$ 13.09
Norwest Mortgage	33.70	24.90	13.89	12.30
Prudential Home Mortgage	43.20	24.17	16.49	5.68
Chase Manhattan Mortgage	15.83	17.44	7.09	5.28
Chemical Residential Mortgage	15.29	16.27	7.43	4.94
Fleet Mortgage Group	22.90	13.90	9.50	5.50
GE Capital Mortgage	12.54	12.06	10.25	0.95
GMAC Mortgage Group	8.17	10.85	5.75	3.32
Bank of America	10.60	9.77	5.73	3.85
North American Mortgage	17.61	9.76	6.54	2.83
Home Savings of America	9.95	8.16	4.15	2.58
Great Western Financial	8.44	7.68	3.58	4.04
NationsBank and affiliates	11.22	6.92	3.91	4.06
World Savings	5.81	6.64	2.60	2.87
PNC Mortgage Corp.	13.17	6.40	4.01	2.31
Director Mortgage Loan	10.50	5.45	N.A.	N.A.
KeyCorp Mortgage	8.19	5.40	N.A.	N.A.
Citicorp and affiliates	5.10	5.11	2.47	1.70
BancBoston Mortgage Corp.	7.81	4.67	4.45	1.31
PHH U.S. Mortgage Corp.	7.85	4.67	2.99	1.82
Total Mortgage Originations	$1,009.30	$753.80	$475.83	$290.43

Source: *Inside Mortgage Finance.*

T A B L E   7–2

Top Mortgage Servicers, 1995 (in millions)

Lender	1993 Volume	1994 Volume	1st Half 1995 Volume
Countrywide Funding	$ 79.94	$ 109.97	$ 121.22
GE Capital Mortgage	64.70	93.58	109.40
Fleet Mortgage Group	69.90	82.20	99.80
Prudential Home Mortgage	68.29	75.47	77.83
Norwest Mortgage	45.67	71.51	100.49
Chase Manhattan Mortgage	47.80	64.53	73.57
GMAC Mortgage Corp.	31.35	58.93	33.18
Chemical Bank and affiliates	33.13	52.69	51.86
Bank of America	46.69	51.70	57.07
Home Savings of America	49.10	50.67	49.50
Citicorp and affiliates	44.00	44.34	40.80
PNC Mortgage Corp.	35.60	42.00	40.00
Great Western Financial	38.97	40.57	42.70
Source One Mortgage	38.40	39.60	28.70
NationsBank and affiliates	29.07	38.96	77.51
BancBoston Mortgage Corp.	26.65	35.81	38.72
First Union Mortgage Corp.	34.76	34.21	37.27
Mellon Mortgage	21.66	30.93	34.00
Lomas Mortgage U.S.A.	27.72	26.61	25.33
KeyCorp Mortgage	22.90	25.46	N.A.
Total Mortgage Originations	$3,144.90	$3,347.51	$3,433.44

Source: *Inside Mortgage Finance.*

joint venture with Coldwell Banker Realty that will provide for a neutral, multi-lender mortgage origination service with 300 Coldwell offices. Customers will be able to evaluate their mortgage options in the Coldwell offices.

PNC has followed in the footsteps of Mellon (Boston Company and Dreyfus) and First Union (Lieber and Co.) in expanding its asset management business through acquisition. To expand its traditional banking business, PNC appears ready to move into Chicago or the middle Atlantic/Southeastern corridor. It is interesting to point out that PNC sold its outlying subsidiaries in Ohio to Banc One in favor of concentrating its efforts on the Cincinnati market, where it ranks fourth in market share.

Since 1991, PNC has completed 12 acquisitions, and excluding Sears Mortgage and BlackRock, the number of employees companywide has remained essentially flat. In March 1995, PNC agreed to buy 84 branches in southern and central
New Jersey (about $3.4 billion in assets) from Chemical Bank. The deal also adds
$2.9 billion in deposits, $1.8 billion in consumer loans, and $500 million in mid-
dle-market commercial loans as well as $297 million in intangibles to PNC's bal-
ance sheet. About 40 percent of the acquired branches are in the suburbs of
Philadelphia, where PNC already owns a bank. The Chemical Bank branch purchase was quickly followed by the purchase of Midlantic Corp., with $13.7 billion
in assets and $10.8 billion in deposits. The purchase price of 2.1 times book value
was considered a bit high. Midlantic will contribute about 18 percent of the combined company's assets, while its shareholders will receive 32 percent of the stock.
The dilution to PNC's book value will be approximately 13 percent after a $190
million pretax restructuring charge. However, Chairman O'Brien claimed that the
deal was actually accretive to earnings per share, adding 7 and 20 cents per share,
respectively, to PNC's 1996 and 1997 net income. PNC was expected to reduce
costs substantially by cutting 18 percent of noninterest expenses from the combined Midlantic, Chemical, and PNC operations, including the closing of 68
branches after the completion of the merger. Additional savings will come from
combining back-office and headquarters operations.

Some analysts feel that the Midlantic acquisition is dilutive to EPS. Midlantic will contribute about 18 percent of the combined company's assets, but its
shareholders will own 32 percent of the stock in the combined company. The earnings dilution is more difficult to measure because of uncertainties regarding the
reaching of cost-cutting and revenue enhancement targets, but the pro forma book
value is easier to calculate. After a $190 million pretax charge (about $0.35 after
taxes), pro forma book value should be about $16.66 per share, roughly 13 percent
lower than the $19.08 reported on March 31, 1995.

Management's claim to saving about 30 percent of Midlantic's expense base
may be difficult to achieve since Midlantic's efficiency ratio was already at 56 percent at the time of the merger announcement. These same analysts are dubious as to
whether management can achieve revenue enhancements of $11 million in 1996 and
$27 million in 1997, respectively, by "driving its products" throughout Midlantic's
customer base.[1] However, these analysts do feel that the acquisition does offer strategic long-run benefits and additional outlets in which PNC can sell its more advanced
products and leverage its technological advances and expenditures (see Table 7–3).

PNC intended to extend its regional reach, increasing consumer core
deposits, which should reduce its heavy dependence on borrowed funds. Generally, consumer deposits are cheaper and less volatile than money market borrowing. PNC's new source of funds and lending base helps the bank change its mix
away from the larger corporate to the consumer and middle-market customer on
both sides of the balance sheet.

T A B L E   7–3

Selected Comparative PNC/Midlantic Numbers

	PNC	Midlantic	Pro Forma
Assets (billions)	$62.1	$13.7	$75.8
Deposits (billions)	$35.0	$10.8	$43.9
Intangibles (millions)	$927.7	$100	$1,027
Branches	530*	338**	N.A.
Employees	23,000*	5,550**	28,550
Net income (millions)	$610	$272	$882
Common equity (millions)	$4,390	$1,409	$5,799
Book value/share	$19.08	$25.93	$16.66
Tangible common equity/assets	5.6%	9.3%	6.1%
NPAs/related assets	1.25%	2.60%	1.50%
Reserves/loans	2.75%	4.10%	3.00%
Reserves/NPLs	325%	217%	288%

* Includes July acquisition of Bank of Old York Road.
** Includes Chemical Banking branches.
Source: Company reports.

Midlantic, founded in the early 1980s with the merger of Midlantic (New Jersey) with Continental Corp. (Pennsylvania), nearly failed in the early 1990s. The company was saved by its new chairman, Gary J. Scheuring, who resorted to the sale of about one-third of the company's assets, generating enough capital to survive. Midlantic sold its credit card and mortgage operations, as well as subsidiary banks. In the postmerger plan, Scheuring will become a PNC director and vice chairman, overseeing the New Jersey and Philadelphia markets and all of PNC's retail banking. Scheuring obtained a premium price for Midlantic's shares (34 percent over market price, 2.2 times book value, and a 15.6 percent premium to core deposits). After squeezing out significant cost savings and improving operating efficiency dramatically, the company could do little else to maintain the momentum in banking profits. Midlantic should benefit from PNC's technological strength. In addition, it will be able to sell PNC advanced and better customer products to its own customer base, especially in the mortgage, credit card, mutual fund, and business service area. PNC benefits from being able to leverage its products over a much larger customer base and from cheaper deposit costs coming from a much larger core deposit base. Midlantic was an attractive takeover target because of the high per capita income of its customer base ($57,000, well above the national average) and the large number of midsize businesses in its banking area.

Investors are often skeptical of cost savings and revenue enhancement forecasts made by acquiring companies. However, there is a good chance that PNC can
revitalize Midlantic's underutilized franchise. The company has raised its merger
charges from $150–$180 million versus the previous estimate of $130 million. The
additional cost is for closing facilities in New Jersey that management did not previously anticipate closing. This should generate more confidence that the $150 mil-
lion cost savings estimate will be met, and possibly exceeded. As the progress of
the integration of Midlantic and the Chemical Banking branches in New Jersey
with PNC unfolds, investors may begin to focus on the longer-term positive impact
of the merger rather than on the shorter-term dilution impact.

TECHNOLOGICAL DEVELOPMENTS

PNC is one of the most technologically advanced banks in the country, one of the
key variables in separating superior banks from average banks. Technologically
driven better service and lower operating costs are key. The bank has several newer
technologies in various implementation stages, including a new branch automation
system, advanced ATM terminals, imaging projects involving file folders, and consumer and student loan processing. The bank added four banking stations, including two at the airport, with automated sales machines in Pittsburgh. These
machines, which cost $150,000 each, allow a customer to do platform transactions
via two-way video by simply entering a booth, sitting down, selecting the product in which he is interested by pushing a button, and picking up an adjacent phone.
The video screen turns on automatically and a trained staff member appears to
answer questions or help with bank transactions. The booths include only a screen,
phone, and printer. The machines are most frequently used to open checking and
savings accounts, apply for auto loans, or buy and sell brokerage products from
PNC-affiliated companies. In addition, the banking stations at the airport provide
traveler's checks and foreign currency exchange. The banking station projects,
which were started in the early 1990s, have provided a good return on investment
and a way to extend the retail banking market to nontraditional locations. PNC
appears to be moving toward client-service technologies. Current efforts in imaging, core systems consolidation, and branch automation reflect this strategy. PNC's
technology is considered among the best in the banking industry.

PNC uses technology to increase the efficiency of its operations. It believes that
the key challenge to serving a broad base of customers profitably is to provide the most
desirable, yet most efficient and effective, delivery channels. PNC has invested more
than $135 million over the last five years to build back-office systems driven from a
single, state-of-the-art computer center now serving the entire organization.

PNC has a world-class telephone banking system whereby a customer can
literally dial from anywhere to open an account or apply for a loan at PNC. PNC's
centralized banking center has been able to handle 86 percent of its customer

questions and problems successfully; the corporate goal is 96 percent. The tele-phone center has the potential to generate 200 branches' worth of sales.

The company has begun to close low-growth, full-service branches, think-ing it can deliver services more efficiently through alternative systems and chan-nels. PNC expects to reap enormous cost savings from the closing of about 200 branches in the next two years. In a pilot program in Philadelphia, PNC is run-ning branches with an enhanced sales culture that features executive sales training and incentives for all employees. Furthermore, by eliminating all paper transac-tions and redundant tasks and truncating processes, PNC cut expenses 25 to 30 per-cent and more than doubled sales.

PNC expects home banking to grow substantially over the next decade, with intelligent televisions offering in-home banking services. They also believe that the cur-rent smart-card technology could be made available through in-home devices loaded with cash. PNC believes that it can combine customer profiles with demographic and other public and behavioral information to enhance sales and marketing decisions.

The electronic delivery system gives PNC's corporate customers access to a myriad of services, including treasury management, investment, and employee benefits products. PNC is leveraging automation internally to streamline commu-nications and processes, including customer service, risk assessment, and credit approval. The result is a higher-quality, improved customer responsiveness and increased productivity.

COST CONTROL

Through PNC's technological infrastructure and disciplined integration process, PNC has eliminated an average of 43 percent of the noninterest expenses of acquired companies. PNC achieved an overhead ratio of 52 percent in 1993, an improvement from the 55.2 percent ratio of 1992, making PNC one of the most efficient banks in the country. Although the overhead ratio was 64 percent in 1994 because of the new acquisitions and losses on sale of securities, compared to 55.4 percent in 1993, this ratio is expected to decline to 52 percent in 1996. Fee busi-nesses, while highly profitable, usually have higher cost structures than banking organizations. PNC expects to close as many as 30 percent of its branches by the end of 1997, helping to reduce its overhead ratio substantially. The company announced a $31 million restructuring charge in the fourth quarter of 1994 to cover the cost of consolidating existing telephone banking centers and continued con-solidations of its branches.

EARNINGS AND OTHER FINANCIAL RATIOS

The combination of increased efficiency, improved credit quality, and increased fee income enabled the bank to generate net income of $725.8 million in 1993, a considerable increase from the $426.9 million of 1992; however, net income declined to $610 million in 1994. During 1994, retail banking contributed 47 percent of earnings, corporate banking contributed 44 percent, and investment management and trust contributed 9 percent (see Figure 7–1 and Table 7–4). PNC achieved an ROE of 18.40 percent and an ROA of 1.44 percent during 1993, considerably improved from ratios of 12.47 and 0.95 percent, respectively, in 1992. But these ratios declined in 1994 to 14.10 and 1.00 percent, respectively, because of management's misjudgment of the direction of interest rates. The ratio of non-performing loans to total loans improved substantially from 2.14 percent in 1992

F I G U R E   7–1

Earnings Contribution by Lines of Business, 1994

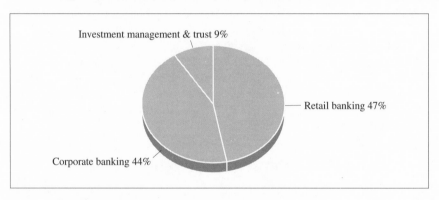

Investment management & trust 9%

Retail banking 47%

Corporate banking 44%

T A B L E   7–4

Line-of-Business Highlights

	Earnings		Average Balance Sheet		Return on Assigned Equity	
	1994	1993	1994	1993	1994	1993
Corporate banking	$292	$294	$14,759	$12,873	16%	17%
Retail banking	314	303	36,791	27,617	16	21
Investment management/trust	67	67	522	480	44	51
Investment banking	(6)	208	10,075	9,115		65
Total	667	872	62,147	50,085	16	24
Adjusted total	$610	$726	$60,896	$50,321	16%	24%

Source: PNC, 1994 *Annual Report.*

to 0.90 percent in 1994. In addition, the bank is well capitalized, with a Tier 1 ratio of 8.6 percent, a total capital to risk-based asset ratio of 11.5 percent, and a leverage ratio of 6.59 percent at year-end 1994.

To enhance earnings and to provide better service, PNC created a corporatewide Private Bank that will focus on serving the unique investment, borrowing, and trust needs of affluent customers. In addition, a Direct Bank was created to focus on more effectively reaching and satisfying contemporary customers, who have demonstrated a strong preference for delivery channels that supplement branch offices. An Asset Management Unit was also created to expand the company's significant product line and more effectively distribute investment services to large institutional investors.

POTPOURRI

On the corporate banking front, PNC has established a leadership market share among smaller and middle-market companies within their operating region with high levels of customer satisfaction. The 1993 loan portfolio was comprised of 40 percent commercial and industrial loans, 27 percent consumer loans, 25 percent residential loans, 3 percent commercial mortgage loans, and 5 percent real estate (see Figure 7–2). PNC has a much higher percentage of commercial and industrial loans in its portfolio than most other superregional banks. In addition, PNC is more of a large corporate lender. Although pricing pressure exists in just about all lending areas, it is worst in the large corporate market area served by the bank.[2]

The company is also a major provider of treasury management products and services, an area in which it enjoys the top market share within the middle market in the region it serves. Through PNC Securities, the company provides full-service

F I G U R E   7–2

Loan Portfolio Composition, 1994 versus 1993

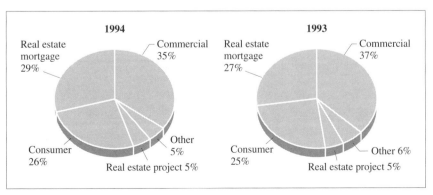

retail brokerage services in more than 10 strategic locations throughout its retail banking network and operates one of the nation's largest bank-affiliated, low-cost brokerage services. PNC Securities is also one of the largest underwriters of revenue bonds for the healthcare industry and for universities and colleges.

PNC is expected to sell to BHC Financial its discount brokerage unit, Trade-Saver, to focus on selling mutual funds and other securities through its licensed branch sales people. PNC recently received approval to sell CNA insurance products across all states and expects to bring more investment and trust products to the roster for cross-selling to customers.

CORPORATE GOALS AND PHILOSOPHY

PNC's first chief executive, Merle Gilliand, set the tone for the company's management style, described as "bottom-up management" and a grassroots approach. The company emphasized quality, not size. Mellon was the bank's premier rival, controlling most of the largest corporate accounts in Pittsburgh. Hence, PNC emphasized small and midsized corporate lending as well as consumer lending. As banking changed over the years, this emphasis on smaller companies favored the growth of PNC as America's corporate giants chose to borrow in the commercial paper market instead of from banks.

Thomas H. O'Brien, who succeeded Gilliand as chairman and CEO, continued with aggressive but conservative leadership, carefully choosing healthy merger partners at the right price. He stated in the company's 1993 annual report to shareholders:

> PNC Bank is a leading superregional bank delivering a broad array of financial services, differentiated from our competition by our performance. We're a hard-working, high-energy, no-nonsense bank, committed to operating at the highest levels of service and profitability. We're tough competitors who have streamlined systems and organized management to provide customers with unmatched products and services. Our dedication to service means we care about and respond to the needs of our customers, employees, and communities. And that's where performance counts . . .
>
> To continue our record of profitable growth, we must become an exceptional marketing company. Everything we do must be with a clear focus on identifying and satisfying our customer's needs and desires in a profitable way. We must grow the businesses by investing in and maintaining a strong and enabling infrastructure, providing products and services of exceptional quality and delivering them efficiently.

The same annual report discusses the philosophy of the bank. "The necessary skills that have helped us achieve a high level of performance for our customers and shareholders include:

- Managing the revenue/expense relationship to improve margins and profitability.
- Planning, negotiating, and integrating acquisitions that increase shareholder value.
- Applying technology to improve effectiveness and efficiency.
- An enhanced ability to manage credit risk and interest rate risk.
- A shared commitment of the entire management team to an organizational vision for growth and the company's single-minded focus on long-term profitability through customer satisfaction."

PNC has strong corporate earning power, derived from a broad array of traditional financial products, fee-based income products, and its state-of-the-art delivery platform. The company is one of the leaders in asset quality (nonperforming assets represented .85 percent of total assets in mid-1994) and among the most efficient of the superregional banks; it continues to make critical infrastructure and technological investments to reduce its operating cost structure. PNC has exhibited the right approach to investing in technology to improve its performance. Management focuses on managing profits by making critical investments in growth businesses such as mortgage banking, investment management and trust, mutual funds, and treasury management, while maintaining high returns in its mature, traditional businesses, such as corporate and retail banking.

PNC has historically maintained a high level of liquidity (loans to average earning assets are lower than many of its peers at 55 percent versus a 70 percent average), while holding about $23 billion in its securities portfolio (about 35 percent of total assets during 1994)[3] (see Figure 7–3). However, the company misjudged the direction of interest rates during 1994. Consequently, its large securities portfolio developed unusually high losses when interest rates rose throughout the year. PNC was already in a liability-sensitive position (negative gap) when rates rose during 1994 because of long maturities in its bond portfolio and $14 billion of receive-fixed, pay-floating interest rate swaps, most of which are amortizing swaps. Unfortunately, such swaps begin to amortize when rates fall and extend maturities when rates rise. Prior to the increase in short-term rates, only 5 percent of the swap portfolio matured after 1996. With the large increase in rates that occurred, virtually the entire swap book matures beyond 1996. In addition, in December 1994, unrecognized losses in the bond portfolio approximated $1 billion (14 percent of equity on an after-tax basis). Unfortunately, even after taking some losses and making some adjustments to the security portfolio in the fourth quarter, the company's gap position is still liability sensitive because $18 billion of the $22 billion securities portfolio is classified as held to maturity. Half of this held-to-maturity portfolio is fixed rate; therefore, PNC is still vulnerable to a rise in short-term rates. This crisis is not life threatening, as PNC is exceptionally well capitalized. However, the bank announced plans to attempt to extricate itself from

F I G U R E   7–3

Securities versus Loans, 1989–1994 (in billions)

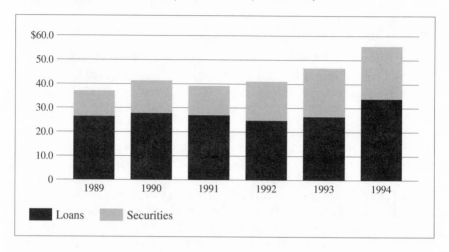

Loans   Securities

this mismatch by neutralizing the off-balance-sheet swaps by buying interest rate caps and countervailing swaps (negatively affecting net income), allowing $2 billion of low-spread corporate loans to run off the books in favor of a higher-spread book of business and exiting from low-return markets and businesses. There is still a lot of interest risk left in the bond portfolio, and normal earnings for the company may not be resumed until 1996 or even 1997.[4]

In addition, management indicated that it would let its securities portfolio run down by up to $6 billion during 1995 to about $17 billion, or 30 percent of earning assets. This would free up capital, but also lower earning assets. PNC's total assets would be reduced by just under 10 percent to about $58 billion by year-end 1995. To offset the negative impact of the portfolio losses, the bank plans a stock buyback program of as many as 24 million shares, close to 10 percent of outstanding stock, during 1995–1996. The securities sales, which have nearly emptied the bank's available-for-sale portfolio, effectively reduced PNC's dependence on high-cost, wholesale borrowed funds, the cost of which had risen during 1994. PNC had utilized such funds to a much greater degree than other superregional banks. Anthony Davis, an analyst at Dean Witter, commented: "We certainly feel better now about the balance-sheet configuration. But I guess we're still a little uncertain as to why they got to that position to begin with."[5]

Management has hinted at taking a one-time charge of roughly $330 million to cover the sale of about $5 billion in securities, previously classified as held for investment, and terminating $3 billion in pay-fixed swaps. The aforementioned securities positions would lower earnings in 1996 by $120 million if action is not taken. The earnings position of the bank would be impacted negatively at least through 1998 as a result of the pay-fixed swaps.

SUMMARY

The price of PNC common shares declined substantially during 1994 as a result of both realized and unrealized losses in their investment securities and swap portfolio. This resulted from the company's misjudgment of the direction of interest rates. PNC addressed part of this problem by selling some fixed-rate securities for a loss of $79 million in the fourth quarter of 1994. This loss was partially offset by a $35 million gain on the sale of mortgage servicing. Because of their negative gap position and expectations of modestly rising interest rates during 1995, the company anticipated a decline in net interest income in 1995 from the level achieved in 1994.

After many years of above average financial ratios, PNC's profitability ratios declined in 1994 to a 1 percent return on assets and a 14 percent return on equity. The company continues to maintain stringent cost controls, low levels of nonperforming assets, and make sensible, nondilutive acquisitions. PNC's highly diversified business lines and geographic locations, and restructuring of its balance sheet, as well as an increase in loan demand should lead to an improvement in the earnings prospects and financial ratios of the bank in 1996 over 1995.

PNC's purchase of Midlantic Corp. and 84 branches from Chemical Banking in southern and central New Jersey gives PNC the number two position in market share in both New Jersey and the Philadelphia area. A larger core deposit base, cheaper retail deposits, and an opportunity to leverage products over a larger and wealthier customer base should help PNC improve its earnings per share and profitability ratios in the years ahead. Long-term EPS growth should approximate 10–12 percent from 1997 onward, primarily as a result of a greater focus on retail banking and the opportunity to market newly acquired retail and corporate customers the more advanced and broader base of products and services offered by PNC. There will also be large cost savings from branch closings and the integration of systems. The new direct bank with over 450 well-trained and experienced bankers with college degrees should also add to fee income in the years ahead. In addition, success of the direct bank could eventually lead to cost reductions through branch consolidations. For example, it looks as if the direct bank should be able to increase consumer loans by over 20 percent within 18 months.

A major emphasis on credit cards with a goal of tripling credit card loans by 1998 should also help increase earnings. Jerry Craft, previous head of Wachovia's highly successful credit card operation, is the new president of Card Issuer Program Management.

Merger activity is likely to slow down for a while as PNC consolidates its Chemical and Midlantic banks into the PNC system. Executive management is likely to eliminate more jobs and close more branches than initially announced to minimize dilution in EPS and to generate higher profitability ratios. However, it will continue to make fill-in acquisitions that can help grow the customer base in wealthy areas. PNC will need a higher P/E ratio to make additional acquisitions without once again diluting earnings.

ENDNOTES

1. C. Kotowski, "PNC Bank," *Oppenheimer & Co.*, July 13, 1995, p. 2.
2. C.S. Berger, "PNC Bank Corp.," *Salomon Brothers Research Report*, November 21, 1994, p. 2.
3. T.H. Hanley, "PNC Bank Corp.," *CS First Boston*, June 2, 1994, pp. 5–6.
4. F.R. DeSantis, "Bank Notes," *Donaldson, Lufkin & Jenrette*, December 5, 1994, pp. 2–5.
5. M. Murray, "PNC Sold Fixed Rate Securtites Last Month at Loss Totaling $79 Million," *The Wall Street Journal*, January 9, 1995, p. B6.

T A B L E   7–5

PNC Bank Corp. Financials

	1990	1991	1992	1993	1994
Earnings per share	$0.37	$1.95	$1.89	$3.04	$2.56
Assets (in millions)	$45,716	$42,793	$44,744	$50,321	$60,896
Net income (in millions)	$70.91	$389.79	$426.94	$725.87	$610.06
Return on assets	0.16%	0.91%	0.95%	1.44%	1.00%

	1994	
	(in millions)	**%**
Average earning assets	$57,187	100
Securities	22,116	39
Loans	33,511	59
Other	1,560	3
Loans	35,407	100
Construction and land	1,628	
Commercial mortgage	1,261	
Highly leveraged	1	
Commercial loans and leases	13,929	
Other foreign	190	
Term LCD		
Credit card receivables	817	
Other consumer	5,681	
Unearned discount		
Corporate	17,009	48
Consumer	6,498	18
Mortgages	11,900	34

	1990	1991	1992	1993	1994
Efficiency ratio	57.15	57.48	57.25	54.41	59.97
Shareholder equity (in millions)	$2,780	$2,795	$3,436	$3,957	$4,336
Preferred	$41	$39	$35	$22	$20
Common	$2,739	$2,756	$3,401	$3,935	$4,316

FIGURE   7–4

PNC Bank Corp. Financial Charts

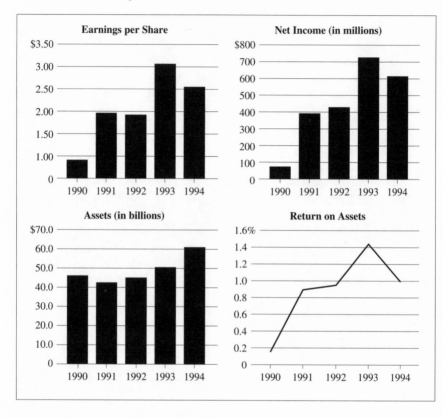

FIGURE 7–5

PNC Bank Corp. Financial Charts

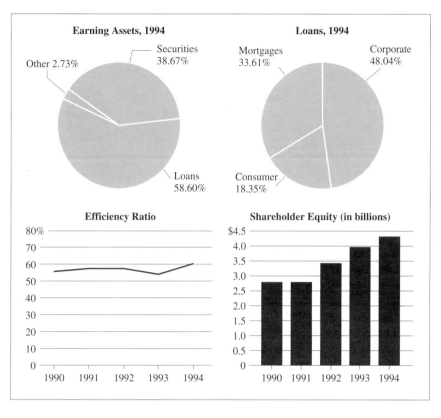

CHAPTER 8

Norwest Corporation

Norwest Corporation, headquartered in Minneapolis, is a nationwide financial services company that was organized in 1929; it owns substantially all the outstanding capital stock of 88 commercial banks serving 16 states (see Table 8–1). Norwest, with 45,000 employees, is a diversified financial services company providing banking, insurance, investment, and other services through more than 3,000 stores in all 50 states, all 10 Canadian provinces, and other countries.

Norwest also owns subsidiaries engaged in various businesses related to banking, principally mortgage banking (network of 781 stores in 50 states, with a

TABLE 8–1

Geographic Distribution of Assets

Banking Group	Total Assets (in billions)	Number of Stores
Twin Cities	$14.0	74
South Central Iowa, Nebraska	6.5	72
Western Arizona, Wyoming, Montana, Colorado, New Mexico, Texas	16.5	309
North Central Greater Minnesota, Indiana, North Dakota, South Dakota, Wisconsin, Ohio, Illinois	13.0	215

Source: Norwest, 1994 *Annual Report.*

mortgage-servicing portfolio of over $100 billion), equipment leasing, agricultural finance, commercial finance, consumer finance (Norwest Financial, a $5.3 billion asset consumer loan company, has 1,030 consumer finance stores in 46 states and 10 Canadian provinces), securities dealing and underwriting, insurance agency services, computer and data processing services, corporate trust services, venture capital investments, and credit card services. Norwest Bank is the 12th largest bank holding company in the United States, with $59.3 billion in assets, and was eighth in market capitalization at $7.8 billion at year-end 1994. The company derived 63 percent of its net earnings from banking, 9 percent from mortgage banking, and 28 percent from the company's high-yield consumer finance subsidiary in 1994 (see Figure 8–1). Breaking down estimated 1995 results even further, Norwest disclosed that 37 percent of earnings would come from pure community banking, 11 percent from investment products, insurance products, and processing earnings, and 14 percent from specialized lending (credit cards, asset-based lending, equipment finance, and corporate).

During 1994, Norwest generated net income of $800 million, accompanied by superb financial ratios. Net income in 1993 was $654 million. This was the seventh consecutive year of record net income. The banking group achieved record annual earnings of $507 million; Norwest Financial reported its 20th consecutive year of record earnings, with net income of $222.5 million; and Norwest Mortgage reported record 1994 earnings of nearly $71 million (see Table 8–2 and Figure 8–2). The company's EPS has averaged 14 percent annual growth from 1990 through 1994, and its average ROE has been 20 percent during that time frame, with higher numbers in 1993 and 1994. Consolidated noninterest income increased

F I G U R E   8–1

Net Income by Segment (in millions)

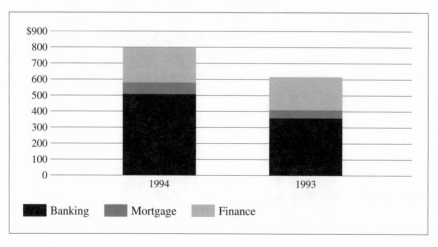

TABLE 8-2

Organizational Earnings*

	1994		1993	
	$ Millions	ROA	$ Millions	ROA
Banking	$507	1.15%	$357	1.13%
Mortgage banking	71	1.35	56	1.02
Norwest financial services	222	3.98	200	4.10
Net income	$800		$613	

* Year ended December 31.
Source: Norwest Corp., *Goldman Sachs, U.S. Research,* July 7, 1995, p. 13.

FIGURE 8-2

Norwest's Return on Assets

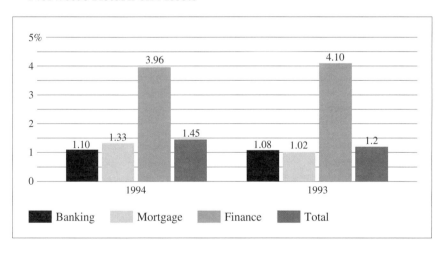

in 1994 despite the company's securities losses of $70.2 million. These securities losses provided an opportunity to reduce future rate risk in an environment of rising rates and to reinvest in shorter maturities at higher yields.

Norwest is the largest bank-owned insurance agency, the second largest automated clearinghouse processor, the third largest farm management firm, the seventh largest ATM switch, the eighth largest stock transfer agent, the ninth largest bank mutual fund manager (over $8.3 billion in proprietary assets under management), and the third largest student loan originator in the United States. All of these sources of revenue help the company generate 37 percent of its revenues from non-interest income (see Table 8–3 and Figure 8–3). Businesses such as Norwest Mortgage, Norwest Cash Management, Norwest Investment Management and Trust, Norwest Investment Services, and Norwest Insurance generated the fee-based revenues that have grown at a compound annual rate of 25 percent from 1989 to 1994.

T A B L E   8–3
Noninterest Income (in millions)

Source of Income	1994	1993
Trust	$ 210	$ 187
Deposit service charges	234	212
Mortgage banking	581	472
Data processing	62	66
Credit card	117	114
Insurance	207	177
Other fee/service charges	182	163
Net investment/mortgage-backed securities	(79)	49
Net venture capital gains	77	60
Other	47	86
Total	$1,638	$1,585

Source: Norwest, 1994 *Annual Report*, p. 40.

F I G U R E   8–3
Norwest's Operating Efficiency Ratio

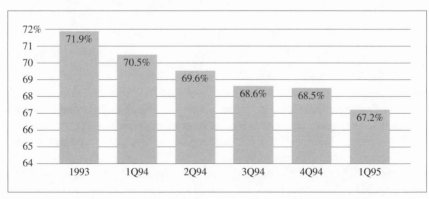

Source: CS First Boston Corp.

The addition in 1994 of Michigan National Bank's mortgage servicing operation with a portfolio valued at $8.6 billion and in 1995 of Directors Mortgage Loan Corporation with a servicing portfolio of $13.7 billion, as well as Barclays American Mortgage Corporation with a servicing portfolio of $15 billion should enable the company to achieve considerable additional fee income, while improving economies of scale and operating efficiency. At $100 billion, its servicing portfolio now ranks as the third largest in the nation, up from the fifth position that it held previously. The company is interested in acquiring all or part of Prudential's $78 million servicing portfolio. Norwest continues to set efficiency standards for the mortgage industry as its employees service 1,300 loans each. Norwest Mortgage should be able to continue to build economies of scale and improve its operating efficiency, critical factors in the highly competitive mortgage business. Norwest Mortgage Company, the largest retail mortgage originator in the nation with over 900 outlets, should continue to generate strong internal growth.

Directors, which ranked 15th nationally in mortgage originations with $4.7 billion in new loans for the year, operates 121 branches in 25 states, one-third of them in California. Norwest had 78 mortgage offices in California prior to the merger. Directors is expected to be run as a free-standing unit that will also offer Norwest credit cards and other banking and financial products.

The company has demonstrated a particularly strong ability to outsell its competition, substantially exceeding industry averages in cross-selling percentages, products per customer, and customer retention. It has an outstanding training program for the sale of company products and an incentive or reward system that works. Norwest sets aggressive goals in these areas to enhance revenue growth and profitability.[1] Morgan Stanley refers to Norwest as a "retailer in bank's clothing."

FINANCIAL RATIOS

Norwest is well known for its extremely conservative financial posture that includes well-diversified revenue sources, long-standing superior credit quality, and a conservative ratio of loan loss reserves to nonperforming assets. Nonperforming loans comprised only 0.4 percent of related assets at the close of 1994, while the firm's loan loss reserves covered 495 percent of nonperforming assets and 2.2 percent of average loans. This high level of excess reserves has enabled Norwest to take loss provisions that are less than net charge-offs (see Figure 8–4). The overhead ratio declined from 72 percent in 1992 and 1993 to 69 percent in 1994 and to 67 percent in the first quarter of 1995 (see Figure 8–3). Norwest expects the overhead ratio to decline to 64 percent by year-end 1996, further improving productivity, through efforts to establish the best operating practices of its most profitable components— branches, regions, consumer finance stores, and so forth—throughout the company.

Norwest is also improving its technological infrastructure and delivery channels, which should improve long-run efficiency. Other drivers of efficiency

FIGURE 8–4

Norwest's Credit Quality

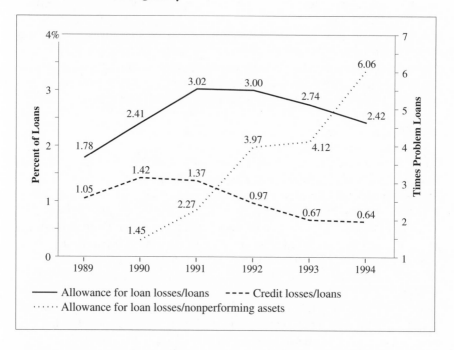

Allowance for loan losses/loans   ---- Credit losses/loans
······ Allowance for loan losses/nonperforming assets

improvement include the reengineering of back-office functions, the continued building of economies of scale, the consolidation of state banks into one bank, and reductions in FDIC fees that took effect September 1995.[2] The strong credit culture, revenue generation, and efficiency improvements should generate an ROA and an ROE of about 1.70 and 22 percent, respectively, by 1996. In 1994, the ROA was 1.45 percent, while the ROE was 21.4 percent (see Figure 8–5). The company has already identified $75–100 million in revenue enhancements and an additional $75–100 million in operating efficiencies that should be obtained by 1996.

Related to Norwest's relatively rapid asset growth, its share buyback program, negative FASB 115 adjustments, and a relatively aggressive program of buying mortgage-servicing rights, the company's tangible assets ratio declined from 5.5 to 4.2 percent from year-end 1993 to 1994, one of the lowest ratios in the superregional universe. However, they do have an exceptionally strong 9.9 percent risk-adjusted Tier 1 capital ratio. The low equity-to-asset ratio may slow down Norwest's ability to grow earnings by acquisitions, share buybacks, and the purchase of mortgage-servicing rights that have all benefited the growth in earnings during the past few years.[3]

FIGURE 8-5

Norwest's ROA and ROE

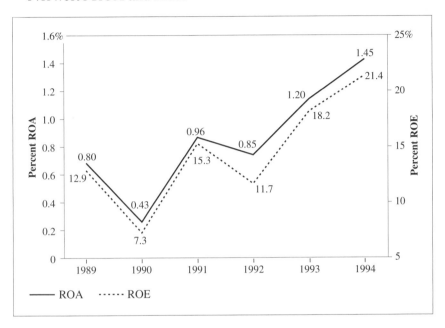

CORPORATE GOALS

According to Richard Kovacevich, CEO, "We want to be recognized as the premier financial services company... and be regarded as one of America's great companies. We want to 'outlocal' the nationals and 'outnational' the locals." The company's financial goals are to achieve EPS growth of at least 10 percent a year, a return on assets of 1.20 percent, and a return on equity in excess of 17 percent. This will be achieved with a conservative financial position measured by asset quality, capital levels, diversity of business, and dispersion of risk by geography, loan size, and industry. Norwest also has three consumer goals:

1. To have 75 percent of its customers view it as the first choice for their next purchase of a financial product.
2. To have at least 50 percent of its customers and prospects, when surveyed, to say they consider Norwest the best financial institution in their community.
3. To achieve levels of service that exceed customer expectations.

HISTORY

The company was incorporated in 1929 as Norwest Bancorporation to acquire controlling interest in banks, trust companies, and other financial institutions operating in the northwestern United States; the name Norwest Corporation was adopted in 1983. BancNorthwestern was formed in 1972 for the purpose of underwriting, distributing, and trading municipal bonds. In the same year, National Bank of Minneapolis (affiliate) formed a leasing company, Lease Northwest, Inc.

During 1973, the holding company acquired Farmers and Merchants State Bank of Stillwater (Minnesota), all the assets of the Krog Agency, Bettendorf Bank and Trust Co. (Iowa), and Security State Bank of Keokuk (Iowa). The holding company also activated Banco Credit Life Insurance Co. to reinsure credit life and accident insurance to loan customers of affiliated banks. In the same year, Northwestern National Bank of Sioux Falls, an affiliate, merged with Parker State Bank (South Dakota) in exchange for shares of stock. During 1974, the holding company formed Banco Financial Corp. (Minneapolis), a wholly owned affiliate offering secured financial services. Later that year, First National Bank of Aberdeen, an affiliate, merged with First National Bank of Bristol (South Dakota).

During 1976, the holding company formed Northwestern Union Trust Co. (Helena, Montana) to combine the fiduciary responsibilities of affiliated banks in Montana and formed First Northwestern Trust Co. of South Dakota (Sioux Falls) to combine the fiduciary responsibilities of affiliated banks in South Dakota.

During 1977, the holding company acquired two Iowa institutions: First National Bank of Ottumwa and First National Bank, Fort Dodge. The company formed First Northwestern Trust Co. of North Dakota (Fargo) to combine the fiduciary responsibilities of affiliated banks in North Dakota, and First Northwestern Trust Co. of Nebraska (Omaha) to combine the fiduciary responsibilities of affiliated banks in Nebraska. In 1978, the holding company acquired First National Bank of Marion (Iowa) and formed Northwestern-Arizona Trust Co. in Scottsdale (Arizona).

During 1979, the holding company acquired 100 percent ownership of Northwest Growth Fund (previously owned 56 percent) and First National Bank of Cedar Falls (Iowa). Northwestern National Bank of Sioux Falls (affiliate) merged with Springfield State Bank (South Dakota).

The holding company acquired Atlantic State Bank (Iowa) in 1980 and the State Bank of Worthington (Minnesota) in 1981. The holding company merged with Dial Corp. in 1982. During 1983, Norwest Bank Sioux Falls (affiliate) merged with the First Mitchell National Bank, while Norwest Bank Owatonna (affiliate) acquired First State Bank of Medford. The holding company acquired First National Bank of Grand Island (Nebraska) and consolidated all affiliate banks in South Dakota into Norwest Bank South Dakota.

In 1985, the holding company sold Residential Funding Corp., Norwest American Bank, and certain mortgage-servicing units of Norwest Mortgage, including the servicing rights of about $11 billion of mortgages. In the same year, all five Norwest Banks and a trust company in Nebraska merged into a single national bank, Norwest Bank Nebraska.

RECENT ACQUISITIONS

During 1988, the holding company formed Norwest Bank Minneapolis through consolidation of the previous 17 banks in Minneapolis and St. Paul; Norwest Bank North Dakota through the consolidation of previous banks in North Dakota; Norwest Bank Minnesota Mesabi through the consolidation of Norwest Bank Ely and Norwest Bank Mesabi; Norwest Bank Minnesota through consolidation of Norwest Bank St. Cloud, Norwest Bank Litchfield, and Norwest Bank Cedar Rapids; Norwest Minnesota Bank through the consolidation of Norwest Bank Duluth, Norwest Bank Grand Rapids, and Norwest Bank Two Harbors; Norwest Bank South Central through the consolidation of Norwest Bank Alberta Lea, Norwest Bank Austin, and Norwest Bank Mankoto; Norwest Bank Lincoln; Norwest Bank Minnesota West through consolidation of Norwest Bank Fergus Falls, Norwest Bank Moorhead, and Norwest Bank Thief River Falls; Norwest Bank Minnesota South through the consolidation of Norwest Bank Fairbult and Norwest Bank Owatonna.

During 1989, the holding company formed Norwest Bank Minnesota Southeast through consolidation of Norwest Bank Dodge Center, Norwest Bank Rochester, and Norwest Bank Winona; formed Norwest Bank Minnesota South Central through the consolidation of Norwest Bank Austin and Norwest Bank Mankato; and acquired all outstanding stock of BankGroup, Inc. (Wagzata, Minnesota).

During 1990, the holding company merged with First Interstate Corp. of Wisconsin, adding $2 billion to assets. In addition, Norwest Corporation acquired Crop Hail Management, Inc., a crop insurance agency located in Kallispell, Montana, and First Minnesota Savings Bank (assets of $2.8 billion).

During 1991, Norwest Corporation acquired Wyoming National Bank Corporation, adding assets of $436 million and banks in Casper, Cheyenne, Gillette, Lovell, Kemmerer, and Wheatland to the banking group. The bank in Kemmerer was later sold. There were three more acquisitions in 1991: Blackhawk Bancorp, a $133 million financial institution headquartered in Waterloo, Iowa; Chalfen Bankshares, Inc., a $235 million financial institution headquartered in Anoka, Minnesota; and MIG Insurance Brokers, an insurance brokerage company in Minneapolis. Also in 1991, the company merged with United Banks of Colorado, Inc., a $5.5 billion financial institution, headquartered in Denver.

During 1992, Davenport Bank and Trust Company (assets of $1.8 billion) was consolidated with Bettendorf Bank, resulting in a subsidiary called Davenport Bank and Trust Co. Norwest acquired United Bancshares, a $174 million holding company in Lincoln, Nebraska.

During 1993, Norwest Corporation acquired the $105 million Rocky Mountain Bancshares, the Bank of Aspen's holding company; the $2 billion Lincoln Financial Corporation, a multibank holding company from Fort Wayne, Indiana; $1.1 billion in retail deposits from Norwest Colorado from Columbia Savings, a subsidiary of First Nationwide; M&D Holding Company, which owned $57.1 million First State Bank of Spring Lake Park, Minnesota; $2 billion in retail deposits and 59 banking locations statewide from Citibank Arizona's banking business for Norwest Bank Arizona; $3.9 billion United Bank Group (New Mexico and Texas); $240 million First National Banks (Colorado); $47 million First American Bank (Colorado); $175 million University Bank (Wisconsin); $119 million St. Cloud National (Minnesota); $99 million Winner Bancshares (South Dakota); $101.1 million Ralston Bank (Nebraska); $57 million Merchants and Miners Bancshares, Inc. (Hibling, Minnesota); Financial Concepts Bancorp, Inc., a $175.5 million bank holding company (Green Bay, Wisconsin); and Borris Systems, Inc., a $6 million data processing/transmission service (East Lansing, Michigan).

In early 1994, the corporation acquired First United Bank Group, a multibank holding company headquartered in Albuquerque, with total assets of $3.9 billion, extending the franchise into New Mexico for the first time, as well as Cooper Bancshares of New Mexico. In addition, the Federal Reserve Board approved the acquisitions of the Bank of Montana system (assets of $807 million), along with two trust offices of Texas Commerce Bank. Norwest acquired Double Eagle Financial Corp. in Phoenix and Land Title Company of Kansas City, further strengthening its position in the title insurance market. The company also acquired a stake in Denver's Crestone Capital Management, which allowed Norwest to expand its investment management role. In addition to the aforementioned bank acquisitions, Norwest acquired a dozen other banks with assets of over $1.3 billion in 1994. In December 1994, Norwest acquired First National Bank of Kerrville, Texas (assets of $206 million) and Texas National Bancshares, Inc., a $188 million-asset banking concern, headquartered in Midland, Texas. As of year-end 1994, Norwest had 15 other acquisitions pending, with total assets of approximately $4.2 billion.

In May 1995, Norwest agreed to acquire two Texas banks: the State National Bank of El Paso ($1.1 billion in assets) and National Bank of Big Springs ($215 million in assets). State National, with eight locations, is the largest bank in El Paso, serving a largely working-class community. These acquisitions boosted Norwest's banking assets in Texas by over 50 percent to $3.3 billion. Norwest also reached an agreement in July 1995 to acquire for $197 million AmFed Financial, a thrift with $1.5 billion in assets. The thrift was acquired at a 24 percent premium to its market price and at 1.4 times its book value.

It is anticipated that Norwest will remain a major acquiror of banks and nonbanks in the future. Historically, the company has often entered new markets via major acquisitions, later filling in gaps with smaller acquisitions to help achieve critical mass. Norwest's current market areas for expansion include Wisconsin, Illinois, and Indiana, where the company does not have a market share among the top five banks. Potential targets include Old National Bancorp and CNB Bancshares, both of Indiana; First Financial Corp., with a $5 billion asset franchise that spans Illinois and Wisconsin; and Society Capital Corp., with a 7.6 percent deposit market share in Milwaukee, almost four times Norwest's market share in that city.[4]

During the second half of 1994, Norwest Mortgage, the largest retail mortgage firm (720 outlets) and one of the largest mortgage servicers in the United States, added to its leading position when Norwest announced agreements to purchase Michigan National Bank's mortgage-servicing operation, with a portfolio valued at $8.6 billion, and Directors Mortgage Loan Corp., with a portfolio of $13.1 billion. Directors, which ranked 15th nationally in mortgage originations with $4.7 billion in new loans for the year, operates 121 branches in 25 states, one-third of them in California. Norwest had 78 mortgage offices in California prior to the merger. Directors is expected to be run as a free-standing unit that will also offer Norwest credit cards and other banking and financial products. Norwest Mortgage also announced in February 1995 that it agreed to purchase the $15 billion servicing portfolio and servicing center of BarclaysAmerican Mortgage Corp. These acquisitions vault Norwest Mortgage from the fifth largest mortgage servicer in the United States to the third spot, with a portfolio in excess of $100 billion. Norwest Mortgage should be able to continue to build economies of scale and improve its operating efficiency, critical factors in the highly competitive mortgage business.

Norwest also agreed to acquire Island Finance from ITT, a business with $1 billion in receivables and 82 branch offices. Island Finance is a highly profitable consumer finance company, with 54 stores in Puerto Rico, 15 in Panama, 5 in the United States Virgin Islands, 5 in the Netherlands Antilles, 2 in Aruba, and 1 in Costa Rica. In addition, Norwest agreed to acquire Community Credit Company, a consumer finance company headquartered in Minneapolis, with 55 stores in six states and $173 million in outstanding loans. Excluding the Island Finance acquisition, the company added 409 banking offices, 626 mortgage-origination stores, and 405 financial stores between 1989 and 1994. Norwest Bank Minnesota has agreed to purchase the mortgage securities administration business of Ryland Group's mortgage subsidiary for $47 million in cash. The Ryland unit, employing 140 people and servicing 546 securities with a balance of $42.8 billion, includes master servicing, securities administration, investor information services, and tax calculation and reporting. Norwest expects the acquisition to be accretive in 1996.

Norwest also agreed to acquire Foothill Group Inc., a Los Angeles–based commercial finance company with receivables of about $750 million, for approximately $441 million. Foothill had earnings of $31.1 million in 1994. The company provides financing to companies that do not meet commercial bank credit standards and that pledge assets such as accounts receivable, inventories, machinery, and equipment for loans. Foothill's operations do not duplicate any part of Norwest's existing business. The acquisition should be completed in the fourth quarter of 1995 and contribute immediately to EPS.

Norwest also announced that it had signed a definitive agreement to acquire Victoria Bankshares, Inc. The transaction will be accounted for as a pooling of interests and should close in the second quarter of 1996. Victoria ($2.0 billion in assets and $1.7 billion in deposits) operated 42 branches and 47 ATMs in the trapezoidal region between Houston, Austin, San Antonio, and Corpus Christi, Texas. Victoria is a healthy bank, with strong credit quality, adequate loss reserves, and an attractive deposit base. The price paid was 1.5 times Victoria's book value, which is below the average price of 1.8 times book value for all announced bank acquisitions through October 1995. Since Victoria operated during 1995 with an efficiency ratio of close to 76 percent, Norwest should be able to reduce Victoria's noninterest expense base by roughly 30 percent given merger expense synergies. If this can be accomplished, this transaction should be modestly accretive germane to EPS. Also, Victoria Bankshares was overcapitalized, with a common-equity-to-assets ratio of 9.6 percent at the end of the third quarter 1995. Not only will this acquisition boost Norwest's book value by $0.20 per share, but it should also free up about $75 million of excess equity that can ultimately be used to repurchase Norwest's common stock. The Victoria acquisition should aid Norwest in establishing a strong banking franchise within Texas that can be used as a platform to complete additional in-market acquisitions.

Norwest and Morgan Guaranty Trust Co. entered into an agreement whereby Norwest bankers would originate long-term, nonrecourse commercial real estate loans between $1 and $15 million, which would then be sold to the unit of JP Morgan. The loans can be for purchasing or refinancing multifamily, office, office-warehouse, or industrial buildings, and hotels, mobile home parks, and nursing homes. After purchasing the loans, Morgan will pool and securitize them with loans from other participating financial institutions. Norwest will earn origination fees and keep the servicing rights for additional fee income.

The revenue growth at Norwest was so strong that the company had securities losses of about $79 million in 1994 and $35 million in the first quarter of 1995, and still showed strong EPS growth. By taking these securities losses and reinvesting the proceeds at higher interest rates, Norwest has positioned itself to perform better within a higher interest rate environment. For example, Norwest sold $1.9 billion of securities with an average yield of 5.9 percent during the third quarter of 1994 and reinvested the proceeds at an average yield of slightly over 8 percent. The increased yield should generate over $38 million in incremental net income annually. Additionally, the net unrealized loss on the company's securities portfolio of $15.4 billion was in excess of $525 million at year-end 1994. In recognizing the aforementioned losses, combined with the first half 1995 bond rally, Norwest has eliminated the unrealized loss in its entire securities portfolio.

As a matter of fact, the book value of Norwest's portfolio rose to close to $11.50 per share at the end of the second quarter of 1995.

TECHNOLOGY

Norwest has spent millions of dollars on technology in the form of (1) customer information files, (2) modernized, front-end branch applications terminals, and (3) the installation of Hogan Systems' ENTER 2000 automated loan and deposit processing systems for both personal bankers and tellers. Similar information and processing systems have been developed for business customers. Norwest has 9,000 PC workstations in place and is training staff on how to use the information and computers to improve cross-selling opportunities with customers. The new hardware and software allow for more than just obtaining account information and other customer information. It also provides "what-if" calculations for financial planning and comparisons with alternative products. The programs can project customer cash flows, college-financing programs, retirement programs, borrowing versus savings liquidation, tax implications, and more. For savings and investment products, one can quickly calculate starting and future values, monthly deposit requirements, taxable versus tax-exempt, returns, and so forth. For loan products, the programs can walk customers through all borrowing options and show the effect of insurance, payment schedules, debt consolidation possibilities, debt versus income and purchase versus lease implications, and so on.

Some sales-prompting and road-mapping tools are automated into the personal computer. On the management side, there is a real-time ability to track daily sales by branch or by banker, allowing for more effective sales coaching and sales follow-up. It provides comparative scoring throughout the Norwest community bank system and establishes an accurate base for compensation incentives.

SUMMARY

Norwest has grown quietly but quickly from regional status to a backyard bank nationwide by adding 1,865 new stores since 1987 (an average of 266 per year). As of March 31, 1995, it had 628 community bank branches, 1,700 ATMs, 1,184 consumer finance stores (including Island Finance), and 744 mortgage banking stores (including Directors Mortgage). The company has just over 2 million customers. It continues to implement aggressively its well-tested formula for adding new stores and increasing profits rapidly. New store expansion will likely continue to be a major engine of revenue growth and profitability. At the end of the first quarter of 1995, Norwest had 13 pending acquisitions with total assets of about $2.7 billion. Early in the third quarter of 1995, Norwest agreed to acquire Amfed Financial Inc., the third largest depository institution in Nevada, for stock valued at about $196 million. The thrift holding company had assets of $1.6 billion and deposits of $1.4 billion. This transaction provides Norwest with entry into the Nevada depository market and offers 43 additional stores for the sale of Norwest products to customers.

Norwest has regionally targeted seven states for acquisitions: Kansas, Idaho, Illinois, Missouri, Oklahoma, Oregon, and Washington. The bank will also look for fill-in opportunities in the 16 states in which it already operates. From 1987 through March 31, 1995, Norwest has acquired 46 banks, rarely using the de novo route to add stores. Most of the 46 acquisitions were accretive in the first full year after acquisition. The average bank branch acquired has come on stream at a 70 basis point profit; it generally takes an average of five years to achieve a 135 basis point level. Although the banking ROA is only 115 basis points as a whole, seasoned banks earn comfortably above 130 basis points, while newer acquisitions anchor the average at the lower end. Norwest has demonstrated an uncanny ability to outsell its competition, substantially exceeding industry averages in cross-selling percentages, products per customer, and customer retention. Norwest continues to set aggressive goals in these areas to enhance revenue growth and profitability.

Norwest has a long-standing philosophy of maintaining an extremely conservative financial posture, which includes exceptionally well-diversified revenue sources, high credit quality, and high capital and loss reserves. This well-run, diversified financial services company is one of the largest mortgage servicers and the largest mortgage originator in the United States. Normal levels of mortgage-servicing sales should help boost Norwest Mortgage's profitability. The company also owns highly profitable Norwest Financial, a $5.3 billion asset, consumer loan company, from which it derived 28 percent of its earnings in 1994. It also has a credit card portfolio of $2.2 billion in outstanding loans housed in Norwest Card Services, placing it among the nation's 25 largest bankcard issuers.

Norwest has demonstrated an ability to deliver financial performance well above industry norms on a consistent basis. The financial institution's geographically diverse franchise allows it to avoid suffering from economic slowdowns in any one region.

Norwest's operating earnings grew more rapidly than most superregional banks over the last five years. The bank should generate EPS growth of at least 13 percent annually over the next few years compared to a regional forecasted average of 8–10 percent for its peers. Norwest should also maintain profitability ratios in the top tier of superregional banks. The performance will be aided by meaningful improvements in operating efficiency and powerful revenue generation at each of the company's core businesses (retail banking, mortgage banking, and consumer finance).[5]

In Figure 3–9, Footnote 17 in the Norwest 1994 *Annual Report* points out that the fair adjusted book value per share is really $42.43 rather than the stated book value of $10.97. As of August 1, 1995, the price-to-book value for Norwest was 210 percent compared to an average of 170 percent for the average superregional bank, while Norwest's price to 1996 earnings (estimated) was 8.7 times compared to 9.1 times for the average superregional. The price-to-adjusted-book value would be about 60 percent.

Norwest is an unusual company. It has more stores than any financial service company in the United States and Canada. It knows how to sell and cross-sell. Norwest focuses on fast-growing, nontraditional lines of business, employing a first-rate retail banking strategy. Its profitability ratios are exemplary as is its management. The company has mastered the art of small bank and thrift acquisitions, most of which are accretive to EPS. Norwest is a disciplined acquiror that delivers consistent earnings. No company does acquisitions better than Norwest. This is likely to continue indefinitely, because Norwest uses a formula that works. However, some institution may desire to merge with Norwest, an institution that would like more sales outlets and customers. KeyCorp is one such player; another is Banc One; a third is NationsBank; a fourth, BankAmerica. If First Bank Systems doesn't acquire First Interstate, First Bank Systems might make a good merger-of-equals candidates for Norwest. However, Norwest has the P/E ratio, the EPS growth, and enough capital strength to remain independent if it wishes. Will it get caught up in the merger frenzy as the number of dance partners dwindles?

ENDNOTES

1. T.H. Hanley, P.J. Carter, and A.B. Collins, "Norwest Corporation," *CS First Boston,* February 2, 1995, p. 2.
2. T.H. Hanley, P.J. Carter, and A.B. Collins, "Norwest Corporation," *CS First Boston,* October 26, 1994, p. 3, and June 9, 1995, p. 6.
3. C. Kotowski, "Banking Quarterly," *Oppenheimer & Co.,* January 27, pp. 115–16.
4. T.H. Hanley, "Bank Consolidation Monthly," *CS First Boston,* October 1994, p. 6.
5. T.H. Hanley, "Norwest Corporation," *CS First Boston,* October 4, 1994, p. 2.

T A B L E   8-4

Norwest Corp. Financials

	1990	1991	1992	1993	1994
Earnings per share	$1.36	$1.46	$1.71	$2.10	$2.41
Assets (in millions)	$34,405	$37,979	$40,536	$47,438	$55,073
Net income (in millions)	$135.80	$422.10	$446.70	$653.60	$800.40
Return on assets	0.39%	1.11%	1.10%	1.38%	1.45%

	1994	
	(in millions)	%
Average earning assets	$49,948	100
Securities	13,662	27
Loans	30,244	61
Other	6,042	12
Loans	32,577	100
Construction and land		
Commercial mortgage	4,158	
Highly leveraged		
Commercial loans and leases	9,152	
Other foreign	130	
Term LCD		
Credit card receivables	2,893	
Other consumer	7,816	
Unearned discount		
Corporate	13,440	41
Consumer	10,709	33
Mortgages	8,428	26

	1990	1991	1992	1993	1994
Efficiency ratio	67.44	67.58	67.80	67.83	68.31
Shareholder equity (in millions)	$2,013	$2,494	$2,907	$3,342	$3,843
Preferred	$35	$208	$345	$342	$344
Common	$1,996	$2,286	$2,562	$3,000	$3,499

F I G U R E   8–6

Norwest Corp. Financial Charts

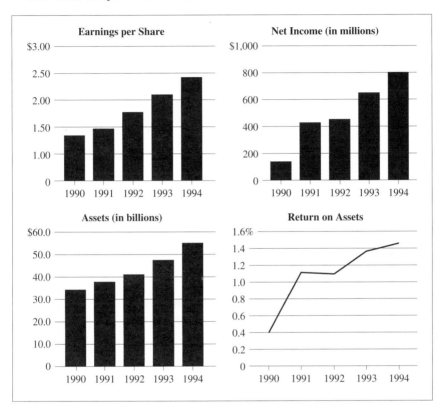

F I G U R E   8–7

Norwest Corp. Financial Charts

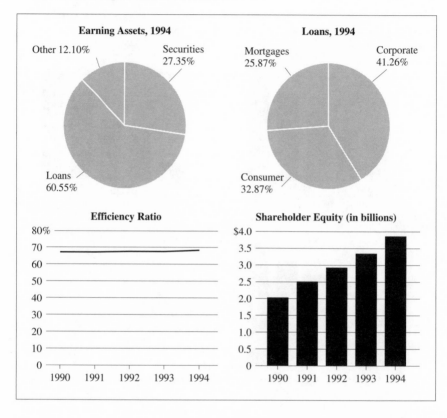

SOUTHEASTERN BANKS

The universe of southeastern superregionals consists of NationsBank, First Union, Wachovia, SunTrust, and Barnett. NationsBank, headquartered in Charlotte, North Carolina, is currently the third largest banking company in the United States and the largest in the South. NationsBank has the largest retail banking franchise in the nation, with close to 2,000 branches in nine states and Washington, DC. Hugh McColl (*American Banker*'s 1993 Banker of the Year) has orchestrated some of the most profitable and largest acquisitions in banking history. Executive management has demonstrated its prowess within the acquisitions arena by completing large deals in Texas, Georgia, Virginia, and Maryland that were creatively structured, competitively priced, and beneficial to existing shareholders. Nations-Bank appears to be shifting from being a credit provider to being a financial advisor/merchant bank as it takes on some of the characteristics of a money center bank. It generated almost 33 percent of its total revenue from fee and noninterest income. Its return on average assets for 1994 was 1.02 percent, while its return on equity was at 16.1 percent. Management is working hard at improving the company's efficiency and credit-quality ratios.

First Union, also headquartered in Charlotte, North Carolina, had almost $113 billion in assets and 2,000 banking offices along the East Coast, from Florida to Connecticut. The company acquired First Fidelity in 1995, a mid-Atlantic retail and middle-market power. First Union's ROA was 1.27 percent, while its ROE was a strong 17.04 percent in 1994. It has focused on leveraging the banking relationship with cross-sales of other products that its customers might need, such as mutual funds, insurance, credit cards, cash management service, or mortgage or home equity loans. It generated 30 percent of its total revenue from fee and noninterest income in the first three quarters of 1995, up substantially from 27 percent

197

in 1994. The service-oriented company is concentrating on reducing noninterest expenses following numerous acquisitions. Until the First Fidelity merger, First Union's acquisitions were usually accretive within 12 months or certainly nondilutive to earnings per share. Both First Union and First Fidelity exhibited strong control of credit quality and kept conservative loan loss reserves. First Union has also developed a highly professional capital markets/investment banking group and would like to resemble a European "universal" bank in the years ahead. The company has grown rapidly over the last decade, primarily by acquisition, to become the sixth largest bank holding company in the United States. Chairman Crutchfield is still acquisition-minded, and analysts anticipate additional fill-in acquisitions along the East Coast.

Wachovia is a much smaller bank ($41 billion in assets with 509 banking offices) than either NationsBank or First Union, but it is considered one of the finest banking organizations in the country. This can be seen by its stellar 1994 financial accomplishments: ROA of 1.46 percent, ROE of 17.41 percent, efficiency ratio of 56 percent, and renowned credit-quality control. The company is also noted for its highly profitable credit card, trust operations, cash management, and operational services.

SunTrust is a superbly managed, conservative banking organization with about $44 billion in assets and a large trust department with close to $43 billion in assets under management. It has about 19,000 employees and 656 full-service banking offices in Georgia, Florida, Tennessee, and Alabama. SunTrust has a strong balance sheet, good control of operating costs, and consistently fine financial ratios. During 1994, the company's ROA was 1.31 percent; its ROE was 17 percent; its efficiency ratio was just under 59 percent; and its ratio of nonperforming assets to total assets was at about 0.64 percent. Active in mergers, the company seems to prefer in-market deals, which enable significant cost benefits through consolidation and branch closings. The motto at SunTrust is "think like a shareholder."

Barnett Banks, headquartered in Jacksonville, is the largest banking organization in Florida, with 621 offices and 18,649 employees. It is the 21st largest bank in the nation. The company has assets of $41 billion, maintaining some form of relationship with 35–40 percent of all households in Florida. It had an ROA of 1.28 percent and an ROE of 16.70 percent in 1994. Barnett has shown marked improvement in both its efficiency ratio and its ratio of nonperforming assets to total loans outstanding during 1993 and 1994, after mediocre performances in 1991 and 1992. The company has recovered from its real estate lending problems and has focused attention on reducing noninterest expenses and acquiring nonbanking companies that generate fee income. It is seeking additional in-market mergers and an asset management company; at the same time, it is a franchise coveted by potential acquirors desiring either to expand into or enter the Florida market.

CHAPTER 9

NationsBank Corporation

Nationsbank Corporation, headquartered in Charlotte, North Carolina, was the third largest bank holding company in the United States with total assets of approximately $170 billion at year-end 1994. It had 1,929 banking centers in 9 states and the District of Columbia and 288 consumer finance offices in 34 states prior to the Bank South acquisition. In addition, it had 10 commercial finance offices. The company provides financial services and products to individuals and businesses in the Southeast, Southwest, mid-Atlantic, and West Coast regions as well as several overseas markets. The main subsidiaries include its general bank, its institutional bank, NationsCredit consumer finance company, and NationsBank CRT, a government securities trading company. The company has established broad functional expertise in both wholesale and retail banking and has moved into nonfinancial services as well. The company generated net income of $1,690 million in 1994, up substantially from $1,301 million in 1993. The improvement in earnings reflected strong loan growth and increased fee income. Continued improvement in operating efficiency and further reductions in credit costs also enhanced earnings.

HISTORY

NationsBank Corporation was formed in North Carolina on December 31, 1991, upon completion of the merger between NCNB Corporation (assets of $66 billion) and C&S/Sovran Corporation (assets of $52 billion). A previous merger attempt by NCNB with C&S had been rebuffed in 1990. However, C&S/Sovran began to have serious problems; and although originally desiring independence, it sought the shelter of a marriage with a financially healthy partner that had a strong leader with a track record of making mergers work. That man was Hugh L. McColl, Jr., chairman of NCNB. Following the merger announcement, it was reported in the *American Banker* that "NationsBank as a whole expects to produce revenues as large as the two predecessor banks with combined expenses that are $350 million lower than the two separate banks." Immediately after the merger, 6,000 employees and numerous redundant branch offices were eliminated.[1]

Management indicated that "the economic and geographic diversity of our market should reduce the company's risk exposure to the individual state economies or specific business sectors. Additionally, product diversity helps protect the company from downturns in any one business segment."[2]

Although other banks walked away from a transaction in 1992 with troubled MNC Financial, Inc. of Baltimore (assets of $17.0 billion), NationsBank announced it had agreed to invest $200 million in MNC through a private placement of newly issued nonvoting stock, with an option to buy the company. In the following year, NationsBank announced it would buy MNC's common stock for a total price of $1.36 billion, of which 49.9 percent would be in cash and 50.1 percent in the company's stock. The acquisition of MNC gave NationsBank a financially attractive means of furthering the company's long-term objective of becoming the leading bank on the East Coast from Baltimore to Miami.

Later that year, NationsBank also announced it would purchase and renovate 11 foreclosed apartment complexes with 2,811 rental units. In October 1992, NationsBank of North Carolina, a subsidiary of NationsBank Corporation, and Dean Witter Financial Services Group, a unit of Sears, Roebuck and Company, announced an alliance to market investment products and services to bank customers within a bank environment. Originally, NationsBank of North Carolina and a subsidiary of Dean Witter each owned 50 percent of the new company, called NationsSecurities. The new company began operations in 1993 as an independent securities brokerage firm acting as an introducing broker for Dean Witter. The customer-broker relationship, including investment advice incidental to the brokerage business, would occur in NationsSecurities, while Dean Witter would act as the clearing broker.

NationsSecurities was located in selected NationsBank branches in North Carolina. The alliance with Dean Witter to form NationsSecurities was intended to fulfill a number of strategic goals: to leverage the company's strength, primarily the extensive delivery system and large customer base, and advance the ability of the company to meet more of its customers' needs.

After just 17 months of operation, NationsBank announced unexpectedly in November 1994 that it was buying out Dean Witter's 50 percent stake in their joint venture. The company was expected to concentrate on the sale of mutual funds and annuities. Although NationsSecurities was plagued with regulatory and public relations problems, this didn't dampen its enthusiasm for selling investment products to its customers. About a week after its announcement to split with Dean Witter, NationsBank announced a new joint venture with Gartmore Capital Management, a London-based investment management concern. The new company will be called Nations Gartmore Investment Management. NationsBank will use its network of branches and sales staff to market an assortment of international mutual funds to be developed by the new venture. The venture will begin business with about $750 million in assets under management, with NationsBank contributing $500 million of business from Panmure Investment Limited (the bank's London-based international investment unit) and Gartmore contributing the $250 million of international business it has developed.

NationsCredit, the consumer finance unit formed as a result of the purchase of Chrysler First, Inc., is headquartered in Allentown, Pennsylvania. Chrysler First is a high-yield consumer and private-label finance company similar in nature to Beneficial Corporation or Norwest Financial. Finance receivables of about $3.7 billion, including $1.5 billion that have been securitized, were acquired. NationsCredit writes and services consumer loans and finances inventory purchases for manufacturers of consumer products. The addition of Chrysler First's assets represented a big step toward the corporate goal of growing consumer-based assets and achieving the critical mass necessary to address a market segment and customer base that has gone historically to nonbank competition. NationsCredit is the second largest bank-owned consumer finance company in the United States.

NationsBank announced the purchase of Chicago Research and Trading Group, Ltd. (CRT) for $225 million in cash. CRT has about 750 employees and $7.2 billion in assets. CRT changed its name to NationsBank CRT, a division of NationsBank of North Carolina. CRT headquarters remained in Chicago, with additional offices in London, Frankfurt, Philadelphia, Osaka, San Francisco, Singapore, Tokyo, and Ridgefield, Connecticut. NationsBank CRT has more than 15 memberships on 19 exchanges. The company trades 75 different options and futures contracts on interest rate equity indexes, petroleum and foreign exchanges, as well as other instruments. It is also a primary dealer of U.S. government securities and gives NationsBank a strong proprietary trading operation.

In addition, NationsBank received approval from the Federal Reserve Board to underwrite and deal in corporate debt and equity securities. The company has aggressively expanded its underwriting expertise by hiring numerous experienced investment bankers. These events broaden substantially the company's ability to serve its extensive corporate client base.

In December 1993, NationsBank acquired U.S. West Financial Services, Inc., a corporate finance subsidiary of U.S. West, Inc., with $2.0 billion in net receivables, a company similar in nature to a mini General Electric Capital Corporation. Through this acquisition and that of Chrysler First, NationsBank has formed the 16th largest nonbank financial services company in the United States.

In 1994, NationsBank agreed to acquire 43 Florida branches ($4.0 billion in deposits) and one branch in Atlanta from California Federal Bank as well as the Consolidated Bank, headquartered in Florida, with 12 branches and assets of about $675 million. NationsBank also acquired Intercontinental Bank of Miami in 1995 in a stock transaction valued at $208 million. The Intercontinental acquisition will add 24 banking centers and more than $1.1 billion in assets. Following on the heels of the Intercontinental acquisition, NationsBank agreed to buy Miami-based CSF Holdings Inc., the largest savings and loan in Florida. CSF has 40 offices in Florida, 8 in California and Virginia, $4.73 billion in assets, and $3.63 billion in deposits. The purchase price was $516 million in cash; a stock swap could have diluted earnings. Industry analysts expect NationsBank to sell the California and Virginia branches and to save from $15–20 million a year by closing about half of the branches in Florida. The acquisition of the assets at Intercontinental and CSF increased NationsBank's assets in Florida to about $28 billion, with over 400 branches, increasing the bank's market share of deposits by 2 percent. In addition, NationsBank agreed to acquire RHNB Corp. of Rock Hill (South Carolina), the $257 million asset, 12-branch parent of Rock Hill National Bank (see Table 9–1).

The acquisition of Atlanta-based Bank South Corp. ($7.6 billion in assets and 149 offices in Georgia, including 60 in-store offices in Kroger supermarkets and the largest number of ATMs in Georgia [267]) for $1.6 billion in stock was for 16 percent over the closing price per share on the day prior to the announcement. (The

T A B L E   9–1

Recent NationsBank Acquisitions

Date	Company	Price (in millions)
February 1993	Chrysler First	$ 100
July 1993	Chicago Research and Trading Group	225
October 1993	MNC Financial	1,360
December 1993	U.S. West Financial Services	85
February 1994	Corpus Christi National Bank	130
August 1994	California Federal Bank (Southeast division)	160
October 1994	Express America Holdings (selected assets)	85
November 1994	Consolidated Bank	N.A.
November 1994	Rock Hill National Bank	53
March 1995	Cypress Financial Corp.	N.A.
March 1995	Source One Mortgage Services	195
March 1995	KeyCorp Mortgage Inc.	500
June 1995	Intercontinental Bank	208
July 1995	CSF Holdings Inc.	516
September 1995	Bank South	1,600

Source: NationsBank press releases.

announcement was made on September 5, 1995.) The price paid was approximately 2.4 times book value and 18.4 times 1994 earnings per share, a hefty price for an acquisition that will dilute NationsBank's book value by $1.30 per share. There will be cost savings on the order of 60 percent of the noninterest expenses of Bank South in this in-market merger in order to prevent any dilution in EPS at NationsBank. Both the price of the acquisition and the suggested cost savings by management are at the high end of the spectrum, suggesting competition for Bank South's hand in marriage. In the past, NationsBank has been known for making relatively cheap acquisitions from the government or buying troubled institutions at a good price. This represents the first time that NationsBank has been willing to pay a rich price for a major acquisition. However, the circumstances and opportunities justify the price from the standpoint of positioning NationsBank to leverage significantly its existing infrastructure in Georgia, thereby improving its revenue growth capacity and operating efficiency throughout the state. NationsBank has estimated that after it has achieved the targeted expense savings, its new (including Bank South) Georgia banking franchise should earn over $200 million more in 1997 than its stand-alone Georgia franchise would have.

The acquisition will reinforce NationsBank's role as the largest bank in Georgia with a 23 percent market share of deposits, as well as the largest bank in Atlanta and its suburbs with a market share of 25 percent. Bank South has a strong franchise and represents a good fit for NationsBank, who will be increasing its retail and small business customer base substantially. NationsBank will be able to leverage its superior and more extensive array of financial products and services to lots of affluent citizens and businesses in Georgia, while cutting overhead substantially at a relatively inefficient Bank South. For example, NationsBank plans to eliminate 100 of the combined banks' 337 Georgia branches. That should trim $174 million in operating costs, making the acquisition a contributor to earnings by 1997. On the retail banking front, Bank South does business with 285,000 households in Georgia, compared to 500,000 households for NationsBank. In addition, Bank South operates a trust and private-banking business with $1.2 billion in assets under management. The opportunity exists for substantial generation of additional revenues from not only the new retail customer base, but from the sale of treasury management, investment banking, capital market, asset management and 401(k) services, leasing, factoring, international banking, asset-backed finance, and venture capital to Bank South's business customer base. NationsBank acquired an extremely healthy bank from a credit perspective (nonperforming assets represented 0.56 percent of total loans and foreclosed real estate), while loan loss reserves covered 396 percent of nonperforming loans and 1.95 percent of total loans.

NationsBank is the largest banking company in the South and Southeast. As a matter of fact, it is bigger than the next three largest banks in the South combined. It has full-service banking centers in Florida, Georgia, Kentucky, Maryland, North Carolina, South Carolina, Tennessee, Texas, Virginia, and Washington, DC (see

Table 9–2). NationsBank has the largest retail banking franchise in the nation with close to 2,000 branches. Subsidiaries in North and South Carolina, Texas, and Tennessee were considered to be high performers in 1994, while the weakest subsidiaries were in Virginia, Maryland, and Washington, DC. The latter group of banks had suffered from serious loan-quality problems in the early 1990s.

NationsBank's product expertise ranges from bread-and-butter commercial and consumer lending to large credit card, mortgage banking, dealer finance, retail brokerage, and money management units (all included within the General Bank) to a growing institutional bank that lends to corporations with revenues over $100 million, trading, and corporate advisory services.

NationsBank also engages in international banking and banking-related operations, with branches in London and Georgetown (Cayman Islands). It also owns a merchant bank and stock brokerage in London (Panmure Gordon and Co.).

NationsBank also provides financial products and services to individuals and businesses in many other states, from New England to the West Coast, and in several overseas markets. At the end of 1993, NationsBank had assets of $158 billion, net income of $1.5 billion, a return on assets of 0.97 percent, and a return on equity of 15.0 percent. Assets grew to $170 billion in 1994, accompanied by net income of $1.7 billion, ROA of 1.02 percent, and ROE of 16.10 percent. In the first half of 1995, NationsBank achieved an ROA of 0.99 percent and an ROE of 16.36 percent. NationsFund, the Trust Group's proprietary family of mutual funds, grew to 47 portfolios and close to $15.0 billion under management in mid-1995.

T A B L E   9–2

Geographical Distribution of Deposits (6/30/94)

Location	Total Deposits	Branches	Deposit Share	Rank
Florida	$18.2	372	14.9	3*
Georgia	8.6	187	13.9	1**
Maryland	10.3	232	25.8	1
North Carolina	8.2	224	13.6	3
South Carolina	5.0	171	22.3	1
Tennessee	4.1	100	8.8	5
Texas	22.9	274	15.8	1
Virginia	9.3	227	16.1	1
Washington, DC	2.2	34	24.2	2

* Upon completion of pending acquisitions, Florida market share will rise substantially and have assets of about $28 billion.

** Upon completion of the Bank South acquisition, the market share in Georgia will rise to 23 percent, with assets of $24 billion.

Source: NationsBank.

NationsBank is among the 10 largest credit card issuers in the country, with more than 5.4 million customers and loans outstanding of $4.8 billion. To increase the volume of outstanding credit cards, NationsBank and *Southern Living* offered a cobranded Visa card to the magazine's 13 million subscribers. The card offers discounts on subscriptions, travel packages, books, house plans, and a one-year subscription to *Southern Living* travel guides. The card has no annual fee if used at least once each year and an introductory low interest rate in the first six months. In another joint venture, NationsBank offered a cobranded card with Exxon, giving cardholders rebates on purchases of gas, auto service, or car accessories at Exxon service stations and 20 merchant partners. Also, the bank, Dean Witter, and Discover have introduced a new MasterCard. Holders of this Prime Option Card will be able to carry new purchases for up to 60 days at the prime rate before the interest rate jumps to prime plus 9.9 percent.

Beginning in December 1995, NationsBank will install 661 ATMs in Stop-N-Go convenience stores in Texas. This venture catapults the bank into second place with 2,900 machines nationally and into first place in the Texas market with 1,013 machines, but substantially behind BankAmerica's 5,600 ATMs.

Vision 95 is NationsBank's new strategic vision for unique retail banking. It includes plans to improve sales performance at branches through work simplification and new staffing models that permit more time for selling retail banking products. To enhance efficiency, branches will use more part-time employees during peak hours. In Texas, for example, 50 percent of all tellers are part time. It is also the goal of NationsBank to service common retail products with common software throughout the holding company.

Hugh McColl (*American Banker*'s 1993 Banker of the Year) has completed some of the most profitable acquisitions in banking history. The senior management at NationsBank has demonstrated its prowess within the acquisitions arena by completing large deals in Texas, Georgia, Virginia, and Maryland that were creatively structured, competitively priced, and beneficial to existing shareholders. The executive management team is adept at deploying excess capital into product-producing revenue streams. Although the company will likely continue to expand its core banking operations, geographic expansion apparently is no longer the primary objective of its acquisitions. NationsBank appears focused on building its functional expertise across broad-ranged financial businesses, capturing a larger share of the total revenues spent on all financial services within North America. Such financial expansion should enable the company to leverage and expand the immense revenue and earnings potential of its large retail and wholesale customer bases. The bank's mandate is to "provide the products [its] customers want in a rapid and reliable manner at a price that is affordable and competitive."

The proclaimed vision for NationsBank is to evolve one step ahead of the banking industry, to meet the broader and more complex needs of its customers, and to gain a significant, if not dominant, position in each of its businesses—building the premier financial services company in the United States. The company plans to strengthen its mix of earning assets by expanding loans as a percentage of earning assets and increasing consumer loans as a percentage of total loans. These should widen margins, better diversify its business, and improve the predictability of credit losses. Nonperforming loans fell to 0.78 percent of total loans outstanding and 0.67 percent of total assets by year-end 1994. The ratio of nonperforming loans to total loans fell even further to 0.75 percent at the end of the third quarter of 1995. Loan loss reserves, which stood at $2.2 billion at the end of 1994, covered 192 percent of nonperforming assets and 2.14 percent of total loans. Net loan charge-offs were 0.33 percent of average loans on an annualized basis. Loan loss reserves were 2.3 percent of average loans and 192 percent of nonperforming assets for 1994. Most analysts feel that loan losses for 1994 are low and that the bank is moderately overreserved. However, over the course of the business cycle, loan losses are expected to average about 0.75 percent of loans. Investors are expected to want banks to maintain loan loss reserves at considerably higher levels (e.g., 2 percent) than they did prior to the previous recession. If loan growth continues to be strong, NationsBank could increase its loan loss reserve to above 2 percent in 1996.[3]

NationsBank has targeted a return on common equity in the 15–18 percent range. Other corporate goals include annual earnings per share and dividend growth of at least 12–15 percent, combined with an efficiency ratio falling below 60 percent by 1996. The company's efficiency ratio was 64 percent in 1993 and 62 percent in 1994, not quite as good as their peer group average. NationsBank eliminated 150 branches and just over 3,000 employees during 1994–95 to help reach its overhead ratio target by 1996. The company expected to close 200 of its least profitable branches by year-end 1995, but it is not just cutting costs, rather, it is working hard on deploying alternative delivery systems. We can expect continuing expense consolidation throughout the retail network and the company's back-office activities, combined with additional spending related to growth-oriented business, product marketing, systems and other revenue enhancing initiatives. NationsBank is working hard on deploying alternative product delivery systems.

Back-office operations by lines of business have been standardized, while all trust operations have been consolidated. The eventual goal is to have one bank across all the states with common systems and products. It is a gigantic and expensive project to organize into one entity all of the banks that have been merged to form NationsBank. The company will continue to consolidate expenses throughout its retail network and back-office functions, and increase investment in growth-oriented businesses, product marketing, banking technology, the Model Banking Center Program, and other revenue-enhancing initiatives. Management at NationsBank is confident that it can save at least $50 million if interstate branching is permitted and it can move to a one-bank structure. NationsBank has targeted an efficiency ratio of 55 percent by mid-1997.

NationsBank appears to be in the midst of shifting from being a traditional credit provider to being a financial advisor/merchant bank. It is in an earlier phase of transition than money center banks. It is expected to continue to invest heavily in employees, skills, and technology—including trading, cash management, and Section 20 distributive capability.

The company, somewhat like Norwest, divides itself into three segments: the General Bank, which serves consumers, small businesses, and middle-market companies; the Global Finance Group, which serves large corporations with annual sales over $100 million; and Nonbank Financial Services, the newest group, which includes its consumer and commercial finance companies. The General Bank accounted for 72 percent of revenues and 64 percent of loans in 1993 and 68 percent of revenues and 62 percent of loans in 1994; the Global Finance Group accounted for 24 percent of revenues and 30 percent of loans in 1993 and 26 percent of revenues and 32 percent of loans in 1994; and the Nonbank Financial Services Group accounted for 4 percent of revenues and 6 percent of loans during 1993 and 6 percent of both revenues and loans in 1994. During 1994, net income and ROE for the General Bank was $932 million and 17 percent, respectively; net income for the Global Finance Group was $631 million, with an ROE of 16 percent; net income for the Financial Services Group was $103 million, while ROE was 13 percent (see Table 9–3).

NCNB ROOTS

NCNB's early ancestor was the Commercial Bank of Charlotte, founded in 1874. Commercial National's future partners were the Southern States Trust Company and Security National Bank. Commercial National, primarily a retail bank, and American Trust, more of a commercial lender, were Charlotte neighbors and agreed to merge in 1957, becoming American Commercial Bank. Once American's cross-state rival Security National merged with Depositors National Bank of Durham, American and Security agreed to merge in 1960, forming North Carolina National Bank with 40 offices and assets of $480 million.

In the decades that followed, NCNB consolidated its position as one of the Southeast's leading financial powers. With a long series of acquisitions, the company grew rapidly throughout North Carolina, reaching 172 offices and assets of $6 billion by 1979. NCNB discovered a loophole in Florida's banking law that allowed it to acquire banks through a subsidiary prior to the establishment of the southeastern reciprocal interstate banking agreement in 1985. NCNB had acquired Florida-based banks with assets in excess of $6 billion by 1985. With its 1988 purchase of bankrupt First Republic Bank of Texas ($26 billion), Chairman McColl quintupled his bank's assets in only five years, elevating the bank to a national powerhouse. In a complicated deal, NCNB received from the FDIC a five-year option to buy all of First Republic's shares, which it did, plus a cash infusion and

TABLE 9-3

Earnings Contribution by Business Function (in millions, except per share data)

	General Bank		Global Finance		Financial Services		Other	
	1994	1993	1994	1993	1994	1993	1994	1993
Net interest income	$3,689	$3,479	$1,180	$1,040	$413	$204	$ 24	
Noninterest income	1,712	1,430	834	626	51	45	0	
Total revenue	5,401	4,909	2,014	1,666	464	249	24	
Provision for credit losses	283	364	(46)	31	73	35		
Gains on sales of securities							(13)	84
OREO expense	8	30	(27)	43	7	5		
Restructuring expense								30
Noninterest expense	3,644	3,342	1,087	798	212	153		
Income before taxes	1,466	1,173	1,000	794	172	56	11	54
Income tax expense	534	433	369	302	69	21	(13)	20
Change in accounting method								
Net income	$932	$740	$631	$492	$103	$35	$ 24	$234
Net interest yield*	4.52%	4.76%	2.81%	3.71%	7.45%	7.80%		
Return on equity	17.0%	16.0%	16.0%	16.0%	13.0%	13.0%		
Efficiency ratio	67.5%	68.1%	54.0%	47.9%	45.6%	61.6%		
Average balances								
Total loans and leases	$58,582	$50,055	$31,109	$26,855	$5,537	$2,622		
Total deposits	77,665	71,967	11,273	8,721	6,064	3,102		
Total assets	86,860	77,976	66,496	44,599				
Year-end balances								
Total loans and leases	63,578	59,591	33,193	28,244	6,380	5,164		
Total deposits	79,905	79,573	13,614	8,926				

*The Global Finance unit's net interest yield excludes the impact of the primary government securities dealer. Including this impact, the net interest yield excludes the impact of the primary government securities dealer. Including this impact, the net interest yield was 1.98 percent in 1994 and 2.66 percent in 1993.

IRS tax breaks worth an estimated $5.5 billion. The Texas acquisition lifted NCNB's assets to about $60 billion.

McColl, "The Commander," is an ex-Marine who has been referred to as the "George Patton of banking"[4] and "the brashest banker in Dixie."[5] McColl has alienated more than a few southern bankers with his attitude, but he has been extremely successful. As McColl has said, "I expect the Herculean."

NCNB Corporation was organized in 1968 to acquire control of North Carolina National Bank, headquartered in Charlotte. In that same year, the company formed NCNB Properties and NCNB Mortgage Corporation. The following year, NCNB acquired Stephenson Finance Co., Inc., now TranSouth Corp.

During 1971, NCNB acquired Factors, Inc. (name later changed to NCNB Financial Services, Inc.) and formed NCNB Tri-South Corp. (disposed of in 1981). In the following year, the company acquired C. Douglas Wilson and Co. (Greenville, South Carolina) and Trust Company of Florida. In 1974, NCNB Mortgage acquired Blanchard and Calhoun Mortgage Co. (Augusta, Georgia). In 1976, Blanchard and Calhoun was merged with C. Douglas Wilson under the name of NCNB Mortgage South, Inc.

During 1979, NCNB acquired from NCNB Mortgage a subsidiary, MAP, Inc., to accelerate the disposition of foreclosed properties. In 1985, TranSouth Financial (sold in 1985) acquired Atlantic Discount Co.

During 1982, NCNB acquired three Florida companies: First National Bank of Lake City, Gulfstream Banks, Inc., of Boca Raton, and Exchange Bancorporation, Inc., Tampa. Gulfstream and Exchange merged into NCNB National Bank of Florida.

During 1984 and 1985, NCNB merged Ellis Banking Corp. of Bradenton (75 branches and assets of $1.8 billion) into NCNB National Bank of Florida. During 1985, NCNB acquired the $2 billion asset Pan America Bank, Inc. (Miami), with 51 offices, and Southern National Bancshares, Inc. (Atlanta). In 1986, NCNB acquired $1.9 billion asset Bankers Trust of Columbia (now NCNB South Carolina), the $108 million asset National Bank of Florida (Miami), seven branches of First American Savings Bank of Gaston County (North Carolina), the Prince William Bank of Dumfires (Virginia), and Hartsville Bancshares (South Carolina). In the same year, NCNB organized NCNB Mortgage Corp. as a subsidiary of NCNB National Bank of North Carolina. In addition, NCNB Mortgage acquired certain assets of Southern National Mortgage Co. (Charlotte).

During 1987, NCNB acquired Centrabank (Baltimore) and the remaining 70.1 percent of Panmure Gordon and Co. (London, England). During 1988 through 1992, NCNB made a series of acquisitions in Texas. It first acquired a 20 percent ownership interest in Texas National Bank, a former subsidiary of First Republic Bank Corp., for $210 million. NCNB purchased the rest of the bank in 1989 in two stages. In the same year NCNB Texas, a subsidiary of NCNB, acquired University Federal Savings Association (Houston) and assumed about $22.3 million in deposits of the former Tyler National Bank, which had been declared insolvent. During

1990, NCNB Texas acquired nine banks with $1.5 billion in deposits from National Bancshares Corp. (San Antonio), and purchased the $8.0 billion mortgage-servicing portfolio of Fundamental Mortgage Corp., a subsidiary of San Jacinto Savings Association.

In 1991, NCNB Mortgage and NCNB Texas Mortgage Corp. were merged under the new name of NCNB Mortgage Corp., a wholly owned subsidiary of NCNB Texas National Bank.

C&S/SOVRAN CORPORATION ROOTS

C&S/Sovran Corporation became the parent holding company of Citizens & Southern Corporation (Atlanta) and Sovran Financial Corporation (Norfolk, Virginia) in 1989. The merger created the nation's 12th largest bank holding company, with $50 billion in assets. Earnings began to decline in 1990 and 1991 as a result of two developments. One was a sharp rise in nonperforming assets, primarily in the metropolitan Washington, DC, area; the second was a decision to identify and charge to earnings some $91 million in nonrecurring expenses, including $69 million in integration and consolidation costs related to continued organizational and technological efficiencies and improvements planned for 1991 and 1992. The troubled C&S/Sovran was acquired by NationsBank in 1991.

What went wrong following the merger of C&S and Sovran? The merger points out that problems can occur when banks of equal size, but from different geographic markets, merge. From a credit perspective, C&S had no idea how troubled Sovran's Washington, DC, real estate loan portfolio really was. In addition, a form of southern golf course etiquette prevented the prompt elimination of unnecessary and expensive top management, as the merged companies operated with dual headquarters and few cutbacks in management. One of the goals of a merger is to create operating and personnel efficiencies. That can't be accomplished with an overabundance of poorly functioning, well-paid executives. In addition, the two companies never succeeded at merging and defining common goals, strategies, and cultural mores. A dual headquarters structure disempowered management from taking the decisive action necessary to address effectively serious performance problems. As management consensus languished, so did the chance for a successful turnaround.[6]

In summary, NationsBank has grown from a multitude of acquisitions. Beginning in 1982, NCNB made major interstate acquisitions in Florida, followed in 1986 by the acquisition of South Carolina-based Bankers Trust. By the end of 1987, year-end assets had reached $28.9 billion. By year-end 1989, assets reached $66.2 billion, following the $23 billion acquisition of First Republic in 1988. By year-end 1991, total assets reached $110.3 billion, with C&S/Sovran accounting for $52 billion. By year-end 1993, assets had reached $157.7 billion, aided by the acquisition of the $15 billion MNC Corp. Assets climbed to close to $170 billion at year-end 1994 as a result of numerous fill-in acquisitions (see Table 9–4). NationsBank's acquisition acumen has always been one of its strengths.

T A B L E   9–4

Asset Size by Year (in billions)

Year	Total Assets
1987	$ 28.9
1989	66.2
1991	110.3
1993	157.7
1994	179.6
1995 (midyear)	184.5

CURRENT ORGANIZATION

NationsBank operates three functional groups: general banking, global finance, and nonbank financial services, all supported by corporatewide functions that include credit policy, marketing, and asset-liability management. The Nonbank Financial Services Group consists of NationsBank Credit (225 offices in 32 states) with $4.6 billion of managed receivables and Greyrock Financial Group with $2 billion in outstandings. The operation was established with the purchase of Chrysler First and U.S. West Financial in 1993. These less regulated entities are targeted for aggressive growth as part of NationsBank's interest in moving to activities outside of the insured deposit and traditional loan arena. The loans in this subsidiary are both nontraditional and high yielding in specialized consumer and corporate niches funded by the money and capital markets. Although Nations-Bank is a relative newcomer to many of these businesses, it should be able to increase market share in them as it continues to attract new talent and builds scale in its operations.

NationsBank Credit specializes in high return, and higher risk, consumer-oriented business by offering products such as secured home loans, home improvement loans, boat loans, and personal lines of credit. Also, NationsBank Credit is the third largest provider of consumer durable goods financing, with inventory-managed finance receivables of $1.4 billion at year-end. Greyrock Group is predominantly a commercial finance company. The group focuses on corporate finance, commercial real estate, equipment finance, and leveraged leasing in the $10–25 million category. Greyrock is also involved in consumer auto financing, manufactured housing, and real estate–secured lending. The goal of NationsBank, with respect to nonbank financial services, is to build its subsidiaries into outstanding companies that can compete with GE Capital on the commercial side and Norwest Financial, Avco, or Beneficial on the consumer side. Additional asset acquisitions can be anticipated to complement internal growth.

The General Bank consists of retail banking operations, electronic banking (ATMs, telephone, and PC banking), commercial lending, national financial products (such as credit cards, mortgages, and indirect consumer lending), trust, investment management, and private banking, and NationsSecurities (see Figure 9–1). NationsBank serves more than 5 million households and 25 percent of the small

F I G U R E   9–1

Future Organizational Structure

NationsBank			
General Bank	**Global Finance**	**Nonbank Financial Services**	**Other People's Money**
Consumer banking • Branch banking • Electronic banking • Insured deposit funding	Corporate finance • Corporate banking • Relationship management • Investment banking • Treasury management • Advisory services	NationsCredit • Consumer finance • Inventory finance	Investment management
Commercial banking		Greyrock Capital • Specialized commercial finance • Specialized consumer finance	Private banking
Small business banking	Specialized finance • Real estate • International • Factoring • Leasing • Business credit		Personal trust
National financial products • Bankcard services • Mortgage banking • Dealer finance	Capital markets • Trading • Structured finance • Public finance • Debt underwriting • Equity underwriting		Retirement services NationsSecurities Insurance

businesses located in the bank's marketing area. Household penetration within its markets is 20 percent, and that rises to 38 percent in the more affluent mid-Atlantic region. NationsBank has one of the most geographically diverse portfolios of any domestic banking company and has no worrisome concentrations. Commercial lending, including middle-market and larger institutional business, represents 43 percent of the portfolio, while residential real estate represents just over 16 percent. It is a corporate goal for consumer loans, including residential mortgages, to reach 50 percent of total loans. At year-end 1994, the consumer loan portfolio stood at about 41 percent of total loans. By region, Texas represents 26 percent, North Carolina 16 percent, and both Florida and Georgia about 10 percent of outstanding loans.

Management implemented technology-based strategy within general banking operations to meet its stated noninterest revenue and efficiency goals. The company has developed an automated platform service system, which will allow for unified procedures, products, and customer information in all NationsBank locations. The system will provide better service and enable the bank to offer customers other products and services that fit their individual profiles, resulting in greater sales per customer contact.[7]

NationsSecurities operates out of 500 branches with 580 full-service account executives. It has more than 140,000 active brokerage accounts and reaches more than 100,000 households, with $8 billion in total client assets. In addition, Nations-Bank Discount Brokerage has 80,000 discount brokerage accounts. Profits for NationsSecurities reached $41 million in 1993 and $44 million in 1994.

NationsBank is still grappling with its revenue-expense equation. The effort will be aided by legal permission to combine Washington, DC, and Maryland banks into a single legal entity. The company has targeted a mid-60s efficiency ratio for the banking group, a considerable improvement from the low-70s level of 1994, but far behind the more efficient Wachovia and Norwest. NationsBank has the second largest ATM network in the country, with 2,900 machines, and one of the largest telephone centers, which responded to 85 million calls during 1994. The increased use of advanced-system ATMs, telephone centers, and computer-based banking should help NationsBank lower its operating costs.

The Global Finance Group encompasses corporate finance (corporate banking, relationship management, investment banking, treasury management, and advisory services), specialized finance (real estate finance, international, factoring, leasing, and business credit), and capital markets (securities trading, derivatives and foreign exchange trading, structured finance, public finance, and debt and equity underwriting). The centerpin is the corporate bank ($18 billion in loans), which performs the relationship management function for this customer segment, actively selling loans and cash management and international services, as well as working with specialized sales forces in capital markets and trust. The investment banking unit generated $138 million in income during 1994, compared to $94 million in 1993 and under $50 million in 1992.

Capital markets include the traditional investment banking products and primary dealer, foreign exchange, and derivative products and trading. The comptroller of the currency is investigating charges that the bank sometimes offers credit only to corporate customers who also hire the NationsBank to underwrite bonds, a potentially illegal practice called *tying*.[8] The real estate bank and specialized lending (factoring, leasing, and business credit) hold a combined total of about $10 billion in loans.

The business segment currently ranks first among U.S. banks in the number of customer relationships. Although this group is an active participant in loan syndications, NationsBank is still behind the lead and co-lead positions in profitability. NationsBank was the third largest syndicator on a global basis by number of deals and fourth in volume, with almost $196 billion during 1994. Germane to investment banking and underwriting, NationsBank is expected to focus on serving its existing corporate banking clients as well as non-Fortune 500 companies that may be overlooked by major Wall Street firms, especially within the bank's marketing area.[9]

FEE-BASED INCOME

NationsBank managed more than $57 billion in client assets and about $164 billion of total assets under administration at year-end 1994. The company also had the third largest family of bank-advised mutual funds and closed-end funds in the nation, with about $15 billion under management.

Fee-based income accounted for almost 33 percent of net revenue in 1994, compared to 31 percent in 1993. Service charges on accounts, trust fees, bankcard income, trading and foreign exchange income, and investment banking income were among the key providers of noninterest revenue in 1994 (see Table 9–5). As the company expands its underwriting powers and builds its distribution network, investment banking revenue should grow rapidly. In the second half of 1994, NationsBank purchased three privately owned mortgage companies in California and the mortgage-servicing business of Express American Holdings Corp., with a $6.5 billion portfolio.

In the first quarter of 1995, Mortgage Corp., a subsidiary of NationsBank Corp., agreed to buy two mortgage-servicing portfolios. The two deals will boost the company's residential-servicing portfolio to about $75 billion, placing it among the top five mortgage servicers in the nation. The first purchase was the $10 billion servicing portfolio from Source One Mortgage Services. The second was the purchase of a $25 billion servicing portfolio from KeyCorp. This should help generate a substantial increase in fee income from the mortgage banking unit at NationsBank. These transactions are part of the holding company's strategy to become a major player in the residential mortgage business. In addition to paying $350 million for the $25 billion servicing portfolio acquired from KeyCorp,

T A B L E   9–5

Noninterest Revenue Comparisons

	1994	1993
Trust fees	$ 435	$ 371
Service charges on deposit accounts	797	681
Investment banking income	138	95
Mortgage servicing and fees	86	77
Fees on factored accounts receivable	74	74
Other service fees	138	118
Bankcard income	280	198
Trading and foreign exchange	273	152
Brokerage income	44	41
Trade finance	67	65
Insurance commissions	49	39
Other	216	191
Total noninterest income	$2,597	$2,101

Source: Company annual reports.

NationsBank paid KeyCorp another $150 million for other servicing-related assets, such as receivables and advances. Mortgage banking income in 1995 should double from the 1994 level of $86 million because of all the mortgage-servicing acquisitions. Bankcard income grew rapidly in 1994 thanks to a growing number of retail merchant accounts, higher activity in these accounts, and the securitization of credit card receivables. NationsBank is among the top 15 bankcard issuers, with more than 5.4 million customer accounts, and is the third largest merchant processor. The bank also entered into a major cobranding relationship with Blockbuster Entertainment Co. that could become a meaningful source of revenue growth.

Increased staffing in the investment banking unit should generate additional revenue, especially in debt and equity underwriting. The acquisition of the Chicago Research and Trading Group, a primary dealer of U.S. government securities and a derivative and foreign exchange trading organization, should boost fee income considerably.

The company's fee-based income was up substantially in the first half of 1995 and was expected to grow by an additional 15 percent in 1996, driven by growth in deposit fees, investment banking fees, acquisition-related mortgage-servicing fees, securities trading income, and miscellaneous income. On the other hand, NationsBank agreed to sell its corporate trust business to Bank of New York for an undisclosed amount of cash. Although this will lower trust fees, it is likely that the corporate trust area did not have enough critical mass to generate much profitability.

ASSET-LIABILITY MANAGEMENT

NationsBank entered the second quarter of 1994 with a slightly liability-sensitive balance sheet that had a $45 billion discretionary portfolio, with $28 billion in securities and $17 billion in receive-fixed interest rate swaps. NationsBank reduced the liability sensitivity of its swap portfolio to a net $8.9 billion by year-end 1994 by adding $8 billion of two-year receive-floating LIBOR swaps in the third quarter, selling $1.5 billion in securities for a $28 million loss, and reinvesting $337 worth of maturing securities. The bank also extended maturities on liabilities by $6 billion by issuing longer-dated foreign time deposits and banknotes. By year-end 1994, the discretionary portfolio was reduced to $35 billion. The portfolio still acted as a drag on net interest income throughout 1994. The negative carry offset the strong growth of the loan portfolio. The $8 billion receive-floating swap portfolio repriced in February 1995, reducing the negative carry on the swap position. In addition, $8 billion of the investment portfolio matured in 1995. When the low-yielding funds were reinvested in two-year Treasury notes, the bank gained an additional $260 million in interest income.[10] The number of common shares outstanding also declined by 5.6 million or 2 percent of the outstanding shares because of the corporate repurchase program.

WHAT DOES THE FUTURE HOLD?

NationsBank's challenge will be to maximize the sales volume of its diverse product lines by leveraging the selling power of its extensive distribution system in the most effective manner. The objectives going forward are improving internal efficiency, optimizing technology infrastructure, and generating revenue from credit cards, mortgage banking, investment management, mutual funds, consumer loans, and commercial finance— "Improve what you've got."[11] The company's operating efficiency is expected to improve in 1995–97 as a result of better technology and a reduction in the number of branches. The overhead ratio is expected to continue its decline from 64 percent and 62 percent in 1993 and 1994, respectively, to 58 percent by 1997. The ratio was at 61.5 percent in the second quarter of 1995 and at 56.7 percent in the third quarter.

To help reduce operating costs, NationsBank has asked federal regulators for permission to combine its operations in Maryland, Virginia, North Carolina, South Carolina, and the District of Columbia into one bank rather than separate entities, each with its own board of directors. The company appears to be moving toward a single-bank structure. Such consolidation would allow about a $50 million reduction in annual operating expenses. NationsBank also expects to close about

150–200 branches, while improving the efficiency of those remaining. Meaningful improvements in operating efficiency should be realized in 1995–96 through the company's efforts to improve its technology infrastructure and streamline its branch network by establishing uniform systems.

Other financial areas that require attention are the credit-quality ratios and the provision for loan losses. Although nonperforming loans increased by $51 million (6 percent) to a total of 0.82 percent of loans outstanding at mid-year 1995, the net charge-off ratio remained low at 31 basis points; but it was $31 million more than the bank's loan loss provision. NationsBank will likely have to increase its loan loss provision to cover both its strong loan growth and its net charge-offs to a more normal level of 50 basis points.

A number of banking analysts have been critical of NationsBank's acquisition of Bank South as "too pricey" and potentially dilutive. However, this acquisition enables the company to leverage its existing infrastructure, improving both its revenue growth capacity and operating efficiency throughout Georgia. On the defensive side, the acquisition of Bank South reduces the growth opportunities for NationsBank's current competitors in Georgia, as well as eliminating a major point of entry for outside competitors seeking to break into the lucrative Atlanta market.

Although the company professes a focus on building up existing business lines, it will likely also expand into other product areas and fill in with some banking or nonbanking acquisitions that will increase market share and revenues in regions where the bank already has a presence. NationsBank has expressed an interest in adding insurance products and services to broaden its nonbanking operations. A major goal at NationsBank is to capture a larger share of the total revenue spent on all financial services, including, but certainly not limited to, traditional banking. The senior management team has proven to be a sophisticated acquiror of both banks and nonbanks, capable of enhancing shareholder value through acquisitions.

Acquisitions are also a possibility as long as they improve market share and are located in large metro areas. BankAmerica, Bank of Boston, and either Wells Fargo or First Interstate are long-shot merger candidates. George Salem, Prudential Securities' bank stock analyst, suggests the following banks for acquisition if the price is right: Signet (Virginia); Hibernia (Louisiana); CoreStates (Pennsylvania); Boatmen's (Missouri); First Interstate (California); and several bank holding companies in Tennessee.[12]

The earnings and image of NationsBank have been controversial. Special tax credits, large securities gains, restructuring charges, purchase acquisitions, and volatile loan loss provisions have created confusion about real earnings, raising questions about whether management is capable of managing the larger organization created by mega-acquisitions. Can management realize the cost savings and create a coherent strategy for one bank from a plethora of acquisitions?[13] The below-average P/E ratio of NationsBank is related to the above issues and the investment community's fear that the bank will make a dilutive acquisition.

However, the company's track record of nondilutive deals is impressive. Actually, management has demonstrated forbearance from expensive deals. For example, NationsBank bid in 1993 or 1994, but did not win, on Dreyfus, Margaretten, and Continental Bank. In addition, those deals that have been accomplished have contributed to earnings either immediately or within one year.[14] The merger-dilution fear factor appears unwarranted. It also looks as if the bank is working hard to become more efficient and to cross-sell its broad base of products throughout its extensive banking network. The company's board of directors also approved a 20 million share stock-repurchase program (almost 7.5 percent of the outstanding shares) beginning in fall 1994. The bank is expected to continue to boost earnings by channeling excess equity to buybacks and acquisitions during the next several years.[15]

Shareholders should benefit from the board's authorization to repurchase an additional 10 million shares in 1995 and 1996. An anticipated decline in FDIC premiums during 1995–96 could lead to $152 million in pretax expense savings (5 percent of EPS) per annum beginning in 1996. However, some portion of the savings may be passed back to consumers in the form of higher deposit rates.[16]

Acquisitions have accounted for a large portion of the company's asset growth. Recent acquisitions have improved its ability to achieve consistent earnings through all phases of a business cycle. Importantly, recent acquisitions have included nonbank financial companies that should allow NationsBank to compete more effectively against the less rigorously regulated financial service companies. Through acquisitions, NationsBank has built a diversified financial services company, establishing or expanding business in consumer finance, corporate finance, retail brokerage, options market making, and primary government security dealing. Many bankers prefer to not be acquired by NationsBank since McColl has a reputation as a ruthless, cost-minded general who tends to replace local managements and eliminate lots of other workers. Although McColl is respected, he is feared as a shrewd takeover artist who can afford to be patient, letting another bank make a first offer on one of his potential prey. Other potential prey include Mellon, with its huge mutual fund franchise, and Bank of Boston, with its successful Latin American operation and specialized commercial lending franchise.

The strengths of the company reside in its diverse franchise; expanding product array; solid, improving asset quality; and sound infrastructure—from which a diversified noninterest income revenue stream can be developed. Concerns from Wall Street analysts center on management's capacity to organize growth and related business risks, as well as additional market risks inherent in trading operations.[17]

ENDNOTES

1. R. Layne, "Partner Shoots for Quick (Exchange of) $350 Million a Year," *American Banker*, July 23, 1991, p. 14.
2. NationsBank, 1991 *Annual Report*, p. 6.

3. L.W. Cohn, "NationsBank," *Paine Webber*, October 31, 994, pp. 1–2.

4. J. Taylor, "The George Patton of Banking," *Forbes*, January 25, 1988, p. 44.

5. J.W. Milligan, "The Brashest Bank in Dixie," *Institutional Investor*, January 1987, pp. 58–60.

6. J. McCoy, L.A. Frieder, and R.B. Hedges, Jr., *BottomLine Banking* (Chicago: Probus Publishing Co., 1994), p. 336.

7. F.W. DeBussey, "NationsBank Corp.," *Fitch*, December 12, 1994, p. 2.

8. D. Greising, "NationsBank: An Excess of Zeal," *Business Week*, November 28, 1994, pp. 104–5.

9. T.H. Hanley, "NationsBank," *CS First Boston*, May 25, 1995, p. 21.

10. S.P. Davis, "NationsBank Corporation," *Goldman Sachs U.S. Research*, January 24, 1995, p. 4.

11. G. Salem, "NationsBank," *Prudential Securities Research*, July 20, 1994, p. 11.

12. Ibid., p. 12.

13. Ibid. p. 3.

14. Ibid., p. 5.

15. T.H. Hanley, "NationsBank," *CS First Boston*, October 19, 1994, p. 1.

16. Davis, p. 5.

17. DeBussey, pp. 1–2.

T A B L E   9–6

NationsBank Financials

	1990	1991	1992	1993	1994
Earnings per share	$3.34	$0.76	$4.52	$5.72	$6.06
Assets (in millions)	$113,692	$115,792	$115,047	$134,400	$166,319
Net income (in millions)	$594.72	$201.85	$1,145.00	$1,501.00	$1,690.00
Return on assets	0.52%	0.17%	1.00%	1.12%	1.02%

	1994	
	(in millions)	%
Average earning assets	$148,381	100
Securities	27,434	18
Loans	95,006	64
Other	25,941	17
Loans	102,367	100
Construction and land	2,981	
Commercial mortgage	7,349	
Highly leveraged		
Commercial loans and leases	47,545	
Other foreign	1,984	
Term LCD		
Credit card receivables	4,752	
Other consumer	17,868	
Unearned discount		
Corporate	59,859	58
Consumer	22,620	22
Mortgages	19,888	19

	1990	1991	1992	1993	1994
Efficiency ratio	64.98	66.58	63.03	62.91	62.54
Shareholder equity (in millions)	$6,222	$6,605	$8,186	$8,651	$10,484
Preferred	$380	$276	$205	$45	$49
Common	$5,842	$6,329	$7,981	$8,606	$10,435

F I G U R E   9–2

Nationsbank Financial Charts

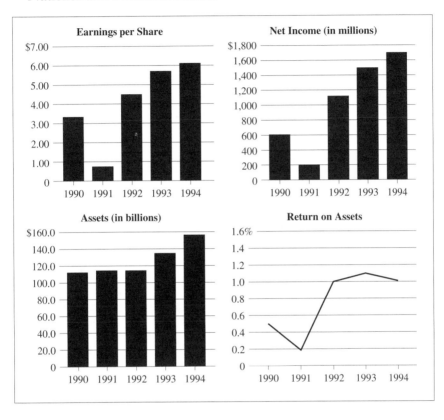

F I G U R E 9-3

NationsBank Financial Charts

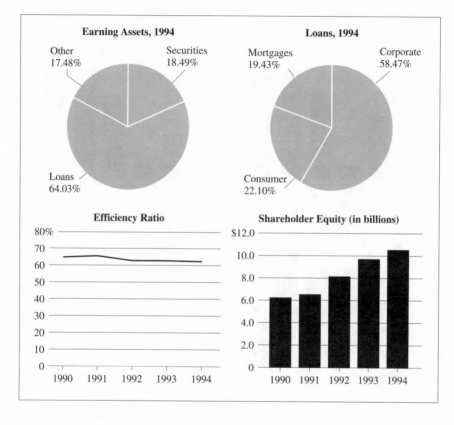

CHAPTER 10

First Union Corporation

First Union, in one of the largest deals in U.S. banking history, agreed to acquire First Fidelity Bancorp for about $5.2 billion in stock in June 1995. First Fidelity, which had 685 branches from Washington, DC, northward, will become, in effect, the northern division of First Union. The merged bank will have close to 2,000 offices and will serve 10.5 million customers from Connecticut to Florida in 14 states and the District of Columbia (see Figure 10–1). First Union will be the sixth largest bank holding company in the country, with assets of $123 billion, an equity capital base of over $8 billion, and a market capitalization in the neighborhood of $13 billion. The merged bank will have its legal and corporate offices in Charlotte, North Carolina. First Union's northern arm will be based in Newark, New Jersey, and Philadelphia, where First Fidelity has dual headquarters.

Chairman Edward Crutchfield felt that First Union, which plowed hundreds of millions of dollars into the bank in recent years to develop new products (such as derivative securities, mutual funds, annuities, and other capital market instruments), would be able to leverage that investment by selling more products to First Fidelity customers. The deal will give First Union entrée into the rich mid-Atlantic and Northeast markets served by First Fidelity. A major attraction for First Union was First Fidelity's concentration on middle-market companies and its 2.5 million customer base. Within the banking community, First Fidelity has one of the leading positions in the country in middle-market business customers.

This is a revenue-driven, out-of-market merger as opposed to a cost-cutting, in-market merger. However, noninterest expenses at First Fidelity will be cut by 19 percent. Since there is so little geographic overlap, just a limited number of branches will be closed initially. Job losses resulting from the merger should be minimal. Job cuts are most likely at corporate offices and in transaction processing centers, where

F I G U R E   10–1

The FTU/FFB Combination at a Glance

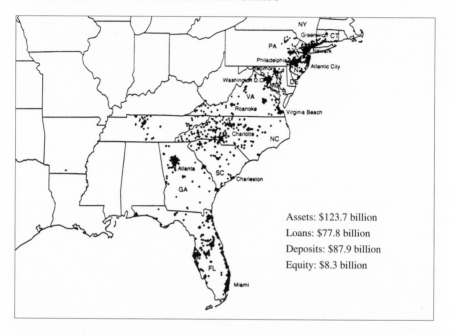

Assets: $123.7 billion
Loans: $77.8 billion
Deposits: $87.9 billion
Equity: $8.3 billion

duplicate functions can be eliminated. Many of the job losses will be through attrition. In some ways, the merger is similar to the Key/Society merger in that Society's more sophisticated products are being sold to Key customers.

First Union paid a premium of 32 percent over the closing price of First Fidelity's stock on the day prior to the announcement. The price-to-book value paid was 190 percent. Based on management's current and prior estimates, the transaction appears 7 percent dilutive to 1995 earnings and 3.7 percent dilutive to 1996 earnings. Edward Crutchfield will remain as chairman and CEO of First Union, while Tony Terracciano, the chairman and CEO of First Fidelity, will become the president of the merged bank, running First Union's northern operations and its capital markets group. John R. Georgious, president of First Union, will become vice chairman and run the southern operations.

The combined company will have about 44,000 employees, 10.5 million customers, 1,930 branches, and a net income of about $1.4 billion. The merger will be dilutive by close to 12 percent to book value per share and by 8 percent to 1995 earnings per share. The deal will not have much of an impact on First Union's financial ratios. Postdeal, tangible common equity will be 5.1 percent of assets, nonperforming assets will be low at 1.1 percent of loans, and the loss reserve will rise to 1.94 percent of loans and 244 percent of nonperforming loans (see Table 10–1).

T A B L E 10-1

Estimated Impact of First Fidelity Acquisition on First Union ($ millions)

	First Union	First Fidelity	First Union Pro Forma	% Change
Balance Sheet (as of March 1995)				
Assets	$77,855	$35,400	$113,25	45%
Loans	55,768	24,093	79,861	43
Intangibles	1,307	778	2,085	60
Common equity	5,491	2,714	7,713*	40
Preferred	0	170	170	
Total equity	5,491	2,884	8,375	53
Tangible common equity/assets	5.5	5.6	5.1	
Tangible total equity/assets	5.5	6.1	5.7	
Shares outstanding, primary	172.1	81.1	274.1	
Book value/share	$31.91	$33.48	$28.14	-12%
Tangible book value/share	$24.31	$23.88	$20.53	-16%
Loan loss reserve	969	581	1,550	
Nonperforming loans	432	204	636	
OREO	145	90	235	
Nonperforming assets	577	294	871	51
NPAs/related assets	1.03%	1.22%	1.09%	
Reserve/loans	1.74%	2.41%	1.94%	
Reserve/NPLs	224%	285%	244%	

Continued on next page

225

Table 10-1—Concluded

	First Union	First Fidelity	First Union Pro Forma	% Change
Terms of the deal				
FTUshare/acquiree share	1.35			
FTU share price at day prior to announcement	$48			
Deal value/acquiree share	$64			
Deal value/book	1.9			
Approximate cost of acquisition	$5,212			
Premium to FFB price	32%			
Date of announcement	6/19/95			
Estimated closing date	12/31/95			
Earnings impact				
Restructuring charge				
After tax	140			
Per share	$0.51			
Cost savings				
After tax	120			
Per share	$0.42			
1995E reported EPS	$5.70	$5.46	$4.71*	–17%
Fully diluted net income	994	464	1,458	
Fully diluted shares	174.4	85.0	279.4	
1996E reported EPS	$6.22	$5.89	$6.08†	–2%
Fully diluted net income	1,114	501	1,727	
Fully diluted shares	179.0	85.0	284.0	

* After restructuring charge and 7.4 million share buyback.

† After cost savings of $64 million and $48 million of revenue enhancements.

Source: Company financial statements: Oppenheimer & Co., Inc. estimates; FirstCall consensus estimates.

First Union increased its restructuring charge to $270 million after taxes ($0.97 per share) from its original $140 million estimate ($0.50 per share) germane to the takeover of First Fidelity. This is related to higher severance and change-of-control charges, real estate write-downs, and service contract terminations. As an experienced acquiror, First Union should have had a better grasp on the restructuring charge and not lost some credibility with its shareholders when it announced its merger with First Fidelity. We have included management's estimate of expense savings and incremental revenue related to the acquisition (see Tables 10–2 and 10–3). In addition, Table 10–4 represents a cost savings and earnings enhancement matrix which gives EPS estimates from 1995–97 for successfully achieving various percentages of its expense targets and revenue goals. For example, if management can produce only 75 percent of its expense savings and 75 percent of its revenue enhancements, EPS would be $5.19 in 1995, $6.00 in 1996, and $6.85 in 1997. This would make the pricing of the deal 6 percent dilutive in 1996 and 2 percent dilutive in 1997.

Prior to the merger announcement with First Fidelity, First Union was the nation's 10th largest bank holding company and was engaged primarily in the general commercial banking and trust business, along with investment banking and capital market products. First Union also provides other financial services, including mortgage banking, home equity lending, leasing, insurance, credit cards, asset-based

T A B L E   10–2

Management's Estimate of Expense Savings (in millions)

	1995	1996	1997	1998
Automation and operations	$4	$37	$55	$68
General banking	3	23	27	33
Capital markets	1	12	16	19
Marketing	2	11	13	17
Consumer lending	2	7	7	9
Corporate real estate	2	6	9	12
Finance	1	3	7	10
Mortgage banking	0	3	7	10
Purchasing	0	3	6	8
Other	1	1	2	3
Total pretax	$16	$106	$149	$189
After-tax	10	64	91	115
EPS impact	$0.03	$0.23	$0.32	$0.40

Source: CS First Boston.

T A B L E   10–3

Management's Estimate of Incremental Revenue (in millions)

	1996	1997	1998
Capital markets products	$ 21	$ 46	$ 65
Risk management products	6	13	19
Dealer division	5	13	19
International	9	10	10
Total capital markets	$ 41	$ 82	$ 113
Capital management/trust	17	18	19
Card products	11	11	11
Insurance	4	4	4
Other	6	7	8
Total pretax	$ 79	$ 122	$ 155
After-tax	48	74	94
Earning per share impact	$0.17	$0.26	$0.33

Source: CS First Boston

T A B L E   10–4

Cost Savings and Earnings Enhancement Matrix

Costs	Revenues	1995E	1996E	1997E
100%	100%	$5.20	$6.10	$7.00
75%	100%	5.19	6.04	6.92
50%	100%	5.18	5.99	6.84
100%	75%	5.20	6.06	6.93
75%	75%	5.19	6.00	6.85
50%	75%	5.18	5.95	6.77
100%	50%	5.20	6.02	6.87
75%	50%	5.19	5.96	6.79
50%	50%	5.18	5.90	6.71
100%	25%	5.20	5.97	6.80
75%	25%	5.19	5.92	6.72
50%	25%	5.18	5.86	6.64
100%	0%	5.20	5.93	6.73
75%	0%	5.19	5.88	6.65
50%	0%	5.18	5.82	6.57

Source: CS First Boston estimates.

financing, securities brokerage services, and merchant banking. With the increased diversification of the bank's wholesale product lines, First Union has created a powerful financial services franchise. Management has made discretionary investments intended to guide the growth of the corporation in today's changing banking environment. First Union should be able to capitalize on significant revenue-generating opportunities that will likely arise from the growing demands of its southeastern customer base for new financial products and services.[1]

The company is well diversified both functionally and geographically, offering products and services to more than eight million customers. At year-end 1994 (prior to the First Fidelity merger announcement), First Union operated 1,338 full-service branches in the South Atlantic states. These branches, or retail stores sell traditional products and any financial product offered by a brokerage house—all under one roof. First Union has the nation's fourth largest branch network and eighth largest ATM network. The company had assets of approximately $77.3 billion at year-end 1994 (compared to $7 billion in 1985) and had 1994 net income of $900 million before and $859 million after a redemption premium on the corporation's Series 1990 preferred stock. This was an increase of 14 percent from net income of $793 million in 1993. First Union's return on assets was 1.22 percent, and its return on equity was a strong 17.4 percent during 1993, while its ROA was 1.27 percent and ROE 17.04 percent during 1994 (see Figure 10–2). During the first half of 1995, First Union achieved an ROA of 1.2 percent and an ROE of 17.2 percent. During the third quarter of 1995, First Union achieved an ROA of 1.25 percent and an ROE of 17.2 percent. The company has achieved above-average profitability ratios over the years.

Through 222 diversified nonbanking offices in 39 states, First Union provides other financial services, including mortgage banking, home equity lending, leasing, insurance, and securities brokerage. The traditional banking markets of First Union include North Carolina, South Carolina, Georgia, Florida, Tennessee, Virginia, and the greater Washington, DC area (see Table 10–5). First Union ranks among the top five banks in market share in the eight states in its marketplace. Following the consummation of the pending acquisitions totaling $6.1 billion in assets of First Florida Savings Bank, American Savings Bank, and Coral Gables FedCorp, First Union will have one-third of its assets in Florida and the second largest deposit share (behind Barnett), with a 16 percent market share. In addition, First Union will have the largest deposit share in North Carolina (21 percent of the market), the third largest deposit share in both Virginia (13 percent) and Washington DC (17 percent), and the third largest deposit share in both Georgia (10 percent) and South Carolina (7 percent).

The loan mix consisted of 46 percent commercial and 54 percent consumer loans in mid-1994. Within the $23 billion commercial portfolio were $5.7 billion in mortgage loans, $1.5 billion in construction loans, and the bulk, $14.1 billion, in a mix of other commercial business loans. Of the $26.5 billion consumer portfolio,

F I G U R E   10–2

Return on Average Assets and Return on Average
Common Equity

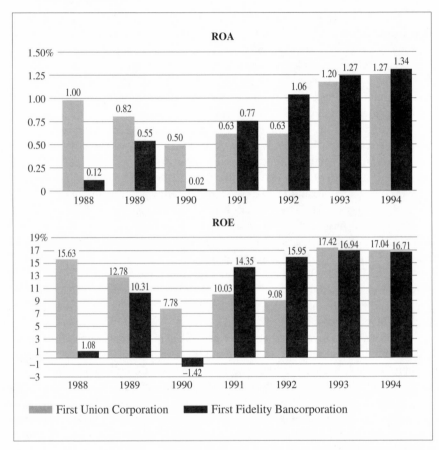

$12.7 billion consisted of installment loans (including credit card), while the remaining $13.8 billion consisted of residential mortgage loans (see Table 10–6). The lending strategy at First Union emphasizes quality growth, diversified by product, geography, and industry. The bank focuses on high-yielding retail products and small-business lending. Germane to geographic diversification, no individual metropolitan market contains more than 7 percent of the commercial loan portfolio. A common credit underwriting structure is in place throughout the bank. In addition, a special real estate credit group reviews large commercial real estate loans prior to approval.

T A B L E   10–5

Full-Service Banking Units by Location on December 31, 1994

Location	Deposits (in billions)	Assets (in billions)	Rank	Branches
North Carolina	$18.0	$23.0	1	276
South Carolina	1.9	2.4	4	66
Georgia	7.2	9.1	3	154
Florida	25.9	31.8	2	552
Tennessee	1.7	2.1	7	54
Virginia	6.2	8.3	3	177
Washington, DC	1.2	1.6	3	33
Maryland	1.0	1.3	10	26

Source: First Union, 1994 *Annual Report*, p. 10.

T A B L E   10–6

Loan Mix, June 30, 1994 (in billions)

Loan Type	Amount
Consumer loans	$26.5
Mortgages	13.8
Installment	12.7
Commercial	22.0
Mortgages	5.7
Construction	1.5
Other business	14.8

Source: Company report.

At year-end 1994, nonperforming assets were at their lowest level since 1991 at $558 million, or 1.03 percent of net loans and foreclosed properties. By the end of the third quarter of 1995, this ratio had improved to 0.91 percent. Seventy-two percent of non-performing loans were collateralized by real estate. The core First Union net charge-off ratio has been lower (better) than average. However, acquisitions with lesser credit quality obfuscated this good track record in the early 1990s.

    First Union has focused on leveraging the banking relationship with cross-sales of other products customers might need, such as mutual funds, insurance, credit cards, credit or cash management services, mortgage loans, or home equity lines of credit. These subsidiary offerings come from units of substance. For example, First Union Mortgage Corporation, the nation's 11th largest mortgage servicer, services a loan portfolio of $34.8 billion. The credit card division had close to $4.5 billion in outstanding loans at mid-year 1995, while the Capital Management Group had $47.6 billion under care, including $23.2 billion of assets under discretionary management at year-end 1994. Of that total, First Union manages $7.2 billion in mutual fund assets under the renamed Evergreen funds, resulting from the acquisition of Lieber and Co., the investment advisor of the Evergreen funds. First Union ranks eighth among banking companies in total assets under management and third in retail fund management. When First Fidelity's $2.5 billion Lexicon Funds are combined, First Union's proprietary mutual funds under management would rise to close to $12.5 billion. This would place First Union in fourth place among bank managers of mutual funds.

STRATEGY AND MISSION

First Union has broadened the definition of full-service financial provider to include many capital market/investment banking products or services. It is a role similar to European style "universal banks." The company's management described it as follows:

> When an individual wants an equity mutual fund, or a corporate treasurer seeks to hedge foreign exchange exposure, or a state or municipality wants to use general obligation bonds, or any customer has any financial need, our vision is for them to think, "I bet First Union offers that." In effect, we are drawing a line in the sand and telling our nonbank competitors: No . . . you will take no more of our good customers.

In essence, the management of First Union is taking Wall Street to Main Street. The strategic priorities of First Union include:

- Providing customers with unparalleled service, convenience, and responsiveness, and through these efforts, becoming the premier provider of financial services in the bank's markets.
- Managing the bank's business in ways that help its customers grow and help build the communities in which it operates.
- Balancing earning power through geographic and product diversity.
- Providing the most innovative capital market and creative financing solutions to its corporate and commercial customers.
- Providing a modern array of products and personal service for its individual customers.

- Increasing the production of its specialty businesses, including capital markets, card products, trust, brokerage, home equity lending, mortgage banking, and insurance.
- Maximizing operating efficiency.
- Emphasizing capital strength and loan quality, with growth in loans, deposits, investment products, and fee income.
- Becoming the first access point for all customers into the financial system.[2]

The mission of First Union is to be the best place for companies and individuals to obtain financial services and products they want: "to delight them with our efforts to help them achieve their specific financial goals." The company is always committed to enhancing value for stockholders and will make every effort to control costs, enhance credit quality, manage risk, and increase sales, leveraging the efficiency and revenue potential in the markets in which it serves, while at the same time providing the finest customer service.

The bank's framework, infrastructure, and franchise provide an excellent foundation for efficiency and increased profitability throughout the second half of the 1990s. The company operates with a standard set of products and a common automation approach. With the installation of a standardized automation system largely behind it, First Union was able to invest in projects to enhance revenues rather than integrating automated systems. These standardized automated systems have allowed the banking company to control costs, introduce new products faster, and provide more complete service and better management information. First Union is well on the way to building a nationally recognized name brand. The bank has streamlined and centralized support functions into service units so that branch personnel can spend more time focusing on customers rather than performing administrative tasks.

One of the largest initiatives at the bank is to improve turnaround and processing time for loan decisions. Since more than 70 percent of the loans outstanding are for those under $250,000, the reduction of processing time from two weeks to three days will substantially free up bank staff to focus on sales.[3]

Mergers and Acquisitions

From November 1985 through January 1990, First Union completed 21 banking acquisitions. From February 1990 through the first quarter of 1994, it acquired another 10 banking organizations, including three major bank holding companies: First American Metro Corp. (VA) and Dominion Bancshares Corp. (VA) and Southeast Bank (FL). From December 1992 through March 1994, the corporation completed a large number of acquisitions that together increased the company's asset size by more than $21 billion prior to consolidation and its deposit base by over $17 billion. Although the prices paid for the acquisitions were often quite attractive, they were usually neither efficient nor robust revenue producers by First Union standards. About 200 of 600 acquired branches have been closed, while the remaining 400 should become more efficient and better revenue producers within two years.

First Union, with a strong appetite for mergers, nicknamed its chairman, Edward A. Crutchfield, "Fast Eddie." First Union, like NationsBank and Banc One, reflects the national trend of strong banks expanding their total share of the retail market at the expense of weaker rivals.[4] However, First Union completed the installation of a standard, multi-state deposit system before some of its competitors, giving it a competitive advantage over most of its peers. Common systems throughout a banking franchise enhance service and convenience to customers and reduce expenses, increasing operating efficiency.

First Union has also embarked on a commercial reengineering project that should be completed before 1996. This should reduce commercial loan turnaround times and improve relationship management with greater documentation and a streamlined approval process more responsive to customers' needs. Eventually, capital market businesses will be included in the information system, which will allow enhanced wholesale cross-selling efforts. This information system will be extremely helpful to the newly hired 100 capital market specialists with specific skills in securitizations, derivative securities, merger and acquisitions advisory, loan syndications, private placements, risk management, and other wholesale market-oriented businesses. The new professionals have joined a support staff of close to 500 bankers who have been retrained and transformed into capital market experts.[5] The capital markets group had pre-tax revenue of $100 million in 1993 and about $150 million in 1994. The revenue contribution of this group is expected to grow to $300 million in 1996 and $400 million in 1997.[6]

This repositioning by management is an attempt to build greater relationships with corporate customers and to generate greater fee-based revenues (see Figure 10–3). The wholesale banking strategy seeks to maintain and expand existing client relationships by offering traditional and non-traditional banking products and services that fulfill all possible financing needs and developing cross-selling at every level of the corporation, which will lead to new business with southeastern middle-market companies that prefer working with an efficient local bank.[7]

TECHNOLOGY

In addition to the aforementioned systems, First Union is rapidly rolling out file-folder image processing technology; however, it is taking a more cautious approach to high-speed check imaging. First Union selected its bank-card business as the pilot program for image processing. Other image processing projects involve brokerage

F I G U R E   10-3

Composition of Revenues (in millions)

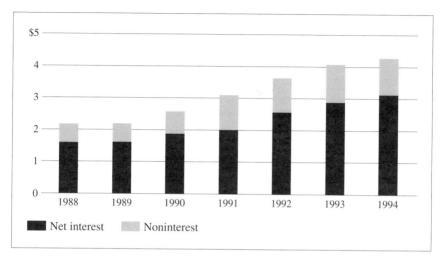

accounts, capital market accounts, retirement reporting, and accounts payable. Also queued up for the new technology are departments such as commercial and consumer loans, corporate real estate, human resources, and mortgages.

The technology utilized at First Union to support retail banking personnel in their sales efforts is reasonably sophisticated. Platform personnel use a prompting system that can lead customers and service representatives through various categories according to customers' interest or needs. Wholesale banking has also benefited from in-house technological developments. For example, turnaround time on small-business loan approvals has been cut from two to four weeks to only 24 hours. In another example of turnaround time, First Union takes only eight minutes to originate a car loan versus 45 minutes for First Fidelity. First Union's significant technological advantage over First Fidelity should facilitate further revenue and productivity gains throughout the organization following the merger of the two companies.

The factor that distinguishes the company from others is its use of a single system for the entire corporation. First Union has one system for all of its business units in each state, including all deposit branches, ATMs, consumer and commercial loans, mortgage loans, general ledger, the capital management group, and human resources. In addition to enhancing target-marketing through screening its massive customer information file from only one system, it also facilitates a much more rapid consolidation of acquired banks. For example, the average conversion time of the company's nine acquisitions during 1994 was just two months.

HISTORY

First Union incorporated in North Carolina in December 1967 as First Union National Bancorp. The name was changed to Cameron Financial Corp. in April 1972 and then to First Union Corp. in April 1975. In November 1977, First Union's subsidiary, Cameron-Brown, sold the assets of the Orlando Hyatt.

In 1981, First Union acquired First National Bank of Catawba County and First National Bank of Albemarle, and in 1983 it acquired Piedmont Corp. In 1985, Atlantic Bancorporation, Northwestern Financial Corp., and Central Florida Bank Corp. were acquired. In 1986, First Union continued to acquire banks, including Southern Bancorporation, Citizens de Kalb, First Bankers Corp., Georgia State Bankshares, First Railroad and Banking Company of Georgia, and Bank of Waynesboro. The year 1987 looks very similar to 1986 in terms of First Union acquisitions, except that there were more. First Union bought Collier Bank, Edison Banks, Inc., Rosewell Bank, Commerce National Bank, First North Port Bancorp., First Sarasota Bancorporation, City Commercial Bank, Sarasota Bank and Trust Co., N.A., First State Bancshares, Inc., Community Banking Corporation, and Bank of Bellevue. In 1988, it acquired Florida Commercial Banks, Inc.

In 1990, First Union acquired Florida National Banks of Florida ($7.8 billion in assets). In 1991, First Union's subsidiary, First Union National Bank of Florida, acquired the deposits of Florida Federal Savings from the Resolution Trust Corp. Also in 1991, another First Union subsidiary, Capital Finance Group Inc., sold its assets and liabilities to the Great Western Consumer Finance Group. Perhaps most important to First Union's future, the company completed a government-assisted purchase of $9.9 billion in assets and 224 branches of Southeast Banks of Miami. As a result, First Union's share of bank deposits in Florida moved up to a strong second place.

In 1993, First Union acquired South Carolina Federal Corp. ($823 million in assets); DF Southeastern, Inc. and its subsidiary Decatur Federal Savings and Loan Association (Georgia's second largest thrift, with $2.6 billion in assets); the $9.4 billion Roanoke-based, Dominion Bankshares Corp.; Georgia Federal Bank FSB ($3.7 billion in assets) from Financial Management Corp.; McLean, Virginia–based First American Metro Corp. ($4.6 billion in assets, $4 billion in deposits); American Commercial Bank; and Enterprise Bank N.A., The Dominion and First American acquisitions gave First Union 380 offices and close to a 15 percent market share in a state in which it previously had no presence. Also in 1993, First Union agreed to acquire Lieber and Co., a New York–based investment management organization that is the advisor to the top-performing Evergreen mutual fund ($3.2 billion in assets under management). With the Lieber acquisition, First Union's family of mutual funds increased to 33 funds. First Union plans to train 2,400 branch employees to sell mutual funds and to allow customers to conduct mutual fund share transactions through ATMs.

In addition, First Union agreed to acquire American Bancshares, Inc., the parent corporation of American Savings Bank Inc. (Monroe, North Carolina), the parent corporation of American Savings Bank, Inc., with assets of $235 million, and Home Federal Savings Bank of Washington, DC. Home operates six branches with assets of $232 million and a mortgage banking company in Annandale, Virginia. The latter acquisition strengthens First Union's retail position in the Washington area, where it is already positioned. In August 1994, First Union completed the acquisition of BancFlorida, a $1.5 billion thrift with 37 offices, headquartered in Naples. This transaction filled in the company's position in southwest Florida, a rapidly growing part of the state. The company's deposit share in the Naples market increased to 20 percent from 3 percent, while its share in the Fort Myers area also increased substantially. First Union's board of directors had authorized the purchase of 17 million shares, approximately the number of shares issued in conjunction with the BancFlorida acquisition. On the negative side, First Union inherited about $95 million in nonperforming assets with the acquisition of BancFlorida. First Union also acquired certain deposits and assets of Chase Manhattan Bank of Florida and of Great Western in Florida. In total, these two acquisitions added $400 million in deposits and additional branch offices. In 1994, First Union completed 10 acquisitions amounting to $4.6 billion in assets, $1.2 million in net loans, and $4.0 billion in deposits.

First Union announced additional in-market acquisitions in the fourth quarter of 1994, including an agreement to purchase Ameribanc Investors Group, headquartered in Annandale, Virginia, for about $108 million, or nearly 150 percent of book value. Ameribanc Investors Group is the parent of $1.1 billion asset Ameribanc Savings Bank, which has 29 branches and four mortgage offices. This acquisition will strengthen First Union's presence in the Washington, DC, area and in Norfolk/Hampton Roads, while giving the bank a toehold in Charlottesville. In its second acquisition, the company agreed to acquire American Savings and Loan Association (Miami), which had assets of $3.5 billion and deposits of $2.24 billion. The stock swap was valued at about $253 million, or close to 114 percent of book value. The acquisition beefed up First Union's market shares in Dade County (where it had a first place share), Broward County (a third place share), and Palm Beach County (a second place share). First Union is expected to cut 25 percent out of American Savings' expense base by consolidating back-office operations, closing branches, and reducing staff. Although the acquisition deletes earnings modestly in 1995, it will be accretive by 1996. First Union also agreed to acquire First Florida Savings Bank of Miami (assets of $101.8 million, deposits of $75 million) for $9.5 million in cash.

In January 1995, First Union also agreed to acquire Coral Gables Fedcorp for about $531 million, or 1.39 times book value. This healthy thrift institution had 34 offices and $2.5 billion in assets and $1.9 billion in deposits at the time of the announcement. First Union should be able to cut more than 30 percent of the thrift's $48 million expense base by consolidating back offices, closing some branches, and cutting some employees. Coral Gables Fedcorp will become part of First Union National Bank of Florida. With this latest transaction, First Union would become the largest banking concern in South Florida. In February 1995, First Union agreed to acquire the United Financial Corporation of South Carolina, Inc., based in Greenwood, for $130.5 million in stock. United Financial has 16 offices and assets of $759 million.

In early 1995, First Union announced plans to acquire Palm Beach Investment Management, which operates the ABT funds ($468 million in assets). The bank will likely incorporate these funds into the Evergreen family of mutual funds. In total, after this merger and the First Fidelity merger, First Union will have more than $10 billion in mutual fund assets under management.

In the second quarter of 1995, First Union agreed to acquire Columbia First Bank (CFFS) of Arlington, Virginia, with about $2.6 billion in assets and $1.5 billion in deposits. Columbia First originated $10 billion in single-family residential mortgages in 1995. The acquisition will cost about $222 million (167 percent of CFFS's year-end book value) in First Union stock and will boost the company's total deposits in the Washington, DC, area to $6.2 billion from $4.7 billion. CFFS operated 33 full-service offices: 9 branches in Virginia, 11 in Maryland, and 13 in the District of Columbia. Following the acquisition, First Union will become the second largest banking organization in the fast-growing District of Columbia region. The acquisition is expected to take place before the end of 1995 and to be accretive to earnings in 1996. First Union indicated it would purchase a number of its own shares equal to at least 50 percent of the number of shares that would be issued in the transaction to avoid diluting share value. Branch consolidation in the DC region would immediately follow the merger, as was the case in First Union's previous thrift acquisitions. First Union is positioned to reap substantial cost savings of about 50 percent of CFFS's $49 million expense base in this combination, while expecting to keep the deposit runoff relatively low at 16 percent. Since the ROA and ROE at CFFS in 1994 were a low 0.45 percent and 9.06 percent, respectively, it must be assumed that First Union entered the transaction in pursuit of customers, deposits, and expense savings.

First Union also agreed to acquire RS Financial Corporation, the parent company of Raleigh Federal Savings Bank, the largest independent savings institution in North Carolina, for $111.6 million in First Union stock. RS Financial had assets of $809.7 million and deposits of $514.4 million as of March 31, 1995. This acquisition enabled First Union to hold on to its slim lead in market share of deposits in North Carolina. Raleigh Federal has 31 branch offices, some in counties in which First Union currently has none (see Table 10–7).

During the fourth quarter of 1995, the bank agreed to acquire Society First Federal Savings, a Fort Meyers (FL) subsidiary of KeyCorp, which has $1.47 billion in assets. By acquiring this savings bank, First Union will snare the top share

T A B L E   10-7

Acquisitions Targeted for Completion in 1995

Company	State	Assets	Loans	Deposits
Ameribanc Investors Group	VA	$ 1,078	$ 600	$ 756
American Savings Florida	FL	3,485	1,920	2,240
Columbia First Bank	VA	2,900	2,200	1,500
Coral Gables Fedcorp	FL	2,464	1,777	1,990
First Florida Savings Bank	FL	92	72	75
Home Federal Savings	GA	194	143	162
RS Financial Corp.	NC	810	516	614
United Financial Corp.	SC	759	619	558
First Fidelity	NJ	35,400	24,000	27,000
Total		$47,182	$31,847	$34,895

Source: *CS First Boston*, June 27, 1995.

of deposits in Fort Meyers, by realizing its strategy of building market share through fill-in acquisitions.

Strengths and Priorities

Core deposits (savings, NOW, money market, noninterest bearing accounts, and consumer time deposits) accounted for $53.2 billion at year-end 1994. Average noninterest-bearing deposits represented 20 percent of core deposits, while higher-rate, other time deposits accounted for 35 percent. Average purchased funds were at 13.3 percent at year-end 1994. The pending retail thrift acquisitions in Florida should reduce the company's need for higher-priced funds.

The company's strengths include a diversified franchise with an expanding array of products, solid and improving asset quality, a demonstrated ability to drive down expenses and to make acquisitions work (synergy), a highly professional capital markets/investment banking group, strong asset-liability management, and sound infrastructure to develop diversified noninterest income revenue streams. Executive management is also impressive; they have developed a sensible game plan, established prudent policies and controls, accumulated strong capital and reserves, and generated solid earnings growth that should continue into the future. Some Wall Street analysts are concerned about management's capacity to coordinate growth and related business risks, as well as the additional market risks inherent in trading operations.

The strategic priorities of the company include building market share within its eastern banking network, controlling expenses, increasing revenues from specialty businesses, and balancing earnings power through geographic and product diversity. First Union believes in solid credit quality with both loan and deposit growth and seeks to outperform competitors in service, convenience, and responsiveness. The company has made considerable progress in reducing its noninterest expenses, as its efficiency ratio has declined to 62 percent in the second quarter of 1995 from 65.37 percent in 1992. This ratio is expected to decline to 58 percent by 1997 when the remainder of the acquired branches can be consolidated. Additionally, the nonperforming asset ratio declined from 4.1 percent in 1991 to 1.95 percent in 1993 and to 0.73 percent in the fourth quarter of 1994, and to 0.72 percent in the third quarter of 1995, while the ratio of reserves to nonperforming assets increased from 71.83 percent in 1991 to 175 percent in 1994, before declining to about 152 percent in 1995. The acquisition of American Savings and Home Federal added about $60 million in nonperforming assets during the third quarter of 1995. Net losses in the credit card portfolio are below 2 percent, half the industry average. On December 31, 1994, the corporation's Tier 1 and total capital ratios were 8.31 percent and 13.64 percent, respectively, while the leverage ratio was at 6.13 percent. Prior to the acquisition of First Fidelity, First Union would have been regarded as well capitalized, conservatively reserved, and ready to make additional meaningful acquisitions. However, the acquisition of First Fidelity has left the company with below-average capital ratios.

First Union has continued to expand its expertise in international banking, primarily to meet the trade, finance, and foreign exchange needs of its domestic corporate customers and to provide commercial banking and capital market products to the U.S. subsidiaries of foreign corporations. The bank has also developed a growing number of partnerships with established banks in 140 countries. First Union processed more than $4 billion in trade transactions and pioneered two new global partnerships during 1994. It signed an agreement with one of the largest South African banks for a credit facility in conjunction with a guaranty by the Export-Import Bank of the United States. The credit facility would be utilized to support the export of capital goods such as mining equipment from U.S. companies. The bank opened an office in Johannesburg in May 1995 to support this activity. During 1994, First Union processed more than $200 million in trade transactions with South Africa. The second partnership was a joint venture with the Hong Kong Chinese Bank (HKCB) to help support U.S. companies with trade in Asia. The company, First Union HKCB Asia Ltd., is expected to process $1.0 billion annually in trade transactions by the year 2000.

First Union expected to issue up to one million smart cards in Atlanta between September 1995 and the start of the Summer Olympics in 1996. The bank also launched a smart card in a closed environment in conjunction with the inaugural season of the Jacksonville Jaguars of the National Football League. These cards will enable fans to purchase concessions and merchandise inside the team's stadium. This will be the initial step toward introducing the open environment smart cards in major metropolitan areas in Florida in 1997. First Union is also expected to introduce its smart cards in the greater Washington, DC, and Richmond areas in 1997, and in Charlotte, Raleigh, Durham, Columbia, Greenville, Spartansburg, and Nashville in 1998. Using a microchip imbedded in plastic that stores cash value, these cards can be used in place of currency and coins in fast-food stores, cafeterias, convenience stores, pay phones, laundromats, and vending machines; they can also be used for buses, taxis, and subways.[8]

To increase fee income, First Union will train 800 of its investment sales specialists to sell insurance annuity products by the end of 1996. First Union Insurance Group has also signed an agreement with Western National Life Insurance Company to develop the first proprietary fixed-annuity product to be offered by First Union to its customers interested in saving for retirement. Western National Life will issue the product and provide marketing and administrative support, while First Union's Capital Markets Group will manage the program's assets. In addition, First Union became the 10th bank holding company to receive approval from the Federal Reserve Board to do debt and equity underwriting through its broker-dealer, First Union Capital Corp.

Fee income as a percentage of total revenue rose to 30 percent in the third quarter of 1995, up from 27.5 percent in the third quarter of 1994. First Union is said to be in negotiations with Prudential Mortgage, which has the fifth largest mortgage servicing portfolio in the nation ($78 billion). With about $36 billion in servicing, First Union ranks as the 16th largest mortgage servicer and could benefit from efficiencies of scale. Purchase of part of the Prudential portfolio is more likely than the entire portfolio. The reason is related to an asking price of about $1 billion for the entire portfolio, a 1.25–1.50 percent premium, or about twice book value. First Union would end up booking about $500 million in goodwill if the company were to be the purchaser of the entire unit. First Union already has $1.5 billion in intangibles, while First Fidelity has $850 million. On a pro forma basis, First Union and First Fidelity have a leverage ratio of about 5.35 percent. Assuming an additional $500 million in goodwill is added with the mortgage servicing transaction, the First Union leverage ratio with First Fidelity and Prudential Mortgage would be approximately 4.95 percent. A ratio of this magnitude would rank lowest among the fifty largest banks in the nation. First Union's pro forma balance sheet could more easily absorb a smaller transaction.

FIRST FIDELITY

First Fidelity, a multibank holding company headquartered in New Jersey, had assets of $36.2 billion and deposits of $28.9 billion at year-end 1994. In 1994, First Fidelity operated 655 branches throughout its six-state franchise, making it the 24th largest bank holding company in the United States and largest in New Jersey in terms of assets. First Fidelity maintained the 13th largest branch network with the 15th largest deposit base in the nation. The bank ranked first in market share in the combined northeastern Pennsylvania and New Jersey regions, second in wealthy Westchester (New York) and Fairfield (Connecticut) counties, and fourth in Philadelphia. The largest shareholder is Banco Santander, a Spanish company, which, prior to the acquisition by First Union, received permission from the Federal Reserve to increase its ownership position to just under 30 percent from about 25 percent. First Fidelity is organized into corporatewide lines of business that serve key customer segments, including wholesale banking, community business banking, trust and private banking, and consumer banking.

After a series of lending problems prior to the ascension of a new management team, the bank maintains a high-quality portfolio, with loans representing about 71 percent of assets and securities 26 percent of assets (see Table 10–8).

T A B L E   10–8

Loan Mix, December 31, 1994

Commercial real estate	16.9%
Residential, one- to four-family loans	25.4
Commercial financial loans	25.8
Consumer loans	22.7
Leasing	8.6
Foreign	0.4

Source: First Fidelity, 1994 *Annual Report.*

HISTORY

When the charter for the Bank of the United States expired in 1811, the New Jersey state legislature enacted the Bank Act of 1812, authorizing the charters for six state banks. With a board of directors consisting primarily of Revolutionary War heroes, the State Bank of Newark opened in that same year. The War of 1812 led to increased business in Newark as government contractors traveled there to procure much needed war materials. Following the war, Newark prospered once again as one of New Jersey's great produce markets and a leading industrial city. The Morris Canal was used to ship large amounts of coal, iron, and even more produce, and industrial development increased as a result of the growth of railroads connecting Newark to Jersey City, Trenton, and Philadelphia. The bank felt threatened by the outbreak of the Civil War because more than half of the sales of Newark merchants were made to southern businesses. However, the war led to orders for war materials from Washington for Newark merchants, and the bank prospered.

The State Bank of Newark was granted a federal charter in 1865 and began business as the National State Bank of Newark. Although the bank's conservative management style helped it weather five depressions, it did not generate much new business. In fact, the Union National Bank, a Newark banking rival, had grown to more than four times the size of National State Bank. With its conservative banking style still in place, however, National State Bank had no difficulty in surviving the Great Depression. It began to grow by seeking new customers and extending long-term credit and loans to an expanding industry during World War II.

In 1949, National State merged with Merchants and Newark Trust Company, bringing the bank its first branch office and first mortgage, personal, and installment loans. In 1950, National State merged with both Orange First National Bank and United States Trust Company. In just 18 months, National State had grown from one of the smallest banks in New Jersey to one of its largest, with assets of just under $170 million. It pursued a merger strategy during the 1950s, acquiring Lincoln National Bank in 1955, and the Irvington Trust Co., First National Bank of Milburn, and Citizens National Bank and Trust Company of Caldwell in 1956 and 1957. The biggest merger took place in 1958 when the bank acquired Federal Trust Company, making it the second largest bank in New Jersey (assets of $418 million). On its 150th anniversary, the bank changed its name to First National State Bank of New Jersey. In 1969, it formed a holding company, First National State Corporation, to aid a program of statewide growth and to participate in certain nonbanking activities.

During the 1980s, the merger of First National Bank of South Jersey and First National Bank of New Jersey increased assets to $6.4 billion, while the merger with Fidelity Union Bancorp brought total assets to $10 billion in 1984. At the time, it was the largest merger in banking history. In 1985, the company was renamed First Fidelity Bancorporation. It quickly acquired Morris County Savings Bank of Morristown.

First Fidelity was formed in 1987, pursuant to the merger of First Fidelity, Inc. (New Jersey) and Fidelcor, Inc. (Pennsylvania). It offers a full range of banking services, including leasing, retail brokerage, insurance brokerage, and mortgage financing. Although headquartered in Lawrenceville, New Jersey, its largest subsidiary banks are in Newark and Philadelphia. Fidelcor was the holding company for Fidelity Bank and Industrial Valley Bank, both of Philadelphia. Although both were primarily full-service retail banks, Fidelity maintained an international banking presence in the wholesale Euro-syndication market. On the wholesale banking front, First Fidelity has a strong market share with regional companies with sales up to about $250 million.

The company made a major investment in new technology and programs to strengthen itself as a relationship bank able to identify and respond to all customer needs. Expansion of the lockbox business through two additional processing points enhanced further the company's position as a major cash manager in the mid-Atlantic states and New England. While the company is active with some Fortune 100 customers, it does business with one out of five smaller businesses in its market area. First Fidelity's corporate trust department is one of the major players in the nation. On the retail banking front, it serves over 1.5 million households. In its market, the bank does business with about one family in five. Total auto loans and leases outstanding exceed $1 billion, placing the company among the top leasing companies in the United States.

New Management Team

The bank began to have major declines in earnings related to a large increase in nonperforming commercial loans. This led to a serious deterioration of the bank's capital ratios, a 40 percent cut in dividends during 1990, and a change in executive management. Anthony Terracciano was hired as chairman and president. He had been president of Mellon Bank, where he served as the right-hand man of Frank Cahouet in solving that bank's problems. In addition, Terracciano had been a vice chairman of Chase Manhattan Bank. Immediately after arrival at First Fidelity, he cut costs dramatically by slashing the number of employees by 20 percent, introduced a new and more efficient standardized process for the bank's loan underwriting program, rebuilt the capital base, expanded into contiguous markets with foothold acquisitions followed by fill-in mergers, and contracted EDS to handle the bank's computer operations. First Fidelity reduced its efficiency ratio from an excessive 70 percent to an impressive 57 percent within three years, while gaining market share in New Jersey and suburban New York City counties. Peter C. Palmieri, vice chairman and chief credit officer, and Wolfgang Schoelkopf, vice chairman and chief financial officer, were the other executives who played major parts in reinvigorating the organization.

Latimer and Buck, the mortgage banking unit that had been a subsidiary of Fidelcor, was sold in 1990, while Fidelcor Business Credit Corp. was sold to the CIT Group in 1991. Since that sale, First Fidelity has been active in acquiring regional retail banks and thrifts, as well as failed financial institutions from both the FDIC and RTC that ranged from Connecticut through New Jersey and Pennsylvania. In 1991, First Fidelity acquired 48 branches of the former City Federal Savings Bank in northern and central New Jersey from the RTC; 53 full-service branch offices and certain assets of First National Bank of Toms River, New Jersey; 3 branch offices from Ensign Federal Savings Bank; and 6 branch offices from Alexander Hamilton Federal Savings and Loan Association.

In 1992, First Fidelity acquired five offices of New York–based American Savings Bank from the FDIC; all 70 branches of the Howard Savings Bank of Newark, New Jersey, from the FDIC; and certain assets and $17 million in deposits of Pitcairn Private Bank of Jenkintown, Pennsylvania. Under a marketing agreement with the bank's Pitcairn Trust Company affiliate, First Fidelity is offering a variety of private banking services to Pitcairn Trust's select group of wealthy customers. Pitcairn Trust's investment funds and tax and asset management services are now available to qualifying First Fidelity customers.

In 1993, First Fidelity entered new markets in Connecticut and New York, providing a contiguous link to existing First Fidelity markets in New York and northern New Jersey. The company completed five acquisitions involving institutions with almost $5 billion in deposits and 116 branches. The holding company acquired Northeast Bancorp of Stamford, Connecticut, and its principal subsidiary, Union Trust Company ($2.7 billion in assets and 61 branches in Fairfield and New Haven counties); 8 branches and $329 million in deposits of Dime Savings Bank of New Jersey in northern New Jersey; 29 branches of Atlantic Financial Savings in Philadelphia; Peoples Westchester Savings Bank (assets of $1.7 billion and 31 branches); and Village Financial Services and its Village Bank subsidiary, operating in Westchester and Riverdale (NY) with $736 million in assets.

In 1994, First Fidelity acquired the Savings Bank of Rockland County, New York ($179 million in assets and 4 branches); Greenwich Financial Corp. and its Greenwich Savings and Loan subsidiary ($408 million in assets); and First InterBancorp of Fishkill and its subsidiary, Mid-Hudson Savings Bank (16 branches, $522 million in assets). The Connecticut and New York acquisitions opened up financially attractive, geographic regions in which First Fidelity can deliver banking services.

In Pennsylvania, First Fidelity acquired First Peoples National Bank of Edwardsville ($101 million in assets). The company acquired Baltimore Bancorp, a $2.2 billion Maryland-based retail bank for about $346 million in cash (213 percent of book value). Cost savings of 40 percent or more are anticipated as the head count is expected to shrink by 300 people, or 27 percent of the acquired staff. To facilitate the purchase, Baltimore Bancorp shifted to a thrift charter, thereby circumventing the southeastern state compact that restricted bank acquisitions by those companies headquartered out of the region.

In mid-1994, prior to the merger with Baltimore Bancorp, First Fidelity purchased from the RTC four branches of the former John Hansen Federal Savings (a failed Maryland-based thrift), with $66 million in deposits. First Fidelity has extended its geographic franchise south into Baltimore, Maryland, and its wealthy suburbs. A similar initial foray into Connecticut established a beachhead into lucrative Fairfield County, which led to a current second place share of market. In addition, First Fidelity announced the acquisition of First State Bank in Delaware, with assets of $38 million in the third quarter of 1994.

First Fidelity's management has consistently acquired financial institutions prudently, paying about 190 percent of book value for its bank acquisitions and 120 percent for its thrifts in 1993–94. These purchase prices were well below the average price paid in the mid-Atlantic region: 202 percent of book value for bank acquisitions and 147 percent for thrift acquisitions.[9]

Bankers Trust and First Fidelity joined forces in 1993 to create a corporation called Global Processing Alliance, Inc. Global sells high-quality, cost-effective check processing and related services to other depository institutions. This venture is expected to reduce First Fidelity's expenses and create a future source of fee income.

Financial Ratios and Potpourri

First Fidelity Bancorp is making good progress in working its way out of its asset problems. As a matter of fact, its ratio of nonperforming assets to total assets fell to 1.06 percent in 1994 from above 4.3 percent in 1991, while its ratio of nonperforming assets to loans and OREO declined from 2.30 percent in 1993 to 1.38 percent at year-end 1994. Its ratio of loan loss reserves to nonperforming assets also grew to a conservative 182 percent at year-end 1994, compared to levels under 100 percent in 1991, while reserve coverage of nonperforming loans rose to 253 percent at the end of 1994 from 159 percent a year earlier. Reserves as a percentage of total loans were 2.52 percent at year-end 1994. First Fidelity's asset-quality team, led by Vice Chairman Palmieri, developed a uniform credit culture and set of policies, established a new risk-rating system and strict limits on loan size and terms, and installed a credit approval process. The new regime's strict credit-quality procedures were critical to the turnaround of the company. Furthermore, First Fidelity is installing a software product that will capture-company-specific data and should enhance management's ability to monitor and control lending risk. The Risk Analysis System (RAS) will assist management in identifying industry or market concentration of loans, generating regulatory reports, and providing support data for sales efforts. In addition, the RAS should help in establishing underwriting guidelines for each loan segment and gauging the riskiness in a particular industry or geographic area.[10]

Commensurate with this improvement in credit quality, the company's ROA increased from 0.77 percent in 1991 to 1.27 percent in 1993 and 1.34 percent in 1994. Similarly, its ROE increased from 14.45 percent in 1991 to 16.9 percent in 1993, before retreating to 16.75 percent in 1994. By year-end 1994, total equity capital had grown to over $3 billion. At the end of 1994, the company's risk-adjusted Tier 1 capital ratio was at 8.74 percent, its leverage ratio was at 6.59 percent, and its total capital ratio was at 11.73 percent. The ratio of shareholders' equity to assets stood at 7.73 percent. All of these ratios were well in excess of what regulators define as a well-capitalized bank. Management raised the company dividend and continued to buy company stock.

First Fidelity's branch network consisted of 520 locations in 1990 and stood at about 700 at the end of 1994. The net branch increase of 142 resulted from the acquisition of almost 430 offices and the consolidation of 285 locations. In January

1995, the bank announced that it would close 40 branches and eliminate 1,000 jobs in 1995–96. Prior to this announcement, First Fidelity had already reduced the number of full-time employees by more than 7,000, from 18,407 to 11,316, while expanding revenue per staff member from $101 million to $165 million.[11]

First Fidelity's management knows how to run an efficient operation and how to make a merger work. The company's merger philosophy includes a zero-dilution game plan within 18 months, that is, the company must earn back any dilution, including special charges, within 18 months. First Fidelity seeks in-market or contiguous-market transactions, where cost synergies are created and redundant capacity and personnel can be eliminated. The company avoids problem franchises and seeks revenue growth opportunities through the cross-selling of existing or new products to newly acquired customers.[12]

Small- and Middle-Market Efforts

First Fidelity currently services about one out of three middle-market companies with $10–250 million in revenues in its geographic area. The company has broadened its involvement with cash management services and introduced trade finance and investment banking products. It is the market leader in New Jersey and eastern Pennsylvania for companies with sales between $1–10 million in revenues, having a relationship with approximately 20 percent of the 50,000 small businesses in the region. In addition, the bank has increased efforts to sell trust banking services to individuals, small businesses, and middle-market companies.[13] The company is making a strong effort to generate fee income and lift its 21.79 percent ratio of noninterest income to net revenue that it achieved in 1994.

Acquisition Summary

From 1990 through the first quarter of 1995, First Fidelity acquired or announced the acquisition of 22 institutions, with just under 5,000 employees, over 400 branches, and a deposit base totaling over $17.5 billion (see Table 10–9). At year-end 1993, the company had fewer employees than it did at the end of 1990.[14]

Its acquisition strategy over the 1990–94 period may be characterized in three ways: government-assisted, in-market, and contiguous-market. The strategy has emphasized deposit gathering first, and then cost-saving opportunities through in-market deals. The company began to make acquisitions in contiguous markets to generate revenue growth from an expanded customer base. Each of the acquisitions has added to earnings per share through the realization of extensive cost efficiencies, improvements in core funding and asset mix, and expansion into affluent growth markets. Every acquisition has been or is expected to be accretive to earnings on a cumulative basis within 18 months of closing.

T A B L E   10–9

Acquisition Summary

Closing Date	Company	Assets	Deposits	Branches
1991	City Savings		$2.7 billion	57
	Toms River Bank	$1.7 billion	1.6 billion	53
	Ensign Bank		130 million	3
	Alexander Hamilton	90 million	180 million	6
	Atlantic Financial		940 million	29
1992	American Savings		335 million	5
	Howard Savings	3.1 billion		70
1993	Pitcairn Private Bank	22 million		
	Northeast Bancorp	2.8 million	2.5 billion	68
	Dime Savings Bank		342 million	8
	Village Financial	813 million	560 million	9
	Peoples Westchester	1.8 billion	1.6 billion	31
1994	Greenwich Financial	412 million		7
	First Peoples National Bank of Edwardsville	102 million	84 million	2
	Savings Bank of Rockland County	186 million	175 million	4
	First InterBancorp	522 million	460 million	16
	Baltimore Bancorp	2.2 billion	2.0 billion	41
1995	First State Bank	32 million		2
	Household Bank, FSB		1.1 billion	24
Total		$17.5 billion		

Source: Company information.

First Fidelity is committed to zero expense growth (adjusted for acquisitions) and remains one of the most disciplined bank acquirors.[15] Following acquisitions, First Fidelity has eliminated duplication in such areas as administration, branch structure, and systems; it has consolidated through legal means and acquired low-cost funding. Cost savings resulting from the bank's in-market acquisitions have been in a range of 52–74 percent; its contiguous transactions have led to cost savings of 40–57 percent.[16] It is expected that at least 10 Bank of Baltimore branches will be closed in 1995, along with 108 additional branches from the core bank. This decision should reduce head count by 7.7 percent, or about 1,000 people. First Fidelity announced a $5 million, severance-related charge for 1995.

Noninterest Income

Noninterest income has grown from $332 million in 1992 to $417 million in 1994. The company's core businesses generate various types of non-interest income, such as charges on deposit accounts, trust income, and other service charges, commissions, and fees (see Table 10–10). As one of the major corporate trust departments in the country, First Fidelity administers about $80 billion of outstanding debt for Fortune 1,000 corporations, public agencies, and government entities.

The bank has initiated programs designed to enhance fee-based income, especially in trust and private banking, consumer banking, and investment products. These programs include the introduction of VISION Banking and new 401(k) and risk management products. VISION Banking, a consumer product that promotes a total bank-customer relationship, encourages customers to consolidate all their banking services with First Fidelity and benefit from the combined balances with free checking, higher rates on savings, discounts on loans, and an all-in-one monthly statement. VISION had more than 130,000 relationships totaling $5.2 billion in deposits at year-end 1994. The program helped grow consumer loans by 21 percent in 1994 over 1993.

T A B L E   10–10

Major Components of Noninterest Income

Component	1994
Trust income	$105.9
Service charges and deposit accounts	145.1
Other service charges, commissions, fees	105.6
Trading revenue	10.1
Net securities transactions	17.7
Other income	32.5
Total	$416.9

Source: First Fidelity, 1994 *Annual Report.*

Acquisition-Minded

Under the leadership of Anthony Terracciano, First Fidelity moved quickly several years ago to address its asset-quality problems, primarily in commercial real estate; to build capital strength; and to control noninterest expenses. Once this was accomplished, First Fidelity bought a series of retail-oriented institutions, weakened by the real estate recession that hit the Northeast with a vengeance, through govern-ment-assisted transactions. Although it might make additional acquisitions, First Fidelity as a part of First Union will also continue to balance carefully the longer-term strategic value and the impact on shareholder value of each transaction. Acquisitions have after all brought the company closer to achieving a major strate-gic goal: extending the franchise to attractive contiguous markets and building the economies of scale and scope necessary for sustained success. Terracciano's skill in cost-cutting, while increasing the asset base of Fidelity, made it the dominant and most profitable bank in New Jersey. He also expanded market share in eastern Pennsylvania, in southeastern Connecticut (14.7 percent market share in Fairfield County and a 12 percent share throughout Connecticut), and in Westchester County, New York, where the bank has the second largest market share.

First Fidelity's initial foray into Maryland is consistent with its long-term goal of offering banking services along the East Coast from Maryland and Wash-ington, DC, through Massachusetts. In February 1995, First Fidelity agreed to buy 24 more branches in Maryland ($1.1 billion in deposits) from Household Bank, a subsidiary of Household Finance Inc., for $76.1 million. The acquisition of First State Bank of Wilmington moved the company into Delaware during 1995, the sixth state in which the bank has a retail branch system. The Delaware operation will have trust and insurance powers.

From late 1990 to the end of 1994, First Fidelity acquired $16.4 billion in assets and $13.7 billion in deposits. The holding company became an industry leader in both productivity and acquisitions.

Why a Merger-of-Equals?

First Fidelity was entering a stage of development in which it required product quality, new products, and considerable investment in technology to compete suc-cessfully. The merger with First Union was a means to obtain a premium price for First Fidelity shareholders and to outsource product growth and development to a stronger partner that not only had the high-quality products desired, but had also made the necessary technological expenditures required to compete successfully.[17] Just prior to the announcement of the merger with First Union, First Fidelity had reached an understanding with Bank of Boston Corporation to merge with no stock premium. However, Banco Santande, the 30 percent owner of First Fidelity, informed Terracianno that it would not agree to a deal without a handsome stock price premium. Hence, a new partner was found.

SUMMARY

First Union is well diversified both functionally and geographically. It is a southeast-ern bank that functions with a strong mid-Atlantic presence, supplemented by national business in mortgages and credit cards. Its capital market initiatives supplement its core commercial banking business. First Union appears well positioned to take advantage of the changing nature of commercial banking, while capitalizing on the fundamental business on which Chairman Crutchfield had built its franchise. Management has demonstrated its commitment to ensuring the profitability of mature businesses while identifying and developing new growth areas. Through a combination of internal growth and acquisitions, First Union is expected to continue its robust growth and financial health as it expands throughout the East. Historically, First Union's earnings grew at a compound annual rate of 20 percent from 1990 to 1994, while enjoying an average ROE of 16 percent and a 1.07 percent ROA over the past 10 years.

The merger of First Union with First Fidelity created a premier retail and middle-market franchise with significant competitive advantages. It created a broader geographic reach and customer base for both banks in two contiguous markets throughout the East Coast. The economies of scale created by the combination should ultimately improve operating efficiency while also allowing for the leveraging of First Union's products and technology.

The combination of superior technology and a renewed focus on revenue generation—all leveraged over a broader base of wealthier customers and a greater concentration of middle-market companies—augurs well for good income growth in the period ahead. The key to success for First Union over the intermediate term lies in its ability to expand the sale of middle-market commercial and consumer products within the company's current operating territory as well as throughout the mid-Atlantic states and in southern New England. Crutchfield believes that within the next decade 10 to 15 major financial institutions will control 50 percent of the nation's banking business.

First Union's strategy calls for growth through acquisitions, thus increasing economies of scale. First Union is expected to continue to make in-market and adjacent-market acquisitions. These acquisitions create diversified deposit sources and commercial customers and provide the opportunity to sell a greater number of well-established products to a new customer base. However, it would not be surprising to see the company acquire an out-of-market bank or nonbanking company that generates substantial fee income. The most likely targets include financial services businesses with a national scope, such as mutual fund, credit card investment management, and insurance/annuity businesses.

Management is promoting a companywide cross-selling effort to leverage customer relationships, technological capabilities, and product expertise. The company will attempt to increase efficiency and fee-based income as it redefines itself as a full-service financial institution, resembling a European-style universal bank. The capital market focus of the wholesale bank should contribute healthy fee-based returns over the medium term. Furthermore, the unparalleled integration of the entire First Union organization, both technological and managerially, positions this powerful franchise to take full advantage of the changing nature of the banking industry.[18] First Union is likely to evolve beyond the confines of a traditional bank into a highly profitable financial services company in which two-thirds of the company will likely be a retail and middle-market commercial bank, while one-third resembles a large nonbanking company.[19]

First Union has had 10 percent compound earnings growth and 14 percent dividend gains since the mid-1980s; in fact, the company has raised its dividend for 18 straight years. The redemption of all outstanding 6.3 million shares of Series 1990 preferred stock by March 31, 1995 should have a positive impact on operating earnings in 1995 and beyond. In addition, Terracciano will likely engineer a series of northeastern bank acquisitions to fill in the Connecticut and suburban New York City franchises and perhaps the southeastern Pennsylvania franchise.

First Union is a well-managed, megaregional bank with good profitability ratios but only average overhead ratios and below-average capital ratios. The takeover of First Fidelity will cause near-term earnings dilution. Expansion in new geographic territories by an aggressive acquisition-minded management could lead to even further dilution in near-term EPS. Given that management has not quantified the amount of near-term earnings dilution it would be willing to incur in any given transaction (as long as the transaction begins to add incrementally to earnings within one year) there is a degree of investor angst present in the market. Also, since First Union is a large derivatives player, the market appears to be paranoid of some hidden charge or substantial artificial inflation of revenue. Overall, the utilization of off-balance-sheet hedging is a more capital and cost-efficient means of neutralizing interest rate risk. First Union's policy regarding interest rate risk is not to allow more than a 5 percent swing in net EPS for a given 200 basis point change in interest rates across the yield curve relative to its base interest rate scenario over a 12-month planning period.[20]

ENDNOTES

1. T.H. Hanley, "First Union," CS First Boston, December 23, 1994, p. 3.
2. First Union, 1994 Annual Report.
3. M.H. Ross, "First Union," Wheat First Butcher Singer, September 14, 1994, p. 3.
4. A. Gart, Regulation, Deregulation, Reregulation: The Future of the Banking, Insurance and Securities Industries (John Wiley & Sons, New York, 1994), p. 346.
5. T.H. Hanley, "First Union Corporation," CS First Boston, July 22, 1994, pp. 11, 18.
6. Ross, pp. 2–6.
7. Hanley, July 22, 1994, p. 11.
8. First Union, First Quarter 1995 Report, p. 4.
9. T.H. Hanley, "First Fidelity," CS First Boston, September 15, 1994, p. 11.
10. Ibid., pp. 8–9.
11. T.H. Hanley, "First Fidelity," CS First Boston, December 7, 1994, pp. 10–11.
12. Ibid., p. 14.
13. Hanley, September 15, 1994, p. 7.
14. C.S. Berger, "First Fidelity," Salomon Brothers Research Report, June 28, 1994, p. 7.

15. R. Albertson, "First Fidelity," *Goldman Sachs Bank Research*, August 17, 1994, p. 1.
16. Hanley, December 7, 1994, p. 18.
17. T.H. Hanley, P.J. Carter, and A.B. Collins, "Bank Stock Consolidation," *CS First Boston*, June 21, 1995, p. 2.
18. T.H. Hanley, "First Union Corporation," *CS First Boston*, October 17, 1994, pp. 3, 5.
19. Hanley, Carter, and Collins, September 18, 1995, p. 3.
20. T.O. McCandless, "First Union Corporation," *Paine Webber Research*, August 1994, pp. 2–7.

T A B L E   10–11

First Union Financials

	1990	1991	1992	1993	1994
Earnings per share	$2.52	$2.55	$3.72	$4.73	$4.98
Assets (in millions)	$52,125	$55,095	$61,146	$68,101	$72,187
Net income (in millions)	$262.37	$348.73	$385.05	$817.52	$925.38
Return on assets	0.50%	0.63%	0.63%	1.20%	1.28%

	1994	
	(in millions)	%
Average earning assets	$65,476	100
Securities	13,276	20
Loans	49,055	75
Other	3,145	5
Loans	54,030	100
Construction and land	1,734	
Commercial mortgage	5,437	
Highly leveraged		
Commercial loans and leases	17,539	
Other foreign	399	
Term LCD		
Credit card receivables		
Other consumer	14,578	
Unearned discount	(672)	
Corporate	25,109	46
Consumer	13,906	26
Mortgages	15,015	28

	1990	1991	1992	1993	1994
Efficiency ratio	63.91	62.52	62.46	60.02	61.84
Shareholder equity (in millions)	$3,244	$3,468	$4,214	$4,839	$5,467
Preferred	$307	$336	$329	$289	$272
Common	$2,937	$3,132	$3,885	$4,550	$5,195

T A B L E   10–11

First Fidelity Financials

	1990	1991	1992	1993	1994
Earnings per share	($0.33)	$3.31	$3.77	$4.58	$5.11
Assets (in millions)	$29,808	$28,727	$29,475	$31,509	$33,742
Net income (in millions)	$(6.13)	$221.24	$313.74	$398.83	$451.06
Return on assets	(0.02)%	0.77%	1.06%	1.27%	1.34%

	1994	
	(in millions)	%
Average earning assets	$30,328	100
Securities	7,984	26
Loans	21,671	71
Other	673	2
Loans	23,802	100
Construction and land	318	
Commercial mortgage	4,035	
Highly leveraged		
Commercial loans and leases	6,454	
Other foreign	110	
Term LCD		
Credit card receivables	385	
Other consumer	3,246	
Unearned discount	(310)	
Corporate	10,917	46
Consumer	3,321	14
Mortgages	9,564	40

	1990	1991	1992	1993	1994
Efficiency ratio	63.64	60.27	56.3	55.98	57.75
Shareholder equity (in millions)	$1,521	$1,617	$2,066	$2,463	$2,806
Preferred	$157	$194	$232	$231	$230
Common	$1,364	$1,423	$1,834	$2,232	$2,576

F I G U R E   10–4

First Union Financial Charts

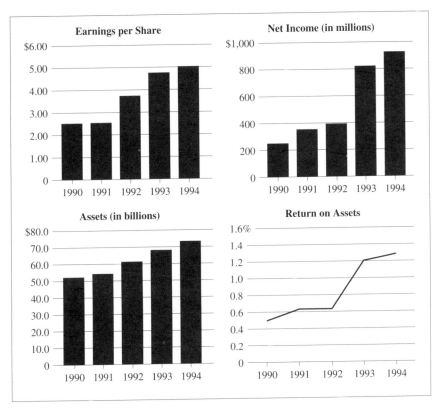

F I G U R E   10–5

First Union Financial Charts

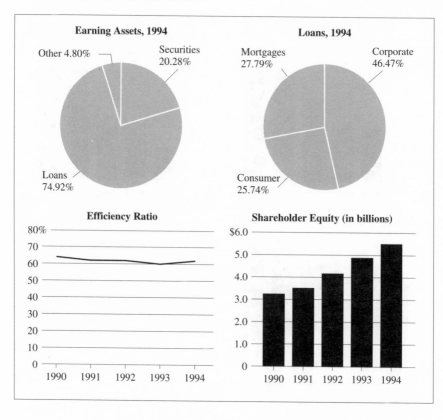

F I G U R E   10–6

First Fidelity Financial Charts

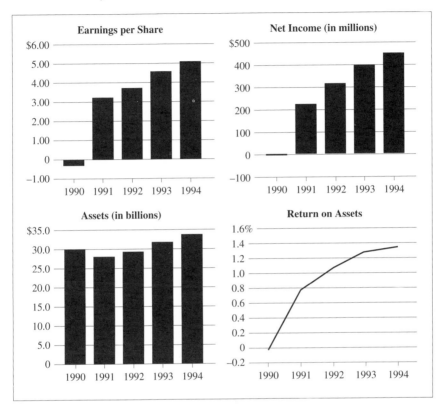

First Fidelity Financial Charts

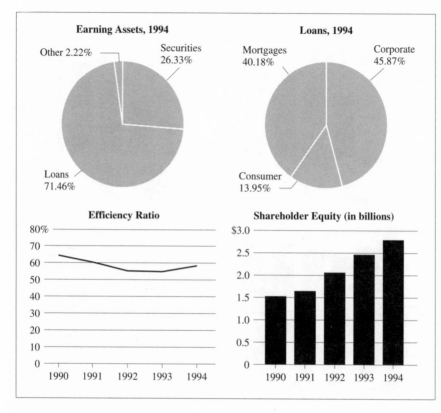

CHAPTER 11

SunTrust Banks

On June 30, 1995, SunTrust Banks Inc., had total assets of $44.2 billion and trust assets under investment management in excess of $40 billion. SunTrust has 19,374 employees and offers complete banking, investment management, and trust services in Georgia, Florida, Tennessee, and Alabama through its 657 full-service banking offices. Its main banking subsidiaries are Trust Company of Georgia, SunBanks, Inc., and Third National Corporation (see Table 11–1). SunBanks is the largest contributor to net income, followed by Trust Company of Georgia and Third National (see Table 11–2).

SunTrust provides corporate finance, investment banking, mortgage banking, factoring, credit cards, discount brokerage, credit-related insurance, and data processing and information services. SunTrust holds the first, second, or third position in 26 out of 36 counties in which it operates in Florida, 23 out of 34 counties in Georgia, and 18 out of 25 counties in Tennessee. The company has a 14 percent deposit share in both Florida and Georgia, with about 363 and 189 offices, respectively.

TABLE 11–1

Total Assets and Deposits by Bank Subsidiary, December 31, 1994 (in billions)

	SunBanks	Trust Company of Georgia	Third National
Total assets	$21.0	$14.9	$6.6
Total deposits	16.8	10.2	5.2

Source: SunTrust, 1994 *Annual Report.*

T A B L E   11–2

Contribution to Net Income (in millions)

	SunBanks	Trust Company of Georgia	Third National
1994	$279.5	$210.8	$81.5
1993	249.9	190.8	70.7

Source: SunTrust, annual reports.

SunTrust has an unusual holding in its investment portfolio that may have a major impact on its future merger and acquisition policy; it holds 24,133,248 shares of common stock in the Coca-Cola Company, with a September 30, 1995, value of about $1.8 billion.

The motto at SunTrust is "think like a shareholder." The philosophy at SunTrust appears to be to concentrate on the things that the company does best. According to its chairman, James B. Williams, "We have never believed nor do we believe now that bigness, in and of itself, is a virtue, and we do not measure our success in terms of size. Our focus at SunTrust remains tightly fixed on quality, profitability and performance."[1] The company has concentrated on acquiring banks within its geographic operating areas without paying the dilutive premiums that other acquiring banks pay.

On June 29, 1984, Trust Company of Georgia (Atlanta), with assets of $5.4 billion, and SunBanks, Inc. (Orlando), with assets of $9.1 billion, announced a reorganization of equals to form SunTrust Banks, Inc., with pro forma assets of $14.5 billion. The combination was made possible by the enactment of regional interstate banking laws in Florida and Georgia. This merger was followed by the 1986 merger of Third National Corporation (Nashville), with assets of $5.0 billion, into SunTrust Banks. The combined company would have assets of $24 billion. At the time of the merger announcement, SunTrust had total assets of $18.8 billion and operated 44 banks with more than 480 offices in Georgia and Florida, as well as nonbank subsidiaries providing mortgage banking, investment and brokerage services, information and data processing services, and other specialized financial activities. Third National operated 12 banks with 134 locations in 17 counties of Tennessee. The biggest affiliates of Third National included Third National Bank in Nashville, American National Bank and Trust Company of Chattanooga, and Third National Bank in Knoxville.

LOAN PORTFOLIO   ·

At year-end 1994, SunTrust's loan portfolio consisted of $9.6 billion of commercial loans, $8.4 billion of one- to four-family mortgage loans, $1.2 billion of construction loans, $4.5 billion of other real estate loans, $3.8 billion of consumer loans, and

$.7 billion of credit card loans (see Table 11–3). The company has targeted residential mortgage and credit card lending for growth in 1995 and beyond. SunTrust is working toward increasing market share of mortgage lending through the branch system, broadening relationships with home builders and realtors and expanding its presence in the wholesale mortgage market. The company's interests lie in originating adjustable rate mortgages and developing products such as "Shortcut Mortgage," featuring an expedited loan approval and closing process. On the credit card front, SunTrust has introduced cobranded credit cards with the PGA Tour and several country music stars. On the debit card front, SunTrust is planning to introduce smart cards in conjunction with the opening of the 1996 Summer Olympic games to be held in Atlanta. In addition, Trust Company of Georgia, best known for corporate banking and personnel trust services, has formed a subsidiary, Personal Express Loans, Inc., to make small loans to credit-impaired consumers. Personal Express will make personal loans in the $3,000–5,000 range. Larger amounts will be loaned on home equity lines. This move follows in the footsteps of KeyCorp and Barnett. Barnett recently purchased a home equity lender, while KeyCorp purchased a company that makes subprime auto loans.

T A B L E   11–3

Loan Portfolio by Loan Type (year-end)

Loan Type	1994	1993	1992
Commercial			
Domestic	$ 9.3	$ 8.2	$ 7.9
International	0.3	0.2	0.2
Real estate			
Construction	1.2	1.1	1.0
One- to four-family	8.4	7.0	5.9
Mortgages			
Other	4.5	4.5	4.5
Lease financing	0.4	0.3	0.4
Credit card	0.7	0.7	0.7
Other consumer	3.8	3.3	2.9
Total	$28.6	$25.3	$23.5

Source: SunTrust, 1994 company reports.

RECENT MERGER ACTIVITY

During 1990, Trust Company Bank of South Georgia, N.A., acquired $165.9 million in assets of Albany First Federal Savings and Loan Association, while $333 million in deposits of Anchor Savings Bank were assumed by Trust Company banks in Atlanta and Savannah. In 1992, Sun acquired Florida Westcoast Banks, Inc., which had assets of $385.6 million.

During 1993, SunTrust completed four bank acquisitions, adding over $2 billion in assets. The company merged HomeTrust Bank of Georgia, located in Gainesville, Georgia ($309.5 million in assets), into a subsidiary, Trust Company Bank of North Georgia; First United Bancorp of Florence, Alabama, parent of First National Bank of Florence ($384.1 million in assets), into a subsidiary of SunTrust; and Flagler Bank Corporation of West Palm Beach, Florida, parent of Flagler National Bank (assets of $452.2 million), into a subsidiary of SunTrust. The company also acquired all the stock of Coast Federal Savings Bank of Sarasota, Florida (assets of $1.1 billion) and agreed to acquire Regional Investment Corporation, the parent of Andrew Jackson Savings Bank located in Tallahassee (assets of $436.8 million). SunTrust also completed the acquisition of Peoples State Bank located in New Port Richey, Florida (assets of $124 million) in May 1995. In addition, the company executed a definitive agreement to acquire Key Biscayne Bankcorp, a $145 million asset institution headquartered in Key Biscayne, Florida.

Following the announcement of the acquisition of Bank South by NationsBank in September 1995, SunTrust announced an agreement to set up small mini-branches in the Georgia stores of Publix supermarkets, which should enable SunTrust to maintain a strong market share throughout Georgia, while becoming more efficient as the company closes 10 of its costly and less profitable full-sized branches.

FINANCIAL RATIOS

SunTrust has a fine reputation for having a strong balance sheet, providing excellent customer service, and maintaining good control of operating costs, all of which are reflected in consistent financial ratios. SunTrust reported an ROA and ROE of 1.32 percent and 17.66 percent, respectively, during 1994, compared to 1.14 percent and 15.0 percent in 1992 and 1.26 percent and 16.5 percent in 1993. During the first half of 1995, SunTrust reported an ROA of 1.35 percent and an ROE of 18.5 percent. Net income reached $522.7 million in 1994, compared with $473.7 million in 1993. The record earnings recorded in 1994 reflected the "positive results of our efforts to grow loans and control expenses . . . A lower provision for loan losses and fewer shares outstanding also contributed."[2]

Its nonperforming assets have been slowly declining, and its ratio of nonperforming assets to average total assets fell to 0.66 percent in the fourth quarter of 1994 from 1.03 percent in 1993. This ratio is expected to decline to close to 0.50 percent by year-end 1996. Loan loss reserves were a strong 345 percent of nonperforming loans and 2.3 percent of total loans during 1994. At June 30, 1995, the company's loan loss reserves as a percentage of nonperforming loans stood at 371 percent, while its ratio of reserves to total loans stood at 2.25 percent. Net charge-offs in 1994 were $60.3 million, or 0.23 percent of average loans, and

$77.5 million below the provision for loan losses for the year 1994; while at mid-year 1995, net charge-offs had fallen to 0.16 percent of average loans. Management opted to book $138 million in loan loss provisions, more than double actual net charge-offs in 1994.

Its ratio of average common equity to assets was a comfortable 9.04 percent as of June 30, 1995, while its efficiency ratio was 58.9 percent during 1994 and 58.2 percent in the second quarter of 1995. This demonstrates that overhead costs are under good control. However, these ratios still lag behind those of industry leader and archrival Wachovia. SunTrust's efficiency ratio should decline to below 56 percent by year-end 1996, as management continues to close branches that do not meet profitability targets. Should regulation permit and management be willing to convert all of the company's independent banks to a common branch system under one bank, there could be an additional cost savings of close to 13 percent of noninterest expenses. From October 1993 through the first half of 1995, the company had repurchased nearly 11 million shares, more than 90 percent of the 12 million authorized in its share repurchase program. The company's share repurchase program lowered the average number of shares outstanding during 1994, helping to increase the ROE; but the program generated a lower equity-to-asset ratio. Its board of directors approved another repurchase program of 10 million shares. Also, SunTrust raised its dividend to $1.44 per share during the fourth quarter of 1994, achieving a dividend payout ratio of 30 percent.

The company initiated a companywide name change resulting in all of its banks adopting the name SunTrust. In addition, SunTrust is devising alternative delivery systems, investing in new technology to streamline processes, and concentrating on relationship banking with both existing and new customers. The use of image technology for corporate banking customers and TeleBank 24, a 24-hour-a-day telephone banking service for retail customers, ensure that SunTrust will have the capabilities to meet and anticipate growing banking needs.

ASSET-LIABILITY MANAGEMENT

The objective of the company's asset-liability management strategy is to optimize net interest income while minimizing the effect of interest rate changes on the net interest margin. As a result of the bank's conservative strategy of maintaining interest rate neutrality, its net interest margin has remained relatively stable. For example, the company's margin moved less than 10 basis points between mid-1993 and year-end 1994, despite large interest rate increases. In addition, the company's margin has remained in a rather narrow 60 basis point range during the last seven years.

The average life of securities in its investment portfolio was about 3.5 years at year-end 1994; however, adjustable rates reduced the average time to repricing to 2.4 years. Mortgage-backed securities accounted for just under 38 percent of the portfolio, while treasury securities accounted for close to 25 percent. Approximately

$11.5 billion in loans repriced within 30 days, while an additional $2.1 billion in loans repriced within 90 days at year-end 1994. SunTrust's board of directors authorized the repurchase of an additional 10 million shares of the company's common stock at the April 1995 meeting.

POTENTIAL FOR ADDITIONAL FEE INCOME

Fee income represented under 25 percent of total income in 1994, a bit lower than the superregional average. Trust income and service charges on deposits were the biggest contributors to fee income (see Table 11–4).

To generate additional fee income and to serve customers better, in 1994, Sun-Trust established a Section 20 subsidiary (Tier 1), SunTrust Capital Markets, Inc. (STCM). The company has authority to engage in underwriting and dealing activities in municipal revenue bonds, commercial paper, mortgage-backed securities, and asset-backed securities secured by consumer receivables. In a few years, once it has developed capabilities and experience, STCM might also apply to the Federal Reserve to offer more sophisticated products and services such as participations and corporate debt financings and equity financing under Tier 2 powers. Over time, STCM will provide relationship managers a single place to call for merger and acquisition advisory, structured finance, and capital sourcing services; acquisition of financing through securities issuance; distribution of securities through trading and sales; and investment of capital for both short- and long-term returns. SunTrust has joined other superregionals, such as BankAmerica, Banc One, Barnett, CoreStates, First Interstate, First Union, NationsBank, Norwest, and PNC, in offering Tier 1 services. BankAmerica, NationsBank, and First Union also offer Tier 2 services.

T A B L E 11–4

Noninterest Income (in millions)

	1994	1993
Trust income	$250.3	$247.0
Deposit service charges	218.4	225.9
Other charges and fees	121.1	142.1
Credit card fees	57.2	57.8
Securities gains (losses)	(2.7)	2.0
Trading account	8.0	11.3
Other income	47.6	40.4
Total	$699.9	$726.5

Source: SunTrust, 1994 *Annual Report.*

SunTrust's overall strategy focuses on affluent and wealthy clients and small to midsize commercial businesses. The company's additional focus on commercial business and value-added cross-selling to retail customers should further enhance earnings. The bank's trust and investment expertise should provide the leverage to penetrate further its client base and enhance business.[3]

SUMMARY

SunTrust's conservative management style of focusing on fee-based revenues, maintaining good control of expenses and credit quality, deploying capital effectively and making in-market, accretive acquisitions has led to consistent double-digit EPS increases over the last decade. This should continue in the future as the company is located in a high-growth region. SunTrust could expand its presence by fill-in mergers as well as moving into other Southeast states such as Alabama, before possibly expanding out of the region. In the meantime, AmSouth (Birmingham), Union Planters (Memphis), and First American (Nashville) represent attractive acquisition candidates. For example, if SunTrust purchased AmSouth at a price of 40 percent above market levels, the company would require only about 12 percent in cost savings/revenue generation for zero dilution. Accordingly, if SunTrust were to purchase First American for a price 40 percent above its current market value, it would need a 16 percent cost savings/revenue generation for zero dilution. SunTrust's acquisition of Union Planters for the same premium above market levels would require only a 2 percent cost savings/revenue generation for zero dilution.

On the other hand, SunTrust would make a marvelous takeover candidate for an out-of-state bank. However, it would take a rich premium to accomplish this. Its total market capitalization is in excess of $6 billion. Therefore, such an acquisition has a low probability of occurring. But, a merger of equals might make more sense if SunTrust decides to give up its independence. There have been rumors in the press of a merger-of-equals between Wachovia and SunTrust. That marriage would appear to be a good strategic fit, while offering cost pruning opportunities of about 25–30 percent of the noninterest expense of Wachovia.

In the meantime, the company is expected to exhibit high-quality, no-surprise, above-average growth in earnings per share for the foreseeable future as a result of improved loan demand and fee income as well as a decline in its efficiency ratio. Also, if SunTrust were to adjust its loan loss provision to its actual loan losses instead of taking its more conservative approach, earnings per share could increase by an additional 10 percent.

In summary, SunTrust's operating fundamentals are strong. Management has demonstrated its ability to maintain a solid, if not pristine, balance sheet through all phases of a business cycle. Conservative loan loss provisioning has continued to restrain bottom-line profitability, but such conservatism allows SunTrust to report consistently solid profits when some of its peers are building reserves in the early stages of an asset-quality downturn. Management has initiated a share repurchase program that should help to sustain EPS growth. This will be counterbalanced by strong internal capital generation. Management could choose to work down reserves slightly if fee-income trends deteriorate. In the meantime, SunTrust's ongoing efficiency and process review should allow for continuation of tight expense control and continued compound annual growth rates in excess of 10 percent for both earnings per share and book value.[4]

ENDNOTES

1. SunTrust Banks, Inc., 1994 *Annual Report.*
2. J.B. Williams, SunTrust news release, January 10, 1995, p. 1.
3. T.H. Hanley, "SunTrust Banks, Inc.," *CS First Boston,* January 11, 1995, p. 2.
4. "Banking Insights," *Duff & Phelps,* March 1995, p. 20.

T A B L E   11–5

SunTrust Banks, Inc., Financials

	1990	1991	1992	1993	1994
Earnings per share	$2.75	$2.90	$3.28	$3.77	$4.37
Assets (in millions)	$30,909	$32,797	$35,356	$37,525	$40,489
Net income (in millions)	$350.37	$370.67	$404.40	$473.73	$522.74
Return on assets	1.13%	1.13%	1.14%	1.26%	1.29%

	1994	
	(in millions)	**%**
Average earning assets	$36,112	
Securities	9,004	24.9
Loans	26,413	73.1
Other	695	2.0
Loans	28,548	
Construction and land	1,151	
Commercial mortgage	4,516	
Highly leveraged	0	
Commercial loans and leases	9,690	
Other foreign	273	
Term LCD	0	
Credit card receivables	690	
Other consumer	3,847	
Unearned discount	0	
Corporate	15,630	54.7
Consumer	4,537	15.8
Mortgages	8,381	29.3

	1990	1991	1992	1993	1994
Efficiency ratio	60.55	60.17	59.22	59.01	58.96
Shareholder equity (in millions)	$2,195	$2,435	$2,698	$2,877	$3,572
Preferred					
Common	$2,195	$2,435	$2,698	$2,877	$3,572

FIGURE   11-1

SunTrust Banks, Inc., Financial Charts

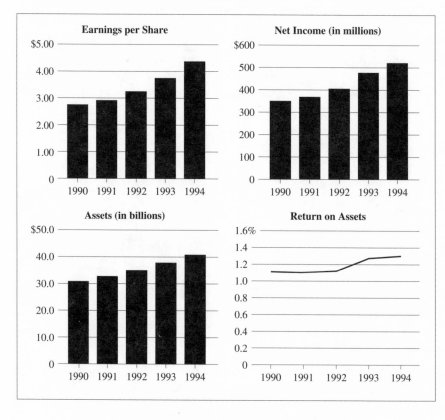

F I G U R E   11–2

SunTrust Banks, Inc., Financial Charts

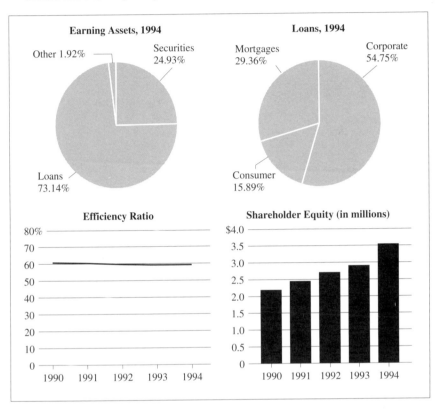

CHAPTER 12

Wachovia Corporation

Wachovia Corporation is a southeastern interstate bank holding company with good diversification and balance of business lines. The company had assets of $39.1 billion at year-end 1994. Its principal banking subsidiaries are Wachovia Bank of North Carolina, Wachovia Bank of Georgia, and Wachovia Bank of South Carolina. Wachovia has consistently produced some of banking's best returns on assets and equity, despite a high level of stockholders' equity, which was 8.4 percent of total assets in 1994, third highest among the 25 largest banks in the United States. In addition to excellent profitability ratios, Wachovia is noted for strong credit controls, good control of operating costs, conservative risk assessment, sound balance sheet management, and consistent production of quality earnings. Wachovia is considered one of the best managed and most profitable banks in the industry.

Wachovia had 493 banking offices in 214 cities throughout its three primary states, with 127 offices in Georgia, 216 in North Carolina, and 150 in South Carolina at year-end 1994 (see Table 12–1). Wachovia also had 625 ATMs, with 297 in North Carolina, 189 in Georgia, and 166 in South Carolina. It also has corporate banking services in New York and Chicago and representative offices in London and Tokyo. There is a foreign branch in Grand Cayman and an Edge Act subsidiary in New York City. In addition, the First National Bank of Atlanta in Wilmington, Delaware, provides credit card operating services for Wachovia's affiliated banks.

In April 1991, Wachovia introduced a credit card prime plus 2.9 percent variable option and with a $39 annual fee. The card, called Prime Plus, has helped generate new accounts and loan outstandings. The company had $1.5 billion in credit card loans when Prime Plus was offered initially. However, at year-end 1994, outstanding credit card loans exceeded $3.5 billion, over 12 percent of total loans.

T A B L E   12–1

Wachovia's Market Share and Branches, September 30, 1994

	North Carolina		Georgia		South Carolina	
	Share	Rank	Share	Rank	Share	Rank
Percent of total bank deposits	15.8	2	10.1	4	21.0	2
Percent of total bank loans	16.5	3	16.1	2	14.8	2
Number of branches	216	5	127	5	150	2

Source: Wachovia Corporation.

Approximately 1.5 million of the 2.5 million accounts were outside of the three home states. Wachovia was the 15th largest bank credit card issuer in the nation in 1994.

Wachovia ranks among the top 10 banks in relationships with the largest corporations in the United States and consistently is rated one of the top three banks in cash management and operational services. More than 1,200 customers use the bank's wholesale lockbox services and over 1,000 corporate customers use its disbursing services. It continues to develop leading technologically based corporate cash management services. As an example, Wachovia offers digitized check imaging to wholesale customers. The bank also uses a check imaging system to expedite the proofing and encoding of checks to other banks for collection.

Wachovia ranked 10th among U.S. banks in master trust assets and 13th in master trust/custodial assets. Wachovia also operates 18 residential mortgage loan offices in its primary markets. It generates additional fee income by providing processing and systems development services for banks. Wachovia is also an underwriter and trader of state and local government securities and provides discount brokerage, foreign exchange, corporate financing, money market, and full personal and corporate trust services. Wachovia's trust function provides services across the nation and has under custody and administration assets totaling about $79 billion, with in excess of $17 billion under discretionary investment management. Also, at year-end 1994, Wachovia had an additional $2.2 billion of in-house mutual fund assets under management in its Biltmore Funds Group. Wachovia earns 31.5 percent of revenues from noninterest income, the largest sources of which are service charges on deposit accounts, trust services, and credit card income (see Table 12–2).

T A B L E   12–2

Noninterest Income (in millions)

Source	1994
Service charges, deposit accounts	$196
Trust services	128
Credit cards	112
Mortgage fees	33
Trading accounts	3
Insurance premiums/commissions	12
Bankers' acceptances/LOC	23
Other service/fee charges	57
Other income	40
Investment security gains	3
Total	$607

Source: Wachovia Corporation, 1994 *Annual Report.*

FINANCIAL RATIOS

Wachovia is best known for the quality of its management, superior financial ratios, exceptionally strong credit quality and cost control of noninterest expenses, applied technology, trust department investments and operations, and a strong capital position. Loan losses were at a minuscule 0.29 percent of average loans in 1994. Credit card net charge-offs were at 1.66 percent of average credit card loans outstanding, well below industry averages. Also, nonperforming assets declined to a low 0.26 percent of assets in 1994. In addition, its ratio of loan loss reserves to nonperforming loans was at 516 percent at year-end 1994. However, Wachovia had reserves of only 1.57 percent of total loans. As loan growth accelerates and higher loan losses accompany higher interest rates, Wachovia may have to increase its provision to loan losses.

Wachovia has a strong capital base, with shareholders' equity as a percentage of assets at 8.39 percent and the Tier 1 capital ratio at 9.89 percent for 1994 (see Table 12–3).

The company posted an overhead ratio of 54 percent in 1994, compared to 56 percent in 1993, among the best in the industry. This was followed by a ratio of 52.7 percent in the first half of 1995. It is expected that Wachovia will improve its efficiency ratio to the 48–50 percent range by 1997. The ratio was at 58 percent in 1992 and 62 percent in 1991. Wachovia ranked among the top 3 banks of the

T A B L E   12–3

Comparison of Capital Levels

	1989	1990	1991	1992	1993	1994 (9 months)
Wachovia	7.25%	7.55%	7.68%	8.16%	8.54%	8.37%
25 largest banks	4.90	4.82	5.13	6.16	6.57	6.98

Source: Wachovia Corporation.

largest 50 in efficiency. The median overhead ratio for the top 50 banks was at approximately 62 percent in the first half of 1994. During 1994, Wachovia's ROE and ROA were 17.40 percent and 1.46 percent, respectively. This compared to an identical ROA and a 17.1 percent ROE in 1993. During the first half of 1995, Wachovia's ROE was 18.48 percent and ROA was 1.52 percent. Net income was $539 million in 1994, compared to $492 million in 1993. Although Wachovia ranked 23rd in asset size, its ROE was 8th and ROA 3rd among the 25 largest banking companies. The dividend payout ratio averaged just under 40 percent. The ratio of noninterest income to net revenue is expected to increase slowly over the next few years, unless a nonbanking acquisition takes place, especially since the bank sold its mortgage-servicing unit.

In a speech before financial analysts on February 3, 1994, in Orlando, Florida, L.M. Baker, Jr., the new CEO, indicated that "Wachovia's guiding principles, forged over more than a century, remain the same in good or hard times. We pursue progressive business strategies within the discipline of strong financial and credit principles. Our dedication to soundness, profitability, and growth remains unchanged." In the passage of leadership from John Medlin to Baker, Wachovia's strong heritage superseded personalities; the organization has done so well historically that there was little to fix. However, the company appears to be streamlining its product delivery by technology, arming employees with state-of-the-art systems that will enable them to become more efficient and smarter, while eliminating as much rework as possible. As efficient as the company has been, Wachovia appears poised to lower cost ratios further while continuing to provide high-quality service. Baker earlier did the same as the head of the North Carolina bank; he is now expanding that effort systemwide.[1]

Wachovia has traditionally maintained a conservative balance sheet. Although the securities portfolio accounted for about 20 percent of assets in 1994, the bank's unrealized securities losses within its held-to-maturity portfolio amounted to less than .5 percent at year-end 1994, compared to an average loss of 3.5 percent among the universe of superregionals.

Wachovia Corporation issued $250 million in 30-year notes during the fourth quarter of 1995. This issue carried a 10-year put option. The security reflects the belief by Wachovia's management that interest rates have reached a low point. Although Wachovia is a premier banking institution in terms of asset quality, capital strength, control of expenses, and earnings quality, it seems to be remaining on the sidelines when it comes to generating additional fee-based businesses and earnings momentum through acquisitions. With a premium valuation relative to other superregionals, it is surprising that Wachovia hasn't sought at least fill-in acquisitions in the Carolinas and Georgia, where cost-cutting and cross-selling of in-house products and services would enhance both short-term and long-term earnings growth. A major strategic acquisition by Wachovia is a strong possibility, with a chance of expansion into Virginia. Most analysts anticipate that Wachovia will initiate some acquisition activity in 1996–97 as the importance of market share in a more difficult earnings environment becomes apparent. However, Wachovia remains a staunch supporter of shareholder value and would not undertake a merger that would erode it. As the earnings environment becomes more difficult for the smaller banks in the Southeast, takeover premiums should lessen, and Wachovia may use such an opportunity to enhance its franchise.[2] Acquisitions are likely to have a role in supporting the growth of the bank's strategic businesses and in helping provide access to more customers. Management is not obsessed with size nor attracted to transactions that dilute shareholder value. Strategic acquisitions or mergers should enhance product capabilities, increase the scale of existing businesses, provide access to a larger base of customers, and increase shareholder value over time. In 1995, it made only one small acquisition. Wachovia agreed to acquire First National Bancshares of Henry County (GA) with assets of $33 million and deposits of $27.3 million.

Business Week and some bank stock analysts have suggested that Wachovia is considering a merger-of-equals with SunTrust Banks. This merger would be a good strategic fit. There would be good cost savings within overlapping branch systems in Georgia and within the two large bank trust departments that could be consolidated into one primary location. Also, Wachovia could easily absorb SunTrust's much smaller credit card group, consolidating that operation in an efficient manner. There is a strong credit quality culture at both banks and good penetration of middle-market and larger corporations on the commercial banking front. Both banks are efficient and well-managed, leaving additional potential for revenue enhancement and modest cost cutting in overlapping areas. The combined bank would benefit from increased geographic and industry diversification of the loan portfolio.

Wachovia sold its $9 billion residential mortgage-servicing portfolio during 1995 to GE Capital Mortgage Services. However, the corporation is committed to enhancing its mortgage origination position. A major resource to support this effort was the introduction of the Wachovia Mortgage Origination System (WMOS), a new automated mortgage application system designed to support branches and mortgage offices. WMOS provides comparisons of mortgage products, reduces application time, and gives lenders immediate cross-selling opportunities.

TECHNOLOGICAL DEVELOPMENTS

The bank initiated a toll-free telephone service that allows retail customers to make banking transactions seven days a week, 24 hours a day. Over 10,000 calls per day are being handled by this phone system. After reaching a Wachovia representative, a customer can ask questions, initiate an account application, obtain rate quotes on savings vehicles and loans, or transfer funds. Wachovia also wants to foster a more aggressive sales-oriented culture throughout the retail bank, from tellers through banking managers. The telephone system frees bank personnel for more effective selling.

Wachovia has also implemented SCORE (strategic credit operation reengineering effort), which consolidates credit operations in 12 cities into Winston-Salem. It is estimated that the company's new branch standardization program will eliminate personnel. On the mortgage front, 14 processing centers are being consolidated into the center at Columbia, South Carolina. In addition, 27 contract buying centers related to sales finance are being consolidated into two centers. Wachovia also initiates a PC-driven mortgage application process, which makes it virtually impossible to make errors, allowing greater cross-selling opportunities. The system also does the documentation automatically for the client. Wachovia has to be included among the leaders in the inevitable change in delivery of financial products and services; the bank will benefit over time because of its use of applied technology to improve service while cutting operating expenses.

Wachovia views technology as a way of adding value to banking products and services. The goal of its information services division is to craft and manage an infrastructure to support business units that will be sufficiently broad and adaptable to avoid reengineering with each advance in technology. Wachovia expects its number of full-service branches to decline substantially in the future as minibranches and technology take their place and as customers make more use of telephones, PCs, and ATMs. Wachovia views the integration of customer information across all functions of the corporation as a key technological advance in retail banking that will allow for more intelligent selling of products and services to targeted prospects. Sharing of customer information across banking functions is extremely important as the banking industry must become more efficient.[3]

For corporate customers, Wachovia offers CD-ROM check imaging. Through this technology, the bank can transfer images of checks onto compact disks for customers. Wachovia also supplies corporate customers with the software to use the CD-ROM disks.

Wachovia spent large sums of money to unify all of its banking operations with an interactive branch automation system and a sophisticated common general ledger system. Future investments will be directed toward growth-enhancing technology designed to create value-added products, facilitate marketing and sales efforts, and provide management with more comprehensive measurement information. There will be an enhanced trust system, products based in image processing, next-generation interactive PC systems for retail customers, and Wachovia Connection, a PC-based gateway to bank information for corporate treasurers. Other technology will be used to develop a more sophisticated system for Wachovia's bankcard, strengthen ATM capabilities, consolidate customer information databases, and expand Wachovia's brokerage capability.

Wachovia has made major organizational and management realignments to help support its strategic initiative and to grow relationships. Two divisions, Corporate Financial Services and General Banking, were formed. Corporate Financial Services includes all credit and noncredit corporate banking services, corporate trust, employee benefit, and charitable trust services. General Banking is charged with implementing a single strategic direction for Wachovia's community banks and more effective coordination of services aimed at the consumer market, including personal trust and investment services. Wachovia seeks more effective selling of products and services. The company has begun to build its sales capability for both corporate and consumer relations. On the corporate front, a 65-member sales team productivity (STP) task force has been established to increase selling effectiveness by positing bankers to bring the best talent to each customer relationship. The shifting of responsibilities under the STP program is expected to double the time available to bankers for selling. On the consumer banking front, 115 investment counselors, approximately one for every four branches, were deployed in key home state areas to sell a full range of investment products.

HISTORY

On December 5, 1985, Wachovia Corp. (about $9 billion in assets) and First Atlanta Corp. ($7 billion in assets) merged to form First Wachovia Corp. Early the next year, the company sold First Atlanta Mortgage Corp. In 1990, Southern First Federal Savings and Loan Association was merged into the First National Bank of Atlanta. The name of the parent company was changed to Wachovia Corporation on May 20, 1991.

Wachovia acquired South Carolina National Corporation ($7.1 billion in assets) later in 1991, becoming the 19th largest bank holding company in the United States. South Carolina National operates under its own name as a wholly owned subsidiary of Wachovia Corporation.

South Carolina National

SC National Corporation was formed in 1971, succeeding South Carolina National Bank. However, the name of the holding company was changed to its current name, South Carolina National Corporation, in 1972. During the period from 1973 through 1991, the company made seven major acquisitions in South Carolina: Bank of Berkeley (Moncks Corner), First Carolina Bank in Beaufort County, Bank of Gaffney, First Bankshares Corp., Bank of Fairfield (Winnsboro), Southern Provident Life Insurance Company, and Atlantic Savings Bank.

SUMMARY

Wachovia is recognized as an industry leader in credit quality, efficiency, and management quality, as reflected in its exemplary financial ratios. The bank has enjoyed a heritage of strong loan quality that spans generations. Wachovia should be able to generate low double-digit EPS increases for 1995 and 1996. However, the company will probably need more distribution outlets or sources of fee income to maintain its superb profitability record over time. Management's approach to acquisitions is highly disciplined and controlled; the company ensures that its own standards are firmly entrenched in an acquired company before purchasing additional targets. Both in-house mergers and significant contiguous-market mergers could provide additional opportunities for cross-selling. Product-driven mergers that increase fee income are also possible. Wachovia carefully studies its market opportunities and is quite sensitive to dilution of EPS in a potential acquisition.

Although the company has no acute problems, it is likely to face intense competition for loans and deposits in North Carolina. These factors could contribute to a decline in margins. Additionally, the bank may need to increase loan loss reserves to meet anticipated charge-offs associated with a strong increase in loan demand and a weak economy. To offset these potential but mild problems, Wachovia will need additional income to remain among the industry leaders.

The key strategies that should help Wachovia maintain a leadership position and outstanding performance include:

- Managing its portfolio of businesses to achieve sound profitable growth.
- Using mergers and acquisitions to complement business development strategies.
- Seeking new markets at home and abroad.
- Becoming more effective in selling products and services, while effectively managing costs.
- Redirecting technology investments to support sales and service capabilities.
- Assessing and prudently managing the use of capital.[4]

ENDNOTES

1. "Bank Stock Valuation Package," *Montgomery Securities Research*, April 11, 1994, p. 15.
2. T.H. Hanley, "Wachovia Corporation," *CS First Boston*, January 17, 1995, p. 3.
3. T.H. Hanley, P.J. Carter, and A.B. Collins, "Separating the Winners from the Losers in the Banking Industry," *CS First Boston*, January 14, 1995, p. 14.
4. Wachovia Corporation, 1994 *Annual Report*, p. 7.

T A B L E   12-4

Wachovia Corporation Financials

	1990	1991	1992	1993	1994
Earnings per share	$2.10	$1.32	$2.48	$2.81	$3.12
Assets (in millions)	$30,469	$32,045	$31,832	$33,620	$37,029
Net income (in millions)	$345.68	$229.54	$433.23	$492.10	$539.06
Return on assets	1.13%	0.72$	1.36%	1.46%	1.46%

	1994	
	(in millions)	%
Average earning assets	$32,794	100
Securities	7,683	23
Loans	24,213	74
Other	898	3
Loans	25,889	100
Construction and land	553	
Commercial mortgage	3,483	
Highly leveraged		
Commercial loans and leases	10,376	
Other foreign	254	
Term LCD		
Credit card receivables	3,969	
Other consumer	3,433	
Unearned discount		
Corporate	14,666	57
Consumer	7,402	29
Mortgages	3,821	15

	1990	1991	1992	1993	1994
Efficiency ratio	58.08	58.51	57.01	55.39	54.36
Shareholder equity (in millions)	$2,237	$2,462	$2,596	$2,872	$3,096
Preferred					
Common	$2,237	$2,462	$2,596	$2,872	$3,096

F I G U R E   12–1

Wachovia Corporation Financial Charts

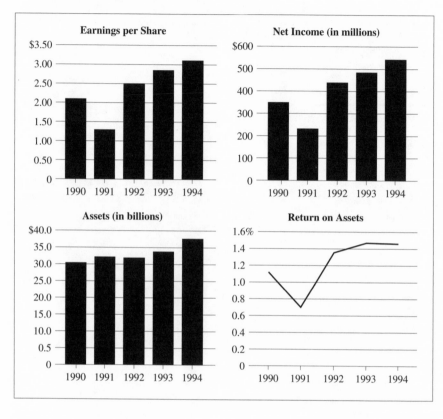

F I G U R E   12–2

Wachovia Corporation Financial Charts

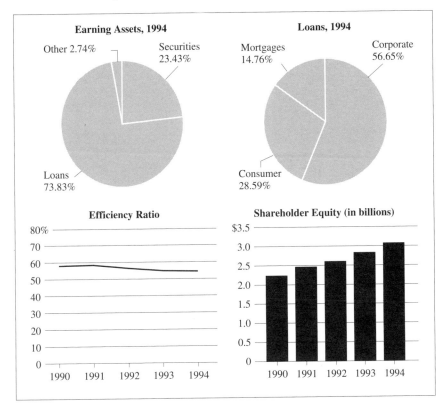

Earning Assets, 1994

Other 2.74%   Securities
                     23.43%

Loans
73.83%

Loans, 1994

Mortgages   Corporate
14.76%   56.65%

Consumer
28.59%

Efficiency Ratio

Shareholder Equity (in billions)

CHAPTER 13

Barnett Banks, Inc.

Barnett Banks, Inc., operated over 628 banking offices and 772 ATMs in Florida and Georgia during 1994. Barnett has the largest ATM network in Florida, with 25 percent more ATMs than its nearest competitor. Headquartered in Jacksonville, the company had total assets of $41.3 billion at year-end 1994, making it the largest bank in Florida and the 25th largest in the United States. Barnett enjoys some form of relationship with 35–40 percent of all households in Florida; yet, this business accounts for only 8 percent of the amount that households spend on all financial services including mutual funds and insurance. The bank leads the Florida marketplace in residential mortgage originations (10 percent market share), corporate middle-market lending (25 percent share), and consumer loans (33 percent share). In addition, the company's retail distribution network is within 10 minutes of 96 percent of the state's households. Barnett also holds high market shares in trust accounts (18 percent), small-business lending (11 percent), and total deposits (20.5 percent including thrifts and 26 percent excluding thrifts).

The company earned $488 million in 1994, with a return on assets of 1.28 percent (the highest in company history) and return on equity of 16.10 percent in 1994 compared to net income of $421 million in 1993, an ROA of 1.13 percent, and an ROE of 15.4 percent. By increasing market share in small-business lending, trust-related activities, residential mortgage lending, and fee income, the company is stimulating revenue growth. Cost containment, declining credit expenses, and accretion from recent acquisitions are also benefiting earnings. ROA is expected to reach 1.32 percent by 1996 (see Table 13–1).

Barnett has made substantial progress in improving its credit quality by reducing its nonperforming asset ratio to 0.76 percent in 1994 from 2.22 percent in 1992. In addition, reserves to nonperforming assets climbed from 65 percent in 1992 to 187 percent in 1994. Barnett also improved its productivity by reducing the overhead ratio to 61.8 percent in 1994 (60.2 percent in the third quarter of 1995) from 65.3 percent in 1993 and 69 percent in 1992. The company has targeted a 58 percent ratio for 1995 and 56 percent for 1996 (see Table 13–2). The company's expense control should be the result of consolidation of operations, reengineering, continuous examination of efficiencies within each of its lines of business, products, and services, as well as technological enhancements. Continuous improvements resulting from the identification and institutionalization of business line "best practices" should pay off in both productivity and market share gains. Although Barnett's estimated efficiency ratios appear to be modest, its decentralized banking structure lends itself to a more elevated expense base than that of Wachovia and other regional peers.[1]

On the positive side, Barnett's overall headcount rose by only 280 in 1994, despite 524 additional full-time equivalent (FTE) employees related to the 1994 acquisitions of Loan America and Glendale Federal's Florida deposit franchise. Further cost containment will come from consolidation, such as lowering head

T A B L E   13–1

Profitability Outlook, 1993–1996

	1993	1994	1995	1996
ROA	1.13%	1.28%	1.29%	1.32%
ROE	15.4	16.1	16.5	17.0

T A B L E   13–2

Productivity Outlook, 1992–1995

	1992	1993	1994	1995*
Overhead ratio as percent of assets	71%	65%	61%	58%
Noninterest expense/average share equity	4.58	4.02	3.57	3.32
Total deposits (in billions)	$34.7	$32.6	$35.1	
Total branches	735	621	628	
Deposits per branch (in millions)	$47	$53	$56	
Employees (FTE)	20,737	18,649	18,929	

* Estimated by authors.

Source: Company reports.

count and increasing back-office efficiency. Barnett closed about 30 of its 628 branches in 1995. Depending on the success of telephone banking and other alternative delivery initiatives, Barnett may close up to 20 percent of its branches in the next few years. The company had more than adequate capital with an equity-to-asset ratio of 7.36 percent and a Tier 1 ratio of 10.74 percent in 1994.

Barnett had $28.5 billion in loans outstanding at year-end 1994. Twenty-seven percent of the loans were classified as commercial, while 73 percent were consumer oriented. This compared with 42 percent commercial and 58 percent consumer in 1990. Of the 1994 total, about 37 percent were in residential mortgages, 28 percent in installment loans, 16 percent in commercial and industrial loans, 8 percent in commercial mortgages, 5 percent in bankcard loans, and 3 percent in construction loans. Consumer loans are dominated by mortgages and car loans (see Table 13–3). Credit quality was not a problem as net charge-offs as a percentage of average loans outstanding was at 0.34 percent for 1994, the best ratio reported since 1985. Barnett intends to increase its small-business market share from 14 percent to 20 percent in three years by reducing underwriting time and expanding offerings to include payroll processing, tax preparation, business credit cards, and other services.

In the 1980s, Barnett grew rapidly by expanding throughout Florida through the acquisition of other banks, followed by branching to capture the growth of those markets. However, Barnett's mission in the 1990s is to create value for owners, customers, and employees. Its goal is to leverage its distribution network by meeting more of its retail customers' financial needs, emphasizing small-business

T A B L E   13–3

Changing Loan Mix

Type of Loan	December 31, 1990	December 31, 1994
Commercial	19%	16%
Construction	9	3
Commercial mortgages	14	8
Total commercial	42	27
Residential mortgages	27	37
Installment	24	28
Bankcard	4	5
Credit lines	2	3
Total consumer	57%	73%
Total loans (in billions)	$28.1	$28.5

Source: Company reports.

banking, and expanding other fee-based businesses. Barnett plans to pursue diversified income opportunities, including internal initiatives, acquisitions, and alliances in attractive markets throughout the country that complement, leverage, and expand the bank's core capabilities.[2]

Barnett intends to enhance customer relationships by expanding its product line, developing new sales and service incentives, and creating new delivery systems that make banking at Barnett more attractive. The bank views information technology as a key to capitalizing on market positions, providing superior customer service, and maintaining competitive cost structures. Barnett employs customer information files (CIFs) to help target-marketing efforts, to meet the evolving needs of customers, to provide improved customer service, and to improve operating efficiencies. Unlike CIFs used by most banks, this CIF determines profitability discretely at the customer and transaction levels and permits predictive modeling. During 1996 and early 1997, two dozen analysts will be using this CIF to develop value propositions to convert the 50 percent of Barnett's customers who are unprofitable into profitable ones.

Barnett is among a handful of banking companies that understand individual customer profitability and customer behavior. Management has just begun to alter strategies based on what it has learned about customer behavior and profitability. Barnett will begin to reduce its expenses by shifting customer demand out of the branches and to lower cost delivery systems such as ATMs and telebanking. There should also be a major revenue impact by 1997 as a result of more focused marketing.

In the 1980s, Barnett's banking sales approach revolved around generating deposit market share; now, however, the company sets sales targets for all products and pays incentives for meeting or exceeding those goals. Basic banking services still remain the core of the business, but Barnett has become a more diversified financial services organization by offering other products, such as mutual funds, stocks, bonds, annuities, and insurance to meet customer needs and to earn fee income. Barnett's goal is to earn consistently 1.2 percent to 1.3 percent on assets, while increasing the percentage of revenues earned by fees and by improving its productivity. The company has also restructured its loan portfolio, emphasizing loans to consumers and small businesses, while reducing commercial real estate loans to less than 12 percent of total loans. Its commercial strategy appears to deemphasize large corporate loans, while targeting small-business and middle-market banking, cash management, and international services. As Charles E. Rice, chairman and CEO, indicated in a January 1995 press release:

> Barnett in 1994 made significant progress toward our strategic goals. We achieved record earnings and profitability while strengthening our core banking business through the acquisition of the Florida franchise of Glendale Savings Bank, and we advanced our diversification strategy through the

acquisition of Loan America Financial Corporation and the pending purchase of EquiCredit Corporation . . . We will continue to develop initiatives to build our traditional banking franchise and diversify our company.

In summary, Barnett's vision for the 1990s focuses on the pursuit of five critically important goals: improving credit quality, increasing efficiency, ensuring business-line profitability, enhancing sales and services, and building a fortress bank. Barnett intends to build customer relationships by selling multiple products and services, backed with strong reserves and capital, within the framework of a dominant franchise that is highly profitable and diversified in its revenue stream. Over the remainder of the decade, Barnett's goal is to become the relationship leader with both product and customer penetration statewide. The strategy has translated into new product development; reengineering of its processes; creation, training, and cultivation of store-based sales forces; use of self-service technology; and the creation of long-term value by increased cross-selling of products and services. The focus on relationship profitability will replace transaction or value growth targets. Barnett is working on strengthening its sales culture and exploring new delivery systems and interactive television. Management will broaden its product line by making, buying, or forming alliances to offer investment products, insurance, and annuities.[3]

Barnett is marketing point-of-sale debit cards to credit card merchants at all levels, especially to supermarkets that do not yet have terminals for credit card acceptance. The bank hopes to capitalize on its 20,000-merchant credit card base in the sale of debit cards. In late 1994, Barnett introduced the Super Card Check Card, a debit card that can be used anywhere Visa is accepted. It can be used to withdraw cash from an ATM machine or to make a purchase at selected point-of-sale terminals in grocery and other stores. The Gator One Card (a debit card/student ID card for the University of Florida) was also introduced.

HISTORY

William B. Barnett established the Bank of Jacksonville in 1877, changing the name to the National Bank of Jacksonville in 1888. The family name became part of the corporate culture when the bank emerged from a reorganization as Barnett First National Bank of Jacksonville in 1908. Although many banks failed during the Great Depression, Barnett National Securities Corporation, a bank holding company, was formed in 1930. The new entity quickly acquired and reopened three banks that had failed.

Barnett Bank stock was sold to the public on a limited basis in the mid-1950s, and the shares were listed in the OTC market in 1962. The bank benefited from the postwar growth of Florida as a retirement haven, where immigrating senior citizens brought their savings and pensions to the financial institutions of the Sunshine State.

Under the leadership of Guy W. Botts, the company acquired eight local banks and opened a ninth in Jacksonville during the late 1960s. Each of these banks was a separate corporation composed of a single full-service banking office. The name was changed first to Barnett Banks of Florida in 1969 and to Barnett Banks, Inc., in 1987. Barnett made two acquisitions in 1988 and four in 1989 in Georgia: it acquired First Federal Savings and Loan Association of Columbus from the FSLIC; Fulton Bancshares of Palmetto; ANB Bancshares of Brunswick; Southern Federal Savings Bank in Thomasville from the FSLIC; FMB Financial Holding, Inc. of Fayetteville; and Investors Trust Financial Corp of Duluth. It also formed Barnett Bank of Atlanta with the consolidation of First Fulton Bank and Trust and Barnett Banks, N.A.

During 1990, Barnett acquired nine troubled financial institutions: First American Bank and Trust, First Federal Savings and Loan Association of the Florida Keys, Tucker State Bank of Jacksonville, and Haven Savings and Loan Association from the FDIC; Financial Processors, Inc.; and First Federal Savings and Loan of Largo, Lincoln Savings and Loan, Royal Palm Savings and Loan, and Empire Savings Bank of America, Florida Division, from the RTC.

RECENT ACTIVITY

During 1992, Barnett acquired CSX Commercial Services, Inc., and United Savings of America. Barnett sold the assets and liabilities of CreditQuick, Inc., and CreditQuick Finance Company to American General Finance, Inc. Barnett outbid three competitors when it acquired First Florida Banks, Inc., with a strong retail presence in the Tampa and Sarasota areas. It was the biggest merger in Barnett history, uniting the two oldest banks in the state.

That acquisition fit many of Barnett's strategic goals by improving the company's risk profile through geographic diversification of assets, increasing noninterest income dramatically through the large trust department of First Florida, and improving productivity through the closing of redundant branches and the elimination of unnecessary employees. Barnett sold the data processing business and the student loan division acquired from First Florida.

In 1993, Barnett swapped its Metro Atlanta banks for Bank South's bank in Pensacola, People's National Bank of Pensacola, plus cash and almost 5 percent of Bank South's common stock. In the following year, Barnett agreed to acquire for about $62 million in cash Loan America Financial Company, the nation's 10th largest mortgage wholesaler. Loan America originated $3.4 billion in mortgages in 1993; these would complement Barnett's originations, which also totaled $3.4 billion in 1993. However, the combined organizations totaled only $4.3 billion in 1994 as mortgage borrowing shrank nationally. In addition, Loan America's servicing portfolio of $3.6 billion will be combined with Barnett's portfolio of $13.1 billion, placing the operation among the top 30 in the country. The purchase provides entry into the wholesale mortgage origination business, which involves making loans through brokers.

Barnett acquired Glendale Federal Bank's Florida operation with retail deposits of about $3.6 billion and 60 branch offices, outbidding several rivals by paying a 6.7 percent premium. Barnett intends to consolidate this bank with its local Barnett Bank, closing redundant branches. The company hopes to generate additional fee income from this merger, while cutting operating costs. Glendale's deposit base is expected to enhance Barnett's deposit market share in at least five important counties. In Dade County (Miami), the new market share will be 12.5 percent, up from 11.0 percent. This places Barnett in second place behind First Union, which had acquired the Southeast Bank Franchise (headquartered in Miami) in the 1980s. Barnett will be number one in market share in four other counties. In Palm Beach County, its pro forma market share will be increased from 14.4 percent to 17.3 percent; in Broward County (Fort Lauderdale), from 11.4 percent to 19.0 percent; in Hillsborough County (Tampa), from 26.4 to 31.8 percent; and in Pinellas County, from 17.8 to 22.8 percent. Barnett will have a 20 percent share of actual deposits as a whole in the Sunshine State. Another positive impact of the Glendale acquisition is that management can replace up to $2 billion in overnight funding with an even greater amount of core deposits paying lower interest rates, on average, of about 175 basis points.

FEE INCOME

In September 1994, Barnett Banks agreed to acquire EquiCredit Corp., a consumer finance company that operates 89 offices in 29 states, with concentrations in Florida, Illinois, California, and Ohio, among others. EquiCredit diversifies Barnett's income stream to a broader geographic customer base and product line.[4]

EquiCredit, headquartered in Barnett's hometown of Jacksonville, sells and services loans secured by first or second mortgages on residential property. The company has a servicing portfolio of $16 billion in residential mortgages, and uses a network of brokers to originate loans, which totaled $602 million in 1993. EquiCredit caters to customers with blemished credit histories and lower incomes than typical commercial bank customers. These clients pay more for credit, bringing potentially higher spreads on loans. EquiCredit's management is experienced and competent as can be seen by the low charge-off ratio for a company in this business line. For example, net charge-offs averaged 0.54 percent in the first half of 1994. The ROE was a healthy 21.2 percent in 1993 and about 23 percent for the first half of 1994. The acquisition also provides cross-selling opportunities through the Loan America broker network and the ability to offer Barnett products, such as credit cards and car loans, to EquiCredit customers. In addition, the acquisition provides opportunities for administrative cost, technology application, and servicing synergy. The transaction should enhance Barnett's fee income through securitization and servicing of mortgage assets.[5]

Barnett agreed to pay $322 million for EquiCredit, about 12 times estimated 1994 earnings. The acquisition should add to Barnett's earnings in 1995 and will be accounted for as a purchase. The acquisition will reduce the tangible equity ratio by about 50 basis points, but even so, capital levels remain strong. This acquisition is in keeping with Barnett's strategy of complementing its core banking business with acquisitions of related financial concerns, such as its previous acquisition of Loan America Financial, a nationwide wholesale mortgage company. Barnett also agreed in early 1995 to acquire Banc Plus, a national full-service mortgage banking company with 54 retail and 9 wholesale offices in 23 states. Banc Plus originated $1.5 billion in loans during 1994 and had a servicing portfolio of $14 billion. After the finalization of the acquisition of Banc Plus, Barnett should be about the 18th largest mortgage servicer with a $32 billion portfolio. Expansion nationally is likely to be pursued through gradual internal growth and small acquisitions. Management seeks to grow Barnett into a top 10 mortgage participant within five years. This would require a servicing portfolio of $75–100 billion. The company also is expected to expand its consumer finance operation to selected national markets in small steps.

The company launched a family of mutual funds called the Emerald Funds to keep customers "inside the Barnett family." To reinforce and support mutual fund sales, Barnett is giving customers with at least $15,000 invested in Emerald Funds access to its Premier Account. This account allows upscale perks such as no-fee credit cards, ATM cards with a $1,000-a-day withdrawal capability, and free checking. Barnett has placed investment representatives in branches who provide a single reference point for information on any investment product, such as mutual funds and annuities.

Barnett ranks 22nd among U.S. banks with credit card outstandings of $1.4 billion and over one million cardholders. The company has experienced good growth as a result of a direct-mail program. Barnett is also one of the first banks to utilize image processing systems at three of its check processing centers, hoping to generate better service for customers and reduce mailing costs, while reaping a return of 15 to 18 percent on its investment in new technology. Barnett's management is leveraging its extensive distribution network throughout Florida and cross-selling a broad variety of products to its current customers and new customers by enhancing service and marketing; the goal is to attract an "increased share of wallet."[6] Armed with a new sales management system that permits the company to gauge profit potential by business line and market, Barnett would like to penetrate further the consumer, small-business, and middle markets in Florida. Barnett should accomplish this as it shifts from being a service-oriented company to focusing on sales using newly designed customer information systems.

The company's greatest challenge will be to boost fee-based revenue. Barnett is still struggling to boost fee income as a percent of total revenues. During 1994, fee-based revenues excluding securities transactions, comprised 25 percent of Barnett's total revenues (see Table 13–4). Although that percentage is likely to rise to 29 percent by 1996, it is well below its peers. The reason behind the weak noninterest income growth is in part related to the sale of several fee-based sources of income (for example, the student loan services and origination business, the bond administration group, and the processing business). On the other hand, the bank is in a relatively strong position and could take advantage of its extensive distribution system to expand fee income.[7] It will certainly generate higher fee income from the Banc Plus acquisition beginning in 1995. Barnett began to diversify its revenue stream through acquisitions of financial service companies with regional or national franchises in complementary lines of business. Barnett's management is expected to focus on enhancing fee income by geographic expansion of product lines. Barnett appears more inclined to deploy the $300 million in capital generated each year into a portfolio of nonregulated companies with growth characteristics more attractive than that available in commercial banking. Mortgage banking and assets management are areas tapped for potential future growth.[8]

Barnett's efforts to generate additional fee income have also been hampered by state law prohibiting banks from selling insurance. Barnett has a case pending before the Supreme Court to overturn the law.

T A B L E   13–4

Fee Income, 1992–1994

Source	1992	1993	1994
Service charges on deposits	$215.8	$22.6	$227.5
Trust income	72.5	82.2	77.4
Credit cards	58.7	55.2	54.4
Mortgage banking	32.8	40.9	33.1
Brokerage	32.7	41.1	30.0
Other service charges/fees	140.5	131.6	104.8
Securities transactions	34.1	(2.1)	(13.1)
Other income	33.3	27.3	28.4
Total fee income	$620.7	$599.0	$542.6

Source: Barnett, 1994 *Annual Report*.

POTPOURRI

Barnett has deployed excess capital into major repurchases of common shares and will continue to do that through April 15, 1996. On that date, the company plans to call in its series A preferred shares. Barnett had previously called its Series C shares in September 1995. The repurchases of both common and preferred stock are additive to EPS.

In addition, Barnett agreed to acquire First Financial Bancshares (Lake Wales, Florida) for $20 million in cash. The acquisition of the $118 million-asset thrift will enable Barnett to solidify its position in the growing Polk County market.

SUMMARY

Barnett has recovered from real estate problems suffered during the 1990–92 recession. The company appears focused on building and diversifying its business. Barnett is expected to continue to focus on the consumer and small-business sectors in Florida. The bank has a 33 percent share of the Florida consumer loan market. Retail banking accounts for 73 percent of Barnett's loans (half of which are residential mortgages) and two-thirds of corporate earnings. Barnett is also strong in the indirect auto business, with a $4.8 billion portfolio (18 percent of total bank loans), a relationship with 59 percent of the auto dealers in Florida, and a 27 percent market share. As a matter of fact, Barnett finances more new cars in Florida than Ford, GM, and Chrysler combined. In addition, Barnett has a 14 percent penetration of the small-business market ($1.3 billion in loans and 5 percent of Barnett's total loan portfolio) and a 37 percent penetration in the middle-market segment. On the other hand, the bank shrank its commercial real estate portfolio from a peak of close to 30 percent in the early 1990s to 12 percent in 1994.[9]

On the fee income side, Barnett hopes to build its mortgage-servicing portfolio from a $32 billion base and would like to buy an asset manager with substantial resources under management to help generate additional fee income. Barnett is expected to shift from a service-oriented culture to a more powerful sales culture. It is currently training personnel to utilize its CIF system effectively to help cross-sell more products and services and to improve the profitability of customer accounts.

Barnett sees a national strategic fit for mortgage banking with the growth of fee income and earning assets, the ability to leverage its franchise, and the ability to build customer relationships. Also, Barnett has a competitive edge in mortgage servicing as it has much lower operating costs, resulting from back-office efficiency, than its peers in that sector. Barnett is expected to limit banking and thrift acquisitions to small in-market deals in Florida. Management has targeted a 12–20 percent internal rate of return from acquisitions. Also, acquisitions must be accretive within 18 months. Chuck Newman, Barnett's chief financial officer, indicated that the company would use its strong capital position and its $75 million in quarterly retained earnings to accomplish the following:

- Grow its loan portfolio.
- Finance acquisitions.

- Fund dividend growth, increasing the payout ratio to 30–40 percent.
- Repurchase shares.[10]

The company announced its intention to repurchase up to 10 million common shares (10 percent of the outstanding shares), enhancing EPS growth. These share repurchases should more than offset the likely conversion to common of Barnett's series A and C convertible preferred stock—which are targeted for redemption after April 15, 1996, and October 15, 1996, respectively.

With the recent removal of the Southeastern compact and the adoption by the Florida state legislature of a nationwide interstate banking bill (effective mid-1995), there will likely be an increase in takeover rumors concerning the Barnett Bank. Although a takeover bid is always a possibility, it is more likely that Barnett will remain independent unless an unbelievably high offer comes along or there is an agreed-upon merger of equals. Barnett's market value is about $5.5 billion, which means a takeover at even a modest premium would cost at least $7 billion. Only the biggest banks with a premium price-to-book value and price-to-earnings ratio could afford such a costly acquisition without considerable dilution. Since SunTrust, First Union, and NationsBank cannot acquire Barnett under current law because of market share dominance considerations following a merger, some analysts suggest that Banc One, Norwest, or BankAmerica might be willing to extend an attractive offer to acquire this retail-oriented bank in order to enter a state with high growth. However, if BankAmerica or Banc One were to acquire Barnett at a price 30 percent above current market, "a premium necessary to attract a reluctant bride," the EPS dilution would be about 12 percent and 11 percent, respectively, as of this writing.[11] On the other hand, regulators might allow SunTrust (number 4 in the Florida market) to acquire Barnett if SunTrust would be willing to divest itself of substantial pieces of the Barnett branch system.

In addition to having the largest ATM and branch networks in Florida and a sophisticated telephone banking service, Barnett is the only Florida bank offering home banking by computer. Barnett is also working on new ways to deliver banking products, including the use of interactive television and a new, more sophisticated ATM that will cash checks and allow bill payments.

In the meantime, although Barnett is a large bank, its focus is that of a community bank with emphasis on retail and small commercial banking. Barnett has a solid, low-cost deposit base with more core deposits than loans. It has relatively few wholesale borrowings and minimal derivatives exposure. The average life of securities in its portfolio was 1.5 years at the end of 1994. The $7 billion securities portfolio was about the same size as its adjustable-rate mortgage (ARM) portfolio. The natural repricing of the ARM portfolio at 150 basis points higher than the 1994 yield should enhance 1995 earnings substantially, as should the reinvestment in either loans or two-year treasuries of the maturing securities portfolio. All in all, the groundwork has been laid for earnings per share to increase by low-double-digit percentages over the next few years as improved operating costs combine with reduced credit-related expenses and better portfolio yields to produce improved ROAs and ROEs. Enhanced information systems and a better marketing focus should enable Barnett to increase customer profitability. Expanding nontraditional businesses (for example, EquiCredit) which grow at a faster rate than traditional banking business should also contribute to faster corporate growth in EPS. "By the year 2000, Barnett will be a fully diversified financial services organization with the acknowledged leadership position in the evolving banking business in its markets and with a diversified group of other financial businesses throughout the nation."[12]

ENDNOTES

1. T.H. Hanley, P.J. Carter, and A.B. Collins, "Barnett Banks," *CS First Boston*, October 13, 1994, p. 4; and November 17, 1994, p. 5.
2. Barnett Banks, 1994 *Annual Report*.
3. C.S. Berger, "Barnett," *Salomon Brothers*, November 17, 1994, pp. 3–5.
4. S. Davis, "Barnett Banks," *Goldman Sachs*, September 27, 1994, p. 2.
5. Berger, p. 6.
6. T.H. Hanley, P.J. Carter, and A.B. Collins, "Banking Weekly," *CS First Boston*, July 20, 1994, p. 4.
7. T.H. Hanley, "Barnett Banks," *CS First Boston*, September 20, 1994, p. 3.
8. J.R. Burke, "Barnett Banks," *Robinson-Humphrey Co., Inc., Research*, February 17, 1995, p. 2.
9. C. Kotowski, "Barnett Banks," *Oppenheimer & Co., Inc., Research*, November 14, 1994, pp. 1–2.
10. Berger, pp. 7–8.
11. J.R. Burke, "Thoughts on Interstate Banking," *Robinson-Humphrey Co., Inc., Research*, August 1994, p. 5.
12. Barnett Banks, 1994 *Annual Report*.

T A B L E   13–5

Barnett Banks, Inc., Financials

	1990	1991	1992	1993	1994
Earnings per share	$1.61	$1.71	$1.97	$4.01	$4.66
Assets (in millions)	$36,122	$37,900	$37,923	$37,356	$38,169
Net income (in millions)	$55.55	$81.44	$207.66	$420.99	$487.97
Return on assets	0.15%	0.21%	0.55%	1.13%	1.28%

	1994	
	(in millions)	**%**
Average earning assets	$34,441	100
Securities	7,554	22
Loans	28,810	78
Other	77	0
Loans	28,519	100
Construction and land	929	
Commercial mortgage	2,379	
Highly leveraged		
Commercial loans and leases	4,349	
Other foreign	96	
Term LCD		
Credit card receivables	1,375	
Other consumer	6,986	
Unearned discount		
Corporate	7,753	27
Consumer	8,361	29
Mortgages	12,405	43

	1990	1991	1992	1993	1994
Efficiency ratio	63.72	65.43	62.94	61.1	60.37
Shareholder equity (in millions)	$2,032	$2,128	$2,511	$2,730	$3,029
Preferred	$1	$119	$216	$215	$215
Common	$2,031	$2,009	$2,295	$2,515	$2,814

F I G U R E   13–1

Barnett Banks, Inc., Financial Charts

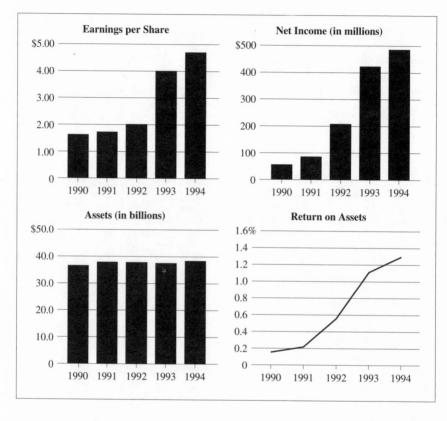

F I G U R E   13–2

Barnett Banks, Inc., Financial Charts

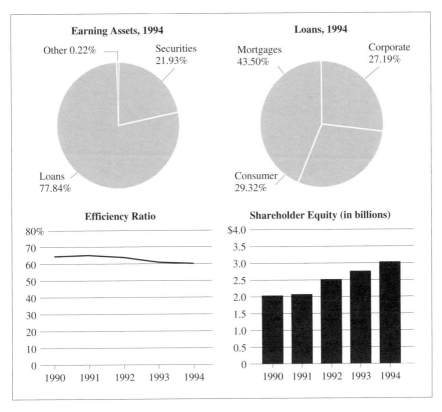

NEW ENGLAND AND MID-ATLANTIC BANKS

The universe of superregional banks for the Northeastern sector of the country consists of Fleet Financial, Bank of Boston, Bank of New York, Mellon, and CoreStates. Even though PNC Corp. is headquartered in Pittsburgh along with Mellon, we have chosen to place it with the Midwestern banks. Some analysts classify Bank of New York as a wholesale, money center bank, and in many ways it is. However, its recent acquisitions of retail banking franchises in the suburbs of New York City and its growing credit card business persuaded us to classify Bank of New York as a special superregional.

The banks in the Northeast were severely affected by the recession that gripped both the nation and particularly that region between 1989 and 1992. Commercial real estate prices tumbled, and the banks with large regional exposures suffered with increased nonperforming loans. Although the recession had a negative impact throughout the industry, some banks found opportunities. Fleet was able to capitalize upon the failure of Bank of New England and the weakened state of Shawmut and Bank of Boston to expand its franchise via a large acquisition campaign. Today, Fleet has in excess of $80 billion in assets, ranking as the ninth largest bank holding company in the United States and the largest bank in New England, with an attractive franchise that stretches throughout New England and New York State. In 1984, Fleet had just under $7 billion in assets. Most analysts feel that after completion of reengineering and massive cost-cutting following its acquisition of Shawmut, Fleet will continue to grow with one more major acquisition out of the region. Nonbanking units or a superregional bank with international capability would be attractive candidates.

Bank of Boston recovered more slowly from the recession. It required some external financing and massive reserving to regain its prerecession health. After being rebuffed by regulators in its bid for the Bank of New England, and later by Shawmut Bank, Fleet, First Fidelity, and CoreStates in bids for those institutions, Bank of Boston sold its Maine and Vermont retail banking franchises and acquired retail banks in Massachusetts and Connecticut. The bank appears to be concentrating its efforts on southern New England, wholesale banking, and Argentina and Brazil, where it owns an extremely profitable franchise. The bank is a major corporate lender and has only recently been a major player in retail banking. Look for continued fill-in acquisitions and perhaps a merger of equals as it looks as if the bank's board of directors would accept a takeover at the "right" price.

Bank of New York has a large network of retail banks in the wealthy suburbs of New York City and in northern New Jersey. It is the sixth largest bank issuer of credit cards and a dominant player in corporate trusts, government securities clearance, American depository receipts (ADRs), mutual fund custody, and unit trusts. It generated 44.26 percent of total revenues from fees or noninterest income, the second largest percentage among superregional banks. Bank of New York is both a retail and wholesale bank and a major bank security processor. It has made nine acquisitions in the last two years of custodial, ADR, and other corporate trust accounts to become one of the top players in the securities processing and custodial industry along with Chase Manhattan Bank and State Street Boston.

CoreStates, headquartered in Philadelphia, is a unique franchise. Following the acquisition of Meridian, it has the largest share of deposits in southeastern Pennsylvania and controls about half of the middle-market business loans in that region. The bank is a leader in technological developments, ATM systems, wholesale banking, and international activities. Executive management has demonstrated skill in making strategic acquisitions within the geographic region it serves, but some of these acquisitions have been dilutive of EPS. The company has excellent asset-liability management skills and a history of outstanding credit controls. CoreStates is in the midst of a dramatic cost-cutting and revenue enhancement campaign that should lead to strong increases in EPS and extraordinary profitability ratios. CoreStates would be a wonderful, but expensive, prize in an acquisition, or even a merger of equals.

Mellon Bank, with its acquisition of Dreyfus and Boston Company, has become the largest bank manager of funds and the second largest asset manager in the United States, behind the Fidelity Investments family of funds. The ratio of noninterest income to total revenue was nearly 50 percent in 1994 and should easily exceed 53 percent by 1997. The bank is also a major wholesale lender throughout the country and a major player in mortgage banking. Mellon also has strong retail franchises in Pittsburgh and in Philadelphia and its suburbs, following the acquisitions of Girard and PSFS/Monitor. Mellon was turned down on a bid to acquire Bank of Boston, so that it may be shopping for a merger-of-equals candidate as well as additional in-market retail banks.

CHAPTER 14

Fleet Financial Group

With a series of major mergers and acquisitions over about a dozen years that included Norstar, Bank of New England, and Shawmut National Corporation, Fleet has grown from a rather innocuous New England bank with assets of under $6 billion to the largest bank in New England and the ninth largest in the United States with assets of more than $80 billion. Moreover, in terms of market capitalization, Fleet should become the seventh largest bank in the country. With the Shawmut merger (announced in February 1995), Fleet became the largest servicer of third-party student loans, the third largest mortgage banking company, the third largest small-business lender, and the tenth largest commercial lender in the nation; in addition, Fleet will have the largest ATM network in the Northeast and the largest market share in New England of personal trust, cash management, private banking, and small-business lending. According to Terrence Murray, who will remain chief executive of the merged company, "This is a superb strategic fit . . . The combined entity will be a financial powerhouse, with critical mass, a broader mix of products and services and an expanded customer base."[1] Joel Alvord, Shawmut chairman, became chairman of the merged company, a title he will pass to Murray in 1998, when Alvord has agreed to leave Fleet.

The Shawmut merger creates an entity that will control 36 percent of banking deposits in Rhode Island, 26 percent in Connecticut, 17 percent in Massachusetts, 18 percent in New Hampshire, and 17 percent in Maine (see Table 14–1). Shawmut's insurance and money management business will provide additional diversification and fee income to Fleet Financial. In fact, Shawmut earned about $400 million in noninterest (fee) income in 1994 (about 26 percent of net revenue), while Fleet earned about $1,116 million in noninterest income during 1994 (about 36.7 percent of net revenue).

T A B L E   14–1

Shawmut and Fleet: Before and after Merger

	Fleet	Shawmut	Combined (Pro Forma)
Assets (in billions)*	$49.0	$32.4*	$81.4
Net income (in millions)	$488.0	$290.7	
Net loans (in billions)	$27.5	$18.7	$46.2
Deposits (in billions)	$34.8	$20.0	$54.8
Total equity (in billions)	$3.6	$2.2	$5.8
Tangible total equity/assets	4.9%	6.3%	5.5%
Employees (in millions)	21,000	9,500	
Branches	843	333	925
Teller machines	893	585	1,500
NPAs/related assets	1.8%	1.54%	1.74%
Reserves/loans	3.46%	2.93%	3.25%
Reserves/NPLs	216%	242%	225%
Book value/share	$22.23	$20.63	$21.44
Mutual fund assets (in billions)	$5.0	$1.3	$6.3
Trust assets (in billions)	$31.8	$24.8	$56.6

* Does not include $3.35 billion in assets of Northeast Federal, whose acquisition by Shawmut is pending.
Source: Derived from company reports.

Prior to the merger announcement, Shawmut held the number one position in middle-market business in both Connecticut and Massachusetts and was second in New England's corporate business market. Additionally, the company had 6,000 middle-market and asset-based lending relationships and 500 national and specialized relationships. On the retail banking front, Shawmut had relationships with one in five households throughout New England and led the market in mortgage originations, small-business banking relationships, and retirement accounts. From its dual headquarters in Hartford and Boston, Shawmut operated 333 banking offices.[2]

Some analysts suggested that although Shawmut's financial condition had improved substantially, the rapid gains in earnings and improvement in financial ratios were over. They also pointed out that Shawmut had paid high prices for recent retail banking acquisitions in New England and had to take a heavy onetime charge. As a matter of fact, Shawmut was one of a few banks whose book value declined in 1994.[3]

Because of the substantial overlap in the franchises of the companies, the merger will allow them to reduce a significant amount of duplicative expenses. Following the

$3.7 billion stock swap, Fleet expects to save at least $400 million a year within 15 months after the deal closes by closing branches, combining processing operations, and cutting the workforce. A total of 4,500 jobs will be cut, at least 3,000 through layoffs, at two institutions that have already undergone huge layoffs and cost-cutting. The combined operation will sell 64 branches and close an additional 150 branches. Fleet expects to have about 925 postmerger branches across New England and New York when the acquisition is finally completed. Fleet will probably close an additional 200 branches by year-end 1997, ending the century with only 50 percent of its 1995 branches.

The company expects $400–500 million in restructuring costs to result from the merger. The merger is also expected to dilute EPS in 1995 by 10 percent and in 1996 by 6 percent, as Fleet paid a 31 percent premium over Shawmut's closing price on the day preceding the merger. Fleet paid 2.4 times Shawmut's tangible book value or 1.8 times book value. In terms of pricing of Fleet's acquisition of Shawmut, this represented one of the least expensive large transactions in 1995. By comparison, First Union acquired First Fidelity for 192 percent of book value, while PNC acquired Midlantic for 2.11 times book value. According to Jeffrey L. Cohn, bank stock analyst at Wainwright & Co., "This is a transaction that is not designed to produce an immediate, as in next year, pickup in earnings. But it gives them significant competitive advantage . . . The acquisition also allows Fleet to assume a much larger customer base."[4]

None of the savings will be realized in 1995 and only part of them in 1996. It will be 1997 at the earliest before the payoff for the acquisition starts to be seen. The accretive potential is more modest than in past megamergers. Both companies have been aggressive in reducing costs on their own. The cost savings will now be spread over a much larger shareholder base, limiting the impact of the cost savings. The cost savings entails the removal of about three-quarters of the incremental branches acquired by Fleet, similar to the BankAmerica/Security Pacific merger. Although the cost savings amounts to about 44 percent of Shawmut's total noninterest expenses in 1995, the savings is only 13 percent of the combined entity.[5] The postmerger company should benefit from broadened management skills, substantial in-market cost savings (for example, the efficiency ratio should decline from 66.8 percent in 1994 to about 53 percent in 1997), a more balanced and diversified loan portfolio, improved pricing dynamics as a result of market dominance, and earnings diversification (see Table 14–2).

Fleet also announced that it would move corporate headquarters from Providence to Boston and sell (especially in Connecticut) at least $3.2 billion in deposits and about $1.0 billion in loans to head off antitrust concerns. Divestitures will reduce total annual revenues by about $100–125 million, while there will be a one-shot gain on sale of divestitures of between $75 and $125 million. While management's $400 million in targeted cost savings remained unchanged, our sense is that this estimate will prove conservative based upon the conversion schedule of

T A B L E   14–2

Selected Financial Projections, 1993–1997E

	1993	1994	1995E	1996E	1997E
Net income (in millions)	$777	$841	$868	$1,360	$1,494
Operating EPS	2.99	3.22	4.00	4.85	5.30
ROA	1.14%	1.16%	1.24%	1.55%	1.58%
ROE	17.66%	17.41%	16.88%	21.02%	21.33%
Efficiency ratio	68.8%	66.8%	62.5%	52.7%	49.9%
Loan loss provisions	327	80	100	150	225
Equity/assets	6.91	7.09	7.42	7.87	8.20

Source: *CS First Boston*, June 19, 1995, p. 4.

the banks. The last back office conversion should be completed over the July 4, 1996 weekend. This implies that about 75 percent of the cost savings can be recouped by the end of September 1996. Therefore, accretion should begin in the fourth quarter, three months ahead of management's initial plan.

Prior to the Shawmut merger announcement, Fleet Financial Group was a $48.8 billion diversified financial services company with 1,200 offices (including 818 branches) across 42 states. Based in Providence, Rhode Island, Fleet had 22,000 employees working at seven banks, with branches throughout New York and New England, where it was the largest banking group (see Figure 14–1). In addition, Fleet has more than 10 major financial service companies located nationwide, including Atlanta, Milwaukee, New York City, Providence, Long Beach, California, and Columbia, South Carolina. The banking subsidiaries accounted for roughly 83 percent of premerger Fleet's balance sheet, while its nonbanking subsidiaries accounted for the remaining 17 percent, or $8 billion in assets. The company operates one of the largest mortgage banking operations in the country, third after Countrywide Funding in mortgage servicing and fifth in mortgage originations. Fleet also owns AFSA Data Corp., the student loan servicing subsidiary. AFSA is the second largest servicer to Sallie Mae, as well as the second largest servicer of student loans. The company services 2.5 million accounts with more than $7 billion in student loans.

Other sources of fee income include Fleet's government banking operations, which won a 10-year contract in 1994 from New York State to process personal income tax returns. Fleet also entered the rapidly growing cobranded credit card arena with the introduction of a Visa card with Caldor, the country's fourth largest discount department store chain. Features of the card include a 1 percent rebate on purchases. Fleet Investment Services (FIS) and Fleet Investment Advisors (FIA),

F I G U R E   14-1

Breakout of State Banking Income, Nine Months Ended September 1994

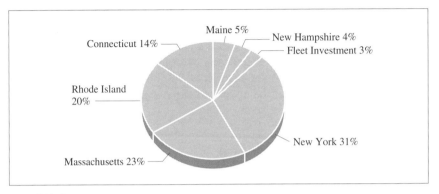

Source: CS First Boston.

which existed prior to the Shawmut merger, offer comprehensive investment, trust, private banking, and brokerage services targeted to affluent customers. FIS/FIA has more than 100,000 investment management relationships and assets under management of $24 billion. Institutional and individual custodial and brokerage activities bring total account relationships to more than 200,000, with almost $45 billion in assets either under management or administration. FIS manages the largest no-load mutual fund family in banking industry, called Galaxy, with 27 funds and $6.1 billion under management as of October 31, 1995. Shawmut should add $1.6 billion in mutual funds under management to bring the total to $7.7 billion. The recent mortgage-servicing acquisitions and merger-related trust assets under management should lead to an increased contribution of fee income in the years ahead (see Table 14–3). The combined Fleet/Shawmut should have a total of $71 billion in trust assets. The old Fleet had $45 billion in trust assets split evenly between managed and custody assets, whereas Shawmut would contribute $26 billion in assets, with $16.5 billion assets in higher-earning managed accounts as of the third quarter 1995. Investment services and catering to wealthy clients in the Northeast could become a major driver of revenue growth.

In the traditional banking business at premerger Fleet, commercial and industrial loans accounted for 48.4 percent of loans outstanding, real estate 27.2 percent, asset-based lending 8.8 percent, leasing 7.6 percent, and communications industry lending 4.7 percent as of June 30, 1994. The credit card portfolio grew to approximately $1.6 billion in outstandings at the end of the third quarter of 1995 and should get even larger with three new cobranded initiatives, namely Gulf Oil, Caldor, and Special Olympic cards.[6] The portfolio, which is geographically broadly based, should gain further as Fleet sells credit cards to the existing customer base. In the postmerger Fleet, commercial and industrial loans will account for about 42 percent of total loans, one- to four-family residential mortgages 19 percent, credit cards 3 percent, other consumer loans 19 percent, and commercial real estate 14 percent. Shawmut brings to the merger particular strength in commercial banking and a specialization in banking for financial institutions. All told, loans will account for about 55 percent of assets and securities 26 percent of assets on a pro forma basis as of year-end 1994 (see Figure 14–2 and Table 14–4).

A detailed breakdown of line-of-business profitability can be seen in Table 14–5. In terms of earnings of the combined organization, commercial banking

T A B L E   14–3

Noninterest Income (in millions)

Source	1992	1993	1994
Mortgage banking	$ 364	$ 414	$ 363
Service charge on deposits	162	173	169
Trust fees	160	174	175
Student loans	61	51	54
Service charges	61	67	87
Other	232	304	326
Total	$1,040	$1,183	$1,174

Source: Derived from Fleet, 1994 *Annual Report.*

F I G U R E   14–2

Pro Forma Loan Concentrations, September 30, 1995

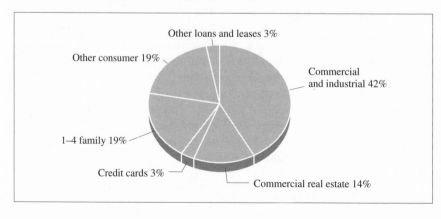

Other loans and leases 3%

Other consumer 19%

Commercial and industrial 42%

1–4 family 19%

Credit cards 3%

Commercial real estate 14%

T A B L E   14–4

Pro Forma Loan Portfolio, September 30, 1995 (in millions)

	Shawmut	Fleet	Pro Forma
Commercial and industrial	$ 9,935	$11,953	$21,388
Commercial real estate	2,632	4,197	6,829
Credit cards		1,569	1,569
1–4 family	5,965	5,135	11,100
Other consumer	3,101	6,389	9,490
Other loans and leases		1,558	1,904
Total	$21,633	$30,801	$52,280

T A B L E   14–5

Return on Average Assets

	Fleet	Shawmut
Commercial banking	1.11%	1.18%
Consumer banking	1.33	1.08
Investment services	4.87	2.93
Financial	1.01	N.A.
Financial institutions	N.A.	1.89
Other	N.A.	0.18
Total	1.27%	0.76%

Source: Derived from company reports.

made up 36 percent of income in 1994, consumer banking 29 percent, investment services 11 percent and other 24 percent.

After recovering from its financial woes of 1991–92, Shawmut was aggressive in acquiring retail banks in New England such as New Dartmouth ($1.7 billion in assets), People's Bancorp of Worcester ($913 million in assets), Gateway Corporation of Connecticut ($1.3 billion in assets), 10 branches from Northeast Savings ($425 million in deposits), Cohasset Savings Bank ($78 million in assets), Old Stone Trust Co. ($417 million), West Newton Savings Bank ($260 million in assets), and Northeast Federal ($3.35 billion in assets). Shawmut also agreed to acquire Barclays Business Credit ($214 million in assets), which provides asset-based financing to middle-market companies. The latter transaction complements

Shawmut's asset-based lending business and provides diversification beyond the New England marketplace.

Improved credit quality, better expense control, and modest revenue generation helped rejuvenate Shawmut. Shawmut's profitability ratios improved substantially. Its ROA increased from 0.33 percent in 1992 to 0.74 percent in 1994, while its ROE increased from 5.99 percent in 1992 to 15.2 percent in 1994. Accompanying Shawmut's better profitability ratios was an improvement in its efficiency ratio from 73 percent in 1992 to 60 percent in the fourth quarter of 1994. Similarly, its nonperforming asset ratio improved from 4.58 percent in 1992 to 0.88 percent in the fourth quarter of 1994. Loan loss reserves as a percentage of nonperforming assets rose to 190 percent at year-end 1994 from 84 percent in 1992, while shareholders' equity as a percentage of assets also grew from 5.16 percent in 1992 to 6.16 percent in 1994.

HISTORY

In 1791, a group of investors led by John Brown, one of New England's most respected merchants, established the Providence Bank. The Providence Bank helped finance the growth of some of America's leading manufacturers. About a decade later, Elkanah Watson and a group of Albany businessmen recognized the need for a bank that could fund the launching points for westward migration. The group established the New York State Bank of Albany in 1803. The State Bank of Albany played an important role in developing New York State and the nation, helping to finance the Great Western Turnpike, the Erie Canal, and several rail lines. Later, the name of the bank was changed to the State Bank of New York, an early predecessor of Norstar. Ironically, Watson was a protégé of Brown, but neither of them could have suspected that their banks would merge almost two centuries later.

Rhode Island Roots

Surviving or acquiring many of their competitors, the Providence Bank and the State Bank of New York became recognized as pillars of their respective financial communities. In 1954, the Providence Union National Bank (the latest incarnation of Brown's original bank) merged with one of Rhode Island's prominent banking institutions, the Industrial Trust Company. Founded in 1886, Industrial Trust was built by businessman-banker Samuel P. Colt, who introduced the European concept of branch banking in the United States. The combination of Rhode Island's most experienced and innovative banks created a full-service financial institution, Industrial National. Throughout the 1950s and 1960s, Industrial National was Rhode Island's banking leader as it expanded its consumer banking services and pioneered state-of-the-art computer automation. Industrial National became one of the first banks to form a one-bank holding company for the purposes of expanding into nonbanking businesses. The holding company, Industrial Bancorp, was listed on the New York Stock Exchange in 1968.

Industrial National's chief executive, John J. Cummings, Jr., envisioned a diversified financial services organization that would enjoy continued growth in both traditional and nontraditional banking functions. In 1972, Industrial National Corp. purchased Ambassador Factors, a New York–based firm that later became Fleet Factors. In 1973, the Southern Discount Co. of Atlanta—subsequently named Fleet Finance—became a corporate subsidiary. The following year, Industrial National acquired Mortgage Associates in Milwaukee. This mortgage banking unit later became Fleet Mortgage Corp. It is now a nationwide company with a substantial servicing portfolio.

Cummings instituted performance incentives that, while commonplace in the industrial sector, were new to the banking industry. One young manager that Cummings attracted was a recent Harvard graduate, Terrence Murray, who played an active role in developing Industrial National's financial services strategy. One of Cummings's last major acts as chief executive at Industrial National was to rechristen the company as the Fleet Financial Group. The Fleet title conveyed Cumming's vision of a corporation that was both bank and nonbank, as it conveyed the image of ships sailing to the same destination. Upon Cummings's death in 1982, Murray, the president, was selected to become chief executive of Fleet Financial Group.

Under Murray's leadership, Fleet Financial continued its expansion both geographically and functionally. Beginning in 1986, Fleet expanded across state lines to acquire regional banks, such as First Connecticut Bancorp (now Fleet Bank, N.A.) and Merrill Trust Co. in Maine (now Fleet Bank of Maine) and in New Hampshire. Fleet's balance sheet grew more than eightfold to $48 billion in 1994 from $5.7 billion at year-end 1983. Subsequently, the company doubled its asset size in a successful nondilutive merger of equals when it combined with New York–based Norstar in 1988. This was followed by its expansion into Massachusetts in 1991 when it acquired the Bank of New England with FDIC assistance. The deal was attractive both from an EPS and balance sheet perspective. Strategically, it also gave the company a strong market share in the most economically important state in New England.

New York Roots

State Bank's management also foresaw the need for geographic and functional diversity in upstate New York. In 1972, the State Bank of Albany and the Liberty National Bank (Buffalo) merged, creating the Union Bank Corp. of New York (UBNY). Prior to the merger, both banks had been soundly managed, becoming major financial players in their respective markets. Both banks had executed a number of important acquisitions in their local markets. UBNY embarked on an aggressive acquisition program that spanned the state under the leadership of Peter D. Kiernan, an Albany insurance executive turned banker. Kiernan's bank achieved record levels of profitability, a new name (Norstar Bancorp), and the first interstate merger in almost 30 years (Maine-based Northeast Bancshare Association).

Fleet/Norstar Merger

Fleet chairman Murray had a reputation as a tough downsizer, firing hundreds of redundant employees from inefficient, acquired firms. The method for increasing productivity was simple. Fleet consolidated the administrative positions of acquired companies into Fleet's existing staff, while folding the diverse computer operations into Fleet's own system. Driven by increasing competition from Bank of Boston and Bank of New England, Murray and Kiernan, the chairman of Norstar (assets of $11 billion), reached agreement on a merger in early 1988. The new corporation was renamed Fleet/Norstar Financial Group. Kiernan and Murray had discussed this merger for a few years before agreeing to the marriage. Kiernan was named chairman and CEO, while Murray was named president. Kiernan's tenure as chairman was cut short by his premature death in September 1988. Murray was then elected chairman, president, and CEO.

Bank of New England Failure

Fleet won a bidding war against BankAmerica and Bank of Boston to acquire Bank of New England (BNE) from the FDIC following BNE's demise in 1991. BNE's crisis began in 1986 when it outbid Fleet for the Conifer Group, a major Massachusetts real estate lender. The real estate portfolio was riddled with failed or shaky deals. As the recession grew worse in New England, so did the performance of BNE's loan portfolio. By 1990, the FDIC was anxious to get rid of BNE and offered generous guarantees against its liabilities. Because Fleet lacked the resources to bid alone for BNE, it combined with Kohlberg Kravis Roberts (KKR) to launch the winning bid. The transaction added close to $13 billion in deposits to Fleet's franchise for a mere 0.83 percent premium to deposits.

　　The acquisition of BNE's banking franchise in New England expanded Fleet/Norstar's size by 40 percent. The former BNE banks in Massachusetts, Connecticut, and Maine were then given the Fleet name. The acquisition of BNE created a retail banking powerhouse in New England and New York State; Fleet surpassed the Bank of Boston as the largest bank in New England. Murray fired about half of BNE's 11,000 employees and consolidated its data centers with those of Fleet. Remaining was a $15 billion institution with the most extensive retail branch network in the region and a large number of stable businesses. The failed bank had been called a toxic waste dump by *Business Week*. BNE was rehabilitated and made profitable sooner than expected. Fleet then returned a number of non-performing loans back to the FDIC as per the contractual arrangement.

RECHRISTENING: FLEET FINANCIAL

In April 1992, the company's name was changed from Fleet/Norstar to Fleet Financial Group, the name originally adopted in 1982 when the company shed its identity as Industrial National Bank. The name change allowed the company to achieve a common identification throughout all of Fleet's major markets.

Fleet continued to expand its banking franchise in 1993 by agreeing to acquire $1 billion asset Sterling Bancshares Corp. (Waltham, Massachusetts) and by assuming the deposits of Jefferson National Bank (Watertown, New York). Fleet also received regulatory approval to acquire $700 million in consumer deposits of 29 upstate New York branches of Chemical Bank. Both the Sterling and Chemical branch acquisitions were consummated in 1994. At the same time, on the basis of an internal study, Fleet announced plans to reduce its number of employees by 7 percent to bring its noninterest expense ratio in line with the best regional banks in the industry. As a result, the company expects ultimately to save some $350 million in operating expenses and add about $50 million in fee revenues. Breaking down the $350 million in savings, personnel expenses should decline by 53 percent, nonpersonnel expenses by 40 percent, and occupancy expenses by 7 percent.

Fleet's efficiency ratio was 69 percent in 1992, 68 percent in 1993, and 64.8 percent in 1994. Its fourth quarter 1994 efficiency ratio was 61.6 percent. Management has targeted a 53 percent ratio for 1997. Although this is an ambitious target, a number of other large branch organizations have achieved this level of efficiency.

The Shawmut Connection

Although the Shawmut roots go back to 1835 in Massachusetts, Shawmut National Corporation was incorporated in 1988 with the merger of Hartford National Corporation, a Connecticut bank holding company, and Shawmut Corporation, a Massachusetts bank holding company. Following the merger, the company maintained dual headquarters in Hartford and Boston, while operating more than 200 branches throughout Connecticut, Massachusetts, and Rhode Island.

The holding company sold Shawmut Mortgage Corp. to National City Corp. in 1989 and sold its credit card portfolio to Norwest Financial Corp. in 1991. In addition, following the devastating New England recession, Shawmut sold approximately one-third of its problem assets for about 66 cents on the dollar to generate nearly $290 million in 1993. The company also declined a merger offer from Bank of Boston and began to acquire retail banks in New England. Shawmut Bank,

N.A. (Massachusetts) had total assets of $12.9 billion at year-end 1993, while Shawmut Bank Connecticut had total assets of $14.5 billion.

Fleet Mortgage

Fleet had operated Fleet Mortgage, Fleet Finance, Norstar, and Fleet Bank on a stand-alone basis until 1992. Since then, the company has moved from a horizontally integrated, geographically organized structure to a vertically integrated, functionally organized structure. There is now one executive in charge of retail banking throughout the company's banks in Rhode Island, Maine, New York, Connecticut, New Hampshire, and Massachusetts. This organizational shift began with a management shake-up in 1993 and culminated with "Fleet Focus," a major restructuring undertaken to enhance efficiency, improve outcome and service, and centralize control.

On the mortgage banking front, Fleet Mortgage Group purchased $3.8 billion of mortgage-servicing rights from undisclosed parties and $5.9 billion from Countrywide Funding in 1994. Fleet also announced a plan to acquire the California-based Plaza Home Mortgage Corporation, with a servicing portfolio of $9.2 billion and annual originations of about $4.5 billion. That acquisition would expand Fleet's mortgage banking operation into western states, especially California, where Fleet had only a modest presence. In addition, the deal would vault Fleet into second place among mortgage-servicing companies, just behind the leader, Countrywide Funding. In May 1995, Fleet Financial Group bought $13.1 billion of mortgage-servicing rights from Household International, Inc., and agreed to service Household's $1.9 billion portfolio of home mortgages. With all of these acquisitions, including the completed tender offer for the remainder of the shares of Fleet Mortgage, Fleet's mortgage-servicing portfolio reached $105 billion.

The enlarged mortgage company has diversified its portfolio and origination channels, while building scale to improve servicing margins. Fleet Mortgage and Banco Mexicano announced their intention to form a venture to develop mortgage banking in Mexico. The new company will attempt to take advantage of the increased demand in Mexico for home ownership and will develop mortgage products to be packaged for sale in the secondary market, initially through private placements and eventually by selling shares to the public. Fleet also reacquired the publicly held shares of Fleet Mortgage Group, its mortgage banking subsidiary.

TECHNOLOGICAL DEVELOPMENTS

Fleet has determined that all of its banks should have a common core architecture and application base to achieve cost savings and consolidate new acquisitions. The focus of technology at Fleet has taken two directions. One focuses directly on the customer; the other is more indirect, providing better support to internal staff so that they in turn can provide better customer service.

Fleet is developing a system of automated workstations, client-server applications that automate staff functions in trust operations, commercial real estate, commercial and industrial lending, asset-based lending, and leasing. The purpose of the system is to increase productivity and improve customer service by providing staff increased power and information systems on their desktop computers. Direct access to centrally kept data reduces customer-response time and alleviates the need for specialized data processing staff to make system inquiries. Fleet is also utilizing work-flow software to streamline processes and better manage productivity. The ability to increase the number of completed transactions through automation will allow the bank's branch staff to concentrate on more customer-specific questions.

Fleet has also installed special automated platform machines, called Quick Touch machines, throughout its New England locations. These systems are self-service terminals that allow customers to perform general ATM functions, such as account inquiry, as well as some transactions that previously were limited to the platform. Fleet expects that the Quick Touch system will do for the platform what ATMs did for the teller function. Quick Touch, aptly named for its touch screen, looks similar to an ATM but has advanced graphic capabilities.

The company introduced a service in all its Northeast markets that allows customers to pay bills to more than 500 national merchants and transfer between Fleet accounts 24 hours a day.

Fleet has also begun to utilize image processing technology, such as the file folder, and is working on improving communication lines, which are currently inadequate, to enable remote access to such technology. In the fourth quarter of 1994, Fleet installed a number of innovative cash management technologies, including imaging applications for commercial accounts. The bank also introduced a cutting-edge deposit reconciliation product, called Fleet Track, which enhances services to cash management customers. For the next few years, Fleet will be looking for ways to leverage its high level of standardization by increasing platform automation, using more intelligent automation, and putting more power and information availability in staff desktops. A by-product of Fleet Focus, the cost-cutting program was the company's realization that it had to make a heavier capital commitment to technology and to utilize a cost-benefit strategy before making those expenditures. Fleet was recognized in *Information Week*'s "1995 Bank Users of Information Technology" as both a leader in technology usage and the best at using information technology to improve corporate productivity.

RECENT MERGER ACTIVITY AND FUTURE SPECULATION

Fleet has been built around a large series of mergers. Prior to the announced reengineering of its operations, the company had not done a great job of integrating the operations of the disparate organizations. Consequently, a large number of inefficiencies were allowed to accumulate throughout the organization. Chairman Murray has also indicated that Fleet should be able to reduce noninterest expenses by an additional $50 million per year once it transforms the independent banks within the holding company into branches following the passage of the interstate banking bill. Although Fleet's core overhead ratio was relatively high in 1992, it should be much more competitive (in the top quartile of banks) following the Focus Program.

In the midst of its sweeping cost-cutting plan, the company announced an agreement in 1994 to acquire NBB Bancorp (New Bedford, Massachusetts), the parent company of New Bedford Institution for Savings. The acquisition adds more than 200,000 customers, 52 offices, $2.5 billion in assets, including $1.3 billion in loans, to the Fleet family, extending its franchise from its headquarters in Providence through southeastern Massachusetts into Cape Cod. Fleet's acquisition of NBB fits in with the company's strategy to fill in its New England franchise. NBB was primarily a deposit and mortgage institution, but it did not offer home equity mortgages or credit cards. Fleet should have a good opportunity to cross-sell a variety of its consumer and small-business products to customers that were previously unavailable from the savings bank. Additionally, NBB had an ROA of 1.24 percent and an ROE of 12.45 percent. Fleet paid 1.7 times tangible book value, half in cash and half in stock. Fleet also received regulatory approval in 1994 to acquire the $1 billion Sterling Bancshares Corp., increasing its retail presence in suburban Boston.

In an internal document, Fleet listed 14 portfolio holdings (each below 5 percent) as "strategic investments" on March 31, 1994. Fleet took a 4.8 percent stake in Summit Bancorp (Chatam, New Jersey). In addition to 84 branch banking offices in northern New Jersey, it had assets of $4.3 billion, including mortgage and insurance units. Fleet also acquired a 3.8 percent stake in Boston-based UST Corp., a bank with $2 billion in assets. UST's presence in Connecticut and Middlesex County (New Hampshire) might fill in some market gaps for the company in New England, should Fleet eventually acquire the institution. Fleet held 795,000 shares of $10.5 billion asset Bay Banks, about 4.2 percent of the company's stock. Bay Banks, headquartered in Massachusetts, has a strong retail franchise and is considered an acquisition candidate by most bank analysts.

In addition, Fleet had acquired small positions in three Vermont banks. The largest stake was a 4.97 percent position in the $1.7 billion asset Banknorth (Burlington); the next largest was a 3.56 percent stake in Chittendon Corp., with $1.2 billion in assets and also headquartered in Burlington; the third Vermont holding was a 4.81 percent position in Brattleboro-based Vermont Financial services, with assets of $940 million. Fleet also took a 4.99 percent stake in $493 million asset Washington Trust Company of Waverly (Rhode Island). Fleet's smallest, but most interesting, positions were taken in Bank of Boston and Shawmut (less than 0.5 percent). Fleet also held stakes in First Fidelity, Amoskeog Bankshares, and First Bankers Trustshares. SEC filings also disclosed holdings in three banks that were acquired by other banks: Multibank Financial Corp., Edgemark Financial Corp., and NEBS Corp. Outside of the merger with Shawmut, none of the other banking stakes have resulted in Fleet acquisitions.

While some analysts view these stock purchases as stakeout positions for potential acquisition, others call them good investments in a region that is experiencing economic recovery after a severe and long-lasting recession. Prior to the announced merger with Shawmut, Fleet held discussions with the Bank of New York and Bank of Boston about the possibility of combining forces, but nothing fruitful developed.

Prior to the Shawmut merger announcement, Murray indicated that a merger of equals would need to include more cost savings than those achieved in the Key-Society merger. Although the Shawmut acquisition makes strategic sense, the target and the price paid are somewhat surprising. Unlike Fleet's first merger of equals with Norstar in January 1988, which doubled Fleet's asset size and diversified its earnings base without dilution, the Shawmut acquisition appears at first blush to be highly dilutive. The combined company looks top heavy as none of either company's top management is departing. Part of this anticipated dilution will be offset by certain divestitures that could bring as much as $100 million; but it is questionable as to how much cost savings there can really be and whether or not the savings can be achieved within the management-targeted 15 months.[7]

By the year 2000, Terrence Murray expects that the bank will be in 25 states. In an all-day investor conference in September 1994 (prior to the Shawmut merger announcement), management reiterated its desire to roughly double its current size and increase its geographic diversity and international presence. Clearly, acquisitions of Bank of New York or CoreStates would accomplish that. Management has frequently indicated its desire to expand beyond the northeastern region. Following the Shawmut merger, the combined company will have more than one-third of its earnings from out of the northeastern region. This merger gives the combined entity the seventh largest market capitalization among United States banks, sufficient for expansion outside the region.[8]

Asset-Liability Management

To reduce its liability sensitivity and neutralize its balance sheet, Fleet reduced its investment portfolio by approximately $6.5 billion between September and year-end 1994. Average earning assets shrank substantially during the fourth quarter. However, since $4 billion of those securities were low-yielding Treasury bills, the company's margins improved in the fourth quarter.

All of Fleet's banks were categorized as well capitalized in 1994. This meant that minimum leverage, Tier 1, and total capital ratios exceeded 5 percent, 6 percent, and 10 percent, respectively. As a whole, Fleet's leverage ratio was 7.77 percent while the Tier 1 risk-based capital ratio was at 10.08 percent, and the total risk-based capital ratio stood at 14.21 percent at year-end 1994.

Looking Ahead

Fleet will have less bricks-and-mortar branches and more ATMs and telephone service centers doing more things. It is experimenting with the idea of using a hub-and-spoke system. The hub would be a 10,000-foot branch with lots of professionals to help customers, while the spokes will be unmanned, electronic branches.[9]

Fleet's strong performance in 1994 was due to a substantially improved efficiency ratio, further reduction in the level of nonperforming assets, and good growth in the loan portfolio. The company is working hard to improve its profitability and price-to-earnings ratios. A premium valuation is important as it allows expansion of the franchise through nondilutive acquisitions. Prior to the New England real estate recession, Fleet had produced superior returns on assets and equity. Since Fleet's ROE was 11 percent in 1992, 16.1 percent in 1993, and 18.8 percent in 1994, with commensurate ROAs of 1.27 percent in 1994, 1.06 percent in 1993, and 0.62 percent in 1992, there was a dramatic turnaround that should be deserving of a higher multiplier. Its fourth quarter 1994 ROA was 1.42 percent, while its ROE was 21.7 percent. In the meantime, the company's nonperforming assets to total loans plus OREO improved to 1.88 percent in 1994 from 2.3 percent in 1993, 3.7 percent in 1992, 6.0 percent in 1991, and 6.8 percent in 1990. The nonperforming asset ratio is among the highest in the superregional universe, reflecting a slow recovery from the economic woes in the region. Reserves to nonperforming assets were at a conservative 166 percent at year-end 1993 and at 184 percent during 1995. Loan loss reserves as a percentage of average loans outstanding for 1995 was a strong 2.85 percent. The bank's loan loss provisioning is below both current charge-offs and long-run expected charge-offs of about 0.85 percent of loans. Although the reduction of the loan loss provision to a level below net charge-offs represents a return of capital to shareholders, it cannot be considered part of the company's normalized earnings base.

Fleet increased its dividend for the fourth time in a year and a half, restoring it to the level attained before being reduced in January 1991 in the midst of the New England real estate crisis. The payout ratio for 1994 approximated 37 percent. Management has indicated that it will move its payout ratio to between 40–45 percent, which implies a dividend of $2.20 per share in 1997, up from $1.72 in 1995.

Following considerable attention in the Focus program to improving efficiency, Fleet's strategic initiatives have also turned toward the revenue side of the equation. The company believes that profits should grow rapidly in the mortgage banking unit and that market share should increase in leasing. Fleet has also centralized support functions in its single-bank approach, creating business utilities like cash management, asset-based lending, and corporate trust. Fleet has identified a pipeline of business prospects and the sales personnel to convert the prospects into multiproduct relationships. The company has discovered that in many areas increased selling to existing customers has proved more profitable than acquiring new ones. Businesses in the consumer franchise with improved prospects include the mortgage company, student loan servicing (in which the company is the primary beneficiary of the government direct loan program), and small-business lending, in which the bank's heavy branch presence should provide the backbone for deeper penetration of the growing, bank-dependent segment. Fleet is also trying to increase market share in the mutual fund, investment management, and credit card businesses. Fleet also expects to leverage its asset collection skills developed at Recoll Management Corp. under an agreement with the FDIC to manage, collect, and liquidate problem loans and assets.[10] By the year 2000, Fleet hopes to develop a diversified revenue stream with one-third of revenues coming from net interest income, one-third from banking fees, and one-third from other fees as it makes more functional acquisitions. Historically, net interest income has accounted for roughly 60–65 percent of Fleet's revenues.[11] For 1994, its ratio of fee income to total revenue was 36.7 percent.

Fleet could take measures to lower ongoing expense accruals (primarily goodwill) as an income statement offset to the $150 million gains from the sale of branches scheduled to close during the first quarter of 1996.

SUMMARY

The proposed Fleet-Shawmut merger is strategically sound and financially disciplined. Although the accretive potential is modest—about 2 percent in 1997, following about a 10 percent dilution in 1995 and a 6 percent dilution in 1996—Fleet had a strategic need to consolidate in-market to gain a larger share and possibly more favorable pricing, while becoming more efficient. Wall Street may have desired more robust accretion to Fleet, but that is not likely for reasons outlined earlier, including roughly $125 million in revenue reduction from divestitures and a combined $273 million in the combined organization. On the other hand, the merger should generate a return on average assets of close to 1.6 percent and a return on average equity of close to 18 percent by 1997, at the high end of our superregional peer group. After all, Shawmut is an extremely attractive franchise because of its distribution system throughout New England, particularly in Connecticut. The company holds the number one position in middle-market business in both Connecticut and Massachusetts and ranks second in New England's corporate business market. Shawmut holds relationships with one in five families in New England and is the market leader in mortgage originations, small-business banking, and retirement accounts. The combination should put Fleet in a lead position in five out of six New England states, establishing market leadership in every strategic sector, including commercial, consumer, small business, investment management, government loans, and cash management.

As we have gone to press, Fleet announced that it had agreed to acquire NatWest's U.S.–based operations for $3.26 billion. National Westminster's U.S.

unit has $31 billion in assets and 330 branches in New Jersey and the New York City area. With this transaction, Fleet Financial Group becomes an even more impressive northeastern regional banking powerhouse. The company expands to 1,225 branches, $70 billion in deposits, 2,000 ATMs, and builds relationships with over four million households. The acquisition of NatWest makes good sense, is nondilutive to Fleet's book value, and increases distribution capability significantly. It also increases Fleet's retail and small/middle market competitive advantages, while creating greater economies of scale, especially in data processing and technology. With this technology, Fleet increases its market share to the number two position in Long Island and stretches its franchise on a continuous line from Maine to New Jersey. The deal was priced well below other major transactions at 1.41 times tangible book value. Fleet expects $200 million in cost savings (23 percent of NatWest's cost base) as a result of the combination.[12] In addition, NatWest has about $22 billion in lower-yielding assets that Fleet is selling. (NatWest is divesting $13 billion in loans before the deal is completed.)

ENDNOTES

1. T.R. Wilke and T. Rebella, "Fleet to Buy Shawmut," *The Wall Street Journal*, February 22, 1995, p. A2.
2. T.H. Hanley, "Shawmut National Corporation," *CS First Boston*, April 25, 1994, pp. 3–4.
3. S. Housell, "Fleet Financial Offers $317 Billion for Shawmut," *New York Times*, February 22, 1995, p. D1.
4. T.D. Glater, "Fleet Financial to Buy Shawmut," *Washington Post*, February 22, 1995, p. 3.
5. S.P. Davis, "Fleet Financial Group," *Goldman Sachs U.S. Research*, February 2, 1995, p. 2.
6. C.S. Berger, "Fleet Financial Group," *Salomon Brothers Bank Research*, October 3, 1994, p. 4.
7. C. Kotowski, "Fleet Financial," *Oppenheimer & Co., Inc., Research Report*, February 24, 1995, pp. 1–2.
8. Davis, p. 2.
9. J.L. Fix, "Deregulation Lets Banks Branch Out," *USA Today*, August 8, 1994, p. 2B.
10. Berger, pp. 1–4.
11. C. Kotowoski, "Fleet Financial," *Oppenheimer & Co., Inc., Research Report*, December 7, 1994, p. 2.
12. T.H. Hanley, P.J. Carter, and A.B. Collins, "The 'New' Fleet Financial Group," *CS First Boston*, December 22, 1995, pp. 3–5.

T A B L E   14–6

Fleet Financial Group Financials

	1990	1991	1992	1993	1994
Earnings per share	($0.51)	$0.67	$1.77	$3.01	$3.75
Assets (in millions)	$34,363	$38,839	$45,166	$45,966	$48,386
Net income (in millions)	($73.69)	$97.67	$279.84	$488.05	$613.02
Return on assets	(0.21)%	0.25%	0.62%	1.06%	1.27%

	1994	
	(in millions)	%
Average earning assets	$43,525	100
Securities	15,438	35
Loans	26,637	61
Other	1,450	3
Loans	27,546	100
Construction and land	509	
Commercial mortgage	3,830	
Highly leveraged		
Commercial loans and leases	11,263	
Other foreign	5	
Term LCD		
Credit card receivables	1,473	
Other consumer	3,148	
Unearned discount		
Corporate	15,607	57
Consumer	4,621	17
Mortgages	7,318	27

	1990	1991	1992	1993	1994
Efficiency ratio	66	69.92	67.83	67.16	62.54
Shareholder equity (in millions)	$2,197	$2,268	$2,885	$3,452	$3,582
Preferred	$125	$186	$605	$553	$398
Common	$2,072	$2,082	$2,280	$2,899	$3,184

F I G U R E   14–3

Fleet Financial Group Financial Charts

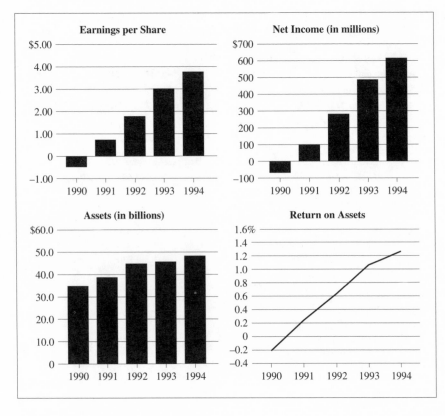

F I G U R E   14–4

Fleet Financial Group Financial Charts

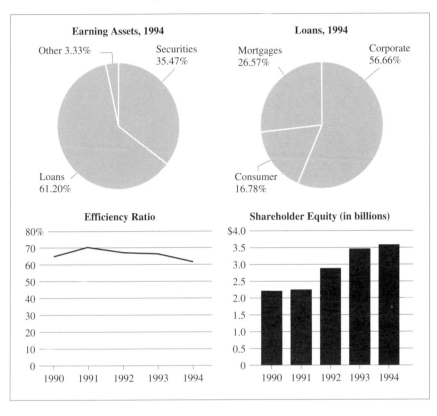

CHAPTER 15

Bank of Boston Corp.

The Bank of Boston, a multibank superregional holding company, had assets at year-end 1994 of $44.6 billion. Although ranked 18th in the nation in total assets, Bank of Boston has the nation's seventh largest commercial and industrial loan portfolio. Through its national and international subsidiaries, the bank provides a wide range of financial services to corporate and institutional customers, governments, individuals, and other financial institutions. Its major banking subsidiaries include the First National Bank of Boston, South Shore Bank, Mechanics Bank, Bank Worcester, and Multibank Financial, all headquartered in Massachusetts; Bank of Boston, Connecticut; and Rhode Island Hospital Trust National Bank (see Table 15–1). Its main branch is located in Boston, Massachusetts, and it operates a network of approximately 325 branches throughout New England where it is the second largest bank to Fleet. Bank of Boston also operates over 150 offices in 23 foreign countries, specializing in Latin American banking with over $7.8 billion in total assets, accounting for about 17 percent of total earning assets in 1994.

The bank wrote off $200 million in Latin American loans in 1987 as the region underwent a severe debt crisis, but it maintains a large branch network in Argentina and Brazil and is the largest foreign bank and third largest private sector bank in Argentina and the second largest in Brazil. Historically, Bank of Boston has been the JP Morgan of Argentina with a heavy emphasis on serving the highest-quality corporate customers in the market as well as governmental units. However, in the last few years, Bank of Boston has developed an important presence in retail banking and middle-market lending. As a matter of fact, approximately one-third of the bank's Argentine loans were to consumer and middle-market customers. This is a different mix of business than that of most U.S. multinational banks, which have traditionally dealt with large multinational corporations and

323

T A B L E   15–1

Selected Breakdown of Assets and Deposits by Location as of
June 30, 1994

	Assets (in billions)	Deposits (in billions)	Branches
BankWorcester	$1.5	$1.3	28
Multibank Financial	2.3	2.0	67
Rhode Island Hospital Trust	3.3	2.6	28
Bank of Boston, Connecticut	4.2	3.2	59
Pioneer Bank	0.8	0.7	20
Argentina	2.0	N.A.	42
Brazil	2.5	N.A.	21

Source: Company reports.

governments as well as in large cross-border transactions. For example, Bank of Boston's loans to government agencies accounted for 16 percent of its loans in Argentina in 1994 compared to about 40 percent in 1987. With expectations of expanding growth of the Argentine banking sector (43 branches in 1994), the bank's number of branches leapfrogged to over 130 in 1995 when it agreed to acquire 93 branch offices and $200 million in assets from the troubled Banco Integrado Departmentel. The Bank of Boston acquired those assets for market value plus a $10 million premium. In addition to the branches, a small government bond portfolio and a modest loan portfolio were acquired. The loans were marked to approximately 50 percent of face value. This acquisition appears to set the stage for another decade of further growth for Bank of Boston in Argentina, giving the company the third largest private sector branch system in the country. Also, the bank is the largest foreign bank manager of mutual funds in Brazil, with assets of $1.6 billion, and it comanages nearly 8 percent of the assets in Argentina's newly privatized pension system through a joint venture with AIG. The combination of its Latin American operation and its sizable commercial and industrial loan portfolio differentiates Bank of Boston from the other superregional banks (see Tables 15–2 and 15–3). Bank of Boston's corporate loans have grown rapidly in South America from $1.2 billion in 1991 to $3.6 billion at year-end 1994, while deposits have grown from $1.3 billion to $3.0 billion during the same time frame (see Tables 15–4 and 15–5). Bank of Boston is geared to private sector lending in Latin America with a strong corporate/institutional base and growing retail and fee-based activities. The bank experienced a nonperforming asset ratio of 0.8 percent in 1994 on its Latin loan portfolio.

T A B L E   15-2

Net Income Analysis (in millions)

	1990	1991	1992	1993	1994
Latin America	$88.3	$41.6	$106.8	$74.2	$ 83
United States	($486.0)	($162.1)	$210.5	$220.3	$323

Source: Bank of Boston, annual reports.

T A B L E   15-3

Return on Assets

	1990	1991	1992	1993
Latin America	3.69%	1.65%	2.60%	1.26%
United States	(1.60%)	(0.28%)	0.85%	0.74%

Source: CS First Boston.

T A B L E   15-4

Latin American Products

	December 1991	December 1994
Corporate loans (in billions)	$1.2	$3.6
Retail loans (in billions)	$0.1	$0.8
Deposits (in billions)	$1.3	$3.0
Credit card holders	32,000	113,000
Global custody (in billions)		$6.4
Mutual funds (in billions)	$0.3	$1.8

Source: CS First Boston.

Lawrence Cohn, Paine Webber bank analyst, estimates the value of the Argentine franchise to be about $900 million, or $8 per Bank of Boston share. During 1994, Argentina represented 52 percent of the bank's Latin American operating income, while Brazil (26 branches in 1994) contributed 30 percent and other Latin American countries contributed 18 percent (see Figures 15–1 and 15–2).

T A B L E   15–5

Latin American Branches (1994)

	Year Entered Market	Assets (in billions)	Branches	Rank
Argentina*	1917	$3.1	43	1 or 2
Brazil	1947	3.2	26	1 or 2
Chile	1979	0.8	9	3
Uruguay	1976	0.4	12	3

* Branches increased to over 130 during 1995.
Source: *CS First Boston.*

F I G U R E   15–1

Breakdown of 1994 Latin American Income, $150 Million Operating Income

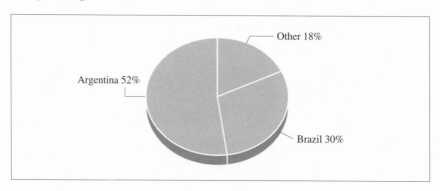

Latin American operations are expected to increase from about 20 percent of the bank's $798 million in pretax income in 1994 to 25 percent by 1997.

The explosive growth of the Latin American operation worries some analysts. Raphael Soifer, Brown Brothers Harriman, points out that "most of the loans that went bad in the 1980s were made in the 1970s, and when they were made everyone pointed to the growing economies." Latin America's historical instability is of great concern. On the other hand, Bank of Boston's return on assets from that region is much higher than in the United States. Executive management at the bank feels that credit quality is high and that the bank has been careful about its credit standards. Also, the portfolio is well diversified. Diane Glossman, Salomon Brothers, agrees that Latin American business is risky, but she points out

F I G U R E   15–2

Bank of Boston's Latin America Operations (in millions)

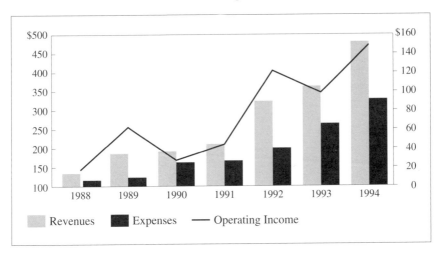

Source: *CS First Boston.*

that the "spreads tend to be bigger to make up for extreme volatility." Since spreads tend to shrink in wholesale lending when economies stabilize, Bank of Boston has been doing more lending to consumers and midsized businesses where the spreads are considerably larger and more stable.[1]

LOAN PORTFOLIO

From December 1989 to December 1994, the bank's total volume of loans grew from $25.1 billion to $31.0 billion. However, there was a shift in asset composition. The percentage of loans from personal, domestic commercial and industrial, and global banking increased significantly, while the percentage of loans in commercial real estate and highly leveraged transactions (HLTs) declined steeply (see Table 15–6). At year-end 1994, the portfolio was comprised of 53 percent domestic commercial loans, 24 percent domestic consumer-related loans, and 23 percent international loans.

In recent years, Bank of Boston has made a concerted effort to shift its strategy away from a high concentration in corporate domestic lending toward personal-related businesses, such as consumer finance, mortgage banking, and private banking. For example, its consumer loans outstanding jumped from $1.7 billion at year-end 1990 to $3.6 billion at year-end 1994. In addition, its mortgage-servicing rights increased to $38 billion at year-end 1994 from $21 billion

T A B L E   15–6

Loan Portfolio Composition

	1994	1989
Personal banking	24%	14%
Global banking	23	12
Domestic commercial and industrial	38	32
Commercial real estate	11	21
HLTs	4	21
Total	100%	100%

Source: Bank of Boston, 1994 *Annual Report*, p. 38.

at year-end 1991. During the same time frame, mortgage originations grew from $5 billion to $15 billion.

The company has recently tried to strengthen its corporate banking area, excluding lending, by bolstering its financial advisory and intermediary role in transactions of midsized corporate customers, wherein lie 80 percent of the bank's 10,000 corporate relationships.

Bank of Boston had little direct exposure to the Mexican currency crisis. Nonetheless, currency and credit risks do exist in other Latin American nations, and any devaluation actions, similar to those in Mexico, would in turn affect the bank's business. However, a near-term major devaluation in Brazil and Argentina, the bank's key Latin American areas of exposure, is not anticipated. Although the local Argentine banking system benefited somewhat from greater liquidity brought about by an easier monetary policy in 1995, some of the provincial banks remain weak. Some of these provincial banks may become privatized in the next few years, and larger, stronger banks, such as Bank of Boston, should continue to benefit from a flight to quality.[2]

Net income for the full year 1994 was $443 million (before extraordinary items and the effect of accounting changes), compared with $322 million in 1993. This represented an increase of 34 percent on a per share basis. On a fully diluted basis, actual net income was $435 million in 1994, compared to $299 million in 1993.

HISTORY

In 1784 a group of Boston merchants created a bank that would help their businesses and their new country grow. These businesses became the bank's first customers and helped establish a customer focus at the heart of the institution. Throughout its over-200-year history, the bank has patterned its business on the needs of its customers, financing the China trade, establishing a presence in

Argentina to serve New England wool merchants, inventing the term loan to meet the needs of Hollywood studios, and offering the first revolving credit product to consumers. "For the history of Bank of Boston is one of relationship banking— of generations of bankers who embraced their customers' goals as their own and worked increasingly to attain them."[3]

Bank of Boston was the first bank in Boston and was founded as the Massachusetts Bank. Its founders were Boston import-export merchants who no longer wished to deal with British banks when sending money abroad and throughout the rest of the colonies. Unfortunately for consumers, the Massachusetts Bank had strict and conservative commercial lending practices, ignoring the man on the street. The bank did not even pay interest on deposits and sometimes charged a fee for keeping deposits. The bank survived a number of economic crises and the War of 1812 and even lent money to support the Union effort during the Civil War.

The bank renamed itself the Massachusetts National Bank following the passage of a national banking system bill in 1864. When the competition began a series of mergers toward the end of the nineteenth century, Massachusetts National decided to merge with the First National Bank of Boston. First National Bank of Boston was founded in 1859 as Safety Fund Bank, changing its name in 1864 when it became a national bank. It rebuffed a merger with Shawmut before going to the altar with Massachusetts National. The First National Bank prospered through World War I and began to open up international offices and extend credit abroad to countries such as Argentina, Britain, and Russia. The bank established its first international office in 1917 in Buenos Aires to facilitate the growing trade in wool between New England textile mills and the rich pampas of Argentina.[4]

The bank grew and prospered during the 1920s and made its first major entry into retail banking in 1923, when it acquired the International Trust Company. In the early stages of the Great Depression, the bank acquired Old Colony Trust Company and the Jamaica Trust Company. Although it survived the depression in relatively strong condition, it did cut its dividend until 1937 and divested its investment banking unit as a result of the passage of the Glass-Steagall Act in 1933. After World War II, Bank of Boston acquired First National Bank (Revere, Massachusetts) and opened a branch office in Rio de Janeiro in 1947.

Bank of Boston continued to prosper during the 1950s, rapidly expanding its foreign business and its factoring business. It was one of the few American banks to withdraw its assets from Cuba before Fidel Castro nationalized the banks. During the 1960s, Bank of Boston internationalized its factoring business and opened a branch in London. By the 1970s, the bank had acquired a reputation as a creative lender that found unconventional solutions to financial problems. Serge Semenenko, the flamboyant Russian-born head of the bank's special industry lending group, contributed greatly to the bank's image by lending to companies such as Hilton Hotels, International Paper, *The Saturday Evening Post*, and Warner Brothers.

The current bank holding company was organized under the laws of Massachusetts on July 1, 1970, as First National Boston Corp., pursuant to a plan of reorganization instituted by First National Bank of Boston, predecessor of the present wholly owned subsidiary of the same name; the present name was adopted in April 1983.

In 1971, the First National Bank of Boston and First Colony, a national subsidiary, became wholly owned subsidiaries of The First National Boston Corporation, the newly formed holding company. In 1972, the bank acquired Cobbs, Allen and Hall Mortgage Co., Inc., now Mortgage Corp. of the South. During the 1970s, a series of bad shipping loans damaged the bank's loan portfolio and consequently reduced earnings considerably.

In 1973, Burlington Bank and Trust Co. (now Bank of Boston–Middlesex), First Bank and Trust Co. of Wellesley (now Bank of Boston–Norfolk), and Holyoke National Bank (now Bank of Boston–Hampden, N.A.) were acquired. In 1976, the bank acquired Invenchek, Inc., of Georgia; in 1977, it acquired the First National Bank of Yarmouth (now Barnstable, N.A.). In 1978, the bank acquired Blackstone Valley National Bank (now Bank of Boston–Worcester) and Marblehead Bank and Trust Co. (renamed Bank of Boston–Essex). During the 1970s and into the early 1980s, the Bank of Boston suffered from poorly performing shipping loans.

In 1980, it acquired Pittsfield National Bank (now Bank of Boston–Berkshire, N.A.) and Southeastern Bancorp, Inc. (now Bank of Boston–Bristol). In 1981, the Bank of Boston acquired the Country Bank, N.A. (renamed Bank of Boston–Franklin, N.A.) and Haverhill National Bank (renamed Bank of Boston–Northern Essex, N.A.). Then, in 1983, the Bank of Boston–Northern Essex was merged into Bank of Boston–Essex; and Bank of Boston–Hampden, N.A. and Bank of Boston–Franklin, N.A. were merged to form Bank of Boston–Western Massachusetts, N.A. Additionally in 1983, the Bank of Boston acquired Stockton, Whatley, Davin and Co., and Fall River Trust Co., which was subsequently merged into the Bank of Boston–Bristol.

Casco-Northern Corp. (Maine) was acquired by the Bank of Boston in 1984 in a stock swap, but was sold to KeyCorp in 1994 when the bank decided to focus its retail banking activities on southern New England. Both Colonial Bancorp Inc. and RIHT Financial Corp. in 1985 were also acquired in stock swaps. RIHT was the parent of Rhode Island Hospital Trust, a large trust and commercial bank headquartered in Providence.

The bank developed a reputation for aloofness, if not arrogance, according to a rival banker who in 1985 told *Business Week* that "they just project an elitist, uncaring attitude." The bank's public image suffered in 1985 when the Justice Department charged it with processing more than $1.2 billion in cash transactions throughout its branch system between 1980 and 1984 of funds belonging to Gennaro J. Angiula, reputed head of New England's largest crime-family, without reporting them to the U.S. Treasury as required by law. After initially denying the accusations, the bank later admitted guilt and paid a substantial fine.

In 1988, the Bank of Boston acquired the Bank of Vermont Corp., which it later sold to KeyCorp in 1994. In 1989, BancBoston Financial Company, a subsidiary, acquired the factoring portfolio of First Union Commercial Corporation, a subsidiary of First Union National Bank of North Carolina. Although the bank recovered from the Angiula affair, it faced some severe financial problems during the 1990–93 recession in New England, particularly from overexposure to the deteriorating commercial real estate market in the region. These problems raised serious questions about the way William Brown ran the bank. Brown was replaced by an Armenian banker, Ira Stepanian (a nonmember of Boston's Beacon Hill society), who became chairman of the holding company. His regime can be credited with turning the bank around, raising substantial amounts of capital, transforming it into a retail bank, and getting it involved in its local community. The new management team realized that it could no longer sit and wait for businesses to come to the bank for their lending and cash management needs, as had been the case under Brahman-like management style of past administrations. Shedding their stuffy and arrogant image, loan officers and executive management began to go out and solicit business under Stepanian. Now, more decision making is in the hands of employees who are close to the customers.

In 1991, Bank of Boston divested itself of Old Colony Trust to NCNB Corp. In that same year, the FDIC sold the failed Bank of New England to Fleet/Norstar rather than either the Bank of Boston or BankAmerica, the other bidders. Shawmut later rejected a buyout offer from the Bank of Boston on January 15, 1993, following close to one year of negotiations, preferring to remain independent after a seeming recovery in earnings. Later in 1993, Bank of Boston acquired $2.4 billion asset Society for Savings Bancorp, Inc. (Connecticut) and $2.4 billion asset Multibank Financial Corp., headquartered in Dedham, Massachusetts. The acquisition of Society, with headquarters in Hartford, propelled Bank of Boston–Connecticut to a position as that state's fourth largest bank. Through Society, the holding company also gained a high-return consumer finance subsidiary, Fidelity Acceptance Corp., with 121 offices in 24 states. With the acquisition of Fidelity, more than 30 percent of the corporation's consumer loan portfolio lies outside of New England. President Charles Gifford has indicated a desire to expand the Connecticut banking franchise into wealthy Fairfield County. The acquisition of Massachusetts-based Multibank Financial strengthened the company's retail banking position in the eastern part of the state. To meet a condition of approval of the merger set by the Federal Reserve Board, the corporation raised approximately $170 million of additional capital. This regulatory capital was required to be maintained exclusively for use in addressing any needs in the corporation's banking subsidiaries.

The company also acquired the $1.5 billion Bank Worcester Corporation, parent company of the 28-branch Worcester County Institution for Savings, giving the bank the leading market share in the second largest city in Massachusetts. These acquisitions brought the bank's total number of branches in the state to 212. Additional acquisitions in Massachusetts that do not dilute EPS can be expected. Bank of Boston must concentrate on additional cost-cutting, closing of redundant and unprofitable branches, and integration of general ledger systems, customer information systems, and a system of demand deposit platforms if it is to lower signigicantly its efficiency ratio.

In June 1993, the company launched the 1784 family of mutual funds, designed to provide investment options complementing customers' savings, money market accounts, and CDs. By year-end 1994, its mutual fund assets stood at $1.4 billion. However, this was a late entry into an industry with intense competition; in addition, in the mutual fund business it takes over $1.5 billion in assets under management to break even. Bank of Boston has also established a broker-dealer subsidiary, 1784 Investor Services, Inc.

During 1994, the company sold its Canadian and U.S. factoring businesses, recording a $32 million pretax gain, and its banks in Vermont and Maine, again at a considerable capital gain. It appears as if Bank of Boston wishes to concentrate its retail banking activities in the southern New England states and Argentina, while still maintaining both a national and international presence in wholesale banking. The Maine and Vermont branch sales to KeyCorp included about $31 million in nonperforming loans and $35 million of goodwill, which should help to strengthen Bank of Boston's balance sheet. The sales also demonstrate management's increasing focus on business-unit profitability, resource allocation, and shareholder returns.[5] The Bank of Boston announced an expansion in highly profitable Argentina with the opening of 10 new branches. In addition, the company acquired Pioneer Bank (Massachusetts), a retail bank with total assets of about $800 million. The company also announced a definitive agreement to acquire Ganis Corporation, a consumer finance company with loan originations of about $380 million annually. Ganis, headquartered in California, specializes in collateral lending for recreational vehicles and boats and should be a valuable complement to Fidelity Acceptance Corporation, a 135-office loan origination network acquired in 1993. On an ongoing basis, Bank of Boston considers possible acquisitions of financial institutions, as well as other assets, to expand according to its business strategy.

The Bank of Boston survived a traumatic recession in New England and has begun to work its way out of its problems. Led by the determined Ira Stepanian, the bank staged a dramatic turnaround from the depths of the 1990–91 period, when it came close to failure. This near fatal collapse was caused by a combination of factors, including a weakened New England economy, a huge portfolio of commercial real estate and construction loans, and questionable asset-quality controls.[6]

Asset quality has continued to improve. Nonperforming loans and assets have declined from a peak of almost $2.3 billion in 1991 to $509 million during the fourth quarter of 1994 (see Figure 15–3). Nonperforming assets to total assets

F I G U R E   15–3

Selected Bank of Boston Financial Ratios (in millions)

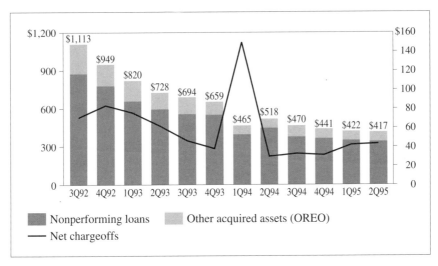

Source: *CS First Boston.*

had declined to about 1.4 percent at year-end 1994 from a peak of close to 8 percent during 1991. During 1994, the company accelerated its disposition of troubled real estate assets. By year-end 1994, its ratio of loan loss reserves to nonperforming assets was at a conservative 134 percent, while the ratio of reserves to average loans was 2.28 percent. Once the company was able to alleviate the enormous burden of poor credit quality in its loan portfolio, it began to reconfigure itself for the future by increasing its capital, expanding into retail banking in southern New England and Latin America, and acquiring mortgage banking and asset management companies. In addition, the company has sold businesses and branches that do not fit into its redesigned strategy, while concentrating on businesses with the highest return and greatest growth potential.

Bank of Boston has made a serious effort to become more of a credit intermediator and less of a purely originating bank in response to the narrowing margins on investment grade lending. The bank is in the process of implementing a discipline that emphasizes risk-adjusted return on capital, which should help the intermediating process. Bank of Boston is also moving toward greater distribution, that is, selling more noncredit products, as well as emphasizing the specialty-industry relationships (media, communications, energy, utilities, transportation, technology, mortgage warehousing loans, and environmental services) where pricing remains better.[7]

At year-end 1994, the Bank of Boston's capital position was comfortable with a 7.0 percent Tier 1 ratio and a 12.0 percent total risk-based capital ratio, well above the 6 percent and 10 percent levels, respectively, that regulators define for a well-capitalized bank.

Bank of Boston's vision is to become a customer-focused, relationship-driven company—to become the bank of choice in the markets it has chosen to serve. It intends to build lasting relationships with customers by understanding their goals, exceeding their expectations, and listening to their many voices. The bank states that it will meet this commitment by demonstrating teamwork, candor, and capability, and by delivering excellent service with efficiency and with integrity. It has also pledged to unleash the energy and imagination of employees to serve its customers.

Bank of Boston has done a good job of improving its efficiency ratio. In the fourth quarter of 1994, the company's efficiency ratio was 59.6 percent, down from 76.2 percent in March 1993. Its goal is to get its efficiency ratio to 57 percent by 1997 (see Figure 15–4). Toward this end, part-time employees represented 14 percent of branch personnel in 1992; this is expected to shift to 55 percent by year-end 1995. Additionally, the bank is working hard to integrate and consolidate its branches and technology.

In the interim, Bank of Boston achieved an ROA of 1.08 percent and an ROE of 14.6 percent in 1994, a considerable improvement over the depressed ratios of 1991 and 1992. Bank of Boston is working hard to improve these subpar returns.

Although the company seems committed to the wholesale lending and regional banking business in Massachusetts, Connecticut, and Rhode Island, it has begun to emphasize the middle-market and small commercial lending businesses,

F I G U R E   15–4

Bank of Boston Efficiency Ratio

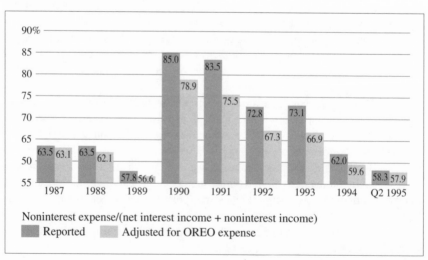

Noninterest expense/(net interest income + noninterest income)
Reported   Adjusted for OREO expense

while also building a consumer banking franchise throughout southern New England. The average deposits per branch of $70 million is considerably higher than those of local banks. The branch network has been an active source for deposit gathering, but it has not been nearly as effective in asset generation. The bank is working to improve this area. In these market segments, loan pricing is typically much higher than in wholesale lending; consequently, returns should be higher along with increased risk.

Profitability and growth have been given a sharper focus by senior management now that the bank's nagging commercial real estate problems are being resolved. Latin American operations will also be fueled for growth. The foreign operations of Bank of Boston place the bank just behind the most active money center banks and easily ahead of all superregional banks. The company anticipates that retail and global banking each will move toward 25–30 percent of total pretax earnings by 1997—from 15 percent in 1994—by outgrowing the expansion in the wholesale business, which currently represents 70 percent of pretax earnings.[8]

The bank also expects to grow revenues in such specialty products as mortgage banking, mezzanine finance and equity investing, personal trust, auto finance, stock transfer, and retail banking. To expand its residential mortgage banking operation, Bank of Boston agreed to purchase the Meridian Mortgage Corporation's $2.5 billion mortgage-servicing portfolio. That acquisition helped Bank of Boston become the nation's eighth largest originator, with $14 billion in new loans during 1993. The mortgage affiliate did business in 49 states and serviced $38 billion in mortgages during 1994, while originating $8 billion in mortgages in that year. In addition, Banc Boston Mortgage announced in May 1995 that it would acquire the Bell Mortgage Co., a privately held company based in Minneapolis. Bell originated about $275 million in residential mortgages during 1994. Banc Boston Mortgage also acquired a branch office in Houston and opened offices in Kansas City, St. Louis, and Gladstone, Missouri. The takeover premiums on mortgage banking operations have begun to shrink. This may help Bank of Boston as the company attempts to expand the mortgage origination and servicing sides of the business to develop greater economies of scale.

Bank of Boston made two other important nonbanking acquisitions in 1995. It acquired Ganis Corporation, a small but highly profitable California-based recreational vehicle and boat financing company. The company has 11 offices and is expected to grow 20–25 percent annually, originating in excess of $400 million in financing per year by 1996. The second acquisition, Century Acceptance Corporation, is a Kansas City–based consumer finance company with 46 branch offices. Bank of Boston should achieve significant cost savings with this acquisition as overlaps with Fidelity Acceptance Corporation are eliminated, resulting in the closing of about 20 branches. Century should add about $1–2 million to the bottom line in 1995 and more than $5 million in 1996 as efficiencies are realized. These acquisitions have also enabled the bank to diversify geographically its consumer loan portfolio, with close to a third of consumer loan assets being booked outside of New England. The bank subsidiaries provide basic consumer lending services, including secured financings of cars, boats, recreational vehicles, and consumer durables through direct loans and second mortgages on residential properties. Despite the slowdown in mortgage banking during 1994, Bank of Boston's personal finance operating income increased to $245 million from $101 million in 1993. In terms of contribution to net income, personal banking expanded from 15 percent in 1993 to 27 percent of total operating income in 1994. This should reach at least 35 percent by 1996. This area should continue to expand both internally and through additional acquisitions for the remainder of the decade.[9]

On the technological front, the bank put into production IBM's high-performance check imaging system for its proof-of-deposit operation. The system accelerates check processing by scanning paper documents and electronically recognizing handwritten dollar amounts of each check, thereby eliminating much of the manual work of bank proof operators.[10]

GLIMPSE OF THE FUTURE

Since its near failure in 1990, the bank has whittled away at its burdensome asset base, while streamlining and diversifying the financial organization. Bank of Boston should have above-average earnings and dividend growth, driven by expense reductions, higher-margin consumer lending, improved asset quality, and redeployment of capital through 1995–96. Management has been concentrating on reducing its core overhead ratio from one of the industry's highest at 74 percent to a much more competitive 59.6 percent in the fourth quarter of 1994 and 57.9 percent in the second quarter of 1995. Bank of Boston is also expected to commit greater resources to higher-return business lines, such as personal and global operations (see Figure 15–5). Therefore, we can expect a switch from a predominantly wholesale banking focus to a more balanced business line with an earnings mix of 35 percent corporate banking, 40 percent personal products, and 25 percent global operations by 1997, from 53 percent, 27 percent, and 20 percent, respectively, in 1994. It is also anticipated that the bank will syndicate and securitize more of its loans rather than leaving the commercial loans that it originates on the balance sheet.[11]

Bank of Boston's balance sheet is interest rate neutral. Additionally, almost 80 percent of the bank's domestic corporate loans are floating-rate loans, repriced off of LIBOR, Eurodollars, or the prime rate. Furthermore, its investment portfolio represents a relatively small 7 percent of earning assets. On the other hand, the bank has one of the highest concentrations of loans to total assets among the 35 largest banks in the country, which could hurt it in a recessionary environment.[12]

We expect to see greater emphasis on fee income, primarily resulting from acquisitions that will complement the bank's existing mortgage banking and finance companies (areas targeted by management) and growth in personal trust, stock transfer, and loan syndication efforts (see Figure 15–6 and Table 15–7). Led by trust and agency fees, financial service fees, foreign exchange trading, mezzanine financing, venture capital, mortgage banking, and loan syndication fees, noninterest income is expected to achieve good growth, exceeding $1.025 billion by 1997.

F I G U R E   15-5

Shifting Business-Line Profitability, 1993–1995E

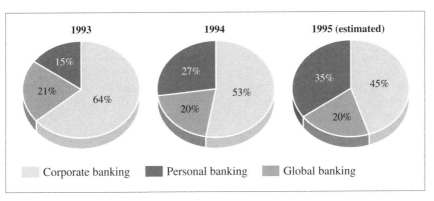

F I G U R E   15-6

Noninterest Income, 1992–1994 (in millions)

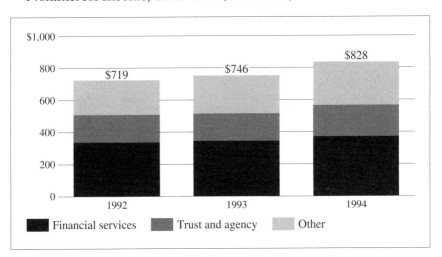

Source: *CS First Boston.*

T A B L E   15-7

Noninterest Income (in millions)

Source	1994	1993
Trust/agency fees	$201	$178
Trading profits/commissions	16	24
Securities gains, net	14	32
Mezzanine/venture capital profits	30	38
Net foreign exchange trading	42	45
Other	102	79
Financial service fees	396	350
Deposit fees	126	122
Letters of credit/acceptances	61	58
Net mortgage-servicing fees	57	6
Loan-related fees	60	45
Factoring fees	4	24
Other	88	95
Total	$828	$746

Source: Bank of Boston, 1994 *Annual Report*, p. 34.

Bank of Boston is a prime acquisition candidate for any bank wishing entry into New England, a larger corporate lending exposure, or a strong franchise in Latin America. It is also a candidate for a friendly merger of equals. Following the merger of Fleet with Shawmut and First Union with First Fidelity, it may become more difficult for Bank of Boston to compete effectively in a more aggressive retail marketing environment. Any problem in Latin America or elsewhere in its operations could bring Bank of Boston to the bargaining table with BankAmerica, Bank of New York, Banc One, NationsBank, CoreStates, Mellon, KeyCorp, First Union, or even Citicorp. Fleet Financial's agreement to merge with Shawmut seemed to act as a catalyst in the acquisition arena. Shawmut had turned down a Bank of Boston merger offer a few years earlier; and there was speculation that Fleet and Bank of Boston were holding merger discussions when the Fleet merger with Shawmut was announced in February 1995 and that First Fidelity almost went to the altar with First Boston in June 1995. CoreStates and Banc One also could not reach an agreement to merge with Bank of Boston in July 1995. Bank of Boston was close to merging with Mellon, but Stepanian persuaded his board of directors to merge instead with CoreStates Financial. However, intense criticism from Wall Street and other Bank of Boston investors concerning a no-premium merger-of-equals offer from CoreStates (thought to be in the $38–40 per share range) was one of the reasons merger discussions broke down. The offer was just too low to satisfy investors.

Also, the deal had limited cost-saving opportunities. Many Bank of Boston investors were hoping for a takeover at or near $50 per share. At the same time Banc One offered $45 per share and then withdrew the offer three days later.

The bank's board of directors has avoided putting the bank up for sale and attracting the highest bid because that would mean losing a Boston-domiciled bank. On July 27, Stepanian resigned from the company, following ill-fated attempts to merge with Shawmut, Fleet, First Fidelity, CoreStates, Mellon, and Banc One. Nancy Bush, a Brown Brothers Harriman analyst, said, "My sense is that it is true that [Stepanian] has bypassed some opportunities . . . Historically, the CEOs of banks have come up through the bank by being good soldiers for 25 years and clawing their way to the top. They see the CEO spot as their reward and are reluctant to let go."[13] There is also the possibility that the detail-minded, often inflexible Stepanian was immovable on too many key issues.

Even though the bank is a leading local institution and may not feel threatened by the in-market merger of its chief rivals, the pressure on Bank of Boston to describe a viable, long-term strategy is coming to a boil. The bank has jettisoned business lines or operations that have not generated meaningful returns and reinvested those proceeds in the historically weak retail operations or in Latin America; however, it is unclear whether management and the board of directors will perceive these steps as sufficient. Bank of Boston can maintain the status quo, continuing to pursue an independent strategy based on gradually improving its existing business mix. The bank would then continue to pare low-return functions and cut operating costs, while continuing to build its retail banking business (with further acquisitions) and the Latin American franchise. A second option might be to take in a joint venture partner for the Latin American operation to gain financing for growth and lessen dependence on this potentially volatile and risky earnings source. A third option could include a merger with one of the aforementioned institutions.

Under Chairman Charles Gifford, president prior to the departure of Stepanian, a new game plan may emerge. If the bank chooses to remain independent, we can expect it to make selective acquisitions to increase its consumer and small-business capabilities, while eliminating any branching overlaps. The company will also be looking for acquisitions to boost fee income, especially in mortgage banking and finance companies. In other words, we can expect fill-in and functional mergers similar to the recent acquisition of Society of Savings and Meridian's Mortgage Banking Company. The bank generally maintains that all mergers or acquisitions must be accretive within two years, unless there is a strong overriding strategic importance to the transaction, such as opening up a new adjacent-marketplace to distribute already existing products and services.[14]

Chairman Gifford announced an agreement to acquire Boston Bancorp, a savings bank with $2.2 billion in assets, in October 1995, a deal former chairman Ira Stepanian was unable to accomplish. Bank of Boston gains 70,000 customers with $1.3 billion in deposits at seven branches, mostly in working class neighborhoods.

The customers of the acquired savings bank have not had access to many bank products, giving Bank of Boston an opportunity to cross-sell many of its more sophisticated consumer banking and investment products. Bank of Boston will swap between $218 to $225 million of its shares to pay for the transaction. Bank of Boston indicated that it would buy back outstanding shares of its stock to pay for the acquisition. The bank will pay Boston Bancorp shareholders a $40 million premium on the adjusted book value of the shares. That value will be affected by the proceeds Boston Bancorp receives from the sale of its $1.6 billion investment portfolio (72 percent of the company's assets), including all of its $130 million commercial loan portfolio. The transaction should be accretive to earnings immediately. It should lower Bank of Boston's cost of funds, as the company is buying $1.3 billion of low cost deposits. Management has also targeted cost savings of $9 million, 30 percent of Boston Bancorp's noninterest expense base. Bank of Boston expects to take a restructuring charge of $6–7 million and will amortize over 10 years $40 million of goodwill. The purchase price of 1.2 times book value is below the average deal price paid for thrifts in 1995.

Just as we were going to press, Bank of Boston announced an agreement to buy BayBanks ($11.5 billion in assets) for $2.2 billion. Following the acquisition of BayBanks, Bank of Boston will have about $58 billion in assets and 500 branches throughout New England. The company will have the dominant position in retail banking in Massachusetts, with a primary relationship with 27 percent of the households and a checking/NOW account with 34 percent of the market. William Crozier, chairman and CEO of BayBanks, will become chairman of Bank of Boston, and Charles Gifford will become president and CEO, assuming the chairmanship upon the retirement of Mr. Crozier in 1998. While the corporation will maintain the Bank of Boston name, the domestic banking franchise will operate under the name of BayBanks.

The indicated purchase price equals 2.16 times BayBank's book value. Pro forma, the deal dilutes Bank of Boston's book value per share by close to 8 percent, including a $240 million pretax restructuring charge. There will be only modest dilution in 1996 earnings per share, assuming $190 million of pretax cost savings, 39 percent of BayBanks costs. The cost savings will come from the closing of 85 branches and from a 2,000-person reduction in head count. (Bank of Boston has 279 branches and 18,000 employees, while BayBanks has 223 branches and 6,500 employees.) The company expects that the realization of cost savings in 1997 and 1998 along with funding advantages from the merger (projected by the company at $24 million after-tax in 1997) should lead to strong earnings per share growth in 1997 and 1998.

This deal gives Bank of Boston the ability to remain independent and be a first-tier player in retail banking in New England. On the other hand, the combined banks themselves are an even more alluring takeover candidate.[15]

Bank of Boston has substantial hidden assets that should help its price in the event of a takeover. These include an overfunded pension plan, undervalued venture capital assets, valuable nonbank assets, and an extremely valuable and profitable Latin American franchise. These factors should result in an upward adjustment to book value of at least $2 per share on a base of approximately $25 per share.

ENDNOTES

1. J. Rebello, "Bank of Boston Reaps Rewards of Its Latin Investment," *The Wall Street Journal*, November 3, 1994.
2. T.H. Hanley, "Bank of Boston Corp.," *CS First Boston*, January 31, 1995, p. 4; and July 3, 1995, p. 7.
3. Bank of Boston, 1993 *Annual Report* (inside front cover).
4. Bank of Boston, 1992 *Annual Report*.
5. S.P. Davis, "Bank of Boston Corporation," *Goldman Sachs U.S. Research*, June 27, 1994, pp. 1–4.
6. T.H. Hanley, "Bank of Boston Corp.," *CS First Boston*, September 20, 1994, p. 5.
7. C.S. Berger, "Bank of Boston—What's Next?" *Salomon Brothers Research Report*, July 29, 1994, pp. 3–4.
8. D. Glassman, "Bank of Boston, Looking Up," *Salomon Brothers Research Report*, June 2, 1994, p. 2.
9. Hanley, July 3, 1995, pp. 5–6.
10. T.H. Hanley, J.P. Carter, and A.B. Collins, "Banking Weekly," *CS First Boston*, October 26, 1994, p. 3.
11. T.H. Hanley, J.P. Carter, and A.B. Collins, "Bank of Boston Corp.," *CS First Boston*, September 22, 1994, p. 8.
12. T.H. Hanley, "Bank of Boston Corp.," *CS First Boston*, December 21, 1994, p. 5.
13. T.L. O'Brien and S. Lipin, "Bank of Boston's Ira Stepanian Resigns after Failed Quests for a Merger Partner," *The Wall Street Journal*, July 28, 1995, p. 3.
14. T.H. Hanley, "Bank of Boston Corp.," *CS First Boston*, September 27, 1994, p. 19.
15. C. Kotowski, "Bank of Boston," *Oppenheimer & Co., Inc.*, December 18, 1995, pp. 2–3.

T A B L E   15–8

Bank of Boston Corp. Financials

	1990	1991	1992	1993	1994
Earnings per share	($5.61)	($0.53)	$2.84	$2.45	$3.61
Assets (in millions)	$36,489	$31,747	$31,675	$38,367	$43,061
Net income (in millions)	($394.52)	($26.60)	$263.10	$299.03	$435.36
Return on assets	(1.08%)	(0.08%)	0.83%	0.78%	1.01%

	1994	
	(in millions)	%
Average earning assets	$38,145	100
Securities	3,510	9
Loans	29,790	78
Other	4,845	13
Loans	31,003	100
Construction and land	354	
Commercial mortgage	3,140	
Highly leveraged	1,272	
Commercial loans and leases	11,981	
Other foreign	7,006	
Term LCD	0	
Credit card receivables	0	
Other consumer	2,462	
Unearned discount	(216)	
Corporate	23,753	77
Consumer	2,246	7
Mortgages	5,004	16

	1990	1991	1992	1993	1994
Efficiency ratio	82.42	72.16	69.59	67.31	60.82
Shareholder equity (in millions)	$1,990	$1,573	$1,916	$2,719	$3,023
Preferred	$208	$208	$297	$508	$508
Common	$1,782	$1,365	$1,619	$2,211	$2,515

F I G U R E   15–7

Bank of Boston Corp. Financial Charts

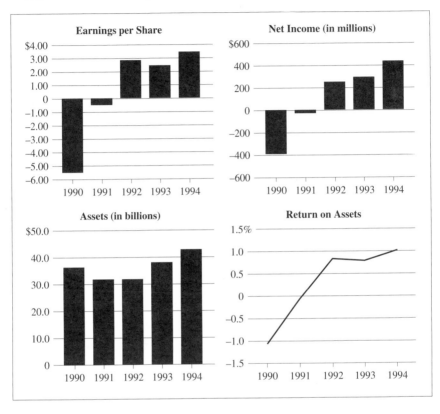

F I G U R E   15–8

Bank of Boston Corp. Financial Charts

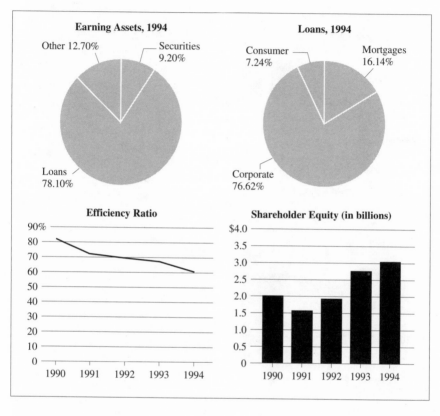

CHAPTER 16

Bank of New York

The Bank of New York Holding Company, Inc., was the 16th largest bank holding company in the United States, with $48.8 billion in assets at year-end 1994. The principal subsidiary, the Bank of New York, provides complete commercial banking, trust, and investment services to banks, corporations, institutions, and individuals in the United States and abroad. The company has transformed itself into a diverse, fee-driven institution. Noninterest income products, such as securities processing and trust and investment, accounted for 39.10 percent of total net revenues in 1994 and 46.84 percent in 1993, while the credit card business is expected to account for close to 22 percent of corporate net income. Bank of New York was the ninth largest bankcard issuer in the nation, with 6 million cards outstanding and receivables of $7.7 billion at year-end 1994.

The management team at Bank of New York, headed by Chairman J. Carter Bacot and President Thomas A. Renyi, is considered one of the finest in the business. The company's culture breeds a customer-driven, highly productive, shareholder-conscious approach to the banking business.[1]

The Bank of New York conducts a national and international wholesale banking business and offers retail banking services throughout New York and northern New Jersey. It also provides a comprehensive range of trust and investment services. In addition to accepting funds for deposit, making loans of all types, and providing personal trust, factoring, corporate trust, and investment counsel services, the Bank of New York issues domestic and foreign letters of credit, transmits funds to domestic or foreign points, buys and sells foreign exchange, issues American depository receipts, and accepts securities and other valuables for safekeeping. The bank holds a total of $3.4 trillion in custody assets. It ranks among the leaders in mutual fund custody (about $300 billion in assets under administration), corporate trust (serving 20,000 public and private issues, with more than $300 billion in principal), and stock transfer agency (more than 7 million shareholder accounts for 350 clients).[2] Bank of New York ranks number one in ADRs (56 percent market share), depository receipts, securities lending, and government securities clearance; it ranks second in mutual fund, custody, and unit trust. First Boston stock analyst Thomas H. Hanley compares Bank of New York to State Street Bank in terms of processing and MBNA or First U.S.A. for credit cards.

The bank also offers international corporate banking services in its foreign offices, including those relating to commercial ventures and activities abroad as well as those related to import-export transactions. Foreign operations income derived from loans continued to decline as a percentage of total revenue, as did the overall foreign contribution which provided 8.1 percent of net income in 1994, 10.6 percent in 1993, 21 percent in 1992, and 37 percent in 1991. On the other hand, the securities and processing business contributed 20 percent of overall net income and more than $530 million (40 percent) of total noninterest income in 1994 (see Table 16–1). With the recent additions of corporate trust and custody businesses (see section entitled "Recent Acquisitions"), the securities processing business should generate more than 25 percent of the bank's overall net income by 1996.

The big revenue drivers in processing continue to be government securities clearance (a continued lack of competition has led to good pricing), ADRs, and corporate trust fees. New sources of fee income are expected to come from the sale of annuities and from three proprietary mutual funds, as well as the acquired corporate trust or ADR processing businesses of NationsBank, JP Morgan, BankAmerica, Meridian, Hibernia, and Cullen Frost. The aforementioned businesses help generate security lending business relating to broker-dealer clearing business. The

T A B L E   16–1

Noninterest Income (in millions)

	1992	1993	1994	1995E	1996E	1997E
Processing fees						
Securities	$ 275	$ 309	$ 359			
Other	148	162	171			
Total	423	471	530			
Trust/investments	121	134	126			
Service charges	437	454	465			
Securities gains	42	64	15			
Other	160	196	153			
Total	$1,183	$1,319	$1,289	$1,345	$1,645	$1,795

Source: Bank of New York, 1994 *Annual Report*, p. 19, and author estimates (E).

settlement network was expanded to 48 countries, while securities lending was expanded to 20 markets, with assets available for lending above $100 billion and average outstandings of $30 billion. In addition, Bank of New York had $14 billion of institutional assets, $12 billion in personal assets, and over $11 billion in custodial assets under management and administration in 1994. Processing, service, trust, and investment fees were the major contributors to noninterest income at the bank (see Table 16–1). This area is expected to show marked revenue improvement in 1996–97 as a result of nine security processing acquisitions made in 1995.

CREDIT CARD BUSINESS

The Bank of New York (Delaware) provides lending and cash management services to corporations primarily located in the mid-Atlantic region. Credit cards contributed approximately 22 percent of the bank's net income in 1994, as outstandings grew to $7.7 billion at year-end 1994 and $8.0 billion at the end of the second quarter of 1995. From a strategic point of view, Bank of New York offers to credit card customers one of the lowest rates in the business. Given its lower cost of doing business, which includes its credit card costs and low charge-off rate of only 3.2 percent in 1993 for the entire credit card portfolio (approximately 100 basis points below the industry average), this line of business has become remarkably profitable. Other credit developments have included the addition of three major unions to the company's successful Union Privilege program: the carpenters' union, the teamsters' union, and the American Teachers Federation. The Union Privilege program accounted for more than 40 percent of cards at year-end 1993 and offered an interest rate on outstanding loans of 5 percent above prime. This is the largest single affinity card in the country. This program is expected to show continued good growth over the next few years.

Bank of New York has continued to demonstrate one of the lowest overheads in the business, with operating costs equaling just 2.3 percent of credit card outstandings in 1993. Only the Bank of New York, among the top 10 bankcard issuers, has adopted a low interest rate strategy. It has also adopted an aggressive solicitation strategy for its credit cards. Over 90 million cards were offered to potential customers during 1994. Response rates on solicitation mailings are four times the industry averages, or 7 percent for union cards and 2.3 percent for other cards. Charge-offs and delinquency rates were much lower than the industry averages.[3]

The bank has begun to offer cobranded Toys "R" Us Visa cards. The no-fee card offers free toys and clothes at Toys "R" Us and points toward free children's travel on airlines and cruises. Cardholders will earn a 3 percent rebate on all purchases at Toys "R" Us and a 1 percent rebate on purchases with the card at other merchants. The Toys "R" Us card could expand credit card outstandings by at least $250 million in 1996.

SPECIALTY LENDING AND BRANCHES

The Bank of New York is based on Wall Street in New York City. It is a leading lender to the communications, entertainment, and publishing industries, with outstanding loans settling in the $2.6–2.9 billion range. It operates just under 380 retail banking offices throughout New York City and its suburbs. This represents the largest retail-oriented market share in the communities surrounding New York City (see Table 16–2). The bank also operates 25 foreign branches and representative offices in Germany, Grand Cayman, Hong Kong, United Kingdom, Japan, Korea, Singapore, Taiwan, Thailand, India, Lebanon, Argentina, Egypt, Turkey, Venezuela, Spain, Philippines, Australia, Italy, France, Mexico, China, and Brazil.

T A B L E   16–2

Branch Locations versus Competition (year-end 1994)

Locations	Bank of New York*	Chemical	Chase	Citibank	Natwest
Long Island	97	74	38	35	68
Northern NYC	136	23	34	30	24
New Jersey	108	120	0	0	132
Total Suburbs	349	217	72	65	224
New York City	36	203	116	154	43
Total	385	420	188	219	267

* As of November, 1995.

Source: Individual company reports.

HISTORY

The Bank of New York, one of the oldest banking organizations in the United States, was founded by Alexander Hamilton and other business associates in 1784. It was opened as a specie bank, based on a metallic monetary system that used coins to back the issuance of paper money rather than land, as in a land bank.

At that time, the country lacked both banks and banking laws. Hamilton devised the constitution for the Bank of New York, the first in New York City, whose policies became the model for most of the banks that followed. Hamilton became U.S. secretary of the treasury in 1789, which aided the bank in enriching relationships with both New York State and the federal government. He sent national business to the bank and protected the institution during difficult times by helping to keep government deposits in the bank. In addition, the bank's original board of directors and investors included many of New York City's leading businessmen and patrician families. The bank's aristocratic heritage helped it gain the confidence of New York's business community and local politicians. It was known in Europe as the largest and safest bank in New York. In 1830, some of the bank's directors assisted in the formation of the New York Life Insurance and Trust Company, another patrician financial services company, which would merge with the Bank of New York almost a century later in 1922.

Its conservatism and image as a safe bank helped it weather a series of financial panics in the United States, which led to the failure of many banks in this country. Because the banks in New York financed most of the cotton and clothing trade between England and the southern states, the outbreak of the Civil War led to some large loan losses. However, the Bank of New York was able to survive this problem, as well as helping the Union finance the Civil War.

In response to the Banking Act of 1863, the Bank of New York shifted to a national charter. It later changed back to a state charter after it merged with the New York Life Insurance and Trust Company. While close to 5,000 banks failed during the Great Depression, the Bank of New York sailed through the largest panic in its financial history with continued profit increases, making dividend payments on time. The bank actively supported President Roosevelt's attempts to stimulate the economy out of the depression and later aided the war effort in the early 1940s.

Following World War II, Bank of New York participated in mergers with Fifth Avenue Bank of midtown Manhattan and with Empire Trust Company (mid-1960s). These mergers brought a different mix of customers to the bank and changed its risk profile. Empire specialized in loans to developing companies, particularly emerging oil and gas companies. The modern day holding company was incorporated in New York on July 8, 1968, as the Bank of New York, Inc. It adopted its present name and commenced operations in 1969 upon the acquisition of six banking subsidiaries: the Bank of New York, Endicott Bank of New York (formerly Endicott National Bank of New York), Exchange Bank of New York (formerly Exchange National Bank of New York), Mechanics and Farmers Bank of Albany, and Metropolitan Bank of Syracuse (formerly Metropolitan National Bank Syracuse).

The bank then acquired Niagara Frontier Bank of New York, which subsequently merged with the Bank of Buffalo in 1975 (assuming the name Bank of Buffalo). In 1972, Mechanics and Farmers Bank of Albany merged with Tanners National Bank of Catskill and took on the name Bank of New York, Albany. Also in 1972, Valley National Bank was acquired and its name changed to Valley Bank of New York. Then in 1974, Valley Bank of New York bought United National Bank of Long Island and subsequently merged.

On January 1, 1976, the company merged all of its eight member banks into the Bank of New York, New York. It is a New York State–chartered trust company and a member of the Federal Reserve system and the FDIC.

In 1980, the bank formed the Bank of New York Life Insurance Co. to provide reinsurance for its installment loan customers. Also in 1980, the bank acquired and merged Empire National Bank into Bank of New York, as well as acquired two mortgage banking subsidiaries: ARCs Mortgage, Inc., and ARCs Mortgage Corp. It also formed BNY Leasing, Inc., a leasing company. In 1981, the Bank of New York Trust Company was formed.

In 1982, J. Carter Bacot became chairman of the bank. Under his vigorous leadership, the holding company underwent dramatic changes. He sold the bank's upstate retail branches, concentrating all of its retail business in the greater New York metropolitan area, especially in suburban Long Island, secondly in Westchester County, and then in northern New Jersey. Bacot also changed the bank's loan philosophy; it began using larger lending limits and making faster decisions. Lending was concentrated in commercial industries, security firms, utilities, and the oil and gas industries. He then began to concentrate the bank's energy on processing the daily transactions of securities brokers. Finally, he initiated a year-long hostile takeover of Irving Trust Company, whose $24 billion in assets were slightly larger than Bank of New York's asset base. This merger expanded substantially the bank's international activities, wholesale banking activities, and corporate trust and processing activities, as well as increasing the amount of trust money under management. The merger increased profitability substantially, in part related to cost savings of close to 35 percent.

Under Bacot, the following new entities and mergers were consummated. In 1983, the bank formed BNY Corp. (Delaware), a bank holding company; its principal subsidiary, the Bank of New York (Delaware), a Delaware banking corporation; the Bank of New York Overseas Finance N.V., a wholly owned subsidiary; and Beacon Capital Management, a wholly owned subsidiary. The bank then sold 36 of its branch offices in 1984. The Delaware bank was chartered primarily to take advantage of that state's lower labor costs and lower taxes.

In 1986, the bank acquired most of the assets of Fidata Trust Company of New York, a subsidiary of Fidata Corp. Also acquired from Fidata Corp. were a trust company in California and a data processing division in Teaneck, New Jersey. Additionally in 1986, the bank acquired a majority interest in RMJ Securities from Security Pacific Corp., and 24.9 percent interest in Leonard Newman, Inc.; it also sold its remaining branches in upper New York State to Norstar Bancorp. In 1987, the bank acquired North American Bancorp, Inc., including its subsidiary Long Island Trust Co.

In 1988, the Bank of New York acquired Irving Bank Corp., a large wholesale bank ($24 billion in assets) with a modest branch system in New York. It was the first time that regulators permitted what was initially a hostile merger of two competing banks. Bacot demonstrated to the banking industry how an in-region merger could be advantageous, as he slashed costs, closed redundant branches, and utilized only one computer and processing system.

In 1989, the Bank of New York divested several of the subsidiaries of the former Irving Bank Corp., including Central Trust Co. (Rochester), Merchants National Bank and Trust Co. (Syracuse), Endicott Trust Co. (Endicott), Union National Bank (Albany), and First National Bank (Moravia). The banks sold had assets of $2.1 billion at year-end 1988 and 72 offices in 17 New York counties. Also in 1989, the Bank of New York sold four upstate New York banks to NBT Bancorp, Inc., of Norwich, New York. The banks sold were the First National Bank of Hancock, Hayes National Bank, Clinton, Fulton County National Bank and Trust Co., and Bank of Lake Placid.

Also in 1989, the bank announced a major change in the organization of its branches in New York. Six new county divisions were created. The bank combined the managements of its own branches in Westchester, Putnam, Queens, Nassau, Suffolk, Dutchess, Rockland, Orange, and Sullivan counties with those of the Bank of Long Island, Dutchess County Bank and Trust Co., Nanuet National Bank, and Scarsdale National Bank and Trust Co.

RECENT ACQUISITIONS

In 1990, the Bank of New York acquired the factoring business of Bankers Trust Co. Also during 1990, the Bank of New York (Delaware) purchased the credit card business of First City Bancorporation of Texas, Inc., and the Dreyfus Consumer Bank's Gold MasterCard portfolio. In 1992, the bank acquired nine branches of American Savings Bank, Riverside Savings Bank, and 62 branches of the banking activities of Barclays Bank of New York, N.A., with $1.8 billion in assets.

In 1993, the Bank of New York acquired National Community Banks, Inc., the seventh largest bank in New Jersey, which is headquartered in Chatham. This 105 branch acquisition ($4.0 billion in assets) brought the company's total number of branches to 383. Although National Community had previously focused on middle-market and small-business clients, Bank of New York has begun to stretch the retail focus of this franchise by offering customers a broader array of products, including 24-hour banking, low-rate credit cards, 60-minute loan approval, and low-cost home mortgages. Bank of New York continued to recognize cost savings from this acquisition related to continued personnel attrition and renegotiated maintenance and branch costs. Of the 1,680 employees in mid-1993, 500 were gone by mid-1994.

During 1993, the company made two important acquisitions in the factoring business. It acquired the factoring businesses of the Bank of Boston and the Canadian Financial Corporation. These two transactions should increase the bank's factoring value from $7.6 billion in 1993 to about $12 billion in 1994. The factoring business can be extremely profitable, provided that the credit quality remains good and proper fraud detection is in place. Bank of New York seems to have a good handle on both of these elements. Consequently, we expect factoring to be one of the major earnings drivers at the company, generating between 8 and 11 percent of earnings, up from 7 percent of total income in 1993. With these acquisitions, BNY Financial Corporation became the second largest factoring operation in the United States and the largest in Canada.

Bank of New York also purchased the corporate trust processing business of Barnett Banks Trust Co. The new relationships acquired in the Southeast should increase the bank's corporate trust business by 10 percent to 16,000 issues, representing over $250 billion in outstanding debt. In addition, Bank of New York announced a decision in the third quarter of 1994 to acquire the corporate and municipal bond administration business of Mercantile Safe Deposit and Trust Co. In all, Bank of New York made four sizable acquisitions of processing businesses during 1993–94, including the corporate trust business of Central Fidelity and Toronto Dominion's New York office. The bank also purchased the ADR business of BankAmerica in January 1995. In addition, Bank of New York signed a definitive agreement with Hibernia Corp. to purchase that company's municipal bond administration business. Bank of New York should receive about 350 municipal bond trustee and agency relationships, with more than $2.7 billion principal amount in outstanding securities. The deal should be accretive to the bank's earnings immediately.

Following its agreement in April 1995 to acquire BankAmerica's processing business, Bank of New York agreed in May 1995 to buy the global securities custody business of JP Morgan for an undisclosed amount (estimated to be $300 million, or about 2.5 times JP Morgan's 1994 revenues from this unit). Bank of New York will take over $800 billion in client assets currently held by JP Morgan in custody accounts, lifting its total assets under custody to about $3.2 trillion, placing Bank of New York's custody business alongside Chase and State Street as one of the biggest in the industry. In June 1995, Bank of New York acquired NationsBank's corporate trust business. There are about 11,500 bond trustee and agency accounts, representing more than $167 billion in outstanding securities. Terms of the deal were not disclosed, but it is estimated that Bank of New York paid about $80 million, or two times NationsBank's 1994 revenue. The NationsBank portfolio consisted of trust and agency appointments for issuers of municipal, corporate, and asset-backed debt instruments. Bank of New York currently has 23,000 corporate trust accounts, with approximately $300 billion in securities. In 1994, and prior to its 1995 acquisition spree, about 20 percent of the company's profits were from the processing business (see Table 16–3). The percentage of total earnings generated from the securities processing business is expected to grow to 25 percent by 1996.

Germane to the JP Morgan custody business, Bank of New York has gained a skilled operations staff and facility in Brussels, to which it will move the existing Bank of New York data center. The bank has the software, hardware, and employee capacity to take on these acquisitions without a bulge in spending or a consolidation charge. The incremental margin on these businesses range from

T A B L E   16–3

Pro Forma Custody and Trust Business, 1994

	Assets (in billions)	Revenue (in millions)
Bank of New York, master trust, custody, securities	$1,650	$107
JP Morgan, global custody	800	136
BankAmerica, domestic custody	462	57
Total	$2,912	$300
BankAmerica, corporate trust	300	123
NationsBank, corporate trust	167	40
Total	$ 467	$163

Source: *CS First Boston*, June 22, 1995, pp. 6–7.

50–90 percent of new revenues because of the elimination of infrastructure costs. Pricing in the industry has begun to stabilize, ending the downward trend in prices. This has positive implications for the bank's existing book of business, bidding on new acquisitions, and pricing on proposal requests.[4]

Bank of New York sold ARCs Mortgage, Inc., with a servicing portfolio of $7.6 billion, to Chase Manhattan Mortgage Co. Bank of New York has indicated that it will remain in the mortgage origination business in the Northeast to service its retail network, but not necessarily elsewhere.

In March 1995, the Bank of New York agreed to acquire Putnam Trust Company, headquartered in Greenwich, Connecticut, for $140 million, or 2.44 times book value. Putnam Trust has eight branches in Fairfield County, with $685 million in assets and $316 million in loans. In 1994, the trust company had an ROA of 0.94 percent and an ROE of 10.82 percent, respectively. Putnam holds over $2 billion in trust assets. The acquisition should be modestly accretive in 1996 with little or no impact on Bank of New York's 1995 earnings, based on 20–30 percent noninterest expense savings.

The bank also announced that it has established its first overseas fund management company. Bank of New York Fund Management Ltd. (Dublin, Ireland) will offer trustee, custody, fund administration and accounting, and transfer agent services to mutual funds in conjunction with Allied Irish Banks. The operations resulted from the bank's following some of its customers who are managing investment funds in Dublin, where several other U.S. banks have set up similar operations. Bank of New York has provided fund management services for U.S. managers operating in Europe since the mid-1980s, but until 1995 it handled such services from New York.

SUMMARY

The bank's net income in 1994 was $749 million, up from $559 million in 1993. It continued to shift its asset mix toward high-yielding assets, showing strong growth in credit card outstandings. The company is also among the leaders in efficiency and productivity. Bank of New York has become a niche player, specializing in at least two areas, credit cards and operation and transaction processing.

If the Bank of New York does not expand nationally in a merger of equals, for instance with another retail or credit card powerhouse like Fleet or CoreStates, it will likely continue to grow its franchise regionally by making sensible retail acquisitions or strategic combinations. Mergers need to be accretive within one year, so price matters. Bank of New York would like to acquire a national diversification, as well as additional processing portfolios, particularly in corporate trust. Its acquisition strategy has been disciplined and focused on building the retail franchise into contiguous markets and on generating more fee income.

The Bank of New York is interested in making further acquisitions; however, acquisitions are not required to fuel the company's growth.[5] With anticipated increases in its credit card and processing businesses and a continued decline in nonperforming loans, the provision for loan losses, and noninterest expense as a percentage of assets, Bank of New York can be expected to generate an ROE above 17 percent and an ROA 1.55 percent in 1996. This compares to an ROE of 15.0 percent and an ROA of 1.21 percent, respectively, in 1993. In 1994, its ROE rose to 18.04 percent, while its ROA improved to 1.46 percent. The company has always been a leader in contracting operating expenses and remains one of the most efficient banks in the country with a 1994 overhead ratio of 54 percent and a 1995 ratio below 50 percent. This ratio has continually declined from a peak of 60.3 percent in 1988. It is expected to decline to about 48 percent by 1996, a sterling performance relative to other banking organizations (see Figure 16–1). The company has a high-quality loan portfolio. Total nonperforming assets were at only 0.72 percent of total assets outstanding in 1994 and close to 65 percent in 1995 (see Figure 16–2). Bank of New York's loan loss reserve as a percentage of nonperforming assets was a conservative 224 percent in 1994 and 236 percent in 1995. Its ratio of loan loss reserve to average loan was also a conservative 2.45 percent for 1994 and just over 2 percent in 1995. The bank was exceptionally well capitalized at year-end 1994, with a ratio of total common equity to assets of close to 8.55 percent, a Tier 1 ratio of 8.45 percent, and a total capital ratio of 13.83 percent. Total capital was strengthened in the fourth quarter of 1994 through the issuance of $300 million of subordinated debentures. Bank of New York has initiated dividend increases and a stock buyback program. The total conversion of warrants issued as part of the Irving Bank merger in 1988 represents a potential increase from 190 to 195 million shares.

The combination of its superior credit card franchise, dominant suburban New York City branch network, growing securities and mutual fund processing

F I G U R E   16–1

Bank of New York Efficiency Ratio

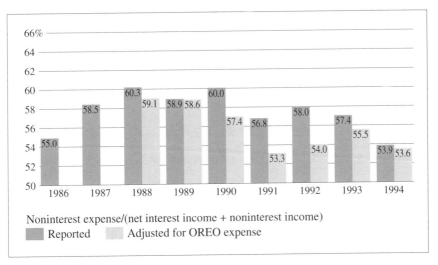

Noninterest expense/(net interest income + noninterest income)
■ Reported   ▒ Adjusted for OREO expense

F I G U R E   16–2

Bank of New York Credit Quality (in millions)

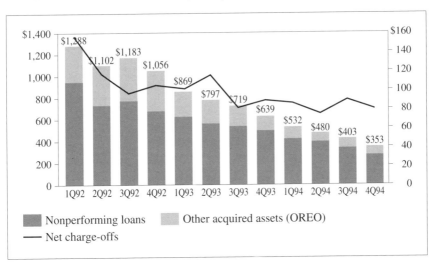

■ Nonperforming loans   ▒ Other acquired assets (OREO)
— Net charge-offs

businesses, international operations, and high productivity distinguish the Bank of New York from its competitors. When excellence in management and strong acquisition and integration skills are added to the other salient characteristics, Bank of

New York should be able to expand earnings per share by low-double-digit numbers in the years ahead because of economies of scale, technological advantages in processing of securities and credit cards, and several successful purchase acquisitions of securities processing businesses.

ENDNOTES

1. T.H. Hanley, "Bank of New York," *CS First Boston*, October 3, 1994, p. 4.
2. D.B. Glossman, "Bank of New York," *Salomon Brothers U.S. Equity Research*, July 22, 1994, p. 8.
3. Hanley, pp. 5–6.
4. D.B. Glossman, "Bank of New York," *Salomon Brothers U.S. Equity Research*, July 21, 1995, pp. 4–5.
5. D.B. Glossman, "Bank of New York—Better than Ever," *Salomon Brothers U.S. Equity Research*, May 11, 1994, p. 2.

T A B L E   16–4

Bank of New York Financials

	1990	1991	1992	1993	1994
Earnings per share	$1.99	$0.64	$2.12	$2.72	$3.70
Assets (in millions)	$53,214	$46,617	$46,227	$46,664	$50,280
Net income (in millions)	$311.00	$134.00	$393.00	$559.00	$749.00
Return on assets	0.58%	0.29%	0.85%	1.20%	1.49%

	*1994**	
	(in millions)	%
Average earning assets	$42,889	100
Securities	5,941	14
Loans	32,029	75
Other	4,919	11
Loans	33,082	100
Construction and land	173E	
Commercial mortgage	2,842E	
Highly leveraged	1,422E	
Commercial loans and leases	14,867E	
Other foreign	4,531E	
Term LCD	163E	
Credit card receivables	0	
Other consumer	6,524E	
Unearned discount	(906)E	
Corporate	23,998	73
Consumer	5,618	17
Mortgages	3,466	10

	1990	1991	1992	1993	1994
Efficiency ratio	56E	55.85	54.87	55.66	54.13
Shareholder equity (in millions)	$3,006	$3,047	$3,405	$3,897	$4,137
Preferred	$395	$395	$409	$334	$157
Common	$2,611	$2,652	$2,996	$3,563	$3,980

*E = estimated.

F I G U R E   16–3

Bank of New York Financial Charts

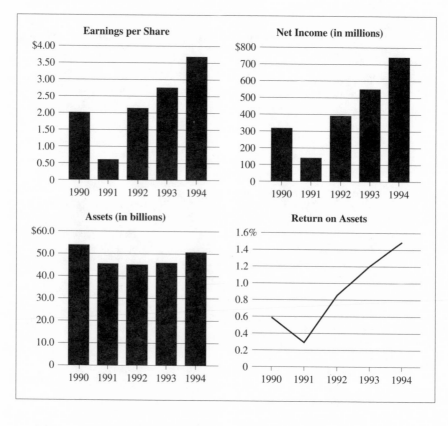

F I G U R E   16–4

Bank of New York Financial Charts

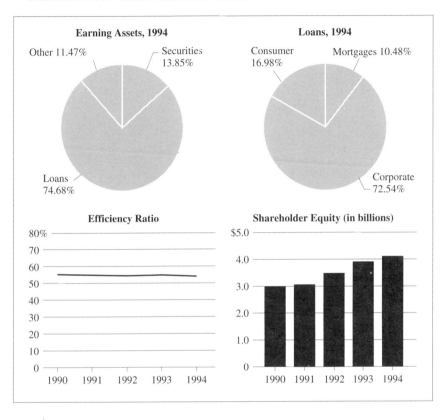

CHAPTER 17

CoreStates
Financial Corp.

CoreStates is a registered bank holding company that was originally incorporated under the laws of Pennsylvania. As of December 31, 1994, CoreStates had assets of $29.3 billion and $2.2 billion in shareholders' equity. However, following the acquisition of Meridian Bancorp for $3.2 billion, the assets of CoreStates should be in the neighborhood of $45 billion with a combined total equity of $3.7 billion, placing the superregional bank among the top 20 bank holding companies germane to asset size. Key performance measures based on operating income continued to improve in 1994 and in the first nine months of 1995 and are among the highest in the banking industry. Returns on average equity and assets were 18.34 percent and 1.50 percent, respectively, in 1994 (excluding one-time charges related to the acquisition of Constitution and Independence Bancorps) compared to 16.49 percent and 1.31 percent, respectively, in 1993. Including the $167 million of one-time after-tax charges, net income in 1994 was $245 million, while ROA was 0.90 percent and ROE was 10.96 percent. For example, third quarter 1995 ROA was 1.85 percent, while ROE was at 22.9 percent. The costs of reserving for problem loans and combining operations of two acquisitions in the first half of 1994 reduced reported earnings substantially in that year. However, after a large decline in operating expenses, these acquisitions should be accretive in 1995.

In mid-1994, CoreStates announced that it had filed an application with the U.S. comptroller of the currency to combine its banking operations in Pennsylvania with those in New Jersey. Like First Fidelity, the CoreStates plan is to merge its dual state operations through a loophole in national banking law by moving its headquarters from Philadelphia to Pennington, New Jersey, across the state line. There CoreStates Bank, N.A., will merge with New Jersey National, creating one legal unit with branches in two states. (The company will keep its corporate headquarters in center-city Philadelphia.) New Jersey law prohibits a bank from operating branches within that state unless it has headquarters there. Upon approval of the application, all of the banks will be consolidated and the name CoreStates Bank will be used for branches, eliminating such venerable names as Philadelphia National Bank, First Pennsylvania Bank, New Jersey National, Germantown Savings Bank, and Hamilton, which have been in the Philadelphia area for more than a century. This move should cut operating expenses by close to 10 percent. In addition, CoreStates customers in Pennsylvania and New Jersey will be able to make deposits to their accounts and have access to all banking services at any CoreStates branch in either state. The company has estimated that it has more than 135,000 customers whose home and work lives cut across the boundaries of both states. Rosemarie B. Greco, president and CEO of CoreStates Bank, N.A., indicated that using one name is the logical accompaniment of moving toward universal branch banking convenience. Terrence Larsen, holding company chairman and CEO, stated: "we will totally refocus ourselves as one bank, with one name and one transcending mission, to exceed our customers' expectations."[1]

Prior to the Meridian acquisition, CoreStates was the nation's 28th largest bank holding company with approximately 450 branch offices and 18 representative offices. Through its subsidiaries, CoreStates provides commercial banking, retail banking, private banking, commercial finance and factoring, trust and investment services, financial services, discount brokerage service, investment and merchant banking, and advisory services to corporations, businesses, financial institutions, and governmental entities. CoreStates provides premier international correspondent and trade-related banking services. With more than 1,200 correspondent banking relationships abroad, CoreStates is one of the most active U.S. financial institutions in these high-potential markets. The company is a top 10 provider of international correspondent banking services, including letter of credit issuance and clearinghouse interbank payment (CHIP) services. During the past seven years, fee income from these activities has grown at an average annual rate of 19 percent. The principal competitors in this area are the large money center banks.

CoreStates is an unusual, high-quality, well-capitalized, corporate and community bank, with outstanding financial ratios. It derives about 25 percent of its revenues from noninterest or fee-related income. The company's overhead ratio is at best average, with an efficiency ratio of 63 percent at year-end 1993, which declined to below 60 percent during the fourth quarter of 1994. On the other hand, its credit quality and reserves for loan losses are strong. Its ratio of nonperforming assets to total assets declined to 1.06 percent of total assets and 1.51 percent of total loans plus real estate foreclosed or in foreclosure during 1994. Its primary source of nonperforming loans has been through acquisitions. At year-end 1994, the bank's ratio of loan loss reserves to nonperforming loans was 203 percent, and its ratio of reserves to total loans was 2.44 percent. CoreStates has more than adequate loan loss reserves. In addition, the company's credit-quality ratios over the business cycle have been less volatile than any of their regional peers. CoreStates tends to avoid unnecessary interest rate risk and has demonstrated skillful asset-liability management. The company uses off-balance-sheet products to enhance its excellent asset-liability process. CoreStates has targeted a dividend-payout ratio of 40 percent, compared to the industry average of 35 percent.

The company benefits from a large base of noninterest-bearing funds, which accounted for about 25 percent of earning assets during 1994. The cash management business and correspondent banking are both large generators of noninterest-bearing funds. In addition, interest rate swaps and other types of derivative instruments (less than $5 billion were utilized during the second quarter of 1994) are used to manage the balance sheet; the company uses swaps only for hedging purposes.

MISSION STATEMENT

The mission statement of CoreStates is as follows:

> To create long-term value for our stakeholders. CoreStates creates value by designing and delivering quality products and services that are responsive to our customers' requirements. We emphasize business lines that generate high returns on equity and strong income growth. Our employees are our most valued strategic advantage . . . [they] are crucial to the development and effective delivery of high-quality customer-driven products. We follow strict standards, financial integrity, manage within prudent risk parameters, and operate under the highest ethical and moral principles. The corporation has a deep commitment to the communities in which we operate. We support and encourage our employees to show that commitment to give of themselves in the communities where they live and work . . . Our actions continue to be guarded by principles that have served us well for more than a decade—a focus on valuing and developing people as a principal competitive edge, on financial soundness, on active risk management, and on applying technology as a competitive tool.[2]

CORPORATE STREAMLINING

In September 1994, CoreStates announced a hiring freeze and a companywide review to boost efficiency and customer service over a 15-month period. In a movement to increase earnings per share, the company is making an effort to lower its relative overhead and increase revenue. These moves are necessary if the company wishes to remain a top-tier superregional; better efficiency ratios and increased fee income can also help increase the company's stock price and P/E ratio.

According to Chairman Larsen, "A lot of our system and procedures were put in place decades ago . . . They do not relate to the future of our organization . . . What we're saying is, 'Step back and look at the needs of your customer, and figure out how that can best be served, starting from scratch.'" Although Larsen has not named specific goals for cutbacks or expense savings, managers have been asked to set "stretch targets" of 40 percent—to cut costs and increase revenues by that amount, at least theoretically. As Larsen explained, "That's not something we're aiming to actually accomplish . . . The idea is to have a number that is large enough to signal a fundamental change in the way we go about our business. We're saying, 'Suppose you got a mandate for that kind of number: What would it take to do it?' Then you look to see whether that makes any sense." For example, a 5 percent reduction in the 1995 expense base yields an estimated 27 cents per share, or an 8 percent addition to forecasted profits. It could also reduce the company's overhead ratio to 55–56 percent. Larsen, who has run CoreStates since 1988, has pushed for systemic change in its corporate culture, calling for more diversity, participation, and flexibility in an organization marked for decades by a rigid hierarchical structure.[3] "We are looking toward the company we think we need to be in the next five years or so," reported Larsen.[4]

Larsen has also moved to streamline management and structure by cutting the size of the holding company's central executive committee from 13 members to 5 and placing all of CoreStates' retail banking decisions under one executive, Rosemarie Greco. He also announced the appointment of Charles L. Coltman as president and chief operating officer. Coltman had previously been assistant to the chairman. CoreStates is also planning to consolidate its various subsidiary banks, giving them a uniform name and marketing identity across Pennsylvania and New Jersey.

In March 1995, CoreStates announced that it would take a $110 million charge in the first quarter as the result of a long-awaited restructuring. The bank planned to fire 890 people, about 6 percent of its workforce, and to close 10 percent of its branches, eliminating 2,800 positions. The remainder of the staff reductions were to come from the elimination of redundancies, attrition, early retirements, a hiring freeze, and automation of processes. Of the $110 million charge, severance costs will account for $72 million, while branch closings, office reorganizations, and miscellaneous items account for the remaining $38 million. CoreStates expects the reengineering to boost annual after-tax earnings by 90 cents a share, or about $210 million pretax by late 1996. This will be comprised of $180 million in net expense savings and $30 million in revenue enhancements. Wholesale banking should generate 43 percent of the expected revenue enhancements, followed by consumer banking with 40 percent and the trust group with 17 percent (see Table 17–1). In addition, the bank indicated it plans to reorganize along geographic lines and will reconfigure in a hub-and-spoke model, with large, full-service branches surrounded by more narrowly focused satellite offices equipped to meet localized needs.[5]

The pretax BEST (Building Exceptional Service Together) impact by business line can be seen in Table 17–1. It suggests improvements of $101 million in wholesale banking (30 percent improvement in profitability over 1994 levels); $89

T A B L E   17–1

BEST Impact by Business Line (in millions)*

	Amount	Percent of Total	Percent Change
Expected Pretax Improvement			
Consumer	$101	48%	30%
Wholesale	89	42	45
Trust	20	10	133
Total	$210	100%	33%
Expected Expense Reductions			
Consumer	$47	26%	13%
Wholesale	41	23	24
Systems and operations	41	23	20
Administration	38	21	21
Trust	13	7	16
Total	$180	100%	15%
Expected Revenue Enhancements			
Consumer	$12	40%	4%
Wholesale	13	43	8
Systems and operations	0	0	0
Administration	0	0	0
Trust	5	17	5
Total	$30	100%	5%

* Improvement in profitability based on 1994 levels.
Source: Goldman Sachs.

million in consumer banking (45 percent improvement); and a $20 million increase in trust pretax profits (133 percent improvement). The program has enhanced decision making accountability, which has been translated into the budget process, accompanied by a stronger ROI discipline.

The cost-savings plan should enable the efficiency ratio to drop from 60 percent during the fourth quarter of 1994 to 52 percent for full-year 1996. It must also be noted that CoreStates has had three significant restructuring charges between the first quarter of 1994 and the first quarter of 1995, with management consequently falling short of hypothetical operating earnings.

In addition to increasing fee income and reducing noninterest costs, another CoreStates goal is to become the bank of choice for small businesses. After an unsuccessful attempt to acquire Rittenhouse Financial Services and Rittenhouse

Trust Company in early 1994, CoreStates is rumored to be searching for a reasonably priced investment company or money management firm to complement its trust department money management activities in order to reach critical mass. CoreStates would prefer to acquire a company with an emphasis on managing common stocks, which generates higher fee income than does managing money market or bond funds. However, the company feels that current asking prices are too high.

HISTORY
Philadelphia Roots

During 1803, Philadelphia businesses were engrossed in forming banks, insurance, turnpike, canal, and bridge companies, while the United States was engaged in the Louisiana Purchase and observing the outbreak of war between England and France. At the time, there were only three banks in Philadelphia: the Bank of North America, the oldest bank in the country; the Bank of the United States, which operated under a federal charter; and the Bank of Pennsylvania, essentially an agency of the Commonwealth of Pennsylvania. The Philadelphia Bank was founded in 1803 to serve people neglected by the three existing banks. These people included small dealers, shopkeepers, and those interested in small loans. Following the passage of the National Banking Act, Philadelphia Bank became a national bank and changed its title to Philadelphia National Bank in 1864.

After more than a half century of banking turbulence, Philadelphia witnessed the merger of the Franklin National Bank with the Fourth Street National Bank in 1926. This merger seemed to act as a catalyst in the merger of the Philadelphia National Bank with the Girard National Bank to form the Philadelphia-Girard National Bank in the same year. Two years later, the Philadelphia-Girard National Bank and the Franklin Fourth Street Bank merged, taking the name of the oldest of the four banks, the Philadelphia National Bank. According to the *Philadelphia Record* of March 3, 1928,

> Philadelphia's tremendous growth in the past decade was fittingly exemplified in the formal approval of the merger by the city's two biggest banks... The consolidation was hailed by business leaders as the greatest single movement in years to attach to Philadelphia the well-earned prestige, as well as the solid financial facilities, consistent with the status of the third largest city in the United States.

Although the Philadelphia Bank was formed to serve neglected parties, it became a wholesale bank. Its customers were principally manufacturers and wholesalers; the bank appeared more interested in large business loans than in personal or retail loans. The Philadelphia National Bank accumulated the cream of the wholesale business in the Philadelphia region and elsewhere. The bank still looks at its large-scale commercial business as essential; however, in recent years it has begun to pay more attention to smaller businesses and retail customers, who were largely the concern of its founders.

As late as 1950, the bank had only three branches: its original location, the former Franklin National headquarters, and a branch in West Philadelphia that tended to take care of the business of the Pennsylvania Railroad, which was situated nearby. Once again, following the merger of two rival Philadelphia banks to form the Girard Trust Corn Exchange Bank, the Philadelphia National Bank merged in 1951 with the Ninth Bank and Trust Company, gaining five branches, a trust business, a savings account business, an active personal loan program, and an entrance into the Kensington and Allegheny section of the city. In the words of the *Philadelphia Inquirer*, "Personal banking will take in a broader scope when Philadelphia's largest bank inaugurates an all-inclusive program of personal banking services which will include neighborhood branches, complete trust services, small loans and special checking accounts."

In 1960, Philadelphia National and Girard Trust Corn Exchange agreed to merge. The merger was approved by the U.S. comptroller of the currency, but the Kennedy administration filed an antitrust suit. The suit failed in the district court, but the merger was turned down by the U.S. Supreme Court in 1963. The Supreme Court ruled that the percentage share of commercial loans and demand deposits of the combined commercial banks would generate too high a share of the market in Philadelphia and the four adjacent counties in Philadelphia.

Recent History

After Philadelphia National Corporation merged with National Central Financial Corporation in 1983, the name was changed to CoreStates to better reflect the new and intended geographic scope of the bank. The main subsidiary of National Central Financial was Hamilton Bank, headquartered in Lancaster, Pennsylvania.

In 1985, CoreStates sold its Colonial Mortgage subsidiaries to General Motors Acceptance Corp. In 1986, CoreStates' subsidiary Congress Financial Corp. acquired James Talcott, Inc., a factoring and commercial finance firm. Additionally in 1986, CoreStates acquired New Jersey National Corp., signifying the first transaction to be closed since Pennsylvania and New Jersey opened their borders to interstate banking.

On March 5, 1990, CoreStates Bank, N.A., acquired First Pennsylvania Corporation ($6.6 billion in assets), winning a bidding war over rival Meridian Bank of Reading, Pennsylvania. Subsequently, in October 1990, CoreStates adopted its present name in connection with the intracorporate merger of Philadelphia National Bank and First Pennsylvania.

In 1992, CoreStates and Associates Corp. of North America completed a sale whereby Associates purchased the assets of CoreStates' subsidiary, Signal Financial

Corp. which included approximately $300 million in receivables. Additionally in 1992, CoreStates acquired First Peoples Financial Corporation, a New Jersey bank with assets of $1 billion, whose principal subsidiary was First Peoples Bank (which was later merged into New Jersey National Bank), and acquired Financial Telesis, a third-party provider of lockbox processing and data-capture services to the commercial banking industry. Third-party remittance processors offer great advantages over traditional bank retail lockbox services because they have better technological capability; thus the service is more efficient and less expensive to corporations. The data-capture division has been a leading provider of data-entry services, specializing in high-volume and time-sensitive applications such as mail orders, subscriptions, physician billing, and marketing surveys. The corporation also sold CoreStates First Pennsylvania's Virgin Island operations (four to six branch offices and associated banking operations) to Banco Popular de Puerto Rico. CoreStates also entered into a joint venture with other superregional banks to create and market electronic payment services (EPS). The joint venture has combined the partners' separate consumer electronic transaction processing businesses and has provided automated teller machine and electronic point-of-sale processing services. CoreStates contributed to EPS its wholly owned subsidiaries Money Access Service, Inc., (MAC), a regional ATM network, and BUYPASS Corporation, a third-party processor of electronic point-of-sale transactions.

RECENT MERGER ACTIVITY

In 1993, CoreStates acquired Inter Community Bancorp in north central New Jersey ($133 million in assets, $110 million in deposits) and combined it with their New Jersey National Bank subsidiary. This acquisition was aimed at strengthening its community banking franchise in the mid-Atlantic region.

In an effort to generate additional fee income, CoreStates formed a new transaction service in September 1993 called Transys, which provides banks and other financial institutions with a full range of check processing, electronic check presenting, and related payment services. CoreStates undertook this initiative to build on its position as a leading provider of third-party payment processing services and to capitalize on the emerging trend among banking institutions to outsource services that are undifferentiated by customers but that require large investments in technology. CoreStates found that such a business would allow many banks to reduce expenses related to check processing and avoid the investment in image technology. Transys processes about 5 million items daily from both CoreStates and other correspondent banks and generates revenues of $75 million. However, it is not yet profitable because it needs a higher volume of check processing and continues to make investments in new processing centers and image-based systems for the proof area. The acquisition of Meridian with assets of $15 billion should provide the additional check processing volume to surpass breakeven.

A related initiative was the November 1993 formation of Synapsys, Inc., a subsidiary offering credit card and merchant processing services for CoreStates and other banks. This is another area in which outsourcing has been the industry trend. Synapsys will serve as one of three development sites for Visa U.S.A.'s next-generation, third-party card processing services for commercial card issuers. Visa is embarking on the introduction of three new commercial credit cards: the Small Business Card, the Corporate Travel and Entertainment Card, and the Purchase Card. All nationwide issuers of these new Visa cards will have to choose between either CoreStates' or First Bank's system to process transactions made with these new corporate cards. The rapidly growing procurement market is estimated at over $430 billion.

CashFlex, CoreStates' lockbox processing business, won Barnett Bank's long-term multimillion dollar processing business. This is another step toward enhancing the company's financial performance through the sale of third-party processing services. Fee revenue from CashFlex has grown from about $10 million in 1992 to approximately $28 million in 1994. Revenues were estimated to be about $100 million by the fourth quarter of 1995. The recent acquisition of Nationwide Remittance Centers, Inc., the largest independent remittance processor in the country, is expected to boost this division's revenue significantly. This strategic acquisition cements CashFlex as the second largest lockbox processor in the nation, increasing CoreStates' critical geographic mass nationwide. Following the acquisition, CashFlex will serve over 60 financial institutions and process over 300 million individual and corporate bill payments annually for several different industries, each with specific billing requirements. The multifaceted transaction processing industry is growing rapidly, as banks continue to outsource various back-office processing functions in efforts to reduce costs and remain competitive. The nationwide cash management industry produces revenues in excess of $7 billion annually and is growing between 5 and 7 percent per year. CoreStates should become a major beneficiary of this outsourcing trend. As a matter of fact, total cash management operations at CoreStates account for about 35 percent of the company's total revenue stream. CashFlex is the second largest lockbox processor, behind Mellon, and generates annual revenues of $75 million.[6]

In 1994, CoreStates acquired Constellation Bancorp, a New Jersey holding company with 49 branches, headquartered in New Brunswick ($2.3 billion in assets, $2.1 billion in deposits), and Independence Bancorp, Inc., a $2.6 billion asset Pennsylvania bank holding company with 54 branches. Independence subsidiaries are Bucks County Bank and Trust Co., Cheltenham Bank, Lehigh Valley Bank, and Third National Bank and Trust Co., Scranton. In addition, CoreStates agreed to acquire the 32-branch Germantown Savings Bank of Bala Cynwyd, Pennsylvania ($1.6 billion in assets, $1.4 billion in deposits). Further, to obtain a full banking charter in Delaware, CoreStates agreed to acquire Clayton Savings and Loan.

The acquisition of Constellation brings CoreState's New Jersey assets to $6.7 billion and its number of New Jersey branches to 153. With this acquisition, CoreStates New Jersey National becomes the fifth largest bank in New Jersey. The acquisition of Independence Bancorp, Germantown Savings Bank (founded in 1854) and Meridian gives CoreStates a 23 percent market share of deposits in the five-county Philadelphia region, making it the market leader in southeastern Pennsylvania, well ahead of second place Mellon's 17 percent share (see Table 17–2). These acquisitions show a strategic move toward building a strong regional community banking presence, emphasizing the consumer, small-business, and middle-market segments, and a further shift toward fee-based income through product-line extensions. Essentially, the recently completed and pending acquisitions will make CoreStates more retail oriented and provide additional opportunities to improve efficiency ratios.

CoreStates is usually successful at growing an acquisition's revenue base and removing 50 percent of its noninterest cost structure over a reasonable period of time. For example, the Germantown Savings Bank (GSB) acquisition should be slightly accretive to 1995 earnings because at least 55 percent of GSB's noninterest expense can be reduced. On the other hand, the Constellation acquisition diluted CoreStates' EPS by about 2 cents in 1994. The Independence acquisition resulted in about a 15-cent dilution to CoreStates' 1994 EPS. CoreStates expected Constellation to contribute positively to earnings in 1995 and for EPS dilution to be eliminated by the fourth quarter of 1995 for the Independence acquisition. The short-term negative impact on earnings, while considerable in 1994, should be offset by CoreStates' aggressive consolidation program. The company expected to realize pretax expense efficiencies of about $35 million annually for each of its

T A B L E   17–2

Selected Completed and Pending Acquisitions

Year	Company	Price (in millions)	Assets (in billions)
1995	Meridian Bancorp	$3,200	$15.0
1994	Germantown Savings Bank	260	1.6
	Independence Bancorp, Inc.	430	2.6
	Constellation Bancorp	300	2.3
1992	First Peoples Financial Corp.	110	1.1
1990	First Pennsylvania	600	6.6
1986	New Jersey National Corp.	300	2.2

Source: Company data.

acquisitions. The acquisitions leave CoreStates in a much stronger position to compete on market visibility, product development, and customer service.

In October 1995, CoreStates announced an agreement to acquire Meridian Bancorp, a $15 billion-asset regional bank, headquartered in Reading, Pennsylvania, in a stock swap valued at $3.2 billion. CoreStates paid 2.13 times book value, with the prices paid in First Union's acquisition of First Fidelity and the UJB acquisition of Summit. On the other hand, adjusted for the United Counties merger with Meridian and a $121 million restructuring charge to be taken at the time the CoreStates merger closes, we estimate Meridian's adjusted book value at $19.70 per share and the price paid by CoreStates at 2.39 times adjusted book value, similar to the price paid by NationsBank to acquire Bank South. Since CoreStates shares were trading at 2.4 times book value prior to the announcement of the acquisition, we do not expect the acquisition to have a noticeable impact on CoreState's book value.

This in-market merger appears to be a good strategic fit for CoreStates since Meridian has 315 branches in eastern Pennsylvania, New Jersey, and Delaware, generally complementing CoreStates' 353-branch network in metropolitan Philadelphia and central New Jersey. Combined, CoreStates and Meridian would rank first in deposit share in 15 of their approximately 50 Delaware Valley counties, in the top 3 in 30 counties, and would be holding a leading 23 percent share in metro Philadelphia, 46 percent in Reading, 33 percent in Trenton, and 27 percent in Allentown-Bethlehem. The company would have a 32 percent penetration of the seven million households in the tri-state region, and a commanding 50–60 percent share of all middle-market business lending. There also exists great potential to cross-sell CoreState's cash management, check/items processing, trade finance, and capital market services to Meridian's customers.

This acquisition provides significant opportunities for cost savings because of the overlapping markets. Also, Meridian has a sizable family of mutual funds and other outside money under management, which should beef up the asset management area at CoreStates. With the addition of the Meridian customer base, the combined customer base at CoreStates will exceed 2.3 million households. In addition, Meridian brings to the CoreStates franchise a solid base of smaller and mid-sized corporate and business customers which complements the lending and cash management strengths at CoreStates. CoreStates projected pretax savings of $186 million annually from the combination and a pretax restructuring charge of $175 million to pay for the closing of some 115 of the combined bank's 667 branches and severance pay for about 2,000 employees. The banks imposed an immediate hiring freeze following the merger announcement. Mr. Larsen will remain chairman and CEO at CoreStates, while Sam McCollough, chairman and CEO at Meridian, will become president and COO at CoreStates. If CoreStates can achieve its forecasted cost savings the merger will not be dilutive and may even be accretive to 1996 EPS (see Table 17–3). The earnings targets set by management for the

T A B L E   17–3

Marriage of Meridian with CoreStates—Pro Forma 1996

	CoreStates	Meridian	Combined
Assets (in billions)	$29.32	$16.5	$45.5
Average loans and leases	$21.82	$10.4	$29.6
Net income (in millions)	$618.3	$221.2	$839.4
Employees	15,745	6,939	N.A.
Shareholders	43,500	26,880	70,300
Branches	353	315	N.A.
Equity	$2.3	$1.4	$3.7
Equity/assets	7.8	8.4	8.1
ROAA	2.0	1.3	1.9
ROCE	23.2%	16.4	22.8
NPAs/related assets	1.2%	1.1%	1.1%
Reserves/loans	2.4%	1.7%	2.2%
Overhead	50.0%	57.4%	52.0%
Noninterest income from trust	$92.1	$75.0	$167.1

Source: Various company press releases and author estimates.

combined banks may be hard to meet since both Meridian and CoreStates are quite efficient operations and both companies will have to curtail stock purchases under pooling-of-interest accounting.

Meridian Bancorp was created when Central Penn Bank (Philadelphia) merged with American Bank (Reading, Pennsylvania) in 1983. Meridian acquired First National Bank of Allentown (1984); First National Bank of Pike County (1986); Delaware Trust Co. (1988); Hill Financial Savings Association (1989); Bell Federal Savings Bank of Philadelphia, Liberty Savings Bank of Pittsburgh, and People's Bancorp of Lebanon (PA) (1992); Cherry Hill National Bank (Cherry Hill, NJ), Commonwealth Bancshares (Williamsport, PA), Provident Savings Bank (Jersey City, NJ), and First National Bank (Bath, PA) in 1993; Grange National Bank of Susquehanna County (Milford, PA), and Security Federal Savings Bank (Vineland, NJ) in 1994; and United Counties Bancorp of Cranford (NJ) (with $1.6 billion in assets in 1995). The Meridian acquisition vaulted CoreStates into a position among the largest 20 banks in the country, while enhancing the bank's role as the dominant financial institution in southeastern Pennsylvania.

The prices CoreStates paid in its transactions have not ventured far from industry norms. In fact, they have generally been at or below the prices paid in truly comparable transactions. In addition, CoreStates has bid low, and lost, in attempted acquisitions of at least five different local banks during 1992–93.[7] Its current acqui-sition parameters specify that any deal must be accretive by the second year and that it must earn a positive shareholder return under a free cash flow analysis. CoreStates' management also considers factors such as credit availability, bank-value dilution, and impact on revenue mix in its acquisition analysis.[8]

KEY BUSINESS SEGMENTS

CoreStates has an evolving portfolio of well-positioned, high-growth businesses. At mid-year 1994, its loan portfolio consisted of 42 percent commercial and indus-trial loans, 18 percent commercial real estate, 16 percent residential real estate, 13 percent consumer loans, 3 percent foreign loans, and 11 percent in other loans such as factoring, leasing, and financial institutions (see Table 17–4). At year-end 1994, CoreStates had $1,374 billion in credit card loans outstanding. Net credit losses on its card portfolio amounted to 2.3 percent of average credit card loans outstanding, much better than industry averages.

The management of credit risk at the bank relies on maintaining a diversified loan portfolio, limiting exposures to a given industry, market segment, geographic region, and borrower concentration, and maintaining its well-established credit cul-ture. For example, management policy is to limit industry concentrations to 50 per-cent of total equity and market segment concentrations to 10 percent of total assets. Early identification of deterioration or problems in the loan portfolio, early recogni-tion of nonperforming assets, maintenance of strong reserves against nonperforming assets, and a credit advisory team process that provides all lenders access to the most senior and experienced credit officers are all important components of CoreStates' credit culture. In addition, the company has a tradition of extensive and ongoing credit training and comprehensive and well-communicated policies and procedures.

T A B L E   17–4

Loan Portfolio Breakdown, June 30, 1994

Type of Loan	Portfolio Percentage
Commercial and industrial	42%
Commercial real estate	18
Residential real estate	16
Consumer loans	13
Foreign loans	3
Other	11

Source: Company reports.

Prior to the bank's major acquisition activity in 1993 and 1994, fee revenue accounted for 40 percent of total revenue. At year-end 1994, that level was 10 percent lower. Nevertheless, fee income is still a prominent and growing business at CoreStates, as can be seen by examining four of the bank's business segments.

Wholesale Banking

This segment accounted for 42 percent of the corporation's operating earnings in the first half of 1994. Commensurate with this, the ROA was 1.27 percent and the ROE 23.65 percent for this unit. The corporate middle-market share in southeastern Pennsylvania approaches 50 percent.

The specialized finance unit has been an area of robust growth, particularly in sectors such as communications, retail trade, healthcare, trucking, real estate, asset-based lending, nonbanking financial institutions, and factoring. Factoring, provided via Congress Financial, generates 22–25 percent of the wholesale banking segment's profits and higher than normal asset yields. Congress is a national asset-based lender with outstanding loans of $2.2 billion and a 15-year compound growth rate of outstanding loans that exceeds 20 percent.

International banking provides about 10 percent of wholesale banking's net income. Philadelphia National Bank, the center of CoreStates' international banking division, is one of the country's leading processors of trade documents and providers of letter-of-credit and collection services. Its well-managed credit facilities are geographically diversified across 46 different markets. In aggregate, nearly $25 billion is extended to major corporations and financial institutions. Based on 1993 volume, CoreStates was the seventh largest letter-of-credit provider. The company's approach to international banking is low risk because of its focus on trade and processing. It conducts international business with 1,200 banks and 150 nonfinancial business customers with home offices or parent companies outside the United States. These nonfinancial companies are based in 13 countries, with most in the United Kingdom, Japan, France, Germany, Sweden, and the Netherlands. Generally, these are large companies that do business with CoreStates because of the bank's relationships with their U.S. operating units or subsidiaries or because they are in industry segments in which CoreStates has specialized knowledge.

The cash management division accounts for about 35 percent of recurring fee income. The division encompasses check clearing, Fedwire transfers, information reporting, account reconciliation, letters of credit, controlled disbursement, international funds transfer, and wholesale and retail lockbox services. CoreStates is one of the few regional banks that compete successfully against money center banks in all of these products. In addition, the company processes more checks than the Federal Reserve Bank of Philadelphia, generating substantial corporate compensating balances in the form of demand deposits that help provide ample liquidity.

Consumer Financial Services

This segment has 420 offices and 482 ATM machines and contains the leading retail bank in the greater Philadelphia market, with a 23 percent market share. It is estimated that up to 40 percent of the 136 new branches from the 1993–94 bank acquisitions might be closed, leaving about 369 branches, as the company has a proclivity for significant cost-cutting and branch consolidation. Consumer financial services accounted for 35 percent of the corporation's operating income in the first half of 1994, with an ROA of 1.62 percent and an ROE of 34.3 percent. This unit's profitability should improve because of increased emphases on credit cards and residential mortgages, higher interest rates, and efficiencies expected to be realized from branch closures.[9]

This business segment has a strong regional credit card division, with 800,000 cardholders and one of the top processing systems in the country. It had $1.37 billion in credit card loans outstanding at the end of 1994, $1.39 billion in installment loans, and more than $175 million in student loans.

Electronic Payment Services, Inc. (EPS)

EPS, the holding company for Money Access Service, Inc. (MAC) and BUY-PASS Corp. MAC, originally owned entirely by CoreStates, is the biggest ATM network in the country (located primarily in the mid-Atlantic states and the Midwest) as measured by monthly transactions volume. Also, BUYPASS is one of the largest third-party electronic data processing companies. Originally owned by CoreStates, Banc One, PNC, and Society, the holding company is now owned by Key, CoreStates, PNC, Banc One, and National City Corp. EPS has 1,400 financial institution members, 14,800 ATMs, and 57,000 point-of-sale terminals. BUYPASS' point-of-sale business is national in scope and currently processes over 650 million transactions annually on 200,000 terminals. BUYPASS processes electronic retail payments, provides transaction authorization information, and routes transactions for settlement. Further growth activities for MAC include expanding the smart card business, acquiring ATM networks, signing up additional banks onto the MAC system, issuing more MAC cards, increasing the usage by those already holding a MAC card, and installing more ATMs.[10]

CoreStates created an umbrella entity, QuestPoint, initially for its Transys check processing unit and its CashFlex remittance processing unit. Acquisition of Nationwide Remittance Centers, Inc., in the first quarter of 1995 made CashFlex the second largest lockbox processor in the United States. CoreStates is planning to consolidate its third-party processing businesses (CashFlex, lockbox processing, Transys check processing, its 25 percent interest in EPS, and Synapsys commercial procurement card processing) under QuestPoint. Management expects QuestPoint's revenues to reach $200 million in 1995, from a 1994 level of $160 million.

Trust and Investment Management

Although exhibiting good investment performance, this is the weakest of the four business segments in terms of net income growth. Personal trust and private banking account for about 50 percent of total division revenues and 75 percent of total fee income. About 50 percent of the personal trust accounts at the lead bank are below standard fee levels. The CoreStates family of mutual funds has assets of about $2 billion under management. The overall mix of total assets under management is heavily skewed toward low-fee liquid-asset and fixed-income products. Only $5 billion in funds under management are in equities; $11 billion are in money markets, and $3.5 billion are in fixed income. Institutional and custody services provide about 25 percent of total division revenues.

Strategically, the company is shifting from being product-based to being regional market/customer-based. The realignment is expected to enhance customer focus and service, while cutting through the bureaucratic boundaries that the line-of-business approach had established. For example, the retail, middle-market, and small-business segments will be serviced through the hub-and-spoke branching model. On the other hand, global financial institutions, specialized industries, and the corporate division will continue to operate as they have in the past, along a line-of-business approach.[11]

SUMMARY

CoreStates is a strongly capitalized bank with shareholders' equity at 8.01 percent of assets, Tier 1 capital at 8.75 percent of risk-adjusted assets, and total capital at 12.5 percent of risk-adjusted assets. In addition, CoreStates is a well-managed bank holding company with outstanding financial ratios in most areas except for its average efficiency ratio. Executive management has addressed the latter ratio with the announced closing of 10 percent of the bank's branches and the elimination of 2,800 jobs. The efficiency ratio should show substantial improvement following the implementation of these cutbacks over the next few years. By 1997, the efficiency ratio could be reduced to 51 percent, which would be among the industry leaders. If this occurs, it is likely that the bank's ROA and ROE would jump to 1.85 percent and 22 percent, respectively.

CoreStates is a niche bank that participates in high-growth businesses. Management's strategic growth objectives remain focused on processing and technology-oriented businesses. CoreStates is well positioned to enjoy above-average revenue growth from the emerging trend in the commercial banking industry toward outsourcing processing services. The bank is revolving away from its traditional corporate banking roots toward both retail and small-business banking and becoming a premier transaction/payments processor.

The bank has exhibited considerable expertise in controlling credit quality, managing assets and liabilities, developing technological capability, and carrying out mergers and acquisitions—all of which help posture it for the future. The bank is likely to continue to make fill-in acquisitions in Pennsylvania and New Jersey at reasonable prices to avoid dilution of earnings. A merger of equals cannot be ruled out. Since the bank sells at a high price-to-book value, an outright takeover is unlikely by another superregional without dilution of that bank's EPS in the short run. On the other hand, a bank that is looking for a strong presence in wholesale and international correspondent banking, a strong retail banking franchise in southeastern Pennsylvania, a solid, dependable base of fee income, and exceptional profitability ratios would do well to think of CoreStates as a merger candidate.

The company has taken minimal interest rate risk in its balance-sheet optimization strategies and does not appear to be at risk from betting on interest rate directions. To remain interest rate neutral, CoreStates utilizes $6 billion of off-balance-sheet products, which are purely for hedging purposes.[12] CoreStates' management of interest rate risk has continued to generate a strong and stable net interest margin. The bank strives to maintain a neutral interest rate risk sensitivity and avoids taking speculative positions on interest rate movements. The company's net interest margin rose in 1994. Only a handful of banks could make that claim. CoreState's unusual business mix allows it to have one of the highest, and most stable, net interest margins in the banking industry.[13]

CoreStates enjoys relationships with nearly one-half of all middle-market companies and has the greatest market share in consumer deposits in the greater Philadelphia area, which should eventually lead to better pricing of products and increased profitability. For example, the bank paid only 1 percent for NOW accounts during 1994, compared to the nearly 2 percent its competition paid, without any noticeable loss of market share.

In addition, it would come as no surprise if CoreStates spun off part of either Congress Financial or EPS, acquired an investment company, or intensified its cost containment effort to help increase earnings per share and the price of its common stock. Management increased the dividend in late 1994 to maintain its targeted payout ratio and to attract investors' interest in the company's stock, which would drive up its price. Additional dividend increases are expected in 1995–96, along with increased authorization to repurchase shares.[14] Management appears focused on improving the price of the common shares and increasing the price-to-earnings ratio. A higher P/E ratio would make it easier for CoreStates to continue to make fill-in acquisitions in Pennsylvania and New Jersey without dilution of earnings per share. EPS growth without acquisitions should exceed 10 percent annually, while the company's ROA and ROE should be greater than 1.50 percent and 17.5 percent, respectively, during 1996. This excellent earnings outlook should translate into additional share buybacks, given the company's large existing capital base and prospectively improved earnings growth. As a matter of fact, in March 1995 the company indicated that it would expand its share repurchase plan from 2 percent of outstanding shares to 5 percent annually, implying that about 7 million shares could be repurchased each year during 1995 and 1996.

Following a number of acquisitions in which management seemed to ignore the importance of dilution (especially to book value), Larsen stated flatly that bank acquisitions are currently at a lower priority than before and that any potential bank acquisition would have to be immediately and strongly accretive to earnings. The most flagrant example of dilution was the bank's acquisition of First Pennsylvania at year-end 1989, when its book value fell 16 percent. In 1994, the bank's book value declined again from 1993 levels as a result of dilution and merger-related restructuring charges from three in-market deals completed during 1994.[15] Essentially, unless a "slam dunk" bank deal comes its way, the likelihood of a bank acquisition during the BEST implementation period is quite low.[16] The "slam drunk" took place with the announced acquisition of Meridian Bancorp. Larsen also indicated that he is interested in building the company's transaction processing business in small accretive steps. An asset management acquisition would also be desirable but is largely unaffordable under current market pricing.[17]

In July 1995, CoreStates almost merged with Bank of Boston. However, that merger was called off most likely because not enough synergies and cost-cutting opportunities could be found to justify the marriage and because Bank of Boston investors were not pleased with a no-premium, merger-of-equals deal. A better strategic investment for CoreStates would be the acquisition of UJB Financial or a merger of equals with Mellon or PNC. However, CoreStates is likely to remain independent unless a highly lucrative offer is made to take over the bank. A merger of equals, for instance, with Bank of New York or National City Corp., is another possibility. CoreStates will most likely continue acquiring banks within its market or in contiguous markets. Additional potential acquisition candidates for the bank include UJB, Wilmington Trust Company, and some smaller banks and thrifts in southern New Jersey and southeastern Pennsylvania. These in-market mergers could give CoreStates the size it needs to make expensive investments in new technology pay off. CoreStates would like to spread the fixed costs of necessary technological advances and improvements over a larger customer base to ensure the profitability of these projects. The bank could also save money by eliminating redundant branches with in-market acquisitions, while keeping new customers happy with a bevy of new products and services.

ENDNOTES

1. A. Cassel, "CoreStates to Go to One Name," *Philadelphia Inquirer*, August 1994, pp. C1–2.
2. "CoreStates," *CS First Boston Global Banking Conference*, April 27, 1994, pp. 4–5.
3. A. Cassel, "Hiring Freeze Begun by the Bank," *Philadelphia Inquirer*, September 13, 1994, pp. D1–2.
4. K. Holland, "Bankers Hours Don't Look So Good," *Business Week*, December 19, 1994, p. 103.
5. T.L. O'Brien, "CoreStates to Take $110 Million Charge in Restructuring," *The Wall Street Journal*, March 30, 1995, p. A4.

6. T.D. McCandless, "CoreStates Financial," *Paine Webber Research*, February 27, 1995, pp. 1–2.

7. T.D. McCandless, "CoreStates Financial Corp.," *Paine Webber Research*, May 31, 1994, p. 2.

8. H.C. Dickson, "CoreStates Financial Corp.," *Smith Barney*, September 6, 1994, p. 13.

9. Ibid., p. 20.

10. McCandless, May 31, 1994, pp. 10–11.

11. J.B. Naschek, "CoreStates Financial—Best Program Unveiled," *Salomon Brothers Equity Research*, April 5, 1995, pp. 4–5.

12. T.D. McCandless, "CoreStates Financial Group," *Paine Webber Research*, December 19, 1994, p. 2.

13. T.D. McCandless, "Regional Banks," *Paine Webber Research*, February 6, 1995, p. 8.

14. T.D. McCandless, "CoreStates Financial Group," *Paine Webber Research*, September 12, 1994, p. 2.

15. C. Swaim, "CoreStates," *Oppenheimer & Co., Inc., Research*, May 19, 1995, p. 2.

16. J.B. Naschek, "CoreStates Financial—Analyst Meeting Solidifies Expectations," *Salomon Brothers Research Report*, June 5, 1995, p. 5.

17. T.D. McCandless, "CoreStates Financial Corp.," *Paine Webber Research*, May 19, 1995, p. 2.

T A B L E   17-5

CoreStates Financial Corp. Financials

	1990	1991	1992	1993	1994
Earnings per share	$1.03	$2.10	$1.57	$2.69	$1.73
Assets (in millions)	$22,642	$22,044	$22,349	$22,825	$27,667
Net income (in millions)	$11.404	$228.14	$181.42	$314.92	$245.36
Return on assets	0.50%	1.03%	0.81%	1.38%	0.89%

	1994	
	(in millions)	%
Average earning assets	$24,303	100
Securities	3,014	12
Loans	19,601	81
Other	1,688	7
Loans	20,527	100
Construction and land	331	
Commercial mortgage	2,979	
Highly leveraged	498	
Commercial loans and leases	10,192	
Other foreign	585	
Term LCD		
Credit card receivables	1,375	
Other consumer	1,387	
Unearned discount		
Corporate	14,585	71
Consumer	2,762	13
Mortgages	3,180	15

	1990	1991	1992	1993	1994
Efficiency ratio	64.55	64.75	68.3	62.51	61.76
Shareholder equity (in millions)	$1,481	$1,460	$1,614	$1,794	$2,270
Preferred					
Common	$1,481	$1,460	$1,614	$1,794	$2,270

F I G U R E   17–1

CoreStates Financial Corp. Financial Charts

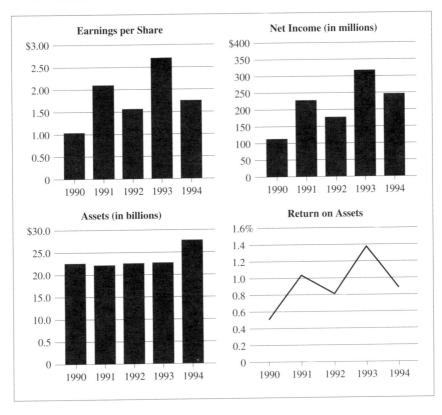

F I G U R E   17–2

CoreStates Financial Corp. Financial Charts

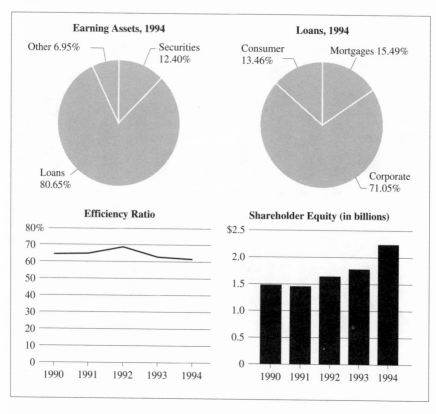

Earning Assets, 1994

Other 6.95%   Securities
                    12.40%

Loans
80.65%

Loans, 1994

Consumer   Mortgages 15.49%
13.46%

Corporate
71.05%

Efficiency Ratio

80%
70
60
50
40
30
20
10
0
    1990   1991   1992   1993   1994

Shareholder Equity (in billions)

$2.5
2.0
1.5
1.0
0.5
0
    1990   1991   1992   1993   1994

CHAPTER 18

Mellon Bank Corporation

Mellon is a Pittsburgh-based diversified financial services company with a bank at its core. It has a good mix of earnings from wholesale and retail banking and numerous fee-based services. The company has often been referred to as the "JP Morgan of the Alleghenies." Management has expanded the breadth of the company's product line to well beyond banks' traditional lending and deposit offerings, generating a balance of fees from nonlending and lending businesses. Mellon generated just over 52 percent of its revenue from noninterest income in 1994, primarily from trust and investment fees, following the acquisition of both the Boston Company and Dreyfus. In addition, Mellon's basic banking business has significantly improved in credit quality, loan growth, and net interest margin.

At year-end 1994, the company had about 20,000 employees and assets of $38.6 billion. With the exception of 1994, profitability has improved continually as the company worked its way out of a history of troubled assets. Mellon achieved a return on assets of 1.14 percent in 1994, compared to 1.29 percent in 1993, and a return on average common shareholders' equity of 9.32 percent in 1994, compared to 1.29 percent in 1993. Net income for 1994 was $433 million compared to $450 million in 1994. During 1994, the company had substantial one-time charges of $130 million (after tax) related to the reimbursement of client funds within its securities lending business, a $479 million after-tax expense related to the merger with Dreyfus, a $10 million after-tax loss on the disposition of securities, and a $16 million charge related to a redemption premium and unamortized issuance costs on its Series H preferred stock. On the other hand, Mellon's preferred dividend cost has been reduced by $17 million annually beginning in 1995. Without those onetime charges, its ROE and ROA were 16.02 percent and 1.71 percent, respectively. The outlook for 1997 and beyond is for a substantial improvement in net income and an ROE in excess of 17 percent and an ROA in excess of 1.7 percent.

Mellon's loan portfolio is of excellent credit quality; nonperforming assets were only 0.62 percent of total assets at year-end 1994, a considerable improvement from the disastrous performance in 1987, when the company reported a loss of $844 million. Most of this loss could be attributed to poor underwriting in the loan portfolio, especially in commercial real estate. The exception to this is the high level of charge-offs on the company's new Cornerstone credit card, which is running about double the industry average. The company has taken corrective action by changing its methods of credit scoring.

Mellon was substantially overreserved in 1994, with a loan loss provision at more than 250 percent of nonperforming assets and 402 percent of nonperforming loans. At year-end, the $607 million reserve represented 2.27 percent of loans. Mellon's current loan practices and loss reserves are exceptionally conservative. In the current environment of low loan charge-offs, Mellon might use a lower loan loss provision, which could boost earnings. The company's quality has become sufficiently pristine (with the exception of the credit card division) that the decision to begin drawing down its reserves appears well within the limits of prudence.[1]

On December 31, 1994, the composition of Mellon's $26.7 billion loan portfolio was 51 percent consumer and 49 percent commercial loans. Of the $13.5 billion in total consumer credit, $8.6 billion was in consumer mortgages and $2.4 billion in credit cards. Credit card loans made up the fastest-growing segment of the portfolio in 1994 and in the first half of 1995. The increase in credit card outstandings was driven by the Cornerstone card, introduced in 1994. The card generated 700,000 new accounts in 1994 and another 300,000 in 1995, with total Cornerstone outstandings of $1.0 billion. Unfortunately, nonperforming credit card assets are running too high and the card has not yet become profitable.

Of the $12.3 billion in commercial loans, $10 billion was domestic commercial, $1.6 billion commercial real estate, and $0.7 billion international loans. Commercial and financial loans represented 37 percent of the total portfolio. Standby letters of credit and foreign guarantees stood at $2.9 billion on December 31, 1993, and December 31, 1994.

Although the overhead ratio was a bit high at 64.5 percent in 1995, it should decline to about 63 percent by 1995 upon total consolidations of Dreyfus (a $1.7 billion acquisition), the Boston Company (a $1.45 billion acquisition), and the branch system. Mellon has targeted an overhead ratio of under 60 percent by 1997. The company also engages in mortgage banking and commercial real estate lending in select domestic markets. Mellon Mortgage Company ranks among the top 20 third-party processors of mortgage-servicing rights in the country. Mellon also generates fee income by handling data processing, bookkeeping, and platform functions, as well as processing credit card transactions and running regional automated teller networks, for small banks. Mellon is also among the top 25 bank issuers of credit cards. During

1995, Mellon purchased the AAA credit card portfolio, with approximately $230 million in receivables, from U.S. Bancorp. Mellon generates additional fee income by being the second largest manager of the cash position of corporations.

Mellon banks do business under the name Mellon Bank, except in the Philadelphia area, where they use the name Mellon PSFS. In December 1992, the corporation acquired selected assets of the former Meritor Savings Bank (formerly called PSFS) in a competitive bid for the deposits and 27 branches in a federally assisted transaction. In 1990, Mellon had acquired 54 branch offices of PSFS in suburban Philadelphia from the troubled Meritor, which at that time gave Mellon the leading market share of retail deposits in the Philadelphia region, the nation's fifth largest city. Previously, in 1983, Mellon had acquired Girard Company, a venerable Philadelphia-based bank holding company with 100 branches and a large trust operation. Mellon also increased its presence in Maryland in 1992 when it acquired eight branches of the former Standard Federal Savings Bank from the RTC. It had previously acquired Community Savings and Loan of Bethesda (Maryland) in 1986.

In 1994, Mellon agreed to acquire Glendale Bancorp, headquartered in Vorhees (New Jersey), a bank holding company with six branches, total assets of $260 million, and deposits of $210 million. This was Mellon's first acquisition in New Jersey; in the 1980s it had been rebuffed by New Jersey regulators in an attempt to acquire an even larger bank. The Glendale acquisition enabled Mellon to conduct retail banking in the New Jersey suburbs of Philadelphia. It appears as if Mellon is interested in acquiring retail banks in the mid-Atlantic states of Pennsylvania, Maryland, Delaware, and New Jersey to complement its national wholesale division and its recent purchase of major fee income generators such as Dreyfus and the Boston Company. It is interesting to note that Mellon had bid too low in an attempt to acquire a large West Virginia bank in 1993.

HISTORY

The company was founded as a private bank in 1869 by Judge Thomas Mellon and called T. Mellon and Sons' Bank. A second bank was formed by Mellon's sons shortly thereafter. The Mellons did not close either bank following the panic of 1873, when more than half the banks in Pittsburgh failed. The Mellons invested their profits in other enterprises, such as Alcoa and Gulf Oil. Andrew Mellon, the son of Thomas Mellon, took over the leadership of the bank. He financed the creation of Union Transfer and Trust Company, joined the national banking system as Mellon National Bank in 1902; formed its first foreign bureau a few years later; and established a tradition of growth through acquisition. The bank established title and trust companies, which are important businesses in the current Mellon sphere. When Andrew Mellon served as U.S. secretary of the treasury under presidents Coolidge, Harding, and Hoover, his brother Richard Mellon became president of the bank. In 1929, Richard Mellon formed Mellbank Security Company to help save many smaller banks during the Great Depression. The Mellon name and the conservatism of the bank helped carry the bank through the depression relatively unscathed. Many panicked customers of other banks withdrew their savings from other banks during the depression and flocked into Mellon with their deposits. Richard Mellon was reported to have muttered, "I told those damn architects to make more room in the lobby."

Richard King Mellon took over the bank in 1933 following the death of his father. He merged Mellon National and Union Trust Company in 1946, forming Mellon National Bank and Trust Company. Mellon also entered into retail banking by increasing its branch network and merging with Mellbank. Mellon began to build a national reputation for trust management and technological innovation in cash management. It controlled one-third of all trust assets in Pennsylvania.

In 1971, the company was incorporated in Pennsylvania as Mellon National Corp. to acquire Mellon Bank, N.A. (successor to Mellon Bank and Trust Co.) effective in 1972. Mellon acquired a series of mortgage and finance companies between 1969 and 1979, including Jay F. Zook, Morrison and Morrison, Inc., Carruth Mortgage Co., Local Loan Co., the Munster, Indiana, office of ITT Thorp Corp., and Mortgage and Trust Co. Most of these companies were merged into Mellon Financial Services Corp.

Internationally, Mellon acquired 25 percent of Banco Bosano, Simsonsen de Investimento, S.A., a Brazilian investment bank, and established Pareto Partners, a London-based advisory firm. It later reduced its ownership interest to 12.5 percent. It also formed Mellon Life Insurance Co. in Wilmington, Delaware, in 1980.

When Pennsylvania expanded its branching laws to allow statewide branching, Mellon acquired a number of banks throughout the state. These included Girard ($4 billion in assets) in 1982. Girard was the second largest bank in Philadelphia, with about 100 branches and a large trust department. Girard's earnings dropped significantly in 1982, but Mellon went ahead with the merger in that year. Mellon appears to have been negligent in its due diligence, not carefully evaluating the quality of the Girard loan portfolio prior to the acquisition. Delinquent loans at Girard cropped up again in 1984, which contributed to a 14 percent decline in the earnings of Mellon. It also prompted Mellon to head to Philadelphia to "Mellonize" the Girard Bank, which previously had a distinguished reputation and a strong retail following in that city and its wealthy suburbs. Mellon fired numerous Girard officers and renamed the bank Mellon Bank (East). This angered many Girard customers, and accounts were lost. The Girard name was revered by Philadelphia's Main Line society and had played a salient role in the city's history. The Girard Savings Institution, later called the Girard Bank, had been founded by Benjamin Woods Richards in 1835. The bank had been named in honor of Stephen Girard, a multimillionaire who left $7 million to Philadelphia to form a school for orphaned boys and who lent money to the federal government to help finance the War of 1812.

Mellon also acquired CCB Bancorp ($570 million in assets), Norwest Pennsylvania Corp. ($700 million in assets), and Commonwealth National Financial Corp. ($1.3 billion in assets). It also created Mellon Bank (Maryland). In addition, Mellon acquired 54 Philadelphia area branches of PSFS, United Penn Bank ($1.5 billion in assets, 33 branches), and the remainder of troubled Meritor Savings Bank ($2.5 billion in assets, $2.7 billion in deposits). When it came to a potential name change for the PSFS branches (PSFS was once the largest savings bank in the United States, and held an account relationship with 25 percent of those with banking accounts in Philadelphia), Mellon did not make the same mistake it made with Girard. All of the Philadelphia-region branches of Mellon were changed to Mellon/PSFS. The branch integration went much more smoothly without alienating the depositor base.

Mellon also enhanced its integrated banking software and data processing systems through the acquisition of Carleton Financial Computations, Inc., and acquired several subsidiaries of the Fidata Corporation that offered securities transfer, pricing, and trust accounting services. By the late 1980s, Mellon was selling its data processing expertise to some 400 small banks across the country.

NEW MANAGEMENT TEAM

In 1987, Mellon recorded its first loss in history. It was related to increased reserves for third-world loans and certain domestic real estate credits in the Pittsburgh area and energy credits in Texas. This loss led to the forced resignation of Mellon chairman J. David Barnes and the closing of about half of Mellon's 20 foreign branches. The corporation then realigned its international operation to focus on multinational corporate credits rather than overseas borrowers. Barnes was replaced with Frank Cahouet, former president of Fannie Mae and the COO responsible for reviving Crocker National prior to its sale to Wells Fargo. Cahouet recruited Anthony P. Terracciano as president and chief operating officer of Mellon, following a successful stint as vice chairman at Chase Manhattan Bank.

Cahouet and Terracciano froze salaries and reduced staff by 10 percent. They formed Grant Street National Bank as a separate entity to hold many of Mellon's weak domestic loans, setting up a good bank, bad bank situation. Management focused attention on the profitable areas that remained in the so-called good bank.

Cahouet's plan was to return Mellon to its original position as a regional bank with a special niche. Mellon has begun to specialize in providing loans and other services to medium-sized corporations, breaking the historic pattern of catering to the Fortune 500 and foreign governments. Mellon has emphasized its trust and investment, data processing, and cash management businesses. The acquisitions of the Boston Company and Dreyfus provide a big boost to the investment management business and the generation of fee income for the mid- to late-1990s. In an effort to maintain its leadership in data processing, the company acquired Backroom

Systems Group, which offers personal computer software designed to automate labor-intensive tasks for financial service companies. Mellon has also continued to develop BancSource, a system that should eventually process all customer loans and deposits. Now Mellon must integrate these developments in data processing throughout its entire system instead of using different systems in branches.

To strengthen further its corporate products and services, Mellon announced a joint venture with Chemical Banking Corporation, called Chemical Mellon Shareholder Services, that will focus exclusively on providing stock transfer and related shareholder services to publicly held companies. This joint venture will be among the largest securities transfer companies in the United States, with more than 13 million shareholder accounts, 2,000 clients, and a large share of companies on both the New York and American stock exchanges. Mellon contributed the assets and business of its Mellon Securities Transfer Services to the joint venture, while Chemical contributed its Geoserve Shareholder Services unit.

PRINCIPAL BUSINESS LINES

The company engages principally in three lines of business:

• *Service Products*—This unit provides a comprehensive range of fee-based services: trust, investment, cash management, and mortgage banking to both a national and international customer base.

• *Retail Financial Services*—This unit provides lending, investment, and deposit products and services to consumers and small businesses in the central Atlantic region, as well as credit cards and other products on a national basis through 406 branch offices, 29 supermarket branches, 586 ATMs, seven loan offices, and a telephone banking center.

Mellon formed a partnership with Acme Markets, the largest grocery store chain in southeastern Pennsylvania, to bring supermarket banking to Acme stores in the Philadelphia region. The company's supermarket offices have proved to be a convenient, cost-effective, and highly successful way to deliver products and services to customers. The Acme partnership marks the biggest supermarket banking effort to date in the Delaware Valley.

• *Wholesale Banking*—This unit serves large corporate customers on a national and select international basis, as well as midsize companies throughout the central Atlantic region. Mellon ranks seventh in the nation among U.S. commercial banks in total number of relationships with large U.S. companies and in the top 12 among large commercial banks in private placements. This unit also provides premium financing to businesses for property and casualty insurance in North America through its AFCO Credit Corporation, furthering a steady source of high-quality collateralized loans. AFCO was purchased from Continental Corporation in December 1993. AFCO has 450 employees and 25 locations in Canada and the United States and gives Mellon the leading market share in the insurance premium financing business.

NONBANKING ACQUISITIONS

The merger with the Boston Company has provided Mellon with a position of sustainable leadership in core trust and investment businesses. Together with the Boston Company, Mellon Trust administers assets of more than $750 billion, including about $125 billion of assets under management, and ranks among the leading providers in each of its core trust businesses: institutional trust services, such as custody or record keeping for employee benefit plans; investment management services for pension and employee benefit plans; administrative services to the mutual fund industry; and private asset management.

The merger with Dreyfus in mid-1994, the largest in company history, represents the biggest merger ever of a banking company with a mutual fund company. With this merger, Mellon became the biggest bank manager of mutual funds and one of the top 10 banks in discretionary trust assets (see Tables 18–1 and 18–2). In fact, Mellon will become the second largest money manager in the United States, with a total of $215 billion in assets under management, behind Fidelity Investments, which manages $250 billion. Mutual fund assets under Mellon's management rose to $73 billion at mid-year 1995. Although Dreyfus added considerable fee income and was a good fit with the rest of the company, the acquisition was dilutive in the short run. However, in the post-Dreyfus period, Mellon should generate

T A B L E   18–1

Bank Mutual Fund Managers, March 31, 1995

Company	Total (in billions)	Mutual Fund Assets			
		Money Market	Fixed Income	Muni	Equity
Mellon/Dreyfus	$68.0	55%	6%	24%	15%
PNC Bank	22.4	84	4	2	11
NationsBank	14.7	60	12	7	22
Wells Fargo	10.6	55	13	7	25
Banc One	9.5	51	15	10	24
BankAmerica	9.4	89	2	2	7
Northern Trust	9.2	75	8	4	14
First Union	8.0	34	9	4	53
Norwest	7.5	55	9	3	34
Chase Manhattan	7.0	56	3	4	38
Average, except Mellon		62%	8%	4%	25%

Source: *American Banker.*

T A B L E   18-2

Top 10 Banks in Discretionary Trust Assets, 1994

	Market Value (in billions)
Bankers Trust	$184.8
Wells Fargo	184.7*
State Street Boston	164.9
Mellon Bank	157.8
JP Morgan	151.1
BankAmerica	101.9
Northern Trust	85.9
Citicorp	73.6
NationsBank	57.4
Chemical Banking	56.6

* Prior to sale of Wells Fargo/Nikko Securities.
Source: *American Banker*.

over $1.75 billion in noninterest revenue during 1996 (about 51 percent of projected 1996 total revenues), compared to an average of about 40 percent at other large commercial banks and 35 percent at superregional banks (see Table 18–3). In addition, Mellon's profitability should be substantially higher and more stable. Investors are usually willing to pay a higher market multiple for more stable earnings and higher profitability ratios. This shift toward a fee-based income represents a conscious effort on the part of Mellon to change its sources of income away from traditional banking activities and interest income.[2] Also, Mellon's capital ratios are strong. Its ratio of common shareholders' equity to assets was 9.54 percent, its Tier 1 capital ratio was 9.5 percent, and its total capital ratio was 12.9 percent at year-end 1994. Mellon's tangible common equity ratio was 7.57 percent at year-end 1994. This suggests that the company has a high level of intangibles on its books, primarily related to its large purchase acquisition of the Boston Company in 1993.

Dreyfus was viewed as a large but lethargic company that had not developed any innovative products in the recent years of extraordinary mutual fund growth; this, in part, explains the decline in the company's market share of mutual fund assets from 5.6 percent in 1985 to 3.6 percent in 1993. However, Mellon viewed Dreyfus as a good strategic fit because it would allow the bank to generate fee income that would offset fluctuations in net interest income from traditional banking operations. Although Mellon had a strong trust department and growing mutual fund business, the company still relied on net interest income for its earnings. The acquisition of Dreyfus would generate fee income for Mellon exceeding 50 percent

T A B L E   18–3

Fee Revenue Composition (in millions)

	1992	1993	1994	1995E	1996E	1997E
Trust/investment management						
Mutual fund management	$ 271	$310	$294			
Administration/custody	23	119	159			
Institutional trust	118	184	223			
Institutional asset management	81	122	143			
Private asset management	91	118	134			
Total trust/investment management	584	$853	$953	$917	$977	$1,050
Cash management/deposit transaction	182	192	197			
Information services	142	152	78			
Mortgage servicing	41	62	78			
Credit card	54	61	72			
Forex/securities trading	21	46	76			
Other	130	172	198			
Total fee income	$1,154	$1,538	$1,652*	$1,664	$1,760	$1,883
Noninterest income/ total revenues	42%	53%	52%	51%	51%	51%

* Prior to announcement of $130 million charge to earnings.

Source: "Mellon Bank Corporation," *CS First Boston*, July 3, 1995, p. 4.

of revenues. Mellon's management also anticipated being able to cut $60 million in operating expenses over the first two years of combined operations.[3] The Dreyfus acquisition in August 1994 diluted Mellon's book value by roughly 14 percent, and earnings fell by 16 percent. However, management expected the initial dilution to be overcome fairly quickly by the increase in high-margin equity products and synergies between the two companies. The Dreyfus contribution in the year since the acquisition did not map out as the company had planned, pushing out the payback period by several years.

One of the initial weaknesses identified with Dreyfus was its underrepresentation in equity and taxable bond funds compared with industry averages. Mellon has publicly stated that it intends to add more equity and international funds to its offerings and to expand its market share of affluent young and middle-aged clients. Equity funds generate much higher management fees than either low-margin money market funds or debt portfolios.[4]

Mellon utilizes numerous means to sell the 150 different Dreyfus products. In addition to print advertising and telemarketing, there are 26 Dreyfus personal financial centers, a few hundred Mellon branches located in Pennsylvania, Delaware, and New Jersey, a wholesaling organization, an institutional sales force, and a defined contribution sales force. Dreyfus intends to add about 10 new funds during 1995–96, primarily equity and high-yield bond funds. Some of the rationale for acquiring Dreyfus in the first place was its high brand name recognition. To unify its image, Mellon has rebranded mutual funds with the Dreyfus name. Mellon used to manage 36 mutual funds, with assets of about $4 billion, through the Boston Company under the Laurel brand name. The sheer size of the Mellon operation, the second largest in the nation after JP Morgan in total trust income ($953 million in 1994) and fourth largest in discretionary assets under management ($158 billion) should allow for economies of scale. The trust business accounts for 24 percent of the organization's total operating income.

Controversy surrounding the Boston Company's institutional asset management business appears to have settled down following the departure of 13 out of 51 institutional asset managers. These personnel departures and the outflow of $14 billion in the period from January 1, 1995, to June 30, 1995, will lead to a decline in fee income at Mellon. Mellon's business does not appear to be impaired and is expected to continue to perform well. Boston Company also hired a team of highly respected international portfolio managers, who brought with them a sizable and growing institutional portfolio. In addition, the president and chief investment officer of Fidelity Management Trust, Alexander Webb III, replaced Desmond J. Heathwood as chief investment officer at Boston Company. It is hoped that Webb will help stem the flow of managed funds out of the company.

Mellon also announced in mid-1994 that it would purchase the public finance business of Sheetz, Smith, and Co., an investment banking firm, with 1993 revenues of about $4 million.

Mellon acquired 50 wholesale and retail mortgage loan origination offices and $3.6 billion in residential loan-servicing rights from U.S. Bancorp for about $75 million in cash. The purchase expanded Mellon's mortgage loan operations from 27 offices in the mid-Atlantic states and New England to 10 states in the Pacific Northwest, the Rocky Mountain region, Hawaii, and the Northeast. The deal will more than double Mellon's origination capability and bolster its loan-servicing business, which currently has a portfolio of $21.5 billion and an annual loan production of around $2.9 billion. In addition, Mellon acquired four Texas-based residential mortgage offices of the former Farm and Home Savings Association of Nevada, Missouri. Two offices are located in Houston and one each in Dallas and Austin. One of the Houston offices also buys loans from third-party originators in 33 states. These offices originated just over $1 billion of loans during 1993.

In July 1995, Mellon Mortgage Co. signed a definitive agreement to acquire Metropolitan Life Insurance Company's residential and commercial mortgage unit, Metmor Finance Inc. (Overland Park, Kansas). Metmor services more than $13 billion in residential and commercial loans. In addition, it operates 24 residential mortgage origination offices in the southwestern and midwestern sections of the country, as well as eight commercial origination offices nationwide. With these mortgage banking acquisitions, Mellon becomes a major player within the industry, servicing $51 billion in mortgages, up from $32 billion a year ago. Mellon also agreed to buy the corporate trust business of Keystone Financial, adding 250 accounts with $3 billion in outstanding principal. Mellon also agreed to acquire the bond services business of KeyCorp with 9 offices in 13 states for an undisclosed sum of money. KeyCorp's bond services portfolio handled 2,700 bond trustee and agency accounts, with outstanding securities valued at more than $27 billion. These fill-in acquisitions enhance Mellon's leadership position in municipal and corporate trust services. Including the above acquisitions, Mellon's corporate trust group will service more than 9,100 trustee and agency accounts, with outstanding securities of more than $146 billion.

Mellon should generate additional fee income in 1996 from a contract that will enable the company to sell mutual funds and other financial services to AAA members. Also, Dreyfus assets under management averaged $77 billion in the third quarter of 1995 compared to $72 billion in the second quarter. This increase is related to market appreciation and higher institutional cash management balances. Increases in the Dreyfus portfolio generate additional fee income as will a new relationship with Golden Gate Bank in San Francisco. Mellon Bank will offer its private-banking services to customers of the California bank, marking the first time that Mellon has offered private banking services (Mellon Private Asset Management) through another bank.

In late November 1994, Mellon announced unexpectedly that it planned to take a $130 million charge to compensate institutional customers at Boston Company for losses suffered in securities-lending funds that Mellon managed and invested. As part of its trust and custody management services, Boston Company lent securities owned by institutional customers to brokers, who put up cash as collateral. In investing the cash, Boston Company gambled on the movement of interest rates and suffered large losses when they continued to increase. Mellon could have passed these losses on to institutional clients, but decided to accept all losses itself, thus protecting the reputations of both Boston Company and Mellon. The portfolio manager in charge was dismissed.[5]

SUMMARY

Mellon's banking franchise is primarily embedded within the Pittsburgh and Philadelphia markets. The company has focused on acquiring financial services businesses and marketing those products to its bank customer base. Consequently, Mellon derives a much larger portion of its income from noninterest sources (fee income) than from net interest sources, compared to its superregional peers.

Although Mellon's efficiency ratio was at 67 percent in 1993, 64.5 percent in 1994, and 63 percent in the first half of 1995, well above those of its peers, it is important to consider that fee-revenue businesses generally pay higher average salaries than traditional banking. Mellon should be able to reduce this ratio to under

60 percent by 1996–97 as it integrates Dreyfus into its trust and internal mutual fund operations. Cost savings begin to appear with the elimination of back-office duplication and consolidation of systems. In addition, Mellon's assumption of the custodial role for the Dreyfus funds, rather than another banking organization, will help its efficiency ratio. On the other hand, fee-based businesses generate higher returns on assets and often require less capital when compared to more traditional banking operations. The transformation of Mellon from a commercial bank into a fee-driven diversified financial services company with a large banking division should allow it to be one of the independent survivors during the upcoming consolidation period. However, a premium offer or a nondiluting merger of equals, with the Mellon team managing the postmerger company, is possible.

Some bank analysts are forecasting that Mellon should be able to generate an ROA in excess of 1.80 percent, perhaps the highest of our universe of superregional banks, and an ROE of at least 17 percent in 1997. These strong profitability ratios should be accompanied by excellent asset quality and strong capital levels, along with a dividend payout ratio in the neighborhood of 42 percent or more.

Mellon is not expected to make any major acquisitions until at least 1996 as a result of restrictions on share repurchases it incurred following the purchase of Dreyfus. However, following the second anniversary of the Dreyfus acquisition, Mellon is expected to begin a major share buyback program. Its stated intention is to reduce its common equity ratio to 7–7.5 percent over the long term, versus about 9.5 percent at year-end 1994. It must also be remembered that Mellon has about $800 million in goodwill that must be subtracted from tangible capital.[6]

Mellon has sharpened its focus on fee-related businesses such as trust services, mutual funds, cash management, and credit cards. Mellon has also continued to strengthen its consumer franchise with a broadened product line and its new Cornerstone credit card. It has also focused greater attention on productivity gains, especially the reduction of its overhead ratio.

On the acquisition front, Mellon is strong enough to stand on its own. However, it may attempt to acquire Bank of Boston, Huntington Bancshares, National City Corporation, or Crestar. On the other hand, a merger of equals with Bank of New York, CoreStates, or some other candidate cannot be ruled out.

ENDNOTES

1. C.S. Berger, "Mellon Bank Corp.," *Salomon Brothers U.S. Equity Research*, February 14, 1995, p. 3.
2. T.H. Hanley, "Mellon Bank Corporation," *CS First Boston*, June 28, 1994, p. 4.
3. T.W. Koch, *Bank Management*, 3d ed. (Fort Worth, TX: The Dreyfus Press, 1995), p. 854.
4. T.H. Hanley, "Mellon Bank Corporation," *CS First Boston*, July 6, 1995, p. 5.
5. M. Murray and G. Putka, "Mellon Bank Plans a Charge of $130 Million," *The Wall Street Journal*, November 29, 1994, p. A2.
6. Berger, p. 6.

T A B L E   18-4

Mellon Bank Corporation Financials

	1990	1991	1992	1993	1994
Earnings per share	$1.89	$3.07	$4.64	$3.09	N.A.
Assets (in millions)	$30,216	$29,050	$29,889	$35,635	$38,106
Net income (in millions)	$174.00	$280.00	$437.00	$361.00	$433.00
Return on assets	0.58%	0.96%	1.46%	1.01%	1.14%

	1994	
	(in millions)	%
Average earning assets	$32,282	100
Securities	5,149	16
Loans	25,097	78
Other	2,036	6
Loans	26,733	100
Construction and land	423	
Commercial mortgage	1,201	
Highly leveraged		
Commercial loans and leases	10,814	
Other foreign	832	
Term LCD		
Credit card receivables	2,381	
Other consumer	2,464	
Unearned discount	(62)	
Corporate	13,270	50
Consumer	4,783	18
Mortgages	8,680	32

	1990	1991	1992	1993	1994
Efficiency ratio	70.76	69.28	65.93	64.29	65.26
Shareholder equity (in millions)	$1,732	$1,904	$2,351	$3,964	$4,277
Preferred	$396	$425	$509	$641	$586
Common	$1,336	$1,479	$1,842	$3,323	$3,691

F I G U R E   18–1

Mellon Bank Corporation Financial Charts

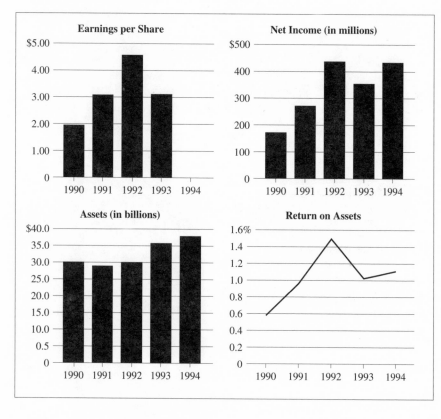

FIGURE   18-2

Mellon Bank Corporation Financial Charts

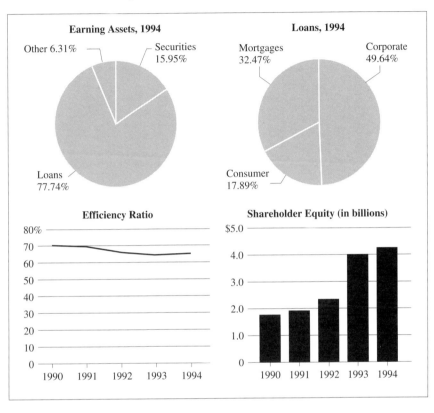

WESTERN BANKS

Superregional banks in the western part of the country performed well in 1994, registering record profits, improving asset quality, and maintaining strong capital positions built up over the past few years. This strong performance mirrored the robust economic expansion in most of the region. The long-awaited turnaround in the California economy also contributed to improved banking conditions and an increase in loan demand. However, the improvement in economic activity was not enough to keep many community banks in California from weak performances, especially those located in southern California, the area hardest hit by the recession. Problem loans continued to be a drag on the performance of small community banks in southern California, which have a high dependency on real estate loans. On the other hand, the three largest banks in the state posted earnings well above the national average.[1]

Three vastly different superregionals dominate western banking: BankAmerica, the third largest bank holding company in the nation with close to $200 billion in assets; First Interstate, headquartered in Los Angeles, but with major banking franchises located in every state west of the Rocky Mountains; and Wells Fargo, an exceptionally well run, $53 billion bank located primarily in California.

BankAmerica has one of the largest branch networks in the United States, with dominant franchises in California, Washington, and Nevada. The bank also has a major network of branches and representative offices abroad. With the acquisition of archrivals Security Pacific and Continental Corp., the bank is truly both a retail bank and a wholesale bank. Executives at BankAmerica have suggested that they would like a major presence on the East Coast and would certainly consider nationwide acquisitions like Bank of Boston or CoreStates. BankAmerica has excellent merger skills and is adept at cost-cutting and integration of acquired franchises.

First Interstate is about one-fourth the size of BankAmerica, but maintains an attractive $56 billion asset franchise throughout the western states. The bank is active in making fill-in mergers and skilled in making them accretive. With good credit controls, strong internal capital generation, and respectable control of non-interest expenses, the bank is a likely acquisition candidate. As a matter of fact, both First Bank Systems and Wells Fargo have made offers to First Interstate to acquire that franchise.

Wells Fargo is also a $53 billion asset bank with exceptional management and a strong internal capital generation rate. The bank is well known for its cost discipline and its money management skills. Wells Fargo would love to acquire First Interstate; however, overtures have been resisted so far. Because Wells Fargo's loan portfolio was primarily California based and concentrated in real estate, it suffered a major increase in nonperforming loans during 1991–92. Previously, it had been regarded as a banking organization with exceptional credit quality. To its credit, Wells Fargo withdrew as a competitive bidder for Security Pacific when the price rose too high and its due diligence work revealed Security Pacific's weakened loan portfolio. Wells Fargo's exemplary financial ratios of the past have returned in 1994, and the bank appears poised for further improvement and growth. It would make an outstanding but expensive acquisition for a bank desiring a nationwide or West Coast presence.

ENDNOTE

1. F. Furlon and G. Zimmerman, "Economy Boosts Western Banking in 1994," *Federal Reserve Bank of San Francisco. Weekly Letter*, January 27, 1995, p. 1.

CHAPTER 19

BANKAMERICA

$\mathbf{B}$ankAmerica was the second largest bank holding company in the United States, with approximately $215 billion in assets, at year-end 1994. The company's franchise runs from the state of Washington in an arc through Texas. In addition, it has a branch system in Hawaii and Alaska and acquired Continental Bank Corp. in Illinois in 1994. In fact, BankAmerica has the largest market share of deposits in the states of California, Washington, and Nevada and has a market share among the top four banks in Texas, Arizona, Hawaii, and Oregon. The company also has 45 foreign branches and 16 representative offices in 36 countries (see Table 19–1).

Prior to 1995 BankAmerica was acquisition-minded; however, there has been limited acquisition activity recently. It has more than 8 million checking account customers and 10 million households with banking relationships. In California, the company's household penetration of at least one noncard product has reached 50 percent. BankAmerica is working hard at cross-selling additional retail products to its current customers through branches and alternative systems.

At the end of 1994, it was the second largest bank in the country, approaching number one Citicorp in asset size. However, with the pending merger of Chemical Banking with Chase Manhattan to form Chase (with $300 billion in assets), BankAmerica will become the third largest bank holding company in the nation in early 1996. With the acquisition of Continental Corp. (renamed Bank of America Illinois), the bank has a healthy balance of retail, foreign, and domestic corporate business. The bank has excellent personal and corporate trust units, and money management operations; it also has a highly successful multistate consumer finance company. Additional acquisitions are likely to include companies that generate fee income from products and services that can be leveraged through close to 2,000 domestic branches, fill-in acquisitions in the western United States, and a couple

T A B L E   19–1

Geographic Distribution of Assets, 1994

	Assets (in billions)	Number of Branches	Deposit Share	Rank
Arizona	$ 8.7	145	25%	2
Alaska	0.2	5	4	5
California	146.0	991	35	1
Hawaii	1.4	33	11	3
Idaho	0.4	20	5	5
Illinois	22.0	1		2
Nevada	4.4	81	34	1
New Mexico	0.8	41	7	4
Oregon	3.1	86	11	3
Texas	9.1	234	6	4
Washington	15.0	271	35	1

of large eastern, midwestern, or southern banks. Since 1988, the bank has made more than 20 acquisitions. More are anticipated once the barriers of interstate banking are removed. More than half the company's earnings now come from corporate or commercial banking, compared with just one-third in 1990.

BankAmerica weathered the severe California recession and its consolidation with weakened Security Pacific by posting an ROA of 1.04 percent and an ROE of 12.9 percent in 1993, followed by an ROA of 1.08 percent and an ROE of 13.2 percent in 1994. During the first half of 1995, the bank's ROA averaged 1.13 percent, while its ROE averaged 14.1 percent. Because of costs associated with the acquisition and consolidation of Security Pacific, the overhead ratio of BankAmerica jumped to 64.0 percent in 1993 and early 1994 from 60.2 percent in 1992. The Security Pacific combination added more branches than any prior bank deal. However, 80 percent of the new branch additions were closed to enhance efficiency, while 96 percent of the accounts and 94 percent of the balances were retained despite the closing of 450 redundant branches. BankAmerica's average California branch size is $65 million in deposits, excluding the 26 largest banking centers within the system. This average is probably the largest in the nation. Since the Security Pacific merger, BankAmerica's transaction accounts have doubled to between 10,000 and 11,000 with about 15 people per branch managing this enormous customer base, down from more than 16 before the merger.[1]

Management expects an overhead ratio of about 58 percent by 1996. This will not be easy to achieve without further consolidation of branches. BankAmerica should benefit greatly from the passage of the interstate banking bill; the company is currently required to carry the additional expense of operating separate banks in separate states. The passage of this legislation should reduce the overhead ratio by 1 percent. However, to capitalize on all of the expense savings opportunities, the company will have to make some initial expenditures in its system.[2] Branch costs are likely to be reduced through the use of alternative delivery channels. Management noted that roughly 70 percent of banking transactions take place outside the branch. Consequently, a 2,000-branch network may not be necessary to maintain customer revenues and funds.

Although credit quality had been a serious problem for the bank in the mid-1980s and following the merger with Security Pacific, it no longer is, as nonperforming loans dropped to under 1.48 percent of total loans in 1994, down from 3.25 percent in 1992. BankAmerica's loan loss reserve stood at 154 percent of its total nonperforming loans at mid-year 1994, a reasonable cushion, given that the company is extremely conservative in classifying even slightly suspect credits as nonperforming. At year-end 1994, its ratio of reserves to loans and leases was at 2.62 percent. With a recovering California, national, and worldwide economy, its nonperforming ratio should decline to around 1.25 percent by 1996. In 1994, the corporation had a ratio of common equity to total assets of 7.34 percent, a Tier 1 risk-based capital ratio of 7.30 percent, and a total risk-based capital ratio of 11.70 percent, well above what the regulators require for a well-capitalized bank.

TECHNOLOGICAL DEVELOPMENTS

BankAmerica has invested heavily in installing and implementing an imaging system for its check processing operations, which process 20 million checks per day. The company expects the system to improve customer service and eventually reduce costs by 35 to 40 percent. It views the imaging system as having enormous potential in terms of internal processing; however, electronic check presentment is more cost-effective currently. Despite working with IBM for many years on a check imaging product, the bank has concluded that its volume of imaging has not yet reached levels that make the technology cost-effective. Additionally, the bank has 36 million customer accounts contained in 23 different bank systems. The bank has developed a 600-gigabyte customer database called the "data warehouse" and software that enables it to reduce the average time spent on difficult customer account inquiries from two hours to five minutes. BankAmerica considers the data warehouse one of its biggest assets and a definite competitive edge. The bank has also introduced a service to help corporate cash management clients combat check fraud. The bank's on-line positive pay service allows clients to access the exception report via personal computers. Clients can review current check serial numbers and dollar amounts, request copies, and initiate pay or no-pay decisions from their own terminals.

Customers are carrying out basic transactions through the bank's 3,500 cash machines and telephone banking. Only about one-third of the bank's 65 million monthly "customer touches," or customer interactions, take place within traditional branches in California. New electronic wall systems are being installed in some malls and retail establishments without any on-site employees. These provide ATM services and customer service telephones, cash depositories for local merchants. In addition, a special banker-on-call service enables customers to arrange personal loans, open mutual funds, obtain credit cards, and so forth with a live banker via keyboard.[3] All required forms and signatures are optically scanned and printed by an interactive computer system. Interactive video looms in the future.

Customers of the bank in the San Francisco area will have the option of placing a color picture of themselves along with their signature on the front of their Master Card and Visa card. This would likely reduce bankcard fraud, which costs the credit card industry more than $1 billion per year.

BankAmerica is considered one of the leading users of technology in the banking industry. Microcomputer technology is a primary focus for technology investment at the bank. Microcomputer technology surrounds various back-end systems that are not expected to be replaced in the near term because they remain efficient and cost-effective. The benefits of microcomputer technology is a responsive system germane to analysis and delivery of information. BankAmerica maintains a huge database of customer information, including demographic data, that is used to support sales and marketing efforts. In 1990–91, the bank introduced a new sales culture meant to enhance bank product sales through bank branches; the branches focus on sales rather than asset size. Branch activities that are not tied to sales or customer services are removed or automated. BankAmerica invested heavily in sophisticated technology in its branches, which includes high-performance PCs linked to the systems that allow customer information to be retrieved rapidly from service desktops, enhancing customer assistance.[4]

HISTORY

The Bank of America was founded in 1904 by Amaedo Peter Giannini as the Bank of Italy. His philosophy of serving "the little fellows" and his dream of national branch banking made Bank of America a controversial bank, especially when it became (temporarily) the world's largest bank only 41 years after it was founded. Giannini's idea of building a branch system so that just about everyone would have access to a bank was an enigma to "big interests" and offended influential members of the patrician financial community, most old-line California bankers, and regulators, who were uncertain about how to respond to this new type of "populous" banking that preferred the bank accounts and loans of farmers and working men rather than the carriage trade. The bank grew rapidly. However, regulations prohibiting Federal Reserve banks from opening new branches stymied expansion.

Giannini cleverly circumvented the regulations by forming separate state banks in northern and southern California in addition to the Bank of Italy and another national bank. Giannini placed four banks under the control of a new holding company, BancItaly. In 1927, California regulations were changed to allow branch banking. Giannini consolidated his four banks into the Bank of America of California. He already owned New York's Bowery and East River National Bank; he then established Bank of America branches in Washington, Oregon, Nevada, and Arizona, again before branch banking was explicitly permitted.

Federal regulators took exception to Giannini's practice of dictating the law and tried to slow down his drive to set up branch banks. In response, Giannini established another holding company in 1928 (Transamerica) to supplant BancItaly and to symbolize what he hoped to accomplish in banking. Transamerica bought Blair and Company, an old-line Wall Street investment banking firm in 1929. In 1930, Giannini consolidated his two banking systems into the Bank of America National Trust and Savings Association, under the control of Transamerica. Because of poor health, Giannini relinquished his presidency of the company to Elisha Walker, the head of Blair, and went to Europe; but he returned to California in 1931 when he heard that Walker was attempting to liquidate Transamerica. Giannini held stockholder meetings throughout California, where three-quarters of the shareholders resided; in a dramatic proxy fight, he warned that "eastern interests" and the "big guys" were trying to ruin the bank. Giannini regained control of the bank. However, the regulators forced him to give up control of the New York banks. Giannini fought political and banking wars against the Federal Reserve, SEC, U.S. Treasury, Hans Morgenthal, and JP Morgan. The enmity Giannini aroused in his war against the establishment cost the bank a chance to have a nationwide branch system as the Federal Reserve attempted to force Transamerica and Bank of America to separate in 1937.

Bank of America grew rapidly during World War II as people flocked to California. By 1945, as it exceeded $5 billion in assets, Bank of America passed Chase Manhattan in size to become at that time the largest bank in the world. Following Giannini's death in 1949, the bank assets still grew rapidly to over $11 billion in assets by 1960. It was the first bank to fund a small-business investment company and to adopt electronic and computerized record keeping. The bank also established the first successful bank credit card, BankAmericard, which later became Visa.

In addition to its major emphasis on retail banking, Bank of America beefed up its international presence and began to pursue wholesale accounts more aggressively. As anticipated, in 1957 the Federal Reserve finally forced the Bank of America to separate from Transamerica. Later, the Bank of America became a stodgy, conservative, inflexible institution, no longer fighting battles for national branching and the man on the street.

BankAmerica Corporation was created in 1968 to hold the assets of Bank of America and to help it expand into nonbank activities. The bank averaged 15 percent in annual growth from 1971 to 1978 under the new CEO A.W. Tom Clausen, earning management great praise. However, when Clausen left the bank in 1981 to head the World Bank, BankAmerica, with $112 billion in assets, began to fall apart. Samuel Armacost, the new CEO, eventually lost his job because of the poor performance of the bank under his tenure. However, all the bad loans in energy, shipping, and agriculture and to third-world countries were put on the books during the fast-growth era of Clausen. The result was that BankAmerica lost money for three straight years, leaving it undercapitalized, illiquid, and unable to raise funds in the money and capital markets. The bank was close to failure. If its name had not been BankAmerica, the regulators would have taken it over. As a matter of fact, for a time BankAmerica's operations were closely supervised by federal banking authorities, under a so-called memorandum of understanding. Although Armacost made an effort to cut costs by closing 187 branches, selling subsidiaries, dropping 3,000 corporate clients, and laying off thousands of employees, nonperforming loans kept cropping up and the institution began to hemorrhage. Its board of directors lost confidence in their leader and were shocked when smaller rival First Interstate made a buyout offer to take over the bank. Armacost was dismissed and replaced with Clausen, who pleaded with investors and regulators to allow the bank to remain independent. Despite an even more attractive offer from First Interstate, Clausen convinced investors to reject the offer.

Clausen, a strong and powerful leader, began restructuring operations. He sold the discount brokerage firm, Charles Schwab, and the bank's Italian subsidiary, both for a substantial profit, helping to restore depleted capital. He made large additional staff cuts and refocused the bank's attention to domestic customers. He extended banking hours, including Saturday, introduced advanced ATMs to lure back retail customers, and paid more attention to the corporate business that the bank had neglected over the last decade. Clausen hired from Wells Fargo and other banks an exceptional new management team, which concentrated on shrinking the bank's nonperforming loans, raising capital, refocusing the direction of the bank on the California division and the Pacific Rim, and controlling noninterest expenses. By the end of 1988, the bank became profitable following three straight years of losses and nearly dying. In 1989, the bank's earnings allowed reinstatement of dividend payments. Retail operations were expanded with acquisitions of Nevada First Bank and American Savings Financial Corporation. The latter institution became a subsidiary of SeaFirst Corp., the largest bank in the Pacific Northwest. SeaFirst was by now an exceptionally profitable bank, but it had been acquired by BankAmerica in 1983, when it got into serious financial difficulty because of many nonperforming energy loans.

Bank earnings exceeded $1 billion in 1990, and acquisitions began to take a higher priority. These acquisitions included Woodburn State Bank of Oregon, Western Savings and Loan branches in Arizona, and Benjamin Franklin and MeraBank Federal Savings, the biggest thrifts in Oregon and Arizona, respectively. The bank also opened a new international branch in Milan, Italy.

It is interesting to point out that its credit problems of the mid-1980s led the bank toward one of the highest-quality loan portfolios in the nation. The earlier weakness helped keep the bank away from high-risk, heavily leveraged transactions and commercial real estate lending, which doomed some large banks during the early 1990s. In 1991, BankAmerica acquired ABQ and Sandia Federal Savings Bank, both in New Mexico, and Village Green National Bank of Houston. BankAmerica also acquired $88 million in assets and 18 branches from Olympic Savings Bank (Washington). During 1991, the acquired assets totaled $5.3 billion. The bank also purchased a subsidiary of GNA Securities that had operated an investment program called Bank of America Investment Services, which offered mutual funds and annuities in the bank's branches since 1988.

Following three years of earnings in excess of $1 billion, BankAmerica acquired its weakened rival Security Pacific Corporation in 1992, the largest merger in banking history, at a cost of $4.6 billion. The merger offered the potential to save $1.2 billion annually for a three-year period by closing 500 redundant branches, consolidating operations and systems, and laying off 12,000 employees. Security Pacific, with assets of close to $60 billion, had been the dominant bank in southern California. The regulatory approval of this merger required divestiture of select assets and liabilities with total deposits of $4.7 billion in California, Washington, Oregon, and Nevada. In addition, BankAmerica agreed to divest certain branches in Arizona with aggregate assets of $1.7 billion. Goodwill recorded in connection with the merger, which represents the excess of the purchase price over the estimated fair value of identifiable net assets at the consummation of the merger, amounted to approximately $3.6 billion. It is interesting to note that Wells Fargo withdrew as a potential acquiror of Security Pacific. Security's loan quality was not up to the standards of Wells Fargo; in addition, it would be difficult for Wells Fargo, with branches concentrated in northern California, to match the cost savings available to BankAmerica, which had a large branch system in Southern California.

Security Pacific and Other Acquisitions

The company's acquisition activity continued with the purchase of 116 Texas branches of Sunbelt Federal Savings; HomeFed, the largest thrift in Hawaii with 30 branches; and Valley Bank of Nevada, which led to BankAmerica becoming the biggest bank in that state.

BankAmerica paid 2.13 times tangible book value to acquire Security Pacific, as well as a price 25 percent higher than agreed to on the announcement date of the marriage. This represents an example of a bank that agreed to be bought out at a time of low stock prices. However, when stock market prices and bank takeover prices rose, so did the closing price of the transaction[5] (see Table 19–2).

The persistent recession in California and problematic assets in Security Pacific's commercial real estate portfolio caused a decline in earnings for 1992. In

T A B L E   19-2

BankAmerica/Security Pacific Transaction

	Announcement, August 21, 1991	Completion, April 22, 1992
Deal value	$4,666.9	$5,832.9
Price per share	$32.89	$41.36
Price/book value	101.51%	213.42%
Price/tangible book value	121.19%	213.42%
Workout period (years)	3	
Price/deposits	8.39%	10.76%
Price/assets	5.80%	7.63%
Premium/core deposits	2.16%	6.85%

Source: SNL Securities, L.P., Charlottesville, VA.

its desire to close the deal, BankAmerica neglected to scrutinize the books carefully, and Security Pacific's portfolio was riddled with bad real estate and commercial loans that became even worse during the extended California recession. Consequently, BankAmerica was forced to write off nearly the entire purchase price of $4.6 billion. However, the impact on earnings was nominal because of accounting wizardry, which includes the use of purchase accounting and the shoving of vast sums onto the balance sheet into categories such as goodwill and net identifiable intangibles. Of course, these intangibles and goodwill must eventually be charged against earnings. BankAmerica will have charges of about $360 million per year against earnings for 25 years.

Despite a decline in earnings in 1992, BankAmerica acquired certain branches and assets and assumed certain liabilities of First Gibraltar of Texas. The company acquired $0.7 billion of consumer loans, $0.2 billion of domestic commercial loans, and $5.9 billion of U.S. government securities and other liquid assets. BankAmerica Texas also assumed deposits with a fair value of $7.1 billion. Unfortunately, earnings from the Texas operations have not worked out as planned. Therefore, management decided to sell these operations or add to critical mass with additional acquisitions to achieve an adequate return on investment.

Prior to the acquisition of Continental Bank, BankAmerica received approval to upgrade its Guangzhou representative office in China to a full-service branch.

RECENT DEVELOPMENTS

The bank was relatively well positioned for the rising interest rate environment of 1994 and had a low exposure to interest rate swaps compared to other large banks. During 1994, BankAmerica announced plans to acquire Continental Bank in a deal valued at about $1.9 billion. The acquisition of a wholesale bank with 2,000 corporate relationships certainly diversified the corporation's customer base. The fundamental value-enhancing motive of BankAmerica was the opportunity to market and distribute its corporate banking products and services to Continental's business customers. Continental conducted banking relationships with 1,600 of the 10,000 largest companies in the United States. Also, BankAmerica has one of the most sophisticated global computer networks, which allows the bank to offer financial services at reduced cost worldwide. Once satisfied with its check clearing, foreign exchange, or cash management service, a company is unlikely to move its business[6] (see Table 19–3 for a brief comparison of salient financial statistics).

Continental provided an extensive range of commercial banking services in the Midwest, the nation, and select international markets. Through its subsidiaries, the company provided business financing, specialized finance and operating services, international trading, and personal banking. The corporation also engaged in equity finance and investing, as both principal and arranger. BankAmerica can almost completely fund Continental's $12 billion portfolio with inexpensive retail deposits from out of state at a savings of about 100 basis points. There should also be savings of about 15 percent in noninterest expenses. BankAmerica has moved the headquarters of its U.S. corporate banking operation to Chicago. The takeover of Continental is expected to generate around $1 billion in excess capital over several years as BankAmerica plans to shrink some $12 billion of the latter's investment portfolio. Even without the Continental acquisition, BankAmerica's position in corporate banking is quite strong; it is tied for fourth place in primary relationships with Fortune

T A B L E   19–3

BankAmerica/ Continental Bank, December 31,1993*

	BankAmerica	Continental
Total assets	$186.93	$22.60
Deposits	$141.62	$13.54
Nonperforming assets	$2.89	$0.50
Net income	$1.95	$0.34
EPS	$4.79	$1.20
ROA	1.05%	1.12%
Total equity	$17.14	$1.92
Employees	96,400	4,200

* All dollar amounts are in billions, except EPS.

Source: Company reports.

1,000 companies (a 29 percent market share). However, the merger with Continental (with a 16 percent market share) would vault BankAmerica past Chemical Banking, the current market leader (a 32 percent market share). In addition to its Fortune 1,000 penetration, Continental brings a strong cash payment product, a midwestern customer orientation, and more middle-market and privately owned companies as customers.[7]

BankAmerica expanded its mortgage banking business with the acquisitions of United Mortgage in Minnesota, the former Margaretten servicing center in Virginia, and in 1995, Arbor National in Uniondale, New York. Arbor, with 20 branches in eight states, services $5.3 billion in mortgages. BankAmerica is among the 10 largest originators and servicers of home mortgage loans. These acquisitions diversified the bank's reach out of California and enabled the organization to increase the efficiency of its mortgage processing operations. The company believes that technology will separate winners from losers in mortgage banking and that only large-scale mortgage banks will be able to make the necessary investments profitably. Banks have been purchasing mortgage banking companies to generate additional fee income through mortgage servicing and originations, and to obtain a source of new customers to whom they can cross-sell other bank products and services.

Approximately 35 percent of BankAmerica's net income in 1994 came from wholesale banking activities such as commercial, corporate, and international lending; payment services; and capital markets. Although California remains its largest market, about half of the bank's loan portfolio came from outside that state. The company's overall return in the corporate and foreign sector in 1994 was below average, but its returns for consumer banking were good and those for middle-market and commercial real estate were outstanding. Its return on average common equity was 16.1 percent for consumer banking, 11.4 percent for U.S. corporate and international banking, 30.4 percent for commercial real estate, 29.4 percent for middle-market banking, and 1.8 percent for non-California banks (see Table 19–4). The diverse business is 60 percent international and 40 percent domestic. In addition, with 30 trading rooms worldwide, BankAmerica has about a 5 percent market share of the world's foreign exchange market.

Noninterest Income

BankAmerica's noninterest income for 1994 was $4.1 billion, representing 34.1 percent of total revenue. Fees and commissions accounted for $2.9 billion, while trading income was $357 million. Foreign exchange trading accounted for $237 of the trading income, while credit card and deposit fees accounted for $343 million and $1.2 billion, respectively, of the total fees and commissions. Trust fees generated $285 million (see Table 19–5). BankAmerica also had about $11 billion in mutual fund assets under management on June 30, 1995. In an effort to increase

T A B L E   19-4

Selected Business Sector Data, 1994*

	Net Income	Average Total Assets	Deposits	ROE
Large corporate and foreign banking	$651	$68	$26	11.4%
Consumer banking	882	65	77	16.1
Commercial real estate	329	9	2	30.4
Middle-market banking	234	14	7	29.4
Private banking/investments	1	3	5	
Other non-California banks	51	24	24	1.8
Other	28	18	6	0.7
Total	$2,176	$201	$147	13.2%

* In billions, except for net income in millions.

Source: BankAmerica, 1994 *Annual Report*, p. 20.

T A B L E   19-5

Noninterest Income (in millions)

Source	1994
Deposit account fees	$1,201
Credit card fees	343
Trust fees	285
Other fees and commissions	1,111
Net trading account	120
Foreign exchange trading	237
Net securities gains	24
Net gains on sales of subsidiaries/operations	85
Net gain asset sales	126
Venture capital activities	136
Other income	479
Total	$4,147

Source: BankAmerica, 1994 *Annual Report*, p. 48.

fee income and to expand internationally, BankAmerica began issuing Visa and MasterCard credit card products in Taiwan. The bank also planned to expand its merchant services business in Taiwan, which currently provides processing to more than 7,000 local merchants. On the other hand, the bank sold its mortgage securities unit (that acts as a trustee and administrator for $24 billion in mortgage-backed securities) to Bankers Trust for an estimated price of between $40 and $50 million. There was not enough critical mass, which limited return on capital, to justify the continued operation of the unit.

While the company has been able to benefit substantially from a reduction in FDIC premiums, it could also suffer from a possible $100 million SAIF assessment to help recapitalize the savings and loan deposit insurance fund.

CORPORATE STRATEGY

BankAmerica's corporate strategy has three components:

- Be as important to its customers as they are to it. Sometimes called *relationship banking.*

- Achieve excellence in select core capabilities or competencies that will make BankAmerica the most important provider for key customer segments.

- Invest shareholders' capital only in those businesses that will create value for shareholders by earning more than the cost of capital.[8]

The company has consistently rejected opportunities to make acquisitions when it believed that prices or risks were too high to create shareholder value. On the other hand, the company will divest businesses in which it cannot create a competitive advantage that will increase shareholder value. The company also intends to buy back about $2.4 billion in equity—$1.9 billion of common, $500 million of preferred—by the end of 1997. It also intends to invest in services that build stronger, more profitable relationships with customers, including investment and asset management; mortgage, credit card, and other consumer lending; raising capital for businesses and distributing and trading securities; commercial finance; and Latin America and Pacific Rim trade finance. BankAmerica also intends to invest in alternative delivery systems such as electronic banking, home banking, in-store branches, and off-site ATMs. BankAmerica's proprietary network of more than 5,700 ATMs is by far the nation's largest. The company has also created a BankAmerica presence on Internet.[9]

Following the lead of Citicorp, BankAmerica opened a full-fledged business office in Hanoi. The branch will offer a wide range of wholesale banking products and services and act as a liaison for BankAmerica customers doing business in Vietnam. The bank has also opened a representative office in Ho Chi Minh City, started a family remittance program for Americans of Vietnamese origin, and became the first U.S. bank to make credit available to Vietnam by participating in a $100 million syndicate.

During August 1995, BankAmerica agreed to sell its corporate trust business to First Bank Systems. BankAmerica chose to leave the corporate trust field, lacking sufficient mass and the commensurate economies of scale to meet its profit targets. In addition, BankAmerica sold 20 of its rural Texas branches to nine various community banks in that state. The branches were originally acquired in 1992 from Sunbelt Federal Savings and First Gibraltar. An additional five branches are expected to be sold before the end of 1995.

BankAmerica has also asked bank regulators for permission to open 285 branches of its thrift subsidiaries in supermarkets and other locations across the country. The plan would extend the bank's retail branch network into all 50 states. BankAmerica currently has retail branches only in California and nine other states. Approximately 188 new branches would be located in Osco/Jewel supermarkets in Illinois, Indiana, Michigan, and Wisconsin. The rest would be located in existing BankAmerica offices around the country, including offices for mortgages and commercial finance.

In October 1995, the board announced plans to retire an additional $250 million in preferred stock, a move which has positive EPS implications. It would not be surprising to see the company redeem the remaining 50 percent of Series J preferred and 83 percent of Series F preferred. These two issues carry coupons of 11 percent and 9.6 percent, respectively, and their redemption should save the company an estimated $25 million annually. In addition, BankAmerica is likely to increase its common stock buyback authorization, which as of November 1995 stood at about $1.9 billion.

SUMMARY

BankAmerica achieved $2,176 million in net income in 1994, up 11 percent from the amount reported in 1993. Although known for its strong retail banking position in the western part of the country, the company has a well-diversified earnings stream, with about one-third of earnings coming from corporate banking, one-third from the California consumer segment, and one-third from other affiliates. In retail banking, BankAmerica is similar to First Interstate in having a branch system throughout the western states. However, BankAmerica had four times the assets of First Interstate at year-end 1995.

BankAmerica's credit exposure in Mexico is about $1.7 billion, half to the public sector and the rest to banks and upscale companies. In addition, the company has about $704 million in Mexican Brady bonds available for sale and $856 million to be held to maturity.

Further fill-in acquisitions are clearly expected. There is speculation that BankAmerica would like to acquire an East Coast connection like Bank of Boston, Bank of New York, Mellon, or CoreStates; a southern partner such as

Wachovia, Barnett, or SunTrust; and a midwestern partner such as Comerica, First Bank Systems, Norwest, or Boatmen's Bancshares. However, the bank is unlikely to pay a large premium to buy big branch systems in other parts of the country. Acquisitions such as those just mentioned would go a long way toward accomplishing founder Giannini's desire to have a nationwide banking system. Richard Rosenberg, chairman, has stated that BankAmerica is more interested in making product acquisitions than branch acquisitions. The most likely near-term acquisition would be that of a mortgage banker in the Southeast.

BankAmerica is once again expanding overseas, particularly in Asia and South America, after it closed down operations in nearly half of the 71 foreign countries in which it operated during the hard times of the 1980s. It has also begun to emphasize fee income from such sources as corporate global payments and cash management, trust, trading, foreign exchange, mortgage servicing, mutual fund sales, investment banking, safe deposit boxes, credit cards, checking, and other branch services.[10] For example, the company announced a new cobranded MasterCard agreement with Sunoco, with no annual fee and an introductory rate of prime plus 2.65 percent, which would move to prime plus 9.9 percent in 1996. The card would give users a rebate equal to 3 percent of Sunoco's gasoline purchases and 2 percent of other purchases. This type of arrangement may help to generate a measure of renewed activity within the bank's card portfolio.

It has also continued to reduce the number of employees, laying off close to 3,500 workers during 1994. In addition, the number of full-time employees declined from 82,100 in 1994 to 80,200 in 1995 despite the fact that assets grew from $202 billion to $227 billion during that period. The massive layoffs of the last 10 years have shredded the old BankAmerica's social contract of lifetime employment. The bank's 5,700 proprietary ATMs (5,000 branches without workers), the largest total in the industry, and the layoffs and should bring its efficiency ratio to under 60 percent, not bad for a bank with a huge branch system. The number of ATMs could readily expand by 50–100 percent and the number of branches could possibly be cut in half as the bank becomes more efficient over the next few years.

BankAmerica officials feel that the loosening of strictures against interstate banking could save the company some $75 million a year, mainly by eliminating the expense of having to maintain separate boards of directors, back offices, and administrative hierarchies at its various state chartered subsidiaries. It is important to point out that the amortization of goodwill of $100 million per quarter adds about 3 percent to the expense ratio. Therefore, BankAmerica's management has to work harder than the typical bank just to achieve average overhead ratios.[11]

The turnaround at BankAmerica is evident. The California economy has begun to improve. Loan demand is growing, while the already strong wholesale bank is about to advance even further with the Continental acquisition. The bank has become more efficient following the Security Pacific merger and has consolidated processing and systems. The non-California banks in Arizona, Texas,

Nevada, and New Mexico—built largely through thrift acquisitions, many of which were troubled or failed franchises that could be fixed—are being reengineered as full-product consumer and small-business banks, with loan systems and merchandising techniques that are being applied throughout the California branch system. BankAmerica has recently begun marketing retail and small-business products in a more comprehensive and aggressive fashion, leveraging their massive branch network and expanding nonbranch, alternative delivery channels. The company is well positioned in the growth markets of Asia and Latin America. It must also be remembered that although BankAmerica had to sell most of its trust business when it came close to failure in the mid-1980s, the noncompete agreement it signed upon this sale has now expired. Meanwhile, a number of the acquired banks have trust businesses to build. The trust area is just part of the natural market in consumer and middle-market businesses that could generate fee income through successful marketing. The aforementioned banking groups in transition should lead to a strong earnings improvement at BankAmerica[12] (see Figure 19–1).

In early 1995, BankAmerica announced a share repurchase program totaling $1.9 billion and a 15 percent dividend hike. Its board of directors also authorized up to $750 million of preferred stock repurchases and redemptions. The company has about $6 billion of intangibles that do not count as Tier 1 capital and are amortized at roughly $90 million per quarter. Under the buyback authorization BankAmerica may repurchase up to $90 million per quarter for the next three years, for a total repurchase of approximately $1.1 billion. The cleverness behind this buyback is that rating agencies and regulators are assured that the company cannot possibly decrease its base of tangible common equity. In addition, the company has the authorization to buy back an additional $2.4 billion as market conditions permit.

F I G U R E   19–1

Transition of BankAmerica's Banking Groups

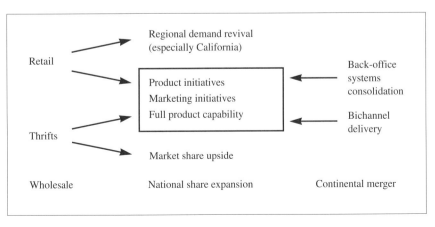

The buyback program, cost-cutting initiatives, and recovery of the California economy should all help the bank increase its return on equity, one of the goals of top management.[13] The reduction in FDIC insurance will also save the bank about $208 million per year.

Richard A. Rosenberg led the bank back to prosperity and was at the helm during the Security Pacific and Continental acquisitions. David Coulter, one of eight vice chairmen, succeeded Rosenberg as chief executive officer in 1996. While Rosenberg's expertise was in retail banking and marketing, Coulter's expertise lies in wholesale banking and international operations. Some Wall Street analysts fear that Mr. Coulter's promotion could lead to departures of several key executives who were disappointed in not being selected as chief executive officer.

ENDNOTES

1. R.B. Albertson, "BankAmerica," *Goldman Sachs U.S. Research,* September 1, 1994, p. 8.
2. T.H. Hanley, "BankAmerica," *CS First Boston,* October 27, 1994, p. 4.
3. T.H. Hanley, P.J. Carter, and A.B. Collins, "Separating the Winners from the Losers in the Banking Industry," *CS First Boston,* February 14, 1995, p. 11.
4. Ibid., p. 11.
5. J.B. McCoy, L.A. Frieder, R.B. Hedges, Jr., *BottomLine Banking* (Probus Publishing Co., 1994), pp. 185–186
6. T.W. Koch, *Bank Management,* 3d ed. (Fort Worth, TX: The Dreyden Press, 1995), p. 652.
7. Albertson, pp. 15–17.
8. BankAmerica, *1994 Annual Report,* p. 2.
9. Ibid., pp. 4–6.
10. J.R. Laing, "Go East, Young Man," *Barron's,* June 6, 1994, p. 31.
11. C. Kotowski, "BankAmerica," *Oppenheimer & Co., Inc., Weekly Research Review,* December 7, 1994, p. 38.
12. Albertson, pp. 2–3.
13. C. Kotowski, "BankAmerica," *Oppenheimer & Co. Research,* February 9, 1995, p. 2.

T A B L E   19–6

BankAmerica Corp. Financials

	1990	1991	1992	1993	1994
Earnings per share	$4.94	$4.78	$4.21	$4.76	$5.33
Assets (in millions)	$107,567	$113,971	$165,828	$185,326	$202,100
Net income (in millions)	$1,115.05	$1,123.72	$1,492.00	$1,954.00	$2,176.00
Return on assets	1.04%	0.99%	0.90%	1.05%	1.08%

	1994 (in millions)	%
Average earning assets	$168,200	100
Securities	23,346	14E
Loans	128,400	76
Other	16,560	10E
Loans	112,098	100
Construction and land	3,616	
Commercial mortgage	10,277	
Highly leveraged		
Commercial loans and leases	38,492	
Other foreign	20,363	
Term LCD		
Credit card receivables	8,020	
Other consumer	26,326	
Unearned discount		
Corporate	72,748	65
Consumer	34,346	31
Mortgages	5,004	4

	1990	1991	1992	1993	1994
Efficiency ratio	62.47	61.32	59.83	62.87	63.45
Shareholder equity (in millions)	$5,971	$7,103	$12,600	$16,285	$17,718
Preferred	$625	$902	$2,144	$2,979	$3,088
Common	$5,346	$6,201	$10,456	$13,306	$14,632

FIGURE 19-2

BankAmerica Corp. Financial Charts

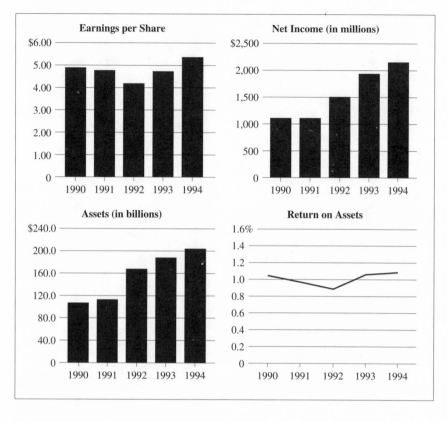

F I G U R E   19-3

BankAmerica Corp. Financial Charts

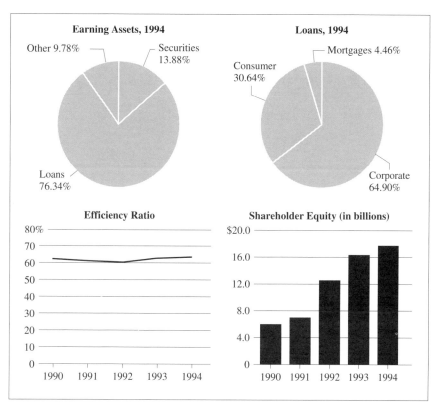

CHAPTER 20

First Interstate Bancorp

First Interstate Bancorp was the 14th largest bank holding company in the nation, with $55.8 billion in assets, at the end of 1994. The company did not incur a loan loss provision in 1994 or 1995. It owns directly or indirectly, through wholly owned subsidiaries, all of the shares of capital stock of 18 banks, which operated over 1,100 banking offices in 13 contiguous states west of the Mississippi River, stretching from Texas to Alaska.

First Interstate is a well-capitalized bank holding company with a tangible common equity ratio of 5.28 percent, a Tier 1 ratio in excess of 7 percent, and a total capital ratio in excess of 10 percent at year-end 1994. In addition, its return on average common equity was 21.6 percent and return on average total assets was 1.38 percent in 1994, placing it near the top of the superregionals in this study. Before the effect of restructuring charges, the ratios were 24.3 percent and 1.55 percent, respectively. The company's net income for 1994 was $733.5 million, including the effect of $141.3 million of restructuring charges.

First Interstate offers all traditional banking services to customers. It also owns an investment banking and a mortgage banking firm. Although the company has a great franchise throughout the western United States, it has been unable to deliver consistent results. For example, in 1990 the bank was almost wiped out by loan losses from acquisitions in Texas and Arizona. Since then, First Interstate has slashed costs, focused on its consumer banking operations, and worked on improving the quality of its loan portfolio. Consequently, at year-end 1994, First Interstate's ratio of nonperforming assets to total assets was among the best of the 25 largest banks at 0.46 percent, down from 3.8 percent in 1989. The company's loan loss reserve was among the highest in the industry at year-end 1994, and it chose not to incur a loan loss provision in that year. The company's loan loss reserve equaled 2.81 percent outstanding loans, while its ratio of the loss reserve to nonperforming assets was 362 percent for 1994. First Interstate is obviously overreserved by any measure of adequacy.

On the other hand, there is considerable room for improvement in operating efficiency. The company is targeting a decline in its efficiency ratio to 59 percent in 1995 and 57 percent in 1996 from a relatively high 65.7 percent in 1993 and 60.8 percent in 1994. Peaking in 1991, its efficiency ratio stood at 70.6 percent (see Figure 20–1). The improvement reflects management's success in consolidating a far-flung organization into a much more efficient regional structure: 21 banks were consolidated into four regional administrative and processing centers, and 11 data centers were consolidated into 2 main data centers. Also, common operating systems were set up throughout the company, while excess costs were squeezed out of acquisitions.[1]

To help cut costs, First Interstate has been aggressive in establishing common systems throughout all of its operations in 13 western states. Also, the company announced a 3,000-person reduction in staff, cutting head count from 28,000 to 25,000, and a $165 million restructuring charge, of which $139 million was realized in the third quarter of 1994 to pay for the staff reductions and other cost-cutting initiatives. In addition, almost 1,900 employees took advantage of the company's early retirement program. Management promises to achieve cost savings of $167 million by the second quarter of 1996. Staff reductions represent $107 million, or 64 percent of the savings, most of which are related to back-office and processing functions. The remaining 36 percent will come from business lines and the risk management group[2] (see Figure 20–2). Although a 57 percent efficiency ratio is an aggressive goal, the current management team has delivered on every

F I G U R E   20–1

Core Efficiency Ratio, 1990–March 1995

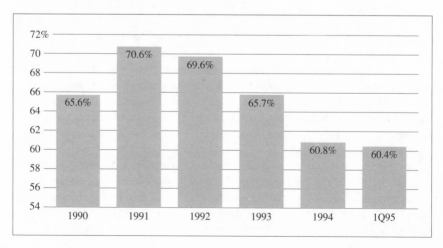

F I G U R E   20-2

Mix of First Interstate's $167 Million Cost Savings

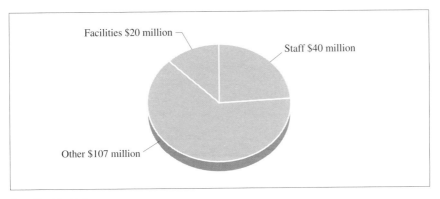

Source: First Interstate Bancorp.

one of its publicly announced performance goals since Edward Carson took over as chairman in 1990. In addition, management has targeted an 18–20 percent ROE. If management is successful in meeting its goals, First Interstate will rank among the most profitable, well-capitalized, and highest-quality banks in the nation.

Upon his retirement, in 1995, Carson passed the CEO reins to Bill Siart. Siart indicated that while the company is in the midst of reducing costs and restructuring, its strategy will be shifted toward relationship banking and superior marketing. Through a program dubbed ROE (redirect our energy or return on equity), management will seek to differentiate First Interstate from other banks in the eyes of customers and attract a greater share of their banking business. For example, bank employees are being asked to generate sales of five consumer or commercial services per customer; the current average is 2.8 services. The focus on customers should enable the bank to maintain its powerful position in the deposit area while growing the revenue contribution of newly developed products and services. The development of a common bankwide deposit system should help retain the core customer deposit base.[3]

LOAN AND DEPOSIT COMPOSITION

The bank has diversified lending and deposit bases. Core deposits, including consumer deposits under $100,000 and noninterest-bearing demand and time deposits, amounted to $46.4 billion (year-end 1994), representing 85 percent of total liabilities. Of that total, in excess of $30 billion were consumer deposits. The huge core deposit base helped earnings in the rising interest rate environment because these consumer rates were much slower in adjusting to money market conditions. Demand and other non-interest-bearing deposits increased to $16.6 billion, or 34 percent of deposits.

On the other side of the balance sheet, there were $31.8 billion in loans outstanding, of which about 38 percent were consumer installment loans, 28 percent real estate mortgages, and 27 percent commercial and industrial loans (see Tables 20–1 and 20–2). It is interesting to point out that First Interstate Bank of California accounted for 45 percent of total assets and 44 percent of total deposits.

T A B L E   20–1

Loan Mix, 1994 (in billions)

Type of Loan	Outstanding
Commercial	$ 8.9
Real estate construction	0.9
Real estate mortgage	9.4
Installment	12.1
Other	0.4
Total	$31.8

Source: First Interstate, 1994 *Annual Report.*

T A B L E   20–2

Liability Funding Mix, 1994 (in billions)

Source	Outstanding
Consumer	
Regular savings	$ 5.9
NOW and DDAs	6.7
Savings (market rate)	11.4
Other	6.3
Total consumer	$30.3
Corporate	
Large CDs and MMDAs	$ 1.4
Short-term borrowings	1.0
Long-term debt	1.3
Total corporate	$ 3.7
Total interest bearing	$33.9
DDAs and noninterest time	16.1
Total core deposits	$46.4

Source: Company reports.

HISTORY

The company known as First Interstate today was once the Western Bancorporation, and before that, First America Corporation, but its roots go back to the origins of Transamerica Corporation in 1904, when A.P. Giannini opened the Bank of Italy in San Francisco.

Transamerica, formed by Giannini to prevent further manipulation of his bank stocks by his banking rivals, became the holding company for the stock of the Bank of Italy based in California and BancItaly based in New York. BancItaly had previously acquired Bank of America, a New York–based bank. Transamerica merged the Bank of America of California and the Bank of Italy, creating the Bank of America National Trust and Savings Association. This hybrid was the fourth largest bank in the United States in 1930, with over $1 billion in assets. Transamerica began to make acquisitions that would eventually form the core of the First Interstate Corporation, including banks and other financial corporations throughout the western states of California, Nevada, Oregon, Washington, and Arizona, as well as New York. Giannini's goal was to unite all of the banks under one umbrella, creating a national branch system as soon as regulation would permit. However, the Great Depression brought with it more restrictive banking regulations. Transamerica divested a majority of its shares in the Bank of America, but continued to add both banking and nonbanking operations during the 1930s. The Federal Reserve filed a suit against Transamerica in 1948, charging that the company had created a potential monopoly with its interstate banking affiliations. However, the U.S. Court of Appeals ruled in 1953 that the holdings were not a monopoly. After the death of Giannini in 1949, Transamerica continued its acquisitions of banks in Colorado, Idaho, Montana, New Mexico, Utah, and Wyoming; it also acquired insurance companies.

The Bank Holding Company Act of 1956 placed additional restrictions on Transamerica. Executive management of Transamerica decided to separate its banking from its nonbanking subsidiaries. Ownership of 23 of Transamerica's banks in 11 western states were transferred to the new FirstAmerica Corporation, whose shares were distributed to Transamerica shareholders. By 1959, the two organizations were totally independent from each other. The company rechristened itself Western Bancorporation in 1961 and adopted its present name in 1981.

In 1959, First America acquired 97.8 percent of the stock of California Bank in exchange for over 5.3 million of its own shares. First Western Bank and Trust Company, an affiliate of which Western Bancorporation owned 74.53 percent, was merged into California Bank in 1961, with the surviving corporate entity named United California Bank. A new wholly owned subsidiary was then formed, named First Western Bank and Trust Co., which purchased from United California Bank the deposits and liabilities of 65 of the 115 banking offices of old First Western

Bank for cash. In 1963, Western Bancorporation sold its holdings in First Western Bank for approximately $63.4 million.

In 1970, National Bank of Washington (Tacoma) and Pacific National Bank (Seattle) were consolidated into one bank under the name of Pacific National Bank. Pacific National Bank was then acquired by Western Bancorp. In 1975, Western Bancorp acquired Western Asset Management Co. and Southern Arizona Bank and Trust Co., a subsidiary, and merged them into First National Bank of Arizona.

In 1978, Western Bancorp reorganized United California Bank and Walker Bank and Trust Co. into wholly owned subsidiaries. In addition, Western Bancorp formed Western Bancorp Venture Capital Co. and Western Credit Corp., also wholly owned subsidiaries. In 1979, it consolidated two Nevada affiliates, First Bank of Nevada and Bank of Nevada, into another wholly owned subsidiary called First National Bank of Nevada.

In 1980, the U.S. comptroller of the currency approved the holding company's consolidation of seven of its affiliated banks: the First National Bank of Oregon (Portland), First National Bank of Arizona (Phoenix), Bank of Idaho, N.A. (Boise), First National Bank of Casper (Wyoming), First National Bank (Fort Collins, Colorado), Conrad National Bank of Kaslispell (Montana), and Santa Fe National Bank (New Mexico). Pacific National Bank of Washington (Seattle) merged with a subsidiary of the holding company. In 1981, the holding company acquired the minority rights in eight affiliated banks and changed its name to First Interstate Bank. In 1982, the company formed First Interstate Commercial Corp. to specialize in asset-based lending to small and medium-sized businesses, and First Interstate Bancard Co., a subsidiary, to consolidate the bankcard activities of its 21 banks into one unit.

In 1983, First Interstate Equities was formed to provide equity capital for growth companies, leveraged buyouts, and special situations, and IntraWest Bank of Denver was merged into First Interstate Bank of Denver. During 1984, First Interstate acquired Continental Illinois Ltd., the London-based merchant banking subsidiary of Continental Illinois Corp. The newly purchased subsidiary was renamed First Interstate Ltd. In the same year, First Interstate Bank of Gallup (New Mexico) was sold to Gallup Bancshares. Also, First Interstate Mortgage Co., a subsidiary of the holding company, acquired Republic Realty Mortgage Corp., which the holding company merged with another acquisition, Commerce Alliance Corp., an independent commercial financing and equipment leasing company.

In 1985, First Interstate Bank of Washington, a subsidiary, acquired Olympic Bank (Everett, Washington). First Interstate Bank, Ltd., was formed in that same year. In 1986, the holding company acquired from RTC certain assets and liabilities of the First National Bank and Trust Co. of Oklahoma City and sold Western Asset Management Company to Legg Mason. In the same year, First Interstate made a bid of $2.78 billion, followed by a second bid of $3.4 billion, to take over the wounded BankAmerica, a company twice the size of First Interstate and the second largest bank in the country. BankAmerica rejected the hostile takeover, with Chairman Clausen rallying BankAmerica's shareholders to allow the bank to remain independent.

During 1988, the holding company acquired Allied Bancshares, Inc. (Houston) and certain assets and liabilities of the former Alaska Continental Bank. The Alaskan bank was renamed First Interstate Bank of Alaska. In the same year, First Interstate sold all of the asset-based loan portfolio of its subsidiary First Interstate Commercial Corp. to Congress Financial Corp. and completed the sale of First Interstate Capital Markets, Inc., a subsidiary of First Interstate Bank, Ltd., to Printon, Kane Government Securities Limited Partnership.

During 1989, First Interstate acquired Alex Brown Financial Group and Jefferson State Bank, while selling Commercial Alliance to Orix Corporation. In 1990, First Interstate sold its consumer lending operation, Nova Financial Services, for $112 million.

During 1991, First Interstate sold three banks in New Mexico to United Financial Corp. for $48 million, one bank in Colorado for $25 million, and First Interstate Bank of Oklahoma to Boatmen's Bancshares for $86 million. These sales helped bolster the bank's capital position, which had deteriorated substantially following combined losses of close to $1 billion in 1989 and 1991.

RECENT ACQUISITIONS

First Interstate announced eight acquisitions totaling $4.0 billion in assets in 1993. The largest was the $2 billion, 53-office San Diego Financial Corp., parent of San Diego Trust and Savings Bank. This acquisition raised First Interstate from ninth to third in market share in San Diego, while making it a leader in trust and mutual funds. The next largest acquisition was Chase Bank in Maricopa (Arizona) with $527 million in assets and 11 banking offices. This acquisition allowed First Interstate to increase penetration of the trust and private banking segments in the upscale Scottsdale area. Chase Trust managed over $250 million in such assets. The third largest acquisition was California Republic Bancorp, Inc., and its sole subsidiary, California Republic Bank, Inc., headquartered in Bakersfield; the bank was then merged into First Interstate Bank of California, the lead bank of First Interstate. This acquisition added 12 branches with $535 million in assets. In addition to adding to market share, the acquisition also enhanced product and service capabilities in such areas as trust, private banking, investment, and cash management. Also, First Interstate sold its international corporate finance, global trading, and distribution businesses to Standard Chartered PLC.

During 1994, First Interstate paid $331 million in cash to purchase the $3 billion asset Sacramento Savings Bank, a unit of Allegheny Corp. Under the terms of the agreement, Allegheny agreed to take back up to $132 million of nonperforming assets. Sacramento Savings is considered generally healthy and has most of its loans in residential mortgages. This acquisition expands First Interstate's operations in California's Central Valley and the northern half of the state. For example, First Interstate increased its mortgage origination capacity in California by 40 percent with 24 newly acquired mortgage lending offices and will now have the second largest market share in the Sacramento area behind BankAmerica. First Interstate is expected to achieve cost savings of nearly 50 percent of Sacramento Savings Bank's expense base by closing 24 redundant branch offices (see Table 20–3). The company also paid $54 million for four banks in Texas, including BankWest Bancorp (assets of $240 million), MNB Bancshares, Inc. ($47 million), Med Center Bank ($143 million), and Park Forest Bank ($23 million).

During the first half of 1995, First Intestate made five additional acquisitions with a total purchase price of $386 million. The acquired banks were Washington-based, 25-office University Savings Bank ($1.27 billion in assets, $929 million in deposits), North Texas Bancshares ($424 in assets, $387 million in deposits), California-based Levy Bancorp ($557 million in assets, $506 million in deposits), Ontario-based First Trust Bank ($197 million in deposits), and Texas-based Tomball National Bancshares ($98 million in assets, $88 million in deposits) (see Table 20–4). These acquisitions are part of an ongoing fill-in strategy, which

T A B L E   20–3

Expense Savings of First Interstate's Acquisitions

	Assets (in billions)	Deposits (in billions)	Expense Savings
California			
Sacramento Savings Bank*	$3.0	$2.8	49%
San Diego Financial	2.0	1.8	42
Levy Bancorp	0.6	0.6	50
California Republic	0.6	0.5	57
Other	0.5	0.5	71
Northwest			
University Savings Bank*	1.1	0.9	41
Other	0.4	0.4	
Southwest			
Chase Bank Arizona	0.5	0.4	70
Texas			
North Texas Bancshares*	0.4	0.4	24
Bancwest Bancorp	0.2	0.2	25
Other	0.3	0.3	41
Total	$9.8**	$8.8	47%

* Acquisition pending consummation as of September 16, 1994.

** Does not foot due to rounding.

Source: First Interstate Bancorp.

T A B L E 20-4

Recent Acquisition Activity (in millions)

Acquisition	Date Closing	Purchase Price	Loans	Assets	Deposits	State
1993						
California Republic Bancorp, Inc.	December 1993	$68	$381	$535	$495	California
1993 total		$68	$381	$535	$938	
1994						
First State Bank of the Oaks	January 1994	$ 23	$ 57	$ 144	$ 130	California
San Diego Financial Corp.	March 1994	340	806	1,939	1,764	California
BancWest Bancorp	April 1994	36	39	240	215	Texas
Chase Bank of Arizona	April 1994	102	356	610	392	Arizona
MNB Bancshares, Inc.	May 1994	5	21	47	41	Texas
Med Center Bank	July 1994	12	53	143	152	Texas
Sacramento Savings Bank	November 1994	337	2,230	3,010	2,598	California
Park Forest National Bank	December 1994	2	13	23	22	Texas
1994 total		$857	$3,575	$6,156	$5,629	
1995						
University Savings Bank	January 1995	$ 205	$ 154	$1,274	$ 929	Washington
North Texas Bancshares, Inc.	January 1995	65	211	424	387	Texas
Levy Bancorp	February 1995	92	266	557	506	California
First Trust Bank	March 1995	16	78	N.A.	197	Ontario
Tomball National Bancshares	July 1995	8	36	98	88	Texas
1995 total		$ 386	$ 745	$2,353	$2,107	
Grand total		$1,311	$4,701	$9,044	$8,674	

Source: CS First Boston.

429

in conjunction with other similar transactions create value for shareholders and utilize excess capital wisely.

The central part of California has escaped with far less damage from the recession and commercial real estate collapse of 1991–93 than the southern part of the state. First Interstate also bought 15 Great Savings Association branches across the state of Washington and the already mentioned University Savings Bank unit in the same state from Glendale Federal. Both purchases complement the holdings of First Interstate in Washington and appear to be part of an aggressive campaign to expand in the Northwest.

These deals are further evidence of First Interstate's turnaround that began in mid-1992 following substantial losses in 1989 and 1991 that were related to bank acquisitions. Rather than agreeing to merge with rivals BankAmerica or Wells Fargo, First Interstate has sought to remain independent by slashing costs, cleaning up its loan portfolio, making excellent acquisitions, and focusing on high-margin consumer banking operations in California and the Northwest. Excellent expense management has played a salient role in the turnaround at First Interstate, along with the installation of a credit culture that has developed an exemplary loan portfolio of high credit quality. The company has deemphasized large corporate and international lending; loans to individuals represented 54 percent of outstandings at the end of the third quarter of 1994.

Senior management is building shareholder value by deploying excess capital into acquisitions and a program to buy back almost 8 million shares of its stock. This adds about 50 cents per share to EPS on an annualized basis. The number of outstanding shares was expected to be reduced to 71 million by the end of 1996. Given the company's robust outlook and stock buyback plan, First Interstate had clearly suggested that it prefered to be an acquiror rather than an acquiree. However, a hostile takeover bid by Wells Fargo has changed the scenario.

A salient part of the company's strategy to increase revenue is improving cross-sales to its growing customer base. First Interstate will continue to seek acquisitions that can add to its strong base of low-cost core deposits, particularly acquisitions in areas of the company's territory that are either fast growing or in which it is underrepresented. The company's overall goal is to be at least in the top three in market share in most of the 49 counties in which it operates. The company also expects to increase fee income from expanded trust and private banking services as well as through the sale of non-FDIC-insured products, including mutual funds, annuities, and fixed-income investments. Through the Westcorp Funds, First Interstate's family of 22 proprietary mutual funds (about $2 billion in assets), along with a menu of a dozen other mutual fund families, the holding company is positioned to meet the changing investment needs of customers who are seeking investment alternatives to conventional bank depository products.

The customers of First Interstate are also benefiting from the company's alliance with Standard Chartered PLC, which is generating benefits for both institutions in areas such as trade finance, corporate finance, foreign exchange, and trade-related activities. In addition, First Interstate introduced a series of new cash management services; the company is now among the top 10 providers of cash management services in the country.

FEE INCOME

First Interstate's noninterest income totaled $1.05 billion in 1994, an increase of $100 million over the prior year. Deposit service charges and trust fees were the biggest contributors, accounting for close to 70 percent of noninterest income. Fee income accounted for approximately 31 percent of total revenues (see Table 20–5). First Interstate has recently reinvigorated marketing efforts for its to trust, asset management, and credit card businesses, which should help generate additional fee income.

T A B L E   20–5

Noninterest Income (in millions)

Source	1994	1993
Deposit service charges	$ 562	$513
Trust fees	193	177
Other charges, commissions	132	149
Merchant credit card fees	40	44
Investment securities gains	21	10
Trading income	17	20
Loan sales gains	3	8
Other income	87	83
Total	$1,055	$954

Source: First Interstate, 1994 *Annual Report.*

TECHNOLOGY

First Interstate has traditionally allowed its subsidiary banks to maintain regional autonomy. Thus, throughout the years the company has invested in technology to support local bank needs and was often in the forefront of industry developments. Each region had its own products, its own processing systems, and its own data center. Consequently, technology expenditures were high and spending was inefficient. The company's first step in lowering overall technology costs was to consolidate the 13 states it served into four regions. Second, it had to consolidate the four regions into using identical applications, eliminating the expense of supporting a structure of 13 systems for each product. First Interstate is relying heavily on technology to reduce the overall cost structure of new acquisitions, integrating them into the First Interstate family of banks. Since the object is to reduce maintenance and fixed costs, the company has shifted from using systems developed in-house to applications purchased from third-party vendors. One of the advantages of total consolidation is that the bank had the advantage of having many existing systems from which to choose. The bank surveyed its entire organization and picked the best technology for each application in the consolidation process.

First Interstate has developed a large centralized telephone sales and service center, which provides improved customer service 24 hours a day. Other alternative delivery systems include supermarket branches, interactive sales kiosks, more extensive ATM coverage, and computer banking.

First Interstate Bank Washington was one of the first banks to implement a check imaging system, and the holding company is exploring the applicability of file-folder imaging applications to a number of business areas such as trust, consumer loans, commercial loans, and human resources. The biggest issue in regard to image processing systems for the company is remote support. First Interstate does not currently have the communications capability to do this, nor does IBM have a solution yet.

In regard to banking technology, First Interstate might be classified as an "aggressive follower," that is, a company wanting to keep up with the competition and consumer demand without incurring the development expenses and risk of being on the cutting edge. The bank seems ready to wait until a technological development has reached the stage at which its risk-reward trade-off is established.[4]

STRATEGIC PLAN

First Interstate's strategic plan is intended to build shareholder value in the dramatically changed banking environment. The company will pursue a back-to-basics approach to capitalize on the wealth of opportunities in its own backyard, focusing on aggressively improving four fundamental areas of business: credit quality, noninterest expense, liquidity, and capitalization. First Interstate's strategy to enhance financial returns and long-term value has the following salient thrusts:

- Refocus energies from managing risk to growing revenues.
- Obtain revenue growth through acquisitions (primarily in California, Texas, and Washington) and from increased sales and marketing efforts.
- Improve customer service.
- Increase commitment to the communities it serves.

The company plans to complement acquisitions with "a continuous stream of initiatives to grow internally and to better meet customer needs by providing banking convenience, innovative products, responsive customer service and support to [its] communities . . . to be a bank with a future, committed to satisfying existing customers, winning new ones, and keeping all of them."[5] The company also announced a 10-year, $2 billion community involvement plan to provide for low- and moderate-income borrowers a range of affordable banking products, including auto, personal, home improvement, and home mortgage loans. The company thinks of itself as a big community bank, that is, a community bank with 500 communities: "Today, we have the financial strength, organizational structure, corporate culture and management team capable of not just responding to emerging challenges, but truly capitalizing on the opportunities they present."[6]

Management believes that First Interstate can be the best regional bank in the country by the year 2000. The company initiated a program to constantly review all lines of business, geographic coverage, and product offerings to ensure that each is meeting its 18–20 percent ROE objective. If it determines that a business line is not enhancing shareholder value and cannot be modified to do so, the company will redirect the capital involved toward opportunities that will.[7]

SUMMARY

First Interstate is a strong and well-diversified superregional franchise with a solid core deposit base, prudent asset-liability management, and conservative credit policies. It is well positioned to take advantage of continued growth opportunities with minimal exposure to liquidity, interest rate, and credit risk.[8]

Management is increasing shareholder value by deploying excess capital into purchase acquisitions, repurchasing common shares, and aggressively restructuring the entire organization. First Interstate should be well positioned to sustain double-digit earnings growth and return on common equity in excess of 20 percent over the 1995–96 period. Aggressive cost-cutting measures and revenue generation are cornerstones of the plan.[9] The company's loan growth in 1995 was funded primarily by the sale of investment securities, as in 1994 when it reduced its securities portfolio by $2.8 billion, or 17 percent, to meet loan demand.

As a result of share repurchases, Tier 1 capital has declined to 6.7 percent from a peak of over 10 percent. With a nearly 20 percent common equity reinvestment rate and asset growth of between 5 and 10 percent, the company's Tier 1 ratio should rise from its current level, which is below average for superregionals. In May 1995, the company announced that the board of directors had approved the repurchase of up to 7.6 million shares, or about 10 percent of its outstanding common share base. These repurchases should reduce First Interstate's common share base to approximately 71 million shares by the end of 1996.

Wells Fargo Bid

In October 1995, Wells Fargo ($52 billion in assets) made an unwelcome offer to acquire First Interstate. Initially, Wells Fargo offered to pay First Interstate 0.625 Wells Fargo shares for each First Interstate share, which on October 18, 1995 equaled $134 per First Interstate share. On a price to book value basis, the offer was at 2.8 times book value, an exceptionally rich opening offer compared to recent takeover premiums that had been no more than 2.5 times book value. First Interstate's ROE is at the high end of the superregional banks (it was at 25.6 percent in the third quarter) and on a price/earnings basis the proposed price was reasonable at only 11.7 times 1996 estimated EPS (14.4 times 1996 EPS normalized for a full loan loss provision). Wells Fargo plans to account for the deal as a purchase in order to preserve the share repurchases it has done in the past and its ability to do share repurchases in the future. This method of accounting would require goodwill of about $400 million a year to be written off through the end of the decade for this merger. However, the cost savings from the merger would soon outstrip the goodwill charge. According to Wells Fargo's projections the deal would be 10 percent dilutive to 1996 EPS, would be neutral in 1997, and 10 percent accretive in 1998. Management would cut $800 million (about 36 percent) from First Interstate's noninterest expense base of $2.2 billion (laying off about 7,500 employees and closing over 100 branches) and lose about $100 million in revenues as a result. After being spurned on its initial offer by First Interstate, the company topped an offer by rival potential acquiror, First Bank System, and offered to swap two-thirds of a share for each First Interstate share, a deal worth $140.92, based on Wells Fargo's share price on November 20, 1995. The second offer is $383 million more than the value of First Bank System's offer of $135.85 per share, based on the exchange of 2.6 First Bank System shares for each First Interstate share.

The First Bank System offer had been accepted originally by the management of First Interstate. The acceptance of a lower offer by the management team at First Interstate raised the eyebrows of some analysts, who claimed that it deprived shareholders of getting a true picture of how the stock market view the proposals and why First Interstate agreed to a deal with First Bank System that carried a lesser value for First Interstate shareholders than the second offer Wells Fargo placed on the table. Was executive management at First Interstate looking out for its own best interests instead of those of shareholders? Among the reasons First Interstate's Siart cited for rejecting the Wells Fargo bid was that close to 9,000 employees would lose their jobs in a merger with Wells, while only 6,000 would lose their jobs in a merger with First Bank Systems. Additionally, the job losses would be spread over several states in the First Bank merger instead of being confined to California under the Wells Fargo merger plan.[10]

A merger between Wells Fargo and First Interstate would establish a bank with over $105 billion in assets with a dominant market share in California and 12 other

Western states. It would also allow the combined banks to cut operating costs dramatically and close redundant branch offices. The second bid would give First Interstate shareholders more than 50 percent of the combined company. Also, the shareholders of First Interstate have a chance of getting bigger annual gains in the value of the combined company's shares than they are likely in the shares of an independent First Interstate. Mr. Hazen, CEO of Wells Fargo, claims that the compelling reason to acquire First Interstate is that EPS can eventually be boosted by 30 percent.[11]

First Bank System's Bid

In considering First Bank System (headquartered in Minneapolis), with $34 billion in assets and 366 banking offices in 11 Midwestern states, we have a bank holding company with stellar third quarter financial ratios: 1.76 percent ROA; 21 percent ROE; 54 percent efficiency ratio; 6.2 percent tangible common equity to assets; and 400 percent reserve coverage on nonperforming loans. The priorities of the bank include the following: cost containment and ongoing reengineering efforts; a focus on niche retail and fee generating businesses (with payment processing continuing to grow into a major fee business and generating 20 percent of revenue in 1995); and acquisitions as a continuing source of growth and driver of scale cost benefits. The bank strongly believes that the 50 percent efficiency plateau can be achieved before the year 2000. First Bank System is also one of the most prolific utilizers of ATMs in the banking industry. Approximately 1,550 (60 percent) of installed ATMs are located directly outside of the company's branches. Many of the other ATMs are installed in either Circle K or 7-Eleven Foods Stores.

First Bank System's management is adept at blending cost control, technology, capital management, and sales incentives. While expanding corporate trust with the recent purchase of BankAmerica's extensive corporate trust business, First Bank System announced it is selling its mortgage banking and title insurance operations because of a lack of economies of scale, the need to upgrade systems, and the volatile earnings of these lines of business. The potential gain is close to $50 million. Trust fees should rise substantially as the BankAmerica transaction doubles the bank's corporate trust fees to $145 million. The bank also expects to achieve 40 percent cost savings by integrating the BankAmerica unit's back office into its own.

The company is also a major repurchaser of outstanding shares of its stock, buying 4.3 million shares in the third quarter of 1995. It is assumed that the bank will repurchase at least 4 million shares each in both the fourth quarter of 1995 and the first quarter of 1996.

The acquisition of First Tier Financial will elevate the bank to the top-market position in Nebraska with a 13.7 percent market share. This acquisition should provide a 15.5 percent internal rate of return, which is lower than First Bank System's current 19 percent return. Hence, this acquisition will be dilutive to ROE until 1997. Upon completion of the pending mergers with First Interstate and First

Tier Financial, the company would have $92 billion in assets and more than 1,500 branches in 21 states in the western half of the United States.

First Bank System has emerged as the potential white knight in an agreement to keep First Interstate out of the hands of Wells Fargo. The combination of First Bank System with First Interstate would have been a no-premium merger of equals. Under the terms of the deal, First Bank System would have issued 2.6 shares for each of the 77.5 million First Interstate shares outstanding. Based on the November 3, 1995 closing price of $51, First Bank System is paying $132 per Interstate share, a modest 4 percent premium to First Interstate's market price. This amounts to 275 percent of First Interstate's book value and 11.5 times 1996 EPS estimate. First Bank System can afford to pay the high price because its stock trades at a high 250 percent of book value. The deal includes lock-up provisions that would cause another buyer of First Interstate to pay $200 million to First Bank System.

Corporate headquarters would remain at least temporarily in Minneapolis and the new company will be called First Interstate. Jack Grundhofer, the highly regarded chairman of First Bank System, would become the CEO of the combined company, while William Siart, First Interstate's CEO, would become president. Most of the lines of business would be run out of First Interstate's Los Angeles headquarters. On a pro forma basis, First Interstate's shareholders would hold 58 percent of the combined company's shares outstanding.

First Bank System has set ambitious cost-cutting targets and anticipates an acceleration in EPS growth in 1997 and beyond. On a pro forma basis, the transaction was roughly 6 percent dilutive to First Bank's book value and 5 percent dilutive to EPS. Management expects to recover the dilution quickly by reducing expenses by $500 million, 25 percent of which was targeted to be realized in 1996. The $500 million was equal to about 22 percent of First Interstate's noninterest cost base and close to 15 percent of the combined company's cost base. The cost savings was ambitious because there is limited geographic overlap between the two companies. First Bank System's management has a strong track record for delivering promised merger savings. About $125 million of targeted cost savings for 1996 will be enough to overcome the dilution. The cost savings, combined with the continuation of an aggressive share repurchase plan led management to project that the deal would be 18 percent accretive to EPS in 1997. In order to maintain the pooling-of-interests accounting treatment for the deal, management would suspend buyback programs in the second and third quarters of 1996 and would repurchase about 10 million shares in the fourth quarter of 1996 and 37 million in 1997. Consequently, average shares would have fallen from 344 million in 1996 to 319 million in 1997. Before restructuring charges, management expected the deal to add roughly $0.04 to EPS in 1996 and $0.94 in 1997. There would have been about a $0.40 charge per share to be taken at the time of the deal. While the reserve recapture was unusual, the company would still have a solid reserve of about 1.75 percent of loans after recapture (see Table 20–6).

T A B L E   20–6

Selected Financials of Merger Candidates

	First Bank System*	First Interstate	Combined
Assets (in billions)	$ 36.5	$ 55.1	$ 91.6
Loans (in billions)	$ 28.1	$ 35.9	$ 64.0
Intangibles** (in billions)	$ 0.9	$ 0.7	$ 2.0
Common equity** (in billions)	$ 3.0	$ 3.6	$ 7.0
Tangible common equity/assets***	5.3	5.4	5.6
Book value/share	$20.33	$47.95	$20.39
Nonperforming assets/ related assets	0.64%	0.57%	0.60%
Reserves/loans	1.81%	2.36%	1.75%
1996E EPS	$4.58	$11.49	$4.65
Approximate cost of acquisition (in billions)		$10.3	
Branches	366	1,148	1,514
ATMs	2,896	1,796	4,692
Retail customers (in millions)	3.1	4.5	7.6
Business customers	0.24	0.23	0.46
Customers/branch	8,470	3,970	5,020

* Pro forma with Tier 1.
** Special merger related adjustments.
*** Adjustments involving Tier 1.
Source: Numerous corporate statements.

While First Bank System's management has an excellent track record in achieving cost savings from acquisitions, the cost cutting will be tougher to realize in this case. Most of First Bank System's past purchases were of problem, inefficient franchises that could be fixed. First Interstate already is an extremely efficient bank holding company that had a 58 percent efficiency ratio in the third quarter of 1995. Moreover, the two merging companies overlap in only Colorado, Wyoming, and Montana.[12]

The combination of First Bank and First Interstate would have potentially created one of the most profitable banks in the United States, earning more than 2 percent on assets and 25 percent on equity by 1997.[13] The two companies have attractive complementary markets and significant funding synergies that should provide important cost savings. Management would have taken a one-time restructuring charge at $475 million, while recapturing $250 million of excess reserves at First Interstate—putting merger-related charges at $225 million on a pretax basis and $140 million on an after-tax basis. With cost savings of $125 million expected to be realized during 1996, book value dilution from the transaction would have been minimal and recaptured quickly.[14]

Phil Heasly, vice chairman of First Bank System, has emphasized that First Bank's core efficiency and effectiveness of operation relative to First Interstate is significant. Regardless of geography, First Bank can elevate a company's performance to its standards, principally by removing costs. For example, First Bank's data facility is run at $130 million per year versus $200 million at First Interstate. At least $80 million in savings could have been found here. First Bank would have also discarded First Interstate's ATM switch in both Arizona and Texas. In addition, First Bank could have brought First Interstate's card processing in-house, saving $5 per account. It has both the facilities and technology to support the First Interstate infrastructure. First Bank processes more efficiently than First Interstate in the back office, which could have saved at least $110 million. First Bank System's management would have eliminated 10–15 percent of the cost of each of the corporate and trust lines of business. Part of the aforementioned cost savings would have come from an average $10,000 salary differential between California employees and those at First Bank System's homeland.[15]

First Bank System announced in early 1996 that the SEC approved its right to treat the proposed merger with First Interstate as a pooling-of-interests accounting. However, if it proceeded along this accounting path, First Bank System would have to suspend its ongoing repurchase program. In fact, it would not be able to repurchase shares for two years following a merger with First Interstate. First Bank System's bid crumbled with this ruling as future post-merger EPS increases were highly dependent upon the ability to buy back outstanding shares. As we went to press, First Interstate agreed to be acquired by Wells Fargo in a deal worth $11.6 billion—the largest merger in U.S. banking history.

Even though First Bank System lost in its bid to acquire First Interstate, the Minneapolis bank holding company will receive $200 million from settlement of a termination provision written into the friendly merger pact. This will result in a tidy profit of about $190 million for First Bank System, which disclosed that it had in the neighborhood of $10 million in expenses in connection with the First Interstate merger.

ENDNOTES

1. T.A. Hanley, "First Interstate Bancorp," *CS First Boston*, July 16, 1995, p. 8.
2. G.M Salem, "First Interstate Bancorp," *Prudential Securities Research*, September 22, 1994, p. 3.
3. T.A. Hanley, P.J. Carter, and A.B. Collins, "First Interstate Bancorp," *CS First Boston*, February 2, 1995, p. 6.
4. T.A. Hanley, "First Interstate Bancorp," *CS First Boston*, July 10, 1995, pp. 8–9.
5. First Interstate Bancorp, 1993 *Annual Report.*
6. Ibid.
7. First Interstate Bancorp, 1994 *Annual Report,* p. 8.

8. T.A. Hanley, P.J. Carter, and A.B. Collins, "First Interstate Bancorp," *CS First Boston*, December 23, 1994, p. 3.

9. T.A. Hanley, P.J. Carter, and A.B. Collins, "First Interstate Bancorp," *CS First Boston*, September 22, 1994, pp. 1–2.

10. S. Lipin, T.L. O'Brien, and R.T. King, Jr., "First Interstate, First Bank to Combine in a Transaction Valued at $918 Billion," *The Wall Street Journal*, November 7, 1995, p. A7.

11. R.T. King, Jr., T.L. O'Brien, and S. Lipin, "A Chance to Cut Costs Drives Wells Fargo Bid for First Interstate," *The Wall Street Journal*, October 19, 1995, p. A13.

12. C. Kotowski, "First Bank System to Merge with First Interstate," *Oppenheimer & Co., Inc.*, November 7, 1995, p. 3.

13. C.S. Berger, "First Bank System—First Interstate Merger Prompts Upgrade," *Salomon Brothers U.S. Equity Research*, November 10, 1995, pp. 8–9.

14. Ibid., pp. 5, 7.

15. C.S. Berger, "War of Words—First Bank System and Wells Fargo Bring Their Case to the Shareholders," *Salomon Brothers U.S. Equity Research*, November 14, 1995, pp. 3–4.

T A B L E   20–7

First Interstate Bancorp Financials

	1990	1991	1992	1993	1994
Earnings per share	$7.30	($5.24)	$3.23	$8.96	$8.71
Assets (in millions)	$54,205	$49,126	$49,031	$49,319	$52,979
Net income (in millions)	$468.75	($288.14)	$282.26	$736.72	$733.50
Return on assets	0.86%	(0.59)%	0.58%	1.49%	1.38%

	1994	
	(in millions)	**%**
Average earning assets	$45,638	100
Securities	16,061	35
Loans	28,644	63
Other	933	2
Loans	33,221	100
Construction and land	933	
Commercial mortgage	4,387	
Highly leveraged		
Commercial loans and leases	9,433	
Other foreign	140	
Term LCD		
Credit card receivables	1,216	
Other consumer	6,781	
Unearned discount		
Corporate	14,893	45
Consumer	7,997	24
Mortgages	10,331	31

	1990	1991	1992	1993	1994
Efficiency ratio	67.76	71.15	69.57	65.94	61.82
Shareholder equity (in millions)	$2,608	$2,766	$2,957	$3,478	$3,599
Preferred	$409	$420	$640	$508	$350
Common	$2,199	$2,346	$2,317	$2,970	$3,249

F I G U R E   20–3

First Interstate Bancorp Financial Charts

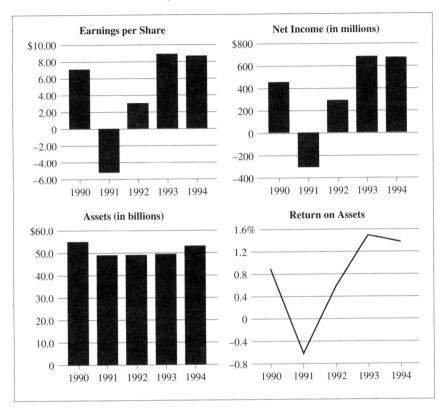

F I G U R E   20–4

First Interstate Bancorp Financial Charts

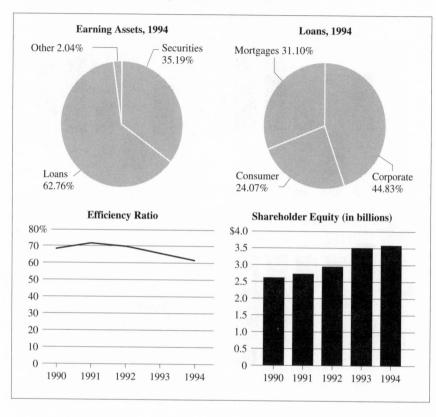

CHAPTER 21

Wells Fargo and Co.

Wells Fargo, a bank holding company, had assets of approximately $53.7 billion at year-end 1994. The company operates one of the largest consumer banking businesses in the country. Besides serving as banker to some 3.5 million California households, Wells Fargo provides a full range of banking services to commercial, agribusiness, real estate, and small-business customers. The company's headquarters is located in the downtown financial district of San Francisco, and it operates just over 600 branches, 1,900 around-the-clock ATMs, and a popular 24-hour telephone banking service throughout California. Wells Fargo owns the land and buildings occupied by 250 of its branches. The company's familiar trademark, the Concord stagecoach, is both a memento of its historic role in the development of the stage line and an enduring symbol of reliability in coming through for its customers, a Wells Fargo hallmark for over 140 years. Wells Fargo was incorporated in Delaware on June 30, 1987, as successor to the company of the same name originally incorporated in California on November 15, 1968.

HISTORY

Wells Fargo Bank is the successor to the banking portion of the business founded by Henry Wells and William G. Fargo in 1852. That business later operated the westernmost leg of the Pony Express and ran stagecoach lines in the western part of the United States. Wells Fargo faced its first crisis in 1855 when the California banking system collapsed as a result of overspeculation. A run on Page, Bacon and Co., a San Francisco bank, began when the collapse of its St. Louis parent was made public. The run spread to other financial institutions, all of which, including Wells Fargo, were forced to close their doors. Wells reopened in sound condition the next week despite a loss of one-third of its net worth. The company was one of a hand-ful of financial and express companies to survive the panic, partly because it kept sufficient assets and liquidity on hand to meet customers' demands rather than transferring most of its assets east. Following the panic, Wells faced little compe-tition in the banking and express business in California and developed a reputation for soundness and dependability. At the turn of the century, Wells Fargo had 3,500 banking and express offices, compared to 436 in 1871. Wells Fargo also began sell-ing money orders in 1885.

Wells Fargo's California banking business was separated from its express business in 1905. Edward H. Harriman, a prominent financier and dominant fig-ure in the Southern Pacific and Union Pacific railroads, had gained control of the company and merged the bank with Nevada National Bank, founded in 1875 by silver moguls James Fair, John Mackay, and William O'Brien, to form Wells Fargo Nevada National Bank. In 1906, the San Francisco earthquake destroyed most of the city's business district, including the Wells Fargo Nevada National Bank build-ing. However, the bank's vaults and credit were left intact and the company rebuilt the bank quickly. As a result of the money that flowed into San Francisco to help rebuild the city, Wells Fargo's deposits increased from $16 million to $35 million within one year. The panic of 1907, which began in New York, followed immedi-ately after the reconstruction boom in San Francisco. Although some New York City banks suffered severe runs, Wells Fargo lost only $1 million in deposits each week for six weeks in a row. Once again, Wells Fargo survived and began to grow slowly. Wells Fargo merged with Union Trust Company to form Wells Fargo Bank and Union Trust Company in 1923. The bank prospered in the 1920s. With con-servative management of its funds, Wells Fargo survived the Great Depression.

The bank was prosperous during the war years. In the 1950s, Wells Fargo began to acquire San Francisco area banks and opened a small branch network around San Francisco. The bank shortened its name to Wells Fargo Bank in 1954, hoping to capitalize on frontier imagery and in preparation for additional expan-sion. Wells Fargo was merged in 1960 with American Trust Company, another of the oldest banks in the western United States. The bank became Wells Fargo Bank, N.A., a national banking association, in 1968. The merger of California's two old-est banks created the 11th largest banking institution in the United States. Fol-lowing this merger, the company opened offices abroad in Tokyo, Seoul, Hong Kong, Mexico City, São Paulo, Caracas, Buenos Aires, and Singapore.

Wells Fargo, together with three other California banks, introduced a Master-Charge card to its customers to help challenge Bank of America in the consumer lending business. During 1968, Wells Fargo completed the acquisition of the Bank of Pasadena, First National Bank of Azusa, Azusa Valley Savings Bank, and Sonoma Mortgage Corporation. In 1973, the company decided to concentrate on medium-sized corporate, consumer, and real estate lending. Beginning in the late 1970s, its investment services grew rapidly, helped along by aggressive marketing, seminars explaining modern portfolio theory, and the availability of indexed funds. The earnings of Wells Fargo declined in the early 1980s, and the bank began to scale down its international operations, concentrating on the California market. Carl Reichardt became chairman in 1983. He cut costs by eliminating 100 branches and 3,000 jobs, while closing down the bank's European offices. Reichardt beefed up Wells Fargo's retail network by actively marketing improved services, like an extensive ATM network.

In 1986–88, Wells Fargo acquired the consumer trust business of Bank of America; rival Crocker National Corp. (headquartered in San Francisco) from Midland Bank for $1.1 billion; and Barclays Bank of California. Crocker was a major bank with $19.2 billion in assets, a branch system concentrated around San Francisco, a good corporate base, and a large trust department, while Barclays Bank was primarily a retail bank with $1.3 billion in assets. As a result of the merger, Wells Fargo doubled its branch network in southern California and increased its consumer loan portfolio by 85 percent. The bank paid only 127 percent of book value for Crocker when other bank acquisitions were averaging 190 percent. Also, Midland Bank kept about $3.5 billion in nonperforming or dubious loans. Following the acquisition, Wells Fargo continued its cost-cutting ways, eliminating redundant branches and 5,700 jobs and selling off unprofitable businesses. In 1987, the company set aside large reserves to cover potential losses on its loans to Brazil and Mexico. This led to a huge drop in net income, but by mid-1989 Wells Fargo had sold or written off all of its medium- and long-term third-world debt. In 1989, Wells divested itself of its last international offices, tightening its focus on domestic commercial and consumer banking activities once again.

During 1990, Wells Fargo completed the acquisition of Valley National Bank of Glendale ($225 million in assets), Central Pacific Corporation of Bakersfield and its subsidiary American National Bank of Bakersfield ($857 million in assets), the Torrey Pines Group of Solana Beach ($443 million in assets), and Citizens Holdings and its two banking subsidiaries of Orange County ($207 million in deposits). In 1990–91, Wells Fargo completed the acquisition of 130 southern California branches with $6.2 billion in deposits from Great American Bank, a federal savings bank. In addition, Wells Fargo acquired 13 branches of the former Santa Barbara Federal Savings from the RTC in 1991. The purchase involved only real estate, no loans or bank deposits.

Wells Fargo also entered into a joint venture (50–50 ownership) with Nikko Securities to form Wells Fargo Nikko Investment Advisers. That company manages approximately $158 billion of investment assets, principally for large corporate and public employee pension funds. The holding company sold Wells Fargo Nikko Investment Advisers in 1995 to gain additional investment funds to pursue a wider global presence.

Wells Fargo's Business and Investment Group is one of the nation's leading managers of personal trust accounts, corporate 401(k) plans, and mutual funds, with approximately $57 billion in assets under management and administration. Of that total, $47 billion consisted of personal trust, employee benefit, and agency assets, while about $11 billion were in the company's Stagecoach and Overland Express family of mutual funds.

Following two years of disappointing performance due to nonperforming, highly leveraged transactions (HLTs) and a large exposure to troubled California commercial real estate, Wells Fargo nearly returned to the levels of profitability it achieved in 1990. Its net income reached $841 million in 1994, compared to $612 million in 1993 and $121 million in 1991. Its ROA reached 1.81 percent in the first half of 1995 and 1.62 percent in 1994, up from 1.2 percent in 1993, 0.54 percent in 1992, and 0.04 percent in 1991, while its ROE rebounded to 26.7 percent in the first half of 1995 from 22.41 percent in 1994, 16.74 percent in 1993, 7.93 percent in 1992, and .07% in 1991 (see Table 21–1). Some analysts anticipate that Wells Fargo's ROA and ROE will exceed 1.70 percent and 27 percent, respectively, in 1997. In 1994, ROEs for specific lines of business were as follows: the Investment Group, 30 percent; the Consumer Lending Group, 28 percent; the Wholesale Products Group, 23 percent; and the Business Banking Group, 22 percent (see Table 21–2).

Under the leadership of Reichart, its former chairman, Wells Fargo weathered a severe storm; and the company appears positioned to achieve record earnings in the years ahead under its new chairman and former president, Paul Hazen. With an improving California economy, its ROA should reach 1.7 percent and its ROE over 27.0 percent by 1997, even with Tier 1 capital in the top quartile at 9.1 percent. During 1989 and 1990, Wells achieved ROAs of 1.26 percent and 1.39 percent and ROEs of 24.49 percent and 25.07 percent, respectively.

The company's higher earnings in 1993–95 resulted from lower or zero loan loss provisions as credit quality improved. Credit-quality problems relating to commercial real estate and HLTs contributed to its depressed financial results in both 1991 and 1992. The prolonged weakness in the California economy and the recession in commercial real estate markets were the culprits. From a peak of $3 billion in September 1992, the company's problem assets fell to under $0.6 billion at the end of 1994, less than 1.6 percent of total loans. Wells Fargo reduced its exposure to both real estate and HLT loans. In fact, its commercial real estate portfolio

T A B L E   21-1

Profitability Ratios, 1992–1994

	1992	1993	1994
ROA	0.54%	1.20%	1.62%
ROE	7.93	16.74	22.41

totaled $9.6 billion at the end of 1994, down from $14.7 billion in March 1991. At the same time, HLT balances fell from a peak of $4.3 billion in 1989 to under $500 million at year-end 1994. Although the company did hold an above-average percentage of commercial real estate loans to total loans (26.5 percent in 1994 and 37 percent in 1992), it held an exceptionally large and conservative investment securities portfolio as a percent of total assets (22 percent in 1994, 25 percent in 1993, and 19 percent in 1992). At year-end 1994, commercial loans accounted for 22 percent, one- to four-family mortgages accounted for 25 percent, other mortgages for 22 percent, real estate construction for 3 percent, consumer loans for 24 percent, and lease financing for 4 percent of total loans (see Table 21–3). The company has

T A B L E   21–2

Lines of Business Results, 1994 (in millions)

Line of Business	Net Income	ROE
Retail distribution	$ 60	17%
Banking business	69	22
Investment	136	30
Real estate	82	13
Wholesale products	156	23
Consumer lending	111	28
Mortgage lending	45	7
Consolidated company	$841	22%

Source: Wells Fargo, 1994 *Annual Report*, pp. 8–9.

T A B L E   21–3

Loan Mix, December 31, 1994

Type of Loan	Percentage
Commercial	22%
One- to four-family mortgages	25
Other mortgages	22
Construction	3
Consumer	24
Lease financing	4

Source: Wells Fargo, 1994 *Annual Report*, p. 20.

reclassified $4 billion of residential mortgages from the loan category to the held-for-sale category in anticipation of exiting the mortgage origination business.

As of December 31, 1994, Wells Fargo's total nonaccrual and restructured loans were 2.3 pecent of total loans, compared with 5.8 percent at the close of the preceding year. At the end of 1994, its ratio of loan loss reserves to nonperforming loans was at a comfortable 329 percent, while its ratio of reserves to nonperforming assets was at 220 percent. The company's net charge-off ratio stood at 0.70 percent for 1994, but was expected to increase slightly in 1995 because of an increase in nonperforming loans. Its allowance for loan losses stood at 5.73 percent of total loans at year-end 1994. The excess reserves at Wells Fargo can be regarded as approximately $16 per share of additional equity. Prior to the third quarter of 1994, Wells Fargo had been incurring quarterly loan provisions at least as high as net charge-offs. As nonperforming loans have declined, the unallocated portion of the company's loan loss reserves grew quickly. Bank management has indicated that the company would incur $0 in loan loss provisions during 1995 to allow a part of its $2.1 billion in loss reserves to reach the equity account by flowing through the income statement. The company's book value will increase, which offsets the dilutive effect of buying back shares at the October 1994 market price of 2.2 times book value.[1]

It is estimated that Wells Fargo's loan losses over the economic cycle will average about 0.75 percent of loans. Thus, on the current loan balance, the bank would ordinarily need a $68 million quarterly provision for loan losses. Its ratio of common equity to assets stood at approximately 6.41 percent and its Tier 1 ratio was at 9.1 percent at year-end 1994, while its internal capital generation rate ran at about a 15 percent pace during that year. The company has announced a further share buyback of up to 10 percent of the existing base, or about five million shares. The reduced number of shares outstanding has helped to raise both EPS and ROE.

On the efficiency front, Wells Fargo is well known for its expense-containment capabilities. Wells should remain among the top three large banks in this ratio. The company achieved an efficiency ratio of 56.6 percent in 1994, down from 57.7 percent in 1993.

Fee Income

Fee income is expected to grow by double digits, led by mortgage banking and mutual fund sales. Fee income as a percentage of total revenue was at 31.35 percent in 1994, compared to 29.21 percent in 1993; it is expected to grow to 33 percent in 1995. Approximately $1.1 billion of noninterest income was achieved in 1993, followed by $1.2 billion in 1994, just about 52 percent of noninterest expense (see Table 21–4). Fee income in 1996 may be negatively affected by the sale of the Wells Fargo Nikko Investment Advisers in the fourth quarter of 1995 to Barclays PLC. In addition, Barclays PLC will also be acquiring MasterWorks, a unit of Wells Fargo

T A B L E   21-4

Noninterest Income, 1993–1994 (in millions)

Source	1994	1993
Service charges, deposit accounts	$ 473	$ 423
Fees and commissions	387	376
Trust/investment services	203	190
Investment securities	8	
Other	129	104
Total	$1,200	$1,093

Source: Wells Fargo, 1994 *Annual Report*, p. 39.

with $6.6 billion of 401(k) assets under management. Wells Fargo should record an after-tax gain of close to $100 million on a total sale price of several hundred million dollars for both units. These funds could be used to acquire additional fee-generating businesses or to accelerate the company's share repurchase plan.

Potpourri

Wells Fargo has good earnings fundamentals as its asset quality has continued to improve with a recovery of the California economy. It has ample liquidity, as represented by its strong and relatively inexpensive core deposit base. The company's average core deposits and stockholders' equity funded 84 percent of its average total assets in 1994. In addition, noninterest deposits accounted for 16 percent of core deposits and almost 24 percent of total deposits.

Wells Fargo reorganized its branch system in mid-1993, deviating from the traditional model employed by most banks. Branch managers' authority was cut, and branch salespeople were assigned to outside product managers rather than branch managers. Salespeople were moved among the branches and divided into four product areas: small business, mortgages, investment products, and upscale consumer banking. At the same time, the sales force was relieved of its traditional customer service responsibilities. Branch managers now supervise only tellers and a small staff of branch customer service specialists. Within each branch, the position of assistant manager was eliminated and the positions of platform and teller employees were combined. There is now only one line for sales and service assistance at most Wells Fargo branches. The branch employees are trained to handle efficiently all basic transactions and sales, identify customer needs, and arrange meetings with product sales specialists for more complicated products. Wells Fargo expects more production from specialization.[2] How has this worked out at the bank? The company has 8 percent fewer branch staff members, handles more transactions than previously, and increased sales across the board by about 30 percent.[3]

Wells Fargo is one of the nation's technological leaders in both retail and wholesale banking. For example, it offers retail banking products nationwide electronically and through the mail. In addition, the bank began nationwide marketing of preapproved small-business loans through the mail. It has directed resources into streamlining its branch system, establishing a state-of-the-art technology infrastructure, profitably segmenting its customer base, and developing alternative product delivery systems. Wells Fargo has made a major move into supermarket banking. At mid-year 1995, the bank was operating 60 fully staffed supermarket bank branches, up from 20 at year-end 1993. It also operated about 101 supermarket branches staffed by only one person, up from 22 in 1994. By contrast BankAmerica operated only 14 supermarket branches in California, though an additional 38 were scheduled to be opened in 1995. BankAmerica also installed 300 automated kiosks in Lucky grocery stores. The addition of supermarket minibranches and full-service branches allowed Wells Fargo to close down 50 traditional branches (see Figure 21–1).

Wells Fargo has become the first superregional bank to offer small businesses a 50 percent discount for using ATM checking accounts, as long as all standard banking attractions are accomplished with ATMs; otherwise, there is a $5 charge per teller visit.

F I G U R E   21-1

Changes in Wells Fargo's Delivery Channels

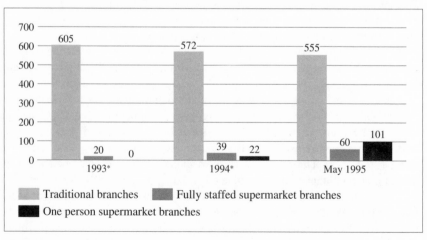

* Year-end.

Source: Donaldson, Lufkin & Jenrette.

Wells Fargo has long been one of the most profitable big banks in the nation. However, this profitability was derived in large part from a heavy emphasis on California commercial real estate lending. Up until 1990, this served the company well. The severe recession in California led to declining real estate values and a large increase in nonperforming loans, shaking the foundations of the company like a California earthquake. Fortunately, the company is both overreserved and overcapitalized. With demands for capital likely to be modest over the next few years and at least $1.5 billion of excess equity in the loss reserves, Wells Fargo will likely, in some combination, increase its dividend, buy back stock, or acquire a West Coast bank. It is expected to repurchase at least one million shares per quarter throughout 1995 and 1996 (up to 10 percent of its share base annually) while keeping its loss provision at $0. The company had an excessively conservative loss reserve of over $2 billion at year-end 1994.[4]

The company will be a major beneficiary of the cut in FDIC premiums. The reduction in FDIC rates during the second half of 1995 should save the company about $72 million annually.

First Interstate Takeover Bids

In February 1994, First Interstate Bancorp declined an offer to merge with Wells Fargo. First Interstate indicated that the Wells Fargo offer was not high enough. First Interstate management was also probably fearful about being pushed aside after the merger.[5] When Chairman Reichart announced his premature retirement about six months later, he indicated that his only career disappointment was the inability to accomplish the merger with First Interstate. He was succeeded by Paul Hazen on January 1995 as chairman and CEO. William Zuendt became president and chief operating officer.

Wells Fargo made an initial unsolicited offer to buy First Interstate in October 1995 for about $10.17 billion or $131 per share, making the takeover bid the largest in banking history. Wells offered a generous 2.8 times book value, while on a price-to-earnings basis the offer was close to a more reasonable 11.7 times estimated 1996 EPS. The stock market responded favorably initially to the Wells Fargo offer as First Interstate's price shot up $34.75 per share (a gain of 33 percent), while the price of Wells Fargo shares jumped $15.375 per share (a 7 percent gain). If the bank succeeds in its bid for First Interstate, the combination of the two California-based banks would create the eighth largest bank in the nation with assets of about $106 billion and about 1,700 branches. Using purchase accounting, the Wells Fargo projections suggest that the deal would be 10 percent dilutive to 1996 EPS, neutral in 1997, 10 percent accretive in 1998, and generate an EPS of nearly 30 percent more in 1999 than would have been the case without the merger. Massive cost-cutting and the repurchase of $7.5 billion of common stock over a five-year period would help earn back dilution rapidly. Management expected to cut

$800 million (about 36 percent) from First Interstate's noninterest expense base of $2.2 billion and expected to lose about $100 million of revenues as a result of over 100 branch closings and 7,500 layoffs. A major attraction of the merger to Wells Fargo is that the bank would be able to close redundant branches and operations in California, while gaining over 6 million customers in 12 western states as well as within California. Wells Fargo estimated that it should be able to enhance revenues by at least $100 million in a few years via the new customer base. Other advantages include a reduction in risk as a consequence of a geographically diversified loan portfolio. There would also be a much larger customer base on which Wells Fargo could spread the technological development costs of state-of-the art computer, communication, and alternative delivery systems along with improved branch operations and information systems (see Table 21–5).

Once again, First Interstate declared that it was not interested in being acquired by Wells Fargo. In response to this hostile bid, First Interstate invited First Bank System, Norwest Corp, and Banc One to examine their books in the hope

T A B L E   21-5

Comparative Statistics

	Wells Fargo		First Interstate	
Assets (% new co./billions of $)	47.6%	$49.9	52.4%	$55.1
Deposits (% new co./billions of $)	44.7%	$38.9	55.3%	$48.2
Earnings (1995 through Sept. 30) (% new co./millions of $)	52.0%	$726.0	48.0%	$669.7
Branches	35.7%	634	64.3%	1,142
Supermarket locations	312			
Equity	50.1%		49.9%	
Employees	19,400		27,901	
Customers (in millions)	3.5		6.1	
Market capitalization (10/18/95)(in billions)	$10.87		$10.62	
ROA (3rd Q 95)	2.07%		1.72%	
ROE	30.1 %		25.6%	
Noninterest income as % revenues	33.8%		30.5%	
Efficiency ratio	54.1%		58.2%	
Equity/assets	6.78%		6.59%	
Nonperforming loans/loans outstanding	1.75%		0.39%	
Reserves/nonperforming loans	312%		603%	

* Most data represents 3rd quarter 1995 results.
Source: Company reports.

of generating a higher bid from a friendly source. At the time of this writing, First Bank System and Wells Fargo are engaged in a bidding war to acquire First Interstate. Wells Fargo raised its offer following a friendly bid by First Bank System. As of mid-November 1995, the Wells offer was worth $139 per share compared to the original offer of $131. This second offer by Wells Fargo is higher than the $135 per share offered by First Bank Systems. Wells Fargo also announced that it could save more money in running First Interstate than its original estimate of $800 million. The savings would amount to just under $1 billion or 45 percent of First Interstate's $2.2 billion of noninterest expenses.[6] The lower offer for First Interstate from First Bank System has been accepted by the board of directors of First Interstate. The acceptance of the offer from First Bank System looks like a senior management job preservation play on the part of First Interstate executives, as well as an attempt to minimize job losses among California branch system employees.

It appears as if Wells Fargo is taking the case to shareholders; the company filed an application with the Federal Reserve Bank of San Francisco to approve a merger with First Interstate, and filed an exchange offer with the SEC. Wells Fargo also filed a complaint against First Interstate's board in Delaware Chancery Court, seeking invalidation of the break-up fees and lock-up options granted First Bank System by First Interstate.[7]

According to Thomas Brown, a banking analyst with DLJ, "…no matter how you cut it, there is more value created with Wells/First Interstate than with First Bank System/First Interstate, or any other deal you can come up with."[8] The problem for Wells Fargo is that shareholders tend to go along with management-backed proposals, suggesting that at this stage First Bank System has an edge. Wells Fargo can always sweeten the offer, hoping to get the support of institutional and large investors, who could place considerable pressure on the board of directors of First Interstate. By raising the exchange ratio, Wells Fargo does little more than create more goodwill (having a negative value for Wells Fargo's shares), transferring more of the value to First Interstate shareholders and accomplishing little to change the long-term value of the offer.[9]

SUMMARY

Wells Fargo won the battle to acquire First Interstate as we went to press, paying $11.6 billion to First Interstate shareholders making it the largest acquisition in U.S. Banking history.

Wells Fargo has devoted considerable internal resources toward streamlining its branch system, establishing a state-of-the-art technology infrastructure, and developing alternative product delivery systems. Wells Fargo emphasizes sophisticated products, a strong sales and service culture, and efficient, customer-oriented product distribution systems. The company should be able to generate ROEs in the range of 22–25 percent and an EPS growth rate of 10 percent over the next few years without the First Interstate merger. For example, in 1995, Wells Fargo reported a 20 percent jump in net income that amounted to a 2.07 percent ROA and a 30.1 percent ROE, the highest levels of profitability reported by any bank with assets in excess of $5 billion. The robust EPS growth would be generated from a low-risk strategy of not growing the balance sheet or net interest income significantly, while repurchasing shares, lowering loan loss provisions, funding new loans out of low-yielding liquid assets, and growing noninterest income.[10]

The bank has plans to sell off $4 billion of thin-margin residential mortgage loans to free additional capital for share repurchases. Additionally, it is growing its credit card portfolio, thereby shifting to a higher-yielding mix of risk-adjusted earning assets that should improve its net interest margin.

The merger with First Interstate is a good strategic fit for Wells Fargo; a major drawback would be a large decline in the ROE of the combined companies because of the huge stock premium paid for First Interstate. Hazen plans to reduce the impact on Wells Fargo's EPS by buying back up to $7.5 billion of shares by the year 2000. Excluding the noncash charges related to goodwill, he predicted that Wells Fargo's cash EPS would jump 30 percent by 1998.[11]

Wells Fargo has opened more than 300 mini-branches in all but one of the big California supermarket chains. With a single person in one of these branches, the bank generates almost half as many new accounts as it does at traditional branches with 11 people. Wells Fargo also watches over its expenses carefully, being among the leaders in efficiency at 54 percent. According to President Zuendt, "What we know how to do is rationalize expense structure."[12]

ENDNOTES

1. T.H. Hanley, "Wells Fargo," *CS First Boston*, October 24, 1994, pp. 4–5.
2. N.C. Deren, "Wells Fargo," term paper, Nova Southeastern University, Ft. Lauderdale, FL, July 9, 1994.
3. T.K. Brown, "Wells Fargo & Co.," *Donaldson, Lufkin & Jenrette*, pp. 24–25.
4. T.H. Hanley, "Wells Fargo," *CS First Boston*, March 27, 1995, pp. 1–2.
5. R. Mitchell, "Wells Back to the Hunt," *Business Week*, March 21, 1994, p. 48.
6. C. Kotowski, "Wells Fargo," *Oppenheimer & Co., Inc.*, November 16, 1995, p. 2.
7. C.S. Berger, "War of Words—First Bank Systems and Wells Fargo Bring Their Cases to the Shareholders," *Salomon Brothers U.S. Equity Research*, November 14, 1995, p. 3.
8. R.T. King, Jr., "First Interstate Spurns Proposal By Wells Fargo," *The Wall Street Journal*, November 13, 1995, p. A4.
9. Berger, p. 4.
10. T.H. Hanley, "Wells Fargo," *CS First Boston*, September 29, 1994, p. 3.
11. R.T. King, Jr., T.L. O'Brian, and S. Lipin, "A Chance to Cut Costs Drives Well Fargo Bid for First Interstate," *The Wall Street Journal*, October 19, 1995, p. A13.
12. Ibid.

T A B L E   21–6

Wells Fargo and Co. Financials

	1990	1991	1992	1993	1994
Earnings per share	$13.39	$0.04	$4.44	$10.10	$14.78
Assets (in millions)	$51,109	$55,022	$52,497	$51,110	$51,849
Net income (in millions)	$711.50	$21.00	$283.00	$612.00	$841.00
Return on assets	1.39%	0.04%	0.54%	1.20%	1.62%

	1994	
	(in millions)	%
Average earning assets	$46,988	100
Securities	12,706	27
Loans	34,039	72
Other	243	1
Loans	36,347	100
Construction and land	1,013	
Commercial mortgage	8,079	
Highly leveraged		
Commercial loans and leases	8,162	
Other foreign	27	
Term LCD		
Credit card receivables	3,125	
Other consumer	6,891	
Unearned discount		
Corporation	17,281	48
Consumer	10,016	28
Mortgages	9,050	25

	1990	1991	1992	1993	1994
Efficiency ratio	53.43	55.72	52.51	55.76	56.35
Shareholder equity (in millions)	$3,137	$3,352	$3,573	$3,996	$4,079
Preferred	$405	$279	$608	$639	$521
Common	$2,732	$3,073	$2,965	$3,357	$3,558

FIGURE 21-2

Wells Fargo and Co. Financial Charts

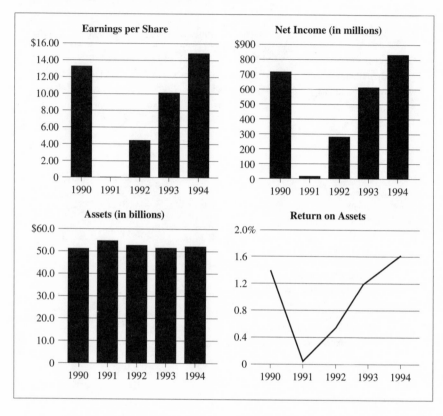

F I G U R E   21–3

Wells Fargo and Co. Financial Charts

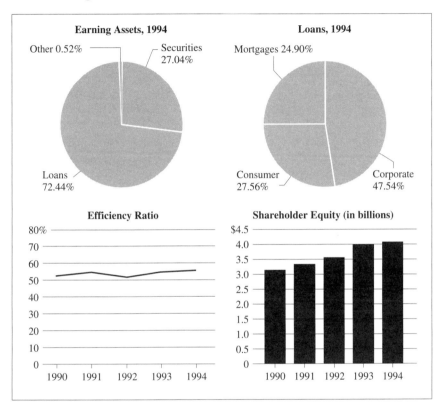

CHAPTER 22

Finale

Although it is entirely possible that we may witness a blockbuster merger or a merger of equals in our universe of superregional banks, it is more likely that most of these banks will try to remain independent. Although the number of bank acquisitions and prices paid for them have accelerated during the first half of the 1990s, the speed at which bank consolidation has taken place has disappointed some analysts. A rebound in bank interest margins and earnings during 1993–94 delayed merger activity as managements' and shareholders' expectations grew. In addition, the reluctance of some CEOs or heirs apparent, who are years away from retirement and not ready to give up power in the event of a merger, has also tempered the pace of merger activity.

REBANKING

Financial institutions have undergone a restructuring during the 1990s that has been brought about by changes in regulation, technology, competition, and the economy. Many banks have changed in nature and refocused their strategies. During the 1980s and early 1990s, regional banks grew rapidly by making acquisitions, adding distribution capability in the process. Some also concentrated on cost-cutting or improving customer service. All worked hard to improve their credit quality and adequacy of capital. The result was near-record earnings, supported by sterling financial ratios. Only 13 banks failed in 1994, compared to an average of over 100 bank failures per year during 1984–92.

Restructuring or reengineering—reducing staff, revamping or removing redundant operations, reconfiguring branch networks, and refocusing businesses toward customers (away from being product-driven companies)—have been part

459

of the banking landscape during the mid-1990s. There were also major increases in dividend payments to shareholders and repurchases of shares in an attempt to enhance shareholder value and reduce excess capital positions.[1]

Successful banks will continue to focus on fee-based income, operating efficiencies, and credit quality. Corporate restructurings will likely be required to continue to improve efficiency ratios. Much progress has been made over the last few years in reducing noncredit-related expenses in spite of the lackluster revenue growth. The widely publicized success of Fleet Financial's Focus program in substantially reducing its overhead ratio may coerce other banks to follow suit.[2] More progress will have to be made in reducing costs for earnings momentum to continue (see Figure 22–1). One of the reasons for this is that credit quality is unlikely to improve further because nonperforming assets and net charge-offs are at low levels (see Figure 2–6 in Chapter 2). There do not appear to be large increases in noninterest revenues on the horizon. Mortgage banking, mortgage servicing, and trust, the largest components of most regional bank fees, remain under significant competitive pressure. After absorbing some losses on derivative securities, banks have also become more cautious, at least in the short run, on risk taking in foreign exchange, swapping, and trading activity.[3]

There are still some banks with excess reserves, for example, Wells Fargo, Fleet, and Norwest. These banks will have greater flexibility on the earnings front in the years ahead. Banks with little or no excess reserves, such as Wachovia, Banc One, NationsBank, and Bank of Boston, will continue to provide loan loss reserves

F I G U R E   22–1

Efficiency Ratios, 1988–1994

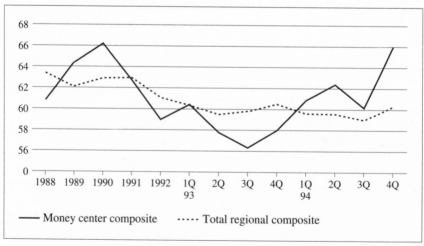

Source: SNL Securities, company reports, and Salomon Brothers Inc.

out of current income to the extent that loan demand remains relatively strong; these banks may possibly come under earnings pressure in 1996 or 1997 should nonperforming loans increase.[4]

Banks have become more skillful in making acquisitions work, limiting dilution in earnings per share. There is a different attitude about mergers in the mid-1990s than in earlier periods of merger activity. (See the section in this chapter entitled "Some Likely Scenarios.")

The revised and more lenient guidelines of the Reagan administration (1982), rising deposit and labor costs, pressures on banks to economize by seeking large-sized and more efficient operations, desires to penetrate new markets to expand bank revenues, and the opportunity to rescue failing depository institutions at relatively favorable prices were catalysts in increasing the size and number of bank mergers. The Reagan Justice Department guidelines and the Garn–St. Germain Act of 1982 made it possible for hundreds of mergers or acquisitions to take place that would have been challenged under the old guidelines.[5] Many analysts feel that the removal of the Glass-Steagall Act will be the next step in banking deregulation. If that 60-year old act dies, it would not be surprising to see regional banks acquire regional brokers as another source of fee income.

Some banks have found special niches, for example, State Street, Northern Trust, Mellon, CoreStates, Bank of New York; others have developed superb banking services or have become low-cost producers via technological strength. Bank managements recognize that relying on old-fashioned large corporate lending as the major source of profitability growth is a thing of the past.

Most of the superregional banks prefer to remain independent and will continue to make small in-market acquisitions, a few will seek a merger of equals in a faster-growing region to sell their well-developed products through new distribution channels. The deep South will be among the most attractive regions for bank merger activity, stimulated by above-average economic growth and below-average salaries in that region and the removal of the Southeastern Compact and the Interstate Banking Bill. Five of the nation's 25 largest bank holding companies are headquartered in the Southeast today, compared to zero in 1980. The Southeastern Compact allowed many relatively small institutions to incubate and grow into superregional bank powerhouses, such as NationsBank and First Union.[6] The Florida market remains highly desirable, with the transfer of wealth to that state. Baby boomers are expected to inherit about $40 billion in 1998, $140 billion in 2004, and $255 billion in 2014. Also, there is more personal net worth in Dade and Broward counties alone (home to Miami and Fort Lauderdale) than in the entire state of Georgia or any other state in the Southeast. Independent banks and thrifts in Florida are being gobbled up by buyers anxious to enter or expand market share in that state. A prize to be captured in Florida is Barnett. NationsBank, First Union, and SunTrust cannot acquire Barnett because of market share considerations; achievement of this objective will required a premium of between 25 and 50 percent of market share price.

Other markets are prime candidates for consolidation because of systemic overcapacity and a lack of economies of scale. Factors like interstate banking and rising interest rates will help sustain and possibly accelerate the consolidation trend within the banking industry. Rising rates could coerce banks to maximize economies of scale to achieve cost savings and revenue growth. States such as California, New York, Pennsylvania, Florida, Illinois, Michigan, Virginia, Connecticut, and Missouri should become prime areas of merger activity.[7]

Branch Closings

During the last decade, banks began moving away from being bricks-and-mortar organizations by either building smaller branches or closing branches after merging with nearby competition, eliminating duplicate locations. The expense of maintaining bank branches has increased while the importance of branches to customers has declined. Customers are making greater use of automated direct deposit services and ATMs. They are doing more business over telephones and computers, methods that cost banks far less than branches (see Figure 22–2). For example, at NationsBank nearly half of the transactions by its eight million customers are now made via telephones or cash machines.

Despite the excellent financial ratios of most banks between 1993 and 1995, banks nationwide are planning to close more branches to lower operating costs in order to compete with banks with cheaper distribution systems. Luke S. Helms, vice chairman of BankAmerica, described the plight of banks as "similar to that of department stores battling low-cost, high-volume specialty stores like Toys "R" Us. The category killers—The Money Store, Charles Schwab, or whatever—have delivery systems that are less expensive than the banks." Banks feel that they can continue to reduce their overhead ratios without a major loss of customers. For example, Chemical Bank closed one of its most troublesome Manhattan branches in 1994. Even though the closest branch was a 10-minute walk from the old one, only 9 percent of the old customers defected to other banks with branches in the neighborhood or where they were employed. The rest remained, with 25 percent now banking entirely by telephone and mail. Additionally, PNC announced plans to close up to 30 percent of its 619 branches between 1995 and 1997. BankAmerica, which merged in 1992 with Security Pacific, its largest California rival, closed 400 branches, leaving it with just a few more offices than either bank before the merger. In 1994, the bank announced its intention to close even more branches.[8]

BANK CONSOLIDATION POTPOURRI

We should continue to see consolidation in many forms:

• The acquisition of smaller banks and thrifts by larger banks.

F I G U R E   22-2

Bank Consumer Transactions*

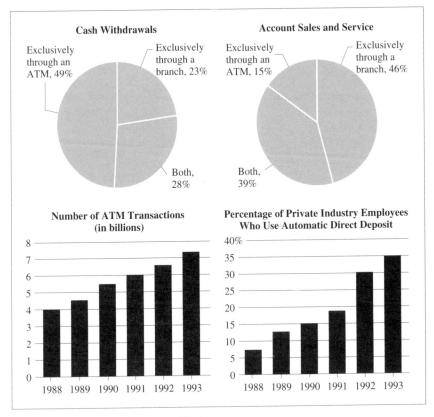

Cash Withdrawals

Exclusively through an ATM, 49%

Exclusively through a branch, 23%

Both, 28%

Account Sales and Service

Exclusively through an ATM, 15%

Exclusively through a branch, 46%

Both, 39%

Number of ATM Transactions (in billions)

1988 1989 1990 1991 1992 1993

Percentage of Private Industry Employees Who Use Automatic Direct Deposit

1988 1989 1990 1991 1992 1993

* Based on a 1993 survey of 90,000 client accounts at 10 banks.

- Acquisitions of nonbank businesses.
- Mergers of equals, where cost savings or revenue enhancements are sufficiently attractive to warrant the combination.[9]

During 1991 through the third quarter of 1995 there were continuous, almost monotonic increases in takeover financial ratios such as price to earnings, price to book, price to assets, and price to deposits (see Tables 22–1 and 22–2). In fact, the average price-to-book ratio for bank transactions has risen from 140 percent in 1991 to 181 percent during the first 220 days of 1995, while thrift prices have jumped from 98 percent to 145 percent over the same period. Some typical bank and thrift acquisition prices during 1993–94 can be seen in Table 22–3.

T A B L E   22–1

Summary Transaction Statistics, 1992 to August, 1995

	1992	1993	1994	1995*
Number of deals	398	477	562	232
Bank	319	372	441	175
Thrift	79	105	121	57
Total deal value (in millions)	$16,111	$23,496	$22,346	$29,891
Bank	11,898	17,820	13,235	25,895
Thrift	4,213	5,676	9,111	3,996
Total assets (in millions)	$164,432	$175,942	$189,931	$226,814
Bank	104,697	127,850	98,259	191,608
Thrift	59,734	48,092	91,672	35,206
Total deposits (in millions)	$133,253	$141,175	$147,363	$164,530
Bank	90,232	103,189	78,478	141,886
Thrift	43,021	37,986	68,886	22,644
Price/book (% average)	143.7%	162.8%	165.3%	170.7%
Bank	150.3	167.9	168.7	180.9
Thrift	119.2	147.1	154.4	145.1
Price/tangible book (% average)	148.9%	166.8%	168.9%	175.1%
Bank	154.0	171.7	172.0	185.2
Thrift	129.7	151.8	158.9	149.7
Price/earnings (median)	14.0%	14.6%	14.4%	15.7%
Bank	14.5	14.9	14.4	15.3
Thrift	12.8	14.1	13.8	16.5
Price/assets (% average)	11.0%	13.8%	14.6%	15.0%
Bank	11.7	14.2	14.8	15.6
Thrift	8.6	12.3	13.8	13.6
Price/deposits (% average)	12.8%	16.1%	16.9%	17.8%
Bank	13.4	16.2	16.9	17.9
Thrift	10.6	15.7	16.9	17.5
Premium/core deposits (median)	4.13%	6.38%	6.68%	7.54%
Bank	4.50	6.88	6.64	8.48
Thrift	1.67	5.19	6.72	5.94
Average 10% WOP (years)	12.3%	12.1%	13.7%	14.3%
Bank	12.6	12.8	14.5	14.4
Thrift	12.0	11.1	12.3	14.2

*Transactions updated as of August 10, 1995.

Source: *CS First Boston.*

From 1991 to 1993, the number of bank mergers grew almost 12 percent, from 260 transactions to 364. During this same time, the number of thrift deals grew from 42 transactions to 105, or 36 percent. Consolidation developments during 1994

T A B L E   22–2

Deal Valuation and Transaction Statistics

	New England	Mid-Atlantic	South-east	Mid-west	South-west	West	Total
Price/book (% average)							
Banks							
1991	89%	140%	114%	141%	125%	153%	140%
1992	100	152	144	153	150	168	144
1993	143	172	168	165	170	178	163
1994	151	186	181	162	173	148	166
1995*	190	167	183	178	181	157	169
Thrifts							
1991	61	74	83	119	100	104	98
1992	117	115	117	118	130	133	119
1993	140	135	150	154	123	146	147
1994	165	154	163	158	140	126	154
1995*	147	165	163	139	N.A.	81	152
Price/earnings (% median)							
Banks							
1991	N.A.	35×	19×	13×	14×	15×	15×
1992	N.A.	47	18	14	11	18	15
1993	18	19	18	14	14	20	15
1994	17	26	17	14	15	18	14
1995*	14	21	15	15	16	14	15
Thrifts							
1991	10×	17×	14×	15×	28×	16×	15×
1992	N.A.	18	13	12	8	9	15
1993	16	17	14	12	7	15	15
1994	16	13	15	15	9	13	14
1995*	13	15	15	20	N.A.	N.A.	14
Number of deals							
Banks							
1991	1	13	43	140	34	26	257
1992	5	21	64	140	66	19	315
1993	5	28	104	130	75	29	371
1994	15	30	97	136	112	44	434
1995*	5	11	21	23	23	14	97
Thrifts							
1991	2	4	13	12	1	8	40
1992	2	13	30	23	7	4	79
1993	12	17	34	32	3	7	105
1994	9	25	31	35	8	13	121
1995*	2	6	9	9	0	2	28

Continued on next page

Table 22–2—*Concluded*

	New England	Mid-Atlantic	South-east	Mid-west	South-west	West	Total
Total deal value (in millions)							
Banks							
1991	$ 8	$2,747	$5,580	$6,839	$ 612	$5,246	$21,031
1992	244	917	3,132	3,169	2,203	2,224	11,889
1993	207	3,985	2,257	8,224	2,103	1,031	17,806
1994	347	2,146	3,790	4,681	1,758	667	13,390
1995*	3,833	168	255	1,678	357	1,831	8,123
Thrifts							
1991	$ 50	$ 192	$ 275	$ 226	$ 5	$ 283	$1,031
1992	217	830	1,379	626	306	858	4,214
1993	1,037	836	1,289	1,958	252	305	5,676
1994	1,099	2,317	1,247	2,384	132	1,935	9,114
1995*	65	660	1,073	279	0	6	2,083

*Year-to-date as of May 17, 1995.

Source: SNL Securities and *CS First Boston.*

included a substantial number of thrift acquisitions. For the first time since 1992, the number of thrift acquisitions substantially outpaced those of banks. During the first seven months of 1995, thrifts were purchased at an average price of 145 percent of book value, while banks commanded a much higher average price of 181 percent of book value (see Tables 22–1 and 22–4). Lower valuation of thrift franchises partly explains the pickup in thrift merger activity. Thrifts have sold at lower prices than banks because a larger percentage of their deposits are in CDs rather than in transaction accounts, and these deposits are more difficult to maintain because of their rate sensitivity. Also, many thrifts sought alliances since they emphasized home mortgage financing as a primary product (50–80 percent of assets) and were beginning to lose the battle for market share to commercial banks, mortgage banks, and other nonbanking institutions. This factor doesn't bode well for the long-term survival and prosperity of the thrift industry. Banks and nonbanks are likely to continue to acquire thrifts for the remainder of the decade because thrifts can provide similar networks for sales of financial products as those of bank acquisition candidates provide and can be purchased at lower premiums. Hence, we are likely to find only the largest and strongest thrifts operating independently by the end of the century.[10] Nonpublic bank and thrift acquisitions have outnumbered publicly traded ones by about five to one over the last few years. However, the sizes of the publicly traded acquirees dwarf those of their nonpublic counterparts by about seven to one (see Table 22–4).[11]

TABLE 22-3
Mergers and Acquisitions of Banks and Thrifts

Announcement Date	Acquirer	Acquiree[*]	Total Assets (in millions)	Deal Value (in millions)	Deal Price/Book	Premium[†]
		Banks				
6/30/94	National Westminster	Central Jersey Bancorp	$1,784	$291	230%	108%
4/15/94	Harris Bankcorp	Suburban Bancorp	1,355	246	242	151
3/21/94	First Fidelity Bancorp	Baltimore Bancorp	2,232	363	213	115
3/21/94	National Westminster	Citizens First Bancorp	2,566	524	238	110
11/22/93	First Chicago	Lake Shore Bancorp	1,203	323	246	104
11/19/93	CoreStates Financial	Independence Bancorp	2,603	513	212	121
11/3/93	Banc One	Liberty National Bancorp	4,847	842	207	113
9/29/93	First Bank System	Boulevard Bancorp	1,517	214	205	115
9/20/93	Marshall & Ilsley	Valley Bancorp	4,337	803	234	111
9/9/93	Comerica	Pacific Western	1,011	133	143	98
8/2/93	CoreStates Financial	Constellation Bancorp	2,350	321	211	114
7/27/93	Norwest	First United Bank Group	3,402	494	209	109
7/27/94	PNC Bank	First Eastern Corp.	2,134	332	196	133
4/2/93	National City	Ohio Bancorp	1,732	224	170	123
3/03/93	Meridian Bancorp	Commonwealth Bancshares	2,036	357	230	134
1/29/93	Bank of New York	National Community Banks	4,003	652	260	130
	Total number of deals	16		$6,631	215%	118%

Continued on next page

467

Table 22–3—*Concluded*

Announcement Date	Acquirer	Acquiree*	Total Assets (in millions)	Deal Value (in millions)	Deal Price/Book	Premium†
		Thrifts				
7/13/94	Astoria Financial Corp.	Fidelity New York	$2,072	$ 160	133%	121%
6/27/94	North Fork Bancorp	Metro Bancshares	1,012	142	171	114
5/9/94	Fleet Financial Group	NBB Bancorp, Inc.	2,441	448	175	105
3/7/94	CoreStates Financial	Germantown Savings	1,637	283	183	115
2/22/94	Summit Bancorp	Crestmont Financial	1,024	91	133	111
1/17/94	First Union Corp.	BancFlorida Financial	1,551	162	162	122
1/11/94	Fifth Third Bancorp	Cumberland Federal	1,135	138	175	131
12/3/93	Roosevelt Financial	Farm and Home Financial	3,775	258	147	140
11/5/93	Shawmut National	Gateway Financial Corp.	1,270	152	172	105
10/25/93	Citizens Financial Group	Neworld Bancorp	1,113	144	164	124
9/22/93	Bank of Boston	BankWorcester Corp.	1,406	248	163	119
9/13/93	AmSouth Bancorp	Fortune Bancorp	2,646	285	151	126
8/17/93	Mercantile Bancorp	United Postal Bancorp	1,267	207	205	129
8/5/93	Southern National Corp.	The First SB, FSB	2,016	181	137	121
7/6/93	ABN-AMRO Holding	Cragin Financial	2,820	563	172	151
5/18/93	Regions Financial	Secor Bank, FSB	2,067	139	159	126
4/14/93	First Fidelity Bancorp	Peoples Westchester	1,797	263	140	102
	Total number of deals	17		$3,863	161%	121%

*Banks and thrifts with $1–10 billion in assets.

†Premium is the announced deal price per share as a percent of the acquiree's stock price the day before the announcement of the deal.

Source: SNL Securities, L.P., Charlottesville, VA.

T A B L E   22–4

Bank and Thrift Merger Transactions, 1991–1994 (in millions)

	Public		Nonpublic	
	Banks	**Thrifts**	**Banks**	**Thrifts**
1991	$9,633	$734	$105	$281
1992	2,860	977	124	530
1993	2,622	729	131	202
1994	2,332	975	117	658

Source: SNL Securities, L.P., Charlottesville, VA.

Some of the reasons for future acquisitions will include:

• The realization on the part of selling bank managements that their organizations are reaching maximum returns on equity and assets.
• The prospects for another round of credit-quality difficulties a year or two out.
• A lack of revenue opportunities when the economy slows.
• The inability or unwillingness to invest properly in technology.
• The fact that acquirors are attempting to reach critical mass and will no longer be restricted by interstate banking laws.
• The effect of the nationwide interstate banking bill in states that currently have restrictive laws and several healthy, sizable bank acquisition candidates.[12]
• The desire or willingness of some CEOs to retire with considerable wealth upon receipt of a hefty takeover premium bid.

SNL Securities completed a study on 12 banks that have been active acquirors over the past few years and are expected to continue to make critical-mass acquisitions. SNL concluded that acquirors electing to increase their size have been willing to pay premiums, counting on consolidation and increased market penetration to conquer any potential earnings dilution. The acquiring banks were willing to pay more for major in-market acquisitions than for banks located in new markets. It was not surprising that SNL found the superregionals to be the most avid in-market acquirors.[13] On the other hand, when some banks have not been able to achieve critical mass in certain geographic markets, they have divested low-market-share branches or subsidiary businesses, as did Bank of Boston with its Maine and Vermont banks. The same was probably true of Banc One's decision to divest four Michigan subsidiaries, since the company has a stated objective to be among the top three in market share in all of its markets.[14]

The number of acquisitions of banks with assets over $10 billion has been below expectations because of a turnaround in bank earnings in 1993–94 and the fact that the integration process is often difficult and time-consuming. Essentially, putting two banks together is easier on paper than in practice. Factors such as the degree of downsizing, the number of employee layoffs and branch closings, the degree of system integration required, the acquiree's sales culture, and the relative sizes of the two organizations make each transaction unique.[15] Following a merger, executive managements often tend to have less time for business development, monitoring the discipline of credit quality and interest rate risk, and long-range and strategic planning. Often, the acquiror loses customers of the acquired bank, who are wooed by higher depository rates or lower loan rates of competitive banks, especially when the original banking officer covering the account has been removed or replaced or when the previously utilized bank branch is closed.

In addition to acquiring banks and thrifts, bank holding companies began acquiring asset management (especially mutual funds) and mortgage banking companies. During 1994, there was a boom in mortgage banking merger and acquisition activity. Commercial bank holding companies acquired 25 out of a total of 31 mortgage banks involved in a takeover. Merger momentum seemed to pick up as the number of home mortgage refinancings declined with rising interest rates, causing weakness in that market. Increasingly, commercial banks are finding mortgage banks to be attractive targets because they generate fee income and provide the opportunity to cross-sell other financial products. Mortgage banking is essentially a scale-driven business that benefits from a critical mass. Those mortgage banks with the largest volumes of both mortgage-generation and mortgage-servicing business are generally the most cost-efficient and successful.

Banks interested in acquiring additional mortgage banks include Norwest, Citicorp, Bank of Boston, Barnett, Mellon, and Fleet, while potentially available mortgage banking companies include Source One Mortgage Corporation, Lomas Mortgage U.S.A., and Express American Mortgage (see Table 22–5 and Figures 22–3 and 22–4).

It is likely that U.S. commercial banks will continue to focus heavily on fee-related businesses. Noninterest income as a percentage of total revenue has grown from a fairly stable 20 percent throughout the 1960s and 1970s to more than 33 percent of total revenue in 1994. This trend is expected to continue for the remainder of the decade. Fee income will help banks remain formidable competitors into the next decade. Banks will also capitalize on a number of advantages, including extensive distribution networks, broad customer bases, an improvement in their ability to cross-sell products and services, and increased productivity. To improve productivity, banks will increasingly utilize technology. Banks have continued to

T A B L E   22-5

Potential Mortgage Bank Acquisition Candidates (in billions)

Servicer	Servicing
Countrywide Funding	$93.62
Source One Mortgage Corp.	38.80
Lomas Mortgage U.S.A.	34.40
North America Mortgage	15.70
PHH U.S. Mortgage	14.93
Ryland Mortgage	9.66
Express American Mortgage	6.80

Source: "Banking Consolidated Monthly," *CS First Boston*, November 1994, p. 6.

F I G U R E   22-3

Top Five Mortgage Originators as of September 30, 1995 (in billions)

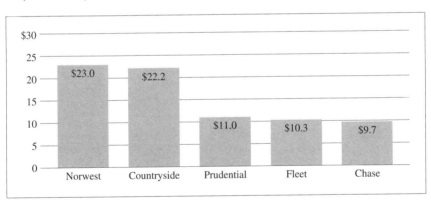

Source: "The 'New' Fleet Financial Group," *CS First Boston*, November 15, 1995, p. 13.

improve their efficiency through technological developments, scale advantages, and improved delivery mechanisms. This trend should continue as banks use acquisitions to derive substantial cost benefits through larger economies of scale and to achieve geographic diversification. Although banks have continued to lose market share in terms of financial assets, growth of fee income and off-balance-sheet activities (for instance, derivative securities) have substantially offset these declines.[16] In addition to niche banks and those that generate a large percentage of their revenue from fee income, the ultimate winners will be banks

F I G U R E   22–4

Top Five Mortgage Servicers as of September 30, 1995
(in billions)

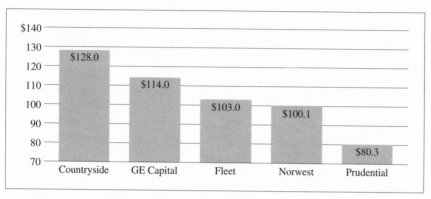

Source: "The 'New' Fleet Financial Group," *CS First Boston*, November 15, 1995, p. 13.

and nonbanking companies that can provide the broadest array of products and services in the most effective manner.

SOME LIKELY SCENARIOS

At year-end 1994, no commercial banking organization was even close to establishing a truly nationwide franchise. Only seven companies had commercial banks in at least 10 states (see Table 22–6). It is likely that a handful of regional banks will do retail banking in a majority of states by the year 2000. NationsBank, Banc One, and KeyCorp fit that description. It is entirely possible that NationsBank might be willing to pay a major premium to acquire Norwest or Wells Fargo before the retirement of its chairman, Hugh McColl.

At present, there is really nothing special that would bring desirable merger candidates such as CoreStates, Barnett, Wells Fargo, Wachovia, or SunTrust to the bargaining table since each is doing particularly well. These banks will not be acquired at bargain-basement prices. Unless there is an unusually attractive offer or an opportunity for the chairman of one of the aforementioned regionals to head the acquiring bank within a few years, there is little incentive for their managements to seek a buyer or merger. However, banking is a cyclical industry. There is likely to be some major problem within the industry before the end of the decade, if history repeats. It may be a classic credit problem, a mammoth problem with derivative securities, or some regional phenomenon that may weaken some banks and bring them to the merger/acquisition bargaining table. Another motivation may be poor growth in shareholder returns resulting from slowed growth in earnings.

TABLE   22–6

State Distribution of Banks, March, 1995

Bank	States	Assets (in billions)
Norwest	15	$ 56
First Interstate	13	59
KeyCorp	12	66
NationsBank	11	174
BankAmerica	11	225
Banc One	11	87
Boatmen's Bancshares	10	32
First Union	9	80
First Bank System	8	26
Citicorp	7	257
Chase Manhattan	7	112
PNC Bank	7	62
Fleet Financial	7	46
South Trust	7	18
Huntington Bancshares	6	18

Source: American Bankers Association.

Historically, the banking industry has participated in boom and bust loan cycles. They were often brought about by banking overcapacity, economic collapse of an industry or region, or the herd syndrome, that is, a rush to book high-margin loans or to participate in lending fads in the same coveted market segments. These loan cycles and fads often resulted in poor credit judgments and large charge-offs, which increased bank failures. This in turn led to an increase in merger activity within the banking industry. For example, some of the lending cycles and fads of the past included REIT loans in the mid-1970s, oil and gas loans in the early to mid-1980s, LDC loans in the mid-1980s, acquisition, development, and construction loans in the mid to late 1980s, and commercial real estate loans in the late 1980s and early 1990s.[17]

Banks made many acquisitions in the 1980s and early 1990s without much concern for EPS dilution. Banks with the highest multiples (P/E ratios) were able to utilize their market premiums to buy institutions that filled in geographic slots with new distribution outlets or added new products and services; or they were able to acquire a wounded or even failing institution from federal regulators at what turned out to be a bargain (for example, Banc One and NationsBank made such acquisitions in Texas). In many cases, these banks were able to return bad loans or a large percentage of them to regulators without having to suffer losses. In some cases, there were even favorable tax consequences in acquiring failing banks because of loss-carry provisions of the federal income tax code.

The goal of the acquisitions was to bring the acquired bank's performance up to the level of the acquiring bank. Banks learned during the 1990s how to cut costs and become efficient institutions. Although some deals were made to acquire additional distributional channels for product-driven firms, thereby increasing revenues, many acquisitions in the 1970s and 1980s seemed to have little strategic merit. Those provided little, if any, revenue enhancement or cost-saving opportunities. Perhaps they were made to increase asset size in an age of the more the merrier, the bigger the better.

Academic research on bank mergers in the period before the 1990s reported the following: Cohen and Reid observed that overall bank size rose, which contributed to the prestige of management but did little for stockholders or the public. Smith found that few changes of any kind followed from the merger of two banks. Although total revenues typically increased after the consummation of a transaction, expenses climbed as well, leaving bank earnings generally unaffected by the merger. In a study by Bacon of 15 bank mergers in Marion County, Indiana, the only substantive results were that shareholders of acquired banks received substantial premiums on the stocks, while management salaries and fringe benefits improved. Two studies by Rose seemed to support the prior findings. One explored the performance of 160 national banks that participated in mergers in 1976–80. Rose found that acquiring national banks were not more profitable and, in fact, averaged somewhat lower ROAs and ROEs than comparably sized nonmerging banks headquartered in the same areas, though none of the differences observed in profitability or risk exposure between merging and nonmerging banks were statistically significant. However, there were major differences in operating efficiency and dependence on local funds between merging and nonmerging national banks. The merger-bound nationals were less efficient and more heavily dependent upon local deposits rather than money market borrowings. A later study by Rose, of 600 mergers in the United States that took place between 1970 and 1985, showed that only a small percentage of them fully achieved their premerger goals. About 60 percent of merging banks believed profits improved following their mergers and less than 50 percent observed significant improvements in their market share or rate of growth.[18] However, it is likely that studies of 1992–95 mergers will show somewhat improved profitability ratios for merged banking institutions.

Commensurate with the recovery of the economy and a multiyear period of low interest rates, both banking margins and return on assets improved dramatically from 1990 to 1994. For example, the average ROA for banks in 1990 was 0.48 percent, while the average ROA in 1994 stood at 1.15 percent. Similarly, ROEs averaged 10–12 percent in 1990–91 and between 14.5–15.5 percent in 1993–94 (see Figure 1–1 in Chapter 1).

With this overall improvement at the industry level, even the weakest of the superregionals had a big turnaround in earnings per share and related financial ratios. Relative major differences in P/E ratios began to disappear. This has had a major impact on slowing down the pace of mergers and acquisitions. For example, the average P/E of a superregional bank was 6 in September 1990, with the highest multiple at about 10 times and the lowest at 4 times. By September 1991, the average P/E of a superregional was 11.3, with the highest more than 13 times and the lowest price just over 6. In September 1992, the average P/E was 11.1, with the highest at more than 13 and the lowest at 6.8. By September 1993, the average P/E was 11.0, with the highest bank multiple at more than 14 and the lowest at about 8. In September 1994, the average superregional P/E stood at 9.4, with the highest at about 11 and the lowest at about 8. By mid-year 1995, the average superregional bank P/E ratio was at 10.3, with the highest at 13.7, the lowest at 8.5 times earnings (see Table 22–7 and Figure 22–5). It is interesting to note that bank stocks

T A B L E   22–7

Price-to-Earnings Ratios of Superregional Banks, June 1995

	P/E	Price/Book
Southeast		
NationsBank	8.5×	1.26
First Union	8.8	1.36
Wachovia	10.5	1.72
SunTrust	12.6	1.68
Barnett	10.2	1.55
Midwest		
Banc One	13.7	1.67
PNC	12.9	1.36
KeyCorp	9.9	1.59
Norwest	11.1	2.23
NBD	8.8	1.40
West		
BankAmerica	9.1	1.16
First Interstate	8.1	1.74
Wells Fargo	10.8	2.59
New England and Mid-Atlantic		
Bank of New York	9.3	1.66
Fleet	9.0	1.37
Bank of Boston	8.7	1.42
Mellon	9.8	1.63
CoreStates	12.4	2.14
Peer average	10.3×	1.66

F I G U R E   22–5

Price/Earnings Multiples for Salomon Brothers 50-Bank Index, 1985–1995

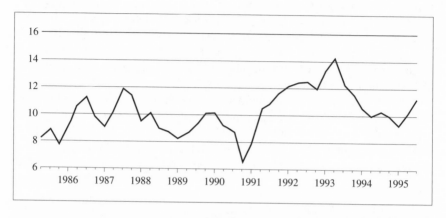

traditionally trade well below those of industrial issues. In only one year in the last four decades (1963) was there general parity between price-to-earnings ratios of banks and industrials. The reasons for the discount include the presence of governmental regulation, perceptions of slow growth, the occasional highly publicized bank failure, the sensitivity of earnings to the business cycle, the emergence of nonbank competition, and credit and interest rate risk.

Not only did relative P/E ratios change, so did stock market forces, which pressured banks into making only those acquisitions that would be accretive within 12 months. Also, many takeover candidates now seem to have stars in their eyes when it comes to acquisition prices. These factors have acted to slow down the pace of merger activity, making it harder to make a merger than it used to be. For example, NationsBank has expressed interest in having a nationwide branch system, but the market will not accord it a high enough market multiple to acquire a bank in a new region without substantial dilution. Unless NationsBank can arrange a no-premium merger of equals or acquire a troubled bank, it may have to be content in the short run to buy smaller banks in its established markets or nonbanks with expanded product offerings.

Goodwill can influence a bank's P/E ratio. Goodwill is an intangible asset that is normally created when an acquired company is purchased for more than its net worth under the purchase method of accounting. Goodwill is written off through amortization of income over a period of years; consequently, it can distort certain financial ratios such as ROE or equity to assets. Practically speaking, it is sensible to ignore goodwill if it equals less than 10 percent of net worth or if it is unmistakably offset by valuable assets of any kind that are unrecognized on the balance sheet. Goodwill in excess of 10 percent of equity may be construed as a weakness in asset quality. On the other hand, quality of earnings should be upgraded because of the amortization penalty on earnings, which could justify a slightly higher P/E ratio.

With the exception of the BankAmerica acquisition of Continental Illinois, merger activity during 1994 was characterized by large regional banks accumulating market share piecemeal by buying smaller banks and thrifts. First Union and First Interstate typified the activity. First Union led the way with five announced mergers, two branch purchases, and four RTC purchases, gathering $7 billion in deposits while building up its franchise in Florida, Virginia, and Washington, DC. First Interstate announced six mergers, one branch purchase, and two RTC transactions, accumulating $5 billion in deposits through California, Washington, and Texas (see Table 22–8). The improvement of market share should help increase the pricing powers of banks as compared to past economic cycles. We can anticipate additional acquisitions of small banks and thrifts that are located in the same geographic region as the buyer. However, over the next few years, the pressures should mount for larger acquisitions when certain banks demonstrate subpar earnings or peaked financial ratios, making them vulnerable to takeover.[19] There may be more announcements similar to the Fleet/Shawmut or First Chicago/NBD agreements to merge.

Interstate consolidation is also occurring rapidly, led by the Southeast region. For the nation as a whole, the three largest institutions in each state now control an average 45 percent of the nation's deposits, up from 37 percent in 1990[20] (see Table 22–9).

T A B L E   22–8

Top Superregional Acquisitions in 1994

Buyer	Purchase Price (in billions)	State
BankAmerica	$9.8	Illinois
First Union	7.0	Florida, Virginia
First Interstate	5.2	California, Washington, Texas
NationsBank	4.9	Florida
Barnett Banks	4.0	Florida
Norwest	3.2	Arizona, Texas
KeyCorp	3.0	Maine, Vermont, Colorado, Oregon
First Fidelity	2.7	Maryland, New York
Fleet Financial	2.2	Massachusetts, Rhode Island

Source: Company reports.

T A B L E   22–9

Market Share of Three Biggest Institutions per State

| | Top Three Share | | |
Selected States	October 1994	December 1993	March 1990
Rhode Island	84.0%	74.2%	63.6%
Maine	56.0	48.3	36.5
Florida	47.7	40.3	28.6
North Dakota	42.9	37.5	33.0
South Dakota	39.8	34.5	33.5
Louisiana	39.7	34.6	29.4
Arizona	77.3	72.9	46.3
South Carolina	46.5	42.3	37.6
North Carolina	46.8	42.9	47.2
Mississippi	40.1	37.1	31.3
Arkansas	31.5	28.5	18.2
National average	44.8	43.1	36.8

Source: Lehman Brothers.

Looking out over the banking horizon for the remainder of the decade, it appears as if most of the money center banks will do well, including Citicorp, Chase, and JP Morgan. In one scenario, they will be joined by the dominant superregional franchises like Fleet and Bank of New York in the Northeast region. NationsBank, First Union, SunTrust, and Wachovia are expected to be dominant franchises in the Southeast, continuing to grow and expand their multistate operations. The Midwest banks that are expected to dominate the landscape include Banc One, Norwest, First Chicago NBD, First Bank System, and KeyCorp; BankAmerica and Wells Fargo are expected to strengthen their West Coast franchises. Some of these superregionals may grow to become megabanks and together control a substantial portion of domestic deposits when the consolidation of the banking industry is completed.[21]

Large banks, such as Banc One and KeyCorp, which have shown little revenue growth from 1993 to 1995, are likely to be acquirors of nonbanking companies to enrich their product offerings or obtain faster-growing specialty businesses, such as credit cards, consumer finance, or asset management. Despite $2 billion in nonbanking acquisitions, Mellon's revenue generation has been lackluster. If management now believes that it has the franchise and management for revenue growth, Mellon might reverse course and make bank acquisitions to expand geographically and to offer their products to a broader customer base.[22]

Florida remains one of the most desirable states in which to establish a franchise, and both North and South Carolina represent attractive growth states. Following the no-premium merger of equals of BBT Financial ($10.6 billion in assets) and Southern National Corp. ($8.2 billion), giving Southern the largest deposit base in North Carolina and the third largest in South Carolina, shareholders of the other Carolina banks can expect to benefit as investor dollars should refocus on the reduced supply of acquirable franchises. The impetus behind the Southern National/BBT deal was the recent legislative change that allowed banks in North Carolina either to acquire or be acquired by banks in approximately 35 other states. Although out-of-state banks may have an interest in the Carolinas, native sons like NationsBank, First Union, and Wachovia may also make preemptive bids for defensive or franchise-filling purposes.[23]

In New England, Bay Banks, a $10.5 billion retail bank headquartered in Massachusetts, remains the prize catch. Another desirable Massachusetts acquisition is UST Corp. ($2 billion). In addition, two Connecticut banks, Centerbank (43 branches, $3 billion in assets) and DS Bancorp (23 branches, $2.2 billion in assets), have recently begun to recover from the weak Connecticut economy and might make desirable acquisition candidates.

In New Jersey, UJB Financial ($20.5 billion) is an attractive acquisition candidate. New York State offers many attractive independent thrifts, while Pennsylvania offers Susquehanna Bancshares ($2.5 billion), Dauphin Deposit ($5 billion), and Keystone Financial ($4.7 billion) as attractive merger candidates. There are three prize franchises left in Ohio: Huntington Bancshares, Inc. ($18.2 billion), Star Banc Corporation ($9.2 billion), and Provident Bancorp, Inc. ($4.8 billion). Virginia offers Crestar Financial Corp. ($14.4 billion), Signet Banking Corp. ($10.5 billion), First Virginia Banks ($7.1 billion), and Jefferson Bancshares ($2.0 billion) as prime acquisition candidates. Riggs National Bank ($4.8 billion) in Washington, DC, and Mercantile Bancshares ($5.9 billion) and Provident Bancshares ($2.3 billion), both headquartered in Maryland, are potential takeover candidates.

Louisiana's Hibernia ($6.55 billion) and Alabama's AmSouth Bancorp ($17.1 billion) and SouthTrust Corp ($15 billion) are attractive acquisition candidates, along with Tennessee's First American ($7.3 billion), National Commerce Bancorp ($2.7 billion), and Union Planter's ($9.7 billion). Another potential candidate is Old Kent Financial ($11.8 billion) in Michigan. Missouri hosts a number of interesting possibilities. They include Boatmen's Bancshares, Inc. ($40 billion), Magna Group ($4.6 billion), and Mercantile Bancorp ($13 billion). KeyCorp has expressed interest in expanding into the St. Louis marketplace. Cullen/Frost ($3.7 billion) is the most likely takeover candidate in Texas now that Victoria Bancshares was acquired by Norwest. First Security Corp ($12 billion) and Zions Bancorp ($5.3 billion) are good candidates in Utah.

Although First Bank System ($35 billion) has been an aggressive acquiror of banks, it is also a strong merger-of-equals, nondilutive acquisition candidate for a bank holding company wishing to expand in the northern Midwest or California. If First Bank System is successful in acquiring First Interstate, then it will obviously no longer be an acquisition candidate. However, if Wells Fargo wins the prize in California, KeyCorp, among others, has expressed an interest in merging with a strong Midwestern franchise. Banc One, NationsBank, Norwest, and BankAmerica are also potential acquirors of First Bank System.

There are two prime jewels headquartered in California that are both strong enough to remain independent but which may choose to become involved in a nondilutive merger of equals. They are Wells Fargo ($52 billion) and First Interstate ($56 billion). A merger of the two would make an almost perfect in-market merger. NationsBank, Banc One, Norwest, BankAmerica, First Bank System, and others would be prime candidates for buying either of the prime jewels if available. At the time of this writing, Wells Fargo and First Bank System are in a battle to acquire First Interstate. Oregon's U.S. Bancorp ($22 billion), Washington Mutual Savings Bank ($16.1 billion), and many California thrifts are additional West Coast acquisition candidates for expansion-minded bank holding companies (see Table 22–10).

There is likely to be a resurgence of bank merger activity during 1996–97 because many smaller banks recognize that they have reached their maximum profitability ratios and measurements. A temporary rise in interest rates during 1994 resulted in large portfolio and lower price-to-earnings ratios for some banks, thus creating takeover candidates. A widening of the spread of price-to-earnings ratios between buyers and sellers may act as a catalyst in increasing the number of mergers.

Another factor is that a number of banks have relatively poor efficiency ratios, making them attractive acquisition candidates. The economics of consolidation are extremely compelling in such cases, particularly in terms of expense savings and earnings enhancements that can be recognized from in-market transactions. For example, if an acquiror can eliminate 40 percent of the cost of a takeover candidate with a 70 percent overhead, the earnings performance of the candidate could be improved by 93 percent (see Table 22–11). Among our takeover candidates in Table 22–10, the efficiency ratios of Liberty Bancorp and Provident Bancshares are above 80 percent, while the efficiency ratios of Cullen/Frost Bankers, Hibernia, and U.S. Bancorp are 70 percent or higher. Bay Banks and Magna Group have efficiency ratios between 67 and 69 percent. Also, the economics of consolidation come into play as banks recognize the growth parameters necessary to achieve consistent returns over time. For example, a single bank achieving a 1.20 percent ROA needs 16.2 percent asset growth to generate comparable returns. The conclusion is that takeovers of both bank and nonbank targets within the financial services industry are likely to increase for the remainder of the decade.[24]

With the announced agreement in May 1995 that Charter One Financial, Inc., would acquire the First Michigan Corporation, forming the ninth largest savings institution in the country (assets of $13 billion, 151 branches in Ohio and Michigan), we must not forget that healthy thrifts can also acquire savings and loans as

T A B L E   22–10

Banking Takeover Candidates, August 3, 1995

	Total Assets (in billions)	Market Cap (in billions)	Price/ Earnings 1995E	Price/ Book 1995E
Banks				
AmSouth Bancorp	$17.1	$2.1	12.3	1.6
Bay Banks	10.5	1.5	12.6	1.8
Boatmen's Bancshares	40.0	4.6	10.4	1.6
Crestar Financial	14.6	1.9	10.3	1.6
Cullen/Frost Bankers	3.7	0.5	11.3	1.5
Deposit Guaranty	5.0	0.7	11.3	1.5
First American	7.3	1.0	10.3	1.5
First Bank System	33.0	4.5	10.4	2.0
First Interstate	55.0	6.6	7.8	1.7
First Security Corp.	12.0	1.4	9.5	1.4
Hibernia	6.7	1.1	8.8	1.5
Jefferson Banshares	2.0	0.3	12.6	1.5
Keystone Financial	4.7	0.7	12.2	1.6
Liberty Bancorp	2.6	0.3	14.4	1.3
Magna Group	4.6	0.6	11.9	1.4
Mercantile Bancshares	5.9	1.1	11.2	1.4
Mercantile Bancorp	13.0	2.0	10.8	1.7
North Fork Bancorporation	2.9	0.4	9.6	1.2
Northern Trust	18.7	2.2	11.1	1.9
Provident Bancshares	2.3	0.2	15.8	1.3
Regions Financial Corp.	12.8	1.7	10.2	1.6
Signet Banking Corp.	10.6	1.4	12.6	1.7
Southern National Corp.	19.9	2.4	10.2	1.7
Star Banc Corp.	9.2	1.5	11.3	1.7
UJB Financial	15.4	1.9	11.4	1.6
Union Planters Corp.	9.7	1.2	9.8	1.5
U.S. Bancorp	31.2	2.7	8.8	1.6
Thrifts				
Cooperative Bank of Concord	0.8	0.1	8.3	0.9
Coast Savings	8.6	0.4	21.6	1.1
Commercial Federal	5.9	0.4	9.3	12.6
Great Financial Corp.	2.1	0.3	15.4	1.1
Leader Financial	2.5	0.3	10.0	1.4
Rochester Community	3.7	0.3	12.9	1.1
Security Capital Corp.	3.0	0.5	21.3	0.9

well as other financial institutions. In fact, there were 121 takeovers in 1994 among U.S. savings institutions.

There are two other groups of potential buyers of regional and superregional banks that we have not discussed: foreign banks and money center banks. Economic

T A B L E   22–11

Earnings Leverage for Mergers and Acquisitions

Expense Savings	Overhead Ratio of Target			
	60%	65%	70%	75%
10%	15%	19%	23%	30%
20	30	37	47	60
30	45	56	70	90
40	60	74	93	120
50	75	93	117	150

Source: "Bank Consolidation Monthly," *CS First Boston*, December 1994, p. 4.

recovery in Europe, the decline of the dollar vis-à-vis major European countries and Japan, and low price-to-earnings ratios on U.S. bank stocks may bring into play several European, Asian, or Australian banks that desire access to U.S. retail dollar deposits or an expansion of their holdings in this country. This was certainly the case for Banco Santander, which received approval from the Federal Reserve Board to increase its ownership in First Fidelity from 24.9 percent to 30 percent in early 1995, prior to the announced acquisition of First Fidelity by First Union. It was also the case for National Australian Bank, which agreed in February 1995 to acquire Michigan National Corp. It is also possible that a money center bank, such as Citicorp, with an improved earnings and capital position may desire increased distribution capability or access to more retail deposits.

The trend for increased acquisition activity should continue, driven by earnings pressure and the need to improve shareholder value. The winners in the consolidation game will be those banks that can leverage their distribution networks and provide the greatest number of products and services across the widest customer base in an efficient manner. In addition, consolidation offers critical mass in many key lines of business. Also, many of the smaller regional banks do not have the capacity or capability to succeed in a more competitive banking environment. It is likely that the economic value of their franchises will erode steadily because of a lack of critical mass, inadequate technological resources, limited product offerings, and overwhelming regulatory burdens.[25]

Most of the mergers will be in-market, allowing for greater operating efficiency. There will also be adjacent-market mergers in new areas allowing for diversification of credit risk across economic regions and additional distribution outlets for company products and services. Banks will purchase nonbanking companies, acquiring mutual fund, mortgage banking, credit card, and other permitted activities that will generate additional fee income and provide economies of scale and critical mass. There will also likely be more megamergers like those between BankAmerica and Security Pacific and Chemical Bank and Manufacturers Hanover (and later Chase Manhattan), as well as mergers of equals that link the leading superregional franchises, fashioned after either the Society/Key (out-of-market) or Fleet/Shawmut (in-market) combinations. According to one banking analyst, "The situation reminds me of my first eighth grade dance, with all the boys on one side and all the girls on the other. As soon as the first couple gets out on the dance floor and breaks the ice, it will be a stampede."[26]

At the time of this writing at mid-year 1995, the merger derby had begun to heat up, with announcements of much bigger acquisitions such as Michigan National ($12 billion in assets), Shawmut ($36 billion), West One ($10 billion), Meridian ($16 billion), First Fidelity ($36 billion), and Midlantic ($13 billion), and the mergers of equals between First Chicago ($72 billion) and NBD ($48 billion) and Chemical Banking ($179 billion) and Chase Manhattan ($119 billion).

In fact, nearly $70 billion of bank mergers were announced in 1995 through mid-December, already exceeding the record set in 1991. The nation's 50 largest banks could consolidate to 15 by the end of the decade. According to Herbert A. Lurie, co-head of financial institutions at Merrill Lynch, "At the end, you'll have maybe 20 money center and superregional banks with assets over $100 billion, a bunch of (very small) community banks, and some niche banks."[27] H. Rodgin Cohen, a prominent bank merger lawyer, feels that "consolidation in this industry has become an economic imperative."[28]

WHAT IS AN INVESTOR TO DO?

Investors who believe in the scenario of consolidation of the banking industry and an increase in merger and acquisition activity throughout the remainder of the decade should put together a portfolio of bank and thrift stocks that are likely takeover candidates (see Table 22–10). However, savvy investors should beware of overvalued stocks with relatively high price/earnings and price/book ratios, where prices have already been bid up to current takeover premiums (see Figure 3–2 and Tables 3–2 and 3–3 in Chapter 3 and Tables 22–1 and 22–2 in this chapter for a guide to takeover prices and premiums).

For those investors wishing to participate in the expected takeover frenzy, but who would rather not choose a portfolio of individual takeover candidates, there is a closed-end mutual fund listed on the New York Stock Exchange that is currently selling at a 15 percent discount to its net asset value. The purchase of shares in the Bank and Thrift Opportunity Fund (BTO), managed by James K. Schmidt of John Hancock Funds, represents a good way to participate in the consolidation of the banking and thrift industries. The fund concentrates on undervalued regional banks and thrifts with healthy earnings prospects and the potential to benefit from industry consolidation. Other bank mutual funds are Pilgrim Regional Banks, Paine Webber Regional Financial Growth, and Fidelity Select Regional Banks.

The long-term outlook for the banking industry is good. Banks tend to do well in a low-inflation, slow-growth economy. With a reduction in FDIC insurance premiums, bank earnings should increase by at least 6 percent in 1996 because of this event alone. Bank stocks also pay above-average dividends and are still selling at just 45 percent of the market multiple. Favorable earnings and continued acquisition activity in the financial services industry augur well for prices of bank stocks.

ENDNOTES

1. C.S. Berger, "Commercial Banks," *Salomon Brothers*, September 7, 1994, p. 1.
2. J.R. Fredericks, "Bank Stock Valuation Package," *Montgomery Securities*, October 11, 1994, p. 3.
3. Berger, pp. 4–9.
4. Ibid., p. 8.
5. P.S. Rose and S.W. Kalari, *Financial Institutions* (Burr Ridge, IL: Irwin, 1995), p. 243.
6. T. H. Hanley, P. J. Carter, and A. B. Collins, "Bank Consolidation Monthly," *CS First Boston*, March 1994, p. 3.
7. T.H. Hanley, P.J. Carter, and A.B. Collins, "Banking Weekly," *CS First Boston*, October 26, 1994, p. 3.
8. *New York Times*, October 23, 1994, p. 14.
9. Berger, p. 2.
10. T.H. Hanley, P.J. Carter, and A.B. Collins, "Bank Consolidation Monthly," *CS First Boston*, September 24, 1994, pp. 2, 6.
11. Hanley, P.J. Carter, and A.B. Collins, October 26, 1994, p. 3.
12. T.H. Hanley, P.J. Carter, and A.B. Collins, "Bank Consolidation Monthly," *CS First Boston*, October 1994, pp. 2–3.
13. Ibid., p. 5.
14. Ibid.
15. T.K. Brown, "Challenging Some of the Traditional Wisdom Surrounding Bank Consolidation," *Bank Notes DLJ*, August 18, 1995, pp. 3–6.
16. T.H. Hanley, P.J. Carter, and A.B. Collins, "The Competitive State of the U.S. Commercial Banking Industry," *CS First Boston*, March 24, 1995, pp. 1, 5.
17. A. Bird, *SuperCommunity Banking* (Chicago: Probus Publishing Co., 1994), p. 3.
18. Rose and Kalari, *Financial Institutions*, p. 243.
19. M.L. Mayo, *Lehman Brothers Research*, January 6, 1995, p. 3.
20. Ibid.
21. Hanley, Carter, and Collins, "Bank Consolidation Monthly," *CS First Boston,* September 1994, pp. 5–6.
22. C.S. Berger, "Bankers in Heat," *Salomon Brothers U.S. Equity Research*, August 16, 1995, p. 12.
23. J.R. Burke, "Thoughts on Interstate Banking," *Robinson-Humphrey & Co., Inc.*, Summer 1994, pp. 2–3.
24. T.H. Hanley, "Bank Consolidation Monthly," *CS First Boston*, December 1994, pp. 4–5.
25. T.H. Hanley, P.J. Carter, and A.B. Collins, "Banking in the 1990s: Who Will Be the Winners by 1997?" *CS First Boston*, 1995 Bank Annual, pp. 16–17.
26. D. Rogers, *The Future of American Banking* (New York: McGraw-Hill, Inc., 1993), p. 293.
27. K. Holland and R.A. Melcher, "Why Banks Bulk Up," *Business Week*, July 31, 1995, p. 67.
28. A. Dunkin, "Investing in a Bank-Eat-Bank World," *Business Week*, July 31, 1995, p. 93.

INDEX

485

NEW FINANCIERS
Profiles of the Industry Leaders Who Are Reshaping Financial Services
Charles B. Wendel

A unique combination of interview and analysis, *The New Financiers* is a virtual summit meeting of financial expertise and strategy. It presents in-depth conversation and interpretive interviews with well-respected corporate chairmen and presidents and leaders who are clearly viewed as "best in the class."
ISBN: 1-55738-908-X $37.50

THE BANKING REVOLUTION
Positioning Your Bank in the New Financial Services Marketplace
Tom Harvey

In order to move forward in the new era of financial services, banks must learn from the lessons of the past, correct the errors of today, and plan a successful course for the future. *The Banking Revolution* offers bankers a unique perspective on their history and more important, their next steps.
ISBN: 1-55738-793-1 $37.50

REENGINEERING THE BANK
A Blueprint for Survival and Success
Paul H. Allen

Reengineering the Bank helps you evaluate your market, your operations, your customers, your balance sheet and your strategies to maximize their value and provide you with the tools to restructure your program.
ISBN: 1-55738-715-X $37.50

BANK MERGERS, ACQUISITIONS, AND STRATEGIC ALLIANCES
Positioning and Protecting Your Bank in the Era of Consolidation
Hazel J. Johnson, Ph.D.

Whether banks are large or small, bankers need to assess their needs and plans for the future. *Bank Mergers, Acquisitions and Strategic Alliances* reviews the processes involved for banks facing any scenario caused by M&A activity.
ISBN: 1-55738-746-X $65.00

THE NEW BUSINESS OF BANKING
Transforming Challenges into Opportunities in Today's Financial Services Marketplace
George Bollenbacher

Now updated for today's changing markets, *The New Business of Banking* takes an eye-opening, positive point of view of banking, focusing on what the winners in the financial services industry are doing, how they are doing it, and how to become a leader in this new era of financial services.
ISBN: 1-55738-771-0 $32.50

The Community Banker Journal

The Community Banker is exactly what the name suggests, a journal created for community bankers by community bankers. It spotlights a different topic in each issue that directly impacts your institution, such as branches, technology, management tools, and the people factor. *The Community Banker* tackles the strategies that are essential to stay competitive and moving ahead in today's volatile banking industry.

A Quarterly Journal by Community Bankers, for Community Bankers.
Order # **CMBK** $225.00 per year

DATE DUE

AUG 2 9 1997		
MAR 2 1 1998	DEC 1 8 2000	
MAY 0 6 1998		
FEB 0 8 2000		
JAN		
APR 0 2 2001		
		Printed in USA